The Social Economics of Poverty

With a formidable lineup of economists, this book provides new insights for understanding social outcomes and for designing innovative policies that cannot be ignored by anyone who claims to be at the frontiers of development economics.

Alain de Janvry, University of California at Berkeley

In *The Social Economics of Poverty*, an eminent team of scholars apply tools of the nascent social economics paradigm to one of the most enduring and frustrating questions in economics: why does poverty persist in a world of abundant resources? Why are some people excluded from growth processes while others are not? Why do some people enjoy access to scarce resources or the efficiency enhancements associated with cooperation while others do not?

Humans do not live in isolation. Observed microeconomic behavior, therefore, depends on people's identities and on the formal and informal social relations that shape their world. These behaviors subsequently affect individual and group identity and relationships, creating a system with dynamic feedback. Such systems commonly lead to low-level, stable states characteristic of poverty traps. Economists are just beginning to explore the consequences of such phenomena.

Individual chapters, written by leading scholars in the field, illustrate how the insights offered by social economics might inform and enhance both the discipline of economics and the design of policies intended to help reduce the incidence and duration of poverty around the world.

Contributors include George A. Akerlof, Lawrence E. Blume, Samuel Bowles, Michael R. Carter, Marco Castillo, Timothy G. Conley, Indraneel Dasgupta, Jean-Yves Duclos, Joan Esteban, Marcel Fafchamps, Hanming Fang, Andrew D. Foster, Tatiana Goetghebuer, Karla Hoff, Ravi Kanbur, Rachel E. Kranton, Eliana La Ferrara, Glenn C. Loury, Jean-Philippe Platteau, Debraj Ray, Arijit Sen, and Christopher R. Udry.

Christopher B. Barrett is International Professor of Applied Economics and Management and co-Director for the African Food Security and Natural Resources Management Program at Cornell University, and Editor of the American Journal of Agricultural Economics.

Priorities in Development Economics
Edited by Paul Mosley
The University of Sheffield

Foreign Trade Reforms and Development Strategy
Jean-Marc Fontaine

Adjustment and Poverty
Options and choices
Frances Stewart

Econometrics and Data Analysis for Developing Countries
Chandan Mukherjee, Marc Wuyts, and Howard White

The Green Revolution in Africa
An economic and political analysis
Paul Mosley

The IMF and the Future
Graham Bird

Poverty and Exclusion in North and South
Essays on social policy and global poverty reduction
Edited by Paul Mosley and Elizabeth Dowler

Food Aid After Fifty Years
Recasting its role
Christopher B. Barrett and Daniel G. Maxwell

The Social Economics of Poverty
On identities, communities, groups, and networks
Edited by Christopher B. Barrett

The Social Economics of Poverty

On identities, communities, groups, and networks

Edited by
Christopher B. Barrett

Routledge
Taylor & Francis Group

LONDON AND NEW YORK

First published 2005
by Routledge
2 Park Square, Milton Park, Abingdon, Oxon OX14 4RN

Simultaneously published in the USA and Canada
by Routledge
270 Madison Ave, New York, NY 10016

Routledge is an imprint of the Taylor & Francis Group

© 2005 editorial matter and selection, Christopher B. Barrett;
individual chapters, the contributors

Typeset in Times New Roman by
Newgen Imaging Systems (P) Ltd, Chennai, India
Printed and bound in Great Britian by
MPG Books Ltd, Bodmin, Cornwall

British Library Cataloguing in Publication Data
A catalogue record for this book is available
from the British Library

Library of Congress Cataloging in Publication Data
A catalog record for this book has been requested

ISBN 0–415–70089–2 (hbk)
ISBN 0–415–70088–4 (pbk)

Contents

Figures

Tables

Contributors

George A. Akerlof is a Nobel Laureate in Economics (2001) and Koshland Professor of Economics, University of California at Berkeley, 549 Evans Hall #3880, Berkeley, CA 94720-3880, USA (akerlof@econ.berkeley.edu).

Christopher B. Barrett is International Professor in the Department of Applied Economics and Management, Cornell University, 315 Warren Hall, Ithaca, NY 14853-7801, USA (cbb2@cornell.edu).

Lawrence E. Blume is Professor in the Department of Economics, Cornell University, 430 Uris Hall, Ithaca, NY 14853, USA and a member of the External Faculty at the Santa Fe Institute (lb19@cornell.edu).

Samuel Bowles is Research Professor and Director of the Behavioral Sciences Program, Santa Fe Institute, 1399 Hyde Park Road, Santa Fe, New Mexico, 87501, USA (bowles@santafe.edu) and Professor of Economics, University of Siena, Siena, Italy (bowles@unisi.it).

Michael R. Carter is Professor in the Department of Agricultural and Applied Economics, University of Wisconsin, Madison, WI 53706, USA (mrcarter@wisc.edu).

Marco Castillo is Assistant Professor in the School of Public Policy, Georgia Institute of Technology, 685 Cherry Street, N.W., Atlanta, GA 30332-0345, USA (marco.castillo@pubpolicy.gatech.edu).

Timothy G. Conley is Associate Professor of Econometrics and Statistics in the Graduate School of Business, University of Chicago, 1101 East 58th Street, Chicago, IL 60637, USA (tim.conley@gsb.uchicago.edu).

Indraneel Dasgupta is Senior Lecturer in the School of Economics, University of Nottingham, Nottingham, NG7 2RD, UK (Indraneel.Dasgupta@nottingham.ac.uk).

Jean-Yves Duclos is Professor in the Département d'économique, Université Laval, Pavillon de Sève, Ste-Foy, Québec, G1K 7P4, Canada (jyves@ecn.ulaval.ca).

Joan Esteban is Director of the Institut d'Analisi Economica, CSIC, Campus UAB, 08193 Bellaterra-Barcelona, Spain (Joan.Esteban@uab.es).

Marcel Fafchamps is Reader in Development Economics, Department of Economics, and Professorial Fellow, Mansfield College, University of Oxford, Manor Road, Oxford, OX1 3UQ, UK (marcel.fafchamps@ economics.oxford.ac.uk).

Hanming Fang is Assistant Professor in the Department of Economics and the Cowles Foundation, Yale University, 37 Hillhouse Avenue, Box 208264, New Haven, CT 06520-8264, USA (hanming.fang@yale.edu).

Andrew D. Foster is Professor in the Departments of Economics and Community Health, Brown University, Box B, 64 Waterman Street, Providence, RI 02906, USA (afoster@brown.edu).

Tatiana Goetghebuer is Research Assistant in the Department of Economics and the Centre for Research in the Economics of Development (CRED), University of Namur, Rempart de la Vierge 8, 5000 Namur, Belgium (tatiana.goetghebuer@fundp.ac.be).

Karla Hoff is Senior Research Economist at the World Bank, 1818 H Street NW, Washington, DC 20433, USA (khoff@worldbank.org).

Ravi Kanbur is T.H. Lee Professor of World Affairs, International Professor of Applied Economics and Management, and Professor of Economics, Cornell University, 309 Warren Hall, Ithaca, NY 14853-7801, USA (sk145@cornell.edu).

Rachel E. Kranton is Professor of Economics in the Department of Economics, University of Maryland, College Park, MD 20742, USA (kranton@ econ.umd.edu).

Eliana La Ferrara is Associate Professor in the Department of Economics, Università Bocconi, Via Sarfatti 25, 20136 Milano, Italy (eliana.laferrara@ uni-bocconi.it).

Glenn C. Loury is University Professor and Professor of Economics, Boston University, 270 Bay State Road, Boston, MA 02215, USA (gloury@bu.edu).

Jean-Philippe Platteau is Professor in the Department of Economics, and Director of the Centre for Research in the Economics of Development (CRED), University of Namur, Rempart de la Vierge 8, 5000 Namur, Belgium (jean-philippe.platteau@fundp.ac.be).

Debraj Ray is Julius Silver Professor of Economics in the Department of Economics, New York University, 269 Mercer Street, New York, NY 10003, USA (debraj.ray@nyu.edu).

Arijit Sen is Associate Professor of Economics in the School of Social Sciences at Jawaharlal Nehru University, New Delhi 110067, India (senarijit@vsnl.net).

Christopher R. Udry is Henry J. Heinz II Professor of Economics in the Department of Economics and Director of the Economic Growth Center, Yale University, PO Box 208269, New Haven, CT 06520, USA (udry@yale.edu).

Acknowledgments

This book represents the fruit of an unusual collaborative effort among 15 economists. In recent years, there have been notable advances within economics in understanding the role of identity, conformity, generalized morality, social networks and norms, and other moral and social dimensions of individual and group behaviors. In essence, economists working in this nascent field of social economics are taking the other social sciences – anthropology, political science, psychology, and sociology – seriously. Members of this team have contributed greatly to these recent advances, some working mainly on theoretical issues, others focusing on empirical research. This project on "The Moral and Social Dimensions of Microeconomic Behavior In Low-Income Communities" has aimed to advance the economics literature further still in this direction.

Whatever progress we have achieved can be attributed to the extraordinary members of the project team. It has been a tremendous pleasure and honor to work with this exceptionally talented set of researchers. I have learned a great deal from Larry Blume, Sam Bowles, Michael Carter, Joan Esteban, Marcel Fafchamps, Andrew Foster, Karla Hoff, Ravi Kanbur, Rachel Kranton, Eliana La Ferrara, Glenn Loury, Jean-Philippe Platteau, Debraj Ray, and Chris Udry. They had each already earned my admiration for the quality and creativity of their prior research. That admiration grew with the opportunity to work with each of them a bit more closely on this project. To each of my fellow team members I extend my personal, sincere thanks for your enthusiastic and inspiring contributions to the team and to the broader research program reflected in this volume. As the only collection of papers from the whole team – subgroups of us have produced or will soon publish special journal issues and individual team members have presented and published their work widely and prominently – this volume serves as a memorial to an unusually productive and stimulating team.

Credit for the idea behind this project really goes to several non-economists. Nathan Hatch and Mike Hamilton of the University of Notre Dame's Christian Scholars Program invited me to form a team of researchers who might individually and collectively investigate issues at the research frontier in economics within a broader, multi-disciplinary effort they designed to explore "the nature of the human person." Generous funding from The Pew Charitable Trusts made it feasible to craft a talented team and to plan a bold and ambitious agenda. Nathan, Mike, Kurt Berends, who succeeded Mike in directing the Christian Scholars Program, and Linda Bergling, who skillfully handled all the administrative details, provided the crucial support necessary to bring that plan to fruition. This book simply would not exist without the vision and encouragement of the Notre Dame team.

We all benefited from the opportunity to present and discuss these chapters at various gatherings. We first met as a group in May 2001 at Cornell University, then again in May 2002 on the outskirts of Rochester, New York. We subsequently organized conference sessions for sub-teams at the 2002 conference of the University of Oxford's Centre for the Study of African Economies, the 2003 annual meetings of the Association of Christian Economists and the American Agricultural Economics Association, and the 2004 American Economic Association annual meetings. Anita Abraham, Kaushik Basu, Arthur Brooks, Indraneel Dasgupta, Gary Fields, Dean Karlan, Dave Richardson, Erik Thorbecke, and session audiences at those events provided numerous valuable comments. We thank them for their intellectual guidance and generosity.

Organizing those events, this volume and the broader research project required skillful support from Quinn Avery, Joy Learman, Andrea Besley, and Cheryl Mrozowski at Cornell. They have each been invaluable. Janet Hou, Jacqueline Murphy, and Emma Stephens did excellent work in proofreading and copy-editing draft chapters. Jason Frasco and Ethan Feldman built, expanded, and maintained an excellent team web site. The editorial staff at Routledge – Rob Langham, Terry Clague, Mike Wendling, and Taiba Batool – have likewise been most helpful and patient.

In closing, I thank and dedicate this volume to my primary social network and inspiration: my lovely wife Clara, and our children, Brendan, Mary Catherine, Joanna, Julia, and Elizabeth. Their patience with and support of me has made this project possible and worthwhile. They are each a blessing from God, providing an invaluable daily reminder that who we are and what we do depends fundamentally on the identities, communities, groups, and networks we build and maintain, starting with our own families.

1 On the relevance of identities, communities, groups, and networks to the economics of poverty alleviation

Christopher B. Barrett

> Most of the people in the world are poor, so if we knew the economics of being poor we would know much of the economics that really matters.
>
> (T.W. Schultz 1980)

1.1 Why social economics?

As T.W. Schultz asserted in the opening sentence from his 1979 Nobel Lecture, that perhaps the most vexing riddle in economics is why some people remain very poor for long periods of time, and why poverty persists across generations. Canonical growth models do not offer convincing explanations of such patterns because the poor should have every incentive to invest in human and physical capital accumulation and to adopt new technologies to improve their lot. Recent efforts to resolve this riddle largely rely on assumptions about exclusionary mechanisms that restrict the ability of certain groups to finance investments, to enjoy the external economies of scale resulting from the investment of others, to cooperate, or a combination of these. Of course, this trick merely displaces the riddle: why are some people excluded and others not? Conversely, why do some people enjoy access to scarce resources or the efficiency enhancements associated with cooperation whereas others do not?

This book aims to advance the understanding of the economists of such questions by exploring how the social and moral identities of individuals affect their membership in communities, groups, and networks, how those identities and social affiliations affect microeconomic behavior, and how the resulting behaviors affect poverty. Humans do not live in isolation – their behavior depends on the relations that shape their world. Variation in relationships can perhaps lead to predictable variation in behaviors and economic outcomes, which, in turn, affect social relationships through subtle feedback mechanisms. Partly as a consequence, the dynamics of human social interactions and the effects on persistent poverty have become a very active area of economic research.

The link between human relationships and behavior can operate through any of several different pathways. We highlight the effect on preferences, rules, and expectations. Individual preferences are not immutably given *deus ex machina*.

Rather, they adapt within the communities to which these individuals belong. Nor are preferences over exclusively material things. People value social relationships, including deviance or conformity, fairness, integrity, friendship, love, etc., and their behaviors manifest the valorization of the intangible (see, e.g., Henrich *et al.* 2004).

Not only preferences but also the rules and expectations governing individuals' interactions are shaped by formal groups and informal networks, be it in contracting for goods and services, in supporting those who suffer adverse shocks, in communicating potentially valuable information, or other interpersonal phenomena. The "ties that bind" create very real constraints on individual choice.

In affecting preferences, rules, and expectations, social forces thus affect both individuals' incentives and the constraints that they perceive. Individuals care not only about pecuniary rewards, but also about intangibles such as prestige, stigma, and fairness. This has implications as well for prices, incomes and other monetary indices of well-being. Whether by influencing preferences or the constraints faced by individual decision makers, the social and moral milieu in which choice occurs plainly matters, as the chapters in this book illustrate.

Furthermore, outcomes affect individuals' endogenous construction and reconstruction of the social environments in which they place themselves or from which they extricate themselves. By changing the costs and benefits of making or maintaining contacts, economic performance necessarily induces updating of the attributes that define identities and communities and of the formal and informal matching processes that define groups and networks. This feedback between individual and group behavior injects a richness into analysis that is too often absent in social science research based excessively on either methodological individualism or cultural determinism. Durlauf and Young (2001, pp. x–1) identify recent advances in this genre as the start of "a new social economics paradigm . . . [that] holds the promise of providing new insights into social and economic dynamics through the explicit study of the interactions that link individual behavior and group outcomes."

This collection of chapters is distinctive in its common focus on persistent poverty. Each of the contributors applies the tools of the nascent social economics paradigm to that most vexing question of economics: why poverty persists in a world of abundant resources. The chapters thus illustrate how the new insights offered by social economics, might inform and improve the design of policies intended to reduce the incidence and duration of poverty around the world.

In this introductory chapter, I begin by highlighting the broad issues in economics and the social sciences to which this volume is addressed. Then I draw brief thematic connections among the individual chapters. Thanks to a generous grant from The Pew Charitable Trusts, through the Christian Scholars Program at the University of Notre Dame, the team of 15 contributors to this volume held two extended workshops. In the first workshop, we discussed general ideas regarding economists' understanding of the nature of the human person – the organizing theme of each of the eight disciplinary teams organized by Notre Dame's Christian

Scholars Program. In the second, we discussed and critiqued early drafts of the chapters that comprise this volume.

1.2   The broad issues

Economic behavior is embedded in a socio-cultural context, although the discipline of economics has been relatively slow to acknowledge this in its models of human behavior. Textbook models posit individuals with immutable, exogenous preferences that reflect no concern for others. Constraints depend only on endowments, technologies, and markets. Economic theory is too often taken to be truly universal in all of its details, although many of the assumptions fundamental to mainstream theory are socio-culturally specific and lack empirical support elsewhere, perhaps especially in poor communities throughout much of the world.

By studying behaviors in communities where the textbook models do not seem to fit as neatly, the contributors to this volume hope to improve not only the relevance of economic research to poor communities, but also the foundational theory and methods of the discipline. We aim to enhance economists' capacity to understand and explain how individuals perceive and adapt their identities and social affiliations and how these identities and affiliations shape social organization and affect the consumption, production and exchange behaviors that constitute economic life.

This effort echoes other recent advances within economics. Behavioral and experimental economists have made great strides in highlighting the inconsistencies between models of pure rational choice and observed human behavior, emphasizing the role of social norms (e.g., of fairness), bounded rationality and behavioral anomalies in understanding microeconomic behavior (Kagel and Roth 1995; Rabin 1998, 2002; Fehr and Falk 2002). The burgeoning fields of behavioral and experimental economics draw heavily on psychology, remaining tightly focused on individual behavior. This volume builds on the rapidly expanding literature in behavioral and experimental economics but aims specifically to situate economic behavior within human communities. In this sense, the work reflected here links closely to cognate disciplines of anthropology, political science, and sociology and to ongoing debates across the social sciences.[1]

There have been numerous earlier efforts in this direction. For example, non-cooperative game theory has now become a nearly universal language for analyzing the strategic interactions that occur among non-anonymous individuals. Advances in evolutionary game theory have been used by both economists and biologists to try to explain seemingly selfless acts and the maintenance of cooperative equilibria in systems that appear vulnerable to manipulation by self-interested agents. By explicating mechanisms of direct and indirect reciprocity, many studies in this strand of the literature effectively serve "to take the altruism out of altruism" (Axelrod 1984; Frank 1988; Bester and Güth 1998; Nowak and Sigmund 2000). One of the core points of this vein of research is that welfare enhancing, cooperative outcomes can be achieved thanks to the complex web of interrelationships that define real societies.

Formal models of interactions among individuals have likewise been used to explain the exercise of coercive power by one or more agents against others (Akerlof 1976; Basu 1986; Bardhan 1991; Naqvi and Wemhöner 1995). The key insight of the economic literature on coercive power is that networks of more than two agents can endow some individuals with the capacity to covertly coerce others into accepting exchanges that predictably leave them worse off and that they would never voluntarily undertake were the powerful member of the network unable to manipulate third parties.

Another strand of the literature that takes a richer view of human relationships than that traditionally considered in economics is the work on social capital. The literature on social capital, which began with the theoretical work of sociologists James Coleman and Mark Granovetter and economist Glenn Loury, treats social networks and social spillovers as *resources* that affect an individual's ability to obtain an education, secure a job, obtain credit, and enforce contracts. After a decade of intense empirical work in this area, there is today a sense that the social capital literature is taking the wrong path to address a real omission in mainstream economics. The Nobel Laureate Ken Arrow (2000) summarized this concern when he wrote: "The concept of measuring social interaction may be a snare and a delusion. Instead of thinking of more and less, it may be more fruitful to think of the existing social relations as a preexisting network into which new parts of the economy . . . have to be fitted." The contributors to this volume would go one step further, emphasizing that social relations are endogenous and dynamic elements of the social systems that underpin economic behavior. Economists need to study more carefully the microlevel processes that generate demonstrable correlations between particular social configurations and material outcomes – such as income, educational attainment, resilience to shocks, traders' profitability, or propensity to adopt improved technologies. A new frontier of work addresses the question: What makes some social states stable, others unstable and therefore transient?

Our common approach to these issues begins with the observable attributes of individuals, what psychologists label "identity." Collective, shared identities – according to ethnicity, gender, lineage, occupation, race, residential location, wealth status, or some other dimension – create communities. Indeed, the word "community" originates with the Latin *communis*, meaning "shared by all or many." Shared identity can lead to salience. Particular attributes become prominent once a population evinces some critical mass that causes people to sort people using that criterion, whether consciously or unconsciously. This sorting may foster affinity among people, causing them to choose to associate with others sharing similar attributes, whether formally, in groups, or informally, in networks. The absence of shared identities can also affect behavior, leading to alienation and social exclusion.

Because individual identities are both cause and consequence of group affiliation, social networks, and the moral codes associated with groups and networks, identities may co-evolve in ways that make it difficult – and perhaps misleading – to separate individual and social level phenomena. The joint determination of many individual attributes and of the social structures that depend on the affinity and alienation induced by identities makes it difficult to isolate the impact of particular attributes or relations, as emphasized in the burgeoning literature on the empirical analysis of social interactions (Manski 1995; Brock and Durlauf 2000; Manski 2000).

Social identity is multidimensional: an individual can belong to multiple communities, groups, and networks. Interlocking networks and groups may reinforce the alienation of some subpopulations and contribute to the persistent poverty of certain social groups; or they may bridge divides. The multidimensional nature of identity is central to understanding social and economic polarization – who feels affinity for whom and who is alienated from whom – as well as the intensity of these positive and negative relations between individuals.

Two core questions emerge naturally from this formulation. The first concerns the evolution of social organization. How do communities, groups and networks form, evolve, and interact? Why do dysfunctional social relationships emerge and what causes them to persist? How should economists define and measure identities, communities, groups, and networks for the purpose of placing individual behavior in its appropriate social context?

Second, how does social organization affect economic outcomes: incomes, information flow, expenditure patterns, productivity, transfers, contracting forms, technology adoption, etc.? Here, the methodological advance of social economics meets the practical concerns of poverty alleviation and social justice. Does the social organization of individuals matter to the welfare of the poor? Does it affect what policy tools are available to and useful for outsiders who might wish to assist disadvantaged people? This is a much richer approach to understanding how the socio-cultural context affects economic outcomes than the sort of scalar-valued stock concept at the root of much of the current empirical work on social capital. Recent theoretical advances – such as the multi-community social interactions model – derive the membership of communities and the nature of local social capital. This literature demonstrates the possibility that market forces may lead to communities with very different levels of social capital, exacerbating initial inequalities among individuals (Bénabou 1996; Hoff and Sen 2005). The promise of social economics is that by marrying the methodological rigor of the economics toolkit with the insights of empirical anthropologists and sociologists, real progress can be made in uncovering some of the structural mechanisms that lead to persistent poverty.

1.3   Key thematic connections among the chapters

The next 14 chapters tackle these two core questions about the nature and evolution of equilibrium social organization and the consequences for economic outcomes. Several themes appear repeatedly: identity and conflict, social norms, and the nature and formation of groups.

Identity and conflict   Following the seminal work of Esteban and Ray (1994), Akerlof and Kranton (2000), and Platteau (2000), several chapters emphasize the role of social and psychological identities in trapping individuals in poverty. Fang and Loury (Chapter 2), Dasgupta and Kanbur (Chapter 6), Akerlof and Kranton (Chapter 8), and Barrett (Chapter 9) study the emergence of individual identities that critically shape behaviors that subsequently reinforce those identities. Moreover, following the identification-alienation framework introduced by Esteban and Ray (1994), identities by multiple individuals create not only communities but, equally, alienation of individuals and groups from one another, at least partly, on the basis of within-group identities. Such alienation can lead to distinct behavioral equilibria and polarized outcomes. Duclos, Esteban, and Ray (Chapter 3) explore the conceptualization and measurement of these patterns in unprecedented depth, illustrating their new measure through the empirical study of polarization in 21 OECD economies.

The economic outcomes that result partly from social identification may in turn become an important dimension of identity, reinforcing patterns of alienation and identification. The key insight of this subset of chapters is thus that the feedback mechanism between identity and individual and group behavior can generate multiple equilibria. The chapters consider a variety of outcomes and social contexts: poor performance in school, low rates of adoption of improved production technologies, the limited provision of local public goods, and others. Although such outcomes are Pareto-inferior to available alternatives, the behaviors that lead to undesirable outcomes can prove individually rational given the reinforcing feedback loop created by the social context in which individuals make behavioral choices. The phenomena that these chapters describe cannot be easily explained using conventional economic models.

Ethnic, racial, and religious conflict is an especially troubling manifestation of the feedback between identity and behavior and the consequences of resulting socio-economic polarization. Notions of identity are shaped by economic outcomes, such as wealth distributions, that affect subpopulations' affinity for others in their community and alienation from those in other communities – where communities are defined by shared, endogenous identities one can distinguish by some measure of social distance. Dasgupta and Kanbur (Chapter 6) show how polarization can breed inter-group conflict, using a different technique to reinforce points made previously by Esteban and Ray (1999). Violence and social instability can result from group enforcement of identities shared with only some others within a population. One of the subtle subthemes to those chapters is the prospective importance of meta-communal public goods – e.g., national identities forged around palpable symbols of national unity, such as an Olympic team, a flag or a national anthem – in reducing multidimensional social distance and thereby helping to bridge communal divides.

Social norms   A second core theme of this volume concerns the emergence of social norms that can perpetuate absolute and relative deprivation. Social norms and other conventions emerge from the aggregate behavior of individuals myopically influenced by their social identities. Blume (Chapter 4) and Bowles (Chapter 5) use evolutionary game theoretic techniques to study the evolution of social norms and the persistence of inequality, respectively. They show how social interactions can lead to durable community norms, some of which may prove exclusionary for some subpopulations. Such norms reflect mutual best responses conditional on individuals' beliefs about others' behavior. There typically exist, however, many possible equilibria, making it difficult to explain the emergence of any particular one and suggesting that there exist multiple tipping points that can lead to rapid shifts between states, what ecologists call "punctuated equilibria." Both Blume and Bowles emphasize that coordination failures need not result from individual myopia and that low-level equilibria can persist for long periods, even if agents are patient.

Carter and Castillo (Chapter 11) empirically document some of the claims that Blume and Bowles advance. Using an unusual data set that blends conventional survey data with experimental results that gauge individual survey respondents' adherence to norms of altruism and trust, Carter and Castillo test whether those characteristics help explain the differential recovery of Honduran households from the damage wrought by Hurricane Mitch. They find strong evidence of persistent social norms of reciprocal and altruistic transfers reinforced by endogenous social interactions. Moreover, these social safety nets favor a subset of relatively privileged households. Their analysis warns against the naive belief that community norms of mutual assistance are equally accessible to all.

Goetghebuer and Platteau (Chapter 15) offer a fascinating account of the feedback mechanism between identity, group membership, and resource allocation in rural Peru. Under traditional property rights regimes, access to land in their study site in rural Peru is reasonably uniform and guaranteed by the social identity that makes one a part of a distinct group, while use of corporate assets, such as land, validates group membership. There results a self-reinforcing equilibrium. Goetghebuer and Platteau study the endogenous evolution of these feedback effects in the face of increasing land scarcity and emerging economic options that shift the institutional mechanisms underpinning resource allocation. Individualization of land tenure and the rise of town-based employment requiring migration combine to reduce both the egalitarian norms that traditionally characterized land allocation and younger adults' identification with their lineage and community, perhaps especially among poorer families. Thus identities, groups and resource allocation mechanisms coevolve and may do so differentially across economic classes.

Hoff and Sen (Chapter 7) study another mechanism through which identities and networks can lead to persistent poverty. They develop a simple but elegant model of a kin system interacting with an expanding market economy. Members can face barriers to entering the market economy, barriers that emanate from the incentives of kin members to engage in workplace nepotism and other sorts of in-kind transfers to meet kin obligations. Facing barriers to good jobs, good housing, or other crucial means to economic advancement, a kin member's response may be to demonstrably sever his kin ties, if he can, in order to improve his modern sector opportunities. That possibility can lead the kin group to respond in a perverse way. If the kin group foresees that it will lose some of its most productive members as the economy opens up, it may take collective action to erect exit barriers. If that occurs, then the kin system – that was once a beneficial arrangement – will become a poverty trap, at least for its most productive members.

The formation and consequences of groups   A third theme concerns the formation and consequences of social aggregates, such as informal farmer networks, trader networks, and self-help groups. Udry and Conley (Chapter 10) show why "households," "firms," and other familiar units of analysis in economics may be inappropriate units of analysis in poor rural villages around the world. Using an unusually rich data set from Ghana, Udry and Conley demonstrate that finance, information, labor, and land flow through social networks that often cleave households. An individual's access to resources is typically conditioned by the network(s) to which she/he belongs, and network-mediated access is typically non-transferable even within nuclear households. The interconnectedness and complementarities among different functional networks (e.g., for information, credit, insurance, etc.) can magnify the importance of each individual link (e.g., for information). Udry and Conley make the case for studying the broad set of networks in poor rural villages, although there remain daunting identification challenges inherent in isolating networks from one another for empirical analysis.

Several other chapters offer strong evidence of the effects on economic performance of group and network membership. Fafchamps (Chapter 12) studies agricultural traders in three African nations (Benin, Madagascar, and Malawi). He finds that individual attributes, such as gender, ethnicity or religion, matter less to access to credit and to information – both key predictors of performance – than do the networks to which a trader belongs. Although his study takes the network structure for granted, Fafchamps' findings suggest that it is the relationships one purposefully builds and maintains – and not the latent relationships prospectively available due to particular shared identities – that may matter most to economic behavior and performance. Fafchamps (2004) makes the broader case that in developing and transition economies with only embryonic legal systems and considerable production risk, markets can be most usefully understood as personal networks that link firms, making possible relational contracting.

Foster (Chapter 13) looks at the determinants of altruism by studying the nutritional status of women in rural Bangladesh, paying careful attention to the biological relationship between the woman and other household residents, and also to the potential selection bias arising from joint residence decisions. Foster finds not only that genetic relationships matter – for example, daughters-in-law fare less well than women biologically related to household heads – but also that individuals care differentially about family members with whom they do and do not live, even controlling for the co-residence decision. In these data, it does not appear true that distance makes the heart grow fonder. These results speak to long-standing concerns about the consequences of patrilocal residence traditions for rural women who face social constraints on activity and mobility.

La Ferrara (Chapter 14) shows how the organization and performance of self-help groups in the slums of Nairobi, Kenya, vary according to the social composition of the group, and how these, in turn, affect the incomes of members. She finds that greater within-group heterogeneity tends to lead to less specialized division of labor and less use of sanctioning mechanisms against free riding behavior. These findings reinforce the point made by others – e.g., Barrett (Chapter 9) and Chwe (2001) – that homophilous groups and networks – i.e., groups whose members possess similar attributes – are more likely to foster inter-household cooperation and social efficiency in the absence of institutional structures expressly designed to manage heterogeneity.

1.4   On social economics and the economics of poverty alleviation

We thus return to the question that opened this introduction: why should scholars and practitioners concerned about poverty reduction pay attention to social economics? What can emerging research in the new social economics paradigm contribute to the practice of poverty reduction? The chapters in this volume point to at least five distinct contributions.

First, the chapters underscore the importance of social context. In many settings, it is essential to consider the identities, communities, groups and networks at play if one seeks to understand the motivations behind individuals' choices regarding the allocation of scarce resources and the standards of living that result. Economic policy operates within a complex social and moral context that varies across cultures and over time. Models are necessarily useful simplifications of a complex reality – as the statistician George Box famously declared, "all models are wrong, some are useful" – but the the reductionism that is useful for modeling one place and time may prove indefensible in another. The research in this volume underscores the caution *caveat utisor*, "user beware!," against injudicious application of models developed in one context to alternative settings.

A second, key implication of social economics is that to make policy recommendations, it is generally important to understand how identities, communities, groups and networks may change in response to interventions. Having recognized the apparent association between social capital measures and economic performance, many development agencies have been aggressively seeking out groups and networks in developing countries, and even creating new groups and networks in the hope that this will stimulate pro-poor growth. Social economics raises important questions about the likelihood of success of ventures that attempt to stimulate the emergence of new groups, versus those aimed at reinforcing preexisting associational structures among the poor. This is a new research frontier about which we still know too little to make policy recommendations with confidence.

This raises a third and closely related point. Although it is true that social groups can sometimes resolve market failures such as imperfect contract enforcement and limited access to insurance and credit, and can thereby facilitate investment and growth, perhaps especially for the poor, so too can groups prove exclusionary, throwing sand in the wheels of progress for excluded individuals and groups. In extreme cases, exclusionary processes turn violent, with the poor suffering a disproportionate share of the resulting hardship, as vividly manifest in recurrent inter-ethnic and inter-faith violence in sub-Saharan Africa and South Asia in recent years.

Fourth, given the self-reinforcing nature of many social groupings and norms, there can be great value in efforts to create meta-identities that bridge social divides and to break down informal and formal exclusionary mechanisms that impede cooperation and accumulation within the poorer segments of a society. Such exclusionary mechanisms are essential to the existence of poverty traps (Carter and Barrett 2005).

Fifth, because social organization is typically characterized by multiple equilibria, small changes in economic conditions can lead to dramatic changes in the behavior of and membership in groups and networks. In systems that appear to function reasonably well this strengthens the case for public safety nets to ensure that covariate shocks associated with natural and human disasters do not so perturb existing social systems as to undermine community mechanisms, such as informal networks that provide critical mutual insurance in the face of household-specific, idiosyncratic shocks.

The application of the emerging tools of social economics to the vexing problem of persistent poverty remains in its infancy. Much remains to be learned. The chapters in this volume help to point the way toward a new era of economic research that maintains greater fidelity to the rich socio-cultural fabric of developing countries and to underprivileged communities in rich nations, and in so doing yields practical advice to policymakers and practitioners struggling to meet the challenge of poverty reduction.

Acknowledgments

I thank Joan Esteban, Karla Hoff, Eliana La Ferrara, and Debraj Ray for helpful comments on an earlier draft. This work was generously supported by The Pew Charitable Trusts and by the United States Agency for International Development (USAID) through grants No. LAG-A-00-96-90016-00 to the BASIS CRSP and HFM-A-00-01-00132-00 to the Strategies and Analyses for Growth and Access (SAGA) cooperative agreement from Africa Bureau. These views, and any errors therein, are purely my own.

Note

1 See, e.g., the fascinating January 2004 special issue of *Journal of Economic Behavior and Organization* on "Evolution and Altruism," featuring a target article by the anthropologist Joseph Henrich and a series of comments by experts from a range of fields.

References

Akerlof, G. (1976) "The economics of caste and the rat race and other woeful tales," *Quarterly Journal of Economics*, 90: 599–617.

Akerlof, G. and R. Kranton (2000) "Economics and identity," *Quarterly Journal of Economics*, 115: 715–53.

Arrow, K.J. (2000) "Observations on social capital," in P. Dasgupta and I. Serageldin (eds), *Social Capital: A Multifaceted Perspective*, Washington, DC: World Bank.

Axelrod, R. (1984) *The Evolution of Cooperation*, New York: Basic Books.

Bardhan, P. (1991) "On the concept of power in economics," *Economics and Politics*, 3: 265–77.

Basu, K. (1986) "One kind of power," *Oxford Economic Papers*, 38: 259–82.

Bénabou, R.J. (1996) "Equity and efficiency in human capital investment: the local connection," *Review of Economic Studies*, 63 (2): 237–64.

Bester, H. and W. Güth (1998) "Is altruism evolutionarily stable?" *Journal of Economic Behavior and Organization*, 34: 193–209.

Brock, W. and S. Durlauf (2000) "Interactions-based models," in J. Heckman and E. Leamer (eds), *Handbook of Econometrics, Volume 5*, Amsterdam: North-Holland.

Carter, M.R. and C.B. Barrett (2005) "The economics of poverty traps and persistent poverty: an asset-based approach," working paper.

Chwe, M.S.-Y. (2001) *Rational Ritual: Culture, Coordination, and Common Knowledge*, Princeton, NJ: Princeton University Press.

Durlauf, S.N. and H.P. Young (eds) (2001) *Social Dynamics*, Washington, DC: Brookings Institution Press.

Esteban, J. and D. Ray (1994) "On the measurement of polarization," *Econometrica* 62: 819–52.

—— (1999) "Conflict and distribution," *Journal of Economic Theory*, 87: 379–415.

Fafchamps, M. (2004) *Market Institutions in Sub-Saharan Africa: Theory and Evidence*, Cambridge, MA: MIT Press.

Fehr, E. and A. Falk (2002) "Psychological foundations of incentives," *European Economic Review*, 46: 687–724.

Frank, R.H. (1988) *Passions Within Reason*, New York: Norton.

Henrich, J., R. Boyd, S. Bowles, C. Camerer, E. Fehr, and H. Gintis (2004) *Foundations of Human Sociality: Economic Experiments and Ethnographic Evidence from Fifteen Small-Scale Societies*, Oxford: Oxford University Press.

Hoff, K. and A. Sen (2005) "Homeownership, community interactions, and segregation," *American Economic Review*, in press.

Kagel, J.H. and A.E. Roth (eds) (1995) *Handbook of Experimental Economics*, Princeton, NJ: Princeton University Press.

Manski, C. (1995) *Identification Problems in the Social Sciences*, Cambridge, MA: Harvard University Press.

—— (2000) "Economic analysis of social interactions," *Journal of Economic Perspectives*, 14: 115–36.

Naqvi, N. and F. Wemhöner (1995) "Power, coercion, and the games landlords play," *Journal of Development Economics*, 47: 191–205.

Nowak, M.A. and K. Sigmund (2000) "Shrewd investments," *Science* 288: 819–20.

Platteau, J.-P. (2000) *Institutions, Social Norms, and Economic Development*, Amsterdam: Harwood Academic Publishers.

Rabin, M. (1998) "Psychology and economics," *Journal of Economic Literature*, 36: 11–46.

—— (2002) "A perspective on psychology and economics," *European Economic Review*, 46: 657–85.

Schultz, T.W. (1980) "Nobel lecture: the economics of being poor," *Journal of Political Economy*, 88: 639–51.

2 Toward an economic theory of dysfunctional identity

Hanming Fang and Glenn C. Loury

2.1 Introduction

Rigorous thinking about the nature and sources of human identity, and about the links between identity and culture, is vitally important for understanding a variety of significant social problems. Students of the subject have pondered why people embrace one identity rather than another, and how their convictions in this regard affect their economic performance. Numerous, conflicting conceptions of identity can be found in the literature. Psychologists draw a fundamental distinction between *social* identity, which deals with how an individual is perceived and categorized by others, and *personal* identity (sometimes called "ego identity"), which invokes a person's answer to the question, "Who am I?"[1] Goffman (1963) describes an individual's social identity as "the categories and attributes anticipated by others during routines of social intercourse in established settings."[2] Social psychologists also use the concept of *collective identity* to ask how a group of distinct individuals might come to embrace a common answer to the "Who am I?" question, and what follows from their having done so.[3] Thinking about *collective* identity leads naturally to a reflection on how social interaction influences the formation and maintenance of personal identities which, in turn, leads naturally into a discussion of "culture."

This chapter explores some connections between identity, culture, and economic functioning. In essence, we will do three things here: propose what we believe to be a novel definition of identity; make precise a sense in which the collective identity of a group of people can be said to be *dysfunctional*; and, describe a specific mechanism of social interaction through which rational individuals could nevertheless choose to embrace a way of thinking about themselves that inhibits their economic functioning.

We are motivated in this pursuit by the commonsense observation that – whether looking within or between countries – economic backwardness, multi-generational poverty, and chronic underdevelopment seem to be connected in some way to the "culture" of those who are disadvantaged, and especially to what may be regarded as their "dysfunctional" notions about identity. Thus, backward groups within many societies (inner-city blacks in the US, low caste people in India, or gypsies (i.e., Roma) in Europe) have been said to languish because they embrace a "culture of poverty," (Banfield 1970), or because they are obsessed with their own victimhood (McWhorter 2000), or due to their adopting an "oppositional identity" (Ogbu 2003). These culture–identity orientations are said to promote economically self-limiting behaviors (regarding education, savings, or occupational choice), and to cause disadvantaged people to "dis-identify" with success in their respective societies.[4] Often, such conjectures about the root causes of "backwardness" are stated imprecisely and supported only by anecdotal evidence. It thus seems desirable to have a more formal way to talk about how an "identity" could be "dysfunctional." We are taking a small step in that direction with this chapter. It is also a commonplace that authors trumpeting the cultural roots of economic backwardness treat "culture" as exogenous. One goal of this exploratory analysis is to consider how strategic interactions among agents in particular environments might incline them to adopt one or another common stance on certain identity questions. In this limited way, at least, we are striving to make "culture" endogenous.

Given the a priori plausibility of their connections to growth and inequality, economists have recently made some interesting attempts to model concepts like "identity" and "culture."[5] Generally speaking, this literature takes what might be called a utilitarian approach to the subject. That is, choices are to be utility-maximizing, but a non-standard utility function is posited – one that has been augmented to incorporate the value of conforming to the norms and expectations associated with a decision-maker's social position. A leading example of this approach is found in the work of Akerlof and Kranton (2000), who model "identity" as a combination of "role" and "prescription." Society is partitioned into a set of "types" – occupants of the various roles. These types have identity-influenced preferences which are biased in favor of certain actions – the ones most consistent with the prescriptions attached to their roles. Both roles and prescriptions are exogenous, given by history. Akerlof and Kranton (2002) go on to delineate a set of role/prescription pairs characteristic of a particular venue of social interactions (secondary schools), and to study how the emergent behaviors of role occupants operating in that venue reflect the prescriptive actions associated with their roles. One limitation of this approach is that, while it explores the implications of individuals having adopted certain identities, it offers no account of how and why people come to have the identities they have. Thus, it cannot guide an assessment of the *efficiency* of people's identity choices.

In contrast, our proposed theory is driven by cognitive, not utilitarian considerations. Building on ideas about racial classification, social cognition, and identity introduced in Loury (2002, chapter 2), and following the categorical approach to cognition pioneered in Fryer and Jackson (2003), we go on to consider the problem of *auto-cognition* – how people see themselves. We ground our approach to identity (and thus, to "culture") in the elemental notions of "categories" and "narratives." Our core idea is that, at its root, personal identity is all about self-perception and self-representation. We are interested in choices about identity made by rational agents anticipating subsequent interaction, who expect their payoffs from this interaction to vary with their identity commitments. Technically, we study a two-stage game in which identity choices are made in the first stage, and agents engage (more or less remuneratively) in some economic interactions in the second stage. Within this framework, we say that a *collective identity* has been adopted when, in subgame perfect equilibrium, individuals make the same first-stage choices. We are particularly interested in showing how a group of people might come to embrace an inefficient, or *dysfunctional* identity.

Using the psychologist's terminology, then, ours is a chapter about *personal not social* identity – albeit in a multi-agent, interactive setting. We formally explore how people with ongoing economic relations might arrive at an answer to the "Who am I?" question. We will say that a person's answer to this question constitutes a "narrative" about personal history – i.e., a summing up of all the events a person has experienced. Yet, for people to tell us who they are, their elaborate stories must be projected onto simpler categories of self-description. A personal history is, necessarily, a *very* complex object. To convey it, an agent must project her richly variegated experiences onto a relatively few descriptors using the limited cognitive resources available.

In the model to be presented here, agents need to "talk" about their personal experiences before realizing potential gains from trade. How they elect to represent themselves to one another affects the productivity of their subsequent economic interactions. Because cognitive resources are limited, they make their representations in a simplified form. An agent's "identity" is the specific method she uses to implement such acts of selective self-representation. A group's "collective identity" is any self-representional mode adopted in common by (most of) the agents in that group. *So, for us, identity choice amounts to a decision about how to articulate a rich life history while using only the limited vocabulary available to a person for conveying who she might be. It is, in other words, the embrace of a way to make selective generalizations about personal experience.* Such generalizing acts unavoidably highlight and retain, for future reference only, that which is most salient. Our "categories" reflect the range of things an agent might take to be salient about herself. Our "narratives" are what results when a complex personal history is mapped onto the categories.[6] These categories, and the narratives to which they lead, are the building blocks of our theory of collective identity. This is potentially a powerful approach, we think, because people who embrace a common identity are predicted to recall their experiences in similar ways, to sort their historical data among the same bins, so to speak. This implication would appear to be testable by direct experimental methods.[7]

To illustrate, consider some hypothetical identity narratives: "I'm an immigrant who came up the hard way"; "I'm a child of the 1960's, and proud of it"; "I'm a working class white male angry at the world for not feeling my pain"; "I'm a tough-minded professional woman determined not to take a back seat to any less qualified man"; "I'm an intellectual who grew up in poverty, unlike those silver-spoon-fed intellectuals who love to talk about the poor but know nothing of them"; "I'm a black man who likes to have sex with other men, but I'm not a 'sissy,' and neither am I 'gay'." (Denizet-Lewis 2003). Each of these hypothetical people – in responding to the question, "Who am I?" – offers us a selective account. Having embraced certain categories of self-representation, they offer a "narrative" about personal experience using their chosen categories. These narratives are their ways of perceiving and representing themselves – their "modalities of self-awareness," if you will.

The key intuition that we strive to capture in our model is that identity choice is a social event, not merely the expression of individuals' values or preferences. In particular, people who interact frequently may end up embracing similar categories of self-representation because they think this leaves them better placed to manage their collective action problems. When this is so, different contexts of social interaction can foster different equilibrium identity configurations, and agents interacting within relatively closed social networks may be inclined to embrace the same or similar identities. But, not all common categorical maps (collective identities) are created equal. Some may be superior to others, in terms of the quality of the interactions to which they give rise. In what follows we show how a "bad" (dysfunctional, self-destructive, victim-based, alienated, oppositional, anti-system) collective identity can be sustained in equilibrium for one group of people and not another, notwithstanding the fact that the "values" of people in the two groups are similar. And, we illustrate why it can be difficult to shift such a problematic pattern of personal identifications using only a marginal intervention: beneficial tacit arrangements may have evolved among the agents, the viability of which turns on their embrace in common of the prevailing identity convention.

We will say that a *dysfunctional collective identity* has been affirmed when an alternative configuration of self-representations exists that would leave everyone better off, and yet no agent wants to embrace any alternative so long as the others with whom she routinely interacts are expected to adhere to the dysfunctional scheme.

In making the arguments to follow, we are inspired in a general way by the distinguished cultural anthropologist, Mary Douglas (2004). Her brilliant essay, "Traditional Culture – Let's Hear No More About It," includes (among many gems!) the following observation, which could readily serve as an epigraph for this chapter:

> Cultural solutions to coordination problems cost time and resources, and . . . need to be grounded in regular personal interaction. Here are two partners who habitually work together, they rely on each other over their lifetimes and help each other in crises, often at personal cost. How does culture enable them to maintain their impressive solidarity? By organizing things so that the benefits pile up on the side of trust. This involves investing personal and political relations with value, such as family, or monarchy; it uses shame to put individuals under heavy obligations of reciprocity; it builds sanctions around the idea of honor and probity; it requires proofs of loyalty to kin, such as wildly ostentatious weddings and funerals to which all kinsfolk must be invited. It controls envy by redistributive institutions which disperse private accumulations and prevent great disparities of wealth. All of this reduces incentives, which is admittedly incompatible with development.

2.2   The model

2.2.1   The basic setup

The formal model we are about to study has three essential features: agents can gain from trading with one another to an extent that depends on what they commonly know about the state of the world. Each agent has some private information about that state. And, by deciding *ex ante* what kind of "face to show to the world," agents determine what features of their private information become public. In this context we propose to study the emergence of dysfunctional collective identities.

More specifically, we consider a simple two-agent, two-stage game of identity choice and repeated risk sharing. Let the agents be indexed by $i = 1, 2$. In the first stage of play each agent makes a once-for-all choice of "identity." In every one of the infinite sequence of periods that constitutes the second stage, the agents receive random income endowments which they might agree to share with one another. We focus initially on what happens in the second stage. Let $y \in Y$ be an endowment realization. We assume that Y is a finite[8] set of non-negative real numbers representing the possible levels of receipt in each period of some perishable consumption good. Because endowments cannot be stored, the sum of agents' consumptions in any period cannot exceed the sum of that period's receipts. Moreover, agents will consume all net resources available to them in each period. To keep things simple, suppose that endowments are independent and identically distributed, both across agents and across periods. Let $p(y)$ be the probability that the endowment y is realized, so: $p(y) > 0$, and $\sum_{y \in Y} p(y) = 1$.

Thus, we have a dynamic game in two stages, with the second stage extending over an infinite sequence of periods. We assume that the agents play non-cooperatively, and that their first-stage identity choices are common knowledge when they enter the second stage. The time line of the model is as follows: before all interactions start, both agents choose their identities. After observing each other's choices in this regard, they engage in an infinitely repeated risk-sharing interaction. We adopt subgame perfection as an equilibrium concept. When agents make a common choice in the first stage of an equilibrium path of play, we think of this as their *collective identity*.

Agents derive utility from consumption over the course of the second stage. They are risk averse, and their identical preferences are additively separable across periods. Indeed, we assume that they are the expected discounted utility maximizers in the second stage, and that they discount the future at a common, constant rate, $\delta < 1$. We denote the utility function by $u: R_+ \to R$, and assume that $u(\cdot)$ is continuous, three-times differentiable, and satisfies (on the relevant range): $u' > 0$, and $u'' < 0$. (We shall see that the sign of u''' figures significantly in the analysis.) This is all we shall have to say about the agents' "tastes" or "values" in this chapter on identity. Note well: in our formulation, agents do not derive utility from their "identities" as such.

Given these preferences, consumption fluctuations are undesirable. So, gains from trade are available to the agents if they can arrange to make interpersonal income transfers in an ongoing manner. This is their collective action problem. Because their second-stage interactions are repeated, by making future dealings contingent on current behavior, agents can exert leverage to enforce compliance with a variety of alternative transfer arrangements. We might even want to think of them as embracing some *custom* or *tradition* in regard to their risk-sharing behavior. Whatever the interpretation, a *risk-sharing arrangement* is defned to be any agreement obligating the agents to make and receive interpersonal transfers to and from one another in some specified manner. We will study some ways that agents' choices about identity affect their risk-sharing prospects.

Before doing so, let us discuss how identity is to be represented in the model. Imagine that the endowment realizations are private information in each period, but that a set of "indicators" is available through use of which an agent can publicly signal her endowment. Let $x \in X$ denote a possible signal. The set of all available signals, X, is a finite collection of indicators, with $|X| \ll |Y|$. (That is, to capture our view that there are many fewer indicators than there are income states, we think of X as being a much smaller set than Y.) Moreover, while the $y \in Y$ are simply numbers – reflecting various levels of the endowment, the $x \in X$ can be more abstract objects – reflecting, for instance, various modes of self-presentation, alternative facial expressions, distinct demeanors, or different verbal cues. To capture our position that it is practically infeasible for an agent to fully describe all aspects of her experience, we require that in every second-stage period each agent makes a public "representation" about her income, $y \in Y$, by "announcing" an indicator, $x \in X$.

We stress that the making of these announcements is not, strictly speaking, a strategic act. We have in mind a situation where, once agents enter the second stage, the signals they emit about their endowments are given off involuntarily, according to some formula or "code" that was adopted by the agent in the first stage of play. It is true that in our model the modes of self-presentation ultimately settled upon by agents do, indeed, emerge from their strategic interactions in the first stage. But, when acting out these behavioral commitments in the second stage the agents ought not to be thought of as engaging in goal-oriented behavior. Rather than trying to take advantage of a risk-sharing arrangement by giving a misleading report, we envision these agents encountering one another during the normal course of their social interactions and, in the context of such encounters, being unable to avoid bearing imperfect witness to their current period's endowment realization. An agent's "identity" in this world is simply her chosen modality for reacting in public to her private (income) experiences.

Accordingly, a function mapping the set of incomes *onto* the set of indicators, $C: Y \to X$, is to be called a *code*. In the first stage of play, agents simultaneously commit themselves to a code. That is, they adopt what might be called a "mode of self-presention" which determines how they publicly react to their privately observed income realizations throughout the second stage. One can think of the agents as using these indicators to construct a "narrative" about their (income) experience. This is what "identity" means in our model. Their behaviors in this regard bind the agents to noisily signal their respective income realizations to one another in a particular manner.

Finally, and this is the key step in our analysis, we posit that any (implicit) income-sharing arrangement adopted by the agents in the second stage must be implemented solely in terms of these "income narratives." That is, consumption smoothing transfers between them can depend only on what is common knowledge between them – namely, their indicators, not their endowment realizations. So, resources move from the one with signal x to the one with signal $\tilde{x}$, but never from the one with income y to the one with income $\tilde{y}$. Intuitively – given the stationary, symmetric, i.i.d. environment that has been assumed – an ideal second-stage risk-sharing arrangement would move resources in each period from the higher-income (y_1, say) to the lower-income (y_2) agent, according to the formula: $t = \hat{T}(y_1, y_2)$, under which transfers come as close as possible to equalizing consumptions, subject to the constraint that the higher-income agent always has an incentive to make the transfer. However, this ideal arrangement is not feasible in our world because the endowment realizations (y_1, y_2) are not publicly observed. Instead, resource flows between agents must be a function of their announced indicators: $t = T(x_1, x_2)$. And, because the indicators are noisy signals of the incomes, a code-constrained income transfer agreement $T(\cdot, \cdot)$ can never perform as well as the full-information ideal, $\hat{T}(\cdot, \cdot)$.[9] How well the code-mediated sharing arrangements actually do perform depends, in a manner to be investigated thoroughly in what follows, on the identity codes embraced by the agents at the first stage.[10]

We do not wish to allow our agents to adopt every conceivable code. In what follows, we assume that only the codes satisfying a property we call *monotonicity* can be considered. For reasons that will become clear, it is desirable that the signaling process preserve the natural order of the endowments. Yet, although the set of possible endowment realizations can be ordered in the natural way, there is in general no meaningful sense in which one indicator (a facial expression or tone of voice, e.g.) is "larger" than another. Monotonicity is the requirement that the sets $\{C^{-1}(x): x \in X\}$ respect the natural ordering on Y in the following sense:

Definition 1. *A code* $C: Y \rightarrow X$ *is* monotonic *if, for every* $\{y, y', y''\} \subset Y$: $C(y) = C(y')$ *and* $\text{Min}\{y, y'\} < y'' < \text{Max}\{y, y'\}$ *implies* $C(y'') = C(y)$.

So, if a code is monotonic then there is a way to assign numbers to indicators such that higher numbers invariably connote higher endowments.

Let C_i denote the first-stage choice of a (monotonic)[11] code by agent i. We will refer to the pair (C_1, C_2) as a *code configuration*. As discussed, a *risk-sharing arrangement* is a way to transfer resources between agents, which depends on what they have to "say" to each other about their incomes, not the incomes themselves. And, such an arrangement is *feasible under a given code configuration* if it can be supported as a subgame perfect equilibrium continuation for the infinitely repeated interactions in the second stage. Given that codes are fixed once and for all at the start of the second stage, that the maximal punishment available for a deviation from any proposed arrangement is (obviously) a reversion to autarky, and that random endowments are i.i.d. across agents and periods, no generality is lost by restricting attention to period-stationary risk-sharing arrangements.[12] In light of the assumed discounting, if no one-shot deviation from a proposed arrangement is beneficial, taking the ensuing punishment into account, then neither can any finite or infinite sequence of deviations be beneficial. Now, let $t \in \Re$ denote a (possibly negative) transfer from agent 1 to agent 2.[13] Reflecting the discussion to this point, we introduce the following formal definitions:

Definition 2. *A* risk-sharing arrangement *is a period-stationary function,* $T: X^2 \rightarrow \Re$, *such that whenever the agents' signals are* (x_1, x_2), *the income transfer between agents is given by:* $t = T(x_1, x_2)$.

Definition 3. *A risk-sharing arrangement* T *is* feasible under a given code configuration *if, for both agents* $i = 1, 2$, *in every second-stage period and for all possible income realizations* $(y_1, y_2) \in Y \times Y$, *no net gain is anticipated for a one-shot deviation from the arrangement that is followed by a reversion to autarky.*

It is worth a moment's reflection at this point on what the model's primitives are supposed to be capturing about the contexts where identity choice occurs. There are four primitives here: the utility function, the discount factor, the set of available signals, and the distribution of random endowments. Using the linguistic conventions of economics, the first two reflect the agents' "tastes," and the last two their "opportunities." As may already be clear, what is most important about the utility function is its degree of risk averse, and how this varies with the level of consumption. The more risk averse are the agents, the greater is their stake in second-stage interactions. The rate of discount in repeated game models usually reflects factors like relationship stability and elapsed time between encounters. Here it is more natural to think of this parameter as capturing the density, or the degree of closure, of the social network mediating agents' second-stage interactions. That is, $\delta \approx 1$ can be interpreted to mean that their encounters are quite frequent because their network is quite dense. Finally, the importance of identity choice varies inversely with the extent to which the available signals can serve as good proxies for the actual endowments. If the set X is quite "small" relative to the set Y, and if the endowments are very noisy, then "wrong" identity choices will have grave consequences. We illustrate the significance of these parameters later in the chapter when we present a numerical comparative statics analysis of the following example.

2.2.2 *An example: the case* $|X| = 2$

To illustrate these ideas, and for the sake of concreteness, we now introduce a simple example to which we shall have occasion to refer throughout this chapter. This example posits that only two indicators are available: $X = \{B, G\}$. So, each second-stage period involves the agents involuntarily signaling to one another, in effect, whether that period's endowment realization has been "good" or "bad." Subsequent transfers between the agents must be based on these binary signals.

This special case is already sufficiently rich to capture the key tradeoff at work in our model. With $|X| = 2$, to choose a code, C, is necessarily to partition the endowment space into realizations with "good" and with "bad" signals: $Y = C^{-1}(B) \cup C^{-1}(G)$. Moreover, monotonic codes are always of the following threshold form: For some $y^* \in Y$, $C(y) = B$ if and only if $y \leq y^*$. To choose a code is thus to decide both about *the frequency of* and *the disparity between* high and low endowment states. There are good reasons to think that the decentralized choices of self-interested agents in this regard will generally not be Pareto efficient. That is, there are good reasons to suppose that the identity configurations emergent in decentralized equilibrium will generally be dysfunctional.

To see the key tradeoff at work here, the following two observations are useful: First, notice that the more widely disparate are the agents' endowment states associated with a given indicator pair, the more profitable are their risk-sharing trades conditional on those signals. Second, observe that the more frequent are the encounters between unequally endowed agents, the greater are their opportunities to engage in profitable risk sharing. Hence, two traits of a code configuration – which we refer to as "mismatch frequency" and "endowment disparity" – are socially desirable. When $|X| = 2$, both traits are simultaneously determined by the choice for each agent of a dividing line between "good" and "bad" endowments, y_i^*. Therefore, in the neighborhood of an optimal choice, one of these desiderata is being traded off against the other at the margin.

2.2.2.1   Three endowment realizations

To begin a more detailed discussion of the case $|X| = 2$, suppose further that only three endowment realizations are possible: $y \in Y = \{l, m, h\}, l < m < h$. In this circumstance, we will denote the endowment probabilities $p(y)$ by p_l, p_m, and p_h, respectively, where $\sum_{k \in \{l,m,h\}} p_k = 1$. A code is simply a map, $C: \{l, m, h\} \rightarrow \{G, B\}$. Under monotonicity, and without further loss of generality, we can restrict attention to the codes, C^P (for "pessimistic") and C^O (for "optimistic"), where

$$C^P(l) = B, \quad C^P(m) = B, \quad C^P(h) = G$$

and

$$C^O(l) = B, \quad C^O(m) = G, \quad C^O(h) = G.$$

Thus, only three code configurations are possible in this two-person society: both are "pessimists" $[\langle C^P, C^P \rangle]$, both "optimists" $[\langle C^O, C^O \rangle]$, or the codes are mixed $[\langle C^P, C^O \rangle$ or $\langle C^O, C^P \rangle]$. In each second stage period the agents' incomes $y_i \in \{l, m, h\}$ are mapped to their signals $x_i \in \{B, G\}$ via one of the two codes, so

$$x_i = C_i(y_i), \quad \text{for } C_i \in \{C^P, C^O\}, \ i \in \{1, 2\}.$$

Risk-sharing transfers are then carried out in each period according to some period-stationary function of the announced indicators, $T(x_1, x_2)$.

Given this setup, the analysis might proceed in two steps: For each code configuration, we would derive the agents' discounted sums of expected utility associated with some feasible transfer arrangement chosen by them in the second-stage continuation. Then, we would study the first-stage code choice as equilibrium behavior in the symmetric, simultaneous move, 2×2 game where actions are the alternative codes $\{C^P, C^O\}$, and payoffs are the agents' respective welfare levels in the implied continuations. Obviously, in this example and in general, many feasible continuations are possible for each configuration since there exist many subgame perfect equilibria of the second stage's repeated interaction. So, to pursue this two-step program we would need to associate a *unique* second-stage welfare level for the agents with each configuration, thereby specifying how the expected utility surplus (relative to autarky) generated by the prospect of risk sharing is to be divided among agents.[14] Once we have done this, the 2×2 first-stage game would be well defined.

Accordingly, throughout this chapter *we posit that the agents adopt as a second-stage continuation that feasible risk-sharing arrangement which maximizes the sum of their expected discounted utilities.*[15]

With this convention about surplus division in hand, we can then characterize first-stage play with a reduced normal form game given by the following matrix:[16]

		Agent 2	
		C^P	C^O
Agent 1	C^P	V_P^*, V_P^*	V_M^{P*}, V_M^{O*}
	C^O	V_M^{O*}, V_M^{P*}	V_O^*, V_O^*

Our interpretation of this 3×2 example is as follows: the signals reflect either a "good" or a "bad" outcome, while the endowments can be either "high," "medium," or "low." So, given the requirement of montonicity, an agent's choice of "identity" amounts to a choice about how to react to an intermediate income realization (whether to code it as a "good" or a "bad" event). One way to talk about this is that, in effect, the agents must choose between being "pessimists" or "optimists." Alternatively, we could envision them as deciding whether, in the event of a middling endowment realization, to view themselves as a "victim" – i.e., as someone who needs a helping hand but who is not in position to lend one.[17] Whatever the interpretation, we can ask whether the "optimistic" configuration $\langle C^O, C^O \rangle$ is better than the "pessimistic" one $\langle C^P, C^P \rangle$, in terms of the potential gains from second-stage risk sharing that it engenders. And, we can inquire whether a mixed configuration – $\langle C^P, C^O \rangle$, say – is inferior to either "collective identity."[18]

Thus, in this example where only two choices of code are possible, we are able to discuss our ideas about dysfunctional collective identities using the basic notions of elementary game theory. If the normal form depicted above is a coordination game (i.e., if $V_P^* > V_M^{O*}$ and $V_O^* > V_M^{P*}$), then strategic forces favor the adoption of *some* collective identity and multiple, Pareto-ranked equilibria exist. Avoiding a dysfunctional identity then becomes a coordination problem for the agents.[19] Alternatively, if this game is a Prisoners' Dilemma (i.e., if $V_M^{P*} > V_O^* > V_P^* > V_M^{O*}$, for instance, so that, although a pessimistic configuration is Pareto inferior to an optimistic one, it is nevertheless a dominant strategy for the agents to be pessimistic), then the two-stage strategic interaction has a "tragedy of the commons" quality about it, and the adoption by rational agents of a dysfunctional identity is all but guaranteed! (In Section 2.4 we use numerical analysis to further explore this case, exhibiting conditions on the primitives of the model under which dysfunctional collective identities are likely (or, bound) to emerge.)

2.2.2.2   A continuum of endowment realizations

We can readily extend this 3×2 example. The assumption of three discrete income realizations, though allowing a colorful interpretation, is incidental to the analysis. When Y is an interval of real numbers and $|X| = 2$, the reduced-form game involves the agents simultaneously choosing thresholds (y_1^*, y_2^*) in the first stage, and reporting a "bad" outcome whenever their endowments are at below our chosen thresholds.[20] This continuum specification is useful because, since the set of alternative thresholds is a bounded interval, and the agents' payoffs are differentiable functions of the threshold pair (assuming a well-behaved endowment distribution), we can use calculus to study the agents' strategic interaction in the first stage. (In Section 2.3.4 we explicitly solve this continuum example, adopting a quadratic utility function and letting the discount factor approach one.)

Now, suppose agent 1 has a lower threshold than agent 2: $y_1^* < y_2^*$. Furthermore, let $\pi_i = \int_{\{y \in Y, \ y \le y_i^*\}} p(y)\,dy$ be the probability that agent i announces "B." So, $\pi_1 < \pi_2$.[21] Then, since the utility function is strictly concave, the endowment disparity between the agents conditional on the event $E = \{y_1 \le y_1^*\} \cap \{y_2 > y_2^*\}$ permits a transfer (from agent 2 to agent 1) with relatively low utility cost to the giver and high utility benefit for the receiver. The more widely disparate are y_1^* and y_2^*, the greater is the social surplus from such a transfer. However, the mismatch frequency for this event is $\Pr\{E\} = \pi_1(1 - \pi_2)$. Thus (as mentioned above) encounters of this kind, though more profitable, occur less often as y_1^* and y_2^* become more widely disparate (since π_1 falls and/or π_2 rises). Moreover, as y_1^* and y_2^* grow further apart, trading opportunities deteriorate in the other "mismatch event," $E' = \{y_1 > y_1^*\} \cap \{y_2 \le y_2^*\}$ (because the endowment ranges conditional on this event overlap more).[22] Thus, at the socially optimal code configuration in this continuum case, the disparity between y_1^* and y_2^* will be such that the benefit of more profitable transfers conditional on E is just balanced by the cost of less profitable transfers conditional on E', plus the cost that E occurs less frequently.[23]

This continuum example can also be used to illustrate why inefficient collective identity choices are to be expected: *the private evaluation of benefits and costs associated with alternative code configurations is likely to differ from this social assessment*. Two countervailing factors can cause private and social valuations to differ in our model.

(i) When contemplating the choice of a higher threshold in the first stage of play, an individual (agent 1, say), takes into account that the second-stage transfer policy will become marginally less attractive for her (because raising her threshold makes her endowment distribution more favorable conditional on either signal, thereby lowering the transfer she receives, or raising the transfer she gives, at every indicator pair). *But this private cost to agent 1 is not a social cost.* Invoking the Envelope Theorem, we know that in the neighborhood of an optimal configuration the net social impact of an induced shift in the transfer arrangement is zero. So, due to this pecuniary externality, agent 1 may tend to set y_1^* *below* its socially optimal level.

(ii) On the other hand, since agent 1's likelihood of giving a transfer declines as y_1^* rises, raising her threshold has a negative effect on her trading partner.[24] *But this social cost is not a private cost to agent 1.* When choosing their thresholds, each agent ignores this impact on the other agent. So, due to this external diseconomy, agent 1 may tend to set y_1^* *above* its socially optimal level.

In general, how the equilibrium and the socially optimal configurations compare depends on the relative magnitude of these two wedges between private and social valuation. In particular, the symmetric equilibrium threshold will exceed the socially optimal level if, when considering a marginal increase in y_1^*, the external diseconomy on agent 2 due to agent 1's lowered frequency of giving a transfer (specified in (ii)) exceeds the pecuniary externality on agent 1 due to the induced decline in her net transfer receipts (specified in (i)). But, using the Envelope Theorem again, any induced negative impact on agent 1 is just offset by an induced positive impact on her trading partner. We conclude that the equilibrium threshold exceeds the socially optimal one if the direct plus the induced impact on agent 2 of a marginal increase in agent 1's threshold is negative.

We can make this point somewhat more formally, while introducing some notation specific to this example that will prove useful later. Thus, with $X = \{B, G\}$ and Y an interval on the non-negative real line, denote by $U(y_1, y_2)$ player one's payoff at the threshold pair, (y_1, y_2). Let $W(y) = U(y, y)$; let U_i be the partial derivatives of U, $i = 1, 2$; let $y^e = y_1^* = y_2^*$ be the agents' common threshold in a symmetric equilibrium, and let y^O be the socially optimal (i.e., the sum-of-discounted − utility-maximizing) common threshold. Then, we have the first-order conditions: $U_1(y^e, y^e) = 0$, and $W'(y^O) = U_1(y^O, y^O) + U_2(y^O, y^O) = 0$.

It follows that $U_2(y^e, y^e) \gtreqless 0$ implies $W'(y^e) \gtreqless 0$ which, in turn, implies $y^e \gtreqless y^o$ (assuming the relevant second-order condition).

We conclude (in the context of this extended example) that the *symmetric equilibrium identity configuration is a spoiled collective identity involving too much pessimism (too much optimism) whenever the net effect of raising one agent's threshold marginally from its equilibrium level is to reduce (increase) the payoff of the other agent!* Thus, the case $|X| = 2$ affords us a tractable context within which to demonstrate the kinship of the "identity coordination problem" being posed here with the classical "tragedy of the commons."

2.3   Analysis

2.3.1   *Notation and preliminaries*

We return now to a discussion of the general model. Imagine that the agents enter the second stage having adopted the (monotonic) code configuration $\langle C_1, C_2 \rangle$. We begin by describing the feasible risk-sharing arrangements available to these agents, and the expected discounted utility surpluses (relative to autarky) that accrue to them from adopting any particular arrangement. Ultimately, we will provide (in Theorem 1) an explicit characterization of the discount factors for which a feasible arrangement can be found that generates positive surplus for both agents. Toward this end, we require some more notation.

For $y \in Y$ an endowment level and $t \in \Re$ a (possibly negative) net transfer, denote the utility change for someone with endowment y who receives a net transfer of t by

$$\Delta u(y,t) \equiv u(y+t) - u(y).$$

Given the distribution of endowments, any code choice induces a distribution of indicators. For $x \in X$, let $q_i(x)$ denote the probability that agent i announces indicator x under code C_i. Then

$$q_i(x) \equiv \sum_{y \in C_i^{-1}(x)} p(y), \quad i = 1, 2.$$

Moreover, for $x \in X$ and $t \in \Re$, consider the conditional expected utility gain over autarky for agent i, given that her indicator realization is x and that her net transfer is to be t. We denote this conditional expected payoff by $v_i(x,t)$, where

$$v_i(x,t) \equiv E\left[\Delta u(y,t) \mid y \in C_i^{-1}(x)\right]$$

$$= \sum_{y \in C_i^{-1}(x)} \frac{p(y)\Delta u(y,t)}{q_i(x)}, \quad i = 1, 2. \tag{1}$$

Analogously, we write $v_i'(x,t)$ to represent the conditional expected *marginal* utility (i.e., the "conditional shadow price") for agent i at indicator x given transfer t. So

$$v_i'(x,t) \equiv E\left[u'(y+t) \mid y \in C_i^{-1}(x)\right] = \frac{\partial v_i}{\partial t}(x,t), \quad i = 1, 2. \tag{2}$$

In what follows we shall be particularly interested in the conditional shadow prices when transfers are zero, $v_i'(x,0)$.

Now, it is obvious that $\{C_i^{-1}(x) : x \in X\}$ is a finite, pairwise-disjoint family of sets that covers Y – i.e., a partition of Y. It is also obvious that when the code C_i is monotonic, these sets are "intervals," in the sense that if $x \neq x'$, then either $\mathrm{Min}\{C_i^{-1}(x)\} > \mathrm{Max}\{C_i^{-1}(x')\}$ or $\mathrm{Max}\{C_i^{-1}(x)\} < \mathrm{Min}\{C_i^{-1}(x')\}$.[25] Given the strict concavity of $u(\cdot)$, we conclude that, for every $x \neq x' \in X$, either

$$v_i'(x,t) > v_i'(x',t) \quad \text{for all } t \in \Re$$

or

$$v_i'(x,t) < v_i'(x',t) \quad \text{for all } t \in \Re.$$

That is, a monotonic code always induces a complete, strict ordering of the marginal valuation schedules, conditional on the elements of X.

Intuitively, given an indicator pair (x_1, x_2) and a level of transfer t, the ratio $v_1'(x_1, -t)/v_2'(x_2, t)$ is the "conditional marginal rate of (utility) substitution" between the agents via adjustments to the transfer at the indicator pair, (x_1, x_2). In particular, efficient risk sharing should entail an effort to equalize these substitution rates, moving resources from agent 1 to agent 2 ($t > 0$) when $v_1'(x_1, 0)/v_2'(x_2, 0)$ is "low," and from agent 2 to agent 1 ($t < 0$) when it is "high." Accordingly, we use $(\tilde{x}_1, \tilde{x}_2)$ and $(\hat{x}_1, \hat{x}_2)$ to denote the special indicator pairs at which the zero-transfer conditional substitution rate takes its largest and its smallest values

$$\frac{v_1'(\tilde{x}_1, 0)}{v_2'(\tilde{x}_2, 0)} \leq \frac{v_1'(x_1, 0)}{v_2'(x_2, 0)} \leq \frac{v_1'(\hat{x}_1, 0)}{v_2'(\hat{x}_2, 0)}, \quad \text{for all } x_1 \in X, \, x_2 \in X.$$

Evidently, $v_1'(x,0)$ is minimized over X at $\tilde{x}_1$ and maximized at $\hat{x}_1$; while, $v_2'(x,0)$ is maximized at $\tilde{x}_2$ and minimized at $\hat{x}_2$. So, again thinking at an intuitive level, the joint indicator realization $(\tilde{x}_1, \tilde{x}_2)$ is the event commonly known to the agents that is most favorable for a marginal tranfer of resources from agent 1 to agent 2 (in the sense that the cost to agent 1 from the transfer is least and the gain from it for agent 2 is greatest at this event). Likewise, the realization $(\hat{x}_1, \hat{x}_2)$ is the event that favors most a marginal transfer of resources from agent 2 to agent 1.

To see how these notions will prove useful, imagine that initially no transfers are taking place and consider the problem of determining whether there is a *marginal transfer arrangement* (i.e., one "near" zero) which leaves both agents better off than under autarky. Clearly, a transfer from agent 1 at $(\tilde{x}_1, \tilde{x}_2)$ that is offset with a transfer in the other direction at $(\hat{x}_1, \hat{x}_2)$ gives the agents their best chance to achieve a Pareto improvement via a marginal arrangement. This is so for two reasons: the size of transfer needed to produce a given increase in the recipient's welfare is least at these realizations; and, the loss in welfare due to making a transfer of given size is also least at these realization. Of course, making both transfers would need to be consistent with incentives if the agents are to achieve a Pareto improvement in this way. But, because the least well-endowed (i.e., most incentive-constrained) giver's cost of a marginal transfer is least at these indicator pairs, if the incentive conditions cannot be satisfied at these realizations then they cannot be satisfied elsewhere. We summarize the discussion to this point in the following Lemma:

Lemma 1. *There is a strict Pareto improving, feasible marginal transfer arrangement only if an arrangement of this kind exists which also satisfies:* $T(\tilde{x}_1, \tilde{x}_2) > 0$, $T(\hat{x}_1, \hat{x}_2) < 0$, *and* $T(x_1, x_2) = 0$ *otherwise.*

2.3.2   Value functions and incentive constraints

Let $V_i(T)$ denote the expected discounted utility surplus (relative to autarky) over the course of the second stage enjoyed by agent i under arrangement T. Given an arrangement, when the announced indicators are (x_1, x_2) agent 1 consumes $y_1 - T(x_1, x_2)$ and agent 2 consumes $y_2 + T(x_1, x_2)$. So, exploiting the stationarity and using equation (1), we can write

$$V_1(T) = (1 - \delta)^{-1} \sum_{x_1 \in X} \sum_{x_2 \in X} q_1(x_1) q_2(x_2) v_1(x_1, -T(x_1, x_2)), \tag{3}$$

and

$$V_2(T) = (1 - \delta)^{-1} \sum_{x_1 \in X} \sum_{x_2 \in X} q_1(x_1) q_2(x_2) v_2(x_2, T(x_1, x_2)). \tag{4}$$

In view of our assumption of risk aversion, it is obvious that the $V_i(\cdot)$ are concave functions of the elements of T.[26]

A transfer arrangement is feasible under a given code configuration if neither agent ever expects to gain by a one-shot deviation from it that is followed by reversion to autarky. So, if under a feasible arrangement T agent i has endowment y and is required to make a transfer to the other agent of magnitude $|t|$, then it must be that

$$u(y) - u(y - |t|) \le \delta V_i(T).$$

Hence, at every indicator pairs (x_1, x_2) the incentive requirements for feasibility are as follows:

Agent 1: $\quad \Delta u[y, -T(x_1, x_2)] \leq \delta V_1(T), \quad$ for all $y \in C_1^{-1}(x_1)$,

and

Agent 2: $\quad \Delta u[y, T(x_1, x_2)] \leq \delta V_2(T), \quad$ for all $y \in C_2^{-1}(x_2)$.

Since $\Delta u(y, t) \gtreqless 0$ as $t \gtreqless 0$, agent 2's inequality holds trivially when $T(x_1, x_2) > 0$, as does agent 1's when $T(x_1, x_2) < 0$. Moreover, since $u(\cdot)$ is a strictly concave function it is clear that if agent i is asked to make a transfer when her indicator is x_i, then the most favorable relevant circumstance for a profitable deviation occurs when $y_i = \text{Min}\{C_i^{-1}(x_i)\}$. So, we may write the $2|X|^2$ incentive conditions (for each agent $i = 1, 2$ and at each indicator pair $(x_1, x_2) \in X^2$) as follows:

$$\delta V_1(T) + \Delta u\left[\text{Min}\{C_1^{-1}(x_1)\}, -T(x_1, x_2)\right] \geq 0, \tag{5}$$

and, likewise

$$\delta V_2(T) + \Delta u\left[\text{Min}\{C_2^{-1}(x_2)\}, T(x_1, x_2)\right] \geq 0. \tag{6}$$

Given $\langle C_1, C_2 \rangle$ and δ, and for the value functions as specified in equations (3) and (4), let $\Im(C_1, C_2; \delta)$ be the set of feasible transfer arrangements under code configuration $\langle C_1, C_2 \rangle$ and discount factor δ:

$$\Im(C_1, C_2; \delta) \equiv \{T \colon X^2 \to \Re \mid T \text{ satisfies5 and 6}\}.$$

Notice that the LHS of inequalities (5) and (6) are concave functions of the $|X|^2$ real numbers, $\{T(x_1, x_2)\}$. Therefore, the set of feasible transfer, $\Im(C_1, C_2; \delta)$, arrangements is convex. Hence, the attainable payoffs for the two players in the second-stage subgame – given a code configuration and discount factor – form a convex subset of $\Re^2$. Since autarky (no transfers and zero surplus for both players) is surely feasible, we have the following result:

Lemma 2. *A feasible transfer arrangement generating a positive surplus for both agents exists if and only if a strictly Pareto improving marginal transfer arrangement exists.*

2.3.3   Gains from trade in the second stage

2.3.3.1   A general result

Given a code configuration $\langle C_1, C_2 \rangle$, we are interested in determining the range of discount factors over which it is possible for both agents to realize a positive surplus from risk sharing in the second stage (relative to autarky). It is clear that for a small enough δ any non-zero risk sharing arrangement is infeasible. Moreover, any arrangement that would yield a positive surplus for both agents becomes feasible when δ is close enough to one. Intuition therefore suggests that for every configuration $\langle C_1, C_2 \rangle$ there is a cut-off level for the discount factor, $\bar{\delta}(C_1, C_2)$, such that no gains from second-stage trade are possible when $\delta \le \bar{\delta}(C_1, C_2)$. This is, indeed, the case. Theorem 1 establishes this fact and provides an explicit characterization of $\bar{\delta}(\cdot, \cdot)$. The significance of this result is that it gives us a way to assess the economic efficacy at relatively low discount factors of alternative identity configurations: The lower is $\bar{\delta}(C_1, C_2)$, the wider is the range of environments under which a positive surplus can be realized, and so (in this specific sense) the greater is the scope for risk sharing afforded by the configuration.

To state and prove the theorem we (unfortunately) need one more bit of notation. For agent i with code C_i and signal $x_i \in X$, consider the most that it could cost that agent to surrender a marginal unit of consumption starting from a situation of zero transfers, and denote this number by ϕ_i. That is

$$\phi_i(x_i) \equiv u'\big[\text{Min}\{C_i^{-1}(x_i)\}\big], \quad i = 1, 2.$$

So, $\phi_i(x_i)$ is the marginal utility of the agent i who has received the lowest endowment level consistent with announcing indicator x_i. (Obviously, $\phi_i(x_i) > v_i'(x_i, 0)$.) We can now state our result.

Theorem 1.   *Given code configuration $\langle C_1, C_2 \rangle$ and discount factor δ, there exists a transfer arrangement $T \in \Im(C_1, C_2; \delta)$ for which $V_i(T) > 0$, $i = 1, 2$, if and only if $\delta > \bar{\delta}(C_1, C_2)$, where $\bar{\delta}(C_1, C_2)$ is the unique solution in the unit interval of*

$$\frac{v_2'(\tilde{x}_2, 0)}{v_1'(\tilde{x}_1, 0)} \cdot \left[1 + \frac{[(1 - \delta)/\delta]\phi_1(\tilde{x}_1)}{q_1(\tilde{x}_1)q_2(\tilde{x}_2)v_1'(\tilde{x}_1, 0)}\right]^{-1}$$

$$= \frac{v_2'(\hat{x}_2, 0)}{v_1'(\hat{x}_1, 0)} \cdot \left[1 + \frac{[(1 - \delta)/\delta]\phi_2(\hat{x}_2)}{q_1(\hat{x}_1)q_2(\hat{x}_2)v_2'(\hat{x}_2, 0)}\right], \tag{7}$$

and where $(\tilde{x}_1, \tilde{x}_2)$ and $(\hat{x}_1, \hat{x}_2)$ are the special indicator pairs defined above, at which the per-period utility substitution rate $v_2'(x_2, 0)/v_1'(x_1, 0)$ takes, respectively, its highest and lowest values on X^2.

Theorem 1 has an intuitive interpretation: it can be understood to say that there are no gains from trade if, with zero transfers taking place, agent 2's marginal welfare cost per unit of agent 1's welfare benefit at $(\hat{x}_1, \hat{x}_2)$ (where it is most favorable for agent 2 to give) exceeds her marginal benefit per unit of 1's cost at $(\tilde{x}_1, \tilde{x}_2)$ (where it is most favorable for agent 1 to give). To see this, notice that the LHS of equation (7) gives the marginal rate of welfare substitution between these agents at zero transfers $([dV_2(T)/dV_1(T)]|_{T=0})$, conditional on the indicator pair $(\tilde{x}_1, \tilde{x}_2)$ and viewed from the perspective of the agent obliged to make a transfer there, for whom the incentive constraint binds. The RHS gives the same welfare substitution rate conditional on $(\hat{x}_1, \hat{x}_2)$. Rates of expected discounted welfare substitution (either side in equation (7)) differ by the indicated multiplicative factors from per-period utility substitution rates $v'_2(x_2, 0)/v'_1(x_1, 0)$. This is because the incentive-constrained giver (the least well-endowed agent 1 at $(\tilde{x}_1, \tilde{x}_2)$ and the least well-endowed agent 2 at $(\hat{x}_1, \hat{x}_2)$) incurs a cost with certainty in the current period, but only with probability $q_1(x_1)q_2(x_2)$ in each subsequent period. So, the term $[(1 - \delta)/\delta]\phi_i(x_i)/q_1(x_1)q_2(x_2)v'_i(x_i, 0)$ represents the current marginal compliance cost per unit of expected discounted future cost, when agent i is the incentive-constrained giver.[27] The larger the δ, the smaller is this term. So, the RHS in equation (7) is strictly decreasing in δ and the LHS is strictly increasing. Moreover, by the definition of $(\tilde{x}_1, \tilde{x}_2)$ and $(\hat{x}_1, \hat{x}_2)$, the RHS is less (greater) than the LHS for δ near one (for δ near zero.) So, equation (7) has a unique solution in the unit interval, as asserted.

Proof. To prove Theorem 1 notice first that, in view of Lemmas 1 and 2, positive surplus for both agents is feasible if and only if there is a feasible marginal risk-sharing arrangement that moves resources from agent 1 to agent 2 only at $(\tilde{x}_1, \tilde{x}_2)$, and from agent 2 to agent 1 only at $(\hat{x}_1, \hat{x}_2)$, such that the outcome of these transfers strictly Pareto dominates autarky. In turn, it is clear (from equations (5) and (6)) that *any* feasible, non-zero transfer arrangement must be a strict Pareto improvement over autarky. Therefore, a positive surplus is possible at the second stage if and only if there exists a pair of positive numbers (t_1, t_2) (representing the magnitudes of the transfers in a marginal arrangement) such that $\hat{T} \in \Im(C_1, C_2; \delta)$, for $\hat{T}$ satisfying

$$\hat{T}(\tilde{x}_1, \tilde{x}_2) \equiv t_1 > 0, \quad \hat{T}(\hat{x}_1, \hat{x}_2) \equiv -t_2 < 0,$$

and

$$\hat{T}(x_1, x_2) = 0 \quad \text{otherwise.}$$

We show that such numbers exist if and only if $\delta > \bar{\delta}(C_1, C_2)$ as defined earlier.

Consider the inequalities (5) and (6). Let us take (t_1, t_2) to be a pair of positive numbers in the neighborhood of $(0, 0)$. For $\hat{T}$ the marginal transfer arrangement specified in terms of (t_1, t_2), define:

$$F_1(t_1, t_2) \equiv \delta V_1(\hat{T}) + \Delta u[\text{Min}\{C_1^{-1}(\tilde{x}_1)\}, -t_1],$$

and

$$F_2(t_1, t_2) \equiv \delta V_2(\hat{T}) + \Delta u[\text{Min}\{C_2^{-1}(\hat{x}_2)\}, t_2].$$

Obviously, there is a feasible marginal transfer arrangement if and only if there is a pair of positive numbers (t_1, t_2) near zero for which $F_i(t_1, t_2) > 0, i = 1, 2$. Totally differentiating the functions $F_i(\cdot, \cdot)$, while bearing in mind that $\partial F_i / \partial t_i < 0$ and $\partial F_i / \partial t_j > 0, i \neq j$, reveals that the inequalities

$$\left[\frac{\partial F_1}{\partial t_1} \right] dt_1 + \left[\frac{\partial F_1}{\partial t_2} \right] dt_2 > 0 \quad \text{and} \quad \left[\frac{\partial F_2}{\partial t_1} \right] dt_1 + \left[\frac{\partial F_2}{\partial t_2} \right] dt_2 > 0.$$

can both hold simultaneously only if

$$-\frac{\partial F_1 / \partial t_1}{\partial F_1 / \partial t_2} < \frac{dt_2}{dt_1} < -\frac{\partial F_2 / \partial t_1}{\partial F_2 / \partial t_2},$$

where the derivatives above are evaluated at $(t_1, t_2) = (0, 0)$. Carrying out the indicated differentiation, one can see that the inequality $-(\partial F_1 / \partial t_1)/(\partial F_1 / \partial t_2) < - (\partial F_2 / \partial t_1)/(\partial F_2 / \partial t_2)$ holds if and only if the LHS exceeds the RHS in equation (7). However, as noted, the LHS increases and the RHS decreases with δ. So, a feasible marginal transfer arrangement can be found which strictly Pareto dominates autarky if and only if $\delta > \bar{\delta}(C_1, C_2)$, as was to be shown.   □

2.3.3.2   *Gains from trade with collective identities*

We now employ Theorem 1 to investigate the scope for risk sharing enjoyed by the agents when they embrace a common code (i.e., a collective identity). Thus, suppose $C_1 = C_2 = C$, and denote by $\bar{\delta}_C \equiv \bar{\delta}(C, C)$ the minimal discount factor consistent with there being positive gains from trade when both agents embrace the same code. Notice that the functions on X defining the distributions of indicators, $q_i(\cdot)$, and the shadow prices, $v_i'(\cdot)$ and $\phi_i(\cdot)$, are now the same for both agents. So, we can drop the subscript i in what follows. Moreover the critical indicator pairs, $(\tilde{x}_1, \tilde{x}_2)$ and $(\hat{x}_1, \hat{x}_2)$ as defined earlier, will in this case be such that

$$(\tilde{x}_1, \tilde{x}_2) = (\hat{x}_2, \hat{x}_1) \equiv (x^H, x^L),$$

where

$$x^H \equiv \text{ArgMin}_{x \in X} \{v'(x, 0)\} \quad \text{and} \quad x^L \equiv \text{ArgMax}_{x \in X} \{v'(x, 0)\}.$$

Here, given a collective identity C, we think of x^H as the "high income" indicator (i.e., the one with the lowest conditional expected marginal utility), and x^L is the "low income" indicator (i.e., the one with highest conditional shadow price), and these are the same for both agents. Define $\phi_C \equiv u'[\text{Min}\{C^{-1}(x^H)\}]$. Then, straightforward manipulation of the formula in equation (7) reveals the following, which we state without proof:

Corollary 1. *If the agents have embraced a collective identity, so that $C_1 = C_2 = C$, then positive gains from trade can be achieved in equilibrium if and only* *if $\delta > \bar{\delta}_C$, where $\bar{\delta}_C$ is given by:*

$$\left(\frac{1 - \bar{\delta}_C}{\bar{\delta}_C}\right) = [q(x^H)q(x^L)] \cdot \left[\frac{v'(x^L, 0) - v'(x^H, 0)}{\phi_C}\right]. \tag{8}$$

Thus, under a collective identity the agents' scope for effective risk sharing depends on three factors: the gap $[v'(x^L, 0) - v'(x^H, 0)]$ in conditional shadow prices between their "worst" and "best" indicator states – this is the social benefit from a marginal transfer; the likelihood $[q(x^H)q(x^L)]$ of an encounter between them when one is in the "worst" and the other the "best" state; and the cost of a marginal transfer to the least well-off person announcing the "best" signal $[\phi_C]$. Equation (8) shows that these various factors combine in an intuitively appealing way to determine whether gains from trade can be attained with the collective identity, C: The term $[v'(x^L, 0) - v'(x^H, 0)]/\phi_C$ gives the ratio of benefits to costs from the best marginal trade, at (x^H, x^L), as viewed by the agent whose incentive constraint binds there. On the RHS of equation (8) this ratio is multiplied by the probability of that particular trading opportunity arising in a later period. Costs are incurred currently, while benefits accrue in perpetuity beginning in the next period. So, $\delta/(1 - \delta) \cdot$ (expected marginal benefit) $>$ (marginal cost) is a necessary condition for a marginal transfer to look profitable to the one who makes it. Equation (8) makes clear that this condition must fail, even for the best marginal transfer, if $\delta \leq \bar{\delta}_C$.

2.3.3.3   *"Optimism" vs. "Pessimism" in the 3×2 case*

Recall now the 3×2 example introduced in Section 2.2.2.1, where identity choice amounts to a decision on whether to code an intermediate endowment state as a "good" (optimist) or a "bad" (pessimist) event. Let $\bar{\delta}_P$ (resp. $\bar{\delta}_O$) denote the critical discount factors below which no surplus is possible, given that a pessimistic (optimistic) collective identity has been adopted by the agents. Then, using equation (8), we conclude that

$$\left(\frac{1 - \bar{\delta}_P}{\bar{\delta}_P}\right) = p_h(1 - p_h) \cdot \left[\frac{\alpha u'(l) + (1 - \alpha)u'(m) - u'(h)}{u'(h)}\right]$$

and

$$\left(\frac{1 - \bar{\delta}_O}{\bar{\delta}_O}\right) = p_l(1 - p_l) \cdot \left[\frac{u'(l) - \beta u'(m) - (1 - \beta)u'(h)}{u'(m)}\right],$$

where $\alpha \equiv p_l/(1 - p_h)$ and $\beta \equiv p_m/(1 - p_l)$. In light of the foregoing discussion, it is obvious that optimism affords a wider scope for risk sharing than does pessimism when $p_l(1 - p_l)/[p_h(1 - p_h)]$ is large, and/or when $|(m - l)/(h - m)|$ is large.

This result is intuitively satisfying. Pessimism conflates low and intermediate endowment states, while optimism conflates intermediate and high states. So, collective optimism will dominate collective pessimism when the information constraint of lumping together high and medium income states is less debilitating to the risk-sharing enterprise than is the constraint of lumping together medium and low states. As an extreme example, as $h - m$ goes to zero, optimism will surely dominate because lumping the h and m endowments entails essentially zero information loss. Just the opposite is the case as $m - l$ goes to zero because lumping the m and l endowments then entails a trivial information loss. Likewise, as p_l goes to zero, pessimism will dominate optimism as a collective identity, and the opposite will be the case as p_h goes to zero. Moreover, as p_m goes to zero, the agents have full endowment information under both pessimism and optimism, so the two collective identities must be equivalent in that case.

Finally, to conclude our discussion of the 3×2 case, suppose the parameters of that example satisfy

$$p_h = p_l \equiv p; \quad p_m = 1 - 2p; \quad \text{and } h - m = m - l \equiv g.$$

We refer to this circumstance, in the context of the 3×2 example, as a *symmetric endowment distribution*. Since asymmetric distributions naturally favor optimism if left-skewed, or pessimism if right-skewed, examining this symmetric case provides a useful benchmark. Under symmetric endowment distributions high and low endowments are equally likely, and the intermediate endowment lies midway between the high and low realizations. Reasoning intuitively, if the endowment distribution is symmetric and if the demand for consumption insurance falls as the level of consumption rises, then a noisy signal at the lower range of endowments should be more of an impediment to welfare-enhancing risk sharing than a noisy signal at the higher range of endowments. So, optimism should dominate pessimism as a collective identity when the endowment distribution is symmetric, if the agent is less risk averse at higher levels of consumption. This is indeed the case, as the following result demonstrates.

Denote by $V_O(t)$ and $V_P(t)$ the agents' common level of welfare in the 3×2 example, under collective "optimism" and collective "pessimism" respectively, given that the transfer arrangement satisfies: $T(G, B) = t \geq 0$. (It is obvious that if both agents adopt the same identity code, then risk-sharing transfers between them will take place only if they announce different indicators.) Then, using equations (3) and (4), a straightforward calculation reveals that

$$\theta \cdot [V_O(t) - V_P(t)] = \{[u(l + g) - u(l)] - [u(l + g + t) - u(l + t)]\}$$
$$- \{[u(l + 2g - t) - u(l + g - t)]$$
$$- [u(l + 2g) - u(l + g)]\},$$

where $\theta \equiv (1 - \delta)/[p(1 - 2p)]$. Using the Fundamental Theorem of Calculus, the above RHS can be written as follows:

$$\text{RHS} = \int_0^g [u'(l + x) - u'(l + t + x)] \, dx$$

$$- \int_0^g [u'(l + g - t + x) - u'(l + g + x)] \, dx$$

$$= \int_0^g \int_0^t u''(l + g + x + w) \, dw \, dx - \int_0^g \int_0^t u''(l + x + w) \, dw \, dx$$

$$= \int_0^g \int_0^g \int_0^t u'''(l + x + w + z) \, dw \, dx \, dz.$$

Accordingly, collective "optimism" dominates collective "pessimism," holding fixed the level of transfer, if the third derivative of the utility function is positive (less risk aversion at higher levels of consumption), while the opposite is true if the third derivative is negative. For a quadratic utility function the two collective identities will be welfare equivalent. Thus, we have the following proposition:

Proposition 1. *Let there be a symmetric endowment distribution in the* 3×2 *example. Then for* δ *sufficiently large, we have that optimism welfare-dominates pessimism* $(V_O^* > V_P^*)$ *if* $u''' > 0$, *while pessimism dominates optimism* $(V_O^* < V_P^*)$ *if* $u''' < 0$.[28]

Proof. From the expression for RHS above, we know that $V_O(t) \gtreqless V_P(t)$ as $u''' \gtreqless 0$, for all t. Moreover, for δ sufficiently large we know that any level of transfer $t = T(G, B)$ that generates a positive utility surplus for the agents is feasible. Hence, by a "revealed preference" argument, the optimal transfer under optimism must generate higher (lower) welfare than the optimal transfer under pessimism when $u''' > 0$ ($u''' < 0$). □

2.3.3.4 Why collective identities promote risk sharing

Equation (7) also provides further insight into the features of a code configuration that tend to be associated with a greater scope for risk sharing (i.e., a lower value of $\bar{\delta}(C_1, C_2)$). Indeed, examining the equation gives us a hint as to why symmetric configurations (collective identities) may foster gainful trade among the agents in a wider range of environments than asymmetric configurations. Let us rewrite the equation as follows:

$$\frac{v_2'(\tilde{x}_2, 0)}{v_1'(\tilde{x}_1, 0)} \cdot [1 + Z(\delta)]^{-1} = \frac{v_2'(\hat{x}_2, 0)}{v_1'(\hat{x}_1, 0)} \cdot [1 + W(\delta)], \tag{9}$$

where

$$Z(\delta) \equiv \frac{(1-\delta)\phi_1(\tilde{x}_1)}{\delta q_1(\tilde{x}_1)q_2(\tilde{x}_2)v_1'(\tilde{x}_1,0)} \quad \text{and} \quad W(\delta) \equiv \frac{(1-\delta)\phi_2(\hat{x}_2)}{\delta v_2'(\hat{x}_2,0)q_1(\hat{x}_1)q_2(\hat{x}_2)}.$$

As mentioned, the functions $Z(\delta)$ and $W(\delta)$ represents current marginal cost per unit of expected discounted future cost, for incentive constrained givers at $(\tilde{x}_1,\tilde{x}_2)$ and $(\hat{x}_1,\hat{x}_2)$, respectively. They are strictly decreasing functions, vanishing as $\delta \uparrow 1$ and growing without bound as $\delta \downarrow 0$. Reasoning informally about equation (9), we note that LHS($\delta = 1$) − RHS($\delta = 1$) = $[v_2'(\tilde{x}_2,0)/v_1'(\tilde{x}_1,0)] - [v_2'(\hat{x}_2,0)/v_1'(\hat{x}_1,0)] > 0$. As δ falls from 1, $Z(\delta)$ and $W(\delta)$ both rise until $\delta = \bar{\delta}$, and the gap between LHS and RHS vanishes. So, the wider is the *endowment disparity* (as measured by the difference $|[v_2'(\tilde{x}_2,0)/v_1'(\tilde{x}_1,0)] - [v_2'(\hat{x}_2,0)/v_1'(\hat{x}_1,0)]|$), other things equal, the smaller is the value of $\bar{\delta}$ at which equation (7) is satisfied. Likewise, the larger are the *mismatch frequencies* (as measured by $q_1(\tilde{x}_1)q_2(\tilde{x}_2)$ and $q_1(\hat{x}_1)q_2(\hat{x}_2)$), and the smaller are the shadow prices $\phi_1(\tilde{x}_1)$ and $\phi_2(\hat{x}_2)$, the smaller will be $\bar{\delta}$.

We can see, therefore, that in general the factors determining the magnitude of $\bar{\delta}$ are the same as those mentioned in Section 2.2.2.2 for the special case, $|X| = 2$: (1) the endowment disparity (i.e., difference of conditional marginal utilities) at the two commonly known events most favorable for trading; (2) the mismatch frequencies (i.e., the probabilities of these events); and (3) the marginal cost of transfers at these events. As mentioned, the endowment disparity is greater when the agents' codes specifically identify widely disparate endowment states (i.e., when very high endowments and/or very low endowments are provided with their own distinct signals so that trade between the agents conditional on these endowment realization becomes possible). On the other hand, allocating separate indicators to very high and very low states uses up cognitive resources while lowering the mismatch frequency (i.e., the probabilities of high/low and low/high indicator realizations fall as the endowment disparity rises). So, as in the example of Section 2.2, a fundamental tradeoff (*endowment disparity* vs. *mismatch frequency*) is involved in the general case. *The basic reason why collective identity configurations afford the agents a greater scope to realize gains from trade is that symmetry between the agents promotes the efficient management of this tradeoff.*[29]

2.3.4   Optimal transfers and dysfunctional identities

2.3.4.1   The general problem

At the start of the second stage the agents adopt a risk-sharing arrangement in anticipation of their infinitely repeated interaction. As mentioned, we assume that they agree to adopt the feasible arrangement that maximizes the sum of their expected discounted utilities. Given a code configuration and a discount factor, denote this optimal arrangement by $T^*[C_1, C_2; \delta]$. Thus

$$T^*[C_1, C_2; \delta] \equiv \text{ArgMax}\{V_1(T) + V_2(T) \mid T \in \Im(C_1, C_2; \delta)\}. \tag{10}$$

Now, observe that (since X is a finite set) a period-stationary transfer arrangement T is simply an array of $|X|^2$ elements that are real numbers. Furthermore, recall that at each indicator pair (x_1, x_2) the LHS of inequalities (5) and (6) (which define feasible transfer arrangements) are strictly concave functions of (the elements of) T. Therefore, since no transfer can exceed the giver's endowment, and since the endowment set Y is bounded, we can identify the set of feasible transfer arrangements $\Im(C_1, C_2; \delta)$ with the points of a compact, convex subset of a finite dimensional Euclidean space. It follows that for every code configuration and discount factor there exists a *unique* (since $V_i(T)$ are strictly concave functions) socially optimal transfer arrangement, as defined by equation (10).

Intuitively, at any indicator pair (x_1, x_2) the optimal arrangement $T^*[C_1, C_2; \delta](x_1, x_2)$ shifts resources from the agent with the lower to the one with the higher conditional shadow price, either until the post transfer conditional marginal valuations have become equal, or until the associated incentive constraint binds. For $\delta \approx 1$, the incentive constraints are guaranteed to hold for any transfer arrangement generating positive surplus for both agents, so in that case the optimal transfer at each indicator pair (x_1, x_2) is simply the unconstrained maximizer of the sum of conditional expected utilities there. Let $\tilde{T}(x_1, x_2)$ denote this best *unconstrained* arrangement. Then:

$$\tilde{T}(x_1, x_2) \equiv \text{ArgMax}\{v_1(x_1, -t) + v_2(x_2, t) \mid t \in \Re\}, \quad \text{for all } (x_1, x_2) \in X^2.$$

Obviously, we must have $v_1'(x_1, -t) = v_2'(x_2, t)$ at $t = \tilde{T}(x_1, x_2)$.

It follows that, with a sufficiently large discount factor, the receiver of an optimal transfer will enjoy higher net consumption than the giver with positive probability. Each pair of indicators (x_1, x_2) is associated with a "rectangle" of endowments, $C_1^{-1}(x_1) \times C_2^{-1}(x_2)$. The unconstrained optimal arrangement equalizes conditional expected marginal utilities at indicator pairs. But then, because utility is strictly concave, when a giving agent consumes least at a fixed indicator pair her marginal utility exceeds the conditional expectation there. And, when a receiving agent consumes most her marginal utility falls short of the corresponding conditional expectation. Thus, for $\delta \approx 1$ the consumption of low endowment givers is always less than that of high endowment receivers at a given indicator pair. This is a useful fact, recorded for future reference as:

Lemma 3. *Given a code configuration $\langle C_1, C_2 \rangle$ there is a δ' sufficiently large such that, for any $\delta > \delta'$ and any indicator pair (x_1, x_2): if the optimal transfer $t = T^*(x_1, x_2) > 0$ then $y_1 - t < y_2 + t$ for some $y_1 \in C_1^{-1}(x_1)$ and $y_2 \in C_2^{-1}(x_2)$, while the opposite inequality obtains if $t < 0$.*[30]

For $\delta \ll 1$ the incentive constraints (5) and (6) become relevant, and the best feasible risk sharing arrangement can no longer be described quite so simply. However, we can readily characterize the optimal transfer arrangement in the general case. (This characterization can be used to compute optimal transfer arrangements in parametric examples, as we do in Section 2.4.) This characterization is derived by adapting to our context an observation familiar from the theory of discounted repeated games: if one knew in advance the overall payoff accruing to each agent from the optimal arrangement, then explicitly deriving the detailed features of that arrangement would be a trivial exercise.

Accordingly, for a given code configuration $\langle C_1, C_2 \rangle$ and discount factor δ, and for arbitrary $w = (w_1, w_2) \in \Re_+^2$, consider the the function $\Psi \colon \Re_+^2 \to \Re_+^2$ defined by

$$\Psi_i(w) \equiv V_i(\hat{T}[w]), \quad i = 1, 2, \tag{11}$$

where $\hat{T}[w]$ solves

$\mathrm{Max}\{V_1(T) + V_2(T)\}$

subject to,

for all $(x_1, x_2) \in X^2$:

$$\delta w_1 \geq -\Delta u\left[\mathrm{Min}\{C_1^{-1}(x_1)\}, -T(x_1, x_2)\right],$$

and

$$\delta w_2 \geq -\Delta u\left[\mathrm{Min}\{C_2^{-1}(x_2)\}, T(x_1, x_2)\right].$$

Thus, $\Psi_i(w)$ is the payoff to agent i associated with the socially most desirable, "pseudo-feasible" transfer arrangement, where "pseudo-feasibility" refers to transfer arrangements that would be feasible if the "psuedo-payoff" w_j were what agent j's anticipated to lose upon reversion to autarky, $j = 1, 2$. Notice that, so long as at least one incentive constraint binds for agent j, then $\Psi_i(w)$ rises and $\Psi_j(w)$ falls as w_j rises, $i \neq j$. This is because raising agent j's pseudo-payoff, w_j, loosens the incentive constraints for transfers going from agent j to agent i, but does not affect the pseudo-feasibility of transfers going from agent i to agent j. So, raising w_j can only lead to an increase in Ψ_i and a decline in Ψ_j.

Now, it is obvious that if $w' = \Psi(w')$, then $\hat{T}[w'] \in \Im(C_1, C_2; \delta)$. (That is, all transfer arrangements $\hat{T}[w']$ associated with the fixed points of $\Psi(\cdot)$ are feasible.) Moreover, it is also obvious that for $w_i^* \equiv V_i(T^*[C_1, C_2; \delta]), i = 1, 2$, we must have $w^* = \Psi(w^*)$. (That is, the payoffs engendered by the optimal transfer arrangement constitute a fixed point of $\Psi(\cdot)$.) Of course, not any fixed point of Ψ will do the trick here, since $(w_1, w_2) = (0, 0)$ (with $\hat{T} \equiv 0$) is always going to be among the "self-generating" payoffs. Nevertheless, we have the following characterization:

Theorem 2. *Fixing the code configuration* $\langle C_1, C_2 \rangle$ *and the discount factor* δ, *let* $\Psi \colon \mathfrak{R}^2_+ \to \mathfrak{R}^2_+$ *be given by equation (11), and define* $\Gamma \equiv \{ w' \in \mathfrak{R}^2_+ \mid \Psi(w') = w' \}$. *Then* Γ *is non-empty and there exists a vector-maximal element,* $w^* \in \Gamma$.[31] *Moreover,* $\hat{T}[w^*] = T^*[C_1, C_2; \delta]$.

Proof. To prove Theorem 2 notice (from the foregoing discussion) that, given a code configuration and discount factor, a unique optimal transfer arrangement T^* exists (maximizing a strictly concave function over a compact, convex set). Moreover, by the definition of optimality, $\langle V_1(T^*), V_2(T^*) \rangle \equiv w^* \in \Gamma$. Thus, we only need to show that w^* is the vector-maximal element of Γ.

So, let $w' \in \Gamma$, with $w' \neq w^*$. Since $\hat{T}[w']$ is feasible and T^* is optimal, it is impossible that $w' \gg w^*$. So, without loss of generality, we assume that $w^*_2 > w'_2$ and then proceed to show that $w^*_1 > w'_1$.

The result is a straightforward consequence of the facts that $\Psi_i(w)$ increases and $\Psi_j(w)$ decreases as w_j rises, $i \neq j$. To see this, observe that: $w^*_1 = \Psi_1(w^*) > \Psi_1(w^*_1, w'_2)$ (since Ψ_1 increases with w_2 and $w^*_2 > w'_2$). Thus,

$$\left[w^*_1 - w'_1 \right] > \left[\Psi_1(w^*_1, w'_2) - \Psi_1(w') \right].$$

At the same time, because Ψ_1 decreases with w_1, we must have that

$$\left[w^*_1 - w'_1 \right] \cdot \left[\Psi_1(w^*_1, w'_2) - \Psi_1(w') \right] < 0.$$

It follows from these two inequalities that $w^*_1 - w'_1 > 0$, as was to be shown. (If the product of two numbers is negative, the larger of these numbers must be positive.) □

2.3.4.2 *Equilibrium in the case* $|X| = 2$, *with quadratic utility and* $\delta \approx 1$

We conclude the analysis of this section by considering the full equilibrium of the two-stage model in the special case where just two indicators are available. To keep the computations tractable, we assume futher that δ is sufficiently large so incentive constraints can be ignored, and that $u(\cdot)$ may be closely approximated by a quadratic function. These are strong assumptions, to be sure. But our goals here are merely illustrative: (i) to show how decentralized, self-interested identity choices by the agents can lead them to embrace a dysfunctional collective identity; and (ii) to see how the bias associated with this inefficient identity choice depends on the fundamentals of the problem.

Thus, for the remainder of this section we study the first stage, reduced-form game under the presumption that the unconstrained optimal transfer arrangement $\hat{T}$ is to be implemented in each period of the second stage. We assume that the utility function can be written as follows:

$$u(y) = \alpha y - \frac{\beta}{2} y^2 + \frac{\gamma}{3} y^3, \tag{12}$$

where α and β are positive constants, and γ is a real number, of either sign, near zero.[32] Endowments y are assumed to be continuously distributed over some bounded interval of $\Re_+$, and the parameters are taken to be such that $u'(y) > 0$ and $u''(y) < 0$ throughout this interval.

We denote the density function of the endowment distribution by $p(y)$ and the cumulative distribution function by $P(y) = \int_{\{v \leq y\}} p(v)\, dv$. The mean endowment is denoted by $\mu = \int yp(y)dy$. For any quantile of the endowment distribution, $z \in [0, 1]$, we denote by $\mu(z) \equiv P^{-1}(z)$ the endowment level associated with that quantile, and we define

$$\mu_z^+ \equiv E[y \mid y > \mu(z)] \quad \text{and} \quad \mu_z^- \equiv E[y \mid y \leq \mu(z)].$$

That is, μ_z^+ (μ_z^-) is the mean endowment conditional on the being above (below) quantile z in the endowment distribution. Obviously, $\mu_z^+ > \mu > \mu_z^-$, and $z\mu_z^- + (1-z)\mu_z^+ \equiv z$ on $[0,1]$. Finally, again for $z \in [0,1]$, we define

$$\rho_z^+ \equiv E[y^2 \mid y > \mu(z)] \quad \text{and} \quad \rho_z^- \equiv E[y^2 \mid y \leq \mu(z)].$$

We will undertake a perturbation analysis of the following form: Staring with $\gamma = 0$, we solve for the (unconstrained) optimal second-stage tranfer arrangement. Holding this arrangement fixed but allowing γ to vary in a neighborhood of zero, we then derive equilibrium and optimal first-stage identity configurations, as functions of γ. That is, we ignore the impact on the optimal transfer arrangement that arises due to a "small" perturbation of the utility function in the neighborhood of a quadratic. This is justified since, for γ near zero, this impact is a second-order effect. The motivation for proceeding in the way will become clear in what follows. For now, it suffices to observe that quadratic utility ($\gamma = 0$) is a "knife-edge" case, where equilibrium and optimal identity configurations coincide, but this is generally not true for the perturbed utility function ($\gamma \neq 0$). So, we can use the perturbation analysis to see how the divergence of equilibrium from optimal configurations depends on the endowment distribution and on (the third derivative of) the utility function.

As mentioned, in the case $|X| = 2$, monotonic codes are defined by thresholds y_i^* such that $C_i(y) = B$ for $y \leq y_i^*$. Equivalently, we can describe such codes by the quantiles of the endowment distribution $z_i \equiv P(y_i^*)$ below which agents report a "bad" outcome. Thus, for the remainder of this section we identify a code configuration with a pair of numbers $(z_1, z_2) \in [0, 1]^2$, and we denote the per-period payoff to agent 1 under such a configuration by $U(z_1, z_2) \equiv (1 - \delta)V_1$. Let (z_1^e, z_2^e) and (z_1^o, z_2^o) denote, respectively, the equilibrium and socially optimal configurations. Then, as discussed in Section 2.2.2.2, the relationship between the equilibrium and the socially optimal configurations is determined by the sign of $U_2(z_1^e, z_2^e)$.

Now, with a quadratic utility function, marginal utility is linear in consumption. So, equating conditional expected marginal utilities between the agents amounts to equating conditional expected consumption levels. Thus, in this case the unconstrained optimal arrangement must be such that the better-off agent transfers to the worse-off agent an amount equal to half the difference in their conditional mean endowments. Moreover, with two indicators, $x \in \{B, G\}$, there are four possible indicator pairs,

$$(x_1, x_2) \in X^2 \equiv \{(B, B), (B, G), (G, B), (G, G)\},$$

and these indicator pairs are realized, respectively, with probabilities

$$q_1(x_1)q_2(x_2) \in \{z_1 z_2, z_1(1 - z_2), (1 - z_1)z_2, (1 - z_1)(1 - z_2)\}. \tag{13}$$

In light of the discussion to this point, it is clear that the unconstrained optimal transfer arrangement in the quadratic, two-indicator case satisfies:

$$T(B, B) = \frac{\mu_{z_1}^- - \mu_{z_2}^-}{2}, \quad T(B, G) = \frac{\mu_{z_1}^- - \mu_{z_2}^+}{2}, \quad \text{and}$$

$$T(G, B) = \frac{\mu_{z_1}^+ - \mu_{z_2}^-}{2}, \quad T(G, G) = \frac{\mu_{z_1}^+ - \mu_{z_2}^+}{2}. \tag{14}$$

We conclude that for $T(x_1, x_2)$ given in equation (14), and for $C_1^{-1}(B) = \{y \leq \mu(z_1)\}$ and $C_1^{-1}(G) = \{y > \mu(z_1)\}$, agent 1's per period expected payoff is given by:

$$U(z_1, z_2) = \sum_{(x_1, x_2) \in X^2} q_1(x_1)q_2(x_2)E\big[\Delta u(y, -T(x_1, x_2)) \,\big|\, y \in C_1^{-1}(x_1)\big]. \tag{15}$$

A simple computation shows that if $u(y) = \alpha y - (\beta/2)y^2 + (\gamma/3)y^3$, then

$$\Delta u(y, t) \equiv u(y + t) - u(y) = u(t) - \beta t y + \gamma(t^2 y + t y^2).$$

Hence, taking conditional expectations above (for $A \subset Y$ an event, and with $\mu_A \equiv E[y \mid A]$ and $\rho_A \equiv E[y^2 \mid A]$), we have that:

$$E[\Delta u(y, t) \mid A] = \alpha t - \beta\left(t\mu_A + \frac{t^2}{2}\right) + \gamma\left(t^2\mu_A + t\rho_A + \frac{t^3}{3}\right). \tag{16}$$

Now, using the formula in equation (15), the expression in (16) (taking conditional expectations at each indicator pair), the transfer arrangement given in (14), and the probabilities as given in (13), we can derive agent 1's payoff via a straightforward but tedious computation (which is omitted here).[33] To state the result compactly, we require just a bit more notation. Thus, for any quantile $z \in [0, 1]$ define

$$\sigma^2(z) \equiv z \left[\mu - \mu_z^-\right]^2 + (1 - z) \left[\mu - \mu_z^+\right]^2 \quad \text{and}$$

$$\sigma^3(z) \equiv z \left[\mu - \mu_z^-\right]^3 + (1 - z) \left[\mu - \mu_z^+\right]^3 .$$

Then, we have the following result:

Proposition 2. *For the utility function $u(\cdot)$ given in equation (12) and the transfer arrangement $T(\cdot, \cdot)$ given in equation (14), the expected per period surplus for agent 1 is*

$$U(z_1, z_2) = \left(\frac{3\beta + 2\gamma\mu}{8}\right) \sigma^2(z_1) + \left(\frac{2\gamma\mu - \beta}{8}\right) \sigma^2(z_2)$$

$$- \left(\frac{5\gamma}{24}\right) \sigma^3(z_1) - \left(\frac{\gamma}{24}\right) \sigma^3(z_2) - \left(\frac{\gamma}{2}\right) H(z_1) + K, \quad (17)$$

where $H(z) \equiv \left[z\mu_z^- \rho_z^- + (1 - z)\mu_z^+ \rho_z^+\right]$ and K is a constant, independent of (z_1, z_2).

We are now in a position to compare the equilibrium and socially optimal collective identities in this "near quadratic utility-two indicator" case. Notice that $U(z_1, z_2)$ is additively separable, so agent 1 has a dominant strategy identity choice in the first stage. Therefore, the unique equilibrium identity choice is the same for both agents in this case, and satisfies:

$$z_1^* = z_2^* = z^e \equiv \text{ArgMax}_{z \in [0,1]} \{(3\beta + 2\gamma\mu)\sigma^2(z)$$

$$- (5\gamma/3)\sigma^3(z) - 4\gamma H(z)\}. \quad (18)$$

By contrast, the unique socially optimal collective identity (which maximizes $U(z, z)$) is given in this case by:

$$z^o \equiv \text{ArgMax}_{z \in [0,1]} \{(\beta + 2\gamma\mu)\sigma^2(z) - \gamma\sigma^3(z) - 2\gamma H(z)\}. \quad (19)$$

For γ in a neighborhood of zero, denote by $z^e(\gamma)$ the solution of equation (18), and let $z^o(\gamma)$ be the solution of equation (19). Then, the following result is immediate:

Corollary 2. *In the exact quadratic utility case ($\gamma = 0$), with $\delta \approx 1$, the equilibrium collective identity is socially optimal: $z^e(0) = z^o(0) = \text{ArgMax}_{z \in [0,1]} \{\sigma^2(z)\}$.*

To carry forward our perturbation analysis, we need to derive the sign of $(d/d\gamma)[z^e(\gamma) - z^o(\gamma)]$ at $\gamma = 0$. If this derivative is positive, then a near quadratic utility function with $\gamma > 0$ yields a dysfunctional collective identity where the agents are too pessimistic (i.e., their probability of announcing a "good" endowment is too low). While, if this derivative is negative then the agents are too optimistic in equilibrium when $\gamma > 0$. (The opposite inferences apply when $\gamma < 0$.) Using the first-order conditions in equations (18) and (19), and applying the Implicit Function Theorem, we conclude that

$$\frac{d}{d\gamma}\left[z^e(\gamma) - z^o(\gamma)\right]\Big|_{\gamma=0} = \frac{(4/3)[d\sigma^3(z^o)/dz] + 2H'(z^o)}{\beta(d^2/dz^2)[\sigma^2(z^o)]}. \tag{20}$$

Since the second-order condition for equation (19) requires the denominator above to be negative, we have the following result:

Corollary 3. *In the near quadratic utility case ($\gamma \approx 0$), with $\delta \approx 1$, the equilibrium identity is too pessimistic (resp., too optimistic) if $\gamma \cdot \{\frac{2}{3}[d\sigma^3(z^o)/dz] + H'(z^o)\} < 0$ (resp., > 0), where $z^o \equiv \text{ArgMax}_{z\in[0,1]}\{\sigma^2(z)\}$.*

The condition (20) is difficult to interpret. We note, however, (as may be easily verified) that when the endowment distribution is uniform the RHS in (20) vanishes. While, if a linear density function is posited, the RHS in (20) is positive when the density is increasing with y (i.e., when the distribution of endowments has a relatively fat right tail), and the RHS is negative when the density is decreasing (i.e., when the distribution of endowments has a fat left tail). From this it follows (assuming linear densities and nearly quadratic utility) that if $u''' > 0$, then the equilibrium identity will be too pessimistic (optimistic) if the endowment distribution has a fat left (right) tail. The opposite conclusion obtains if $u''' < 0$.

2.4 Numerical analysis of the 3 × 2 case

We return now to the 3 × 2 example. We will employ a parametric class of utility functions $u(\cdot)$ to explore the comparative statics of that case. Consider the constant relative risk aversion (CRRA) family of utility functions

$$u(y) = \frac{y^{1-\rho}}{1-\rho}, \quad \text{with } \rho \in (0, 1],$$

when $\rho = 1, u(y) = \ln y$. Given this utility function, the outcome in our model is determined by the distribution of random incomes, the discount factor, δ, and the risk aversion parameter, ρ. Note that CRRA utilities satisfy $u''' > 0$. Thus, the set

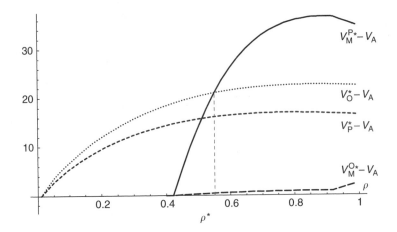

Figure 2.1 The value differences from the autarky value V_A as functions of ρ:
$p_l = 0.5, p_m = 0.2, l = 1, m = 6, h = 10, \delta = 0.99$.

of economic environments within which we work is defined as follows:

$$\left\langle \left(\{k, p_k\}_{k \in \{l,m,h\}}, \delta, \rho \right) : l < m < h, p_k \in (0, 1), \right.$$

$$\left. \sum_{k \in \{l,m,h\}} p_k = 1, \delta \in (0, 1), \rho \in (0, 1] \right\rangle.$$

In what follows, we study how equilibrium identities chosen in the first stage depend on the discount factor and the degree of risk aversion. We do this by calculating numerically the second-stage continuation values under autarky, under the "optimistic" and "pessimistic" collective codings, and under the mixed coding. We then examine how these continuation values vary with the pair of parameters, (δ, ρ). Our numerical results are summarized in Figures 2.1–2.4.

2.4.1   *Risk aversion and collective identities*

We first consider how the equilibrium coding choices are affected by the relative risk aversion parameter ρ. As ρ gets larger, the agent becomes more risk averse, which means (of course) that risk sharing becomes more valuable to them, other things equal. Thus, one way of interpreting the comparative statics exercise is to think of an increase in the risk-aversion parameter as reflecting a raising of the stakes for the agents in their second-stage interactions. The equilibrium coding depends on the relative value of V_M^{O*} as compared with V_O^* and V_P^*. Figure 2.1. shows the differences between $(V_P^*, V_O^*, V_M^{P*}, V_M^{O*})$ and the autarky value V as ρ varies. Note the figure depicts a threshold ρ^* such that when for any $\rho \in (0, \rho^*)$, we have the following inequalities:

$$V_O^* - V_A > V_M^{P*} - V_A$$
$$V_P^* - V_A > V_M^{O*} - V_A.$$

The first equality implies that if the other agent is choosing C_O, I will be better off by choosing C_O, which will secure myself a value of V_O, than choosing C_P – which will only yield a value of V_M^P for *me* since we would be at a mixed code equilibrium. Therefore, the first equality implies that $\langle C_O, C_O \rangle$ is an equilibrium. Analogously, the second inequality implies that the other agent is choosing C_P, I am better off choosing C_P than C_O, because a choice of C_P yields value of V_P and a choice of C_O a value of V_M^O.

Therefore when $\rho \in (0, \rho^*)$, we are *multiple* equilibria collective identities. Moreover, the equilibria are Pareto-ranked: the "optimistic" equilibrium $\langle C_O, C_O \rangle$ Pareto dominates the "pessimistic" equilibrium $\langle C_P, C_P \rangle$. When $\rho > \rho^*$, Figure 2.1 shows that

$$V_O^* - V_A < V_M^{P*} - V_A, \quad \text{but} \quad V_P^* - V_A > V_M^{O*} - V_A.$$

Therefore, the unique equilibrium collective identity is the "pessimistic" identity $\langle C_P, C_P \rangle$. It is worth noting that if both agents can commit to choose the "optimistic" coding, both agents' value would be higher than the equilibrium value V_P^*. The "optimistic" coding does not constitute an equilibrium due to forces similar to the familiar "Prisoner's Dilemma."

2.4.2 *Discount factors and collective identities*

The second comparative statics we do in this numerical exercise is with respect to the discount factor δ. A discount factor can capture many things in repeated game models, including expected stability of the relationship or the length of time elapsing between the repeated encounters. Here it is natural to think of the discount factor as capturing the density of the social network within which the agents interact, follow their identity choices. That is, a large discount factor (near one) can be interpreted to mean that the repeated encounters are quite frequent, and thus the social network within which agents are embedded is dense.

Figure 2.2 shows three curves $V_P^* - V_M^{O*}$, $V_O^* - V_M^{P*}$, and $V_O^* - V_P^*$, all as functions of the discount factor δ, under a risk aversion parameter $\rho = 0.5$. Note that both $V_P^* - V_M^{O*}$ and $V_O^* - V_M^{P*}$ are strictly positive for all values of δ plotted. This indicates that there are two equilibrium coding for $\rho = 0.5$. The reason is simple. When $V_P^* - V_M^{O*}$ is positive, it means that, if the other agent is choosing a code C_P, I will be better off choosing C_P to secure a value of V_P^* than choosing C_O and obtain value V_M^{O*}. When $V_O^* - V_M^{P*}$ is positive, it means that, if the other agent is choosing a code C_O, then I will be better off choosing C_O to secure a value of V_O^* than choosing C_P and obtain value V_M^{P*}. Also note from Figure 2.2 that $V_O^* - V_P^*$

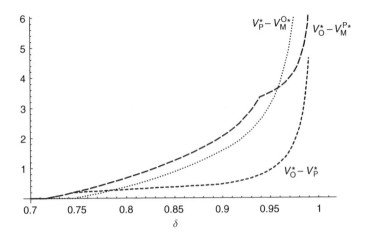

Figure 2.2 Relevant value differences as function of δ: $p_l = 0.5, p_m = 0.2,$ $l = 1, m = 6, h = 10, \rho = 0.5.$

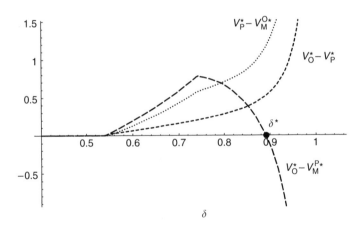

Figure 2.3 Relevant value differences as function of δ: $p_l = 0.5, p_m = 0.2,$ $l = 1, m = 6, h = 10, \rho = 0.8.$

is also strictly positive for all values of δ plotted. This means that the "optimistic" coding equilibrium Pareto dominates the "pessimistic" coding equilibrium.

Figure 2.3 also shows three curves $V_P^* - V_M^{O*}$, $V_O^* - V_M^{P*}$, and $V_O^* - V_P^*$, all as functions of the discount factor δ, but under a risk aversion parameter $\rho = 0.8$. Note that, for this case, while $V_P^* - V_M^{O*}$ is strictly positive for all values of δ plotted, $V_O^* - V_M^{P*}$ is only positive when δ is less than a threshold δ^*. That is, communities with high degree of isolation, which implies a higher level of δ tend to have difficulty forming "optimistic" codes. Note that, a negative value of $V_O^* - V_M^{P*}$ when δ is high does not mean that V_O^* and V_M^{P*} are low, it just means

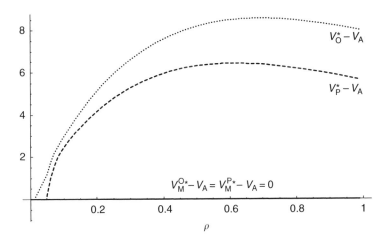

Figure 2.4 The value differences from the autarky value V_A as functions of ρ: $p_l = 0.3, p_m = 0.4, l = 2, m = 6, h = 10, \delta = 0.99$.

that there is a profitable deviation when the other agent is choosing C_O. At all levels of δ, the simulation shows that $V_O^* > V_P^*$, i.e., agents are better off under the "optimistic" code.

2.4.3   Income generating processes and collective identities

Figures 2.1–2.3 are simulated from a particular income generating process characterized by (p_l, p_m, p_h, l, m, h). In general, the exact set of equilibrium collective identities will depend on the fine details of the income generating process. Here we show some simulation result for a symmetric environment to illustrate the results in Section 2.3.3.3. Consider a symmetric environment in which $p_l = p_h = 0.3$, $p_m = 0.4, l = 2, m = 6, h = 10$. In Figure 2.4, we let $\delta = 0.99$ and depict the difference between $V_P^*, V_O^*, V_M^{P*}, V_M^{O*}$ and the autarky value V_A. It turns out that under this particular income generating process, there is no scope for risk sharing under mixed codes. Thus $V_M^{O*} = V_M^{P*} = V_A$. Figure 2.4 shows that there are two equilibrium collective identities and the optimistic identity dominates the pessimistic identity, confirming our prediction in Proposition 1 because $u''' > 0$ for CRRA utility functions. Figure 2.5 shows the relevant payoff differences, as a function of δ, with ρ fixed at 0.8. It turns out the "Prisoner's Dilemma" like situation does not arise under this symmetric income generating process.

2.5   Discussion and next steps

We now offer a few observations about our general approach and its limitations, as well as some suggestions for further work. The risk-sharing problem studied here is simply a laboratory within which to explore our main idea – which is modeling

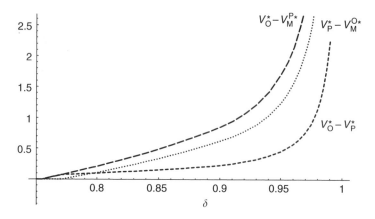

Figure 2.5 Relevant value differences as function of δ: $p_l = 0.3, p_m = 0.4,$
$l = 2, m = 6, h = 10, \rho = 0.8.$

identity as the "coding" of personal history into a simplified form.[34] One nice
thing about the risk-sharing formulation, though, is that it easily accomodates an
analysis of some classic identity oppositions – the "optimist" vs. the "pessimist,"
for instance; or, one with a "wide" vs. a "narrow" sense of what constitutes her
"victimization." This framework also makes it easy to get an intuitive grasp of
how identity choice interacts with economic behavior: in our model, choosing
an identity is equivalent to deciding upon a way to limit the information that is
publicly available about one's (income) experience. Studying the consequences of
such endogenous restrictions on public information is a relatively easy thing to do
in a risk-sharing context, and the resulting model is rich with implications.

We have derived results in our simple, two-person setting about when the strategic interaction leading to collective identity choice is a coordination game, and
when it is a prisoner's dilemma, based on the size of the discount factor and the
degree of risk aversion. The numerical analysis (which assumed constant relative
risk aversion) showed that when risk aversion is below a threshold, the simultaneous choice of identity in the first stage is a coordination game; when it is above
a threshold, and when the discount factor is high enough, then we have a prisoner's dilemma with "pessimistic" coding being the only equilibrium, although it
is Pareto dominated by the "optimistic" coding. This seems to us a very interesting
finding. The degree of risk aversion may be taken as a proxy for the importance of
the economic interactions that are being influenced by identity choices. The more
risk averse are the agents, the more is at stake in their risk-sharing interactions.
This finding from our numerical analysis, therefore, can be interpreted as saying
that when a great deal is at stake in their risk-sharing interactions, "pessimism"
(or, embracing a "wide," not "narrow," sense of what constitutes "victimization")
is likely to emerge as a dysfunctional collective identity. We also find that, when
the risk aversion is low, first-stage identity choice is a coordination game for

all discount factor. Thus, when the stakes are not very high for the economic interaction, multiple equilibria are likely. This means that two similarly situated but socially isolated populations could end up making widely different (though equally "rational") identity choices.

While we believe the approach to "identity" offered here is promising, we recognize that our analysis has some serious limitations. Our model endogenizes the choice of identity, but this is a once-and-for-all choice. We allow for no evolution of identities, no chance for agents to "invest" in remaking their identities (through education, relocation, sex change operations(!), etc.). In reality, of course, identities can evolve. One vexing question is why this malleability of identity is greater in some "cultures" than in others.[35] Relatedly, suppose agents cannot perfectly observe each other's identities, but they can learn about each other over time. To revisit some examples mentioned in the introduction: Is he gay or not? Is she a single-minded career woman, or not? Is that white guy over there really angry? In reality, the first-stage identity choice game would not be in normal form. And, this being the case, it is far from clear that the multiple equilibria we find to exist in a static identity choice setting would survive the dynamics of equilibrium selection if agents' identities were imperfectly observed, but agents could learn about each other over time.

Our theory (but also, common sense) emphasizes that "identity" is endogenous, and is shaped by social contacts. So, the question arises: What kind of social networks in which people might be embedded lead to what kinds of choices about identity? This is a particularly interesting question for someone studying race, culture, and social inequality in the US. One implication of our theory, in a slightly expanded model allowing for the assortative matching of agents from distinct groups before playing the second-stage repeated game, is that distinctive patterns of identity choices by individuals in distinct groups is more likely if patterns of social interaction are more group-segregated. This leads us to speculate that anyone who believes "culture" is important in sustaining racial inequality in a society like the US should look seriously at the linkages between identity and social integration. Casual empiricists make much of the observable differences in "values" between distinct groups. But, our analysis points toward a recognition of the fact that such cultural difference may be parasitic upon a pre-existing disparity in the structures of social interaction.[36] If group inequality is partly due to cultural differences, if cultural variation is partly a matter of distinct identity choices, and if identity choices diverge in part because of segregated social networks, then social *integration* of some sort might be an antidote for inequality.

But, what kind of integration would be most important, and which egalitarian interventions might be most effective? Consider, for instance, the distinction emphasized by political scientist Robert Putnam between "bridging" and "bonding" social connection.[37] "Bridges" are connections between people belonging to different (racial/ethnic) groups; "bonds" are connections between people in the same group. In general, a social network is characterized by its "nodes" (people) and its "links" (connections), where the links might be thought of as coming in these two flavors – bridges and bonds.[38] All of this suggests what might be a useful way of thinking about the connection between culture and inequality. Whether or not a given (possibly dysfunctional) pattern of behavior becomes normative within an economically backward, socially isolated group (so that conformity pressures favoring that behavior can develop) could depend in interesting ways on what might be called the *architecture* of the social network in which the group is embedded – i.e., on the density and relative frequency of these two types of bonds. Our approach could be extended in this direction, perhaps even to include the study of endogenously generated racial identities.[39] We plan to pursue this possibility in future work.

In another vein that we intend to pursue, our conceptualization of identity seems to be similar to *language* in the following sense: saying that different communities can embrace different collective identities (in the sense that states of the world are understood differently due to the limited cognitive capacity) is isomorphic to saying that different communities can adopt different languages.[40] That is, while one community may have a word to describe a particular state of the world, in another community no word may exist to specifically describe that state of world. So, our framework (extended to incorporate moral hazard in the endowment generating process) might be useful for asking why we do not observe complete languages – i.e., languages in which a different word exists to describe each possible state of nature. One reason could be that ambiguity is sometimes useful in a world where there is a tradeoff between effort incentives and risk sharing. More specifically, it may be true that, given any fixed income generating process, a complete vocabulary could achieve better risk sharing; but, if incomes are endogenous, then this completeness might undermine incentives to take income-enhancing effort.

Finally, we wish to discuss informally one more possible extension of this line of inquiry. It is an implication of Lemma 3, as applied to the 3×2 case, that when the discount factor is sufficiently large the post-transfer consumption of an agent with the intermediate income will be greater than that of an agent with the high income under "pessimism," but less than that of an agent with the low income under "optimism." This finding could have interesting implications when the model is extended to allow for endogenous efforts. It suggests that an effort disincentive could exist under either type of collective identity, and that the nature of this disincentive might depend on the precise way that effort shifts the distribution of random incomes.

Thus, consider the following speculative argument: let the parameters be such that the identity choice game is a coordination game. Modify the game by inserting an (unobservable) effort choice prior to the realization of incomes in each period of the second stage. Effort is costly, but it makes higher-income realizations more likely to occur. If the result of more effort is to raise the probability of a high income and to lower the probability of an intermediate income, leaving the probability of a low income unchanged, then the "pessimistic" coding (which makes post-transfer consumption lower for the high than for the intermediate income agent) may lead to an overall equilibrium with low effort, compared to the "optimistic" coding. That is, *"pessimism" could be a dysfunctional collective identity when it is difficult to reduce the chance of poverty but possible to increase the chance of becoming rich through high effort.* Similarly, if the result of effort is mainly to raise the probability of an intermediate income and to lower the probability of a low income, leaving the probability of a high income unchanged, then the "optimistic" coding (which makes post-transfer consumption lower for the middle than the low income agent) may lead to equilibrium with low effort, compared to the "pessimistic" coding. In this case, *"optimism" could be a dysfunctional collective identity when it is difficult to increase the chance of becoming rich but possible to reduce the chance of being poor through high effort.*

Of course, this is all just conjecture at this point. But these conjectures, based on the interaction between collective identity and the technology of income improvement, seem quite intriguing to us. Note that in both of these speculative instances, a certain monotonicity property fails: higher effort does not increase the likelihood ratio of every income level relative to all lower-income levels. What the discussion suggests is that incentive problems may cause a collective identity choice to be inefficient when this non-monotonicity overlaps with the clustering of income states under a code. That is, a dysfunctional collective identity may come about when effort causes the higher-income state within a code to become relatively less likely than the lower income state. We will be looking at this possibility in the next phase of this research program.

2.6   Conclusion

Managing collective action problems is itself a collective action problem. In our model, two agents need to share resources in order to smooth consumption over time. This is their collective action problem, and how the agents manage it depends on how they interpret their personal experiences to one another. We imagine that agents decide on a way to publicly render their private experiences, mindful of the fact that any subsequent transactions between them must be framed in terms of those renderings. This framework implies a non-cooperative game of identity choice, where "identity" is understood to be a way of rendering "the self" to others. We have shown that, under a wide range of conditions, the strategic forces of this game favor the agents adopting a common, collective identity in equilibrium. Moreover, we have also shown that when the density of their interactions and their potential gains from trade are sufficiently great, the equilibrium of this implied identity game has a "tragedy of the commons" character, and a universally superior way exists for agents to render their experiences to one another. So, under these conditions their collective identity can be said to be *dysfunctional.* This classical economic insight is a principle benefit of the approach to "identity" that we are proposing here.

Acknowledgments

The authors thank Chris Barrett, Stephen Coate, Roland Fryer, Antonio Merlo, Stephen Morris, and Andrew Postlewaite for helpful discussions. We remain solely responsible for any errors. We gratefully acknowledge the financial support of The Andrew W. Mellon Foundation and The Pew Charitable Trusts.

Notes

1 See, e.g., the useful survey on "The Self" in the *Handbook of Social Psychology* (Baumeister 1998).
2 Goffman (1963) uses yet another distinction – between "virtual" and "actual" social identities. The former is a social artifact, an identity constructed "from the outside" via social imputations based on a person's physical presentation. While the latter is relatively objective, an identity constructed "from the inside" via the accumulation of facts specific to a person's biography. Goffman's analysis of "stigma" is all about the interesting drama that unfolds when virtual and actual identities diverge systematically in the social experience of a given individual.
3 Sidanius and Pratto (2001) and Aronson *et al.* (2003) are interesting illustrations of how the "collective identity" concept has been used in the social psychology literature.
4 One popular version of this hypothesis is the suspicion that native-born black Americans fare poorly in school because many think that the doing of academic work is "acting white" (see, e.g., Ronald Ferguson's chapter in the Loury *et al.* volume (2005)).
5 See, e.g., North (1981), Grief (1994), Bernheim (1994), Akerlof (1997), Akerlof and Kranton (2000, 2002), and Fryer (2003). Fryer's work on "cultural capital," which also studies an infinitely repeated game as a laboratory for investigating the economic consequences of "culture," is the most similar to our own.
6 All of this is very much in the spirit of Fryer and Jackson (2003). To reduce a person's full experience to a relatively few descriptors is akin to associating an object's "attributes" with the "prototypes" discussed by Fryer and Jackson.
7 Some experimental work in this spirit has already been undertaken. Hoff and Pandey (2003) study the effects of caste identity on the cognitive performance of youngsters in an Indian village. Burns (2004) studies the impact of racial identity on trust in post-Apartheid South Africa.
8 We make Y finite here to ease the exposition of the general case. Nothing of consequence turns on this. Later in the chapter, when we study the special case where $|X| = 2$, it is convenient to let Y be an interval of real numbers (permitting use of the calculus).
9 As we shall see, the ideal code-mediated arrangement moves resources in each period from the "higher-indicator" (x_1, say) to the "lower-indicator" (x_2) agent, according to the formula: $t = T(x_1, x_2)$, where transfers attempt to equalize conditional expected marginal utilities of consumption, subject to incentive constraints. (The notions of "higher" and "lower" indicators are sensible for "monotonic" codes, as per the definition later.)
10 One might think that cooperative risk sharing would be easier to sustain in an equilibrium continuation of the second stage, infinitely repeated interactions, if the agents have adopted the same codes in the first stage. This conjecture is basically correct, and in what follows it is verified in the context of our model.
11 While non-monotonic codes are conceivable, it is intuitively obvious that, given the nature of the subsequent income-sharing problem, they are informationally inefficient when compared to some alternative monotonic code that uses "the same" (in a sense that could be made precise) cognitive resources. So, practically speaking, we do not see this monotonicity condition as entailing any real loss of generality.
12 That is, we consider only those arrangements where transfers depend, in the same manner each period, on that period's indicators alone.
13 When $t > 0$ we will speak of agent 1 "giving" and agent 2 "receiving" a transfer of size $|t|$, and conversely when $t < 0$.

14 Sometimes we shall be interested only in the question of whether, for a given configuration, there exists any surplus whatsoever in the second stage, in which case the issue of surplus division does not arise.

15 To be sure, other methods of surplus-splitting can be imagined – Nash bargaining, for instance. But our assumption here seems quite plausible. For, if both agents have chosen the same code, the utility possibility frontier for the second-stage continuation is symmetric about the 45° line, in which case our selection method coincides with the Nash bargaining outcome. On the other hand, given the *ex ante* symmetry of this strategic situation, it makes sense to think that each agent is "equally likely" to end up on either side of a mixed configuration. So, rational agents viewing the surplus division problem from behind a "veil of ignorance" well might agree to adopt the equilibrium selection method we have proposed.

16 Here we are using the obvious notation; so, V_M^{O*} is the payoff to the optimistic agent under a mixed configuration, while V_P^* is either agent's payoff under a pessimistic configuration, etc.

17 On this interpretation the example permits us to ask, in the habit if not in the spirit of McWhorter (2000), whether an expansive sense of one's victimization constitutes a "dysfunctional collective identity!"

18 Stating this more provocatively, the example permits us to investigate whether the agents spread their joint-income risks more effectively when they embrace a common "narrative of victimization!"

19 As the literature on finitely repeated games makes clear (e.g., Benoit and Krishna 1985), in principle this coordination problem could be easily "solved." In our two-stage setup, given that autarky is always an equilibrium continuation at the second stage, coordination on the efficient equilibrium in the reduced normal form could be enforced by threatening the autarkic risk-sharing continuation if either agent embraces the "wrong" identity. Exploiting this insight, one might argue that a dysfunctional identity ought not to emerge in cases where the reduced normal form is a coordination game if the agents use all of the strategic resources available to them.

We do not find this argument convincing. The prospect of renegotiation seriously undermines the credibility of any such threat. ("If you turn out to be the 'wrong' kind of person, then I won't have anything to do with you" is a threat lacking credibility in most social networks!) And while the same claim could be made about reversion to autarky as a threat supporting any risk sharing *within* the second stage, we think that the renegotiation of a risk-sharing arrangement after a deviation on identity choices has been observed, but before any risk sharing has actually taken place, is a much easier thing to envision than the renegotiation of such an agreement after its own terms have just been violated. This admittedly informal reasoning nevertheless suggests that we might plausibly impose "renegotiation-proofness" between *stages*, but not between *periods* within the second stage, which would leave the agents still facing the coordination difficulty that we are discussing here.

20 It is natural here, in keeping with the intuition from the 3×2 case, to associate a higher threshold y_i with a "more pessimistic" identity choice by agent i (or, with the agent adopting a "more expansive sense of her victimization"), since a higher threshold makes it less likely that a "good" signal is announced.

21 Hereafter, if Y is an interval of real numbers we take $p: Y \to \Re_+$ to be a probability density function, with

$$\int_Y p(y)\, dy = 1 \quad \text{and} \quad \int_Y y p(y)\, dy < \infty.$$

22 Notice that $\Pr\{E'\} = \pi_2(1 - \pi_1) > \Pr\{E\}$, since $\pi_2 > \pi_1$.

23 Of course, if the agents embrace a collective identity then they share a common threshold, and the disparity between y_1^* and y_2^* is zero.

24 With $y_1^* < y_2^*$, the likelihood of agent 1 (resp., agent 2) giving a transfer is $\pi_2(1 - \pi_1)$ [resp., $1 - \pi_2(1 - \pi_1)$].

25 So, the choice of a monotonic code amounts to deciding upon a way to partition the range of incomes into "connected" subsets of Y, with there being as many cells in the partition as there are elements of X.

26 We stress that the functions $q_i(x_i)$, $v_i(x, t)$, and $V_i(T)$ very much depend on the code C_i, and that our notation suppresses that dependence.

27 This interpretation may be verified by observing that, from the point of view of the least well off giving agent at $(\tilde{x}_1, \tilde{x}_2)$ (say), the expected marginal cost of a transfer is $\phi_1(\tilde{x}_1)$ in the current period, plus $q_1(\tilde{x}_1)q_2(\tilde{x}_2)v_1'(\tilde{x}_1, 0)$ starting in the next period and continuing in perpetuity. Moreover, the importance of a cost incurred in a single current period, relative to a cost incurred in perpetuity starting next period, is $(1 - \delta)/\delta$.

28 It does *not* follow from this result that optimism is an equilibrium collective identity when $u''' > 0$. That would require $V_O^* > V_M^{P*}$. Indeed, as demonstrated in Figure 2.1 (see Section 2.4), under constant relative risk aversion (so $u''' > 0$), if the agents are sufficiently risk averse then the collective identity of pessimism is a dominant strategy Nash Equilibrium of the reduced-form first stage game, even though the optimistic configuration welfare dominates the pessimistic one.

29 To see this, it may help to consider the following problem: Let $\tilde{y}$ be any random variable continuously distributed on some interval of real numbers, Y. Find sets of "high" and "low" realizations of $\tilde{y}$ for the two agents, respectively denoted Y_i^H and Y_i^L, $i = 1, 2$, so as to

$$\text{Max}\left\{\sum_{i \neq j}\left[E\left(u'(\tilde{y}) \mid Y_i^L\right) - E\left(u'(\tilde{y}) \mid Y_j^H\right)\right] \text{s.t. } \sum_{i \neq j}\Pr\{Y_i^L\}\Pr\{Y_j^H\} \geq \theta\right\}.$$

So the sets (Y_i^H, Y_i^L), $i \in \{1, 2\}$, are to be chosen to maximize the average difference in conditional marginal utilities of the agents across high/low indicator realizations, subject to keeping the probability of a high/low realization above some bound, θ. A little thought and a bit of algebra (which we leave to the reader) reveals that, for numbers $y^H > y^L \in Y$, the solution for this maximization problem entails

$$Y_1^H = Y_2^H = \left\{y \in Y \mid y \geq y^H\right\} \quad \text{and} \quad Y_1^L = Y_2^L = \left\{y \in Y \mid y \leq y^L\right\},$$

where y^H and y^L are such that

$$u'\left(y^H\right) - E\left[u'(\tilde{y}) \mid \tilde{y} \geq y^H\right] = E\left[u'(\tilde{y}) \mid \tilde{y} \leq y^L\right] - u'\left(y^L\right)$$

and

$$2\left[\sum_{y \geq y^H} p(y)\right]\left[\sum_{y \leq y^L} p(y)\right] = \theta.$$

Thus, for a given sum of mismatch frequencies, the following symmetric configuration yields the widest endowment disparity (and thus the greatest potential gain from the marginal trade): both agents are assigned identical "high" and "low" events at the upper and lower ends (respectively) of the endowment distribution. The two boundaries defining these events must be such that a high/low realization occurs with the required frequency, and such that the spread between the average shadow price of consumption and the shadow price at the boundary is equated across events. (Otherwise, one could widen the disparity in average shadow prices while maintaining the frequency of low/high encounters by adjusting the boundaries of the high and the low events.) Note that this argument is general, and does not depend on the assumption that $|X| = 2$, nor (if random signaling is allowed) on the assumption that Y is an interval of real numbers.

30 Strictly speaking, this should be a weak inequality, since consumption levels must be identical when both of the sets $C_i^{-1}(x_i)$ are singletons. But, that occurence is not to be expected in equilibrium, given that $|X| \ll |Y|$.

31 That is, w^* is such that $w^* \gg w'$, for all $w' \in \Gamma$, $w' \neq w^*$.

32 That is, the term $(\gamma/3)y^3$ is a perturbation of the quadratic utility function. We will examine how equilibrium and socially optimal identities vary with γ in a neighborhood of zero.

33 Details of this computation are available from the authors upon request. The "trick" is to rewrite the optimal transfer (at indicator pair (B, B), say) as

$$T(B, B) = \frac{\mu_{z_1}^- - \mu_{z_2}^-}{2} = \left(\frac{1}{2}\right) \left[(\mu - \mu_{z_2}^-) - (\mu - \mu_{z_1}^-) \right],$$

and to use the identity

$$z \left(\mu - \mu_z^- \right) + (1 - z) \left(\mu - \mu_z^+ \right) \equiv 0,$$

when evaluating the expectation over indicator pairs of the various terms in equation (16).

34 For instance, we might just as well have studied a repeated "Prisoner's Dilemma" – with pairwise random matching of agents to play in each period, and public but noisy signals about each agent's history of play depending on her choice of code. Or, we could have pursued our agenda in a market setting – an exchange economy, say, with many heterogenous agents whose preferences depend on code-mediated narratives about their "types." Then, the aggregate demand function would vary with the distribution of adopted codes in the population, and market-clearing prices would both depend on but also help to determine the equilibrium distribution of codes. One can surely think of other interactions where the coordinated choices of identities have economic consequence. All of this makes for a fit subject for further research.

35 This question is taken up by Chris Barrett in his contribution in Chapter 1 of this volume.

36 After all, one hears very little about collective identities based on hair length, eye color, or shoe size. This may be due to the fact that segregated patterns of social interaction along such lines as these are virtually non-existent!

37 See the article describing Putnam's recent work in *The Economist*, February 26, 2004.

38 An interesting and accessible discussion of the mathematics of such networks, emphasizing the importance of this kind of qualitative distinction between different types of links, is Barabási (2002).

39 Sociologist Mary Waters (2001) provides an interesting illustration of the complexity of racial identity choice among black Americans. Based on her extensive interviews with first- and second-generation West Indian immigrants, she draws a rich and enlightening contrast between the self-definitions adopted by these subjects vs. those embraced by the more indigenous black American population.

40 This interpretation and possible extension of our work has been suggested to us by Antonio Merlo of the University of Pennsylvania.

References

Akerlof, George (1997). "Social Distance and Social Decisions," *Econometrica*, 65(5): 1005–27.

Akerlof, George and Rachel Kranton (2000). "Economics and Identity," *The Quarterly Journal of Economics*, 115(3): 715–53.

——(2002). "Identity and Schooling: Some Lessons for the Economics of Education," *Journal of Economic Literature*, 40(4): 1167–201.

Aronson, Joshua, Claude M. Steele, M.F. Salinas, and M.J. Lustina (2003). "The Effects of Stereotype Threat on the Standardized Test Performance of College Students," in E. Aronson (ed.), *Readings about the Social Animal*, 8th edition, New York: Freeman.

Banfield, Edward (1970). *The Unheavenly City: The Nature and Future of Our Urban Crisis*. Boston, MA: Little Brown.

Barabási, Albert-László (2002). *Linked: How Everything is Connected to Everything else and What it Means*. New York: Perseus Books Group.

Barrett, Christopher (2005). "Smallholder Identities and Social Networks: The Challenge of Improving Productivity and Welfare," in Christopher B. Barrett (ed.), *The Social Economics of Poverty: On Identities, Communities, Groups, and Networks*. London: Routledge.

Baumeister, Roy (1998). "The Self," in Daniel T. Gilbert, S. Fiske, and G. Lindzey (eds), *Handbook of Social Psychology* (2 volumes), Oxford: Oxford University Press. Vol (1), pp (680)–740.

Benoit, Jean-Pierre and Vijay Krishna (1985). "Finitely Repeated Games," *Econometrica* (July): 905–22.

Bernheim, Douglas (1994). "A Theory of Conformity," *Journal of Political Economy*, 102(5): 841–77.

Burns, Justine (2004). "Race and Trust in Post Apartheid South Africa," unpublished manuscript. New Mexico: Santa Fe Institute.

Denizet-Lewis, Benoit (2003). "Double Lives on the Down Low," *The New York Times Sunday Magazine* (August 3, 2003).

Douglas, Mary (2004). "Traditional Culture – Let's Hear No More About It," in Vijayendra Rao and Michael Walton (eds), *Culture and Public Action*. Stanford, CA: Stanford University Press, pp (85)–109.

The Economist (2004). "The kindness of strangers?" February 26, 2004.

Ferguson, Ronald (2005). "Why America's Black-White School Achievement Gap Persists," in Glenn C. Loury, Tariq Modood, and Steven M. Teles (eds), *Ethnicity, Social Mobility and Public Policy*, Cambridge: Cambridge University Press.

Fryer, Roland (2003). "An Economic Approach to Cultural Capital," unpublished manuscript. Cambridge, MA: Harvard University.

Fryer, Roland and Matt Jackson (2003). "Categorical Cognition: A Psychological Model of Categories and Identification in Decision Making," unpublished manuscript. Cambridge, MA: Harvard University.

Goffman, Erving (1963). *Stigma: Notes on the Management of Spoiled Identities*. New York: Simon & Schuster.

Grief, Avner (1994). "Cultural Beliefs and the Organization of Society: A Historical and Theoretical Reflection on Collectivist and Individualist Societies," *The Journal of Political Economy*, 102(5): 912–50.

Hoff, Karla and P. Pandey (2003). "Why are Social Inequalities So Durable?" Discussion Paper. Washington, DC/Pennsylvania: World Bank and Pennsylvania State University.

Loury, Glenn C. (2002). *The Anatomy of Racial Inequality*. Cambridge, MA: Harvard University Press.

Loury, Glenn C., Steven Teles, and Tariq Modood (eds) (2005). *Ethnicity, Social Mobility and Public Policy in the US and the UK*. Cambridge: Cambridge University Press.

McWhorter, John (2000). *Losing the Race: Self-Sabatoge in Black America*. New York: The Free Press.

North, Douglas (1981). *Structure and Change in Economic History*. New York: W.W. Norton & Company.

Ogbu, John (2003). *Black Students in Affluent Suburbs: A Study in Academic Disengagement*. Mahwah, NJ: Lawrence Erlbaum.

Sidanius, James and Felicia Pratto (2001). *Social Dominance: An Intergroup Theory of Social Hierarchy and Oppression*. Cambridge: Cambridge University Press.

Waters, Mary (2001). *Black Identities: West Indian Immigrant Dreams and American Realities*. Cambridge, MA: Harvard University Press.

3   Polarization

Concepts, measurement, estimation

Jean-Yves Duclos, Joan Esteban,
and Debraj Ray

3.1   Introduction

Initiated by Esteban and Ray (1991, 1994), Foster and Wolfson (1992) and Wolfson (1994), there has been a recent upsurge of interest in the measurement of polarization[1] and in the use of such measures as a correlate of different aspects of socioeconomic performance. It seems fairly widely accepted that polarization is a concept that is distinct from inequality, and that – at least in principle – it could be connected with several aspects of social, economic, and political change.[2]

Following Esteban and Ray (1991, 1994), we rely almost exclusively on what might be called the *identification–alienation* framework. The idea is simple: polarization is related to the alienation that individuals and groups feel from one another, *but such alienation is fuelled by notions of within-group identity*. In concentrating on such phenomena, we do not mean to suggest that instances in which a single isolated individual runs amok with a machine gun are rare, or that they are unimportant in the larger scheme of things. It is just that these are not the objects of our enquiry. We are interested in the correlates of organized, large-scale social unrest – strikes, demonstrations, processions, widespread violence, and revolt or rebellion. Such phenomena thrive on differences, to be sure. But they cannot exist without notions of group identity either.

This brief discussion immediately suggests that inequality, inasmuch as it concerns itself with interpersonal alienation, captures but one aspect of polarization. To be sure, there are some obvious changes that would be branded as both inequality- and polarization-enhancing. For instance, if two income groups are further separated by increasing economic distance, inequality and polarization would presumably both increase. However, *local* equalizations of income differences at two different ranges of the income distribution will most likely lead to two better defined groups – each with a clearer sense of itself and the other. In this case, inequality will have come down but polarization may be on the rise.

The purpose of this chapter is two-fold. First, we develop the measurement theory of polarization for the case in which the relevant distributions can be described by density functions. There are many such instances, the most important being income, consumption and wealth – regrouped under "income" for short. The reason for doing so is simple: with sample data aggregated along income intervals, it is unclear how to provide a statistically satisfactory account of whether distributive measures (based on such data) are significantly different across time or entities. Indeed, a rapidly burgeoning literature on the statistics of inequality and poverty measurement shows how to construct appropriate statistical tests for such measures using disaggregated data (see, e.g., Beach and Davidson 1983; Beach and Richmond 1985; Bishop *et al.* 1989; Kakwani 1993; Anderson 1996; and Davidson and Duclos 1997, 2000). A rigorous axiomatic development of the polarization concept in the "density case" is then a prerequisite for proper statistical examination of polarization.

In this chapter we concentrate on the axiomatics and estimation of "pure income polarization," i.e., of indices of polarization for which individuals identify themselves only with those with similar income levels. (However, Section 3.4 does contain several preliminary remarks on the broader concept of "social polarization.") With this settled, we turn to issues of estimation. The main problem is how to estimate the size of the groups to which individuals belong. Again, using arbitrary income intervals would appear somewhat unsatisfactory. Instead, we estimate group size non-parametrically using kernel density procedures. A natural estimator of the polarization indices is then given by substituting the distribution function by the empirical distribution function. Assuming that we are using a random sample of independently and identically distributed observations of income, the resulting estimator has a limiting normal distribution with parameters that can be estimated free of assumptions on the true (but unknown) distribution of incomes. Distribution-free statistical inference can then be applied to ensure that the orderings of polarization across entities are not simply due to sampling noise.

It is useful to locate this chapter in the context of the earlier step in the measurement of polarization in Esteban and Ray (1994) – ER from now on. The measure derived in ER was based on a discrete, finite set of income groupings located in a continuous ambient space of possible income values. This generated two major problems, one conceptual and the other practical. At the conceptual level we have the drawback that the measure presents an unpleasant discontinuity. This is precisely due to the fact that ER is based on a population distributed over a discrete and distinct number of points.[3] The practical difficulty is that the population is assumed to have *already* been bunched in the relevant groups. This feature rendered the measure of little use for many interesting problems.[4] As mentioned earlier, the present chapter addresses both problems and provides what we hope is a useable measure.

In addition, the main axioms that we use to characterize income polarization are substantially different from ER (though they are similar in spirit). In large part, this is due to the fact that we are dealing with a completely different domain (spaces of densities). We therefore find it of interest that these new axioms end up characterizing a measure of polarization that turns out to be the natural extension of ER to the case of continuous distributions. At a deeper level, there are, however, important differences, such as the different bounds on the "polarization-sensitivity" parameter α that are obtained.

In Section 3.2 we axiomatically characterize a measure of pure income polarization and examine its properties; this is the conceptual heart of the chapter. We then turn in Section 3.3 to estimation and inference issues for polarization measures and subsequently illustrate the axiomatic and statistical results using data drawn from the Luxembourg Income Study (LIS) data sets for 21 countries. We compute the Gini coefficient and the polarization measure for these countries for years in Wave 3 (1989–92) and Wave 4 (1994–7), and find *inter alia* that the two indices furnish distinct information on the shape of the distributions. Section 3.4 summarizes the results and discusses an important extension. All proofs are relegated to an appendix.

3.2   Measuring income polarization

The purpose of this section is to proceed toward a full axiomatization of income polarization.

3.2.1   *Starting point*

The domain under consideration is the class of all continuous (unnormalized) densities in $\mathbb{R}_+$, with their integrals corresponding to various population sizes. Let f be such a density; we are interested in its *polarization $P(f)$*. We first describe the notions of "alienation" and "identification" for each individual with income located in the support of f.

We presume that an individual located at x feels alienation *vis-à-vis* another located at y, and that this alienation is monotonic in distance $|x - y|$. This notion is commonplace in the literature on the conceptual foundations of inequality (see, e.g., Sen 1997).

At the same time, the "identity–alienation framework" we adopt (referred to as IA henceforth) emphasizes that alienation *per se* is not the end of the story: for alienation to be translated into effective voice, action, or protest, the individual must – to greater or lesser degree – *identify* with others in society. In this chapter, we presume that an individual located at income x experiences a sense of identification that depends on the density at x, $f(x)$.

Taken in a broader context, the identification assumption is obviously quite specific. For instance, one might consider the possibility that individuals have a nondegenerate "window of identification" (though the foundations for the width of such an identification window appear unclear). We address this issue (and others) in our discussion of identification in Section 3.2.4, but recognize that a full analysis of the behavioral foundations of identification is beyond the scope of this chapter.

As in ER, we are interested in the *effective antagonism* of x toward y (under f). In its most abstract form, we may depict this as some nonnegative function

$$T(i,a),$$

where $i = f(x)$ and $a = |x - y|$. It is assumed that T is increasing in its second argument and that $T(i, 0) = T(0, a) = 0$, just as in ER. (This last condition asserts that while the consequences of an isolated individual's sense of alienation might be important, this is not the focus of our exercise.) We take polarization to be proportional to the "sum" of all effective antagonisms:

$$P(F) = \iint T(f(x), |x - y|) f(x) f(y) \, dx \, dy. \tag{1}$$

This class of measures is neither very useful nor operational, though at this stage it it incorporates the structure of the IA assumptions. In particular, much depends on the choice of the functional form T. In what follows, we place axioms on this starting point so as to pin down this functional form.

3.2.2 Axioms

Densities and basic operations   Our axioms will largely be based on domains that are unions of one or more very simple densities f that we will call *basic densities*. These are unnormalized (by population), are symmetric and unimodal, and have compact support.[5]

To be sure, f can be *population rescaled* to any population p by simply multiplying f pointwise by p to arrive at a new distribution pf (unnormalized). Likewise, f can undergo a *slide*. A *slide to the right by x* is just a new density g such that $g(y) = f(y - x)$. Likewise for a slide to the left. And f with mean μ' can be *income rescaled* to any new mean μ that we please as follows: $g(x) = (\mu'/\mu) f(x\mu'/\mu)$ for all x.[6] These operations maintain symmetry and unimodality and therefore keep us within the class of basic densities.

If we think of slides and scalings as inducing a partition of the basic densities, each collection of basic densities in the same element of the partition may be associated with a *root*, a basic density with mean 1 and support $[0, 2]$, with population size set to unity. That is, one can transform any basic density to its root by a set of scalings and slides. (This concept will be important both in the axioms as well as in the main proof.) Two distinct roots differ in "shape," a quality that cannot be transformed by the given operations.

Finally, we shall also use the concept of a *squeeze*, defined as follows. Let f be any basic density with mean μ and let λ lie in $(0, 1]$. A λ-*squeeze* of f is a transformation as follows:

$$f^\lambda(x) \equiv \frac{1}{\lambda} f \left[\frac{x - (1 - \lambda)\mu}{\lambda} \right]. \tag{2}$$

A (λ-) squeeze is, in words, a very special sort of mean-preserving reduction in the spread of f. It concentrates more weight on the *global* mean of the distribution, as opposed to what would be achieved, say, with a progressive Dalton transfer on the same side of the mean. Thus a squeeze truly collapses a density inwards toward its global mean. The following properties can be formally established: (a) for each $\lambda \in (0, 1)$, f^λ is a density; (b) for each $\lambda \in (0, 1)$, f^λ has the same mean as f; (c) if $0 < \lambda < \lambda' < 1$, then f^λ second-order stochastically dominates $f^{\lambda'}$; and (d) as $\lambda \downarrow 0$, f^λ converges weakly to the degenerate measure granting all weight to μ.

Notice that there is nothing in the definition that requires a squeeze to be applied to symmetric unimodal densities with compact support. In principle, a squeeze as defined could be applied to any density. However, the axioms to be placed below acquire additional cogency when limited to such densities.

Statement of the axioms   We will impose four axioms on the polarization measure.

Axiom 1   If a distribution is composed of a *single* basic density, then a squeeze of that density cannot increase polarization.

Axiom 1 is self-evident. A squeeze, as defined here, corresponds to a *global* compression of any basic density. If only one of these makes up the distribution (see Figure 3.1), then the distribution is globally compressed and we must associate this with no higher polarization. Viewed in the context of our background model, however, it is clear that Axiom 1 is going to generate some interesting restrictions. This is because a squeeze creates a reduction in inter-individual alienation but also serves to raise identification for a positive measure of agents – those located "centrally" in the distribution. The implied restriction is, then, that the latter's positive impact on polarization must be counterbalanced by the former's negative impact.

Our next axiom considers an initial situation (see Figure 3.2) composed of three disjoint densities all sharing the same root. The situation is completely symmetric, with densities 1 and 3 having the same total population and with density 2 exactly midway between densities 1 and 3.

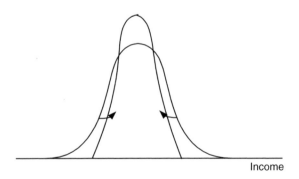

Income

Figure 3.1 A single squeeze cannot increase polarization.

Figure 3.2 A double squeeze cannot lower polarization.

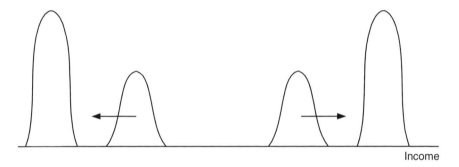

Figure 3.3 A "symmetric outward slide" must raise polarization.

Axiom 2   If a symmetric distribution is composed of three basic densities with the same root and mutually disjoint supports, then a symmetric squeeze of the *side* densities cannot reduce polarization.

In some sense, this is the defining axiom of polarization, and may be used to motivate the concept. Notice that this axiom argues that a particular "local" squeeze (as opposed to the "global" squeeze of the entire distribution in Axiom 1) must not bring down polarization. At this stage there is an explicit departure from inequality measurement.

Our third axiom considers a symmetric distribution composed of *four* basic densities, once again all sharing the same root.

Axiom 3   Consider a symmetric distribution composed of four basic densities with the same root and mutually disjoint supports, as in Figure 3.3. Slide the two middle densities to the side as shown (keeping all supports disjoint). Then polarization must go up.

Our final axiom is a simple population-invariance principle. It states that if one situation exhibits greater polarization than another, it must continue to do so when populations in both situations are scaled up or down by the same amount, leaving all (relative) distributions unchanged.

Axiom 4   If $P(F) \geq P(G)$ and $p > 0$, then $P(pF) \geq P(pG)$, where pF and pG represent (identical) population scalings of F and G, respectively.

3.2.3   *Characterization theorem*

Theorem 1. *A measure P, as described in (1), satisfies Axioms 1–4 if and only if it is proportional to*

$$P_\alpha(f) \equiv \iint f(x)^{1+\alpha} f(y)|y - x|\, dy\, dx, \qquad (3)$$

where $\alpha \in [0.25, 1]$.

3.2.4   *Discussion*

Several aspects of this theorem require extended discussion.

Scaling   Theorem 1 states that a measure of polarization satisfying the preceding four axioms has to be *proportional* to the measure we have characterized. We may wish to exploit this degree of freedom to make the polarization measure scale-free. Homogeneity of degree zero can be achieved, if desired, by multiplying $P_\alpha(F)$ by $\mu^{\alpha-1}$, where μ is mean income. It is easy to see that this procedure is equivalent to one in which all incomes are normalized by their mean, and (3) is subsequently applied.

Importance of the IA structure   The theorem represents a particularly sharp characterization of the class of polarization measures that satisfy *both* the axioms we have imposed *and* the IA structure. It must be emphasized that both these factors play a role in pinning down our functional form. In fact, it can be checked that several other measures of polarization satisfy Axioms 1–4, though we omit this discussion for the sake of brevity. The IA framework is, therefore, an essential part of the argument.

Partial ordering   At the same time, and despite the sharpness of the functional form, notice that we do *not* obtain a complete ordering for polarization, nor do we attempt to do this.[7] A range of values of α is entertained in the theorem. The union of the complete orderings generated by each value gives us a partial order for polarization. Pinning down this order completely is an open question.

Identification   A full behavioral foundation for the identification postulate is not within the scope of this chapter. However, we make two remarks on the particular specification used here.

First, our axioms imply that identification increases with group size. A well-known problem of collective action (due to Pareto 1906; and Olson 1965) suggests, however, that smaller groups may sometimes be more effective than larger groups in securing their ends. This argument has been explored by several authors, but perhaps most relevant to the current discussion is Esteban and Ray (2001), which shows that if social conflict arises over the provision of *public goods* (or even if the good is partially private but the cost function for the supply of lobbying resources has sufficient curvature[8]), then larger groups are more effective *in the aggregate*, even though each individual in such groups may be less active owing to the free-rider problem. This finding is consistent with our implication that identification increases with group size.

Second, we remark on our choice of basing identification on the point density. We may more generally suppose that individuals possess a "window of identification" as in ER, Section 3.4. Individuals within this window would be considered "similar" – possibly with weights decreasing with the distance – and would contribute to a sense of group identity. At the same time, individuals would feel alienated only from those outside the window. Thus, broadening one's window of identification has two effects. First, it includes more neighbors when computing one's sense of identification. Second, it reduces one's sense of distance with respect to aliens – because the width of the identification window affects the "starting point" for alienation.

These two effects can be simultaneously captured in our seemingly narrower model. Let t be some parameter representing the "breadth" in identification. Suppose that this means that each individual x will consider an individual with income y to be at the point $(1 - t)x + ty$. (Thus t is inversely proportional to "breadth.") The "perceived density" of y from the vantage point of an individual located at x is then

$$\frac{1}{t} f \left(\frac{y - (1 - t)x}{t} \right),$$

so that if $t < 1$, the sense of identification is generally heightened (simply set $x = y$ above). Thus a small value of t stands for greater identification.

It can be easily shown that the polarization measure resulting from this extended notion of identification is proportional to our measure by the factor $t^{1-\alpha}$. Therefore, broadening the sense of identification simply amounts to a re-scaling of the measure defined for the limit case in which one is identified with individuals having exactly the same income.

It is also possible to directly base identification on the average density over a non-degenerate window. It can be shown that when our polarization measure is rewritten to incorporate this notion of identification, it converges precisely to the measure in Theorem 1 as the size of the window converges to zero. Thus an alternative view of point-identification is that it is a robust approximation to "narrow" identification windows.

Asymmetric alienation   In ER we already pointed out that in some environments our implicit hypothesis of a symmetric sense of alienation might not be appropriate. It can be argued that while individuals may feel alienated with respect to those with higher income or wealth, such sentiments need not be reciprocated. For the extreme case of purely one-sided alienation the appropriate extension would be

$$P_\alpha(f) \equiv \int f(x)^{1+\alpha} \int_x f(y)(y-x)\,dy\,dx.$$

(This is not to say that we have axiomatized such an extension.)

This approach would create a change in the polarization ordering, and depending on the context, it may be a change worth exploring further. The main difference is that (relative to the symmetric case) larger humps or spikes at the lower end of the wealth distribution will be given more weight. In particular, maximal polarization would not be achieved at some symmetric bimodal distribution but at some bimodal distribution that exhibits a larger (local) mode at the bottom of the distribution. This issue is discussed in more detail in ER.

Remarks on the proof, and the derived bounds on α   The proof of Theorem 1 is long and involved, so a brief roadmap may be useful here. The first half of the proof shows that our axioms imply equation (3), along with the asserted bounds on α. We begin by noting that the function T must be (weakly) concave in alienation (Lemmas 1 and 2). Axiom 2 yields this. Yet by Lemmas 3 and 4 (which centrally employ Axiom 3), T must be (weakly) convex as well. These two assertions must imply that T is linear in alienation, and so is of the form $T(i,a) = \phi(i)a$ for some function ϕ (Lemma 4 again). Lemma 5 completes the derivation of our functional form by using the population invariance principle (Axiom 4) to argue that ϕ must exhibit constant elasticity.

Our measure bears an interesting resemblance to the Gini coefficient. Indeed, if $\alpha = 0$, the measure *is* the Gini coefficient. However, our arguments ensure that not only is $\alpha > 0$, it cannot go below some uniformly positive lower bound, which happens to be 0.25. Where, in the axioms and in the IA structure, does such a bound lurk? To appreciate this, consider Axiom 2, which refers to a double-squeeze of two "side" basic densities. Such squeezes bring down internal alienations in each component density. Yet the axiom demands that overall polarization not fall. It follows, therefore, that the increased identifications created by the squeeze must outweigh the decreased within-component alienation. This restricts α. It cannot be too low.

By a similar token, α cannot be too high either. The bite here comes from Axiom 1, which decrees that a single squeeze (in an environment where there is just one basic component) cannot increase polarization. Once again, alienation comes down and some identifications go up (as the single squeeze occurs), but this time we want the decline in alienation to dominate the proceedings. This is tantamount to an upper bound on α.[9]

The previous arguments are made using Lemmas 6 and 7, which also begin the proof that the axioms are *implied* by our class of measures. The various steps for this direction of the proof, which essentially consist in verifying the axioms, are completed in Lemmas 8 through 11.

The approach to our characterization bears a superficial similarity to ER. Actually, the axioms *are* similar in spirit, dealing as they do in each case with issues of identification and alienation. However, their specific structure is fundamentally different. This is because our axioms strongly exploit the density structure of the model (in ER there are only discrete groupings). In turn, this creates basic differences in the method of proof. It is comforting that the two approaches yield the same functional characterization in the end, albeit with different numerical restrictions on the value of α.

3.2.5   Comparing distributions

The fundamental hypothesis underlying all of our analysis is that polarization is driven by the interplay of two forces: identification with one's own group and alienation *vis-á-vis* others. Our axioms yield a particular functional form to the interaction between these two forces. When comparing two distributions, which should we expect to display the greater polarization? Our informal answer is that this should depend on the separate contributions of alienation and identification and on their joint co-movement. Increased alienation is associated with an increase in income distances. Increased identification would manifest itself in a sharper definition of groups, i.e., the already highly populated points in the distribution becoming even more populated at the expense of the less populated. Such a change would produce an increase in the variability of the density over the support of the distribution. Finally, when taken jointly, these effects may reinforce each other in the sense that alienation may be highest at the incomes that have experienced an increase in identification, or they may counterbalance each other.

To be sure, it is not possible to move these three factors around independently. After all, one density describes the income distribution and the three factors we have mentioned are byproducts of that density. Nevertheless, thinking in this way develops some intuition for polarization, which we will try and put to use in Section 3.3.2.

To pursue this line of reasoning, first normalize all incomes by their mean to make the results scale free. Fix a particular value of α, as given by Theorem 1. (More on this parameter later.) The α-*identification* at income y, denoted by $\iota_\alpha(y)$, is measured by $f(y)^\alpha$. Hence, the *average* α-identification $\bar{\iota}$ is defined by

$$\bar{\iota}_\alpha \equiv \int f(y)^\alpha \, dF(y) = \int f(y)^{1+\alpha} \, dy. \tag{4}$$

The alienation between two individuals with incomes y and x is given by $|y-x|$. Therefore, the overall alienation felt by an individual with income y, $a(y)$, is

$$a(y) = \int |y - x| \, dF(x), \tag{5}$$

and the average alienation $\bar{a}$ is

$$\bar{a} = \int a(y) \, dF(y) = \iint |y - x| \, dF(x) \, dF(y). \tag{6}$$

(Notice that $\bar{a}$ is twice the Gini coefficient.) Now conduct a completely routine exercise. Define ρ as the *normalized covariance* between identification and alienation: $\rho \equiv \mathrm{cov}_{\iota_\alpha,a} / \bar{\iota}_\alpha \bar{a}$. Then,

$$
\begin{aligned}
\rho \equiv \frac{\mathrm{cov}_{\iota_\alpha,a}}{\bar{\iota}_\alpha \bar{a}} &= \frac{1}{\bar{\iota}_\alpha \bar{a}} \int [\iota_\alpha(y) - \bar{\iota}_\alpha][a(y) - \bar{a}] f(y) \, dy \\
&= \frac{1}{\bar{\iota}_\alpha \bar{a}} \left[\int f(y)^{1+\alpha} a(y) \, dy - \bar{a} \bar{\iota}_\alpha \right] \\
&= \frac{P_\alpha(f)}{\bar{\iota}_\alpha \bar{a}} - 1,
\end{aligned}
$$

so that,

$$P_\alpha(f) = \bar{a} \bar{\iota}_\alpha [1 + \rho]. \tag{7}$$

This is a more precise statement of the informal idea expressed at the start of this section.

There is one dimension, however, along which this decomposition lacks intuition. It is that α unavoidably enters into it: we make this explicit by using the term α-identification (though we will resort to "identification" when there is little risk of confusion). This sort of identification is not intrinsic to the density. Yet the formula itself is useful, for it tells us that – all other things being equal – greater variation, "spikiness," or multimodality in the density is likely to translate into greater polarization for that density, this effect making itself felt more strongly when α is larger. The reason is simple: the main ingredient for α-identification is the function $x^{1+\alpha}$ (see equation (4)), which is a strictly convex function of x.

The connection with spikiness or multimodality ties in with our graphical intuitions regarding polarization. We reiterate, however, that this is only one factor of several, and that often it may not be possible to change this factor in the direction of higher polarization without infringing the *ceteris paribus* qualification. For instance, if a unimodal density is altered by the introduction of two or more local modes, such multimodality *per se* may not bring higher polarization with it. This is because the existence of several modes may *also* bring average alienation down. In particular, a highly skewed distribution with a single mode may still exhibit greater polarization relative to other bimodal distributions. Nevertheless, the connection with "variability" may be helpful in some situations, and we will invoke it in the empirical discussion of Section 3.3.2. Indeed, in unimodal situations (which present the most subtle problems as far as polarization is concerned), these factors can act as guides to simple visual inspection.

3.3   Estimation and illustration

3.3.1   Estimation and statistical inference

We now turn to estimation issues regarding $P_\alpha(F)$ and associated questions of statistical inference. The details of this discussion may be found in the addendum to this chapter. First note that for every distribution function F with associated density f and mean μ, we have that

$$P_\alpha(F) = \int_y f(y)^\alpha a(y)\, dF(y), \tag{8}$$

with $a(y) \equiv \mu + y(2F(y) - 1) - 2\int_{-\infty}^y x\, dF(x)$. Suppose, then, that we wish to estimate $P_\alpha(F)$ using a random sample of n i.i.d. observations of income y_i, $i = 1, \ldots, n$, drawn from the distribution $F(y)$ and ordered such that $y_1 \leq y_2 \leq \cdots \leq y_n$. A natural estimator of $P_\alpha(F)$ is

$$P_\alpha(\hat{F}) = n^{-1} \sum_{i=1}^{n} \hat{f}(y_i)^\alpha \hat{a}(y_i), \tag{9}$$

where $\hat{a}(y_i)$ is given as

$$\hat{a}(y_i) = \hat{\mu} + y_i[n^{-1}(2i - 1) - 1] - n^{-1}\left(2\sum_{j=1}^{i-1} y_j + y_i\right), \tag{10}$$

$\hat{\mu}$ is the sample mean, and where $\hat{f}(y_i)^\alpha$ is estimated non-parametrically using kernel estimation procedures.[10] These procedures use a symmetric kernel function $K(u)$, defined such that $\int_{-\infty}^\infty K(u)\, du = 1$ and $K(u) \geq 0$ – a Gaussian kernel is used in the illustration. The estimator $\hat{f}(y)$ is then defined as $\hat{f}(y) \equiv n^{-1} \sum_{i=1}^n K_h(y - y_i)$, with $K_h(z) \equiv h^{-1}K(z/h)$ and h being a bandwidth parameter. A common technique to select an "optimal" bandwidth h^* is to minimize the mean square error (MSE) of the estimator, given a sample of size n. A "rule-of-thumb" formula that can be used to do this in our context is approximately given by:

$$h^* \cong 4.7\, n^{-0.5}\, \sigma\alpha^{0.1}. \tag{11}$$

Easily computed, this formula works well with the normal distribution since it is then never farther than 5% from the h^* that truly minimizes the MSE. For skewness larger than about 6, a more robust – though more cumbersome – approximate formula for the computation of h^* is given by

$$h^* \cong n^{-0.5} IQ \frac{3.76 + 14.7\sigma_{\ln}}{(1 + 1.09 \cdot 10^{-4}\sigma_{\ln})^{7268+15323\alpha}}, \tag{12}$$

where IQ is the interquartile and $\sigma_{\ln}$ is the variance of the logarithms of income.

It can also be shown (under certain mild regularity conditions) that $n^{0.5}[P_\alpha(\hat{F}) - P_\alpha(F)]$ has an asymptotic limiting normal distribution $N(0, V_\alpha)$, with

$$V_\alpha = \underset{f(y)}{\text{var}} \left[(1 + \alpha) f(y)^\alpha a(y) + y \int f(x)^\alpha \, dF(x) \right.$$

$$\left. + 2 \int_y^\infty (x - y) f(x)^\alpha \, dF(x) \right]. \tag{13}$$

This result is distribution-free in the sense that everything in the above can be estimated consistently *without* having to specify the population distribution from which the sample is drawn.

3.3.2   An illustration

We illustrate the above results with data drawn from the LIS data sets[11] on 21 countries for each of Wave 3 (1989–92) and Wave 4 (1994–7). Countries, survey years and abbreviations are listed in Table 3.1. We use household disposable income (i.e., post-tax-and-transfer income) normalized by an adult-equivalence scale defined as $s^{0.5}$, where s is household size. Observations with negative incomes are removed as well as those with incomes exceeding 50 times the average (this affects less than 1% of all samples). Household observations are weighted by the LIS sample weights times the number of persons in the household. As discussed in Section 3.2.4, the usual homogeneity-of-degree-zero property is imposed throughout by multiplying the indices $P_\alpha(F)$ by $\mu^{\alpha-1}$ or equivalently by normalizing all incomes by their mean. For ease of comparison, all indices are divided by 2, so that $P_{\alpha=0}(F)$ is the usual Gini coefficient.

Tables 3.2 and 3.3 show estimates of the Gini (P_0) and four polarization indices (P_α for $\alpha = 0.25, 0.5, 0.75, 1$) in 21 countries for each of the two waves, along with their asymptotic standard deviations. The polarization indices are typically rather precisely estimated, with often only the third decimal of the estimators being subject to sampling variability. Using a conventional test size of 5%, it can be checked that around 90% of the possible cross-country comparisons are statistically significant, whatever the value of α. Tables 3.2 and 3.3 also show the country rankings, with a high rank corresponding to a relatively large value of the relevant index, and with countries displayed by their order in the Gini ranking.

Polarization behaves differently from inequality   Observe first that P_0 and $P_{0.25}$ induce very similar rankings. But considerable differences arise between

Table 3.1 LIS country codes

Countries	Abbreviations	Years	Sample sizes
Australia	as	1989/1994	16 331/7441
Belgium	be	1992/1997	3821/4632
Canada	cn	1991/1994	21 647/40 849
Czech Republic	cz	1992/1996	16 234/28 148
Denmark	dk	1992/1995	12 895/13 124
Finland	fi	1991/1995	11 749/9263
France	fr	1989/1994	9038/11 294
Germany	ge	1989/1994	4187/6045
Hungary	hu	1991/1994	2019/1992
Israel	is	1992/1997	5212/5230
Italy	it	1991/1994	8188/8135
Luxembourg	lx	1991/1994	1957/1813
Mexico	mx	1989/1996	11 531/14 042
Netherlands	nl	1991/1994	4378/5187
Norway	nw	1991/1995	8073/10 127
Poland	pl	1992/1995	6602/32 009
Republic of China/ Taiwan	rc	1991/1995	16 434/14 706
Russia	ru	1992/1995	6361/3518
Sweden	sw	1992/1995	12 484/16 260
United Kingdom	uk	1991/1995	7056/6797
United States	us	1991/1994	16 052/66 014

P_0 and P_1. For instance, for Wave 3, the Czech Republic has the lowest Gini index of all countries, but ranks 11 in terms of P_1. Conversely, Canada, Australia, and the US exhibit high Gini inequality, but relatively low "P_1-polarization." The correlation across country rankings for different αs clearly falls as the distance between the αs increases. The lowest Pearson correlation of all – 0.6753 – is the correlation between the Gini index and P_1 in Wave 3. Clearly, polarization and inequality are naturally correlated, but they are also *empirically* distinct in this dataset. Moreover, the extent to which inequality comparisons resemble polarization comparisons depend on the parameter α, which essentially captures the power of the identification effect.

Alienation and identification   Recall the decomposition exercise carried out in Section 3.2.5, in which we obtained equation (7), reproduced here for convenience:

$$P_\alpha = \bar{a}\bar{\iota}_\alpha[1 + \rho].$$

Table 3.4 summarizes the relevant statistics for all Wave 3 countries, decomposing polarization as the product of average alienation, average identification and (one plus) the normalized covariance between the two. Consider $\alpha = 1$. Note that the bulk of cross-country variation in polarization stems from significant variation in average identification as well as in average alienation. In contrast, the covariance between the two does not exhibit similar variation across countries. Some

Table 3.2 Polarization indices and polarization rankings (Rkg) from LIS Wave 3

Country	α = 0		α = 0.25		α = 0.50		α = 0.75		α = 1	
	Index	Rkg	Index	Rkg	Index	Rkg	Index	Rkg	Index	Rkg
cz92	0.2082	1	0.1767	1	0.1637	2	0.1585	4	0.1575	11
	0.0023		0.0014		0.0011		0.0011		0.0012	
fi91	0.2086	2	0.1782	2	0.1611	1	0.1505	1	0.1436	1
	0.0017		0.0010		0.0007		0.0005		0.0005	
be92	0.2236	3	0.1898	4	0.1699	4	0.1571	3	0.1484	3
	0.0028		0.0018		0.0012		0.0010		0.0010	
sw92	0.2267	4	0.1888	3	0.1674	3	0.1543	2	0.1459	2
	0.0019		0.0012		0.0008		0.0006		0.0006	
nw91	0.2315	5	0.1919	5	0.1713	5	0.1588	5	0.1505	5
	0.0029		0.0017		0.0013		0.0011		0.0011	
dk92	0.2367	6	0.1964	6	0.1744	6	0.1603	6	0.1504	4
	0.0026		0.0015		0.0011		0.0010		0.0011	
lx91	0.2389	7	0.2002	7	0.1787	8	0.1652	8	0.1563	10
	0.0051		0.0032		0.0024		0.0022		0.0023	
ge89	0.2469	8	0.2019	8	0.1779	7	0.1634	7	0.1540	7
	0.0048		0.0028		0.0021		0.0020		0.0021	
nl91	0.2633	9	0.2122	9	0.1859	9	0.1700	9	0.1596	16
	0.0054		0.0031		0.0024		0.0024		0.0025	
rc91	0.2708	10	0.2189	10	0.1902	11	0.1723	14	0.1603	17
	0.0019		0.0011		0.0009		0.0008		0.0009	
pl92	0.2737	11	0.2193	11	0.1894	10	0.1706	11	0.1577	13
	0.0032		0.0019		0.0014		0.0012		0.0013	
fr89	0.2815	12	0.2229	12	0.1912	12	0.1715	12	0.1580	14
	0.0033		0.0019		0.0014		0.0013		0.0014	
hu91	0.2828	13	0.2230	13	0.1913	13	0.1719	13	0.1587	15
	0.0066		0.0039		0.0028		0.0026		0.0027	
it91	0.2887	14	0.2307	15	0.1968	15	0.1741	15	0.1577	12
	0.0028		0.0016		0.0012		0.0011		0.0012	
cn91	0.2891	15	0.2301	14	0.1945	14	0.1701	10	0.1523	6
	0.0018		0.0011		0.0008		0.0006		0.0006	
is92	0.3055	16	0.2421	17	0.2051	17	0.1804	18	0.1626	18
	0.0036		0.0021		0.0016		0.0015		0.0015	
as89	0.3084	17	0.2421	16	0.2023	16	0.1750	16	0.1549	8
	0.0020		0.0012		0.0008		0.0007		0.0008	
uk91	0.3381	18	0.2607	18	0.2185	19	0.1911	19	0.1716	19
	0.0053		0.0028		0.0023		0.0023		0.0025	
us91	0.3394	19	0.2625	19	0.2140	18	0.1802	17	0.1551	9
	0.0019		0.0012		0.0008		0.0006		0.0006	
ru92	0.4017	20	0.2957	20	0.2400	20	0.2046	20	0.1797	20
	0.0066		0.0035		0.0029		0.0029		0.0031	
mx89	0.4909	21	0.3462	21	0.2802	21	0.2432	21	0.2202	21
	0.0055		0.0034		0.0030		0.0032		0.0036	

Note
Standard errors appear on every second line.

Table 3.3 Polarization indices and polarization rankings (Rkg) from LIS Wave 4

Country	$\alpha = 0$		$\alpha = 0.25$		$\alpha = 0.50$		$\alpha = 0.75$		$\alpha = 1$	
	Index	Rkg	Index	Rkg	Index	Rkg	Index	Rkg	Index	Rkg
fi95	0.2174	1	0.1832	1	0.1661	2	0.1564	2	0.1506	6
	0.0027		0.0016		0.0012		0.0011		0.0012	
sw95	0.2218	2	0.1845	2	0.1652	1	0.1549	1	0.1498	3
	0.0019		0.0012		0.0008		0.0007		0.0008	
lx94	0.2353	3	0.1978	4	0.1764	4	0.1633	7	0.1549	8
	0.0043		0.0028		0.0021		0.0017		0.0019	
nw95	0.2403	4	0.1970	3	0.1750	3	0.1616	3	0.1527	7
	0.0049		0.0029		0.0024		0.0023		0.0024	
be97	0.2496	5	0.2061	5	0.1796	5	0.1616	4	0.1486	1
	0.0029		0.0018		0.0012		0.0010		0.0010	
dk95	0.2532	6	0.2073	6	0.1808	6	0.1632	6	0.1504	5
	0.0026		0.0015		0.0011		0.0011		0.0011	
nl94	0.2558	7	0.2094	7	0.1812	7	0.1624	5	0.1491	2
	0.0029		0.0018		0.0012		0.0009		0.0010	
cz96	0.2589	8	0.2104	8	0.1854	9	0.1709	10	0.1618	13
	0.0017		0.0010		0.0008		0.0007		0.0008	
ge94	0.2649	9	0.2133	9	0.1846	8	0.1669	8	0.1553	10
	0.0048		0.0030		0.0023		0.0021		0.0022	
rc95	0.2781	10	0.2234	10	0.1931	10	0.1742	11	0.1614	12
	0.0021		0.0013		0.0009		0.0009		0.0010	
cn94	0.2859	11	0.2289	12	0.1933	11	0.1687	9	0.1504	4
	0.0011		0.0007		0.0005		0.0004		0.0003	
fr94	0.2897	12	0.2284	11	0.1963	12	0.1766	13	0.1634	14
	0.0031		0.0018		0.0014		0.0013		0.0014	
as94	0.3078	13	0.2433	14	0.2033	14	0.1757	12	0.1553	9
	0.0028		0.0016		0.0012		0.0010		0.0011	
pl95	0.3108	14	0.2389	13	0.2023	13	0.1799	14	0.1645	15
	0.0024		0.0014		0.0011		0.0010		0.0011	
hu94	0.3248	15	0.2486	15	0.2087	15	0.1852	15	0.1700	18
	0.0081		0.0048		0.0037		0.0035		0.0038	
is97	0.3371	16	0.2598	17	0.2159	17	0.1871	18	0.1666	17
	0.0044		0.0025		0.0019		0.0018		0.0020	
it95	0.3406	17	0.2596	16	0.2148	16	0.1856	16	0.1647	16
	0.0037		0.0021		0.0016		0.0015		0.0016	
uk95	0.3429	18	0.2622	18	0.2193	18	0.1925	19	0.1741	19
	0.0041		0.0022		0.0018		0.0018		0.0020	
us94	0.3622	19	0.2747	19	0.2223	19	0.1868	17	0.1610	11
	0.0010		0.0006		0.0004		0.0004		0.0004	
ru95	0.4497	20	0.3222	20	0.2566	20	0.2164	20	0.1889	20
	0.0061		0.0035		0.0028		0.0028		0.0030	
mx96	0.4953	21	0.3483	21	0.2826	21	0.2464	21	0.2237	21
	0.0046		0.0028		0.0025		0.0027		0.0030	

Note
Standard errors appear on every second line.

Table 3.4 Alienation and identification – LIS Wave 3

Country	$\alpha=0$ Gini	$\alpha=0.25$ $\bar{i}$	c^a	$\bar{i}\cdot c^a$	P	$\alpha=0.50$ $\bar{i}$	c^a	$\bar{i}\cdot c^a$	P	$\alpha=0.75$ $\bar{i}$	c^a	$\bar{i}\cdot c^a$	P	$\alpha=1$ $\bar{i}$	c^a	$\bar{i}\cdot c^a$	P
as89	0.3084	0.8508	0.9227	0.7851	0.2421	0.7440	0.8815	0.6559	0.2023	0.6627	0.8562	0.5675	0.1750	0.5984	0.8394	0.5023	0.1549
be92	0.2233	0.9110	0.9327	0.8497	0.1897	0.8518	0.8931	0.7608	0.1699	0.8105	0.8678	0.7034	0.1571	0.7811	0.8506	0.6643	0.1484
cn91	0.2891	0.8634	0.9219	0.7960	0.2301	0.7658	0.8784	0.6727	0.1945	0.6916	0.8509	0.5885	0.1701	0.6332	0.8321	0.5269	0.1523
cz92	0.2081	0.9504	0.8935	0.8492	0.1767	0.9337	0.8423	0.7865	0.1637	0.9364	0.8132	0.7615	0.1585	0.9526	0.7944	0.7567	0.1575
dk92	0.2367	0.9051	0.9169	0.8298	0.1964	0.8415	0.8759	0.7370	0.1744	0.7952	0.8519	0.6774	0.1603	0.7598	0.8361	0.6352	0.1504
fi91	0.2086	0.9227	0.9259	0.8543	0.1782	0.8747	0.8829	0.7723	0.1611	0.8440	0.8547	0.7214	0.1505	0.8248	0.8345	0.6882	0.1435
fr89	0.2815	0.8782	0.9015	0.7917	0.2229	0.7978	0.8514	0.6792	0.1912	0.7406	0.8224	0.6091	0.1715	0.6979	0.8041	0.5612	0.1580
ge89	0.2469	0.9021	0.9066	0.8179	0.2019	0.8398	0.8583	0.7208	0.1779	0.7984	0.8290	0.6618	0.1634	0.7707	0.8094	0.6238	0.1540
hu91	0.2828	0.8797	0.8965	0.7887	0.2230	0.8007	0.8451	0.6767	0.1913	0.7451	0.8157	0.6078	0.1719	0.7042	0.7972	0.5614	0.1587
is92	0.3055	0.8626	0.9188	0.7926	0.2421	0.7663	0.8761	0.6714	0.2051	0.6944	0.8505	0.5906	0.1804	0.6384	0.8337	0.5322	0.1626
it91	0.2887	0.8676	0.9212	0.7993	0.2307	0.7745	0.8802	0.6817	0.1968	0.7046	0.8558	0.6030	0.1741	0.6501	0.8404	0.5463	0.1577
lx91	0.2389	0.9088	0.9222	0.8381	0.2002	0.8490	0.8807	0.7477	0.1787	0.8081	0.8557	0.6915	0.1652	0.7798	0.8392	0.6544	0.1563
mx89	0.4909	0.8343	0.8453	0.7052	0.3462	0.7302	0.7817	0.5707	0.2802	0.6588	0.7520	0.4954	0.2432	0.6090	0.7366	0.4486	0.2202
nl91	0.2633	0.8952	0.9003	0.8059	0.2122	0.8280	0.8526	0.7059	0.1859	0.7822	0.8255	0.6457	0.1700	0.7499	0.8084	0.6062	0.1596
nw91	0.2315	0.9128	0.9082	0.8290	0.1919	0.8581	0.8623	0.7400	0.1713	0.8216	0.8347	0.6859	0.1588	0.7970	0.8158	0.6502	0.1505
pl92	0.2737	0.8837	0.9067	0.8013	0.2193	0.8068	0.8575	0.6919	0.1894	0.7526	0.8278	0.6230	0.1705	0.7129	0.8081	0.5762	0.1577
rc91	0.2708	0.8883	0.9099	0.8083	0.2189	0.8152	0.8616	0.7024	0.1902	0.7645	0.8323	0.6362	0.1723	0.7281	0.8130	0.5919	0.1603
ru92	0.4017	0.8300	0.8868	0.7361	0.2957	0.7138	0.8369	0.5974	0.2400	0.6282	0.8108	0.5094	0.2046	0.5622	0.7960	0.4475	0.1797
sw92	0.2267	0.9077	0.9177	0.8330	0.1888	0.8499	0.8691	0.7387	0.1674	0.8126	0.8376	0.6807	0.1543	0.7889	0.8159	0.6436	0.1459
uk91	0.3381	0.8521	0.9047	0.7709	0.2607	0.7498	0.8618	0.6461	0.2185	0.6737	0.8390	0.5652	0.1911	0.6145	0.8258	0.5074	0.1716
us91	0.3394	0.8298	0.9320	0.7734	0.2625	0.7063	0.8930	0.6307	0.2140	0.6116	0.8685	0.5311	0.1803	0.5364	0.8520	0.4571	0.1551

Note
a $c = (1 + \rho)$.

countries (Finland, Sweden, and Denmark) rank low both in terms in inequality and polarization, due in large part to low average alienation. Some countries, most strikingly Russia, Mexico, and the UK rank consistently high both in terms of inequality and polarization – even though average identification for the three countries is among the lowest of all. Average alienation is very high in these countries. Yet other countries show low inequality but relatively high polarization, while others exhibit the reverse relative rankings.

While maintaining the same average alienation, the UK density exhibits higher variability than its US counterpart – see the upper panel in Figure 3.4. The US distribution shows a remarkably flat density on the interval [0.25, 1.25] of normalized incomes and so has thick tails. In contrast, the UK displays a clear mode at $y = 0.4$ and thinner tails. Because – as already discussed in Section 3.2.5 – the identification function f^α times the density f is strictly convex in f, the country with the greater variation in identification will exhibit a higher value of average identification, *with the difference growing more pronounced as α increases*. To be sure, variations in identification find their starkest expression when distributions are multimodal, but even without such multimodality, variation is possible.

Remember that variation in identification is only one of several factors. In particular, we do not mean to suggest that the country with the greater variation in identification will invariably exhibit greater polarization as $\alpha \to 1$. For instance, our notion of a squeeze increases the variability of identification, but polarization must fall, by Axiom 1 (this is because alienation falls too with the squeeze). See the discussion at the end of Section 3.2.5 for another illustration of this point.

Sensitivity to α As α increases from 0.25 to 1, the cross-country variation in the value of average α-identification goes up. This increase in cross-country variability produces frequent "crossings" in the ranking of countries by polarization. Such crossings can occur at very low values of α (below 0.25) so that for *all* $\alpha \in [0.25, 1]$ the polarization ranking opposes the inequality ranking. This is the case (for Wave 3) for Belgium–Sweden, Italy–Canada, and Israel–Australia. Crossings could – and do – occur for intermediate values of $\alpha \in [0.25, 1]$. To be sure, they may not occur for any $\alpha \leq 1$, thus causing the polarization ordering to coincide with the inequality ordering. This is indeed a most frequent case for pairwise comparisons in Wave 3. Finally, in Wave 4 we also observe "double crossings" in the cases of Canada–France and Australia–Poland. In both cases, the first country starts with higher inequality, P_0, followed by a lower value of $P_{0.25}$, but later returning to higher values for larger values of α.

UK inequality is very close to US inequality; for all intents and purposes the two have the same Gini in Wave 3. Indeed, the UK ranks eighteenth and the US nineteenth – this is true for any $\alpha < 0.33$. However, as α increases beyond 0.33 up to 1, the UK retains the nineteenth position, while the US descends to ninth in the rankings. That fall in rankings occurs mostly when α increases beyond 0.75.

The Czech–US densities provide additional visual support to this sensitivity – see the lower panel in Figure 3.4. Here, the basic inequality comparison is unambiguous: the Czech Republic has lower inequality than the US. But the Czech

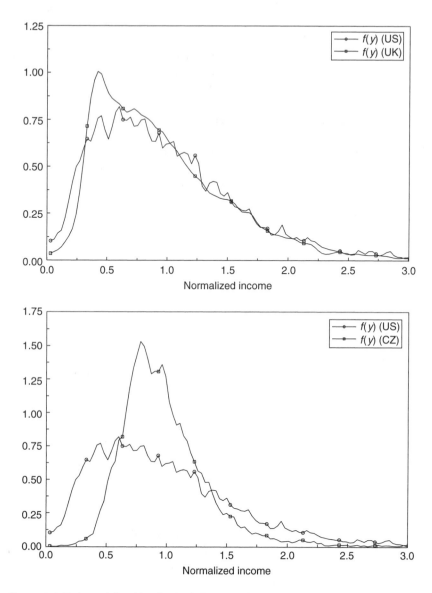

Figure 3.4 Estimated densities for the US, UK, and Czech Republic, Wave 3.

Republic has a spikier density with greater variation in it. This "shadow of multimodality" kicks in as α is increased, so much so that the Czech Republic is actually deemed equally or more polarized than the US by the time $\alpha = 1$.

Partial ordering   One might respond to the above observations as follows: our axiomatics do *not* rule out values of α very close to 0.25. Hence, in the strict sense of a partial order we are unable to (empirically) distinguish adequately between inequality and polarization, at least with the dataset at hand. In our opinion this response would be too hasty. Our characterization not only implies a partial ordering, it provides a very clean picture of how that ordering is parameterized, with the parameter α having a definite interpretation. If substantial variations in ranking occur as α increases, this warrants a closer look, and certainly shows – empirically – how "large" subsets of polarization indices work very differently from the Gini inequality index.[12]

3.4   Final remarks, and a proposed extension

In this chapter we present and characterize a class of measures for income polarization, based on what we call the identification–alienation structure. Our approach is fundamentally based on the view that inter-personal alienation fuels a polarized society, as does inequality. Our departure from inequality measurement lies in the notion that such alienation must also be complemented by a sense of identification. This combination of the two forces generates a class of measures that are sensitive (in the same direction) to both elements of inequality and equality, depending on where these changes are located in the overall distribution.

Our characterization, and the alternative decomposition presented in equation (7), permit us to describe the measure very simply: for any income distribution, polarization is the product of average alienation, average identification, and (one plus) the mean-normalized covariance between these two variables. We also discuss estimation issues for our measures as well as associated questions of statistical inference.

We wish to close this chapter with some remarks on what we see to be the main conceptual task ahead. Our analysis generates a certain structure for identification and alienation functions *in the special case in which both identification and alienation are based on the same characteristic*. This characteristic can be income or wealth. In principle, it could be any measurable feature with a well-defined ordering. The key restriction, however, is that whatever we choose the salient characteristic for identification to be, inter-group alienation has to be driven by the very same characteristic. This seems obvious in the cases of income or wealth. Yet, for some relevant social characteristics this might not be a natural assumption. Think of the case of ethnic polarization. It may or may not seem appropriate here to base inter-ethnic alienation as *only* depending on some suitably defined "ethnicity distance." In the cases of socially based group identification we find it more compelling to adopt a multi-dimensional approach to polarization, permitting alienation to depend on characteristics other than the one that defines group identity. In this proposed extension, we liberally transplant our findings to the case of social polarization, but with no further axiomatic reasoning. In our opinion, such reasoning is an important subject of future research.

Suppose, then, that there are M "social groups," based on region, kin, ethnicity, religion .... Let n_j be the number of individuals in group j, with overall population normalized to one. Let F_j describe the distribution of income in group j (with

f_j the accompanying density), unnormalized by group population. One may now entertain a variety of "social polarization measures."

3.4.1 Pure social polarization

Consider, first, the case of "pure social polarization," in which income plays no role. Assume that each person is "fully" identified with every other member of his group. Likewise, the alienation function takes on values that are specific to group pairs and have no reference to income. For each pair of groups j and k denote this value by Δ_{jk}. Then a natural transplant of equation (3) yields the measure

$$P_s(\mathbf{F}) = \sum_{j=1}^{M} \sum_{k=1}^{M} n_j^\alpha n_k \Delta_{jk}. \tag{14}$$

Even this sort of specification may be too general in some interesting instances in which individuals are interested only in the dichotomous perception Us/They. In particular, in these instances, individuals are not interested in differentiating between the different opposing groups. Perhaps the simplest instance of this is a pure contest (Esteban and Ray 1999), which yields the variant[13]

$$\tilde{P}_s(\mathbf{F}) = \sum_{j=1}^{M} n_j^\alpha (1 - n_j). \tag{15}$$

3.4.2 Hybrids

Once the two extremes – pure income polarization and pure social polariza- tion – are identified, we may easily consider several hybrids. As examples, consider the case in which notions of identification are mediated not just by group membership but by income similarities as well, while the antagonism equation remains untouched. Then we get what one might call *social polarization with income-mediated identification*:

$$P_s(\mathbf{F}) = \sum_{j=1}^{M} (1 - n_j) \int_x f_j(x)^\alpha \, dF_j(x). \tag{16}$$

One could expand (or contract) the importance of income further, while still staying away from the extremes. For instance, suppose that – in addition to the income- mediation of group identity – alienation is also income-mediated (for alienation, two individuals must belong to different groups *and* have different incomes). Now groups have only a demarcating role – they are necessary (but not sufficient) for identity, and they are necessary (but not sufficient) for alienation. The resulting measure would look like this:

$$P^*(\mathbf{F}) = \sum_{j=1}^{M} \sum_{k \neq j} \int_x \int_y f_j(x)^\alpha |x - y| \, dF_j(x) \, dF_k(y).$$ (17)

Note that we do not intend to suggest that other special cases or hybrids are not possible, or that they are less important. The discussion here is only to show that social and economic considerations can be profitably combined in the measurement of polarization. Indeed, it is conceivable that such measures will perform better than the more commonly used fragmentation measures in the analysis of social conflict. But a full exploration of this last theme must await a future paper.

Appendix

Proof of Theorem 1

First, we show that Axioms 1–4 imply equation (3). The given lemma follows from Jensen's inequality; proof omitted.

Lemma 1. *Let g be a continuous real-valued function defined on* $\mathbb{R}$ *such that for all* $x > 0$ *and all* δ *with* $0 < \delta < x$,

$$g(x) \geq \frac{1}{2\delta} \int_{x-\delta}^{x+\delta} g(y) \, dy.$$ (18)

Then g must be a concave function.

In what follows, remember that our measure only considers income *differences* across people, so that we may slide any distribution to left or right as we please.

Lemma 2. *The function T must be concave in a for every i > 0.*

Proof. Fix $x > 0$, some $i > 0$, and $\delta \in (0, x)$. Consider three basic densities as in Axiom 2 (see Figure 3.1) but specialize as shown in Figure 3.5; each is a transform of a uniform basic density. The bases are centered at $-x$, 0, and x. The side densities are of width 2δ and height h, and the middle density is of width 2ϵ and height i. We shall vary ϵ and h but to make sure that Axiom 2 applies, we choose $\epsilon > 0$ such that $\delta + \epsilon < x$. A λ-squeeze of the side densities simply contracts their base width to $2\lambda\delta$, while the height is raised to h/λ. For each λ, decompose the measure equation (1) into five components. (a) The "internal polarization" P_m of the middle rectangle. This component does not vary with λ so there will be no need to explicitly calculate it. (b) The "internal polarization" P_s of each side rectangle. (c) Total effective antagonism, A_{ms} felt by inhabitants of the middle toward each side density. (d) Total effective antagonism A_{sm} felt

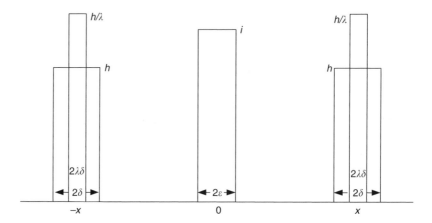

Figure 3.5 Three basic densities.

by inhabitants of each side toward the middle. (e) Total effective antagonism A_{ss} felt by inhabitants of one side toward the other side. Each of these last four terms appear twice, so that (writing everything as a function of λ),

$$P(\lambda) = P_m + 2P_s(\lambda) + 2A_{ms}(\lambda) + 2A_{sm}(\lambda) + 2A_{ss}(\lambda). \tag{19}$$

Now we compute the terms on the right-hand side of equation (19). First,

$$P_s(\lambda) = \frac{1}{\lambda^2} \int_{x-\lambda\delta}^{x+\lambda\delta} \int_{x-\lambda\delta}^{x+\lambda\delta} T(h/\lambda, |b' - b|)h^2 \, db' \, db,$$

where (here and in all subsequent cases) b will stand for the "origin" income (to which the identification is applied), and b' the "destination income" (toward which the antagonism is felt). Next,

$$A_{ms}(\lambda) = \frac{1}{\lambda} \int_{-\epsilon}^{\epsilon} \int_{x-\lambda\delta}^{x+\lambda\delta} T(i, b' - b)ih \, db' \, db.$$

Third,

$$A_{sm}(\lambda) = \frac{1}{\lambda} \int_{x-\lambda\delta}^{x+\lambda\delta} \int_{-\epsilon}^{\epsilon} T(h/\lambda, b - b')hi \, db' \, db.$$

And finally,

$$A_{ss}(\lambda) = \frac{1}{\lambda^2} \int_{-x-\lambda\delta}^{-x+\lambda\delta} \int_{x-\lambda\delta}^{x+\lambda\delta} T(h/\lambda, b' - b) h^2 \, db' \, db.$$

The axiom requires that $P(\lambda) \geq P(1)$. Equivalently, we require that $(P(\lambda) - P(1))/2h \geq 0$ for all h, which implies in particular that

$$\lim_{h \to 0} \inf \frac{P(\lambda) - P(1)}{2h} \geq 0. \tag{20}$$

If we divide through by h in the individual components calculated above and then send h to 0, it is easy to see that the only term that remains is A_{ms}. Formally, equation (20) and the calculations above must jointly imply that

$$\frac{1}{\lambda} \int_{-\epsilon}^{\epsilon} \int_{x-\lambda\delta}^{x+\lambda\delta} T(i, b' - b) \, db' \, db \geq \int_{-\epsilon}^{\epsilon} \int_{x-\delta}^{x+\delta} T(i, b' - b) \, db' \, db, \tag{21}$$

and this must be true for all $\lambda \in (0, 1)$ as well as all $\epsilon \in (0, x - \delta)$. Therefore we may insist on the inequality in equation (21) holding as $\lambda \to 0$. Performing the necessary calculations, we may conclude that

$$\frac{1}{\epsilon} \int_{-\epsilon}^{\epsilon} T(i, x - b) \, db \geq \frac{1}{\epsilon} \int_{-\epsilon}^{\epsilon} \int_{x-\delta}^{x+\delta} T(i, b' - b) \, db' \, db, \tag{22}$$

for every $\epsilon \in (0, x - \delta)$. Finally, take ϵ to zero in equation (22). This allows us to deduce that

$$T(i, x) \geq \int_{x-\delta}^{x+\delta} T(i, b') \, db'. \tag{23}$$

As equation (23) must hold for every $x > 0$ and every $\delta \in (0, x)$, we may invoke Lemma 1 to conclude that T is concave in x for every $i > 0$. $\square$

Lemma 3. *Let g be a concave, continuous function on $\mathbb{R}_+$, with $g(0) = 0$. Suppose that for each a and a' with $a > a' > 0$, there exists $\bar{\Delta} > 0$ such that*

$$g(a + \Delta) - g(a) \geq g(a') - g(a' - \Delta), \tag{24}$$

for all $\Delta \in (0, \bar{\Delta})$. Then g must be linear.

The proof is straightforward and is omitted.

Lemma 4. *There is a continuous function $\phi(i)$ such that $T(i,a) = \phi(i)a$ for all i and a.*

Proof. Fix a and a' with $a > a' > 0$, and $i > 0$. Consider four basic densities as in Axiom 3 (see Figure 3.3) but specialize as shown in Figure 3.6; each is a transform of a uniform basic density. The bases are centered at locations $-y$, $-x$, x, and y, where $x \equiv (a - a')/2$, and $y \equiv (a + a')/2$. The "inner" densities are of width 2δ and height h, and the "outer" densities are of width 2ϵ and height i. We shall vary different parameters (particularly x) but to ensure disjoint support we assume throughout that $\epsilon < x$ and $\delta + \epsilon < y - x - \bar{\Delta}$ for some $\bar{\Delta} > 0$. Again, decompose the polarization measure equation (1) into several distinct components. (a) The "internal polarization" of each rectangle j; call it P_j, $j = 1, 2, 3, 4$. These components are unchanged as we change x so there will be no need to calculate them explicitly. (b) Total effective antagonism $A_{jk}(x)$ felt by inhabitants of rectangle j toward rectangle k (we emphasize dependence on the parameter x). Thus, total polarization $P(x)$ is given by

$$P(x) = \sum_{j=1}^{4} P_j + \sum_{j}\sum_{k \neq j} A_{jk}(x) = \sum_{j=1}^{4} P_j + 2A_{12}(x) + 2A_{13}(x)$$
$$+ 2A_{21}(x) + 2A_{31}(x) + 2A_{23}(x) + 2A_{14},$$

where the second equality simply exploits obvious symmetries and A_{14} is noted to be independent of x. Let us compute the terms in this formula that do change with x. We have

$$A_{12}(x) = \int_{-y-\epsilon}^{-y+\epsilon} \int_{-x-\delta}^{-x+\delta} T(i, b' - b)ih\,db'\,db,$$

$$A_{13}(x) = \int_{-y-\epsilon}^{-y+\epsilon} \int_{x-\delta}^{x+\delta} T(i, b' - b)ih\,db'\,db,$$

$$A_{21}(x) = \int_{-x-\delta}^{-x+\delta} \int_{-y-\epsilon}^{-y+\epsilon} T(h, b - b')ih\,db'\,db,$$

$$A_{31}(x) = \int_{x-\delta}^{x+\delta} \int_{-y-\epsilon}^{-y+\epsilon} T(h, b - b')ih\,db'\,db,$$

and

$$A_{23}(x) = \int_{-x-\delta}^{-x+\delta} \int_{x-\delta}^{x+\delta} T(h, b - b')h^2\,db'\,db.$$

Now, the axiom requires that $P(x + \Delta) - P(x) \geq 0$. Equivalently, we require that $[P(x + \Delta) - P(1)]/2ih \geq 0$ for all h, which implies in particular that

$$\lim_{h \to 0} \inf \frac{P(x + \Delta) - P(x)}{2ih} \geq 0.$$

Using this information along with the computations for $P(x)$ and the various $A_{jk}(x)$'s, we see (after some substitution of variables and transposition of terms) that

$$\int_{-y-\epsilon}^{-y+\epsilon} \int_{x-\delta}^{x+\delta} [T(i, b' - b + \Delta) - T(i, b' - b)] \, db' \, db$$

$$\geq \int_{-y-\epsilon}^{-y+\epsilon} \int_{-x-\delta}^{-x+\delta} [T(i, b' - b) - T(i, b' - b - \Delta)] \, db' \, db.$$

Dividing through by δ in this expression and then taking δ to zero, we may conclude that

$$\int_{-y-\epsilon}^{-y+\epsilon} [T(i, x - b + \Delta) - T(i, x - b)] \, db$$

$$\geq \int_{-y-\epsilon}^{-y+\epsilon} [T(i, -x - b) - T(i, -x - b - \Delta)] \, db,$$

and dividing this inequality, in turn, by ϵ and taking ϵ to zero, we see that

$$T(i, a + \Delta) - T(i, a) \geq T(i, a') - T(i, a' - \Delta),$$

where we use the observations that $x + y = a$, and $y - x = a'$. Therefore the conditions of Lemma 3 are satisfied, and $T(i, \cdot)$ must be linear for every $i > 0$ since $T(0, a) = 0$. That is, there is a function $\phi(i)$ such that $T(i, a) = \phi(i)a$ for every i and a. Given that T is continuous by assumption, the same must be true of ϕ. □

Lemma 5. $\phi(i)$ *must be of the form* Ki^α, *for constants* $(K, \alpha) \gg 0$.

Proof. As a preliminary step, observe that,

$$\phi(i) > 0 \quad \text{whenever } i > 0, \tag{25}$$

otherwise Axiom 3 would fail for configurations constructed from rectangular basic densities of equal height i. We first prove that ϕ satisfies the fundamental

Cauchy equation

$$\phi(p)\phi(p') = \phi(pp')\phi(1) \tag{26}$$

for every $(p, p') \gg 0$. To this end, fix p and p', and define $r \equiv pp'$. In what follows, we assume that $p \geq r$.[14] Consider a configuration with two basic densities, both of width 2ϵ, the first centered at 0, and the second centered at 1. The heights are p and h (where $h > 0$ but soon to be made arbitrarily small). A little computation shows that polarization in this case is given by

$$P = ph[\phi(p) + \phi(h)] \left\{ \int_{-\epsilon}^{\epsilon} \int_{1-\epsilon}^{1+\epsilon} (b' - b)\, db'\, db \right\}$$

$$+ [p^2\phi(p) + h^2\phi(h)] \left\{ \int_{-\epsilon}^{\epsilon} \int_{-\epsilon}^{\epsilon} |b' - b|\, db'\, db \right\}$$

$$= 4\epsilon^2 ph[\phi(p) + \phi(h)] + \frac{8\epsilon^3}{3}[p^2\phi(p) + h^2\phi(h)], \tag{27}$$

where the first equality invokes Lemma 4. Now change the height of the first rectangle to r. Using equation (25) and $p \geq r$, it is easy to see that for each ϵ, there exists a (unique) height $h(\epsilon)$ for the second rectangle such that the polarizations of the two configurations are equated. Invoking equation (27), $h(\epsilon)$ is such that

$$ph[\phi(p) + \phi(h)] + \frac{2\epsilon}{3}[p^2\phi(p) + h^2\phi(h)]$$

$$= rh(\epsilon)[\phi(r) + \phi(h(\epsilon))] + \frac{2\epsilon}{3}[r^2\phi(r) + h(\epsilon)^2\phi(h(\epsilon))]. \tag{28}$$

By Axiom 4, it follows that for all $\lambda > 0$,

$$\lambda^2 ph[\phi(\lambda p) + \phi(\lambda h)] + \frac{2\epsilon}{3}[(\lambda p)^2\phi(\lambda p) + (\lambda h)^2\phi(\lambda h)]$$

$$= \lambda^2 rh(\epsilon)[\phi(\lambda r) + \phi(\lambda h(\epsilon))] + \frac{2\epsilon}{3}\{(\lambda r)^2\phi(\lambda r) + [\lambda h(\epsilon)]^2\phi(\lambda h(\epsilon))\}. \tag{29}$$

Notice that as $\epsilon \downarrow 0$, $h(\epsilon)$ lies in some bounded set. We may therefore extract a convergent subsequence with limit h' as $\epsilon \downarrow 0$. By the continuity of ϕ, we may pass to the limit in equations (28) and (29) to conclude that

$$ph[\phi(p) + \phi(h)] = rh'[\phi(r) + \phi(h')] \tag{30}$$

and

$$\lambda^2 ph[\phi(\lambda p) + \phi(\lambda h)] = \lambda^2 rh'[\phi(\lambda r) + \phi(\lambda h')]. \tag{31}$$

Combining equations (30) and (31), we see that

$$\frac{\phi(p) + \phi(h)}{\phi(\lambda p) + \phi(\lambda h)} = \frac{\phi(r) + \phi(h')}{\phi(\lambda r) + \phi(\lambda h')}. \tag{32}$$

Taking limits in (32) as $h \to 0$ and noting that $h' \to 0$ as a result (examine (30) to confirm this), we have for all $\lambda > 0$,

$$\frac{\phi(p)}{\phi(\lambda p)} = \frac{\phi(r)}{\phi(\lambda r)}. \tag{33}$$

Put $\lambda = 1/p$ and recall that $r = pp'$. Then equation (33) yields the required Cauchy equation (26). To complete the proof, recall that ϕ is continuous and that equation (25) holds. The class of solutions to equation (26) (that satisfy these additional qualifications) is completely described by $\phi(p) = Kp^\alpha$ for constants $(K, \alpha) \gg 0$ (see, e.g., Aczél 1966, p. 41, theorem 3). □

Lemmas 4 and 5 together establish "necessity," though it still remains to establish the bounds on α. We shall do so along with our proof of "sufficiency," which we begin now.

Lemma 6. *Let f be a basic density with mass p and mean μ on support $[a, b]$. Let $m \equiv \mu - a$, and let f^* denote the root of f. Then, if f^λ denotes some λ-squeeze of f,*

$$P(F^\lambda) = 4kp^{2+\alpha}(m\lambda)^{1-\alpha} \int_0^1 f^*(x)^{1+\alpha} \left\{ \int_0^1 f^*(y)(1 - y) \, dy \right.$$

$$\left. + \int_x^1 f^*(y)(y - x) \, dy \right\} dx \tag{34}$$

for some constant $k > 0$.

Proof. Recall that a slide of f has no effect on the computations, so we may as well set $a = 0$ and $b = 2m$, where $m = \mu - a$ is now to be interpreted as the mean. Given equation (3),

$$P(F) = k \iint f(x)^{1+\alpha} f(y)|y - x| \, dy \, dx \tag{35}$$

for some $k > 0$. Using the fact that f is symmetric, we can write

$$P(F) = 2k \int_0^m \int_0^{2m} f(x')^{1+\alpha} f(y')|x' - y'| \, dy' \, dx'$$

$$= 2k \int_0^m f(x')^{1+\alpha} \left\{ \int_0^{x'} f(y')(x' - y') \, dy' + \int_{x'}^m f(y')(y' - x') \, dy' \right.$$

$$+ \left. \int_m^{2m} f(y')(y' - x') \, dy' \right\} dx'. \tag{36}$$

Examine the very last term in equation (36). Change variables by setting $z \equiv 2m - y'$, and use symmetry to deduce that

$$\int_m^{2m} f(y')(y' - x') \, dy' = \int_0^m f(z)(2m - x' - z) \, dz.$$

Substituting this in equation (36), and manipulating terms, we obtain

$$P(F) = 4k \int_0^m f(x')^{1+\alpha} \left\{ \int_0^m f(y')(m - y') \, dy' \right.$$

$$+ \left. \int_{x'}^m f(y')(y' - x') \, dy' \right\} dx'. \tag{37}$$

Now suppose that f^λ is a λ-squeeze of f. Note that equation (37) holds just as readily for f^λ as for f. Therefore, using the expression for f given in equation (2), we see that

$$P(F^\lambda) = 4k\lambda^{-(2+\alpha)} \int_{(1-\lambda)m}^m f\left(\frac{x' - (1 - \lambda)m}{\lambda}\right)^{1+\alpha}$$

$$\times \left\{ \int_{(1-\lambda)m}^m f\left(\frac{y' - (1 - \lambda)m}{\lambda}\right)(m - y') \, dy' \right.$$

$$+ \left. \int_{x'}^m f\left(\frac{y' - (1 - \lambda)m}{\lambda}\right)(y' - x') \, dy' \right\} dx'.$$

Perform the change of variables $x'' = [x' - (1 - \lambda)m]/\lambda$ and $y'' = [y' - (1 - \lambda)m]/\lambda$. Then it is easy to see that

$$P(F^\lambda) = 4k\lambda^{1-\alpha} \int_0^m f(x'')^{1+\alpha} \left\{ \int_0^m f(y'')(m - y'') \, dy'' \right.$$

$$+ \left. \int_{x''}^m f(y'')(y'' - x'') \, dy'' \right\} dx''.$$

To complete the proof, we must recover the root f^* from f. To this end, first population-scale f to h, where h has mass 1. That is, $f(z) = ph(z)$ for all z. Doing so, we see that

$$P(F^\lambda) = 4kp^{2+\alpha}\lambda^{1-\alpha}\int_0^m h(x'')^{1+\alpha}\left\{\int_0^m h(y'')(m - y'')\,dy''\right.$$
$$\left. + \int_{x''}^m h(y'')(y'' - x'')\,dy''\right\}dx''.$$

Finally, make the change of variables $x = x''/m$ and $y = y''/m$. Noting that $f^*(z) = mh(mz)$, we get equation (34). $\quad\square$

Lemma 7. *Let f and g be two basic densities with disjoint support, with their means separated by distance d, and with population masses p and q respectively. Let f have mean μ on support $[a, b]$. Let $m \equiv \mu - a$ and let f^* denote the root of f. Then for any λ-squeeze f^λ of f,*

$$A(f^\lambda, g) = 2kdp^{1+\alpha}q(m\lambda)^{-\alpha}\int_0^1 f^*(x)^{1+\alpha}\,dx, \tag{38}$$

where $A(f^\lambda, g)$ denotes the total effective antagonism felt by members of f^λ toward members of g.

Proof. Without loss of generality, let f have support $[0, 2m]$ (with mean m), and g have support $[d, d + 2m]$ (where $d \geq 2m$ for disjoint supports). Using equation (35),

$$A(f, g) = k\int_0^{2m} f(x)^{1+\alpha}\left[\int_d^{d+2m} g(y)(y - x)\,dy\right]dx$$

$$= k\int_0^{2m} f(x)^{1+\alpha}\left[\int_d^{d+m} g(y)(y - x)\,dy\right.$$

$$\left. + \int_{d+m}^{d+2m} g(y)(y - x)\,dy\right]dx$$

$$= k\int_0^{2m} f(x)^{1+\alpha}\left[\int_d^{d+m} g(y)2(m + d - x)\,dy\right]dx$$

$$= kq\int_0^{2m} f(x)^{1+\alpha}(m + d - x)\,dx$$

$$= 2dkq\int_0^m f(x)^{1+\alpha}\,dx,$$

where the third equality exploits the symmetry of g,[15] the fourth equality uses the fact that $\int_d^{d+m} g(y) = q/2$, and the final equality uses the symmetry of f.[16] To be sure, this formula applies to any λ-squeeze of f, so that

$$A(f^\lambda, g) = 2dkq \int_0^m f^\lambda(x')^{1+\alpha} dx'$$

$$= 2dkq\lambda^{-(1+\alpha)} \int_{(1-\lambda)m}^m f\left(\frac{x' - (1-\lambda)m}{\lambda}\right)^{1+\alpha} dx',$$

and making the change of variables $x'' = [x' - (1-\lambda)m]/\lambda$, we may conclude that

$$A(f^\lambda, g) = 2dkq\lambda^{-\alpha} \int_0^m f(x'')^{1+\alpha} dx''.$$

To complete the proof, we must recover the root f^* from f. As in the proof of Lemma 6, first population-scale f to h, where h has mass 1. That is, $f(z) = ph(z)$ for all z. Doing so, we see that

$$A(f^\lambda, g) = 2dkp^{1+\alpha}q\lambda^{-\alpha} \int_0^m h(x'')^{1+\alpha} dx''.$$

Finally, make the change of variables $x = x''/m$. Noting that $f^*(z) = mh(mz)$, we get equation (38). $\qquad\square$

Lemma 8. *Define, for any root f and $\alpha > 0$,*

$$\psi(f, \alpha) \equiv \frac{\int_0^1 f(x)^{1+\alpha} dx}{\int_0^1 f(x)^{1+\alpha} \left\{\int_0^1 f(y)(1-y)\, dy + \int_x^1 f(y)(y-x)\, dy\right\} dx}.$$
(39)

Then – for any $\alpha > 0$ – $\psi(f, \alpha)$ attains its minimum value when f is the uniform root, and this minimum value equals 3.

Proof. It will be useful to work with the inverse function

$$\zeta(f, \alpha) \equiv \psi(f, \alpha)^{-1}$$

$$= \frac{\int_0^1 f(x)^{1+\alpha} \left\{\int_0^1 f(y)(1-y)\, dy + \int_x^1 f(y)(y-x)\, dy\right\} dx}{\int_0^1 f(x)^{1+\alpha}\, dx}.$$

Note that $\zeta(f,\alpha)$ may be viewed as a weighted average of

$$L(x) \equiv \int_0^1 f(y)(1-y)\,dy + \int_x^1 f(y)(y-x)\,dy \tag{40}$$

as this expression varies over $x \in [0,1]$, where the "weight" on a particular x is just

$$\frac{f(x)^{1+\alpha}}{\int_0^1 f(z)^{1+\alpha}\,dz}$$

which integrates over x to 1. Now observe that $L(x)$ is *decreasing* in x. Moreover, by the unimodality of a root, the weights must be nondecreasing in x. It follows that

$$\zeta(f,\alpha) \le \int_0^1 L(x)\,dx. \tag{41}$$

Now

$$\begin{aligned}
L(x) &= \int_0^1 f(y)(1-y)\,dy + \int_x^1 f(y)(y-x)\,dy \\
&= \int_0^1 f(y)(1-x)\,dy + \int_0^x f(y)(x-y)\,dy \\
&= \frac{1-x}{2} + \int_0^x f(y)(x-y)\,dy.
\end{aligned} \tag{42}$$

Because $f(x)$ is nondecreasing and integrates to $1/2$ on $[0,1]$, it must be the case that $\int_0^x f(y)(x-y)\,dy \le \int_0^x (x-y)/2\,dy$ for all $x \le 1$. Using this information in equation (42) and combining it with equation (41),

$$\begin{aligned}
\zeta(f,\alpha) &\le \int_0^1 \left(\frac{1-x}{2} + \int_0^x \frac{x-y}{2}\,dy \right) dx \\
&= \int_0^1 \left(\int_0^1 \frac{1-y}{2}\,dy + \int_x^1 \frac{y-x}{2}\,dy \right) dx \\
&= \zeta(u,\alpha),
\end{aligned} \tag{43}$$

where u stands for the uniform root taking constant value $1/2$ on $[0,2]$. Simple integration reveals that $\zeta(u,\alpha) = 1/3$. $\qquad\square$

Lemma 9. *Given that $P(f)$ is of the form equation (35), Axiom 1 is satisfied if and only if $\alpha \le 1$.*

Proof. Simply inspect equation (34). $\qquad\square$

Lemma 10. *Given that $P(f)$ is of the form equation (35), Axiom 2 is satisfied if and only if $\alpha \geq 0.25$.*

Proof. Consider a configuration as given in Axiom 2: a symmetric distribution made out of three basic densities. By symmetry, the side densities must share the same root; call this f^*. Let p denote their (common) population mass and m their (common) difference from their means to their lower support. Likewise, denote the root of the middle density by g^*, by q its population mass, and by n the difference between mean and lower support. As in the proof of Lemma 2, we may decompose the polarization measure equation (35) into several components. First, there are the "internal polarizations" of the middle density (P_m) and of the two side densities (P_s). Next, there are various subtotals of effective antagonism felt by members of one of the basic densities toward another basic density. Let A_{ms} denote this when the "origin" density is the middle and the "destination" density one of the sides. Likewise, A_{sm} is obtained by permuting origin and destination densities. Finally, denote by A_{ss} the total effective antagonism felt by inhabitants of one side toward the other side. Observe that each of these last four terms appear twice, so that (writing everything as a function of λ), overall polarization is given by

$$P(\lambda) = P_m + 2P_s(\lambda) + 2A_{ms}(\lambda) + 2A_{sm}(\lambda) + 2A_{ss}(\lambda). \tag{44}$$

Compute these terms. For brevity, define for any root h,

$$\psi_1(h, \alpha) \equiv \int_0^1 h(x)^{1+\alpha} \left\{ \int_0^1 h(y)(1 - y)\,dy + \int_x^1 h(y)(y - x)\,dy \right\} dx$$

and

$$\psi_2(h, \alpha) \equiv \int_0^1 h(x)^{1+\alpha}\,dx.$$

Now, using Lemmas 6 and 7, we see that

$$P_s(\lambda) = 4kp^{2+\alpha}(m\lambda)^{1-\alpha}\psi_1(f^*, \alpha),$$

while

$$A_{ms}(\lambda) = 2kdq^{1+\alpha}pn^{-\alpha}\psi_2(g^*, \alpha).$$

Moreover,

$$A_{sm}(\lambda) = 2kdp^{1+\alpha}q(m\lambda)^{-\alpha}\psi_2(f^*, \alpha),$$

and

$$A_{ss}(\lambda) = 4kdp^{2+\alpha}(m\lambda)^{-\alpha}\psi_2(f^*,\alpha),$$

(where it should be remembered that the distance between the means of the two side densities is $2d$). Observe from these calculations that $A_{ms}(\lambda)$ is entirely insensitive to λ. Consequently, feeding all the computed terms into equation (44), we may conclude that

$$P(\lambda) = C\left[2\lambda^{1-\alpha} + \frac{d}{m}\psi(f^*,\alpha)\lambda^{-\alpha}\left(\frac{q}{p}+2\right)\right] + D,$$

where C and D are positive constants independent of λ, and

$$\psi(f^*,\alpha) = \frac{\psi_2(f^*,\alpha)}{\psi_1(f^*,\alpha)}$$

by construction; see equation (39) in the statement of Lemma 8. It follows from this expression that for Axiom 2 to hold, it is necessary and sufficient that for *every* three-density configuration of the sort described in that axiom,

$$2\lambda^{1-\alpha} + \frac{d}{m}\psi(f^*,\alpha)\lambda^{-\alpha}\left(\frac{q}{p}+2\right) \qquad (45)$$

must be nonincreasing in λ over $(0,1]$. An examination of the expression in equation (45) quickly shows that a situation in which q is arbitrarily close to zero (relative to p) is a necessary and sufficient test case. By the same logic, one should make d/m as small as possible. The disjoint-support hypothesis of Axiom 2 tells us that this lowest value is 1. So it will be necessary and sufficient to show that for every root f^*,

$$\lambda^{1-\alpha} + \psi(f^*,\alpha)\lambda^{-\alpha} \qquad (46)$$

is nonincreasing in λ over $(0,1]$. For any f^*, it is easy enough to compute the necessary and sufficient bounds on α. Simple differentiation reveals that

$$(1-\alpha)\lambda^{-\alpha} - \alpha\psi(f^*,\alpha)\lambda^{-(1+\alpha)}$$

must be nonnegative for every $\lambda \in (0,1]$; the necessary and sufficient condition for this is

$$\alpha \geq \frac{1}{1+\psi(f^*,\alpha)}. \qquad (47)$$

Therefore, to find the necessary and sufficient bound on α (uniform over all roots), we need to minimize $\psi(f^*, \alpha)$ by choice of f^*, subject to the condition that f^* be a root. By Lemma 8, this minimum value is 3. Using this information in equation (47), we are done. □

Lemma 11. *Given that $P(f)$ is of the form (35), Axiom 3 is satisfied.*

Proof. Consider a symmetric distribution composed of four basic densities, as in the statement of Axiom 3. Number the densities 1, 2, 3, and 4, in the same order displayed in Figure 3.6. Let x denote the amount of the slide (experienced by the inner densities) in the axiom. For each such x, let $d_{jk}(x)$ denote the (absolute) difference between the means of basic densities j and k. As we have done several times before, we may decompose the polarization of this configuration into several components. First, there is the "internal polarization" of each rectangle j; call it P_j, $j = 1, 2, 3, 4$. (These will stay unchanged with x.) Next, there is the total effective antagonism felt by inhabitants of each basic density toward another; call this $A_{jk}(x)$, where j is the "origin" density and k is the "destination" density. Thus total polarization $P(x)$, again written explicitly as a function of x, is given by

$$P(x) = \sum_{j=1}^{4} P_j + \sum_{j}\sum_{k \neq j} A_{jk}(x)$$

so that, using symmetry,

$$P(x) - P(0) = 2\{[A_{12}(x) + A_{13}(x)] - [A_{12}(0) + A_{13}(0)]\}$$
$$+ [A_{23}(x) - A_{23}(0)]. \tag{48}$$

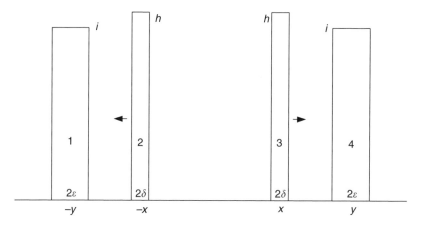

Figure 3.6 Four basic densities.

Now Lemma 7 tells us that for all i and j,

$$A_{ij}(x) = k_{ij}d_{ij}(x),$$

where k_{ij} is a positive constant which is independent of distances across the two basic densities, and in particular is independent of x. Using this information in equation (48), it is trivial to see that

$$P(x) - P(0) = A_{23}(x) - A_{23}(0) = k_{ij}x > 0,$$

so that Axiom 3 is satisfied. $\square$

Given equation (35), Axiom 4 is trivial to verify. Therefore Lemmas 9, 10, and 11 complete the proof of the theorem.

Addendum

This addendum contains details and proofs of the estimation and statistical inference results that are reported at the beginning of Section 3.3.

Estimating $P_\alpha(F)$

The following rewriting of $P_\alpha(F)$ is useful:

Observation 1. *For every distribution function F with associated density f and mean μ,*

$$P_\alpha(F) = \int_y f(y)^\alpha a(y)\, dF(y) \equiv \int_y p_\alpha(y)\, dF(y), \qquad (49)$$

with $a(y) \equiv \mu + y(2F(y) - 1) - 2\mu^*(y)$, where $\mu^*(y) = \int_{-\infty}^y x\, dF(x)$ is a partial mean and where $p_\alpha(y) = f(y)^\alpha a(y)$.

Proof of Observation 1. First note that $|x - y| = x + y - 2\min(x, y)$. Hence, by equation (3),

$$P_\alpha(f) = \int_x \int_y f(y)^\alpha [x + y - 2\min(x, y)]\, dF(y)\, dF(x).$$

To prove equation (49), note that

$$\int_x \int_y x\, f(y)^\alpha\, dF(y)\, dF(x) = \mu \int_y f(y)^\alpha\, dF(y), \qquad (50)$$

and that

$$\int_x \int_y f(y)^\alpha \min(x, y) \, dF(y) \, dF(x)$$

$$= \int_x \int_{y=-\infty}^{y=x} yf(y)^\alpha \, dF(y) \, dF(x) + \int_x \int_{y=x}^\infty xf(y)^\alpha \, dF(y) \, dF(x).$$

$$(51)$$

The first term in equation (51) can be integrated by parts over x:

$$\int_{y=-\infty}^{y=x} yf(y)^\alpha \, dF(y) F(x) \Big|_{-\infty}^\infty - \int xf(x)^\alpha F(x) \, dF(x)$$

$$= \int yf(y)^\alpha \, dF(y) - \int xf(x)^\alpha F(x) \, dF(x)$$

$$= \int yf(y)^\alpha [1 - F(y)] \, dF(y).$$

$$(52)$$

The last term in equation (51) can also be integrated by parts over x as follows:

$$\int_x \int_{y=x}^\infty xf(y)^\alpha \, dF(y) \, dF(x) = \int_x \int_{y=x}^\infty f(y)^\alpha \, dF(y) \, x \, dF(x)$$

$$= \mu^*(x) \int_{y=x}^\infty f(y)^\alpha \, dF(y) \Big|_{x=-\infty}^{x=\infty}$$

$$+ \int_x \mu^*(x) f(x)^\alpha \, dF(x)$$

$$= \int_y \mu^*(y) f(y)^\alpha \, dF(y),$$

$$(53)$$

where $\mu^*(x) = \int_{-\infty}^x z \, dF(z)$ is a partial mean. Adding terms yields equation (49), and completes the proof. $\qquad \square$

Suppose that we estimate $P_\alpha(F)$ using a random sample of n i.i.d observations of income y_i, $i = 1, \ldots, n$, drawn from the distribution $F(y)$, and ordered such that $y_1 \le y_2 \le \cdots \le y_n$. As in equation (9), a natural estimator of $P_\alpha(F)$ is $P_\alpha(\hat{F})$, given by substituting the distribution function $F(y)$ by the empirical distribution function $\hat{F}(y)$, by replacing $f(y)^\alpha$ by a suitable estimator $\hat{f}(y)^\alpha$ (to be examined below), and by replacing $a(y)$ by $\hat{a}(y)$:

$$P_\alpha(\hat{F}) = \int \hat{f}(y)^\alpha \hat{a}(y) \, d\hat{F}(y) = n^{-1} \sum_{i=1}^n \hat{f}(y_i)^\alpha \hat{a}(y_i),$$

$$(54)$$

with $\hat{p}_\alpha(y_i) = \hat{f}(y_i)^\alpha \hat{a}(y_i)$. Note that y_i is the empirical quantile for percentiles between $(i-1)/n$ and i/n. Hence, we may use

$$\hat{F}(y_i) = \frac{1}{2}\left(\frac{i-1}{n} + \frac{i}{n}\right) = 0.5n^{-1}(2i-1), \tag{55}$$

and

$$\hat{\mu}^*(y_i) = n^{-1}\left(\sum_{j=1}^{i-1} y_j + \frac{i-(i-1)}{2}y_i\right), \tag{56}$$

and thus define $\hat{a}(y_i)$ as

$$\hat{a}(y_i) = \hat{\mu} + y_i(n^{-1}(2i-1)-1) - n^{-1}\left(2\sum_{j=1}^{i-1} y_j + y_i\right), \tag{57}$$

where $\hat{\mu}$ is the sample mean.

Observe that adding an exact replication of the sample to the original sample should not change the value of the estimator $P_\alpha(\hat{F})$. Indeed, supposing that the estimators $\hat{f}(\cdot)^\alpha$ are invariant to sample size, this is indeed the case when formulae (9) and (57) are used. We record this formally as,

Observation 2. *Let* $\mathbf{y} = (y_1, y_2, \ldots, y_n)$ *and* $\tilde{\mathbf{y}} = (\tilde{y}_1, \tilde{y}_2, \ldots, \tilde{y}_{2n})$ *be two vectors of sizes n and 2n respectively, ordered along increasing values of income. Suppose that for each* $i \in \{1, \ldots, n\}$, $y_i = \tilde{y}_{2i-1} = \tilde{y}_{2i}$ *for all* $i = 1, \ldots, n$. *Let* $P_\alpha(F_{\mathbf{y}})$ *be the polarization index defined by (9) and (57) for a vector of income* $\mathbf{y}$. *Then, provided that* $f_{\mathbf{y}}(y_i) = f_{\tilde{\mathbf{y}}}(y_i)$ *for* $i = 1, \ldots, n$, *it must be that* $P_\alpha(F_{\mathbf{y}}) = P_\alpha(F_{\tilde{\mathbf{y}}})$.

Proof of Observation 2. It will be enough to show that $2a_{\mathbf{y}}(y_i) = a_{\tilde{\mathbf{y}}}(\tilde{y}_{2i-1}) + a_{\tilde{\mathbf{y}}}(\tilde{y}_{2i})$ since we have assumed that $f_{\mathbf{y}}(y_i) = f_{\tilde{\mathbf{y}}}(\tilde{y}_{2i-1}) = f_{\tilde{\mathbf{y}}}(\tilde{y}_{2i})$ for all $i = 1, \ldots, n$. Clearly, $\mu_{\mathbf{y}} = \mu_{\tilde{\mathbf{y}}}$. Note also that $a_{\tilde{\mathbf{y}}}(\tilde{y}_{2i-1})$ can be expressed as,

$$a_{\tilde{\mathbf{y}}}(\tilde{y}_{2i-1}) = \mu_{\mathbf{y}} + y_i\{(2n)^{-1}[2(2i-1)-1]-1\}$$

$$- (2n)^{-1}\left(2\sum_{j=1}^{2i-2} \tilde{y}_j + \tilde{y}_{2i-1}\right). \tag{58}$$

Similarly, for $a_{\tilde{\mathbf{y}}}(\tilde{y}_{2i})$, we have,

$$a_{\tilde{\mathbf{y}}}(\tilde{y}_{2i}) = \mu_{\mathbf{y}} + y_i\{(2n)^{-1}[2(2i) - 1] - 1\} - (2n)^{-1}\left(2\sum_{j=1}^{2i-1}\tilde{y}_j + \tilde{y}_{2i}\right). \tag{59}$$

Summing equations (58) and (59), we find

$$a_{\tilde{\mathbf{y}}}(\tilde{y}_{2i-1}) + a_{\tilde{\mathbf{y}}}(\tilde{y}_{2i}) = 2\left\{\mu_{\mathbf{y}} + y_i[n^{-1}(2i-1) - 1]\right.$$
$$\left. - n^{-1}\left(2\sum_{j=1}^{i-1}y_j + y_i\right)\right\}$$
$$= 2a_{\mathbf{y}}(y_i). \tag{60}$$

Adding up the product of $f_{\mathbf{y}}(\tilde{y}_j)a_{\tilde{\mathbf{y}}}(\tilde{y}_j)$ across j and dividing by $2n$ shows that $P_\alpha(F_{\mathbf{y}}) = P_\alpha(F_{\tilde{\mathbf{y}}})$. □

When observations are weighted (or "grouped"), with w_i being the sampling weight on observation i and with $\bar{w} = \sum_{j=1}^n w_j$ being the sum of weights, a population-invariant definition of $\hat{g}(y_i)$ is then:

$$\hat{a}(y_i) = \hat{\mu} + y_i\left[\bar{w}^{-1}\left(2\sum_{j=1}^i w_j - w_i\right) - 1\right]$$
$$- \bar{w}^{-1}\left(2\sum_{j=1}^{i-1} w_j y_j + w_i y_i\right). \tag{61}$$

Equation (57) is a special case of equation (61) obtained when $w_i = 1$ for all i. For analytical simplicity, we focus on the case of samples with unweighted i.i.d. observations.

$f(y_i)^\alpha$ and the sampling distribution of $P_\alpha(\hat{F})$

It will be generally desirable to adjust our estimator of $f(y_i)^\alpha$ to sample size in order to minimize the sampling error of estimating the polarization indices. To facilitate a more detailed discussion of this issue, first decompose the estimator

$P_\alpha(\hat{F})$ across its separate sources of sampling variability:

$$P_\alpha(\hat{F}) - P_\alpha(F) = \int [\hat{p}_\alpha(y) - p_\alpha(y)] \, dF(y) + \int p_\alpha(y) \, d(\hat{F} - F)(y)$$

$$+ \int [\hat{p}_\alpha(y) - p_\alpha(y)] \, d(\hat{F} - F)(y). \tag{62}$$

The first source of variation, $\hat{p}_\alpha(y) - p_\alpha(y)$, comes from the sampling error made in estimating the identification and the alienation effects at each point y in the income distribution. It can be decomposed further as:

$$\hat{p}_\alpha(y) - p_\alpha(y) = [\hat{f}(y)^\alpha - f(y)^\alpha] a(y) + f(y)^\alpha [\hat{a}(y) - a(y)]$$

$$+ [\hat{f}(y)^\alpha - f(y)^\alpha][\hat{a}(y) - a(y)]. \tag{63}$$

As can be seen by inspection, $\hat{a}(y) - a(y)$ is of order $O(n^{-1/2})$. Assuming that $\hat{f}(y)^\alpha - f(y)^\alpha$ vanishes as n tends to infinity (as will be shown in the proof of Theorem 2), the last term in equation (63) is of lower order than the others and can therefore be ignored asymptotically.

This argument also shows that $\hat{p}_\alpha(y) - p_\alpha(y) \sim o(1)$. Because $F(y) - \hat{F}(y) = O(n^{-1/2})$, the last term in equation (62) is of order $o(n^{-1/2})$, and can also be ignored. Combining equations (62) and (63), we thus see that for large n,

$$P_\alpha(\hat{F}) - P_\alpha(F) \cong \int [\hat{f}(y)^\alpha - f(y)^\alpha] a(y) \, dF(y) \tag{64}$$

$$+ \int f(y)^\alpha [\hat{a}(y) - a(y)] \, dF(y) \tag{65}$$

$$+ \int p_\alpha(y) \, d(\hat{F} - F)(y). \tag{66}$$

The terms in equations (65) and (66) are further developed in the proof of Theorem 2 below.

We thus turn to the estimation of $f(y)^\alpha$ in equation (64), which we do non-parametrically using kernel density estimation. This uses a kernel function $K(u)$, defined such that $\int_{-\infty}^\infty K(u) \, du = 1$ (this guarantees the desired property that $\int_{-\infty}^\infty \hat{f}(y) \, dy = 1$) and $K(u) \geq 0$ (this guarantees that $\hat{f}(y) \geq 0$). It is also convenient to choose a kernel function that is symmetric around 0, with $\int u K(u) \, du = 0$ and $\int u^2 K(u) \, du = \sigma_K^2 < \infty$. The estimator $\hat{f}(y)$ is then defined as

$$\hat{f}(y) \equiv n^{-1} \sum_{i=1}^n K_h(y - y_i), \tag{67}$$

where $K_h(z) \equiv h^{-1}K(z/h)$. The parameter h is usually referred to as the bandwidth (or window width, or smoothing parameter). One kernel function that has nice continuity and differentiability properties is the Gaussian kernel, defined by

$$K(u) = (2\pi)^{-0.5} \exp(-0.5u^2), \tag{68}$$

a form that we have used in the illustration.[17]

With $f(y)^\alpha$ estimated according to this general technique, we have the following theorem on the asymptotic sampling distribution of $\hat{P}_\alpha$.

Theorem 2. *Assume that the order-2 population moments of y, $p_\alpha(y)$, $f(y)^\alpha$, $\int_{-\infty}^y zf(z)^\alpha \, dF(z)$, and $y\int_{-\infty}^y f(z)^\alpha \, dF(z)$ are finite. Let h in $K_h(\cdot)$ vanish as n tends to infinity. Then $n^{0.5}[P_\alpha(\hat{F}) - P_\alpha(F)]$ has a limiting normal distribution $N(0, V_\alpha)$, with*

$$V_\alpha = \underset{f(y)}{\mathrm{var}}(v_\alpha(y)), \tag{69}$$

where

$$v_\alpha(y) = (1+\alpha)p_\alpha(y) + y\int f(x)^\alpha \, dF(x)$$
$$+ 2\int_y^\infty (x - y)f(x)^\alpha \, dF(x). \tag{70}$$

Proof of Theorem 2.   Consider first equation (64). Note that

$$\int [\hat{f}(y)^\alpha - f(y)^\alpha]a(y)\,dF(y) \cong \int \alpha f(y)^{\alpha-1}[\hat{f}(y) - f(y)]a(y)\,dF(y)$$

$$= \alpha \int p_{\alpha-1}(y)n^{-1}\sum_{i=1}^n K_h(y - y_i)\,dF(y)$$

$$- \alpha \int p_\alpha(y)\,dF(y)$$

$$= \alpha n^{-1}\sum_{i=1}^n \int p_{\alpha-1}(y)K_h(y - y_i)\,dF(y)$$

$$- \alpha \int p_\alpha(y)\,dF(y). \tag{71}$$

Taking $h \to 0$ as $n \to \infty$, and recalling that $\int K_h(y - y_i)\, dy = 1$, the first term in equation (71) tends asymptotically to

$$\alpha n^{-1} \sum_{i=1}^{n} \int p_{\alpha-1}(y) K_h(y - y_i)\, dF(y) \cong \alpha n^{-1} \sum_{i=1}^{n} p_{\alpha-1}(y_i) f(y_i)$$

$$= \alpha n^{-1} \sum_{i=1}^{n} p_\alpha(y_i).$$

Thus, we can rewrite the term on the right-hand side of equation (64) as,

$$\int [\hat{f}(y)^\alpha - f(y)^\alpha] a(y)\, dF(y) \cong \alpha n^{-1} \sum_{i=1}^{n} [p_\alpha(y_i) - P_\alpha] = O(n^{-1/2}).$$

Now turn to equation (65). Let I be an indicator function that equals 1 if its argument is true and 0 otherwise. We find:

$$\int f(y)^\alpha [\hat{a}(y) - a(y)]\, dF(y)$$

$$= \int f(y)^\alpha \{[\hat{\mu} + y(2\hat{F}(y) - 1) - 2\hat{\mu}^*(y)] - a(y)\}\, dF(y)$$

$$\cong \int f(y)^\alpha \left(n^{-1} \sum_{i=1}^{n} \{y_i + y[2I(y_i \le y) - 1]\right.$$

$$\left. - 2y_i I(y_i \le y)\} - a(y) \right) dF(y)$$

$$= n^{-1} \sum_{i=1}^{n} \int f(y)^\alpha \{y_i[1 - 2I(y_i \le y)] + 2yI(y_i \le y)\}\, dF(y)$$

$$- \int f(y)^\alpha [\mu + 2yF(y) - 2\mu^*(y)]\, dF(y)$$

$$= n^{-1} \sum_{i=1}^{n} \left(\int f(y)^\alpha\, dF(y)\, y_i - 2y_i \int_{y_i}^{\infty} f(y)^\alpha\, dF(y) \right.$$

$$\left. + 2\int_{y_i}^{\infty} yf(y)^\alpha\, dF(y) \right) - \int f(y)^\alpha [\mu + 2yF(y) - 2\mu^*(y)]\, dF(y)$$

$$= O(n^{-1/2}).$$

Now consider equation (66):

$$\int P_\alpha(y)d(\hat{F} - F)(y) = n^{-1}\sum_{i=1}^{n}[f(y_i)^\alpha a(y_i) - P_\alpha] = O(n^{-1/2}).$$

Collecting and summarizing terms, we obtain:

$$P_\alpha(\hat{F}) - P_\alpha(f) \cong n^{-1}\sum_{i=1}^{n}\left((1+\alpha)f(y_i)^\alpha a(y_i) + \int y_i f(y)^\alpha \, dF(y)\right.$$

$$+2\int_{y_i}^{\infty}(y - y_i)f(y)^\alpha \, dF(y)\right) - \left((1+\alpha)P_\alpha(f)\right.$$

$$+\int f(y)^\alpha(\mu + 2(yF(y) - \mu^*(y)))\, dF(y)\right).$$

Applying the law of large numbers to $P_\alpha(\hat{F}) - P_\alpha(f)$, note that $\lim_{n\to\infty} \mathbf{E}[n^{0.5}(P_\alpha(\hat{F}) - P_\alpha(f))] = 0$. The central limit theorem then leads to the finding that $n^{0.5}[P_\alpha(\hat{F}) - P_\alpha(f)]$ has a limiting normal distribution $N(0, V_\alpha)$, with V_α as described in the statement of the theorem. □

Observe that the assertion of Theorem 2 is distribution-free since everything in equation (69) can be estimated consistently *without* having to specify the population distribution from which the sample is drawn. $P_\alpha(\hat{F})$ is thus a root-n consistent estimator of $P_\alpha(F)$, unlike the usual non-parametric density and regression estimators which are often $n^{2/5}$ consistent. The strength of Theorem 2 also lies in the fact that so long as h tends to vanish as n increases, the precise path taken by h has a negligible influence on the asymptotic variance since it does not appear in equation (69).

The minimization of sampling error

In finite samples, however, $P_\alpha(\hat{F})$ is biased. The bias arises from the smoothing techniques employed in the estimation of the density function $f(y)$. In addition, the finite-sample variance of $P_\alpha(\hat{F})$ is also affected by the smoothing techniques. As is usual in the non-parametric literature, the larger the value of h, the larger the finite-sample bias, but the lower is the finite-sample variance. We exploit this tradeoff to choose an "optimal" bandwidth for the estimation of $P_\alpha(\hat{F})$, which we denote by $h^*(n)$.

A common technique is to select $h^*(n)$ so as to minimize the MSE of the estimator, given a sample of size n. To see what this entails, decompose (for a given h) the MSE into the sum of the squared bias and of the variance involved in estimating $P_\alpha(F)$:

$$\text{MSE}_h(P_\alpha(\hat{F})) = (\text{bias}_h(P_\alpha(\hat{F})))^2 + \text{var}_h(P_\alpha(\hat{F})), \tag{72}$$

and denote by $h^*(n)$ the value of h which minimizes $\text{MSE}_h(P_\alpha(\hat{F}))$. This value is described in the following theorem:

Theorem 3. *For large n, $h^*(n)$ is given by*

$$h^*(n) = \sqrt{-\frac{\text{cov}(v_\alpha(y), p''_\alpha(y))}{\alpha\sigma_K^2 \left(\int f''(y)p_\alpha(y)\,dy\right)^2}} n^{-0.5} + O(n^{-1}). \tag{73}$$

Proof of Theorem 3. Using equations (64)–(66), we may write $\text{bias}_h(\hat{F}_\alpha) = E[P_\alpha(\hat{F}) - P_\alpha(f)]$ as:

$$E[P_\alpha(\hat{F}) - P_\alpha(f)] \cong \int E[\hat{f}(y)^\alpha - f(y)^\alpha]a(y)\,dF(y)$$

$$+ \int f(y)^\alpha E[\hat{a}(y) - a(y)]\,dF(y)$$

$$+ \int p_\alpha(y)\,dE[\hat{F} - F](y)$$

$$= \int E[\hat{f}(y)^\alpha - f(y)^\alpha]a(y)\,dF(y), \tag{74}$$

since $\hat{a}(y)$ and $\hat{F}(y)$ are unbiased estimators of (y) and $F(y)$, respectively. For $E[\hat{f}(y)^\alpha - f(y)^\alpha]$, we may use a first-order Taylor expansion around $f(y)^\alpha$:

$$E[\hat{f}(y)^\alpha - f(y)^\alpha] \cong \alpha f(y)^{\alpha-1}E[\hat{f}(y) - f(y)].$$

For symmetric kernel functions, the bias $E[\hat{f}(y) - f(y)]$ can be shown to be approximately equal to (see, e.g., Silverman 1986, p. 39)

$$0.5h^2\sigma_K^2 f''(y), \tag{75}$$

where $f''(y)$ is the second-order derivative of the density function. Hence, the bias $E[P_\alpha(\hat{F}) - P_\alpha(f)]$ is approximately equal to

$$E[P_\alpha(\hat{F}) - P_\alpha(f)] \cong 0.5\alpha\sigma_K^2 h^2 \int f''(y)p_\alpha(y)\,dy = O(h^2). \tag{76}$$

It follows that the bias will be low if the kernel function has a low variance σ_K^2: it is precisely then that the observations "closer" to y will count more, and those are also the observations that provide the least biased estimate of the density at y. But the bias also depends on the curvature of $f(y)$, as weighted by $p_\alpha(y)$: in the absence of such a curvature, the density function is linear and the bias provided by using observations on the left of y is just (locally) outweighed by the bias provided by using observations on the right of y. For the variance $\mathrm{var}_h(P_\alpha(\hat{f}))$, we first reconsider the first term in equation (71), which is the dominant term through which the choice of h influences $\mathrm{var}(P_\alpha(\hat{f}))$. We may write this as follows:

$$
\alpha n^{-1} \sum_{i=1}^{n} \int p_\alpha(y) K_h(y - y_i)\, dy = \alpha n^{-1} \sum_{i=1}^{n} \int p_\alpha(y_i - ht) K(t)\, dt
$$

$$
\cong \alpha n^{-1} \sum_{i=1}^{n} \int K(t)\big[p_\alpha(y_i) - ht p'_\alpha(y_i)
$$

$$
+ 0.5 h^2 t^2 p''_\alpha(y_i) \big]\, dt
$$

$$
= \alpha n^{-1} \sum_{i=1}^{n} \big(p_\alpha(y_i) + 0.5\sigma_K^2 h^2 p''_\alpha(y_i) \big),
$$

$$
(77)
$$

where the first equality substitutes t for $h^{-1}(y_i - y)$, where the succeeding approximation is the result of Taylor-expanding $p_\alpha(y_i - ht)$ around $t = 0$, and where the last line follows from the properties of the kernel function $K(t)$. Thus, combining equations (77) and (69) to incorporate a finite-sample correction for the role of h in the variance of $\hat{f}_\alpha$, we can write:

$$
\mathrm{var}_h(P_\alpha(\hat{f})) = n^{-1} \underset{f(y)}{\mathrm{var}} \left(0.5\alpha\sigma_K^2 h^2 p''_\alpha(y) + v_\alpha(y) \right) = O(n^{-1}).
$$

For small h, the impact of h on the finite sample variance comes predominantly from the covariance between $v_\alpha(y)$ and $p''_\alpha(y)$ since $\mathrm{var}(0.5\alpha\sigma_K^2 h^2 p''_\alpha(y))$ is then of smaller order h^4. This covariance, however, is not easily unravelled. When the covariance is negative (which we do expect to observe), a larger value of h will tend to decrease $\mathrm{var}_h(P_\alpha(\hat{f}))$ since this will tend to level the distribution of $0.5\alpha\sigma_K^2 h^2 p''_\alpha(y) + v_\alpha(y)$, which is the random variable whose variance determines the sampling variance of $P_\alpha(\hat{f})$. Combining squared-bias and variance into equation (72), we obtain:

$$
\mathrm{MSE}_h(P_\alpha(\hat{f})) = \left(0.5\alpha\sigma_K^2 h^2 \int f''(y) p_\alpha(y)\, dy \right)^2
$$

$$
+ n^{-1} \underset{f(y)}{\mathrm{var}} \left(0.5\alpha\sigma_K^2 h^2 p''_\alpha(y) + v_\alpha(y) \right).
$$

$h^*(n)$ is found by minimizing $\mathrm{MSE}_h(P_\alpha(\hat{f}))$ with respect to h. The derivative of $\mathrm{MSE}_h(P_\alpha(\hat{f}))$ with respect to h gives:

$$
h^3 \left(\alpha\sigma_K^2 \int f''(y) p_\alpha(y)\,dy \right)^2 + n^{-1}\alpha\sigma_K^2 h \int \Big[\big(0.5\alpha\sigma_K^2 h^2 p_\alpha''(y) + v_\alpha(y)\big)
$$
$$
- \Big(0.5\alpha\sigma_K^2 h^2 \int p_\alpha''(y)\,dF(y) + \int v_\alpha(y)\,dF(y)\Big) \Big]
$$
$$
\times \Big[p_\alpha''(y) - \int p_\alpha''(y)\,dF(y) \Big]\, dF(y).
$$

Since $h^*(n) > 0$ in finite samples, we may divide the above expression by h, and then find $h^*(n)$ by setting the result equal to 0. This yields:

$$
h^*(n)^2 = -\frac{n^{-1}\mathrm{cov}\left(v_\alpha(y), p_\alpha''(y)\right)}{\alpha\sigma_K^2\left[\left(\int f''(y) p_\alpha(y)\,dy\right)^2 - 0.5 n^{-1}\mathrm{var}\left(p''(y) p_\alpha(y)\right)\right]}. \tag{78}
$$

For large n (and thus for a small optimal h), $h^*(n)$ is thus given by

$$
h^*(n) = \sqrt{-\frac{\mathrm{cov}\left(v_\alpha(y), p_\alpha''(y)\right)}{\alpha\sigma_K^2\left(\int f''(y) p_\alpha(y)\,dy\right)^2}} \, n^{-0.5} + O(n^{-1}). \tag{79}
$$

This completes the proof. $\square$

It is well known that $f''(y)$ is proportional to the bias of the estimator $\hat{f}(y)$. A large value of $\alpha\sigma_K^2\left(\int f''(y) p_\alpha(y)\,dy\right)^2$ will thus necessitate a lower value of $h^*(n)$ in order to reduce the bias. Conversely, a larger negative correlation between $v_\alpha(y)$ and $p_\alpha''(y)$ will militate in favor of a larger $h^*(n)$ in order to decrease the sampling variance. More importantly, the optimal bandwidth for the estimation of the polarization index is of order $O(n^{-1/2})$, unlike the usual kernel estimators which are of significantly larger order $O(n^{-1/5})$. Because of this, we may expect the precise choice of h not to be overly influential on the sampling precision of polarization estimators.

To compute $h^*(n)$, two general approaches can be followed. We can assume that $f(y)$ is not too far from a parametric density function, such as the normal or the log-normal, and use equation (73) to compute $h^*(n)$ (for instance, in the manner of Silverman (1986, p. 45) for point density estimation). Alternatively, we can estimate the terms in equation (73) directly from the empirical distribution, using an initial value of h to compute the $f(y)$ in the $v_\alpha(y)$ and $p_\alpha(y)$ functions. For both of these approaches (and particularly for the last one), expression in equation (73) is clearly distribution specific, and it will also generally be very cumbersome to estimate.

It would thus seem useful to devise a "rule-of-thumb" formula that can be used to provide a readily computable value for h. When the true distribution is that of a normal distribution with variance σ^2, and when a Gaussian kernel (see equation (68)) is used to estimate $\hat{f}(y)$, h^* is approximately given by:

$$h^* \cong 4.7 \, n^{-0.5} \, \sigma \alpha^{0.1}. \tag{80}$$

Easily computed, this formula works well with the normal distribution[18] since it is never farther than 5% from the h^* that truly minimizes the MSE. The use of such approximate rules also seems justified by the fact that the MSE of the polarization indices does not appear to be overly sensitive to the choice of the bandwidth h. Equation (80) seems to perform relatively well with other distributions than the normal, including the popular log-normal one, although this is less true when the distribution becomes very skewed. For skewness larger than about 6, a more robust – though more cumbersome – approximate formula for the computation of h^* is given by

$$h^* \cong n^{-0.5} \text{IQ} \frac{(3.76 + 14.7\sigma_{\ln})}{(1 + 1.09 \cdot 10^{-4}\sigma_{\ln})^{(7268+15323\alpha)}}, \tag{81}$$

where IQ is the interquartile and $\sigma_{\ln}$ is the variance of the logarithms of income – an indicator of the skewness of the income distribution.

Acknowledgments

In this chapter, we reproduce our paper published in *Econometrica* 2004, with an addendum containing the proofs of the estimation and statistical inference results that are reported in Section 3.3.1.

This research was funded by The Pew Charitable Trusts, CRSH, FQRSC, the Chair of Canada in Social Policies and Human Resources, and National Science Foundation 0241070 (Ray). Duclos and Ray thank the Instituto de Análisis Económico (CSIC) for hospitality during the startup phase of this project. Esteban is a member of Barcelona Economics and thanks the support from the General-itat de Catalunya, the Instituto de Estudios Fiscales, the European Commission CIT2-CT-2004-506084, and the MCYT SEC-2003-1961. We thank Oliver Linton, Patrick Richard, a Co-Editor, and two anonymous referees for useful comments. Finally, we are grateful to Nicolas Beaulieu for his excellent research assistance.

Notes

1 See Esteban and Ray (1991, 1994), Foster and Wolfson (1992), Wolfson (1994, 1997), Alesina and Spolaore (1997), Quah (1997), Wang and Tsui (2000), Esteban *et al.* (1998), Chakravarty and Majumder (2001), Zhang and Kanbur (2001), and Rodríguez and Salas (2002).

2 See, for instance, D'Ambrosio and Wolff (2001), Collier and Hoeffler (2001), Fajnzylber *et al.* (2000), Garcia-Montalvo and Reynal-Querol (2002), Gradín (2000),

Knack and Keefer (2001), Milanovic (2000), Quah (1997), and Reynal-Querol (2002). See also Esteban and Ray (1999) for a formal analysis of the connections between polarization and the equilibrium level of conflict in a model of strategic interaction.

3 ER (section 4, p. 846) mention this problem.

4 In Esteban *et al.* (1998) we presented a statistically reasonable way to bunch the population in groups and thus make the ER measure operational. Yet, the number of groups had to be taken as exogenous and the procedure altogether had no clear efficiency properties.

5 By symmetry we mean that $f(m-x) = f(m+x)$ for all $x \in [0,m]$, where m is the mean and by unimodality we mean that f is nondecreasing on $[0,m]$.

6 The reason for this particular formulation is best seen by examining the corresponding cumulative distribution functions, which must satisfy the property that $G(x) = F(x\mu'/\mu)$, and then taking derivatives.

7 Indeed, it is possible to impose additional requirements (along the lines explored by ER, for instance) to place narrower bounds on α. But we do not consider this necessarily desirable. For instance, the upper value $\alpha = 1$ has the property that all λ-squeezes of any distribution leave polarization unchanged. We do not feel that a satisfactory measure *must* possess this feature. This is the reason we are more comfortable with a possible range of acceptable values for α.

8 Esteban and Ray prove that if the cost function has enough curvature so that it is "at least" quadratic, then larger groups are more effective even if the conflict is over purely private goods.

9 One might ask: why do the arguments in this paragraph and the one just before lead to "compatible" thresholds for α? The reason is this: in the double-squeeze, there are cross-group alienations as well which permit a given increase in identification to have a stronger impact on polarization. Therefore, the required threshold on α is smaller in this case.

10 The literature on kernel density estimation is large – see for instance Silverman (1986), Härdle (1990), and Pagan and Ullah (1999) for an introduction to it.

11 See http://lissy.ceps.lu for detailed information on the structure of these data.

12 One would expect these distinctions to magnify even further for distributions that are not unimodal (unfortunately, this exploration is not permitted by our dataset). For instance, one might use our measures to explore the "twin-peaks" property identified by Quah (1996) for the world distribution of income. But this is the subject of future research.

13 See Reynal-Querol (2002) for a similar analysis. D'Ambrosio and Wolff (2001) also consider a measure of this type but with income distances across groups explicitly considered.

14 If $r \geq p$, simply permute p and r in the given argument.

15 That is, for each $y \in [d, d+m]$, $g(y) = g[d + 2m - (y - d)] = g(2d + 2m - y)$. Moreover, $(y-x) + [(2d + 2m - y) - x] = 2(d + m - x)$.

16 That is, for each $x \in [0,m]$, $f(x) = f(2m - x)$. Moreover, $(m + d - x) + [m + d - (2m - x)] = 2d$.

17 Note that the Gaussian kernel has the property that $\sigma_K^2 = 1$.

18 Extensive numerical simulations were made using various values of $n \geq 500$, σ, and $\alpha = 0.25$ to 1.

References

Aczél, J. (1966) *Lectures on Functional Equations and Their Applications*, New York: Academic Press.

Alesina, A. and E. Spolaore (1997) "On the number and size of nations," *Quarterly Journal of Economics*, 113: 1027–56.

Anderson, G. (1996) "Nonparametric tests of stochastic dominance in income distributions," *Econometrica*, 64: 1183–93.

Beach, C. and R. Davidson (1983) "Distribution-free statistical inference with Lorenz curves and income shares," *Review of Economic Studies*, 50(4): 723–35.

Beach, C. and J. Richmond (1985) "Joint confidence intervals for income shares and Lorenz," *International Economic Review*, 26(2): 439–50.

Bishop, J.A., S. Chakraborti, and P.D. Thistle (1989) "Asymptotically distribution-free statistical inference for generalized Lorenz curves," *The Review of Economics and Statistics*, 71: 725–7.

Chakravarty, S.R. and A. Majumder (2001) "Inequality, polarization and welfare: theory and applications," *Australian Economic Papers*, 40: 1–13.

Collier, P. and A. Hoeffler (2001) "Greed and grievance in Civil War," mimeo., World Bank, Washington, DC.

D'Ambrosio, C. and E. Wolff (2001) "Is wealth becoming more polarized in the United States?," Working Paper 330, Levy Economics Institute, Bard College.

Davidson, R. and J.Y. Duclos (1997) "Statistical inference for the measurement of the incidence of taxes and transfers," *Econometrica*, 65(6): 1453–65.

—— (2000) "Statistical inference for stochastic dominance and for the measurement of poverty and inequality," *Econometrica*, 68: 1435–65.

Esteban, J. and D. Ray (1991) "On the measurement of polarization," Working Paper 18, Institute for Economic Development, Boston University.

—— (1994) "On the measurement of polarization," *Econometrica*, 62: 819–52.

—— (1999) "Conflict and distribution," *Journal of Economic Theory*, 87: 379–415.

—— (2001) "Collective action and the group size paradox," *American Political Science Review*, 95: 663–72.

Esteban, J., C. Gradín, and D. Ray (1998) "Extensions of a measure of polarization, with an application to the income distribution of five OECD countries," mimeo., Instituto de Análisis Económico.

Fajnzylber, P., D. Lederman, and N. Loayza (2000) "Crime and victimization: an economic perspective," *Economia*, 1: 219–78.

Foster, J.E. and M.C. Wolfson (1992) "Polarization and the decline of the middle class: Canada and the U.S.," mimeo., Vanderbilt University.

Garcia-Montalvo, J. and M. Reynal-Querol (2002) "Why ethnic fractionalization? Polarization, ethnic conflict and growth," mimeo.

Gradín, C. (2000) "Polarization by sub-populations in Spain, 1973–91," *Review of Income and Wealth*, 46: 457–74.

Härdle, W. (1990) *Applied Nonparametric Regression*, Cambridge: Cambridge University Press.

Kakwani, N.C. (1993) "Statistical inference in the measurement of poverty," *Review of Economics and Statistics*, 75(3): 632–9.

Knack, S. and P. Keefer (2001) "Polarization, politics and property rights: links between inequality and growth," mimeo., World Bank, Washington, DC.

Milanovic, B. (2000) "A new polarization measure and its applications," mimeo., Development Research Group, World Bank, Washington, DC.

Olson, M. (1965) *The Logic of Collective Action*, Cambridge, MA: Harvard University Press.

Pagan, A.R. and A. Ullah (1999) *Nonparametric Econometrics*, Cambridge: Cambridge University Press.

Pareto, V. (1906) *Manual of Political Economy*, New York: A.M. Kelley, 1927 edition.

Quah, D. (1996) "Twin peaks: growth and convergence in models of distribution dynamics," *Economic Journal*, 106: 1045–55.

—— (1997) "Empirics for growth and distribution: stratification, polarization and convergence clubs," *Journal of Economic Growth*, 2: 27–59.

Reynal-Querol, M. (2002) "Ethnicity, political systems, and civil wars," *Journal of Conflict Resolution*, 46: 29–54.

Rodríguez, J.G. and R. Salas (2002) "Extended bi-polarization and inequality measures," mimeo., Universidad Complutense de Madrid.

Sen, A. (1997) *On Economic Inequality*, Second Edition, Oxford: Oxford University Press and Clarendon Press.

Silverman, B.W. (1986) *Density Estimation for Statistics and Data Analysis*, London: Chapman and Hall.

Wang, Y.Q. and K.Y. Tsui (2000) "Polarization orderings and new classes of polarization indices," *Journal of Public Economic Theory*, 2: 349–63.

Wolfson, M.C. (1994) "When inequalities diverge," *American Economic Review*, Papers and Proceedings, 84: 353–8.

—— (1997) "Divergent inequalities: theory and empirical results," *Review of Income and Wealth*, 43: 401–21.

Zhang, X. and R. Kanbur (2001) "What difference do polarisation measures make? An application to China," *Journal of Development Studies*, 37: 85–98.

4 Evolutionary equilibrium with forward-looking players

Lawrence E. Blume

4.1 Social norms and coordination

Conventions and norms are the glue that holds society together. When social outcomes appear to be coordinated or predictable, the cause is most often not a remarkable correlation of taste or concerted collective action, but individual adherence to well-understood and shared guides to normative behavior. This is not to say that social order is explained by norms and conventions; instead, an explanation of social order is rooted in an understanding of their origins and consequences.

In this chapter, I summarize the case for evolutionary game theory as a framework for the investigation of the origins and persistence of norms and conventions. One problem with evolutionary models is that individuals are not forward-looking, a property which lies at the heart of the arguments over the application of rational choice theory to the problem of social order. I demonstrate here one way to address this problem, and also some of the consequences of taking the future seriously.

4.1.1 Homo economicus vs. homo sociologicus

Homo economicus and *homo sociologicus* are the two straw men of social science.[1] For *homo economicus*, each social act is a considered choice, an exercise in naked self-interest. For *homo sociologicus* there is no choice. Man is a boat without rudder, drifting at the mercy of the powerful tides of social forces.

The substantive question underlying these caricatures is the scope of instrumental behavior. Each of us at different times pursue material gain, consciously follow social custom, act reflexively from habit or tradition, and respond to emotions. Weber (1947) developed a typology of action which distinguished *affectual choice*, seated entirely in emotional responses; *traditional actions*, rooted in social custom; *value-rational* or *axiological choice*, which flows from assertions of belief, regardless of consequences; and *instrumental choice*, behavior whose purpose is to produce particular outcomes in order to achieve specific goals. The domains of these types are fluid. What was once rational becomes customary; and what was customary or emotionally determined can be reexamined rationally.

The answer to the question of when and why individuals feel and act upon social obligations, or act in altruistic ways, is contested by these two explanatory traditions. Some rational choice theorists argue that obedience to norms is a direct expression of self-interest. Norm obedience directly generates utility. For example, Riker and Ordeshook (1968) and Tullock (1967) eliminate the paradox of voting by having the act of voting itself generate utility beyond its (negligible) instrumental effect on the outcome. Others, such as Ellison (1994) and Kandori (1992), view social norms as implicit long-term contracts. When social interaction is recurrent, reciprocity is rational. These explanations are not without problems. Making norm obedience an argument of a utility function simply pushes back the explanatory problem. How did norms get there? Why do some social prescriptions become normative while others do not?[2] The long-term contracting explanations are based on what some might regard as a weakness of dynamic game theory. When social interaction is recurrent, reciprocity is rational if individuals are sufficiently patient. But there are many distinct self-consistent social formations. Nearly every outcome is rational, if individuals are sufficiently patient. This is the content of the so-called "folk theorems" for repeated games. Now the problem is pushed back to equilibrium selection. Why (or when) do we observe those equilibria which are norm-respecting and not some others?

Homo sociologicus offers a different set of answers. Much effort has been expended demonstrating that commitment to norms is complementary to, rather than consequent of, instrumental behavior.[3] As put succinctly by Durkheim, "It is therefore in the nature of society itself that we must seek the explanation of social life."[4] I will not attempt to summarize this vast and varied literature here, but I claim that any such survey would conclude that what is being rejected by this tradition is not the rational action *per se*, but the methodological individualism.[5] Thus this tradition is not only at odds with rational choice theory, it is also in opposition to exchange theorists such as Homans, whose individualist views were developed from behaviorist rather than utilitarian principles. The methodological holist position does not preclude understanding the functionality of social norms, and thus, to some degree, their persistence, for any truly dysfunctional norm would adversely affect the future of any society that took it up. But it is less helpful in understanding the origins of norms, and functionality alone cannot explain persistence.

Having given up on explanations of adherence to norms that are based solely on individual incentives, some social scientists who hold to the holist tradition nonetheless recognize that the active agents in the society are individuals, and that norms emerge as an aggregate of their activities. Durkheim writes:[6]

> society is not the mere sum of individuals, but the system formed by their association represents a specific reality which has its own characteristics. Undoubtedly no collective entity can be produced if there are no individual consciousnesses: this is a necessary but not a sufficient condition. In addition, these consciousnesses must be associated and combined, but combined

in a certain way. It is from this combination that social life arises and consequently it is this combination which explains it. By aggregating together, by interpenetrating, by fusing together, individuals give birth to a being, psychical if you will, but one which constitutes a psychical individuality of a new kind.

(1982 (1895), p. 129)

For Durkheim, social life, and in particular, the "collective consciousness," is an emergent property of a system of interacting individuals.[7] Evolutionary game theory offers one approach to the study of emergent properties in systems of interacting agents. The evolutionary game theory program is to replace or supplement highly detailed explorations of individual rationality in a social environment with an examination of the social interactions and rough descriptions of adaptive behavior. The outcome of an evolutionary game theory analysis is a description of equilibrium as a population state, that is to say, as an emergent property of the system whose interactions are captured in the evolutionary model.[8] As a method for modeling emergence, evolutionary game theory is one bridge across the individualism/holism gap.

4.1.2   *Emergence and equilibrium selection*

In the context of evolutionary game theory, social norms are often understood as solutions to coordination problems which arise in a population of individuals large enough that most members never directly interact with one another, thus precluding the possibility of effective collective action. The process of norm emergence has been modeled in the evolutionary game theory as a population of individuals engaging in multiple strategic interactions in which some actions are thought of as "norm adhering" and others as "norm defecting." Generally speaking, the more a norm is adhered to, the greater is the cost which is borne by any individual who breaks the norm (although individual choice behavior is loosely specified and idiosyncratic). Thus the strategic interaction is a coordination game. Evolutionary dynamics then describes the pattern of norm adherence through time.[9] The simplest coordination games to study are the two-by-two games, where two players each choose from among two actions.

Elementary evolutionary game theory, which is to say, static equilibrium concepts such as evolutionarily stable strategies, and deterministic dynamic models such as replicator dynamics, has little to say about coordination games beyond the observation that polymorphic (mixed) equilibria may not be robust. In particular, these models cannot distinguish the different pure coordination outcomes. In the last decade, however, game theorists have come to understand the importance of agent heterogeneity and idiosyncratic behavior for selecting among equilibria. Blume (1993), Kandori *et al.* (1993), and Young (1993), among others, have shown how, with different microdynamics and different kinds of strategic interaction, small amounts of randomness in individuals' decision processes have a large impact on the determination of *which* equilibrium is most likely to appear.

Stochastic adjustment models like these have four distinguishing characteristics: A *matching technology*, which describes how individuals in the population interact with one another; *myopic agents*, who do not value the future at all but consider only the present in making a choice; *inertia in choice*, which is to say that agents cannot continually revise their choice but are to some degree locked in to their current action; and *noisy choice* which is a consequence either of random idiosyncratic utility or limited rationality. Inertia and noisy choice in particular speak of some of the issues raised by critics of rational choice theory. Inertia is the force of habit and tradition. Only occasionally are choices rationally examined for their instrumental value, and payoff perturbations or simple noise in choice are a first pass at accounting for a non-instrumental component in choice.

The cost of focusing on interactions in evolutionary game theory models has been the oversimplification of the individual. Indeed utility maximization is a component of choice, but the optimization problem is so spare that it is hard to say that the decision model is in any sense rational. In particular, the contrast between *homo economicus* and *homo sociologicus* is often posed as a contrast between forward-looking and backward-looking behavior. *Homo economicus* is concerned with beliefs about the effects of present intentions on future consequences, while *homo sociologicus* looks backwards to pre-existing social structure. But the actors in most evolutionary game theory models have no concept of a future. Beliefs about where the social process may be headed have no impact on current choice. The purpose of this chapter is to bring consideration of the future into the evolutionary analysis of two-by-two games, and to examine its implications for emergence.

The surprising finding of this chapter is the effect of patience on equilibrium selection. The natural conjecture is that, while the distribution of play is centered on the risk-dominant action when individuals are myopic, payoff-dominance would emerge from the actions of patient individuals. This is not the case for a reasonable class of equilibria. I investigate *monotonic equilibria*, which suits those with the property that individuals follow: As more individuals play a given choice, the more likely a given decision-maker will make the same choice. I show that when there is a unique risk-dominant outcome in the static game, the dynamic game with sufficiently patient individuals has a unique equilibrium in which all individuals *always* choose the risk-dominant choice. In games where risk- and payoff-dominance differ, I conclude that the unique monotonic equilibrium has all the individuals always coordinating on the low-payoff outcome. This finding defeats the intuitive analysis that suggests coordination failure is a consequence of myopia.

4.2 The model

The model envisions a population of individuals who are matched at random moments for an instantaneous strategic interaction, just as two billiard balls might collide while both are in motion. The payoffs from the match are determined by the actions the two individuals hold at the instant of the match. At other distinct random moments, individuals can revise their strategic choice.

Although the model as described is quite abstract, applications of this idea to economics are manifold; for instance, the Menger–Kiyotaki–Wright model of monetary exchange,[10] and some versions of Diamond's (1982) search equilibrium model.

Models in the population game literature have been implemented in three ways. Canning (1992), Kandori *et al.* (1993), Samuelson (1994), and Young (1993) all implement the evolutionary story as a discrete time Markov chain. Foster and Young (1990), and Fudenberg and Harris (1992) implement this model as a Brownian motion. Blume (1993, 1995, 2003) implements this model as a continuous-time jump process. In particular, when all individuals are *ex-ante* identical, this formulation is a continuous-time birth–death process. Binmore *et al.* (1995) use a birth–death chain approximation to analyze a model with more complicated Markovian evolution. Birth–death models have an advantage over those models in which at any date many individuals may revise their strategy; and they are significantly easier to analyze. In particular, they make possible the study of the dynamic programming problems necessary to understand forward-looking behavior. Consequently I will use the continuous-time construction with discrete events and random matching as developed in Blume (2003).

A *stochastic strategy revision process* is a population process which describes the distribution of a set of strategies among a population of individuals. The population has N individuals. Given too is a payoff matrix for a 2×2 symmetric coordination game G with strategy set $\{\alpha, \beta\}$. Each individual is labeled with a strategy. The *state* of the population process at time t is the number M_t of individuals choosing α.

From time to time each individual has an opportunity to revise her strategy. An individual's *policy* is a map that assigns to each state a probability of choosing α if given the opportunity to revise her strategy, at an instant when the process is in that state (β will be chosen with the complementary probability). Formally, a policy is a map $\pi : \{0, \ldots, N-1\} \to [0, 1]$ with the interpretation that $\pi(M)$ is the probability that the decision-maker chooses α when M of the $N-1$ other individuals in the population are already choosing α. The constraint that the optimal policy depends only upon the current state, that policies are *Markovian*, will be justified in equilibrium.

The phrase "from time to time" has a very specific meaning. An event that happens "from time to time" is an event which happens at random intervals whose evolution is described by a Poisson alarm clock. Consider the arrival of strategy revision opportunities for individual n. Associated with player n is a collection $\{x_{nl}\}_{l=1}^{\infty}$ of independent random variables, each distributed exponentially with rate parameter σ (mean $1/\sigma$). The variable x_{n1} is the waiting time until the first strategy revision opportunity, x_{n2} is the interarrival time between the first and second strategy revision opportunity, and so forth. Thus the waiting time until the mth strategy revision opportunity for individual n is $\sum_{l=1}^{m} x_{nl}$.

When an individual's expected utility calculation indicates that a particular action is best, that choice may not in fact be implemented. Fix an ϵ strictly between

0 and 1. With probability $1 - \epsilon$ the nominal expected-utility-maximizing choice is realized, and with probability ϵ the new choice is chosen by a draw from the distribution which assigns probability q to α. The probability that a decision-maker using policy π will choose α is

$$\rho_\pi(M) \equiv (1 - \epsilon)\pi(M) + \epsilon q .$$

The probability that a β-chooser will choose to remain with β is $\rho'_\pi(M + 1) = 1 - \rho_\pi(M + 1)$. One can think of the deviation from notional expected utility maximization as either the effect of an idiosyncratic random utility term or as the consequence of boundedly rational choice. In the latter case, ϵ measures the deviation from rationality.

Matches are treated similarly. For each pair of individuals (m, n) with $m < n$ there is a collection of independent rate $\delta/(N - 1)$ exponentially distributed random variables $\{x_{mnl}\}_{l=1}^\infty$, where x_{mnl} is the interarrival time between the $l - 1$th and lth match of individuals m and n. It follows from the properties of independent, distributed random variables that the interarrival time between the $l - 1$th and lth matches of individual n with anybody is exponentially distributed with rate parameter δ. Notice that matching cannot be independent across individuals (although for large N it is approximately so). This does not matter. The only independence requirements are the independence of revision opportunities and matches, and the independence of revision opportunities across individuals.

When individuals are matched, each receives a utility determined by the actions each of the pair employs at the moment of the match, according to the payoff matrix G.

Each individual discounts the future at rate r. Given the policies of other individuals, the expected present discounted value of the payoff stream from a policy for any individual can be computed. Each individual chooses a policy to maximize that expected present discounted value. A stochastic strategy revision process is an *equilibrium strategy revision process* if each individual's policy is the ϵ-mixture of the expected present discounted value maximizing policy π^* and the random policy q.

In summary, the decision problem dynamics are described by three parameters which are common to all individuals in the population: r, the intertemporal discount rate; δ, the arrival rate of new matches; and σ, the arrival rate of strategy revision opportunities. As expected, myopic play arises as individuals become impatient, as r becomes large. More surprising is that myopic behavior emerges for any discount rate when the arrival rate of revision opportunities σ, is sufficiently small. This includes situations wherein all individuals are extremely patient.

Now come the details. Suppose the population contains N individuals. Choose an individual, say, individual 1, and suppose she is at a *strategy revision opportunity* – an instant of time at which she may revise her choice. Her policy, or strategy, is denoted by π_1. The argument of π_1 is the number of individual 1's $N - 1$ fellow individuals who are currently using strategy α. The value of π_1 is the probability she chooses strategy α. The stochastic process which describes the evolution of the opponents' behaviors is called the *opponent process*. Typically the current choice of individual 1 will affect the evolution of opponents' play, and so the evolution of the opponent process will be contingent upon the current choice of individual 1.

I will describe the individual choice problem through its value function. I construct the value for individual 1 in state M and currently using α by computing the value of the next event. Many events can happen to individual 1. Strategy revision opportunities arrive to her at rate σ, and to everyone else at rate $(N-1)\sigma$. She receives matches at rate δ. (The matches of others are not payoff relevant to her.) So the aggregate arrival rate of events is $N\sigma + \delta$. When an event arrives, with probability $\sigma/(N\sigma + \delta)$ it is a strategy revision opportunity. With probability $\delta/(N\sigma + \delta)$ it is a match. With probability $(N - M - 1)\sigma/(N\sigma + \delta)$, it is an updating opportunity for another individual currently choosing β. In this case the state of the opponent process increases by one with probability $\rho_\pi(M + 1)$ and remains the same with probability $\rho'_\pi(M + 1)$. With probability $M\sigma/(N\sigma + \delta)$ the event is an updating opportunity for another individual currently choosing α. In this case the state of the opponent process decreases by one with probability $\rho'_\pi(M)$ and remains the same with probability $\rho_\pi(M)$.

When individual 1 is matched, the probability that she meets an opponent playing strategy l is proportional to the number of individuals choosing strategy l in the current state α. Thus her expected return from a match when the opponent process is in state m and she uses action k is

$$v(k, \alpha) = \frac{m}{N-1} G(k, \alpha) + \frac{N-1-m}{N-1} G(k, \beta). \tag{1}$$

To construct the value function, let τ denote the time to the next event. The random variable τ is exponentially distributed with parameter $N\sigma + \delta$. The value function is given by the Bellman equation. For the individual currently choosing α in state M of the opponent process,

$$
\begin{aligned}
V(\alpha, M) = E\Bigg\{ e^{-r\tilde{\tau}} \Bigg[&\frac{\delta}{N\sigma + \delta} \big(v(\alpha, M) + V\alpha, M\big) \\
&+ \frac{\sigma(N - M - 1)}{N\sigma + \delta} \big(\rho_\pi(M + 1)V(\alpha, M + 1) \\
&+ \rho'_\pi(M + 1)V(\alpha, M)\big) \\
&+ \frac{\sigma M}{N\sigma + \delta} \big(\rho'_\pi(M)V(\alpha, M) + \rho_\pi(M)V(\alpha, M - 1)\big) \\
&+ \frac{\sigma}{N\sigma + \delta} \max_\pi \big(\rho_\pi(M)V(\alpha, M) + \rho'_\pi(M)V(\beta, M)\big) \Bigg] \Bigg\}. \tag{2}
\end{aligned}
$$

A computation shows that

$$
\begin{aligned}
V(\alpha, M) = {} & \frac{\delta}{r + \sigma N}\, v(\alpha, m) \\
& + \frac{\sigma(N - M - 1)}{r + \sigma N} \big[\rho(M + 1) V(\alpha, M + 1) \\
& + \rho'(M + 1) V(\alpha, M) \big] \\
& + \frac{\sigma M}{r + \sigma N} \big[\rho(M) V(\alpha, M) + \rho'(M) V(\alpha, M - 1) \big] \\
& + \frac{\sigma}{r + \sigma N} \big[\rho(M) V(\alpha, M) + \rho'(M) V(\beta, M) \big],
\end{aligned}
\tag{3a}
$$

and

$$
\begin{aligned}
V(\beta, M) = {} & \frac{\delta}{r + \sigma N}\, v(\beta, m) \\
& + \frac{\sigma(N - M - 1)}{r + \sigma N} \big[\rho(M) V(\beta, M + 1) + \rho'(M) V(\beta, M) \big] \\
& + \frac{\sigma M}{r + \sigma N} \big[\rho(M - 1) V(\beta, M) + \rho'(M - 1) V(\beta, M - 1) \big] \\
& + \frac{\sigma}{r + \sigma N} \big[\rho(M) V(\alpha, M) + \rho'(M) V(\beta, M) \big].
\end{aligned}
\tag{3b}
$$

Standard contraction mapping arguments show that the Bellman equation has a unique solution which is the value function for individual 1's dynamic programming problem. The optimal strategy for individual 1 requires that when a strategy revision opportunity arises in state m she chooses the probability π to maximize $\rho_\pi(M) V(\alpha, M) + \rho'_\pi(M) V(\beta, M)$. Notice that individual 1's Bellman equation accounts for the possibilty of a noisy perturbation in choice.

4.3   Equilibrium

The equilibrium concept introduced here is closely related to Nash equilibrium. It differs only in the presence of the perturbations. Essentially, a rational population equilibrium as defined below is a Nash equilibrium of a perturbed game wherein all strategies are required to be minimally mixed.[11]

Definition 1. *A rational population equilibrium is a strategy π such that for all states a of the opponent process and policy functions π', $E_{\pi(a)} V(\tilde{k}, a) \geq E_{\pi'(a)} V(\tilde{k}, a)$. An equilibrium strategy revision process is the stochastic strategy revision process which results from a rational population equilibrium.*

The existence of equilibrium is straightforward because the dynamic program-ming problems are well-behaved.

Theorem 1. *A rational population equilibrium exists.*

Proof. For both the dynamic programs the solution correspondence will be non-empty-, convex- and compact-valued, and upper hemi-continuous with respect to the parameters of the opponent processes. These parameters are in turn continuous with respect to the opponents' policy, so a standard fixed-point argument proves the existence of equilibrium.   □

The equilibrium strategy revision process is constructed from the equilibrium policy function π in just the way the opponent process was constructed. The state space is $\{0, N\}$, and the state variable counts the number of α-choosers. The process is a birth–death process, and the birth and death rates in state M are, respectively,

$$\lambda(M) = (N - M)\sigma\rho_\pi(M),$$

$$\mu(M) = M\sigma\rho'_\pi(M).$$

The possibility of idiosyncratic choice implies that all states are reachable from one another regardless of what the equilibrium strategy actually is. The Markov process of population states is irreducible, and so the process is ergodic. The invariant distribution is easily computed from the birth and death rates:[12]

Corollary 1. *For any equilibrium π, the corresponding equilibrium strategy revision process is ergodic. The invariant distribution is characterized by the relations*

$$\frac{v(M)}{v(0)} = \binom{N}{M} \prod_{m=1}^{M} \frac{\rho_\pi(m-1)}{\rho'_\pi(m)}.$$

In Blume (1993) I suggested that one source of random noise is random util-ity. That is, in evaluating outcomes each player draws from a payoff distribution. Distributions are known, but the value of a draw is observed only by the player making the draw, and only at the moment of a match. The numbers in the pay-off matrix are means of the payoff distributions. For the specific cases studied in Blume (1993, 2003) the random utility model sets up very well, but I do not have an existence proof at any level of generality. The problem is with the single-person decision problem. The random utility model would require that the probability distribution q depend upon the values $V(k, a)$. One would hope that something like the Bellman equation would determine these values. Unfortunately, with dependence on the $V(k, a)$, the Bellman equation no longer needs to have a unique fixed point. Fundamentally, the problem lies in developing a random utility choice theory which is consistent with some form of backwards induction – an interesting and perhaps important exercise, but beyond the scope of this chapter.

One interesting class of equilibria is the *monotonic equilibria*, which is defined by the property that π is non-decreasing in its argument. Monotonic equilibria are the most natural equilibria of the games discussed in this chapter, since they reflect the basic intuition of coordination games. The more the people choose α, the bigger is the payoff advantage to choosing α over β, and therefore the more likely β-choosers are to switch to α; and vice versa. In the next section it will become apparent that all equilibria are monotonic when r is large or σ is sufficiently small. In the following section I will show that monotonic equilibria exist for large enough N, and small enough r and ϵ. Likely a proof of the existence of monotonic equilibria for all parameter values can be constructed along the lines of the proof of Theorem 1 in Blume (2002), but this is not pursued here.

Finally, standard arguments also prove:

Corollary 2. *The correspondences from parameters r, δ, and σ to equilibrium strategies and to the invariant distributions for the equilibrium strategy revision process are upper hemi-continuous.*

4.4 Myopic behavior

Myopic behavior emerges when the value function becomes proportional to the payoff function in every state. When such proportionality occurs, the solution to the intertemporal optimization problem is identical to that of maximizing immediate expected returns on the supposition that a match will take place before the opponent process changes. Not surprisingly, myopic behavior emerges as the discount factor r gets large. In addition, myopic behavior emerges as the arrival rate of strategy revision opportunities becomes small. In this case, even when looking far into the future, one expects the state of the opponent process to remain unchanged with high probability, so that the future looks just like the present.

Theorem 2. *For any discount rate r and matching rate δ, the myopic limit $V(k, a) \propto v(k, a)$ is reached as σ becomes sufficiently small. For any σ and δ, the myopic limit is reached as r becomes large.*

Proof. Manipulate the Bellman equations (3). Let

$$D = r + \sigma(N - 1 - M)\rho_\pi(M + 1) + \sigma M \rho_\pi'(M) + \sigma .$$

One can derive from equations (3) that

$$
\frac{rV(\alpha, M)}{v(\alpha, M)} = \frac{\sigma(N-1-M)\rho_\pi(M+1)}{D} \frac{rV(\alpha, M+1)}{v(\alpha, M)}
$$
$$
+ \frac{\sigma M \rho'_\pi(M)}{D} \frac{rV(\alpha, M-1)}{v(\alpha, M)}
$$
$$
+ \frac{\sigma \, r \, \max_{\pi(M)}[\rho_\pi V(\alpha, M) + \rho'_\pi(M)V(\beta, M)]}{D} \frac{1}{v(\alpha, M)} + \frac{\delta r}{D}. \qquad (4)
$$

The value function is uniformly bounded across states. Let v^* and v_* denote the upper and lower bounds, respectively, for the payoff function v (which in turn are the largest and smallest entries in the matrix G). The value function is bounded above by the value of a reward process which pays out at every match v^*. This upper bound is

$$
V^* = E[e^{-r\tau}(v^* + V^*)],
$$

where τ is the waiting time until the next match. Computing,

$$
V^* = \sigma \int_0^\infty e^{-(r+\sigma)t}(v^* + V^*) \, dt
$$
$$
= \frac{\sigma}{r+\sigma}(v^* + V^*)
$$
$$
= \frac{\sigma}{r} v^*.
$$

Similarly, a lower bound is $V_* = (\sigma/r)v_*$. It follows that each of the rV/v terms in equation (4), including the max term, is bounded above by $\sigma v^*/v_*$ and below by $\sigma v_*/v^*$.

Taking limits as $r \to \infty$ and making use of the bounds, it is easily seen that $rV(\alpha, M)/v(\alpha, M) \to \delta$. A similar argument gives the same conclusion as $\sigma \to 0$. The same arguments apply when α is replaced with β in the arguments of V and v. □

Notice that slowing down the arrival rate of strategy revision opportunities is not the same thing as speeding up the matching rate. As δ grows, $\delta^{-1}V(\alpha, M)/v(\alpha, M)$ converges to r/D, which is not independent of M.

The consequences of myopic play in this model have been developed in a number of papers. Two natural questions to investigate are the model's large population behavior and its small noise behavior. The small noise results discussed below parallel the earlier results of Blume (1993), Kandori *et al.* (1993), and Young (1993).

Coordination games exhibit strategic complementarities, i.e., the more likely it is that a player's opponent will play a particular strategy, the higher the payoff for the player to choose that strategy. Operationally, this implies the existence of a probability p^* such that if the percentage of the population playing α exceeds p^*, α will be the unique best response (and β will be the unique best response if the fraction playing α is below p^*). The range $(p^*, 1]$ is the basin of attraction for the action α and the range $[0, p^*)$ is the basin of attraction for β. The following corollary is an immediate consequence of Theorem 2 and Corollary 2:

Corollary 3. *For fixed r and δ there is a $\sigma(r, \delta)$ and for fixed δ and σ there is an $r(\delta, \sigma)$ such that for all (r, δ, σ), such that $r > r(\delta, \sigma)$ or $\sigma < \sigma(r, \delta)$, the only rational population equilibrium is the myopic equilibrium in which $\pi(M) = 1$ if $M/(N-1) > p^*$ and $\pi(M) = 0$ for $M/(N-1) < p^*$.*

The key concept for understanding equilibrium emergence in the long run is the risk-dominance. Risk-dominance of an action can be stated in several different ways. Most convenient for our purposes is the following:

Definition 2. *Action α in the two-by-two coordination game with payoff matrix G is risk-dominant iff $p^* < 1/2$.*

That is, α is risk-dominant if it is a best response when some fraction less than half of the population is using it. For instance, in the game depicted in Figure 4.1, the strategy α is payoff-dominant because among all the Nash equilibria of the game it gives the highest payoff, but the strategy β is risk-dominant because if α and β are equally likely, β is the best response. Intuitively, the higher payoff from coordinating on α is offset by the higher cost of playing α in the event that coordination fails.

The consequences of equilibrium selection for emergence are striking because they demonstrate how social interaction extends and transforms the logic of individual decision-making. Suppose that α is risk-dominant, so $p^* < 1/2$. Rescale the population states so that, instead of measuring absolute numbers they measure population fractions (i.e., divide by N). Thus for all processes the state space can be taken to be $[0, 1]$.

	α	β
α	3, 3	−2, 0
β	0, −2	2, 2

Figure 4.1 A coordination game.

Theorem 3. *For fixed* (r, δ, σ) *such that* $r > r(\delta, \sigma)$ *or* $\sigma < \sigma(r, \delta)$:

1   For fixed $\epsilon < p^*$, *as* $N \to \infty$ *the invariant distribution converges to point mass at* $1 - \epsilon$.

2   For fixed N *large enough, as* $\epsilon \to 0$, *the invariant distribution converges to* 1.

The first result, a strong law of large numbers for social interaction models, is proved in Blume and Durlauf (2003), and the second is proved in Blume (2003). The answers to the two natural questions raised earlier in this section are simply put. Coordination on the risk-dominant action emerges in the myopic limit. This interpretation is clearly true for the second result. For the first, it can be shown that the short run dynamics of the model can be characterized by a differential equation which has two stable states, one at ϵ and one at $1 - \epsilon$. These are the two candidate states where the invariant distribution can pile up as N becomes large. The Theorem shows that the invariant distribution will concentrate around the limit point in the basin of attraction of the risk-dominant equilibrium.

4.5   Patient players in two-by-two coordination games

This section characterizes monotonic equilibria in two-by-two coordination games when players are patient. When players are myopic, the only rational population equilibria have invariant distributions which pile up on those states in which nearly all individuals choose the risk-dominant choice, even when it is not payoff dominant. The inability to reach the payoff-dominant outcome is sometimes regarded as a consequence of myopia. If individuals were sufficiently patient, it is argued, they would pay the penalty of high short-run deviations from equilibrium in order to achieve higher long-run gains from payoff-dominance. This argument is false. The striking result is that for small r and ϵ, the only monotonic equilibrium is one in which all individuals *always* choose the risk-dominant choice. Patience strengthens the barriers against the risk-dominated equilibrium, even when it is payoff-dominant.

Some of the intuitions behind the result are straightforward. Payoff-dominance does have a distinguished role in the $\beta = 1$ limit: When players care about the time-average of payoffs, "always play α" and "always play β" are both rational population equilibria. The subtle feature of the result is that the intuition about payoff-dominance fails for β near 1. The theorem really demonstrates a failure of lower-semicontinuity of the equilibrium correspondence at $r = 0$, and the fact that some small amount of discounting occurs is crucial to the result.

A computation shows that always playing the risk-dominant strategy is an equilibrium. Another possibility is an equilibrium with a threshold state M^* above which all players play α and at or below which all players choose β. This is ruled out because at the threshold – either the last α state or the first β state, some players will have the option to move the process across it – an α player in the first case, and a β player in the second. If ϵ is sufficiently small, the process will move very, very quickly to the sink of the basin of attraction in which the pivotal player puts it, and it will stay there for a very, very long time. In this circumstance, the patient pivotal player will always want to choose the payoff-dominant outcome. Consequently M^* cannot be the threshold.

The remaining possibility is all players always choosing the risk-dominated equilibrium. Here the proof comes down to a calculation. It is easily seen that the benefit of deviating to the risk-dominant strategy in any state is small, and shrinks to 0 as r becomes small. But the benefit is strictly positive.

Theorem 4. *Suppose that the game G has a unique risk-dominant action. For all δ and σ, for r and ϵ sufficiently small and N sufficiently large, choosing the risk-dominant strategy in every state is the unique monotonic equilibrium.*

In particular, choosing the non-risk-dominant action in every state, even when it is payoff-dominant, is not a rational population equilibrium. A simple calculation shows the following:

Corollary 4. *Under the conditions of Theorem 4, the invariant distribution for the equilibrium strategy revision process is the binomial distribution $b(N, 1 - \epsilon)$.*

Proof. The proof technique is to specify a ρ, take appropriate limits of parameters, and check the value function given in equations (3) to see if the optimal policy generates the ρ that began the calculation.

The first calculation shows that for small enough r and ϵ, $\pi(M) \equiv 1$ (always choosing α) is an equilibrium if α is risk-dominant, and is not if α is risk-dominated. Let $\Delta(M) = V(\alpha, M) - V(\beta, M)$, and let $\Delta_v(M) = v(\alpha, M) - v(\beta, M)$. The optimal policy π assigns positive probability to α only if $\Delta(M) \geq 0$. Computing,

$$
\begin{aligned}
\Delta(M) = {} & \frac{\delta}{r + \sigma N} \Delta_v(M) + \frac{\sigma(N - M - 1)}{r + \sigma N} \\
& \times \big[\rho(M + 1)V(\alpha, M + 1) - \rho(M)V(\beta, M + 1) \\
& \quad + \rho'(M + 1)V(\alpha, M) - \rho'(M)V(\beta, M) \big] \\
& + \frac{\sigma M}{r + \sigma N} \big[\rho(M)V(\alpha, M) - \rho(M - 1)V(\beta, M) \\
& \quad + \rho'(M)V(\alpha, M - 1) - \rho'(M - 1)V(\beta, M - 1) \big]
\end{aligned}
$$

The policy $\pi(M) \equiv 1$ is an equilibrium if and only if when $\rho(M) \equiv 1 - \epsilon$, $\Delta(M) \geq 0$ for all M. When $\rho(M) \equiv \rho$,

$$
\begin{aligned}
\Delta(M) = {} & \frac{\delta}{r + \sigma N} \Delta_v(M) + \frac{\sigma(N - M - 1)}{r + \sigma N} \\
& \times [\rho \Delta(M + 1) + (1 - \rho)\Delta(M)] \\
& + \frac{\sigma M}{r + \sigma N} [\rho \Delta(M) + (1 - \rho)\Delta(M - 1)].
\end{aligned}
$$

First, suppose $\epsilon = 0$. Then $\rho = 1$ and the difference equation becomes

$$
\Delta(M) = \frac{\sigma(N - M - 1)}{r + \sigma(N - M)} \Delta(M + 1) + \frac{\delta}{r + \sigma(N - M)} \Delta_v(M).
$$

Then

$$
\lim_{r \to 0} \Delta(M) = \frac{\delta}{\sigma(N - M)} [\Delta_v(M) + \cdots + \Delta_v(N - 1)].
$$

It is easy to see that the right-hand side is positive for all $M \geq \max\{0, (2p^* - 1)(N - 1)\}$ and negative otherwise if N is large enough. The difference function $\Delta_v(M)$ is linear in M and equals 0 at $p^*(N - 1)$. Therefore the claim is true so long as N is large enough that $(2p^* - 1)(N - 1) < 1$ if $p^* < 1/2$. (Strict inequality rules out indifference at the boundary state.) Thus $\pi(M) \equiv 1$ is optimal for all r sufficiently close to 0 if $p^* < 1/2$, and is not optimal if $p^* > 1/2$. Finally, the solution to the difference equation is continuous in ϵ at $\epsilon = 0$, so for given r sufficiently small there is an $\hat{\epsilon}$ such that for all $\epsilon < \hat{\epsilon}$, if α is risk-dominant then $\pi(M) \equiv 1$ is optimal, and if α is risk-dominated, then $\pi(M) = 1$ is not optimal.

The only other possibility for a monotonic equilibrium is the existence of an M^* between 0 and $N - 1$, such that $\pi(M) = 0$ for $M < M^*$ and $\pi(M) = 1$ for $M \geq M^*$. For this the normalized value functions are solved. Suppose $\epsilon = 0$, so that $\rho(M) = 1$ for $M \geq M^*$ and $\rho(M) = 0$ for $M < M^*$. Calculations show

$$
\lim_{r \to 0} rV(\alpha, M) = \begin{cases}
\delta v(\alpha, N - 1) & \text{if } M \geq M^*, \\
\dfrac{N - M^* + 1}{N} \delta v(\alpha, N - 1) & \text{if } M = M^* - 1, \\
\quad + \dfrac{M^* - 1}{N} \delta v(\beta, 0) & \\
\delta v(\beta, 0) & \text{if } M < M^* - 1,
\end{cases}
$$

and

$$\lim_{r \to 0} r V(\beta, M) = \begin{cases} \delta v(\alpha, N - 1) & \text{if } M > M^*, \\ \dfrac{N - M^*}{N} \delta v(\alpha, N - 1) + \dfrac{M^*}{N} \delta v(\beta, 0) & \text{if } M = M^*, \\ \delta v(\beta, 0) & \text{if } M \leq M^* - 1. \end{cases}$$

Therefore

$$\lim_{r \to 0} r \Delta(M^*) = \frac{M^*}{N} \delta \left[v(\alpha, N - 1) - v(\beta, 0) \right],$$

and

$$\lim_{r \to 0} r \Delta(M^* - 1) = \frac{N - M^*}{N} \delta \left[v(\alpha, N - 1) - v(\beta, 0) \right].$$

Both of these have the same sign, so it is not possible that $\pi(M^*) = 1$ and $\pi(M^* - 1) = 0$ unless $v(\alpha, 0) = v(\beta, N)$. Again the conclusions remain valid for r sufficiently small and for ϵ sufficiently small given r. □

4.6   Conclusion

This chapter studies the evolution of play in a population of players continually interacting with one another. Players are repeatedly and randomly matched against opponents. Players revise their strategic choices only at discrete random moments, each player independent of the others. The model is built from Poisson processes in continuous time, but individuals interact at discrete random moments. Individual rationality alone would suggest that some kind of coordination would occur. But the dynamics of social interaction limit what kind of coordination can occur. For the pairwise coordination problems studied here, the only emergent state is risk-dominant coordination.

This chapter has extended the stochastic evolutionary paradigm by considering forward-looking agents. Extensions in other directions are required to develop a full-fledged theory of the emergence of social norms. One direction has to do with the topology of social interaction. Here we have considered global random matching. Everyone is equally likely to interact with anyone else. At the other extreme, myopic random matching with a restricted subset of neighbors has been examined by Blume (1993, 1995) and Morris (2000). Other matching models have not been considered.

More generally, different kinds of interaction may generate different incentives for coordination. Stigma, for instance, depends upon individuals being labeled as different and then being punished for wearing that label. Labeling and the ability to react to labels is a complexity not treated here.[13] Other interaction models have yet to be explored in depth, but there is no reason to believe that risk-dominant selection is universal. Mailath *et al.* (2001), for instance, have shown that in at least some models where matching is endogenous, payoff-dominant selection can obtain. The challenge for evolutionary game theory is to identify emergent properties for a rich class of interaction mechanisms and to allow for more complex individual behaviors. The promise of this work is an account of the emergence of social order, of Durkheim's "collective entity," that satisfies the constraint of methodological individualism but which is not trivially reductive.

Acknowledgments

This research was supported by the National Science Foundation, the John D. and Catherine T. MacArthur Foundation, and The Pew Charitable Trusts. It was begun during visits to the Institute for Advanced Studies at the Hebrew University and the Department of Economics at Tel Aviv University.

Notes

1 This is not to say that each discipline is characterized by diametrically opposed views of individual behavior. Modern versions of exchange theory invoke rational choice models to explain social life. And while rational choice models have dominated economics for the last 50 years, the discipline certainly has a rich and internally respected tradition which thinks of individuals as embedded in social structures, going back to Adam Smith.
2 There is a tendency in the literature to see all social norms as productive social capital, as "goods." But normative behaviors such as norms of racial or ethnic discrimination are clearly not productive social capital. So explanations based on the efficiency-inducing aspects of social prescriptions fail. See Durlauf (2002) and Portes (1998).
3 Parsons (1937) is a prominant example. Also Elster (1989).
4 Durkheim (1982 [1895], p. 128).
5 In a footnote to the quotation cited below, Durkheim (1982 [1895], n. 17, p. 145) writes, "In this sense and for these reasons we can and must speak of a collective consciousness distinct from individual consciousnesses."
6 Durkheim (1982 [1895], p. 129).
7 See *supra* n. 4.
8 I use the phrase "emergent property" quite precisely to mean a behavior of the system that exists on a temporal or spatial scale different from the scale at which the equations defining the behaviors of the individual agents who comprise the system are defined. I thank Jim Crutchfield for this succinct definition.
9 See Skyrms (1996) for a discussion of distributive justice using elementary evolutionary game theory arguments.
10 Menger (1892) and Kiyotaki and Wright (1989).
11 Trembling hand perfect equilibria in finite games are the limit of such equilibria as the minimal mixing bound goes to 0, an exercise.
12 See Blume (2003) for details.
13 See Blume (2002) for a model of this process in the spirit of evolutionary game theory.

References

Binmore, Ken L., Larry Samuelson, and Richard Vaughn. (1995) "Musical chairs: modelling noisy evolution." *Games and Economic Behaviour*. 11, 1 (October): 1–35.

Blume, L.E. (1993) "The statistical mechanics of strategic interaction." *Games and Economic Behaviour.* 4 (July): 387–424.

——(1995) "The statistical mechanics of best response strategy revision." *Games and Economic Behaviour.* 11 (November): 111–45.

——(2002) "Stigma and social control." Institut für Hohere Studien, Wien. Also online at http://econwpa.wustl.edu/eps/game/papers/0312/312002.pdf

——(2003) "How noise matters." *Games and Economic Behaviour.* 44 (August): 251–71.

Blume, L.E. and Steven Durlauf. (2003) "Equilibrium concepts for social interaction models." *International Game Theory Review.* 5, 3 (September): 193–210.

Canning, D. (1992) "Average behavior in learning models." *Journal of Economic Theory.* 57 (August): 442–72.

Diamond, Peter. (1982) "Aggregate demand management in search equilibrium." *Journal of Political Economy.* 90 (October): 881–94.

Durkheim, Emile. (1982 [1895]) *The Rules of Sociological Method,* New York: The Free Press.

Durlauf, Steven N. (2002) "Bowling alone: a review essay." *Journal of Economic Behavior and Organization.* 47, 3 (March): 259–73.

Ellison, G. (1994) "Cooperation in the prisoner's dilemma with anonymous random matching." *The Review of Economic Studies.* 61 (July): 567–88.

Elster, Jon. (1989) *The Cement of Society,* Cambridge: Cambridge University Press.

Foster, D. and H.P. Young. (1990) "Stochastic evolutionary game dynamics." *Theoretical Population Biology.* 38 (October): 219–32.

Fudenberg, D. and C. Harris. (1992) "Evolutionary dynamics with aggregate shocks." *Journal of Economic Theory.* 57, 2 (August): 420–41.

Kandori, Michihiro. (1992) "Social norms and community enforcement." *The Review of Economic Studies.* 59, 1 (January): 63–80.

Kandori, M., G. Mailath, and R. Rob. (1993) "Learning, mutation and long run equilibrium in games." *Econometrica.* 61 (January): 29–56.

Kiyotaki, N. and R. Wright. (1989) "On money as a medium of exchange." *Journal of Political Economy.* 92 (August): 927–54.

Mailath, George, Larry Samuelson, and Avner Shaked. (2001) "Endogenous interactions." In Antonio Nicita and Ugo Pagano (eds), *The Evolution of Economic Diversity,* New York: Routledge, pp. 300–24.

Menger, C. (1892) "On the origin of money." *Economic Journal.* 2 (June): 239–55.

Morris, Stephen. (2000) "Contagion." *Review of Economic Studies.* 67, 1 (January): 57–78.

Parsons, Talcott. (1937) *The Structure of Social Action,* New York: McGraw-Hill.

Portes, Alejandro. (1998) "Social capital: its origins and applications in modern sociology." *Annual Review of Sociology.* 24: 1–24.

Riker, William H. and Peter C. Ordeshook. (1968) "A theory of the calculus of voting." *American Political Science Review.* 62, 1 (January): 25–42.

Samuelson, Larry. (1994) "Stochastic stability in games with alternative best replies." *Journal of Economic Theory.* 64 (October): 35–65.

Skyrms, Brian. (1996) *Evolution of the Social Contract,* Cambridge: Cambridge University Press.

Tullock, Gordon. (1967) *Toward a Mathematics of Politics,* Ann Arbor, MI: University of Michigan Press.

Weber, Max. (1947) *The Theory of Social and Economic Organization*; being Part I of *Wirtschaft und Gesellschaft*, translated from the German by A. R. Henderson and Talcott Parsons, London: W. Hodge.

Young, H. Peyton. (1993) "The evolution of conventions." *Econometrica*. 61, 1 (January): 57–84.

5 Is inequality an evolutionary universal?

Samuel Bowles

5.1 Introduction

Hernán Cortés' long letters to King Charles of Castile describe the exotic and unusual customs he and his armed band encountered as they advanced toward Temixtitan in 1519. But in light of the thirteen millennia or more that had passed since there had been any sustained contact between people of the Old World and the New, what is striking about his account of Mexico is how familiar it all was. Upon reaching Temixtitan (modern day Mexico City), he wrote:

> There are many chiefs, all of whom reside in this city, and the country towns contain peasants who are vassals of these lords and each of whom holds his land independently; some have more than others . . . And there are many poor people who beg from the rich in the streets as the poor do in Spain and in other civilized places.
>
> (1986, pp. 68, 75)

He remarks also that "the orderly manner which, until now, these people have been governed is almost like that of the states of Venice or Genoa or Pisa."

Some scholars, like Cortés, are impressed by the similarity of institutions in quite differing environments and have postulated a set of social arrangements that are favored by historical evolutionary processes. Talcott Parsons (1964) termed these *evolutionary universals*, namely, those ways of ordering society which crop up with sufficient frequency in a variety of circumstances to suggest their general evolutionary viability. Parsons offered vision as a biological analogy to these evolutionary universals. Another biological example would be sexual reproduction. Both have emerged under a wide variety of circumstances and in a great many species. Among the human examples that Parsons identifies as evolutionary universals are money, bureaucracy, and "social stratification."

Are inegalitarian institutions evolutionary universals? Some types of inegalitarian social arrangements seem to be highly persistent and yet to offer no advantages in productive efficiency. Leading examples are the monopolization of political rights by elites, the caste system, the exclusion of all but the well to do from entrepreneurial pursuits, and blocked access to basic education and medical care.

The purpose of this chapter is to see what light evolutionary theory coupled with the theory of collective action can shed on such questions as: Why have institutions that implement highly unequal divisions of the social product been so ubiquitous since the domestication of animals and plants 11 millennia ago? Why do they persist when they convey no clear efficiency advantages over other feasible social arrangements?

Institutions that implement widespread poverty and that persist over long periods despite their lack of productive superiority over alternative more egalitarian institutions are what I term *institutional poverty traps*. Some institutional poverty traps implement low average incomes for the populations which they affect.

An example, due to Banerjee and Iyer (2002), also illustrates the way that institutions can induce poor aggregate economic performance with poverty as its correlate. One effect of British rule in India was a growing entrenchment of the power and property rights of powerful landlords. Their influence was already substantial under the Mughal rulers before the British, but during the Bengal Presidency it was greatly strengthened by the Permanent Settlement of 1793. This act of the colonial rulers conferred de facto governmental powers to the landlords (the *zamindars*) by giving them the right to collect taxes (keeping a substantial fraction for themselves). The fact that British taxation and land tenure policy was not uniform throughout the Raj provides a natural experiment to test the importance of institutions. Banerjee and Iyer compared the post-Independence economic performance and social indicators of districts of modern-day India in which landlords had been empowered by the colonial land tenure and taxation systems with other districts where the landlords had been bypassed in favor of the village community or direct taxation of the individual cultivator. They found that the landlord-controlled districts had significantly *lower* rates of agricultural productivity growth stemming from lower rates of investment and lesser use of modern inputs. The landlord-controlled districts also lagged significantly in educational and health improvements.[1] These findings suggest that enduring poverty can result from the persistence of an institutional innovation occurring a century or more earlier.

The institutional poverty traps studied by Banerjee and Iyer and Engerman and Sokolof concern the ways that institutions result in low levels of *aggregate* economic performance: even the relatively well to do in the *zamindari* regions of India are not well off. Here, I will investigate another type of institutional poverty trap, namely one in which poverty results due to the unequal division of output between classes – i.e., individuals with different structural positions in the economy, such as landlords and share croppers or employers and workers. Examples of such divisions include social structures in which a single landlord claims half or more of the crop of ten or more tenants, thus receiving an order of magnitude more income than the average tenant while putting in substantially less effort. Another example is the class structure of the classical capitalist firm, in which an owner pays wages equivalent to two-thirds of the value added that is produced by each of a hundred or more workers he employs, resulting in an income difference of 50 : 1. An important question to be explored is: does the persistence of these highly unequal divisions require that the associated institutions be productively superior in some sense to alternative social arrangements? Or may their persistence be explained by other evolutionary advantages they possess?

In these two examples, an institution may be represented as one of a number of possible conventions, i.e., equilibria in which members of a population typically act in ways that maximize payoffs given the actions taken by others and in which individuals' beliefs about what others will do support continued adherence to these conventional actions. A convention is thus an outcome in which it is in the interest of people to adhere to the convention as long as they believe that most others will do the same. This property is what justifies the term "mutual best response" to describe a convention. A common noneconomic example of a convention is driving on the right or on the left. Examples of distributional conventions include simple principles of division such as "finders keepers" or "first come first served," as well as more complicated principles of allocation such as the variety of rules which have governed the exchange of goods or the division of the products of one's labor over the course of human evolution.

Because a convention is one of many possible mutually best responses, institutions are not environmentally determined, but rather are of human construction (but not necessarily of deliberate design). Conventions are self-enforcing (i.e., they are evolutionarily stable) as a result of the positive feedbacks associated with the members' conforming to a common strategy. As a result of this, institutions that take the form of conventions will display inertia, and transitions among them will occur rapidly but infrequently, displaying a pattern that biologists call *punctuated equilibria* (Eldredge and Gould 1972).

To explore why institutional poverty traps are seemingly common, we need to understand the birth, diffusion, and eclipse of institutions and the process by which one institution supplants another. This will require an account of how characteristics of institutions contribute to their evolutionary success. Institutions may proliferate as the result of the ability of the groups governed by them to be victorious in wars, or to survive ecological crises when others perish. But to some extent the evolutionary success of institutions depends on how likely a group is to "hit upon" differing social arrangements, and, once hit upon, how resilient an institution is to pressures for change from the members of the group. Here, I will set aside the effects of between-group competition and differential group survival to focus on the within-group processes that make some institutions easy to "hit upon" and resilient once in place. Two quite distinct approaches to the within-group processes bringing about institutional innovation may be identified.

The first, similar to the biologist Sewall Wright's use of drift to explain a movement from one fitness peak across a fitness valley to another peak (Wright 1931), is that proposed by stochastic evolutionary game theory pioneered by Foster and Young (1990). In this Darwin-inspired approach, change occurs through the chance bunching of individuals' mutation-like idiosyncratic behavior. If in a given period a sufficient number of people do not adhere to the convention, then adhering to the convention will no longer be a best response, and so the convention will unravel. If this happens, a new convention may be established, much as a neighborhood may "tip" from being mostly of one race to mostly of another. Changes in language use, the racial composition of neighborhoods, contractual shares, market days, and etiquette have been modeled in this manner.

The second approach, initiated by Marx, stresses asymmetries among the players and explains institutional innovation by the changing power balance between those who benefit from differing conventions. In this framework, revolutionary change in institutions is likely when existing institutions facilitate the collective action of those who would benefit from a change in institutions, and when, because existing institutions are inefficient by comparison to an alternative, there are substantial potential gains to making a switch. This collective-action-based approach has been used to model conflicts among classes, resulting in a basic transformation of social organization, such as the French, Russian, and Cuban revolutions, as well as more gradual changes in institutional arrangements such as the centuries-long erosion of European feudalism.

Do these approaches allow us to say anything about the characteristics of evolutionarily successful institutions? Though the underlying causal mechanisms are different, the Marx-inspired approach shares with Darwin-inspired stochastic evolutionary game theory the prediction that institutional arrangements which are both inefficient and highly unequal will bear an evolutionary disability and will tend to be displaced in the long run by more efficient and more egalitarian institutions.[2] This is quite an arresting claim in light of the long-term historical persistence of social arrangements which would appear to be neither efficient nor egalitarian. But the only formal model supporting this claim – the stochastic evolutionary game theory model due to Young (1998) – may be of limited relevance to real historical processes. The reason is that the "tipping" events that alter institutions are not generally induced by mutation-like accidents of behavior, but are rather the result of the intentional collective action of people who are not making mistakes, but rather are trying to better their condition.

Thus to address questions of institutional persistence, evolutionary theory must be coupled with the theory of collective action. A plausible account of collective action, combined with the fact that the classes are often of quite different sizes – many sharecroppers, few landlords, e.g. – leads to a conclusion at odds with that of stochastic evolutionary game theory: while more efficient and more equal institutions are indeed favored by plausible evolutionary processes under some conditions, it is also true that inefficient and unequal institutions can persist over very long periods of time.

5.2   Evolutionary models of institutional transformation

Structural and social engineering approaches to the rise, persistence, and fall of institutions study constitution-making as a deliberate process, whereby powerful groups or farsighted planners implement the rules that govern social interactions, seeking thereby to further their own or the public's interest. By contrast, evolutionary approaches represent institutions as an emergent property arising from the uncoordinated actions of members of a population, of which none are seeking to implement aggregate outcomes. The genes accounting for the design of the bird's wing were not trying to fly, but only to replicate. In like manner, in models of social evolution, the actions that sustain many customs, norms, and other aspects of social are motivated by other goals, these structures being unintended byproducts. The approach developed later is evolutionary in spirit and formal methods, but it incorporates the fact that when people act in ways that change institutions they are often attempting to do just that, even if the resulting processes do not reflect their objectives.

Because nothing of importance concerning the main points given later is lost in taking an especially simple case, I confine myself to the analysis of the evolutionary dynamics governing transitions between two conventions in a two-person two-strategy game in a large population of individuals subdivided into two groups, the members of which are randomly paired to interact in a non-cooperative game with members of the other group.

Individuals' best-response play is based on a single-period memory, and they maximize their expected payoffs based on the distribution of the population in the previous period. The two population subgroups, initially assumed to be of equal size, are termed As and Bs. When either is paired with a member of the other group, they may choose action 1 or 0, with the A's payoffs, a_{ij}, representing the payoff to an A-person playing action i against a B-person playing action j, and analogously for the B's. If the members of the pair choose the same action they get positive benefits, while if they chose different actions they get nothing. For concreteness, suppose the subgroups are economic classes selecting a contract to regulate their joint production, which will only take place if they agree on a contract. Payoffs are shares of the joint surplus of the project, with the no-production outcome normalized to zero for both. The payoffs, with the As as the row player, and the Bs as column player, are given in Figure 5.1.

To capture the conflict of interest between the two groups, let us assume that $b_{00} > b_{11} = a_{11} > a_{00} > 0$ so the Bs strictly prefer the outcome in which both play 0 and the As prefer the equal division outcome which results when both play 1.[3] Both of these outcomes are strict Nash equilibria, and thus both represent conventions, which I will denote E_0 and E_1 (or $\{0, 0\}$ and $\{1, 1\}$). Both populations are normalized to unit size, so I refer equivalently to the numbers of players and the fraction of the population, abstracting from integer problems.

	B offer contract 1	B offer contract 0
A offer contract 1	$a_{11}b_{11}$	0 0
A offer contract 0	0 0	$a_{00}b_{00}$

Figure 5.1 Payoffs in the contract game.

The state of this population in any time period t is $\{\alpha_t, \beta_t\}$, where α is the fraction of the As who played 1 in the previous period and β is the fraction of the Bs who played 1. For any state of the population, expected payoffs a_i and b_i for the As and Bs respectively playing strategy i, depend on the distribution of play among the opposing group in the previous period, or dropping the time subscript:

$$a_1 = \beta a_{11}, \quad a_0 = (1 - \beta)a_{00}, \quad b_1 = \alpha b_{11}, \quad b_0 = (1 - \alpha)b_{00}.$$

The relationship between the population state and the expected payoffs to each action is illustrated in Figure 5.2.

Individuals take a given action – they are 1-players or 0-players – and they continue doing so from period to period until they update their action, at which point they may switch. Suppose that at the beginning of every period some fraction ω of each sub-population may update their actions. (This might be due to the age structure of the population, with updating taking place only at a given period of life, in which case the "periods" in the model may be understood as "generations." Of course, updating could be much more frequent.) The updating is based on the expected payoffs to the two actions; these expectations are simply the payoffs which would obtain if the previous period's state remained unchanged (the population composition in the previous period being common knowledge in the current period). While this updating process is not very sophisticated, it may realistically reflect individuals' cognitive capacities and it assures that in equilibrium – when the population state is stationary – the beliefs of the actors formed in this naive process are confirmed in practice.

I will analyze the single-period change in the population state $(\Delta\alpha, \Delta\beta)$ under the assumption that individual updating of strategies is monotonic in average payoffs so that $\Delta\alpha$ and $\Delta\beta$ have the signs respectively, of $(a_1 - a_0)$ and $(b_1 - b_0)$.

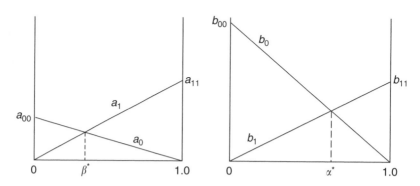

Figure 5.2 Expected payoffs depend on the distribution of play in the previous period.

Note
The vertical axis is in payoff units. A's payoffs depend on β the fraction of B's offering contract 1, while the B's payoffs depend on α the fraction of A's offering contract 1. Because $b_{00} > b_{11} = a_{11} > a_{00}$, the convention E_1 (i.e., $\alpha = 1 = \beta$) is preferred by the As while E_0 is preferred by the Bs.

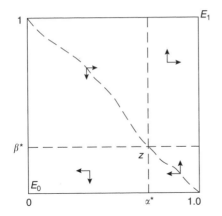

Figure 5.3 The state space. The arrows give the direction of change at every point.

Note
E_1 and E_0 are stable equilibria; z is a saddle.

The resulting population dynamics are illustrated in Figure 5.3, where the relevant regions are defined by:

$$\alpha^* = b_{00}/(b_{11} + b_{00}),$$
$$\beta^* = a_{00}/(a_{11} + a_{00}),$$

with these two population distributions equating the expected payoffs to the two strategies for the two sub-populations, respectively. These values of α and β define best response functions: for $\alpha < \alpha^*$ B's best response is to play 0, and for $\alpha \geq \alpha^*$ B's best response is to play 1, with β^* interpreted analogously.

For states $\alpha < \alpha^*$ and $\beta < \beta^*$ (in the southwest region of Figure 5.3) it is obvious that $\Delta\alpha$ and $\Delta\beta$ are both negative and the state will move to $\{0,0\}$. Analogous reasoning holds for the northeast region. In the northwest and southeast regions of the state space, we may define a locus of states from which the system will transit to the interior equilibrium α^*, β^*, with states below that locus transiting to $\{0,0\}$, and above the locus to $\{1,1\}$. The area below the dashed downward-sloping line in Figure 5.3 is the basin of attraction of $\{0,0\}$ if a population governed by the above dynamic finds itself in this region it will move to the $\{0,0\}$ convention. If a population governed by the above dynamic finds itself in this region it will move to the $\{0,0\}$ convention, absent further perturbations. The size of the basin of attraction of $\{0,0\}$ varies with $\alpha^*\beta^*$. While the interior equilibrium $\{\alpha^*, \beta^*\}$ is an unstable Nash equilibrium (a saddle), the outcomes $\{0,0\}$, and $\{1,1\}$ are absorbing states of the dynamic process, meaning that if the population is ever at either of these states, it will never leave. There being more than one such absorbing state, the dynamic process is *non-ergodic*, i.e., its long-run average behavior is dependent on initial conditions.

The critical values α^* and β^* will be important in what follows. Suppose the reigning convention is $\{0,0\}$ and the As would like to induce a shift to $\{1,1\}$, which is more favorable to them. If some fraction of the As greater than α^* were to "strike," refusing to accept a_{00} and insisting on a_{11} instead, then Figure 5.2 confirms that in the next period the Bs, having encountered these idiosyncratic As would best respond by switching to the 1-contract, thereby tipping the population from $\{0,0\}$ to $\{1,1\}$. Thus α^* is a "collective action threshold" indicating the minimum number of deviant As required to displace the $\{0,0\}$ equilibrium. It is easy to see (from Figure 5.2) that were the $\{0,0\}$ convention to become even more unequal (by increasing b_{00}), the effect would be to increase α^*, thereby raising the collective action threshold for the As.

Similar reasoning holds for the Bs of course. If the status quo convention were $\{1,1\}$, the Bs might wish to induce a shift to $\{0,0\}$, which they could do if $(1-\beta^*)$ of them deviated from the best response, "locking out" any As unwilling to transact according the 0-contract. The effect on the Bs collective action threshold of the 0-contract becoming even more unequal (lowering a_{00}) can also be seen from Figure 5.2: it lowers β^* and hence makes it more difficult for the Bs to induce a tipping event to bring about a shift to the convention they would prefer.

The important point here is that were the 0-contract more unequal, it would make it more difficult for the As to induce a shift away from this convention to the $\{1,1\}$ convention they prefer; but it also makes it more difficult for the Bs to induce a shift away from the 1-contract to the $\{0,0\}$ convention that they prefer. The result is that increasing the inequality of the more unequal convention makes it more likely that the population will be "stuck" in one convention or the other. But we cannot say whether greater inequality in the $\{0,0\}$ convention will result in the population being more likely in the long run to be there as opposed to the $\{1,1\}$ convention. To do this we need to consider the set of feasible contracts rather than just two, and we need to be more specific about the process by which deviant play occurs.

5.3   A taxonomy of contracts

Suppose contracts differ in their distributional shares and also in the level of total surplus (sum of payoffs) they yield. Some contracts are, in this sense, more efficient than others. This might occur if the use of a particular technology required a distinct set of property rights, which in turn supported a particular equilibrium contract. An example of this technology-institutions mapping is the relationship between the production of sugar and precious metals extraction in the early history of the New World and the exclusive and coercive institutions that prevailed there (Sokoloff and Engerman 2000). Another is the rise of agriculture and the emergence of individual property rights ten or so millennia ago (Bowles and Choi 2002).

Analysis of the 2×2 contract game is facilitated if we write $a_{11}=1, b_{11}=1$ and $a_{00}+b_{00}=\rho$, so $\rho/2$ is a measure of the relative efficiency of the $\{0,0\}$ convention; when ρ takes the value of 2, the two conventions produce the same joint surplus. Further, let the A player's share of joint surplus in the B-favoring

	B offer Contract 1	B offer Contract 0
A offer Contract 1	$a_{11} = 1$ $b_{11} = 1$	0 0
A offer Contract 0	0 0	$a_{00} = \sigma\rho,$ $b_{00} = (1-\sigma)\rho$

Figure 5.4 Modified contract game payoffs.

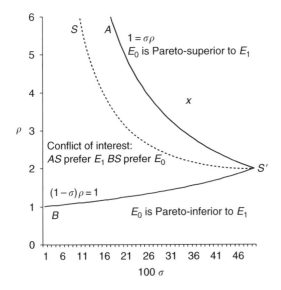

Figure 5.5 Contrasting contracts. Each point represents the efficiency and distributional share of the Alternative contract supporting the equilibrium E_0.
Contracts above $S'A$ are Pareto-superior to the Benchmark contract with
$\rho = 2$ and $\sigma = \frac{1}{2}$. Contracts below $S'B$ are Pareto-inferior to the
Benchmark contract.

$\{0, 0\}$ equilibria be $\sigma \frac{1}{2}$, with $(1-\sigma)$ the share gained by B. The payoffs are shown
in Figure 5.4.

The contract space shown in Figure 5.5 depicts a set of Alternative contracts
defining convention E_0. Point S' is the benchmark contract (with $\rho = 2$ and
$\sigma = \frac{1}{2}$). Thus if the two possible contracts are represented by points S' and x, both
groups will prefer the Alternative contract because both $\sigma\rho$ and $(1-\sigma)\rho$ exceed 1
under its terms. Contracts above AS' are Pareto-superior to the benchmark. (Ignore
the locus $S'S$ for the moment.)

Conflict of interest between the two groups is confined to the contracts lying below *AS* and above *BS*. This does not ensure that the *S'* would be eclipsed by an alternative contract like *x*. The reason is that while *x* is Pareto-superior to the *S'*, adherence to *S'* is a mutual best response and so will only be dislodged by non-best response actions such as the strikes or lockouts mentioned earlier. Our intuition, however, says that Pareto-inferior conventions must be at a disadvantage in a stochastic environment.

If non-best response actions (also called "idiosyncratic") occurred by chance, with each person best responding with probability $(1 - \varepsilon)$ and adopting the other strategy with probability ε, we can use the results of stochastic evolutionary game theory to make some strong predictions. A striking theorem due to Peyton Young (1998) demonstrates that populations evolving according to this dynamic will spend most of their time at conventions that are not only efficient but also egalitarian. Under some innocuous restrictions on the updating process, Young's "Contract Theorem" shows that the most persistent convention (called the stochastically stable state) is the one which maximizes the relative payoffs of the group with the lowest relative payoff.

The reason is that conventions that are egalitarian in this sense have larger basins of attraction than more unequal conventions. For this reason, the chance bunching of a sufficiently large number deviant players tipping the population into the basin of attraction of such a convention is likely to happen sooner than for a convention with a smaller basin of attraction. Thus, such conventions are *accessible*. It is also true that such conventions are also *robust*, in that they are unlikely to be unraveled by non-best response play, because having a large basin of attraction means that it takes a large fraction of one population or the other to unravel the convention. The combination of accessibility and robustness is what determines the persistence of a convention. If we consider an Alternative contract in Figure 5.5 and compare it with the Benchmark $\{1, 1\}$ contract, the two basins of attraction will be of the same size if $a_{00}b_{00} = a_{11}b_{11}$, which using the payoffs in Figure 5.4 requires that

$$\sigma(1 - \sigma)\rho^2 = 1.$$

If the alternative convention is such that $a_{00}b_{00} > a_{11}b_{11}$ (meaning $\sigma(1 - \sigma)\rho^2 > 1$) then the alternative will be the more persistent of the two conventions. It is clear from this condition that both relative efficiency and equality of shares contribute to stochastic stability of a convention (the term $\sigma(1 - \sigma)$ is maximized for $\sigma = \frac{1}{2}$).

Figure 5.5 illustrates a novel kind of efficiency-equality tradeoff. It depicts the relationship between efficiency and equality as determinants of persistence: *SS'* is the locus of combinations of ρ and σ such that $\sigma(1 - \sigma)\rho^2 = 1$. Thus *SS'* is the locus of Alternative contracts such that both conventions are equally persistent. Alternative contracts above *SS'* are more persistent when the other convention is based on the Benchmark contract. For Alternative contracts below *SS'* the Benchmark contract is more persistent. Calculations using the model just described confirm that more efficient and more equal conventions are likely to be more persistent. We can explore the long run behavior of the system by assuming that $\{0, 0\}$ is the status quo and then calculating the expected waiting time (number of periods) before idiosyncratic chance actions of either the As or the Bs induce a tipping event, propelling the population from $\{0, 0\}$ to $\{1, 1\}$. Using the same method we then calculate the expected waiting time for a transition back to $\{0, 0\}$. The fraction of the "round trip" – i.e., the waiting time from $\{0, 0\}$ to $\{1, 1\}$ and back – that the population spends at each equilibrium can then be calculated.

Figure 5.6 gives the results of this calculation for various values of σ and ρ, where the two sub-populations each have 12 members. The height of each bar gives the expected fraction of time the population will spend at the convention in question if the Benchmark contract is $\{1, 1\}$ as before. Where E_0 is identical to $E_1(\rho = 2$ and $\sigma = \frac{1}{2}$ indicated by the dark bar at these coordinates) the population spends half of its time at each convention as one would expect. One can see a band of conventions (similar to the locus SS' in Figure 5.5) which like $\rho = 2$ and $\sigma = \frac{1}{2}$ generate equal average waiting times (e.g., $\rho = 2.5$ and

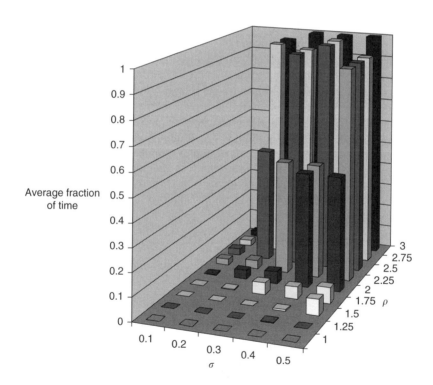

Figure 5.6 Efficient and equal conventions are persistent when deviant behavior is unintentional.

Note
The Benchmark convention is E_1 for which $\rho = 2$ and $\sigma = \frac{1}{2}$.

$\sigma = 0.2$ generates this result, as does $\rho = 2.25$ and $\sigma = 0.3$). The population will spend virtually all of the time at conventions more efficient or more equal than these.

The reason that more equal conventions are favored in this framework is as follows: consider an Alternative contract with $\rho = 2$ and $\sigma < \frac{1}{2}$. An increase in the distributional share of the As in the Alternative contract has two effects. First, it lowers α^* and thus it requires fewer instances of idiosyncratic play by the As to disrupt the Alternative Contract, inducing a movement to the Benchmark (which they prefer). The reason is that when the Alternative is *less unequal*, it takes fewer idiosyncratic As to induce the Bs to switch to the Benchmark. The second effect of an increase in σ is to raise β^*, thus reducing the minimal fraction of non-best-responding Bs (namely $(1 - \beta^*)$) required to induce the As to abandon their preferred Benchmark contract in favor of the Alternative. The two effects of a more equal Alternative contract work in opposite directions, the first leading to a shorter waiting time for a transition from the Benchmark to the Alternative, and the second leading to a shorter waiting time for the reverse transition. But for $\sigma < \frac{1}{2}$ the second effect is larger, so the population will spend more time at the Alternative, the more equal it is.

It is easy to see why efficient conventions would be favored in this setup. For at least one group, offering the efficient contract must be risk dominant in the standard sense that if one believes that the other will offer the two contracts with equal probability, then the best response is to offer the more efficient one. Inefficient conventions are not accessible because it takes a large amount of non-best-response play to induce best responders to shift from an efficient to an inefficient convention. Note that this is not because best responders anticipate the consequences of their switching for the population level dynamics. Rather, their response is purely individual and based on past (not anticipated future) population states; no individual is attempting to implement the more efficient convention. Inefficient conventions are not persistent for analogous reasons.

Less transparent is the result that highly unequal conventions are not good candidates for persistence. This is a consequence of the fact that they are easily unraveled, because as Young (1998, p. 137) puts it: "it does not take many stochastic shocks to create an environment in which members of the dissatisfied group prefer to try something different." Note that in this example it is the idiosyncratic play of the *privileged* group that unravels the unequal convention, i.e., the convention from which they benefit disproportionately. Note also, that the more unequal the convention is, the more easily is it unraveled by this means.

If deviant behavior is indeed just accidental, then this account is correct. But the plausibility of the illustrations given earlier – the "strike" and the "lockout" – rested on the idea that deviant behaviors are undertaken deliberately and not by mistake. Indeed, it typically is the deviant behavior of the disadvantaged group that induces institutional transitions. It was not a fortuitous piling up of unlikely accidents on the part of Communist Party officials that doomed Communism, but rather a combination of chance events and the deliberate and coordinated actions taken by those seeking to live under other institutions.

5.4 Collective action

We therefore need to study how the distributional share of a contract (σ) might affect the vulnerability to the collective action of those seeking to improve their share. When intentional non-best response play is introduced in the form of collective action by those trying to displace the status quo convention, the dynamic of institutional innovation is substantially altered. It is no longer generally the case that the persistent states are egalitarian and efficient. In particular, if the rich are few and the poor many, unequal, and inefficient institutions can be very persistent. The reason is that when non-best response play is intentional there is just one way (rather than two) that a convention can be overturned (by the actions of those who would benefit more at the other convention), and the larger numbers of the poor militate against a sufficient fraction of them adopting a non-best response to displace the equilibrium under which they do poorly.

The collective action approach requires some modifications in the earlier model. First, the players must be assumed to recognize the possibility of transitioning to a new institutional setup, and have the ability to anticipate the consequences of their actions on the actions of others. Thus, rather than restricting individuals to backward-looking updating, I now introduce a limited capacity to look forward. By *collective action*, I mean the intentional joint action toward common ends by members of a large group of people who do not have the capacity to commit to binding agreements prior to acting (i.e., they act non-cooperatively). Examples are strikes, ethnic violence, insurrections, demonstrations, and boycotts.[4]

To clarify the underlying processes, I will first analyze a degenerate case in which individuals participate in a non-best response collective action when it is in their individual interest that the action take place. Suppose that there is a probability ε that each person is "called to a meeting" at which those attending consider undertaking a non-best response action. For example, assume the B-favorable convention $\{0, 0\}$ obtains and some fraction of Bs (resulting from the "call") are considering switching to offer a 1-contract instead. But they cannot benefit from switching because they prefer the status quo convention, and destabilizing it – should enough of the other possible B-innovators also switch – could propel them to the alternate convention under which they would be worse off. These potentially idiosyncratic players would thus decline the opportunity to innovate.[5]

By contrast, imagine that a group of As were randomly called for deliberation of the merits of a switch away from the governing convention $\{0, 0\}$, and suppose that should they all adopt a non-best response, this will be common knowledge. Each then might reason as follows. If they are sufficiently numerous and if all of them switched, the best response for the Bs would be to switch as well. Knowing this, should they all switch, they would anticipate the Bs response and so would persist in offering 1-contracts in the next period. As a result, the A-unfavorable convention $\{0, 0\}$ would be displaced.

Suppose there are n members of the A population (previously normalized to unity). Because if fewer than $n\alpha^*$ As were called, there could be no benefit to collective action even if it were uniformly successful, let us analyze the case for which the number called, η, exceeds this critical level, i.e., $\eta \geq n\alpha^*$. To lend some concreteness to the case let us say that switching means to engage with other As in a strike, refusing to accept any outcome less than a_{11} (all this means is to offer a 1-contract, so the strategy set is unchanged). We can then calculate the expected waiting time before sufficiently many As are "called" so that a tipping event (a strike) occurs. Unlike Figure 5.6 we do not include the possibility that the B's idiosyncratic actions would induce a "tip" because if sufficiently many of them were "called" they would recognize that they would not benefit from disrupting the status quo convention. Then, supposing that the population has been tipped to the $\{1, 1\}$ convention by the A's strike, we calculate the expected waiting time before enough Bs are "called" to allow a tipping event back to the B-favorable convention $\{0, 0\}$. As in Figure 5.6 the fraction of the "round trip" – the waiting time from $\{0, 0\}$ to $\{1, 1\}$ and back – that the population spends at each equilibrium is then calculated.

The height of the columns in Figure 5.7 gives the fraction of time spent at each of a number of Alternative conventions when the benchmark is as before $\{1, 1\}$ and the unequal Alternative conventions are characterized by differing levels of efficiency. The figure shows the effect of assuming sub-populations of different size (retaining

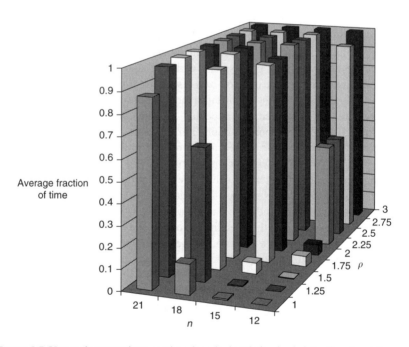

Figure 5.7 Unequal conventions persist when deviant behavior is intentional and the poor outnumber the rich.

Note
Total population is 24; the Benchmark convention is E_1 ($\sigma = \frac{1}{2}, \rho = 2$). E_0 is characterized by the values of ρ indicated and $\sigma = 0.3$.

the degenerate model of collective action) for an alternative contract with $\sigma = 0.3$ and with the ρ values as shown. By contrast to the equal sub-population size case depicted in Figure 5.6, when population sizes differ, unequal and quite inefficient conventions may be highly persistent. For example, in the equal population size case, a convention with $\sigma = 0.3$ needed a ρ of 2.25 to be equally persistent to E_1; but if the A's number 18 and the B's 6, the two conventions are equally persistent when the unequal convention is much *less* efficient than the benchmark, i.e., $\rho = 1.25$. Where there are 21 As (and 3 Bs) the population will spend most of the time in the unequal convention even if its level of efficiency is half that of the equal convention. Note that the level of inequality measured by the average income of B's relative to A's is $n(1 - \sigma)/\sigma(24 - n)$, each B interacting with more As as their relative share of the population increases. Thus, at the convention E_0 if $\sigma = 0.3$ and the As and Bs are equally numerous, the Bs have an income 2.33 times the As but when there are 21 As and 3 Bs, the ratio is 16.33. Thus highly unequal distribution of income may result from unequal sub-population sizes, and may be persistent because of the unequal sub-population sizes.

The evolutionary success of unequal and inefficient conventions benefitting the smaller class is readily explained. As long as the rate of idiosyncratic play is less than the critical fraction of the population required to induce a transition (which I assume), smaller groups will more frequently experience "tipping opportunities" when the realized fraction of the population who are "called" by chance exceeds the expected fraction (ε itself). The theory of sampling error tells us that the class whose numbers are smaller will generate more "tipping" possibilities. Small size does not facilitate collective action if more than the critical number are "called."

5.5   Persistent inequality

So far I have abstracted from the problem of collective action by assuming that whenever a sufficient fraction of a sub-population is "called" they will adopt a non-best response if they (and their group) would benefit if all of those called adopted the non-best response. But this was just a pedagogical device permitting a sequential presentation of the main aspects of a unified causal mechanism. Thus, what is needed is a model of the coordination problem posed by collective action, nested in the larger population game representing institutional evolution. Taking account of the intentional nature of collective action will provide an explanation of why highly unequal conventions may be vulnerable to unraveling, while moderately unequal conventions may be highly persistent, even if they are not particularly efficient.

Because collective actions generically take the form of n-person public goods games in which the dominant strategy is non-participation if preferences are wholly self-regarding, the extended model must address incentives for each to free ride when others act in pursuit of commonly shared objectives. A second desideratum is that the model should reflect the fact that opportunities for collective action often arise by chance, or at least in ways too complex to tractably model, examples being economic depressions, wars, price shocks, booms, and natural disasters. Finally, unlike idiosyncratic play, participation in collective action is not only intentional (rather than accidental) but is also conditional on one's beliefs about the likelihood and consequences of a substantial number of one's kind changing behaviors. For this reason, facts about global rather than simply local payoff (i.e., payoffs both in the present convention and in the alternative, rather than those in the neighborhood of the current population state alone) may have a bearing on the outcomes.[6]

Engaging in this collective activity yields in-process benefits of two types. First, irrespective of the consequences of the action, conformism (or punishment of non-conformists) may impose a cost on those not adopting the most common action. So, let c be the cost of being a sole non-conformist, and the conformism costs to those striking being $(1 - s)c$ where s is the fraction of those "called" who strike. The costs to the non-strikers is sc. Further, there are net benefits or costs associated with the action that may be independent of the numbers participating, including both the time, resources, and possibly risk of harm associated with the collective action as well as the positive value of participating, or what Wood (2003) terms the "pleasure of agency."[7]

It is reasonable to suppose that these subjective benefits depend on the magnitude of the gains to be had if the action is successful, not primarily because these gains are a likely consequence of one's individual participation (which is very unlikely in large groups) but because the magnitude of the gains to be had is plausibly related to the strength of the norms motivating the action. The pleasure of participating in a collective action that would, if successful, transform the conditions of one's class from squalor to abundance is likely to be greater than the pleasure of acting for a wage increase of a few cents more an hour.

So let the net subjective benefits for an A engaging in a collective action to displace convention $\{0, 0\}$ be:

$$\delta = \delta(a_{11} - a_{00}),$$

where δ is a positive constant, reflecting the fact that joining a collective action in pursuit of an institutional change from which one and one's peers will not benefit nor confers any benefits. If the strike fails (because too few participate in it) the status quo convention will persist, and all As will get a_{00} in subsequent periods independently of whether they participated in the strike or not. Likewise, if the strike succeeds, all As will get a_{11} in subsequent periods, irrespective of their actions this period. Thus the relevant comparison is between the single period net benefits to striking (insisting on contract 1, refusing contract 0) or abstaining are:

$$u_1 = \delta(a_{11} - a_{00}) - (1 - s)c,$$

$$u_0 = a_{00} - sc.$$

These payoff functions are illustrated in Figure 5.8, from which it is clear if those involved believe that at least s^* of their fellows will join in, then strikers' expected

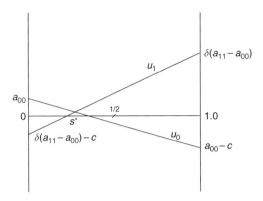

Figure 5.8 The collective action problem.

Note
If $s^* < \frac{1}{2}$ the risk dominant equilibrium is universal participation in the non-best response action.

payoffs will exceed those of non-participants, and hence all will elect to strike the critical value, s^* equates u_0 and u_1:

$$s^* = \tfrac{1}{2} - [\delta(a_{11} - a_{00}) - a_{00}]/2c.$$

How might A's beliefs be formed? The simplest supposition consistent with the given model is that having no information about what the others will do, each believes that the likelihood of each of the others participating is $\frac{1}{2}$, so the expected fraction participating is $\frac{1}{2}$, and all will participate if s^* less than one half.[8] In a game of this type, the strategy that maximizes expected payoffs when one attributes equal probability to the others' choice of a strategy is termed the risk dominant strategy, and the result of all following a risk dominant strategy is termed the risk dominant equilibrium.

Thus, unanimous participation (of those "called") will occur if striking is the risk dominant equilibrium of the collective action game, requiring that the numerator of the bracketed term on the right hand side of the equation above for s^* be positive, or that the "pleasure of agency" outweighs the loss of a single period's income. (Note that while inferior payoffs in the status quo convention ($a_{11} - a_{00} > 0$) is a necessary condition for participation, it is not sufficient, as it does not insure that $\delta(a_{11} - a_{00}) - a_{00} > 0$.)

The properties of the dynamical system are substantially altered by modeling idiosyncratic play as intentional collective action. Notice that if $\delta(a_{11} - a_{00}) - a_{00} < 0$ collective action will not take place (irrespective of the numbers of randomly drawn potential innovators), so the A-unfavorable convention $\{0, 0\}$, if ever attained, will persist forever (it is an absorbing state). Thus in the dynamical system with collective action as the form of non-best response, institutional lock-ins are possible, with initial conditions determining which of the two conventions will emerge, and then persist forever. To see that this must be the case for a finite "pleasure of agency" parameter δ, consider an unequal convention with $a_{11} - a_{00} = \Delta$. Letting Δ become arbitrarily small must make $\delta(a_{11} - a_{00}) - a_{00} < 0$, so collective action by As will not occur and E_0, should it ever occur, will persist forever. Thus there must exist a set of conventions, less equal than E_1 and no more efficient, that will persist forever. These conventions are examples of inequality resulting from institutional lock-in.

How are we to interpret these persistent unequal states? Over relevant time scales, the parameters of the model are likely to change due to cultural and political changes affecting δ or technical or other changes affecting the payoffs to the relevant contracts. Suppose some unequal Alternative contract defines the status quo convention (E_0), and it represents an absorbing state. If technical change made the $\{1, 1\}$ contract progressively more efficient by comparison to $\{0, 0\}$, then $\delta(a_{11} - a_{00})$ would eventually exceed a_{00}. As a result, the conditions for collective action would obtain, and a transition from E_0 to E_1 would eventually take place. Transitions in the reverse direction would become more unlikely over time as the increase in a_{11} raises the minimum number of non-best responding Bs required to unravel E_1. Thus, the institutional demands of new technologies may account for the emergence of new contractual conventions. A cultural change enhancing the pleasure of agency, δ – a role played by liberation theology in some parts of Latin America, by the spread of democratic ideology in South Africa and the former Communist countries – would have the same effect. This is very roughly Marx's account which sees history as a progressive succession of "modes of production," each contributing to "the development of the forces of production" for a period, then becoming a "fetter" on further technological advance and being replaced through the collective action of the class that would benefit by a shift to a new convention more consistent with the new technologies.

5.6 Conclusion

The above reasoning suggests that unequal institutions may persist over long periods due to the nature of these arrangements as self-enforcing conventions and the difficulty faced by the poor in coordinating the types of collective action necessary to "tip" a population from an unequal to a more equal set of institutions. Very unequal institutions would be quite vulnerable to unraveling if the actions inducing the change were the idiosyncratic non-best response actions of members of the class that benefits from these institutions. But this process obviously does not capture the dynamics of most historical transitions. By contrast, in the more empirically relevant case institutional tipping takes place through the deliberate refusal of those disadvantaged by the status quo convention to abide by its terms. In this case, highly unequal conventions are difficult to dislodge: the more unequal the status quo is, the greater the number of deviant actions of the least well off are required to tip the population to a more egalitarian alternative. Taking account of the intentional nature of deviance, and the fact that it takes the form of collective action introduces the central question of motivation. The main result is thus that moderate levels of inequality may be insufficient to motivate collective action by *any of the poor*, while conventions characterized by extreme levels of inequality can only be displaced through collective actions endorsed by *very large fractions of the poor*.

Institutions differ in evolutionarily relevant ways not captured in this model by measures of efficiency, distributional shares, and relative group size, of course. Some institutions may facilitate collective action of the disadvantaged, while others make it more difficult to coordinate the actions of the poor. Marx, and many since, have believed that the social conditions of industrial capitalism constituted a schoolhouse of revolution, by contrast with earlier institutions of sharecropping, tax farming in societies of independent peasants, and slavery, e.g. By contrast, Moore (1966), Mao (1953), Markoff (1996), Scott (1976), Wood (2003), and others, with perhaps greater accuracy, have seen patron-client relationships in agrarian societies and highly unequal systems of land holding as especially vulnerable to revolutionary overturns. These extensions of the basic model may be represented in the differing net benefits of collective action, δ, subscripted by the conventions to which they apply.

Whether the persistence of institutions that implement high levels of inequality can be explained by such a model is of course an open question, one awaiting the necessary theory-building, and empirical investigation. A plausible alternative explanation of institutional evolution makes success in intergroup competition – victory in warfare, access to favorable environments, heightened rates of population increase and the like – a key arbiter of the rise, diffusion, and demise of institutions. These processes were implicit in Talcott Parson's description of evolutionary universals, and explicit in the related thinking of Frederich Hayek (1988). Models along these lines suggest that some egalitarian institutions – such as food sharing among non-relatives or monogamy – may contribute to group success and thus, to their own persistence (Bowles *et al.* 2003). More adequate models would encompass both the within-group dynamics modeled here and these and other forms of between-group competition. (An example is provided in Bowles and Choi (2002).)

Acknowledgments

Thanks to Karla Hoff, Steven Durlauf, Ugo Pagano, Yong-jin Park, Bae Smith, Elisabeth Wood, Jorgen Weibull, and Peyton Young for valuable contributions to this chapter, and to The Pew Charitable Trusts and the Santa Fe Institute for financial support. The formal mathematical analysis of the processes described here can be found in Bowles (2004).

Notes

1 The causal connection between landlord control and these subsequent results remains to be explored. Because colonial practices changed over time in response to events such as the revolt by Indian soldiers in 1857 and over space in response to the idiosyncracies

of local administrators, Banerjee and Iyer were able to identify independent sources of variation in the land tenure and taxation policies not due to pre-existing conditions.

2 Efficient institutions yield a larger joint surplus, while in a more equal convention, the share of the least well-off is larger.

3 I refer to $\{1, 1\}$ as the "equal" convention as a shorthand. The levels of well-being attained by the As and Bs cannot be determined without additional information. (For example, if the As are share croppers who interact with only one B (a landlord), while Bs interact with many As, the "equal" convention would exhibit unequal incomes of the two groups.)

4 The proviso that play is non-cooperative excludes the degenerate case (with which I begin for purposes of illustration) of groups whose structure allows the assignment of obligatory actions to each of its members. While most successful collective actions include a wide range of selective incentives and sanctions to deter free riding, few if any groups have the capacity to simply mandate group-beneficial behaviors by individual members.

5 Favored groups, like the Bs in convention $\{0, 0\}$ may deploy informal or governmental sanctions to minimize idiosyncratic play of their own members. Examples include the shunning and more severe sanctions imposed on whites offering favorable contracts to non-whites in racially stratified societies such as apartheid South Africa and the US South prior to the Civil Rights Movement.

6 This means that individuals are forward looking to the extent that they can anticipate the consequences of successful collective action.

7 Compelling evidence from the histories of collective action (e.g., Moore 1978; Wood 2003) anthropology (Knauft 1991; Boehm 1993), experimental economics (Fehr and Gaechter 2002), and agent-based models of cultural and genetic evolution (Boyd *et al.* 2003; Bowles and Gintis 2004) suggests that individuals knowingly engage in costly actions to punish violations of norms, even when these actions cannot otherwise benefit the individual.

8 The choice of $\frac{1}{2}$ is conventional but arbitrary; individuals may have prior beliefs of the fraction likely to participate based on previous similar situation and the like. If individuals then apply their reasoning to each of the others (each, supposing that half will participate, will also participate), they would then correctly predict that $s = 1$; but while this second round of induction may determine whether the individual expects the collective action to be successful in displacing the convention, it is not relevant to the individual's behavior, as the relative payoffs of participating or not are independent of the success of the action.

References

Banerjee, Abhijit and Lakshmi Iyer (2002) "History, institutions and economic performance: the legacy of colonial land tenure systems in India," MIT Working Paper 02–27.

Boehm, Christopher (1993) "Egalitarian behavior and reverse dominance hierarchy," *Current Anthropology*, 34(3): 227–54.

Bowles, Samuel (2004) *Microeconomics: Behavior, Institutions, and Evolution*, Princeton, NJ: Princeton University Press.

Bowles, Samuel and Herbert Gintis (2004) "The evolution of strong reciprocity: cooperation in a heterogeneous population," *Theoretical Population Biology*, 65: 17–28.

Bowles, Samuel and Jung-Kyoo Choi (2002) "The first property rights revolution," *Santa Fe Institute Working Paper 02-11-061.*

Bowles, Samuel, Jung-Kyoo Choi, and Astrid Hopfensitz (2003) "The coevolution of individual behaviors and group level institutions," *Journal of Theoretical Biology*, 223(2): 135–47.

Boyd, Robert, Herbert Gintis, Samuel Bowles, and Peter Richerson (2003) "The evolution of altruistic punishment," *Proceedings of the National Academy of Science (USA)*, 20: 123–43.

Cortes, Hernan, translated and edited by Anthony Pagden (1986) *Letters From Mexico*, New Haven, CT: Yale University Press.

Eldredge, Niles and S.J. Gould (1972) "Punctuated equilibria: an alternative to phyletic gradualism," in T.J.M Schopf and J.M. Thomas (eds), *Models in Paleobiology*, San Francisco, CA: Freeman, Cooper, pp. 82–115.

Fehr, Ernst and Simon Gaechter (2002) "Altruistic punishment in humans," *Nature*, 415: 137–40.

Foster, Dean and H. Peyton Young (1990) "Stochastic evolutionary game dynamics," *Theoretical Population Biology*, 38: 219–32.

Hayek, F.A. (1988) *The Fatal Conceit: The Errors of Socialism*, Chicago, IL: University of Chicago Press.

Knauft, Bruce M. (1991) "Violence and sociality in human evolution," *Current Anthropology*, 32(4): 391–428.

Mao, Zedong (1953) *Report of an Investigation into the Peasant Movement in HUNAN*, Peking: Foreign Languages Press.

Markoff, John (1996) *The Abolition of Feudalism: Peasants, Lords and Legislators in the French Revolution*, University Park, PA: Pennsylvania State University Press.

Moore, Barrington Jr (1966) *Social Origins of Dictatorship and Democracy, Lord and Peasant in the Making of the Modern World*, Boston, MA: Beacon Press.

——(1978) *Injustice: The Social Bases of Obedience and Revolt*, White Plains: M.E. Sharpe.

Parsons, Talcott (1964) "Evolutionary Universals in Society," *American Sociological Review*, 29(3): 339–57.

Scott, James C. (1976) *The Moral Economy of the Peasant: Rebellion and Subsistence in Southeast Asia*, New Haven, CT: Yale University Press.

Sokoloff, K. and S. Engerman (2000) "Institutions, factor endowments, and paths of development in the New World," *Journal of Economic Perspectives*, 14(3): 217–32.

Wood, Elisabeth (2003) *Insurgent Collective Action and Civil War in El Salvador*, Cambridge: Cambridge University Press.

Wright, Sewall (1931) "Evolution in Mendelian populations," *Genetics*, 16: 97–159.

Young, H. Peyton (1998) *Individual Strategy and Social Structure: An Evolutionary Theory of Institutions*, Princeton, NJ: Princeton University Press.

6 Bridging communal divides

Separation, patronage, integration

Indraneel Dasgupta and Ravi Kanbur

6.1 Introduction

Simmering communal tensions between relatively well-defined social groups divided along racial, religious, linguistic, or ethnic lines are a pervasive feature of most societies. In both developed and developing countries, such tensions often spill over into open and widespread conflict, including large-scale violence. While the recent history of countries such as India, Indonesia, the Philippines, Rwanda, and Yugoslavia bear extreme testimony to this phenomenon, few societies, if any, past or present, have been completely free of non-class communal divisions. Indeed, one of the major challenges facing both individual countries and supra-national institutions today appears to be the problem of holding inter-group conflicts in check.[1]

At a very broad level, one can observe at least three major types of individual responses to the existence of sharp non-class identity cleavages in society along, say, ethnic, religious, racial, or linguistic lines. We can term these responses "separatist," "syncretist," and "integrationist." The separatist response consists of an exclusive, celebratory assertion of one's own communal identity and a conscious rejection of other possible forms of communal identity. The syncretist response involves attempts by some members of one community to relate to members of another community through active engagement with the identity markers of the latter. The integrationist response, on the other hand, is constituted by attempts on the part of members of one community to relate to members of another community via activities or commitments that do not appear, a priori, to be exclusively, or even primarily, associated with either community.

One example of separatist practices is provided by strong espousal of restrictions on social interaction among different caste groups in India. More generally, activities associated with identity politics and "community" or "self-help" initiatives along ethnic, linguistic, racial, or religious lines can be thought of as examples of separatist responses. "Acting black," "going native," participating in ethnic or religious activities of another community, contributing to the development of a different language, contributing to the study of another culture or civilization, etc. all provide common examples of syncretist practices. As examples of integrationist responses, one may cite activities such as inter-ethnic or inter-religious marriage, supporting a racially mixed sports club or political party, cheering for the national cricket team, etc.

In light of the pervasive nature of all three types of responses highlighted, two questions naturally suggest themselves to economists. First, what is the relationship between a given wealth distribution across communities and the pattern of these alternative responses to pre-existing notions of communal distinctiveness? Second, what implications do these individual responses carry, when aggregated, for the nature and extent of communal tensions? The answer to the first question would provide an understanding of how individual responses to historically given notions of identity and communal distinctiveness are shaped by inequalities in wealth distribution. The answer to the second would explicate conditions under which inequalities in wealth distribution have the potential to generate social strife and distributive conflict between communities. The purpose of this chapter is to address these issues.

Studies by economists, as well as other social scientists, have explored various aspects of identity and inter-group conflict.[2] Recently, Dasgupta and Kanbur (2001, 2002) have developed a public (or rather, "club") good-based interpretation of community identity and membership, and analyzed its implications for inequality, income distribution, and class conflict. They begin from the premise that what seems to define communities as communities is the presence of something (a) to which all members have common access, and (b) through which members acquire social access to each other. Thus, one way of formalizing the notion of *belonging* to a community is by positing access to a community-specific local public good. For example, belonging to a religious community can be interpreted to imply (a) common access to that community's places of worship and religious activities, and (b) access to social interaction with other members of the community through common participation in worship and collective religious activities. Similarly, the right to participate in ethno-linguistic festivals and rituals can be considered constitutive of the ethnic identity of an individual, and participation in such activities may provide a platform where members of the ethnic group come together to interact socially. At a slightly different level, the presence of local or neighborhood public goods (such as parks, roads, libraries, concert halls, auditoria, museums, sports clubs, safety, etc.) and the social interaction which is brought about as an indirect consequence of accessing and using such public goods, can be considered as defining that which constitutes a *community* out of a collection of individuals living in geographical proximity to each other.

What each individual in a community enjoys is the aggregation of individual level activities that constitute the community. But the aggregation is made up of each individual participating in the community and contributing to it. How much each individual contributes to community activity depends on her resources and her preferences, and of course on how much other individuals are already contributing. Thus, the equilibrium of a game of voluntary contributions to the community-specific public good seems a natural way to model how individual choices lead to community outcomes.

In their analysis, Dasgupta and Kanbur (2001, 2002) assume a tight connection between an individual and a community. Each individual is associated with one community and its public good, and either does not have access to or does not value the public good of another community. No individual contributes to any public good other than that constitutive of her own community *qua* community. Thus, their investigation is entirely confined to the "separatist" case, and does not incorporate different patterns of separatist, syncretist, or integrationist responses as a function of the distribution of wealth across communities. Our chapter generalizes and extends that earlier, more restrictive framework to analyze the richer set of possibilities. In so doing, we also contribute to the formal analysis of voluntary contributions to multiple public goods, an issue that has been largely neglected in the literature.[3]

Section 6.2 sets up the basic model. We consider two communities of equal size defined by community-specific public goods. Each community consists of some *core* members, who do not derive positive utility from the other community's public good, and some *fringe* members, who do. All members of a community are assumed to have identical wealth endowments, though wealth endowments can vary across communities. Individuals play a Cournot game of voluntary contributions toward the two public goods. Section 6.3 investigates the conditions under which fringe individuals in one community will contribute toward the public good constitutive of the other's community self-definition *qua* community. Specifically, we analyze how the extent of wealth inequality across communities determines whether individuals will engage in separatist or syncretist activities. We show that a relatively egalitarian cross-community wealth distribution makes for separatist responses on the part of every individual in society. If one community is significantly wealthier than the other, then fringe individuals in the richer community will engage in syncretist activities. However, all individuals in the poorer community will turn separatist. Section 6.4 examines the implications of these results for distributive conflicts between communities. We show that separatism generates incentives for all individuals to support the expropriation of the other community, and, thereby, provides grounds for communal conflict. Except in a special case, such grounds exist *even* in a syncretist equilibrium. Section 6.5 expands the analysis by incorporating a "meta-communal" element to an agent's self-identity, i.e., a public good that is "common" to all communities. We show that both communities undertake integrationist activities, i.e., contribute to this meta-communal public good, when the wealth gap between communities is relatively low. In such an equilibrium, while communities remain separated at the level of the public good constitutive of a community's self-identity, no individual has any incentive to support expropriation of the other community. This is so because what an individual would gain in terms of additional wealth would be exactly compensated by a corresponding reduction in the other community's contribution to the meta-communal public good. However, large wealth gaps imply that only individuals in the richer community will contribute to the meta-communal public good. This once again provides grounds for distributive conflicts between communities. Section 6.6

discusses some concrete illustrations of our theoretical analysis and provides concluding remarks.

6.2 The basic model

Consider a society consisting of two communities, A, B, defined by the presence of the community-specific public goods A and B, respectively. All individuals are born into, and grow up in, one of these two communities. Thus, by $i \in A$, we shall denote an individual born into community A, and similarly for individuals born into the other community. There are n individuals in society, $n \geq 4$. We shall assume that the communities are equal in size, so that $n_A = n_B = n/2$.

For any individual i born into community $\alpha, \alpha \in \{A, B\}$, preferences are given by an additively separable, homothetic utility function:

$$u_i^\alpha = u^{\alpha,i}(x_i, y_A, y_B), \tag{1}$$

where y_A, y_B denote the amounts of the two public goods A and B, respectively, while x_i denotes the amount of the private good. It follows from the assumptions of separability and homotheticity that the marginal rate of substitution between any two goods is a function only of the ratio of their quantities. We shall assume that the ratios of the marginal utilities have the following form:

$$\left[\left(\frac{\partial u^{\alpha,i}}{\partial x_i} \right) \Big/ \left(\frac{\partial u^{\alpha,i}}{\partial y_\alpha} \right) \right] = \left(\frac{y_\alpha}{x_i} \right)^\varepsilon,$$

$$\left[\left(\frac{\partial u^{\alpha,i}}{\partial y_\alpha} \right) \Big/ \left(\frac{\partial u^{\alpha,i}}{\partial y_\beta} \right) \right] = \theta_i^{-1} \left(\frac{y_\beta}{k y_\alpha} \right)^\varepsilon, \tag{2}$$

where $\varepsilon \in (0, 1]$, $k \in (0, 1)$, $\beta \in [\{A, B\} - \{\alpha\}]$ and $\theta_i \in \{1\} \cup \Re_-$ ($\Re_-$ denoting the set of all non-positive real numbers).

To illustrate, one may assume preferences to have Cobb–Douglas or CES representation. Thus, e.g., preferences of individuals i, j belonging to communities A and B, respectively, may have the following form:

$$u^{A,i} = x_i^\gamma + y_A^\gamma + \theta_i k^{1-\gamma} y_B^\gamma,$$
$$u^{B,j} = x_j^\gamma + y_B^\gamma + \theta_j k^{1-\gamma} y_A^\gamma,$$

where $\gamma \in (0, 1)$, so that $\varepsilon = 1 - \gamma$.

The essential idea that we wish to capture through our restrictions on preferences is the following. All individuals, by virtue of having grown up within a particular community, acquire a particular community *identity* as an integral part of their psychological make-up. However, attitudes toward the other community vary among individuals within the same community. Each community contains some *core members*, who grow up to be indifferent, or even hostile, to that which is constitutive of the very identity of the other community. Formally, we define core members as such by virtue of the fact that the other community's public good provides zero, or, possibly even negative, utility to them. We model these individuals by ascribing $[\theta_i \leq 0]$ to them. For example, some members of one religious community may find the other community's places of worship of no value whatsoever. This possibility is captured in our model by ascribing a value of 0 to θ_i. Core members of one religious community may even find the religious practices of the other community abhorrent. We can incorporate this case by means of a negative value of θ_i, a larger absolute value of θ_i implying a stronger degree of abhorrence for the public good that is constitutive of the other community. Each community also contains some *fringe members* who have a dual character. Like core individuals, fringe individuals also have historically given communal identities. Thus, fringe individuals also have a preference bias against the public good constitutive of the other community, reflecting their personal history and upbringing. Given identical amounts of the two public goods, they would be willing to give up less than one unit of their own community's public good in exchange for an additional unit of the other community's public good. The preference bias of these individuals against the public good definitive of the other community is, however, contingent and not absolute. They relate to the other community in a positive way. If the other community's public good is sufficiently low compared to that of their own community, fringe individuals would be willing to give up more than one unit of their own community's public good in exchange for an additional unit of the other community's public good. We model such individuals by ascribing a value of 1 to θ_i, and by assuming $0 < k < 1$.

We shall assume all prices to be unity for notational simplicity. To explicate further the nature of restrictions imposed by our specification of preferences, we note the following. Since all prices are unity, if an individual i happened to own the entire wealth endowment of society, then i would purchase identical amounts of her private good and her own community's public good. Additionally, if i happened to be a fringe individual born into, say, community A, then she would purchase $k y_A$ amount of *community B's* public good (and zero amount of community B's private consumption good). If, however, i happened to be a core individual in community A, and happened to own the entire society's wealth, then she would allocate her entire wealth equally between her own private consumption and the public good A, spending nothing on B.[4]

Let $\underline{A} = \{i \in A | \theta_i \leq 0\}$, $\underline{B} = \{i \in B | \theta_i \leq 0\}$, $\bar{A} = [A - \underline{A}]$ and $\bar{B} = [B - \underline{B}]$. Thus, the set $\underline{A}$ represents the group of *core* members of community A. The set $\underline{B}$ is interpreted analogously. $\bar{A}, \bar{B}$ are the groups of fringe members in communities A and B, respectively. $[\bar{A} \cup \bar{B}]$ is thus the collection of all individuals in society who can possibly engage in syncretist activities, and, thereby, act as a *bridge* between the two communities. The numbers of individuals belonging to the different groups are $n_{\bar{A}}, n_{\bar{B}}, n_A, n_B$, respectively; $n_{\bar{A}}, n_{\bar{B}}, n_A, n_B \geq 1$. For every $j \in \{A, B\}$, the wealth of an individual belonging to community j is I_j. Thus, all agents within a community have identical wealth, but wealth ownership may vary across communities. We abstract from wealth differentials within a community in order to focus on wealth differentials across communities.[5]

Individuals simultaneously choose their contributions to the public goods. Thus, we model the problem as a Cournot game involving voluntary contributions to the two community-specific public goods.

Given any $\alpha \in \{A, B\}$, for every $i \in \alpha$, the problem is

$$\underset{x_i, y_A, y_B}{\text{Max}} \; u^{\alpha, i}(x_i, y_A, y_B), \tag{3}$$

subject to the budget constraint

$$x_i + y_A + y_B = I_\alpha + y_{-i,A} + y_{-i,B}, \tag{4}$$

and the additional constraints

$$\text{for all } \chi \in \{A, B\}, \quad y_\chi \geq y_{-i,\chi}, \tag{5}$$

where $y_{-i,\chi}$ represents the total amount spent on community χ's public good by all individuals in society except i.

Our assumed restrictions on preferences suffice to guarantee the existence of a Nash equilibrium. We shall use the superscript N to denote the Nash equilibrium values of variables, whereas $y_{\alpha\beta}^N$ will denote the total contribution by group α to community β's public good in a Nash equilibrium, where $\alpha \in \{\underline{A}, \underline{B}, \bar{A}, \bar{B}, A, B\}$ and $\beta \in \{A, B\}$.

It is easy to see from equations (1) to (5) that any two agents belonging to the same group must make identical *total* contributions to the two public goods. It is clear that neither any $\underline{A}$ individual, nor any $\underline{B}$ individual will ever contribute to the other community's public good, since by assumption $\theta_i \leq 0$ for such individuals. It follows that all core individuals in a community must make identical contributions to that community's public good in a Nash equilibrium. If the total contribution from the set of all fringe individuals in a community is zero for one public good, then it follows that all fringe individuals in that community must contribute identical amounts to the other public good in that Nash equilibrium. However, if the total contribution from the set of all fringe individuals in a community happens to be positive for both public goods, then one has multiple Nash equilibria. There will exist Nash equilibria where two fringe individuals in the same community contribute different amounts to the two public goods (though their total individual expenditures on the two public goods must be identical and uniquely determined, as must be the total amounts of the two public goods provided). In our discussion, we shall focus on the symmetric equilibrium for such cases, where all fringe individuals in a community contribute identical amounts to each public good.

6.3 Syncretism as patronage

We now proceed to investigate the conditions under which different groups of agents will be contributory to the different public goods. More specifically, we focus on the nature and determinants of syncretist activities, i.e., contribution to the public good constitutive of the other community. Recall that no core individual can ever engage in such activities. When will fringe individuals do so? What determines the community identity of such fringe individuals who, by engaging in syncretist activities, become actual, rather than merely potential, *bridge individuals*?

In order to organize our discussion of these issues, we first introduce the notion of *communal separation*.

Definition 1. Two communities, A and B, will be said to be *separated* in a Nash equilibrium if and only if in that Nash equilibrium, $y_{AB}^N, y_{BA}^N = 0$. They will be called *connected* otherwise.

Thus, two communities are "separated" if no individual in either community contributes to the public good definitive of the other community. Note that, in this construction, "separated" communities need not necessarily be "segregated" in any standard sense. For example, communities can live in the same neighborhood, attend the same workplace, use the same public facilities, or enter into economic relations with one another, and yet be considered separated according to our definition. What is key to our notion of communal "separateness" is the non-contribution, by members of the other community, to that which is constitutive of one community's specific identity, *qua* community. Thus, e.g., two ethnic groups may live and work together in the same neighborhood, yet neither may contribute toward the expenses for collective assertions/celebrations of the other's sense of ethnic self, such as ethnic rituals and festivals. While one would not, typically, describe such a situation as ethnic segregation, one would still seem to feel intuitively that the two communities are "separated" in an important way. It is this intuitive understanding that we seek to capture in our formal definition. Of course, communities can be both segregated in the standard sense and separated in our sense.

On the other hand, if individuals born into one community contribute to the public good constitutive of the identity of the other community *qua* community, we shall consider the two communities to be "connected." Within the class of Nash equilibria where communities are connected, the nature of their connectedness may, however, be varied. One a priori possibility is that fringe members of both communities will become bridge individuals, i.e., contribute to one another's public good. Alternatively, one community may be connected to another by virtue of the fact that fringe individuals of only one community contribute to the other community's public good. We term such a Nash equilibrium "patronizing."

Definition 2. A Nash equilibrium is *patronizing* if and only if there exists $\alpha \in \{A, B\}$ such that $\lfloor y_{\alpha\beta}^N > 0, y_{\beta\alpha}^N = 0$, where $\beta \in [\{A, B\} - \{\alpha\}]\rfloor$ in that Nash equilibrium. Then, community α will be called the *patron* community and community β the *client* community in that Nash equilibrium.

Remark 1. Every *connected* Nash equilibrium is necessarily *patronizing.*

To see this, note that, if $y_{\widetilde{A}B}^N > 0$, then $[ky_A^N \geq y_B^N]$. A symmetric claim is true when $y_{\widetilde{B}A}^N > 0$. Since $k < 1$, it immediately follows that, in a Nash equilibrium, $y_{\widetilde{A}B}^N, y_{\widetilde{B}A}^N$ cannot both be positive. Thus, in our framework, communities can only be either separated or exist in a patron – client relationship.[6] In light of this finding, it is natural to examine the conditions under which one community will patronize another.

Proposition 1.

(i) *Communities A, B are separated in a Nash equilibrium if and only if $[kI_B \leq I_A \leq (I_B/k)]$.*
(ii) *For all $\alpha \in \{A, B\}$, community α patronizes community β, $\beta \in [\{A, B\} - \{\alpha\}]$, if and only if $\lfloor I_\beta < kI_\alpha \rfloor$.*

Proof. See the Appendix. □

Proposition 1(i) provides necessary and sufficient conditions for communities to be separated in the Nash equilibrium. Given our assumption that the two communities are identical in size, the requirement essentially is that all individuals have roughly similar wealth holdings. Thus, broadly, the communities must be relatively close in terms of total community wealth for them to be separated.[7] *An egalitarian wealth distribution between communities makes for division.*[8]

Proposition 1(ii) implies that if a community has much higher per capita wealth holdings, it will patronize the other.[9] Thus, a sharply inegalitarian distribution of wealth across communities actually binds the communities together, albeit in an unequal relationship of dominance and dependency, with the subaltern community (the one with the smaller amount of total wealth holding) becoming the client of the dominant community.

The act of patronage *differentiates* the patron community: in a patronizing Nash equilibrium, every fringe individual in the patron community contributes *less* to her own community's public good than any core individual of that community. In light of Proposition 1, it is easy to check that the following must hold.

Proposition 2. *For all $\alpha \in \{A, B\}$, (i) $[(y_{\alpha\alpha}^N/n_{\underline{\alpha}}) > (y_{\bar{\alpha}\alpha}^N/n_{\bar{\alpha}})]$ if $\lfloor I_\beta < kI_\alpha \rfloor$, and (ii) $[(y_{\alpha\alpha}^N/n_{\underline{\alpha}}) = (y_{\bar{\alpha}\alpha}^N/n_{\bar{\alpha}})]$ otherwise; where $\beta \in [\{A, B\} - \{\alpha\}]$.*

It can be easily seen that client communities cannot be differentiated: core and fringe individuals will all contribute identical amounts to the community's own public good within such a community.

Patron–client relationships can be of various kinds. First, one can distinguish between Nash equilibria marked by *active* and *passive* client communities. By *active* clients, we mean communities which, while receiving contributions from the patron community, also make positive contributions themselves toward their own public goods. *Passive* client communities do not, depending entirely on the patron community for the provision of the public good which defines their own community. The construction of the community identity of passive client communities is thus completely parasitical on the syncretist behavior of fringe individuals born into the patron community.[10] Second, we can make a parallel demarcation with reference to the patron community. We call a patron community *loose* if the fringe individuals in that community contribute only to the public good of the client community, depending entirely on the contributions of core members within their community for provision of their own community's public good. A patron community is *compact* if all individuals born into that community contribute toward its own public good.

A client community is passive when its per capita wealth is significantly less than that of the patron community. The larger the fringe group within the patron community, the smaller the wealth differential that suffices to make a client community passive. More formally, we have the following result, which follows immediately from equations (3) to (5), once we note that, in any Nash equilibrium, it must be the case that, for any community, say A, $y_A^N \geq [kn_{\bar{B}}I_B/(n_{\bar{B}} + 1 + k)]$.

Proposition 3. *For any $\alpha \in \{A, B\}$, $\lfloor y_{\alpha\alpha}^N > 0 \rfloor$ only if $[I_\alpha > (kn_{\bar{\beta}}I_\beta)/(n_{\bar{\beta}} + 1 + k)]$, where $\beta \in [\{A, B\} - \{\alpha\}]$.*

We now proceed to investigate the conditions which determine whether a patron community will be loose or compact.

Proposition 4. *Consider $\beta \in \{A, B\}$, and let $\alpha \in [\{A, B\} - \{\beta\}]$.*

(i) *Suppose $\lfloor n_{\bar{\beta}} > kn_\beta \rfloor$. Then there exist $p \in (1/(1 + k), 1)$ such that:*

    (a) *if $I_\beta \in ((I_A + I_B)/(1 + k), p(I_A + I_B))$, then β is a compact patron community, and α an active client community, in the (symmetric) Nash equilibrium, and*

    (b) *if $I_\beta \in [p(I_A + I_B), (I_A + I_B)]$, then β is a compact patron community, and α a passive client community, in the (symmetric) Nash equilibrium.*

(ii) *Suppose $\lfloor n_{\bar{\beta}} < kn_\beta \rfloor$. Then there exist $q_1, q_2 \in (1/(1 + k), 1)$, $q_1 > q_2$, such that:*

    (a) *if $I_\beta \in ((I_A + I_B)/(1 + k), q_2(I_A + I_B))$, then β is a compact patron community, and α an active client community, in the (symmetric) Nash equilibrium,*

    (b) *if $I_\beta \in [q_2(I_A + I_B), q_1(I_A + I_B))$, then β is a loose patron community, and α an active client community, in the Nash equilibrium, and*

    (c) *if $I_\beta \in [q_1(I_A + I_B), (I_A + I_B)]$, then β is a loose patron community, and α a passive client community, in the Nash equilibrium.*

(iii) *Suppose* $\lfloor n_{\bar{\beta}} = kn_{\beta} \rfloor$. *Then there exist* $p \in (1/(1+k), 1)$ *such that:*

(a) *if* $I_{\beta} \in ((I_A + I_B)/(1+k), p(I_A + I_B))$, *then* β *is a compact patron community, and* α *an active client community, in the (symmetric) Nash equilibrium, and*

(b) *if* $I_{\beta} \in [p(I_A + I_B), (I_A + I_B)]$, *then* β *is a loose patron community, and* α *a passive client community, in the Nash equilibrium.*

Proof. See the Appendix. □

Suppose the per capita wealth holding of one community, say A, is much lower than that of the other community, B. Then Proposition 4 essentially implies that the patron community B will be *loose* if it contains a large number of core individuals, but relatively few fringe individuals, i.e., if patronage activity happens to be undertaken by a relatively small proportion of community members. The patron community will be *compact* if patronage activities are widespread in the community.

Consider now the case where the client community, say A, is active, and the patron community, B, is compact, in the Nash equilibrium. Then we must have:

$$[x_A^N = y_A^N = ky_B^N = kx_B^N],$$ (6)

which yields:

$$y_B^N = \frac{\sum_{\alpha \in \{A,B\}} n_{\alpha} I_{\alpha}}{(1 + n_B) + k(1 + n_A)}.$$ (7)

Using equations (6) and (7), we get the following.

Remark 2. Consider two Nash equilibria, generated by two different wealth distributions, such that the client community is active, and the patron community compact, in both Nash equilibria. Then the consumption bundle of every individual in society must be invariant in the two Nash equilibria.

6.4   Separation, patronage, and communal conflicts

We now proceed to analyze the implications of the results presented in Section 6.3 for the nature of distributive conflicts between communities, where members of one community seek to dispossess the members of another community of their wealth. For analytical clarity, we think of such conflicts as proposals to *reduce* the wealth of every member of one community, say B, by some given amount ΔI_B, and distribute the total proceeds equally among the members of the other community, A, so that every member of the latter community receives a wealth *increment* $\Delta I_A = \Delta I_B$. Let the initial, status quo distribution of wealth be $\langle I_A^*, I_B^* \rangle$.

First consider the case where the two communities are separated in the Nash equilibrium before, as well as after, such a redistribution of wealth. It can be easily checked that, in any Nash equilibrium where the two communities are separated,

$$\left[x_A^N = y_A^N = \frac{n_A I_A}{n_A + 1} \right] \quad \text{and} \quad \left[x_B^N = y_B^N = \frac{n_B I_B}{n_B + 1} \right].$$

Then, if a total amount T is taken away from community B and distributed amongst the members of community A, for every individual born into that community, total money value of her consumption of the private good and the public good A increases by $[2T/(n_A + 1)]$. For every individual born into community B, total money value of her consumption of the private good and the public good B decreases by the same amount (since the communities are identical in size). Clearly, therefore, such a redistribution makes all core individuals in the winning community A better off, and all core individuals in the losing community B worse off. Fringe members of A also effectively gain an amount $[2T/(n_A + 1)]$, but the reduction in the amount of the public good B (by $[T/(n_A + 1)]$) reduces their gain. Thus, fringe members of A are better off overall as well.[11] Analogously, all members of B are worse off. We summarize this analysis in the following Proposition.

Proposition 5. *Suppose that the two communities are separated in the Nash equilibrium corresponding to some initial wealth distribution $\langle I_A^*, I_B^* \rangle$. Consider a proposal to alter the wealth distribution to $\langle I_A^* + \Delta I_A, I_B^* - \Delta I_B \rangle$, such that: (a) $\Delta I_A = \Delta I_B > 0$; and (b) the communities would remain separated in the Nash equilibrium corresponding to $\langle I_A^* + \Delta I_A, I_B^* - \Delta I_B \rangle$. Then, if the proposal is implemented: every member of A will be better off, while every member of B will be worse off.*

Recall that, by Proposition 1, the two communities will coexist in a separated equilibrium when the distribution of wealth across communities is roughly equal. Proposition 5 implies that such a distribution may be inherently fragile and conflict-laden, in that it generates incentives for individuals in both communities to support political entrepreneurs, formations or agendas which seek to dispossess the other community. Core individuals in either community will always have an incentive to support such divisive proposals. Even fringe individuals will join the bandwagon when the two communities are not too dissimilar numerically. Consequently, communal separation, stemming from an egalitarian cross-community distribution of wealth, has the potential to generate mass support in both communities for sectarian political platforms, and thus for communal strife.

By Proposition 1(ii), an unequal distribution of wealth across communities connects communities in a patron–client relationship. Does such syncretist behavior by fringe individuals in the patron community reduce individual incentives to support proposals to dispossess the other community? A straightforward comparison of the Nash equilibrium levels of public goods yields the following conclusions.

If the per capita wealth gap between the two communities is extremely large, then by Proposition 3, the poor community, say B, will become the passive client of the rich community A. In this case, every member of the rich community is better off if that community can expropriate any part of the wealth of the poorer community. Thus, every individual born into A, whether core or fringe, has an incentive to support expropriation of the poor community, B, and thereby, further extend the degree of its impoverishment.[12] On the other hand, every core member of the client community has an incentive to oppose the expropriation of her own community (and support expropriation of the patron community).[13] Interestingly, fringe members of the poor community may (though not necessarily) support the expropriation of their *own* community. Thus, under some parametric configurations, fringe members of the poor community may turn *comprador*, supporting the dispossession of their own community, even though they themselves also stand to lose wealth directly from such dispossession.[14] Under other parametric configurations, however, the interests of fringe individuals in the poor community will be in line with those of core members of their own community. In either case, core individuals in the client community have an incentive to support expropriation of the fringe in their own community.

Now consider the case where the per capita wealth gap between the two communities is large, so that the rich community A patronizes the poor community B, but not exceedingly so, in that the client community is active.

First consider the sub-case where the rich community A consists largely of core individuals, so that the patron community is loose (see Proposition 4(ii)). In this case, every core individual in the patron community would support measures to expropriate the client community. In fact, such individuals would support measures to expropriate fringe, "heretical," "liberal," or "cosmopolitan" members of their own community as well. However, fringe members of the patron community may now acquire incentives to oppose the expropriation of the client community. On the other hand, every core member of the client community benefits from an expropriation of the patron community. As before, fringe members of the client community have a dual character: they may or may not benefit from an expropriation of the patron community. However, irrespective of the political interests of the fringe in the client community, the core in that community no longer has any interest in dispossessing its own fringe.[15]

Lastly, given an active client community B, consider the sub-case where the patron community contains a significant proportion of fringe individuals, and is therefore compact (see Proposition 4(i)). In this case, since the consumption bundle of any individual in society in a Nash equilibrium depends only on total wealth of society as a whole, and not on its distribution (see Remark 2), no A individual has any incentive to support agendas of wealth redistribution, unless they involve an expropriation large enough to turn the client community passive in the new Nash equilibrium. Otherwise, gains that core individuals in A make would be exactly neutralized through a reduction in spending by fringe individuals in A on that community's public good. Similarly, gains that fringe individuals in A make would be exactly negated through a corresponding reduction in spending by the client community B on its own public good. Thus, only in this case does patronage generate incentives that provide even a limited degree of protection to the poor community from political agendas that seek to further impoverish that community. Analogously, no individual in B has any incentive to support relatively small expropriations of the patron community. Any gains that B individuals make would be exactly negated by a reduction in spending by fringe A individuals on community B's public good.[16]

6.5   Integration via meta-community

The analysis of inter-community conflicts provided in Section 6.4 does not appear to provide any ground for optimism regarding the incentives individuals may have for opposing distributive conflicts with another community. Syncretist activities, which necessarily take the form of patronage, can restrain inter-community conflicts, but only under quite special conditions, namely if (i) the act of patronage is widespread in the patron community, and (ii) the wealth holding of the client community is relatively close to that of the patron community, so that the client community is active in the Nash equilibrium. For egalitarians, in particular, the prospects are grim. Communities will be separated when their wealth holdings are roughly similar, providing the greatest incentive for individuals to support agendas of communal conflict.[17]

Can communities be brought together through the presence of a public good which stands "above" particular communities? In most multi-ethnic, multi-religious, or otherwise fragmented, societies, one can perceive a strand within the public discourse which urges individuals to relate to a "broader" identity, an overarching public good of sorts, which is not specific to one's own "narrow" community. "The Nation," of course, is a common example, as are its variants such as "American values," "Britishness," or the national sports team.[18] But so are the calls to the poor to relate as a class, to Muslims to relate as the Umma, to Catholics to relate as members of the Church, etc.

How does one incorporate such a non-sectarian, or "*meta-communal*," public good within our framework? One way of doing this seems to be to assume that the marginal rate of substitution between such a meta-communal public good and the private good is identical for individuals who consume identical amounts of the two goods, regardless of their communal identity.

We then have, for any individual i born into community $\alpha, \alpha \in \{A, B\}$, preferences are given by an additively separable, homothetic utility function,

$$u_i^\alpha = u^{\alpha,i}(x_i, y_A, y_B, z),$$

where z is the amount of the meta-communal public good, Z,

$$\frac{u_x^{\alpha,i}}{u_z^{\alpha,i}} = \left(\frac{z}{\lambda x_i}\right)^\varepsilon,$$

$\lambda \in (0, 1]$, and the other restrictions on preferences are as specified earlier in Section 6.2.

Definition 3. A Nash equilibrium is meta-communally integrated if and only if both communities contribute a positive amount to the meta-communal public good Z in that Nash equilibrium.

Proposition 6. *A Nash equilibrium is meta-communally integrated only if that Nash equilibrium is separated.*

Proof. See the Appendix. □

Proposition 6 states that communal separation is necessary for meta-communal integration.

Remark 3. In light of Proposition 6, it can be easily checked that, in a meta-communally integrated Nash equilibrium, the amounts of the two community-specific public goods must be equal. Furthermore, all members of society must consume identical amounts of the private good. Thus, meta-communal integration generates complete identity in terms of consumption bundles, in spite of possible wealth differences, and actual preference differences, across communities.

Remark 4. If community A patronizes community B in the sphere of communal identity, it must patronize community B in the meta-communal sphere as well. However, community A may patronize community B in the meta-communal sphere, and yet the two communities may remain separated in the communal sphere. Furthermore, all core individuals in the patron community must spend a positive amount on the patron community's public good and the meta-communal public good, taken together.[19]

When will two communities be meta-communally integrated? Consider first the benchmark case of equal wealth distribution, where $I_A = I_B = \bar{I}$. It is easy to show that, in this case, the communities will be separated in the communal sphere, but integrated at the meta-communal level. Each community will provide $z/2$ amount of the meta-communal public good. Then, since $[x_A^N = x_B^N = y_A^N = y_B^N = (z^N/\lambda)]$, we have:

$$z^N \left(\frac{n + 2 + \lambda}{\lambda} \right) = n\bar{I},$$

which yields

$$\bar{\omega} = \frac{z^N}{n} = \frac{\lambda \bar{I}}{(n + 2 + \lambda)}.$$

Using the well-known neutrality property of Cournot games with voluntary contributions to public goods (Bergstrom *et al.* 1986), we immediately get the following.

Proposition 7. *A Nash equilibrium is meta-communally integrated if and only if for some* $\alpha \in \{A, B\}, [I_\alpha \in (\bar{I} - \bar{\varpi}, \bar{I} + \bar{\varpi})]$ *where* $\bar{I} = (I_A + I_B)/2$ *and* $\bar{\varpi} = \lambda \bar{I}/(n + 2 + \lambda)$.

Proposition 7 states the necessary and sufficient condition for communities to be meta-communally integrated when they are of the same size numerically. Essentially, this is the requirement that the cross-community wealth distribution be relatively equal.[20] It follows (from the neutrality property) that, if communities are meta-communally integrated, then no individual in either community has any incentive to support measures to expropriate the other community, so long as those measures are relatively small, in that they would leave the two communities meta-communally integrated even after implementation.

Thus, in a society where sharp wealth inequalities exist between communities, even non-communal forms of identity, such as nation, class, or language, would become identified with the dominant community, and would not have the capacity to hold distributive conflicts in check. On the other hand, such meta-communal identities can in fact remove individual incentives to support distributive conflicts across communities when inter-community wealth disparities are relatively low.

Figure 6.1 shows how patterns of patronage change with changes in the distribution of a given amount of wealth across communities. In the region PQ,

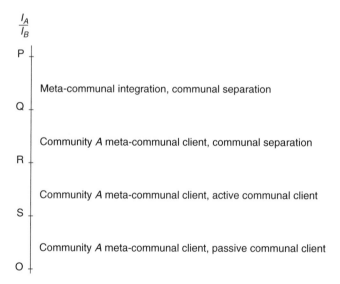

Figure 6.1 OP $= 1$.

the distribution of wealth is relatively equal, though *B* is the richer community. The two communities are separated at the communal level, but integrated at the meta-communal level. No individual has any incentive to support political proposals to dispossess the other community (nor, indeed, other members of her own community) in this zone. As the wealth distribution changes in favor of community *B*, in the zone QR, only community *B* contributes to the meta-communal public good, while the two communities remain separated at the level of communal identity. All members of both *A* and *B* now acquire incentives to dispossess the other community. However, no member of any community has any incentive to support expropriation of other members. Thus, the two communities are directly pitted against one another. Further enrichment of *B* however turns it into a patron community, while *A* becomes an active client community. In the zone RS, distributive conflicts will be held in check provided fringe individuals in *B* contribute to at least two public goods, which need not be the case unless patronage activities are widespread in the richer community. Otherwise, the patron community will turn loose. In that case the core in the patron community will acquire incentives to expropriate both the client community and the patron fringe. No individual in the client community, however, can benefit from expropriating other members of her own community. Lastly, no *B* individual, whether fringe or core, has any incentive to oppose measures to dispossess *A* when community *B*'s relative wealth rises further. Intra-community conflicts in *B* will persist in this zone if *B* happens to be loose. Additionally, all individuals in the client community now stand to benefit directly from expropriating other members of their own community. It is also possible that fringe members of *A* will benefit if *B* expropriates *A*, but that core members of *A* will be worse off from such expropriation. Thus, core and fringe groups in the client community may be pitted against one another. In sum, an egalitarian distribution of wealth across communities provides the most effective check against conflicts between communities (zone PQ). However, this is associated with separation between the communities at the level of communal identity.

6.6   Discussion and conclusion

The formal propositions of this chapter can serve to anchor a discussion of the nature of communal tensions, and of the relationship of these tensions to the distribution of wealth across communities. The theoretical insights gained warn us not to expect a simple monotonic relationship between wealth disparities and communal tensions, the complications arising precisely because of the very nature of the activities that define community. The theoretical analysis also highlights the importance of meta-communal activities, as opposed to simply cross-communal engagement by a fringe of individuals, in reducing communal tensions.

When there are no meta-communal public goods, cross-communal engagement depends on "fringe" individuals in a community, who value positively the public good that defines the other community. But putting a value on a public good, and contributing to its upkeep, are two very different things. Who contributes to which public good is the outcome of an interaction between and within communities. We show that when the two communities' wealth levels are similar, the fringe individuals from each community, who get utility out of the other community's public good, will nevertheless free ride and will not contribute to this public good, although they will contribute to the public good of their own community, along with the "core" members of their community. There is thus a clear separation, and no engagement, across the two communities.

Such separation breeds communal tension in the sense that we have formalized the notion here. Proposals to expropriate the wealth of the other community will find willing listeners in either community. Expropriation of the wealth of the other community generates net gains for those expropriating, because no one from either community is engaging with, i.e., contributing to, the public good of the other community. It may seem paradoxical that such communal tension is the outcome in a world where wealth differences are not large, but it is precisely communal equality which leads to lack of cross-communal engagement. Lack of significant engagement between middle-class black and white communities in the United States, or between middle-class Asian and white communities in Britain, might be understood in these terms. As wealth disparities between the communities grow, a form of engagement does develop. Fringe individuals of the wealthier community begin to contribute to the public good of the less wealthy community – they act as patrons to the poor community's clientist role. Might this engagement reduce or eliminate communal tensions? The answer to this question turns out to depend subtly on the relationship between fringe and core individuals inside the dominant community, and on the magnitude of the wealth differential. If the fringe individuals in the wealthy community are sufficiently numerous so that they contribute to both their own and the other community's public good, and all individuals in the client community contribute to their own public good, then all individuals in society are linked together in a web of relationships that ensure that neither community can gain from expropriating the other, since what is gained in the transfer of private resources will be lost in the supply of some public good. Cross-community engagement of significant numbers of white individuals at the height of the US civil rights movement, who were nevertheless very much part of the white society, is the picture conjured up here to illustrate how linkages can reduce communal tensions.

But this happy state of affairs is a special case that requires a particular configuration of the relative numbers of core and fringe individuals in the dominant community. Deviations will reintroduce communal tension. Thus, if the wealthy community's fringe is not contributing to its own public good but only to the public good of the other community, so that there is no linkage between core and fringe in the wealthy community, proposals to expropriate the wealthy community will find willing listeners in the less wealthy community. And proposals for wealth transfers from the poorer community to the richer community will always have support in the majority core of the richer community. During British rule in India, a small number of the white ruling community "went native" and not only put value on, but also contributed to, the development of the sense of history and culture of India. But these individuals were few and far between, had little connection to the heart of the community they came from, and were seen as outcasts. There was indeed cross-communal engagement through this fringe as it helped create a new sense of "Indianness" among the Indians, but communal tensions were not thereby reduced. Indians still resented the power and wealth of the white community and were willing, in our terms, to expropriate it.

When the fringe in the richer community free rides on the contributions of the core from its own community, and the poorer community free rides in turn on the former, then, in addition to cross-communal tensions, tensions are generated within each community. The core in each community now has an interest in expropriating its own fringe. These tensions are recounted in the history books and novels of the Empire. The *comprador*, or "collaborationist," Bengali intelligentsia of the early nineteenth-century India, engaged as it was in acquiring and learning the culture of the ruling British, as well as benefiting from the indigenous Bengali identity, was vulnerable to attack from its own conservative core, since (i) it was not contributing significantly to Bengali identity, and (ii) it stood to benefit from further enrichment and consolidation of the British community. Thus, e.g., the Westernized rebel "Young Bengal" of Calcutta were subjected to much scorn, ridicule, and attack in their own community. Similarly, the fringe of the British ruling community were vulnerable to attack from their own core, and were reviled for "going native," since they were contributing to the sense of Indian identity in their own fashion, but were free riding on the contribution of their own core to British identity. These conflicts between British and Indian communities, as well as between core and fringe in each community, during the later period of British rule in India are well depicted, e.g., in E.M. Forster's novel *A Passage to India*.

It should perhaps not be surprising that with community-specific public goods it is difficult to eliminate communal tensions, although the intricate patterns of when and how they emerge as wealth gaps vary produces many surprises. But what of meta-community activities, activities to which all can contribute and from which all can benefit? Varshney (2002) talks of two forms of engagement between communities – "associational" and "everyday." The distinction is that the former requires an organizational setting, a platform on which there is an interaction between the two communities, and he gives many concrete examples. In our terminology, the hope is that if such cross-communal public goods emerge, or are created, they could act to reduce communal tension because now expropriating the other community serves to reduce its capacity to contribute to the public good that both communities value.

But the logic of individual interactions in the supply of the meta-public good, in the presence of interactions on the community-specific goods, and in the context of cross-community difference in wealth, produces an intricate set of patterns. When the two communities are relatively equal in wealth, they are separated at the community level but integrated at the meta-community level. Despite the separation at the community level, in the sense that no individual in either community contributes to the public good of the other community, there is no communal tension, in the sense that there is no incentive for one community to propose an expropriation of the wealth of the other. When both communities contribute to the meta-public good, which happens when they are relatively equal in wealth, communal tensions are minimized. Thus in a multi-ethnic nation, ethnic tensions are greatly reduced when two things happen simultaneously – a strong sense of national identity is developed, and wealth gaps between ethnic groups are reduced. It can be argued that this is the strategy that has been followed successfully in Malaysia and in Singapore. On the other hand, despite attempts at developing a national identity in Indonesia, ethnic tensions have remained strong because of the continuing wide wealth disparities among ethnic groups.

As wealth disparities between communities grow, there comes a point where only the wealthy community contributes to the meta-communal public good, while no individual in either community contributes to the public good of the other community. This state of affairs creates an incentive for each community to expropriate the other. The wealthy community gains resources from the poorer community which was in any case not contributing to the meta-communal public good. The poorer community gains resources, loses some supply of the meta-communal public good, but benefits overall from expropriating the wealthier community. This is an account of ethnic tensions which many will find illustrative of Indonesia.

Further increases in wealth disparities lead to a state of affairs where not only is the wealthy community the sole contributor to the meta-public good, but the fringe individuals in the wealthy community contribute to the public good of the poorer community as well. In this state of patronage, as we have labeled it, there is a possibility that communal tensions will reduce. This will occur if (i) the fringe in the wealthy community contributes to both its own community-specific public good and that of the poorer community, and (ii) the poorer community contributes to its own public good. But outside this special case, which disappears as the wealth distribution gets even more unequal, communal tensions increase with wealth inequality across communities.

The central message from this analysis is the simultaneous importance of two factors – a meta-communal public good, and cross-community equality in wealth. Both are needed in order to eliminate communal conflict. Either on its own is not enough. Equality of wealth on its own will lead to separation of the two communities and communal tension. A meta-communal good with great communal inequality will lead to patronage and communal tension. But equality *and* meta-communal public goods jointly produce a situation of reduced communal tension, in the sense that they eliminate the incentive for individuals in either community to expropriate the wealth of members of the other community.

Purposive creation of meta-community public goods *and* purposive equalization of cross-communal wealth gaps thus holds the key to communal harmony in societies with deep divisions of race, ethnicity, religion, or language. Of course, this analysis only opens up more questions. What exactly is the nature of communal tension, which we have captured simply as the gain from expropriating wealth from the other community? Such expropriation is not costless, and itself involves collective action problems within the community. It will be important to model these costs explicitly to get a better handle on the gains from expropriation, which in turn goes into our concept of communal tension. At the same time, if it was costless to "create" meta-communal public goods, and the return from such creation was a reduction in communal tension, why do we not see so many of these goods that communal tensions are reduced to zero? Clearly, there are costs to the creation of public goods, and these have to be balanced against the benefits. Such an analysis needs to be developed if we are to better understand why we see certain meta-communal public goods and not others (for a start in this direction, see Clark and Kanbur 2002). Finally, we have, of course, abstracted from wealth difference within each of the communities. Examination of the relationship between class and community tensions, an analysis begun in Dasgupta and Kanbur (2001), will merit much closer attention.

Appendix

Proof of Proposition 1. (i) First consider the case where $\lfloor y_{AB}^N, y_{BA}^N = 0 \rfloor$. Then, noting that Nash equilibria must be symmetric, it is easy to check that

$$\forall \alpha \in \{A, B\}, \lVert y_\alpha^N = n_\alpha I_\alpha / (n_\alpha + 1) \rfloor, \text{ and } \lfloor y_\alpha^N \geq k y_\beta^N \rfloor,$$

$$\text{where } \beta \in [\{A, B\} - \{\alpha\}].$$

The required inequality follows. Now suppose, without loss of generality, that $\lfloor y_{BA}^N > 0 \rfloor$. Then $\lfloor y_{AB}^N = 0 \rfloor$ (see Remark 1). It follows that $[k y_B^N \geq y_A^N > n_A I_A / (n_A + 1)]$. Furthermore, $[y_B^N \leq n_B I_B / (n_B + 1)]$. Noting that $n_A = n_B$, part (i) of Proposition 1 follows.

(ii) Suppose now, without loss of generality, that $[I_A < k I_B]$. Then, from Proposition 1(i), either $\lfloor y_{BA}^N > 0 \rfloor$, or $\lfloor y_{AB}^N > 0 \rfloor$. The latter possibility is ruled out by an argument exactly analogous to that presented in the preceding paragraph. □

To prove Proposition 4, we shall use the following result.

Lemma N.1. *Suppose, for some* $\alpha \in \{A, B\}$, $\lfloor y_{\alpha\alpha}^N = 0 \rfloor$. *Then, for* $\beta \in [\{A, B\} - \{\alpha\}]$, $[y_{\beta\beta}^N > 0]$ *if and only if* $\lfloor n_{\bar\beta} > k n_\beta \rfloor$.

Proof of Lemma N.1. Suppose $y_{\beta\beta}^N = 0$. Then we have: $[y_\beta^N = n_\beta I_\beta / (n_\beta + 1)]$, and, (noting that $y_{\alpha\alpha}^N = 0$ by assumption), $[y_\alpha^N = (k n_{\bar\beta} I_\beta) / (n_{\bar\beta} + k)]$. Noting that $k y_\beta^N \geq y_\alpha^N$, we thus get: $\lfloor n_{\bar\beta} \leq k n_\beta \rfloor$. Hence, if $\lfloor n_{\bar\beta} > k n_\beta \rfloor$, then $y_{\beta\beta}^N > 0$. Now suppose $y_{\beta\beta}^N > 0$. Then $[y_\beta^N > n_\beta I_\beta / (n_\beta + 1)]$. However, (noting that $y_{\alpha\alpha}^N = 0$), we have $\lVert I_\beta + y_{\beta\beta}^N + [(n_{\bar\beta} - 1) / n_{\bar\beta}] y_\alpha^N + [(n_{\bar\beta} - 1) / n_{\bar\beta}] y_{\beta\beta}^N \rfloor (2 + k)^{-1} = y_\beta^N \rfloor$, and

$[y_\alpha^N = ky_\beta^N]$, which, together, yield: $[(n_{\bar{\beta}} I_\beta)/(n_{\bar{\beta}} + k) > y_\beta^N]$. Hence, if $y_{\beta\beta}^N > 0$, then $\lfloor n_{\bar{\beta}} > kn_\beta \rfloor$.   □

Proof of Proposition 4. Without loss of generality, suppose $I_B > I_A$. First consider the benchmark case where $I_A = kI_B$. By Proposition 1(i), the communities must be separated in the Nash equilibrium. It can be easily checked that each individual in A will spend an amount $k(I_A + I_B)/(n_A + 1)(1 + k)$ on the public good A, while each individual in B will spend an amount $(I_B + I_A)/(n_B + 1)(1 + k)$ on the public good B. Consider now an income redistribution such that every individual in A loses an amount r, while every individual in B gains this amount (since, by assumption, $n_A = n_B$). By Proposition 1(ii), any such redistribution will turn A into the client of B. The transfer to B can be conceptualized as: (i) a prior gain of $n_B r/n_{\bar{B}}$ by every fringe individual in B, and (ii) a subsequent loss of $rn_B/n_{\bar{B}}$ by every fringe individual in B, with r gained by every core individual in B.

Note first that, if $n_{\bar{B}} > kn_B$, then, for any $0 < r < [k/(n_A + 1)][(I_A + I_B)/(1 + k)]$, $(rn_B/n_{\bar{B}}) < [1/(n_B + 1)][(I_A + I_B)/(1 + k)]$. It immediately follows from the neutrality result that, if $0 < r < [k/(n_A + 1)][(I_A + I_B)/(1 + k)]$, then B will be a compact patron, and A an active client, in the post-redistribution Nash equilibrium. It is easy to check that, if $r \geq [k/(n_A + 1)][(I_A + I_B)/(1 + k)]$, then A must become a passive client. It immediately follows from Lemma N.1 that B must remain compact for such redistributions as well. This completes the proof of part (i) of Proposition 4.

Now suppose $n_{\bar{B}} \leq kn_B$. It is obvious that there must exist $q_1 \in (1/(1 + k), 1)$ such that A would be a passive client community if and only if $I_B \in [q_1(I_A + I_B), (I_A + I_B)]$. That B must be loose for such cases follows from Lemma N.1. Now note that, if $n_{\bar{B}} \leq kn_B$, then, for $r^* = [k/(n_A + 1)][(I_A + I_B)/(1 + k)]$, $(r^* n_B/n_{\bar{B}}) \geq [1/(n_B + 1)][(I_A + I_B)/(1 + k)]$. It immediately follows from the neutrality result for Cournot games of voluntary contributions to public goods that, if $0 < r < [n_{\bar{B}}/n_B][1/(n_B + 1)][(I_A + I_B)/(1 + k)]$, then B will be a compact patron, and A an active client, in the post-redistribution Nash equilibrium. However, if $r \geq [n_{\bar{B}}/n_B][1/(n_B + 1)][(I_A + I_B)/(1 + k)]$, then B must become a loose patron. For values of r sufficiently close to $[n_{\bar{B}}/n_B][1/(n_B + 1)][(I_A + I_B)/(1 + k)]$, A must remain active if $n_{\bar{B}} < kn_B$. Part (ii) of Proposition 4 follows. Lastly, if $n_{\bar{B}} = kn_B$, then for all $r \geq [n_{\bar{B}}/n_B][1/(n_B + 1)][(I_A + I_B)/(1 + k)]$, A must become passive. That B must be a loose patron for these cases follows from Lemma N.1, yielding Part (iii).   □

Proof of Proposition 6. First consider a Nash equilibrium which is connected, and therefore, patronizing (Remark 1). Suppose, without loss of generality, that, in this equilibrium, $y_{AB}^N > 0$. Then $[(z^N/\lambda) \geq y_A^N \geq (y_B^N/k)]$, which implies $[(z^N/\lambda) > y_B^N]$. Now suppose community B contributes to Z. Then $[y_B^N \geq (z^N/\lambda)]$.   □

Acknowledgments

We thank Chris Barrett, Richard Cornes, Junichi Itaya, Daniel Seidmann, and seminar audiences at CSSS Calcutta, Birkbeck, Tulane, and Duke for helpful comments. Financial support from The Pew Charitable Trusts is gratefully acknowledged.

Notes

1 See, e.g., Gurr (1993), Hardin (1995), Uvin (1998), and Esman and Herring (2002).
2 The anthropological literature on community identity is large. Akerlof and Kranton (2000) and Bowles and Gintis (2004) are recent examples of contributions by economists. The link between public goods provision and ethnic divisions has been explored in Alesina *et al.* (1999). There is also a psychological literature on group identity, as exemplified by Wetherell (1996). Hardin (1995) is a recent analytical contribution to issues surrounding identity and group conflict.
3 Exceptions include Kemp (1984), Bergstrom *et al.* (1986), and Cornes and Schweinberger (1996). Some of the formal results presented here are similar to those arrived at in a general theoretical setting by Cornes and Itaya (2003).
4 The restriction on preferences that generates an optimal ratio of 1 : 1 between private consumption and own community's public good consumption is purely for notational simplicity. We can allow any optimal ratio between these two goods without qualitatively altering our results. Separability and homotheticity are not crucial either. In essence, we need two assumptions: given any $\langle y_A, y_B \rangle$ (i) the maximum amount of community A's public good that fringe individuals in A are willing to give away for an additional unit of community B's public good is always *lower* than the corresponding amount for fringe individuals in B, and (ii) the maximum amount of community A's public good that fringe individuals in A are willing to give away for an additional unit of community B's public good is always *higher* than the corresponding amount for core individuals in A, and similarly for community B. These weaker restrictions on preferences, however, make the exposition cumbersome without adding any insight.
5 We leave out the possibility that for some individuals the two public goods are perfect substitutes. This might be the case, e.g., for atheists when communities are defined along religious lines. These "rootless" individuals do not possess any particular community identity in a substantive sense, even though they are born into some particular community. Since they don't belong, they are irrelevant in our present context.
6 If all fringe individuals engage in syncretist activities, then, in such a Nash equilibrium, the marginal rate of substitution between the public goods A and B must be identical for fringe individuals in both communities. However, this would seem to intuitively imply that the community origins of fringe individuals become irrelevant to their sense of identity at the margin. The situation we are focusing on is one instead where individuals always maintain their communal identity, so that, e.g., a fringe Hindu such as Gandhi remains a Hindu nevertheless, even at the margin, and thus different from a fringe Muslim such as Moulana Azad. Formally, this feature is embedded into our model by the assumption that, for any arbitrary (positive) consumption bundle, the amount of community A's public good that fringe individuals in A are willing to give away for an additional unit of community B's public good is always lower than the corresponding amount for fringe individuals in B. See note 4.
7 This generalizes to the case where the communities differ in size. If individuals born into one community have much larger wealth holdings than those born into the other, then this must be compensated by a correspondingly significant numerical advantage on part of the poorer community in a separated equilibrium.

8 Note that, if k is small, i.e., if even fringe individuals in a community have a sharp preference bias against the identity marker of the other community, then a relatively large wealth gap can co-exist with communal separation. Segregated societies such as the American South, apartheid South Africa and Israel would seem to present examples of such "separate but *unequal*" social equilibria.

9 Unless, in the general case (see note 7), the poorer community has a countervailing advantage in numbers.

10 Contributions by "orientalist" historians and archaelogists from Europe to the reconstruction of Asian history in the nineteenth and early twentieth centuries can be interpreted along these lines. See Said (1978, 1993).

11 If the communities are of different size, then, while core individuals in A must necessarily be better off, fringe individuals in A can possibly be worse off. The necessary (but not sufficient) condition for this is $n_A > 2n_B + 1$. Thus, fringe members of A may have an incentive to oppose expropriation of B only when B is numerically much smaller than A. Conversely, fringe members of B may have an incentive to support the expropriation of their own community, or oppose that of the other community, only when A is numerically much smaller than B.

12 This is in line with the fact that many "Orientalist" scholars of European extraction were also staunch imperialists.

13 That client communities are "ungrateful" is a comment often heard from members of the patron community. Rudyard Kipling's notorious poem "The White Man's Burden" provides a succinct expression of this understanding, with its associated strains of exasperated martyrdom: "Take up the White Man's burden-/ And reap his old reward:/ The blame of those ye better, / The hate of those ye guard . . . " (Kipling 1996, p. 18). Kipling wrote the poem in 1899 following the colonization of the Philippines by the United States.

14 Dasgupta and Kanbur (2001) and Cornes and Sandler (2000) discuss related cases where individuals directly *lose* wealth from redistribution, but nevertheless benefit overall (because of the additional public goods provision generated by redistribution).

15 The nineteenth-century Indian poet Mirza Galib, himself a fringe Muslim, captured well the dual and self-contradictory responses of fringe individuals: "Eeman mujhey rokey hai jo kheenchey hai mujhey kufr/ Kaba mere peechey hai kaleesa mere agey" "If faith checks me, paganism attracts,/ Kaba is behind me, a temple in front" (trans. Joshi 1998, Couplet 87).

16 This is an immediate implication of the well-known neutrality result for Cournot games of voluntary contributions to public goods. See Bergstrom *et al.* (1986) and Cornes and Sandler (1996). Bernheim and Bagwell (1988) present a similar result in the context of interlinked "dynastic" families.

17 Liberal white "Third Way" politicians in the United States and United Kingdom often project "cultural understanding," i.e., individual syncretism, as a key strategy for reducing social tensions. Our analysis suggests this strategy would be ineffective unless associated with other measures that reduce the wealth gap between white and non-white communities. Perhaps paradoxically, this multi-culturalist strategy would also be ineffective if the wealth gap is entirely eliminated. Gitlin (1995) provides an insightful account of social tensions generated by "multiculturalist" identity politics in contemporary America.

18 "The identification of the citizen with the republic as a common enterprise is essentially the recognition of a common good" (Taylor 1995, pp. 191–2). The British Conservative politician Norman Tebbit once famously demanded of British South Asians that they actively support the English national cricket team against their Indian or Pakistani rivals.

19 Note that the claims stated in Proposition 6, Remark 3, and Remark 4 are all valid irrespective of the numerical sizes of the two communities.

20 This result can be easily generalized, at the cost of some notational complexity, to cover the possibility of the two communities being dissimilar numerically.

References

Akerlof, George A. and Kranton, Rachel E. (2000) "Economics and Identity," *QJE*, 115 (August): 715–53.

Alesina, Alberto, Baqir, Reza, and Easterly, William (1990) "Public Goods and Ethnic Divisions," *QJE*, 114 (November): 1243–84.

Bergstrom, T.C., Blume, Larry, and Varian, Hal (1986) "On the Private Provision of Public Goods," *J. Public Econ.*, 29 (February): 25–49.

Bernheim, B. Douglas and Bagwell, Kyle (1988) "Is Everything Neutral?" *JPE*, 96 (April): 308–38.

Bowles, Samuel and Gintis, Herbert (2004) "Persistent Parochialism: Trust and Exclusion in Ethnic Networks," *J. Econ. Behav. Organ.*, 55 (September): 1–23.

Clark, Simon and Kanbur, Ravi (2002) "Samuelson Machines and the Optimal Public Private Mix." Working Paper No. 31/02 (October). Ithaca, NY: Dept. App. Econ. Management, Cornell Univ.

Cornes, Richard and Itaya, Junichi (2003) "Models with Two or More Public Goods." Discussion Paper No. 03/21 (October). Nottingham: Sch. Econ., Univ. Nottingham.

Cornes, Richard and Sandler, Todd (1996) *The Theory of Externalities, Public Goods and Club Goods*. 2nd edn. Cambridge: Cambridge Univ. Press.

——(2000) "Pareto-Improving Redistribution and Pure Public Goods," *German Econ. Rev.*, 1 (May): 169–86.

Cornes, Richard and Schweinberger, Albert S. (1996) "Free Riding and the Inefficiency of the Private Production of Pure Public Goods," *Canadian J. Econ.*, 29 (February): 70–91.

Dasgupta, I. and Kanbur, R. (2001) "Class, Community, Inequality." Working Paper No. 24/01 (December). Ithaca, NY: Dept. App. Econ. Management, Cornell Univ.

——(2002) "How Workers Get Poor Because Capitalists Get Rich: A General Equilibrium Model of Labor Supply, Community and the Class Distribution of Income." Working Paper No. 16/02 (June). Ithaca, NY: Dept. App. Econ. Management, Cornell Univ.

Esman, Milton and Herring, Ronald (eds) (2002) *Carrots, Sticks and Ethnic Conflicts: Rethinking Development Assistance*. Ann Arbor, MI: Univ. Michigan Press.

Gitlin, Todd (1995) *The Twilight of Common Dreams: Why America is Wracked by Culture Wars*. New York: Metropolitan Books.

Gurr, Ted R. (1993) *Minorities at Risk: A Global View of Ethnopolitical Conflicts*. Washington, DC: U.S. Institute of Peace Press.

Hardin, Russell (1995) *One For All: The Logic of Group Conflict*. Princeton, NJ: Princeton Univ. Press.

Joshi, Umesh (1998) *Galib: The Man and His Couplets*. Delhi: Variety Book Depot.

Kemp, M.C. (1984) "A Note on the Theory of International Transfers," *Econ. Letters*, 14 (January): 259–62.

Kipling, Rudyard (1996) *If*. London: Phoenix Paperback.

Said, Edward (1978) *Orientalism*. New York: Random House.

——(1993) *Culture and Imperialism*. New York: Knopf.

Taylor, Charles (1995) *Philosophical Arguments*. Cambridge, MA: Harvard Univ. Press.

Uvin, Peter (1998) *Aiding Violence: The Development Enterprise in Rwanda*. West Hartford, CT: Kumarian Press.

Varshney, Ashustosh (2002) *Ethnic Conflict and Civic Life: Hindus and Muslims in India*. New Haven, CT: Yale Univ. Press.

Wetherell, Margaret (1996) "Group Conflict and the Social Psychology of Racism," In Margaret Wetherell (ed.). *Group Conflict and the Social Psychology of Racism*. Thousand Oaks, CA: Sage Publications.

7 The extended family system and market interactions

Karla Hoff and Arijit Sen

The question of the relation between the profit motive and social customs is a very old one in economics. In one view, that of standard neoclassical economics, social customs do not play any independent role. While different cultures are characterized by different regularities in behavior, these regularities reflect different conditions and change when it becomes an advantage to everyone to change them. "Social customs follow the money," as some sociologists put it.

But there is another view according to which social customs that are harmful to every individual can nonetheless fail to be overturned by self-interest. This view rests on two points. First, social customs can affect economic outcomes. (For example, the custom of treating people according to a norm of fairness affects economic performance because it is costly, or simply infeasible, to specify all possible outcomes of an interaction.) Second, individuals' choices of good and bad customs are influenced by the choices of others in their social network: good customs may spread; so may bad. The present chapter inscribes itself in the line of this second view.[1]

The social custom that this chapter considers is the *extended family system* (*kin system*, for short). By definition, it is "a system of shared rights and obligations encompassing a large number of near and distant relatives" (Wolf 1955). We model it as a *social contract* for mutual insurance within an extended family. We think of the kin system as a pre-existing network into which new market opportunities have to be fit and address the question, can the kin system outlast its usefulness?

Arnott and Stiglitz (1991) show that one possibility is that an informal insurance arrangement mitigates moral hazard problems in the formal insurance market and so raises welfare; the arrangement exploits monitoring devices not available to the market. Another possibility is that an informal insurance arrangement exacerbates moral hazard problems and lowers welfare; the arrangement provides individuals too much insurance and thus lessens care to avoid accidents. In this chapter, we show that the latter concern about the worsening of moral hazard in formal markets applies much more generally:[2] the kin system can exacerbate moral hazard problems in markets that have nothing to do with insurance. In markets where monitoring and utilization are costly, the kin system can lead to lower wages, blocked employment possibilities, or higher prices charged to individuals in subcultures characterized by the kin system. It can thus change the way an entire subculture, with a pre-existing kin system, becomes integrated into a market economy.

The central argument of this chapter is that the kin system provides individuals with incentives that they would not otherwise have to exploit the asymmetric information in markets. One example is *nepotism*. Once a member of a kin group is in a managerial position with power to recruit and promote, other members of the kin group exert pressure on him for favors and can enter into side-contracts through which transfers required under the kin system are fulfilled in-kind. Labor market evidence supports the view that ethnic loyalties introduce new constraints into organizational performance (Collier and Garg 1999). Another example occurs where an individual in a kin group who becomes rich enough to leave his village and rent a city apartment fulfills his obligations to his kin at least partly through sharing his home.[3] These behaviors impose costs on the employer and landlord. Kin groups entail a web of reciprocal obligations that can be a menace in modern, market-based settings because they aggravate the problem of moral hazard. As a result, individuals from a subculture in which the kin system is widespread may find that they face less favorable terms in the market than individuals from subcultures in which the kin system is not practiced.

The idea that the kin system can distort behavior in markets has long been recognized. As evidence of this point, consider the following passages from pioneering books in development economics:[4]

> Where the extended family system exists, any member of the family whose income increases may be besieged by correspondingly increased demands for support from a large number of distant relations . . . A strong sense of family obligation . . . may cause a man to appoint relatives to jobs for which they are unsuited . . . it may be fear, rather than affection, which drives them to nepotism.
>
> (Lewis 1955, p. 114)

> Demands to provide jobs for a wide range of kin, irrespective of their qualifications, and requests for cash donations or gifts of varying amounts from a stream of 'visitors' are probably the most frequent claims [on businessmen in Africa].
>
> (Kennedy 1988, p. 169)

which leads to a predictable response:

> [The extended family system] adds to the reluctance of foreign firms to employ members of the local population in positions of trust and responsibility.
>
> (Bauer and Yamey 1957, p. 66)

But there does not exist a theory of equilibrium outcomes when agents simultaneously interact through the kin system and through the market, and without a theory it is difficult to make welfare evaluations of the system.

This chapter offers a simple theory. In this theory, families in some subcultures have the ability to choose whether or not to participate in an extended family system. In making that choice, they take the market environment as given (since a single family is only a small part of the subculture). But in response to the informal insurance arrangements of the kin groups in a subculture, market opportunities do change. An individual's subculture conditions his opportunities in the market. We show that the kin system – which may have had decisive importance for survival in high-risk peasant societies – may be harmful once a market system is created.

We then distinguish two sets of forces that may cause a dysfunctional kin system to persist. One set of forces operates at the level of the individual. An individual might want to commit to an employer or landlord that he will not participate in the kin system. But if the only means to do that is social assimilation to another subculture, the cost to the individual may be too high. Another set of forces, which depend on collective action, are, paradoxically, improvements in future prospects for earning income that would benefit the best of the kin group and cause them to exit. Their exit would make the rest of the kin group worse off. When abilities to profit from future opportunities differ, improvements in future average utility prospects may trigger collective opposition to the new prospects, a form of status quo bias.[5]

The idea that the group may vigorously oppose a new opportunity that selects the best from the kin group is captured by Carol Stack (1974) in *All our Kin*. This study of a poor African-American kin group in a US city shows that the group exerts various forms of social control to reduce the ability of members to exit. The following passage reports details of a woman's story that were substantiated by Stack's discussions with many other people:

> Me and Otis could be married, but they all ruined that. Aunt Augusta told Magnolia that he was no good. Magnolia was the fault of it too. They don't want to see me married! Magnolia knows that it be money getting away from her. I couldn't spend the time with her and the kids and be giving her the money that I do now. I'd have my husband to look after. I couldn't go where she wants me to go. I couldn't come every time she calls me, like if Calvin took sick or the kids took sick, or if she took sick. That's all the running I do now. I couldn't do that. You think a man would put up with as many times as I go over their house in a cab, giving half my money to her all the time? That's the reason why they don't want me married. You think a man would let Aunt Augusta come into the house and take food out of the icebox from his kids? ...

> (Carol Stack 1974, p. 114)

The remainder of this chapter is divided into three sections. The next section provides evidence for the view of culture as a control mechanism, one that could permit people in an extended family to enter into a social contract for mutual insurance. Section 7.2 develops, by means of examples, aspects of the moral hazard problem that the kin system may create in labor and housing markets. Section 7.3 analyzes forces that may cause a dysfunctional kin system to persist.

7.1   Culture as a control mechanism

According to Clifford Geertz, "culture is best seen not as complexes of concrete behavior patterns . . . but as a set of control mechanisms – plans, recipes, rules, instructions . . . for the governing of behavior" (quoted in Becker 1996, p. 16). Our work builds on Geertz' view of culture. In some cultures, a use to which such control mechanisms are put is the enforcement of egalitarian insurance arrangements. According to Scott (1976) and Platteau (1991, 1996), in cultures where kin-based mutual insurance arrangements are important, including cultures in Africa, the Philippines, and Vietnam, egalitarian norms and ethical values prescribing the right to subsistence are widespread. Sanctions for those who shirk the obligations of the kin group system may entail economic consequences (loss of employment or destruction of property), stigma, social ostracism, or violence (see, e.g., Sahlins 1965, pp. 208–13; Colson 1947, pp. 44–50). Religion can also enforce social obligations, as the case below describes:

> [I]n a celebrated Kenyan court case, a successful Luo man left a will specifying that he was to be buried by his wife in Nairobi rather than by his kin group in his home district. The kin challenged the right of the wife to conduct such a burial. The Kenyan high court overturned the will, siding with the kin group. This decision was important because the kin group's ultimate sanction against recalcitrant members is to bury them near their ancestors, who can be expected to exact retribution. The Kenyan high court was upholding the social obligations inherent in kin group membership.
>
> (Collier 2001, p. 298)

Modern social groups can also *create* such control mechanisms. In the extended family system described by Stack (1974) in *All our Kin*, African–American households in a low-income community in a US city enter into temporary child exchange as a symbol of mutual trust, and the bonds that develop between adults and children reinforce the adults' incentive to honor their commitments to the extended family (pp. 28–9). This network shares the central features that we take to define a kin system: it is a durable, kin-centered, nonmarket insurance arrangement, and it is enforced through social control mechanisms.

7.2   Market discrimination as a response to the kin system

The population is divided into two groups. The first group is a single kin system – each member of this group will be called a *K*-individual. The second group is a set of "independent" individuals who are not bound by any kinship ties – the *I*-individuals.

We posit that each *K*-individual is committed to abide by the following *mutual assistance norm:* if the individual gets a white-collar job in the modern sector, then he has to help raise the well-being of one (or more) pre-identified member(s) of the kin group.[6]

Our purpose in this section is to address the following questions: (a) When a *K*-individual obtains a good job in the modern sector, will he find it privately optimal to meet his mutual assistance obligation *in cash* or *in kind*? (b) If he finds it optimal to make in-kind transfers, will such behavior be socially inefficient?

We will present two examples that will clarify the conditions under which a *K*-individual will make in-kind transfers that will have adverse consequences for the parties with whom he contracts in the market. We will then conclude that if they can identify him as a *K*-individual at the time of contracting, they will be reluctant to enter into a contract on the same terms as for an *I*-individual, and that this will constitute a barrier to a *K*-individual's entry into the modern-sector labor market.

7.2.1 *Example 1 – nepotism*

In this example, an agent undertakes a productive activity on behalf of a principal and in doing so, hires an assistant. By *nepotism*, we mean favoritism toward relatives in hiring at a cost in terms of the quality of employees. Some nepotism can be prevented by rules barring the hiring of family members. But when employees have obligations to an extended family, it is difficult for an employer to identify nepotism because members of the group may include distant relatives.

7.2.1.1 *The model*

Consider a sector in which the production process requires a senior worker and a production team consisting of many junior workers. Both jobs are unionized: the senior worker has to be paid a base salary of $\bar{w}$ and the junior worker has to be paid $\underline{w}$, with $\bar{w} > \underline{w}$. There are many firms and in some of them, the "match quality" among the workers in the production team affects the level of output. If a vacancy on the team is filled with a junior worker who is a good match, output is equal to $\bar{\pi}$, and if it is bad, output is equal to $\underline{\pi}$, where $\bar{\pi} > \underline{\pi}$. Only the senior worker can ascertain the quality of the match, and so the responsibility of selecting the junior worker is delegated to him. If the senior worker picks an arbitrary individual (or his nephew) to be the junior worker, then the match quality will be good with probability $\lambda \in \{0, 1\}$. On the other hand, if the senior worker expends search effort c – e.g., by holding interviews and conducting a trial run with a prospective new employee and the rest of the team, then the senior worker will find a good match with probability 1.

Because the senior worker has to be paid a baseline wage of $\bar{w}$ whether or not he searches, the firm may institute a bonus scheme, where the senior worker is paid $\bar{w} + \beta$ when $\pi = \bar{\pi}$ in order to induce him to search for a good match. We now characterize the optimal bonus scheme for an *I*-agent and a *K*-agent.

We write an individual's utility function as $u(y) - e$, where e is the effort expended in searching (so e is equal to c or 0). Under a bonus scheme β, an

I-agent will search if and only if

$$u(\bar{w} + \beta) - c \geq \lambda u(\bar{w} + \beta) + [1 - \lambda]u(\bar{w})$$

i.e., he will search if and only if the bonus is at least β^I, where β^I solves the above with equality. The firm's expected payoff is thus $\bar{\pi} - \bar{w} - \beta^I$ if it offers that bonus scheme, and $\lambda\bar{\pi} + [1 - \lambda]\underline{\pi} - \bar{w}$ if it does not offer a bonus scheme. We assume that λ is sufficiently small and $\bar{\pi} - \underline{\pi}$ sufficiently large that the former exceeds the latter. Thus, if the firm hires an I-agent as the senior worker, the optimal wage contract is to offer him a bonus β^I when output is high.

Now consider a K-individual as a senior worker. The moment that this individual is chosen (at random, since all K-individuals are *ex ante* identical) for the job at $\bar{w}$, that determines the level of his transfer to his kin group. We assume that the transfer is determined by his permanent wage $\bar{w}$ and not by any subsequent bonus that he might receive (i.e., we assume that firm output is not common knowledge). We also assume that $\bar{w}$ is sufficiently high in relation to the individual's *ex ante* expected income that to obtain a job as a senior worker puts him near the top of the income distribution in the extended family.

Every K-individual has a nephew in his kin group who, on his own, has a probability $\mu < 1$ of getting a job as a junior worker. If the K-agent who is a senior worker engages in nepotism by giving his nephew the junior job, that is construed by the extended family as making an in-kind transfer of value $[1 - \mu]\underline{w}$. We now define two variables: let τ denote the transfer owed to his kin group, and let δ denote the net amount of the in-kind transfer that the senior worker who hired his nephew would owe to his kin group:

$$\delta \equiv \tau - [1 - \mu]\underline{w}.$$

Now consider a K-agent who has been hired as a senior worker. He will obtain utility

$$u(\bar{w} + \beta - \tau) - c,$$

if he searches, and expected utility

$$\lambda u(\bar{w} + \beta - \delta) + [1 - \lambda]u(\bar{w} - \delta),$$

if he does not search and engages in nepotism. Thus, the minimal bonus that induces him to search is β^K, such that[7]

$$u(\bar{w} + \beta^K - \tau) - c = \lambda u(\bar{w} + \beta^K - \delta) + [1 - \lambda]u(\bar{w} - \delta).$$

Note that if δ is arbitrarily close to zero, then evaluated at $\beta = \beta^I$, the left-hand side is less than the right-hand side. This implies that for δ small, $\beta^K > \beta^I$. This means that when a K-agent can meet a large part of his kin obligations by nepotism, he has to be given a larger bonus than an *I*-agent in order to induce him to search for a "good match."

To summarize, the following inequalities hold for δ sufficiently small: (a) Hiring an *I*-manager with bonus β^I *is preferred to* hiring anyone with no bonus scheme, and (b) Hiring an *I*-manager with bonus β^I *is preferred to* hiring a *K*-manager with bonus β^K. It follows that if a *K*-manager can fulfill a sufficiently large part of his transfer obligations to his kin group by nepotism, no firm will hire a *K*-individual in lieu of an *I*-individual.

7.2.2   Example 2 – home-sharing

In the preceding example, an agent undertook production activities on behalf of a principal. In the next example, an agent rents a durable good from a principal. We focus on housing, but similar problems arise for a principal who rents any durable good for which both utilization and monitoring are costly.

7.2.2.1   The model

We employ the simplest model in which moral hazard is present. There are two locations, the city and the surrounding villages. In the city, there are a set of housing units. A set of agents holds jobs in the city. A requirement of the job is that the job-holder rent a housing unit in the city. (For example, punctual attendance may require that the individual has assured housing near his job.) The agent's utility function is

$$u(m) - v(n),$$

where m is the numeraire good and n is the number of residents, in addition to the household, who share the housing unit. The functions u and v are increasing and strictly concave, and $v(\cdot)$ denotes the agent's disutility from sharing his apartment with kin outside his household.[8]

To a landlord, the opportunity cost of renting a housing unit is (i) the opportunity cost, F, of his fixed capital and the depreciation (wear and tear) when the home is occupied by one household, and (ii) the additional depreciation $C(n)$ when the renting household has n kin members sharing the unit. We take $C(n)$ to be an increasing convex function. While a landlord would like to specify the value of n in the rental contract, we assume that is not possible. For example, the law may bar the landlord from making spot checks of the apartment at night. Thus, a household can only be charged a lump-sum rental rate, denoted by R, independent of how many kin members it shares the unit with. (We address the issue of determining the value of R below.)

Access to housing in the city is valuable to someone who lives in a village. For example, it could save a student the cost of commuting to a school in the city, or increase an individual's probability of finding a city job. Let H denote the monetary value of access to city housing, e.g., a place on the floor of an apartment.

Consider a K-agent who rents a housing unit at R, has realized an income y_i, and has to make a transfer τ to his extended kin. In general, τ could be negative or positive: any transfers that the household makes in-kind could be compensated through transfers from the extended family system. Let m_i denote the own consumption of the numeraire good, and let m_k denote transfers (which also could be negative or positive) of the numeraire good to kin. The agent's problem is:

$$\underset{\{n,m_i,m_k\}}{\text{Max}} \ u(m_i) - v(n),$$

subject to

$$y_i \geq m_i + m_k + R \quad \text{(income constraint)}$$
$$\tau \leq m_k + nH \quad \text{(transfer constraint)}$$

or, equivalently,[9]

$$\underset{n}{\text{Max}} \ u(y - R - \tau + nH) - v(n).$$

His choice of n solves

$$u'(m_i)H = v'(n).$$

This equation means that the individual will increase the number of kin members whom he shelters until the marginal transfer benefit is equal to the marginal disutility of sharing his apartment with another member of his extended kin. Since there is a benefit to the extended kin to be housed in the city, the left-hand side is strictly positive. Thus, for $v'(0)$ small enough, a tenant in an extended family system will always share his housing unit: $n^* > 0$.

We have implicitly made a stark assumption. Only a K-agent makes side-contracts for use of his rented home. We can easily relax that assumption. Our qualitative result requires only that the extended family system increases the "gains from trade" from such a side-contract. That effect could spring from many sources: e.g., an explicit contract in which a renter sublets housing could be illegal and therefore unenforceable; the extended family system may create bonds that make sharing one's apartment less burdensome ($v(n)$ shifts down for a K-agent); or the fact that an extended family system creates multiplex bonds and limited privacy among a wide group of extended kin increases the scope for punishing an individual who harms his host.

We are now ready to consider the landlord's problem in determining R. In a competitive market with perfect foresight, when a landlord rents to a K-agent with income y_i, the landlord will recognize that such an agent will share the housing unit with n^* kin members. The competitive rent that the landlord will charge is

$$R = F + C(n^*).$$

Thus, although the K-tenant does not directly pay the marginal depreciation cost of sharing, he indirectly pays the cost of increased utilization through the higher rental rate.

In general, when landlords do not have precise information as to whether their potential tenants are K-agents or not, they will use membership in a subculture as an *indicator*; the rental rate will be conditioned on subculture. If $\bar{n}$ is the average value of n for an agent in subculture s', from which K-individuals are drawn then a landlord will wish to condition the rent on the tenant's subculture (denoted $R_{s'}, R_s$), and the equilibrium rental prices will satisfy

$$R_{s'} - R_s = C(\bar{n}).$$

Although the tenant chooses n on the basis of zero marginal costs, he pays the true costs in the form of higher contractual rents, as shown in this section. In aggregate, renters in the subculture bear the full social cost of the use of housing. But since they face a distortion in the marginal cost of housing, the allocation is inefficient. The break-even condition of the landlords requires that $R_{s'}$ be varied to satisfy

$$dR_{s'} = C'd\bar{n}.$$

The utility of a tenant who is a K-agent is $u(y - R - \tau + nH) - v(n)$. The change in that utility level for the typical agent as n varies is

$$u'[Hd\bar{n} - C'd\bar{n}] - v'd\bar{n},$$

which, for the tenant who chooses to shelter the average number of kin ($n^* = \bar{n}$), is equal to

$$-C'd\bar{n} < 0.$$

The renter shares housing with too many kin members; the marginal utility of taking on the last kin member is negative. The implication is that the practice of transfers in-kind rather than in cash must generate utility losses for some K-agents in the economy.

If price discrimination on the basis of the renter's subculture is prohibited, then (since the break-even price for a K-individual exceeds that for an I-individual), no landlord will be willing to rent to a K-individual.[10]

7.3   Can a dysfunctional custom persist?

In this section, we argue that the social custom of the extended family system can persist even when the custom lowers welfare. We begin with three definitions. By a *subculture*, we mean a set of shared concepts, beliefs, and commitment devices of a group of individuals exhibiting physical markers, speech, or other behaviors that distinguish the group from others. Let s' denote a subculture with control mechanisms to enforce commitments for mutual insurance within an extended family. Let s denote another subculture in which the set of shared concepts does not permit such enforcement.

In this section, we will briefly consider three cases, in turn:

1   The individual can change his behavior, but not his subculture.
2   The individual can change his behavior *and* assimilate to a different subculture.
3   The subculture can take a collective action to reinforce adherence to custom.

7.3.1   Group reputation

We first assume that an individual's subculture is based only on birth and hence is non-elective. An individual of subculture s' has a choice whether or not to participate in the extended family system. That choice is known within his subculture, but it cannot be credibly signaled to others in the market economy.

Let $U_{s'}^K$ denote his expected utility if he participates in the extended family system, and let $U_{s'}^I$ denote his expected utility if he does not. If

$$U_s^I > U_{s'}^K > U_{s'}^I,$$

then the individual in subculture s' will choose to participate in an extended family system, even though, could he have shed his social identity as a member of a subculture with the extended family system, he would have been better off. The extended family system that was once optimal is no longer optimal, but is maintained because individuals cannot signal to the market that they do not participate in the extended family system. Not being able to signal this, they are better off belonging to an extended family system than not. And thus the group reputation for sharing is inherited by each new generation in the subculture.[11] A population's vulnerability to risk leads to a social custom, the extended family system, and that custom may outlast its usefulness and perpetuate poverty when valuable market opportunities emerge.

7.3.2   Exit costs

Next consider a case more supportive of change. Suppose that an individual can signal that he is not part of an extended family system – e.g., by socially assimilating to another subculture by adopting its religion and language. Platteau (2000) argues that this process has occurred all over the world, but that in some highly traditional societies,

> principles of equity are so adverse to change [that] a single individual, even when endowed with special qualities and powerful psychological resources, cannot successfully defy the conventions of the society. He will unavoidably ... be squashed by various forms of opposition, especially when his economic success depends on his behavior as a hard-nosed businessman in dealing with fellow tribesmen. To break through, he needs the protection afforded by the deviant actions of a *sufficient number* of other innovators in his locality. Rising economic opportunities alone will usually not suffice to generate dynamic entrepreneurs in the absence of *a critical mass of cultural energies harnessed towards countering social resistance* ... Experience shows that a critical mass of return migrants who have been exposed to outside opportunities for a sufficiently long time are likely to form a core dissident group able to call customary norms and values into question. They may then act as role models dragging other villagers into opposition ...
>
> (Platteau 2000, emphasis added)[12]

Let ρ be the fraction of the population of subculture s' that does not participate in the extended family system. Let $U_s^I - E(\rho)$ be the utility associated with signaling that one does not participate in the extended family system. The first term reflects the individual's access to the market opportunities of an individual of subculture s, and the second term is the cost of defying customary norms (E stands for "exit"), which is decreasing in the fraction of the subculture that defines the convention: $E' < 0$. Let $U_{s'}^K(\rho)$ be the utility associated with participation in the kin system. This utility is decreasing in ρ since the fewer the participants, the more limited are the gains from pooling risks.[13] Each individual chooses the behavior that yields him greater utility, taking ρ and the market prices associated with subcultures s' and s as given. If most people choose to participate in the extended family system, the insurance benefits may be high and the cost of defying the social norms will also be high. But if most people defy the convention, then both the insurance benefits of participation and the cost of exit will be low, rendering that also an equilibrium. An interior equilibrium (where ρ is between 0 and 1) is a fraction ρ^* that solves the equation

$$U_s^I - E(\rho) = U_{s'}^K(\rho),$$

and there may be multiple equilibria. "Corner" equilibria where all agents make the same choice may also exist – one entailing full participation if

$$U_s^I - E(0) < U_{s'}^K(0),$$

and another entailing no participation if[14]

$$U_s^I - E(1) > U_{s'}^K(1).$$

Thus, both the cases where all participate in the kin system and where all exit the kin system may be Nash equilibria; and the traditional solution concepts in game theory do not provide a basis for determining the circumstances under which each will result in an equilibrium. Evolutionary game theory models, pioneered by the theoretical biologist Maynard Smith (1982), and adapted to describe the evolution of human conventions among populations of boundedly rational individuals by Axelrod (1984), among others, shed light on this question. A slight variant of this model can be used to explore the idea that payoff differentials will exert evolutionary pressure on the population composition in a setting similar to ours.[15]

Consider the population of subculture s'. Assume that the K- and I-strategies are choices that an individual will adopt for the current period. After each period, he observes with noise the payoffs to the alternative strategy. Because of the presence of noise, he may not always make the correct decision and the likelihood that he makes the correct one is larger, the larger the payoff gap between the two strategies. This implies that the rate of change of the population composition ($d\rho/dt$) will be faster, the greater the gap in the payoffs to the two strategies.

We can now ask whether an outcome, e.g., universal adherence to the kin system in any given period, is "evolutionarily stable," in the sense that if all members of the population adopt it, then no mutant strategy could invade the population.[16] Suppose that exposure to modern influences causes a perturbation (a "mutation") in the initial outcome so that now a proportion m of subculture s' are I-individuals, and a proportion $1 - m$ are K-individuals (m is for mutant). Then $\rho = 0$ (all participate in the kin system in a given period) is an evolutionarily stable outcome if there exist values for m sufficiently small that the proportion of K-individuals approaches 1 as the number of periods over which the society evolves approaches infinity. The set of points $m_0 \in [0, m^*)$ such that a trajectory through m_0 approaches 0 is called the *basin of attraction* of the outcome where all participate in the kin system.

Figure 7.1 depicts the case where the strategy that would be best for all, if all adopted it, is the I-strategy. But the I-strategy gives payoffs lower than the K-strategy if most individuals do the K-strategy, because social sanctions for exiting the traditional kin system are high. The basin of attraction of the K-strategy is $[0, m^*)$. Any mutation above m^* is in the basin of attraction of the I-strategy. The proportion $\rho = m^*$ is also an equilibrium, but it is unstable since

$$\frac{d}{d\rho}\{U_{s'}^K(\rho) - [U_s^I - E(\rho)]\} < 0.$$

In words, the expected return to the K-strategy relative to the I-strategy is falling everywhere as more exit the kin system. Since the payoffs to the two strategies are equal at $\rho = m^*$, the returns to the I-strategy must be superior to the returns

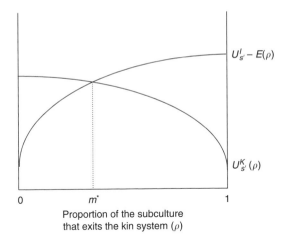

$U_{s'}^I - E(\rho)$

$U_{s'}^K (\rho)$

0   m^* 1
Proportion of the subculture
that exits the kin system (ρ)

Figure 7.1 The basin of attraction of the kin system is $[0, m^*)$.

to the *K*-strategy for values of ρ above m^*. Thus, more will exit. There are three equilibrium population fractions, $0, m^*$, and 1, and only the corner equilibria are evolutionarily stable.

This simple model provides a framework for thinking about changes in initial conditions and policy that over a long period of time may have a large effect on a subculture. Drivers of cultural transformation include technological innovation and the expansion of the market system, which would tend to increase the market opportunities foregone as a result of the extended family system. Factors that lower the return to participation in the extended family system include a fall in non-covariate risk (e.g., a fall in the risk of disease), an increase in mobility that raises the cost of enforcing the kin system, and exposure to new ideas that weakens the hold of traditional norms and religious beliefs that support the informal insurance arrangement. Figure 7.2 illustrates the basic insight: any increase in the payoff to the *I*-strategy relative to the *K*-strategy increases the basin of attraction of the *I*-strategy equilibrium.

7.3.3 *Collective conservatism*

Up to now we have abstracted from differences in the ability to benefit from market opportunities. It is plausible that in practice, such differences are large. Improvements in opportunities to earn income in the modern sector will tend to attract the best of the kin group and cause them to exit. Their exit would make the rest of the kin group worse off. It might thus trigger opposition to the new opportunities from the extended family. The extended family system might become an active instrument of stagnation – an instrument that it would be in no one's interest to wield absent the tight network of mutual dependence which the extended

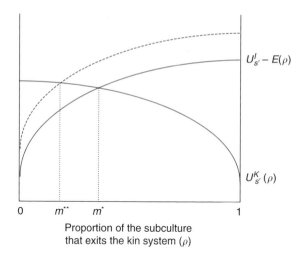

$U^I_{s'} - E(\rho)$

$U^K_{s'}(\rho)$

0   m^{**} m^* 1

Proportion of the subculture
that exits the kin system (ρ)

Figure 7.2 An increase in market opportunities foregone as a result of the kin system
decreases the basin of attraction of the kin system is $[0, m^*)$ to $[0, m^{**})$.

family system creates. This is an example of what Kuran (1995) calls "collective
conservatism." A formal analysis is in Hoff and Sen (in print).

7.4   Conclusion

In this chapter, we developed a set of simple models of the extended family system
as a nonmarket insurance arrangement that is enforceable in some subcultures but
not in others. By widening the scope for side-contracting among individuals in a kin
group, the extended family system can exacerbate problems of moral hazard in all
markets with asymmetric information. Thus, individuals from different subcultures
may face quite different market opportunities. The chapter offers a new perspective
on the difficulties of the transition to a market-based economy for a subculture
initially characterized by the extended family system.

A subculture that has mechanisms to enforce insurance arrangements might
also have the potential to use these mechanisms – information sharing, social
sanctions, and norms – to reduce opportunism in lending and productive activities
jointly undertaken within the extended family. Whereas this chapter has emphasized the adverse effects of the extended family system on the efficiency of market
interactions and, as discussed, there is little evidence of positive effects of the
extended family system on productive activities even of family-owned firms in
Africa, it is widely argued that in East Asia the extended family system has spurred
entrepreneurship. The question of how the extended family system may evolve
in response to the new economic opportunities is one of several difficult issues
regarding the effect of the culture on economic development on which this chapter
makes only a start.

Acknowledgments

We thank Larry Blume, Quy-Toan Do, Maitreesh Ghatak, Vijayendra Rao, and workshop participants at Cornell, the Santa Fe Institute, and the World Bank for helpful comments.

Notes

 1 Studies of dysfunctional social institutions include Akerlof (1976) (the caste system), Greif (1994) (collectivist enforcement), Young (1998) (an evolutionary approach to the emergence of customs), and Mahoney and Sanchirico (2001) (an accessible, non-technical review of the evolutionary approach).
 2 We do not focus in this chapter on the former concern, namely, that the willingness of members of an extended family system to pool risk may *mitigate* moral hazard in markets because, e.g., it elicits peer monitoring. Research on the nineteenth century US and on developing countries supports this thesis for capital markets (e.g., Lamoreaux 1994; Fafchamps 2002), but the evidence is mixed for the ongoing operations of family-owned firms. For example, Grazer's (2001) study of manufacturing firms in Ghana finds that relatives are not clearly more productive than non-relatives.
 3 In urban apartments in developing countries, it is common for an entire bank of mail boxes to display not a single name. The usual explanation is that people fear unending demands to provide shelter to a large number of distant relations, and so try to reveal where they live only to a chosen few.
 4 These passages and other similar ones are cited in Platteau (2000, pp. 20–2).
 5 A survey of sources of such bias is Kuran (1988).
 6 We do not explicitly model how such a mutual assistance rule is enforced. It could be self-enforcing in a scenario of repeated interactions, or it could be enforced by the kin-group by threats of social sanctions, as discussed above.
 7 We abstract from all other features of the relationship between the senior worker and his nephew that could affect performance. For example, shared information within an extended family could lower search costs or raise the likelihood (λ) of a good match even without search, while the bonds of kinship could have an ambiguous effect on output – either lowering it because discipline would be harder to impose, or raising it because, when people trust each other, communication and transaction costs are reduced.
 8 For simplicity, we treat n as a continuous variable.
 9 The constraints always bind at a solution to this problem; otherwise, the individual could lower the transfers while still fulfilling his obligations and, thus, be better off.
10 One could express the same idea with a more general model. Suppose individuals in the village who want to live in the city each chooses between renting a housing unit from an owner, or not, and that K-agents have the additional option of entering into a side-contract with a renter in the kin group to share. For a K-individual, the rental price of housing is high and only a few people can afford apartments in the city. For an I-individual, the rental price is low and many people can afford apartments in the city. In the first case, the need for insurance (lest one be one of those who cannot afford a city apartment) is high; in the second case, it is low. There may be simple examples of utility functions, income distributions, and $C(n)$ such that, for some parameter values, the extended kin system increases *ex ante* welfare, while for others it lowers it.
11 Formal models of the persistence of behaviors which lead to a group reputation that makes everyone worse off are Stiglitz (1974) and Tirole (1996).
12 We quote this passage at length as a corrective to the view, implicit in some recent work on informal insurance arrangements, that the central problem raised by informal insurance arrangements is that of enforcement. While this is true in some settings, in

traditional peasant societies the obstacle to efficiency may not be lack of enforcement but instead may be too much enforcement – the power of the group to sustain an informal insurance arrangement whose cost in foregone market opportunities exceeds the benefits.

13 For simplicity, we treat the special case where each extended family is identical, but the qualitative results do not depend on this assumption.

14 One might suppose that the inequality in the text below would always be satisfied: there can be no insurance benefits if no one pools risks. But if the motives relevant to the individual's decision include a concern to respect traditional norms, then $E(1) > 0$. The inequality in the text would be violated for $E(1)$ sufficiently large.

15 At first glance, the analysis here may seem unrelated to the canonical analysis in Maynard Smith and much of evolutionary game theory, which focuses on two-person games in which individuals are matched with a single partner in each period. Our under-lying game form is not a two-person interaction, but rather interactions in the informal insurance scheme and in the market where the size of the population that is character-ized by a particular strategy determines payoffs. However, Maynard Smith (1982, p. 24) himself notes that the standard analysis extends readily to the case where an individual's success depends, "not on a series of individual opponents, but on some average property of the population s as a whole, or some section of it." Maynard Smith describes this case as "playing the field" as opposed to playing a two-person game.

16 A formal definition for the case where payoffs depend directly on the fraction of the population that has adopted each strategy, is in Maynard Smith (p. 24).

References

Akerlof, George (1976) "The economics of caste and of the rat race and other woeful tales." *Quarterly Journal of Economics*. 90: 599–617.

Arnott, Richard and Stiglitz, Joseph E. (1991) "Moral hazard and nonmarket institu-tions: dysfunctional crowding out or peer monitoring?" *American Economic Review*. 81: 179–90.

Axelrod, Robert (1984) *The Evolution of Cooperation*. New York: Basic Books.

Bauer, Peter T. and Yamey, B.S. (1957) *The Economics of Under-Developed Countries*. Cambridge, UK: Cambridge University Press.

Becker, Gary S. (1996) *Accounting for Tastes*. Cambridge, MA: Harvard University Press.

Collier, Paul (2001) Comment on "Distributive conflicts, collective action, and institutional economics," by Pranab Bardhan, in G. Meier and J. Stiglitz (eds), *Frontiers of Devel-opment Economics: The Future in Perspective*, New York: Oxford University Press, pp. 296–9.

Collier, Paul and Garg, Ashish (1999) "On kin groups and wages in the Ghanaian labour market." *Oxford Bulletin of Economics and Statistics*. 61: 133–57.

Colson, E. (1947) *Tradition and Contract: The Problem of Order*. Chicago, IL: Aldine.

Fafchamps, Marcel and Minten, B. (2002) "Returns to social network capital among traders." *Oxford Economic Papers*. 54: 173–206.

Grazer, Garth (2001) "The firm and the family network: measuring the relative productivity of relatives." Manuscript. New Haven, CT: Yale University.

Greif, Avner (1994) "Cultural beliefs and the organization of society: a historical and theoretical reflection on collectivist and individualist societies." *Journal of Political Economy*. 102: 12–50.

Hoff, Karla and Arijit Sen (in print) "The kin system as a poverty trap?" in Samuel Bowles, Steven Durlauf, and Karla Hoff (eds), *Poverty Traps*, Princeton, NJ: Princeton University Press.

Kennedy, P. (1988) *African Capitalism – The Struggle for Ascendancy*. Cambridge: Cambridge University Press.

Kuran, Timur (1988) "The tenacious past: theories of personal and collective conservatism." *Journal of Economic Behavior and Organization*. 143–71.

——(1995) *Private Truths, Public Lies: The Social Consequences of Preference Falsification*. Cambridge, MA: Harvard University Press.

Lamoreaux, Naomi (1994) *Insider Lending: Banks, Personal Connections, and Economic Development in Industrial New England*. Cambridge, UK: Cambridge University Press.

Lewis, W. Arthur (1955) *The Theory of Economic Growth*. London: George Allen & Unwin.

Mahoney, Paul G. and Sanchirico, Chris W. (2001) "Competing norms and social evolution: Is the fittest norm efficient?" *University of Pennsylvania Law Review*. 149: 2027–62.

Maynard Smith, John (1982) *Evolution and the Theory of Games*. Cambridge, UK: Cambridge University Press.

Platteau, Jean-Philippe (1991) "Traditional systems of social security and hunger insurance." in E. Ahmad, J. Dreze, J. Hills, and A. Sen (eds), *Social Security in Developing Countries*, Oxford: Clarendon Press, pp. 112–70.

——(1996) "Traditional sharing norms as an obstacle to economic growth in tribal societies." CRED working paper no.173, Facultes universitaires Notre-Dame de la Paix, Namur, Belgium.

——(2000) *Institutions, Social Norms, and Economic Development*. Amsterdam: Harwood Publishers.

Sahlins, M.D. (1965) "On the sociology of primitive exchange." in B. Banton (ed.), *The Relevance of Models for Social Anthropology*, London: Tavistock Publications, pp. 139–236.

Scott, James C. (1976) *The Moral Economy of the Peasant – Rebellion and Subsistence in Southeast Asia*. New Haven, CT and London, UK: Yale University Press.

Stack, Carol (1974) *All our Kin: Strategies for Survival in a Black Community*. New York: Harper & Row.

Stiglitz, Joseph E. (1974) "Theories of discrimination and economic policy." in G. von Furstenberg, Ann R. Horowitz, and Bennett Harrison (eds), *Patterns of Racial Discrimination*, Lexington, MA: D.C. Heath, Lexington Books, pp. 5–26.

Tirole, Jean (1996) "A theory of collective reputations (with applications to the persistence of corruption and to firm quality)." *Review of Economic Studies*. 63: 1–22.

Wolf, Charles (1955) "Institutions and economic development." *American Economic Review*. 45: 867–83.

Young, H. Peyton (1998) *Individual Strategy and Social Structure: An Evolutionary Theory of Institutions*. Princeton, NJ: Princeton University Press.

8 Social divisions within schools

How school policies can affect students' identities and educational choices

George A. Akerlof and Rachel E. Kranton

8.1 Introduction

Why do many minority students and students in poor communities perform badly and spend less time in school? This question plagues educators, policy makers, and researchers alike. There are many possible economic answers. Schools in minority communities have fewer resources, parents have less time and ability to help with homework, children move from school to school as their parents follow different job opportunities, children have to contribute to household chores or family income, etc. All of these factors almost certainly contribute to lower educational outcomes of minority and poor students. But studies that control for such economic characteristics still find strikingly lower outcomes.[1] These findings indicate that something may be missing from the standard economic model of education. Inspired by work outside economics, we bring social dimensions to the economic analysis of school policy.[2]

This chapter considers how school policies can affect social divisions among students and thereby influence students' academic achievement. In our analysis we depart from the typical economic view of students and schools. In a typical economic model, students choose effort (or time) in school to balance its discounted return with its opportunity cost, and school quality is determined by its resources and its academic offerings. In Akerlof and Kranton (2002), we introduce a model of education which explores two aspects of schooling which have thus far eluded economic analysis. First is a sociological view of the student as the primary decision maker. Second is the conception of the school as a social institution. This chapter elaborates this model and explores in detail how school policies can influence students' identities and change academic outcomes.

We first present a model of student decision-making where a primary concern is the student's self-image. In this model, students act like children as described by sociologists and psychologists: they want to fit in.[3] A student gains utility when her actions and those of others enhance her *self-image*. Her self-image, or *identity*, is associated with the social environment. That is, a student thinks of herself and others according to different *social categories*. Social categories include racial and ethnic designations, such as black and Hispanic, and in the school context include such groups as "jock" and "nerd." Students also have ideas about how people in these groups should behave. We call these notions *prescriptions*, and the prescriptions give the *ideal*, or stereotypical physical attributes and behavior, of people in each category. Students then gain or lose utility insofar as they belong to social categories with high or low social status and their attributes and behavior match the ideal of their category.[4]

In our modeling, schools face a tradeoff that captures the historical and ethnographic accounts of schooling in the United States. In our framework, schools are social institutions. As in these accounts, schools not only impart skills, they impart an image of the ideal student in terms of appearance, language, comportment, and accent. These accounts, and our model, see the school as having a choice between promoting a student ideal closer to economically useful cultural norms and skills and an ideal closer to the students' social backgrounds.[5] It may seem strange to an economist that such a tradeoff exists. But sociologists' accounts reveal that skills, and business norms of dress and comportment, are not socially neutral. Even such skills as proficiency in English and mathematics are associated with particular social categories, and a curriculum can be seen to privilege certain social groups. In this case, the promotion of certain skills and prescriptions for behavior can alienate students from different social backgrounds.[6]

This chapter elaborates three possibilities for school policy.

We first consider schools that promote a single social category. This case captures assimilationist American schools of the early twentieth century as described by historians. In these schools, immigrant students were expected to shed their native cultures, languages, and habits. According to David Tyack (1974), turn-of-the-century public schools demanded "total assimilation . . . [and] creat[ed] a sense of shame at being 'foreign'" (p. 234).[7] In our model, a student at such a school can choose between two possible identities. The student can identify with the school and try to fit its ideal image. The student could instead reject the school. Historians describe this choice as particularly difficult for immigrant students whose backgrounds and religions did not match the school's ideal. We see similar emotions among African–American students, Hispanic students, and other minorities in studies as recently as the 1990s.[8] We show how the existence of this school ideal affects educational attainment. We see how an ideal that does not match the demographics of the student population can lead many students to reject the school and have low levels of academic achievement.

We then consider a school policy to adjust its ideal to the student population. This model captures schools in the latter part of the twentieth century, as described by educators; schools adjusted their policies and curricula in response to school integration.[9] In our interpretation, school administrators face a tradeoff between promoting a single ideal or offering students a choice. With choice, more students in a diverse population find ways to identify with the school. The outcome is more "democratic" in that more students are engaged in the school, but some students acquire lower skills.

Finally, we consider school reform programs that strive to reduce the salience of social differences among their students. In many reform programs we see how administrators and teachers spend considerable resources to create a school community; i.e., create a school category that is distinct from the outside social environment. The staff delineate prescriptions for student behaviors and work to ensure that students identify with the school and its ideals. Prominent examples include the Central Park East Elementary and Secondary Schools in Harlem and the Comer Schools in New Haven.[10] We see these schools, in our economic terminology, as devoting resources to change students' identities and their relationships with the school. The schools reduce the initial social differences among the students and create a community, with an ideal of academic excellence. The framework we develop thus suggests a synthesis of the sociological and economic viewpoints, providing a new economic model of how resources can affect educational outcomes.[11]

The chapter is organized as follows. In the next section we review our general model of student utility and identity, and build a particular model of utility and schools as a social institution. In Section 8.3 we consider students' choices of identity when attending a school promoting a single social category. In Section 8.4, we ask how schools might modify the categories and associated ideals to better match their student population. In Section 8.5, we consider the possibility that schools can devote resources to reduce the salience of social difference. We then conclude.

8.2   A model of students, schools, and identity

In this section we review our basic model of utility, students, and schools. In this model, students derive utility from two sources. The first source is the standard utility from effort in school and income found in the economics literature. The second source is the student's self-image, or identity. Furthermore, schools have both economic and identity aspects. As in a standard economic model, schools complement students' efforts in school in the production of marketable skills. Here we add the possibility that schools are also social institutions that affect students' identities.

8.2.1   General model of student utility and identity

We first outline the general ingredients of a model of student utility where identity, or self-image, is salient. As in a standard model of education, a student's utility could depend on her effort in school and the pecuniary returns to this effort.[12] Let e_i be student i's effort in school, and let $k(e_i)$ be the pecuniary benefits of e_i, which derive from the returns to skills in the labor market. A standard utility function would posit i's utility as a function of $k(e_i)$ and the pecuniary and opportunity costs of effort, e_i.

As for utility from identity, as in Akerlof and Kranton (2000), we begin with a set of social categories, $\mathbf{C}$. These categories may include racial and ethnic designations, gender, and in the school context could include, e.g., "jocks" and "nerds."

Prescriptions, **P**, give the ideal characteristics and behavior for each category. An individual i assigns himself to a category, and we denote this assignment c_i. i's self-image, M_i, depends on the match between his behavior e_i and characteristics, denoted ϵ_i, with the ideals for his category. Student i's utility is then

$$U_i = U_i(k(e_i), e_i, M_i),$$

where

$$M_i = M_i(e_i, c_i; \epsilon_i, \mathbf{P}).$$

We use the word identity to describe both a student's assigned category and the payoffs associated with self-image. Thus, we speak of gains or losses in identity, which are the gains or losses in utility derived from the term M_i.

This model captures findings of social psychology experiments, conducted with school-age children as well as adults. These experiments reveal that assigned social categories can influence behavior. Consider the classic Robbers Cave experiment.[13] In this experiment, two groups of randomly selected 11-year-old boys were taken to a park in Oklahoma, where they were kept apart for a week. During this week, researchers found the boys developed a sense of belonging to their group. When they met for a tournament in the second week, the 11-year old equivalent of war broke out, complete with name-calling and stereotyping. Minimal group experiments show that competition is not necessary for category assignments to affect behavior (Tajfel and Turner 1979). Experiments, with both children and adults, show that subjects are more likely to give rewards to those assigned the same label than to others, even when the assignment is random, recipients are anonymous, and there is no impact on own payoffs.

Outside of experiments, we see that school-age children understand notions of appropriate and inapproriate behavior for different types of people. Children are aware of gender categories, and beyond the ages of 5 or 6, self-segregate into groups of boys and girls. Even very young children may have some understanding of the social categories and prescriptions for "blacks" and "whites." Lisa Delpit (1995, p. 48) tells of the new black first-grader who asked her black teacher why she was speaking in a different voice, a voice blacks use when interacting with whites: "Teacher, how come you talkin' like a white person? You talkin' just like my momma talk when she get on the phone."

8.2.2 *A particular model of student utility and identity*

To capture the workings of students' social systems in schools, we construct a specific model of utility and identity based on the general model earlier. In this model students choose effort in school and divide themselves into different social groups.[14] A student derives utility from two sources: income and identity. For simplicity, we will specify each of these utilities separately and then add them to comprise a student's overall utility. This linear model parsimoniously melds much of the sociology and psychology of identity with the economic model.

Consider a population of students normalized to size one. Each student i chooses a level of effort e_i to exert in school. We suppose that the pecuniary returns to a student's effort in school, k_i, depend on effort, e_i, according to some function $k_i = k_i(e_i)$, and the student's pecuniary cost of effort is $c(e_i)$. This cost of effort includes any direct cost of exerting effort in school and any opportunity cost of this effort. The student's overall economic utility is simply $k_i(e_i) - c(e_i)$, and throughout the chapter we let $c(e_i) \equiv \frac{1}{2}(e_i)^2$.

We now specify utility from identity. Each student has an ascriptive social characteristic ϵ_i, such as class, ethnicity, or other social attribute, which does not directly affect the production of skills. We assume that ϵ_i is independently and uniformly distributed on $[m - \sigma/2, m + \sigma/2]$, where m is the mean and σ represents the diversity of the student population.[15] The students' social system is represented by a finite set of social categories **C**. Each social category can be associated with a particular point in the space of attributes, and this point gives the ideal characteristic for that particular category. For example, if the social categories are jocks and burnouts (as in Eckert 1989) and ϵ represents skin color or ethnicity, then the ideal jock could be described by a particular skin color or ethnicity. We denote the ideal characteristic for social category c to be $\epsilon^*(c)$. Each social category is also associated with an ideal level of effort in school. We denote the ideal effort level for social category c to be $e^*(c)$. In our analysis, the set of social categories, **C**, and their associated ideal attributes, $\epsilon^*(c)$, and effort levels, $e^*(c)$, are potentially objects of school policy.

The student's utility from her self-image or identity, M_i, depends on her chosen category and the match between her effort level, her characteristic, and the ideals for her category. For a simple specification of utility from identity, let the utility the agent derives from belonging to social category c be a constant amount I_c and the utility he loses by diverging from the ideal effort level be $\frac{1}{2}(e_i - e^*(c))^2$. The student further loses utility by the extent to which his given attributes do not match the ideal for his category. We specify these losses to be a function $g(\epsilon^*(c), \epsilon_i, t)$ where t is a parameter that captures the importance of fitting in with the group to utility. This parameter t is critical to this and subsequent models. It measures how difficult it is for students with different ascriptive characteristics to fit in a group. That is, t measures the extent to which ascriptive characteristics, such as skin color and ethnicity, affect identity utility.

We can now fully specify a student's utility function, which consists of both the standard economic utility and utility from identity. A student i with characteristic ϵ_i who chooses to be in category c earns utility

$$U_i = p\left[k_i(e_i) - \tfrac{1}{2}e_i^2\right] + (1-p)\left[I_c - g\left(\epsilon^*(c), \epsilon_i, t\right) - \tfrac{1}{2}(e_i - e^*(c))^2\right],$$

$$(1)$$

where p is the weight a student places on economic utility and the remainder, $(1 - p)$, is the weight on identity utility.

8.2.3 School as a social institution

We next model the school as a social institution. We suppose schools represent a social category and have an ideal student, in terms of characteristics ϵ and effort e. Anthropologists, historians, and social psychologists describe the various ways schools impart this ideal. School rituals – pep rallies, homeroom announcements, assemblies – and day-to-day interactions in classrooms, hallways, and gymnasiums reveal the nature of this ideal.[16] We posit a school social category S, associated with a point on the spectrum $[m - \sigma/2, m + \sigma/2]$ that describes the ideal characteristic of a student in the school. We denote this ideal characteristic as s; that is, $\epsilon^*(S) \equiv s$. With the utility function earlier, students with characteristic ϵ close to s would earn high identity payoffs from being in the school social category S. Those with characteristic ϵ far away would earn lower payoffs, as they do not fit in so easily.

We further assume that s, the school ideal, affects marketable skills. In particular, the greater is s, the more skills a student will obtain for a given effort level in school. This assumption reflects associations between certain social categories and the curriculum, behavioral prescriptions, and other aspects of economic success.[17] Let the production function take the form $k_i = se_i$, so that income is increasing in s and e_i, and s is complementary to a student's effort in school.

We have now specified a utility function with identity and schools as a social institution. In the next section we examine how students, with these utility functions, choose whether or not to identify with the school. We will see how the school ideal s, the distribution parameters of the student population m and σ, and the extent to which ascriptive characteristics matter to identity, t, all can affect educational attainment.

8.3 Social divisions in school and educational attainment

We consider here student divisions into social groups when the school has a single social category S with exogenous ideals for this category of s and $e^*(S)$. This case represents historians' view of assimilation in US schools earlier in the twentieth century. The solution serves as a building block for the modeling later, where we allow the school to both choose the number of social categories (one or two) and choose the associated ideals.

When the school promotes a single social category S, there are two social categories that students can choose from. They can choose to identify with the school and try to live up to the ideals of s and $e^*(S)$. Or they can choose to not identify with the school, and thus avoid any losses from not fitting the ideals. We label this second social category B for "burnouts," a commonly used word to describe students who reject their schools' ideals and disobey their rules. Burnouts have no particular ideal in the space of attributes $[m - \sigma/2, m + \sigma/2]$, but their ideal level of effort in school, $e^*(B)$, is set to zero.

Following the model earlier for students' identity utilities, we specify the following identity payoffs for students in each category. A student i who identifies with the school category, S, earns $I_S - t(s - \epsilon_i)$ for $\epsilon_i \leq s$ and earns I_S for $\epsilon_i > s$. A student suffers an identity loss $\frac{1}{2}(e_i - e^*(S))^2$ for diverging from the ideal effort level $e^*(S)$. A student i who does not identify with the school, a "(B)urnout," earns identity payoffs I_B. Furthermore, B will also lose identity utility of $\frac{1}{2}(e_i)^2$ for deviating from the prescribed effort level of zero.

With these assumptions, a student i who choose to be S or B would have utility, respectively,

$$U_i(S) = \begin{cases} p\left[s \cdot e_i - \frac{1}{2}e_i^2\right] + (1-p)\left[I_S - \frac{1}{2}(e_i - e^*(S))^2\right] & \text{for } \epsilon_i > s \\ p\left[s \cdot e_i - \frac{1}{2}e_i^2\right] + (1-p)\left[I_S - t(s - \epsilon_i) - \frac{1}{2}(e_i - e^*(S))^2\right] & \text{for } \epsilon_i \leq s \end{cases}$$

$$U_i(B) = p\left[s \cdot e_i - \frac{1}{2}e_i^2\right] + (1-p)\left[I_B - \frac{1}{2}e_i^2\right].$$

$$(2)$$

To maximize utility, each student chooses a social category and his or her effort level.

We analyze the division of students into groups and the educational outcomes in the special case of $p = 0$, as suggested by ethnographies and other studies of student motivation.[18]

In this case, any student who chooses to be S will choose effort level $e^*(S)$, and any student who chooses to be B will choose an effort level of zero. A student then chooses between S and B to balance the relative social status of identifying with the school, I_S vs. I_B, with any loss in utility from not fitting in, $t(s - \epsilon_i)$. That is, for a student who chooses S, utility is

$$U_i(S) = \begin{cases} I_S & \text{for } \epsilon_i > s \\ I_S - t(s - \epsilon_i) & \text{for } \epsilon_i \leq s. \end{cases}$$

$$(3)$$

For a student who chooses B, utility is

$$U_i(B) = I_B.$$

Since $I_S > I_B$, any student for whom $\epsilon_i > s$ will choose to be S. For the remainder of the students $\epsilon_i \leq s$, we set $U_i(B) = U_i(S)$ to find the student with the characteristic, denoted $\bar{\epsilon}$, that makes him just indifferent between choosing S and B. We have

$$\bar{\epsilon} = s - \frac{I}{t},$$

where $I \equiv I_S - I_B$. Solving for the fraction of students with characteristics below $\bar{\epsilon}$, we find the number of burnouts, i.e., the number of students who do not identify with the school. Let β denote this fraction of students. We have

$$\beta = \frac{1}{2} + \frac{s - m - I/t}{\sigma}. \tag{4}$$

Since burnouts do not exert effort in school, and S students exert effort level $e^*(S)$, the mean skill acquisition of the student population, which we denote as K, is

$$K = s \cdot e^*(S) \cdot \left(\frac{1}{2} - \frac{s - m - I/t}{\sigma} \right). \tag{5}$$

From this simple model, we gain three key insights into the effect of identity and schools on student academic achievement.

First, we see a direct effect of social difference, t, on skill acquisition. For a given school ideal s, average skills are declining in t. When t is higher, it is harder for students with different social backgrounds to fit in the school. Hence, more students reject the school and exert low levels of effort.

Proposition 1. *For a fixed school ideal, when ascriptive characteristics become more important – t is higher – average skill of the student population is lower.*

Proof. Simple examination of $\partial K / \partial t$ shows that $\partial K / \partial t < 0$ for all s.   □

Second, when social differences are sufficiently salient, i.e., t is sufficiently high, a higher ideal s corresponds to a decrease in the level of skill acquisition. The ideal s is a complement to students' efforts in producing skills, but when s is high there are more burnouts. The greater number of burnouts overwhelms the direct effect of s on students' skill acquisition.

Proposition 2. *For t sufficiently high, there exists an ideal type for the school $\tilde{s} < m + \sigma$ such that for all $s > \tilde{s}$, average skill K declines in s. This critical ideal type is $\tilde{s} \equiv (m + \sigma + I/t)/2$. As s increases above $\tilde{s}$, more students reject the school, reducing the total skill level.*

Proof. Differentiating K with respect to s we have

$$\frac{\partial K}{\partial s} = \frac{1}{2} + \frac{s + m + I/t}{\sigma} - \frac{2s}{\sigma},$$

which is negative for $s > \tilde{s} \equiv (m + \sigma + I/t)/2$. Comparing the upper bound of the distribution, $m + \sigma$, to this value, we see that $m + \sigma > (m + \sigma + I/t)/2$ for $t > I/m$. Hence, for $t > I/m$, there exists a critical ideal type $\tilde{s} < m + \sigma$ such for all $s > \tilde{s}$, $\partial K / \partial s < 0$.   □

Finally, we see that the negative effect of s is more pronounced the greater is the diversity of students σ. With a more diverse student population, the greater the potential number of students who will not identify with the school. Hence, a higher school ideal corresponds to a greater number of burnouts when σ is high.

Proposition 3. *For all $s > \tilde{s}$, the rate at which skills decrease in s is increasing in σ. Hence, an increase in s decreases average skills more when the student population is more diverse (σ is high).*

Proof. Examining the cross-partial derivative $\partial K / \partial s \partial \sigma$ we have

$$\frac{\partial K}{\partial s \partial \sigma} = \frac{2s}{\sigma^2} - \frac{m + (I/t)}{2\sigma^2},$$

which is positive for $s > (m+I/t)/2$. Since $\tilde{s} \equiv (m+\sigma+I/t)/2$, this cross-partial is positive for all values of $s > \tilde{s}$. □

8.4   School policy and student social divisions

In this section we consider how school policy can affect students' choices and educational outcomes. In the analysis earlier, the key variables – the school ideal, s, and the salience, t, of ascriptive attributes – were taken as given. We now consider the possibility that the school can choose these variables optimally to maximize overall academic achievement.

We first consider a school that has a single social category and chooses an ideal s. We then consider a school that can choose to have two social categories and two associated ideals. In each case, we assume the school makes this selection to maximize the total skills, K.[19]

The first exercise captures how schools can adapt to their student population, as many schools did in the latter part of the twentieth century in response to civil rights and integration. Consider the changes at "Hamilton High," a school in northern New York State, which educators argue reflect general trends in US education. *The World We Created at Hamilton High* by Gerald Grant (1988) describes a school that changed its ideals in response to a dramatic change in the demographics of its student population. In the 1950s and early 1960s, Hamilton High served a largely homogenous, white, middle-class population. The school's ideal matched the student population; the principal had few doubts that his job was to "enforce middle-class standards of courtesy and respect, emphasize a college preparatory curriculum and put winning teams on the Hamilton field." In the late 1960s, under orders of forced integration, a significant number of poor black students entered Hamilton High. In terms of our model, the diversity, σ, of the student population increased. There was a great deal of discord, even rioting which closed the school for some time. As the story of Hamilton High continues, we see the school adjusting to its diverse student body. Gradually, the school of Greek-letter clubs and a capella choruses faded away. A new school emerged, whose defining feature was tolerance.

The second case – where a school can promote two social categories – represents a leading view of contemporary public schools in the United States. In these schools, students are free to choose among different courses and academic tracks. As in the continued story of Hamilton High, and in other schools throughout the country, students in the 1970s were granted greater rights, including the right to choose their curriculum. Even though formal tracking was eliminated, students now tracked themselves. This transformation of Hamilton High conforms to educators' descriptions of typical US high schools across the country (Hampel 1986). Powell *et al.* (1985) call these high schools "shopping malls," where students are treated as customers. The schools give them what they want, making little or no attempt to change their values. The Shopping Mall High School appears not to be just the result of changes in the 1960s as reported by Grant and Hampel, but rather to be the much longer evolutionary outcome of continued changes of US schools, where earlier in the century nonacademic subjects ("life skills" curricula) were introduced for the non-college-bound students (see Goldin and Katz 1997).

We begin with a school that optimally chooses an ideal for its single social category.

8.4.1   *The school chooses optimally a single ideal*

Suppose now that a school has a single social category S and it can choose s to maximize the average skill attainment of its students. Let K_1 be the average skill attainment in this case, where the subscript 1 indicates the school has a single social category. As we have already seen earlier, $K_1 = s \cdot e^*(S) \cdot (1 - \beta)$, where β is the fraction of burnouts. As we saw in Proposition 2, an increase in s can involve a tradeoff: increasing s increases skills directly, but increases β, the number of burnouts. The optimal s balances these effects. Solving for the school ideal s^{**} that maximizes average student skills K_1, we have:

$$s^{**} = \min\left[m + \frac{\sigma}{2}, \frac{1}{2}\left(m + \frac{\sigma}{2} + \frac{I}{t} \right) \right].\tag{6}$$

This simple maximization exercise gives us an important insight on how schools might modify their policies and curriculum to better match the student demographics and increase the number of students who feel comfortable in school. When the social parameter t is high, the optimal ideal s^{**} is decreasing in t. The more social differences matter to students' identities, the more the school must reduce its ideal to engage students in the school and increase skills.[20] Similarly, the greater the diversity of the student population (σ), the more a school must reduce its ideal. With a diverse student population, more students are likely to become burnouts. A school compensates by choosing a lower s.

Proposition 4. *The more important are students' social backgrounds (higher t) or the more diverse the student population (higher σ), the more a school promoting a single category will reduce its ideal (s), sacrificing a direct input into skill attainment in order to encourage students to identify with the school.*

Proof. Simple examination of $\partial s^{**}/\partial t$ and $\partial s^{**}/\partial \sigma$ gives the result.   □

This result mirrors the debates over curriculum and textbooks in many parts of the United States, in particular with respect to African American and minority schools. One side of the debate argues that certain literatures, histories, and skills are standard and important for students entering college or the work world. The other side of the debate argues that these same literatures, histories, and skills are demeaning to their students. When forced to attend a school with such curricula, students, at best, "turn off" and, at worst, disrupt the school. Schools then must adjust their curricula and presentation of the material to match their population better.[21]

8.4.2   The school chooses optimally two ideals

We now consider the possibility that a school can give students a choice between different categories. Instead of one category, the school can promote two social categories with different ideals. As discussed earlier, this exercise captures educators' views of many contemporary US public school systems. Schools do not impose or promote a single ideal. Rather, they provide different alternatives, some emphasizing academic achievement, the others not.

We summarize these categories with two possibilities: H for Honors Students and M for Middle Students. The school correspondingly chooses two ideals s_H and s_M, where $s_H \geq s_M$ and s_H is associated with higher academic achievement. Middle students are a prominent category in Theodore Sizer's (1984) description of US' public schools, as well as Powell *et al.*'s *Shopping Mall High School*. These students are largely uninspired; they make their way through the school day without being prompted to investigate, learn, or question.

When the school promotes two categories, the students have three social categories from which to choose: (H)onors students, with ideals s_H and $e(H)$; (M)iddle students with ideals s_M and $e(M)$, and (B)urnouts, with ideal effort level $e(B)$, where $e(H) > e(M) > e(B) \equiv 0$.

As before, a student's identity depends on the match between his or her own characteristics and behavior and the ideal of his or her category. We again consider students' choices of effort and category for $p = 0$. A student i choosing category $c_i = H, M$ then earns utility

$$U_i(S) = \begin{cases} I_S & \text{for } \epsilon_i > s \\ I_S - t(s - \epsilon_i) - \frac{1}{2}(e_i - e(c_i))^2 & \text{for } \epsilon_i \leq s. \end{cases} \quad (7)$$

Burnouts earn the utility of the previous model.

Finding the students who are just indifferent between H and M and those just indifferent between M and B, we see following division of students:[22]

$$(1/\sigma)(m + (\sigma/2) - s_H) \qquad H \text{ students}$$
$$(1/\sigma)(s_H - s_M + (I/t)) \qquad M \text{ students} \qquad (8)$$
$$(1/\sigma)(s_M - (I/t) - m + (\sigma/2)) \quad B \text{ students.}$$

Notice that the higher is s_H, the fewer the number of H students. Less students fit the ideal of the high category. Notice further that the higher is the difference $(s_H - s_M)$, the greater the number of M students. When s_H is relatively high and s_M relatively low, more students are closer to the middle student ideal. Of course, the greater is s_M, the greater the number of burnouts. Fewer students have characteristics that fit the ideals of the school. With students divided into groups in this way, mean skills as a function of s_H and s_M are

$$K_2 = s_H \left[\frac{1}{2} + \frac{m - s_H}{\sigma} \right] e(H) + s_M \left[\frac{s_H - s_M}{\sigma} + \frac{I}{\sigma t} \right] e(M), \qquad (9)$$

where the subscript 2 in K_2 indicates the school has two categories rather than one.

When setting s_H and s_M, the school faces two tradeoffs. First, raising ideals s_H and s_M directly increases skill attainment, but increases the number of burnouts. Second, there is competition between the categories. Increasing $(s_H - s_M)$ increases the skills of the honor students, but more students will opt for the middle category, with lower educational attainment.

The following analysis solves for s_H^* and s_M^*, the values that maximize K_2. We will see how the absolute levels of s_H^* and s_M^* depend on the social parameters of the model – the diversity of the student population (σ) and the extent to which social differences matter to students' identities (t). We will also examine the relative magnitudes of s_H^* and s_M^*. We will see that the distance $(s_H^* - s_M^*)$ increases with t and σ. When t and σ are high, s_H^* is far from s_M^*, and middle students are receiving quite a different input to their education than honor students. Hence, greater diversity and social differences translate into larger differences in educational outcomes.

We first observe that there is a minimum value of the optimal s_M. The school will never find it optimal to set the ideal s_M below the value $I/t + m - \sigma/2$. Given the outcome of student choices described in line (8), setting s_M below $I/t + m - \sigma/2$ does not change the number of students in each group. At $s_M = I/t + m - \sigma/2$, there are exactly zero burnouts. Hence, it can never enhance average achievement to set s_M at a lower level, and it is never an optimal choice for the school.

Lemma 1. *For all levels of m, t, and s, the optimal ideal s_M for middle students is at least $I/t + m - \sigma/2$.*

Proof. To see this suppose the contrary. Suppose the school chooses some $s_H \geq s_M$ such that $s_M < m - \sigma/2 + I/t$. The school can increase attainment by increasing s_M to some s'_M so that $s'_M = m - \sigma/2 + I/t$. The number of honors, middle, and burnout students does not change. (There are no burnouts in either case.) The school, however, increases the skill attainment of the middle students by increasing their ideal type. □

We continue our analysis by observing that schools face a tradeoff between the students at the top and the students at the bottom of the distribution. We find there are two optimal vectors of s_H and s_M, each for different levels of the social parameters m and σ. For high levels of diversity or a mean student characteristic, the optimal value of s_M is strictly above its minimum $I/t + m - \sigma/2$. In this case, the school sets an optimal s_M where some students choose to be burnouts. The population mean or diversity level is high enough so that the school finds it optimal to sacrifice the education of the students at the bottom of the distribution to increase the education level of students at the top. When the population has a low mean or low diversity level, the school will choose a level of s_M at $I/t + m - \sigma/2$. There is less of a tradeoff between students at the top or bottom of the distribution, and the school optimally sets s_M so that there are no burnouts.

Proposition 5. *For m high enough or σ high enough, $(s_H^*, s_M^*) = (s'_H, s'_M)$ and for lower values of m or σ, $(s_H^*, s_M^*) = (s''_H, I/t + m - \sigma/2)$ where*

$$s'_M = \left(m + \frac{\sigma}{2}\right)\left(\frac{e(H)}{4e(H) - e(M)}\right) + \left(\frac{I}{t}\right)\left(\frac{2e(H)}{4e(H) - e(M)}\right)$$

$$s'_H = \left(m + \frac{\sigma}{2}\right)\left(\frac{2e(H)}{4e(H) - e(M)}\right) + \left(\frac{I}{t}\right)\left(\frac{e(H)}{4e(H) - e(M)}\right)$$

$$s''_H = \max\left[\frac{m}{2}\left(\frac{e(H) + e(M)}{e(H)}\right) + \left(\frac{\sigma}{4}\right)\left(\frac{e(H) - e(M)}{e(H)}\right) + \frac{I}{2t}\left(\frac{e(M)}{e(H)}\right),\right.$$

$$\left.\frac{I}{t} + m - \frac{\sigma}{2}\right].$$

Hence, for higher levels of diversity or mean student characteristic, the school sets high ideals and some students will not identify with the school. For lower levels of these demographic parameters, the school chooses ideals where all students will identify with the school.

Proof. Let us ignore for the moment that we know the optimal s_M must be at least $m - \sigma/2 + I/t$ and solve for the values of s_H and s_M that maximize

$$\Pi = s_H\left(\frac{1}{2} + \frac{m - s_H}{\sigma}\right)e(H) + s_M\left(\frac{s_H - s_M}{\sigma} + \frac{I}{t\sigma}\right)e(M).$$

The first order conditions are:

$$\frac{\partial \Pi}{\partial s_H} = \left(\frac{1}{2} + \frac{m - s_H}{\sigma}\right) e(H) - \frac{s_H}{\sigma} e(H) + \frac{s_M}{\sigma} e(M) = 0$$

$$\frac{\partial \Pi}{\partial s_M} = \left(\frac{s_H - s_M}{\sigma} + \frac{I}{t\sigma}\right) e(M) - \frac{s_M}{\sigma} e(M) = 0.$$

These two conditions give us the optimal position of s_H in relation to s_M and vice versa:

$$s_H(s_M) = \frac{m}{2} + \frac{\sigma}{4} + \frac{s_M}{2} \left[\frac{e(M)}{e(H)}\right]$$

and

$$s_M(s_H) = \frac{I}{2t} + \frac{s_H}{2}.$$

Solving for the s_H and s_M that maximizes Π we have:

$$s'_H = \left(m + \frac{\sigma}{2}\right) \left(\frac{2e(H)}{4e(H) - e(M)}\right) + \left(\frac{I}{t}\right) \left(\frac{e(H)}{4e(H) - e(M)}\right)$$

$$s'_M = \left(m + \frac{\sigma}{2}\right) \left(\frac{e(H)}{4e(H) - e(M)}\right) + \left(\frac{I}{t}\right) \left(\frac{2e(H)}{4e(H) - e(M)}\right).$$

Note that when $s'_M \geq I/t + m - \sigma/2$, s'_H and s'_M not only maximize Π, they maximize K_2. When $s'_M < I/t + m - \sigma/2$, however, the school could get greater skills by setting $s_M = I/t + m - \sigma/2$ and setting s_H optimally given $s_M = I/t + m - \sigma/2$.

Let us check the conditions under which $s'_M \geq I/t + m - \sigma/2$. Comparing s'_M and $I/t + m - \sigma/2$, we have $s'_M \geq I/t + m - \sigma/2$ when

$$\frac{\sigma}{2} > m \left(\frac{3e(H) - e(M)}{4e(H) - e(M)}\right) + \frac{I}{t} \left(\frac{2e(H) - e(M)}{4e(H) - e(M)}\right).$$

Here it is clear that, for any values of m and I/t, there exists some σ sufficiently small (but still positive) such that the inequality is not satisfied. In this case, s'_H and s'_M do not maximize Π. Instead, the school can generate higher skills by setting $s_M = I/t + m - \sigma/2$ and set s_H optimally given this s_M.

Label these values s_H'' and s_M''. To find s_H'', we evaluate the function $s_H(s_M)$ at $s_M = I/t + m - \sigma/2$ which gives us

$$\frac{m}{2}\left(\frac{e(H)+e(M)}{e(H)}\right) + \frac{\sigma}{4}\left(\frac{e(H)-e(M)}{e(H)}\right) + \frac{I}{2t}\left(\frac{e(M)}{e(H)}\right).$$

We then have

$$s_H'' = \max\left[\frac{m}{2}\left(\frac{e(H)+e(M)}{e(H)}\right) + \left(\frac{\sigma}{4}\right)\left(\frac{e(H)-e(M)}{e(H)}\right) + \frac{I}{2t}\left(\frac{e(M)}{e(H)}\right),\right.$$
$$\left.\frac{I}{t} + m - \frac{\sigma}{2}\right].$$

Note that $s_H'' = I/t + m - \sigma/2$ when

$$\frac{\sigma}{2} > m\left[\frac{e(H)-e(M)}{3e(H)-e(M)}\right] + \frac{I}{t}\left[\frac{2e(H)-e(M)}{3e(H)-e(M)}\right].$$

Combining two inequalities, we have $s_H'' > s_M'' = I/t + m - \sigma/2$ for

$$m\left(\frac{3e(H)-e(M)}{4e(H)-e(M)}\right) + \frac{I}{t}\left(\frac{2e(H)-e(M)}{4e(H)-e(M)}\right)$$
$$> \frac{\sigma}{2} > m\left(\frac{e(H)-e(M)}{3e(H)-e(M)}\right) + \frac{I}{t}\left(\frac{2e(H)-e(M)}{3e(H)-e(M)}\right).$$

This range is non-empty for reasonable conditions on I/t and m. For σ yet lower, we have $s_H'' = s_M'' = I/t + m - \sigma/2$. Hence, there exists a $\bar\sigma \geq 0$ such that for all $\sigma > \bar\sigma$, $(s_H^*, s_M^*) = (s_H', s_M')$ and (s_H', s_M') are increasing in σ. For all $\sigma < \bar\sigma$, $(s_H^*, s_M^*) = (s_1'', I/t + m - \sigma/2)$. We have similar results for m. As m increases, (s_H', s_M') increase. But the lower bound of the distribution increases faster. (To see this examine the inequality that must be satisfied for $s_M' > (I/t) + m - (\sigma/2)$. It is harder to satisfy for higher m.) Eventually, for sufficiently high m we have $s_M' < I/t + m - \sigma/2$, so $(s_H^*, s_M^*) = (s_H'', I/t + m - \sigma/2)$.   □

Thus we see how a school balances the education levels of the students at the top of the distribution with the education level at the bottom of the distribution. When m or σ is high enough, the school finds it optimal to set high ideals. The students at the top of the distribution have higher educational outcomes, but the students at the bottom become burnouts. When m or σ is low, the school finds it optimal to set lower ideals. There are no burnouts, but the students at the top of the distribution have lower educational attainment.

8.4.3 Should the school promote one or two categories?

In the previous two sections we examined two different school policies. The first policy was a single category; the second policy was two categories. Both policies have their benefits and costs. With one category s, there are almost always students who choose to become burnouts. But students who identify with the school have a high input to their education. With two categories, the second ideal type allows students at the bottom of the distribution to identify with the school. While this second policy setting sounds like it would always dominate the first, it does not. There is competition between the Honors category and the Middle category. When the school sets a second ideal, some students from the upper end of the distribution will decide not to be H students, but to become M students. These students have lower academic achievement.

In this section, we ask when is it optimal for a school to not give students a choice between two ideals, and instead promote a single ideal. Comparison of the total skills for one category, s^{**}, and of two, s_H^* and s_M^*, shows that when the social distinctions are large (t is large or σ is large), the school achieves higher skills by providing two categories. Having two categories increases the number of students who identify with the school. When the social distinctions are small (t is small or σ is small), students are more likely to identify with the school, and a school will maximize skills by eliminating choice and providing a single standard.

Let us consider σ sufficiently small such that $s_H^* = s_M^* = I/t + m - \sigma/2$. (Note that this σ is strictly positive.) To show that it is optimal to have one type in this case, compare the value of $K_2(s_H^*, s_M^*)$ with $K_1(s_H^*)$. We have:

$$K_2(s_H^*, s_M^*) = s_H^* \left(\frac{1}{2} + \frac{m - s_H^*}{\sigma} \right) e(H) + s_M^* \left(\frac{s_H^* - s_M^*}{\sigma} + \frac{I}{t\sigma} \right) e(M)$$

and

$$K_1(s_H^*) - K_2\left(s_H^*, s_M^*\right) = \frac{I}{t\sigma} \left(s_H^* e(H) - s_M^* e(M) \right) - s_M^* \left(\frac{s_H^* - s_M^*}{\sigma} \right) e(M).$$

For σ such that $s_H^* = s_M^* = I/t + m - \sigma/2$, this difference becomes:

$$K_1\left(s_H^*\right) - K_2\left(s_H^*, s_M^*\right) = \frac{I}{t\sigma} \left(\frac{I}{t} + m - \frac{\sigma}{2} \right) (e(H) - e(M)).$$

We can see that this difference is strictly positive for a sufficiently small σ, given $e(H) > e(M)$.

This difference has an interesting interpretation: when σ is small, there is a large loss in creating two types. When another type is introduced below the first, at the margin many students are choosing to become M students rather than H students. It is better not to give the students this choice.

Notice that there is a similar result for m. Given all the other parameter values, select m sufficiently large so that $s_H^* = s_M^* = I/t + m - \sigma/2$. (The critical inequality under which s is strictly greater than $I/t + m - \sigma/2$ is harder to satisfy with larger m.) As m increases, eventually $s_M^* = I/t + m - \sigma/2$. For yet larger m, we have both $s_H^* = s_M^* = I/t + m - \sigma/2$. In this case, it is optimal to have one type. We record these findings and prove them formally in the following Proposition.

Proposition 6. *For any $e(H) \geq e(M) > 0$, for σ sufficiently high, the school will attain higher average skills when the school promotes two ideals. The optimal school will have $s_H^* > s_M^*$ and yield higher skill attainment than with a single type. However, for σ low enough, providing students a choice can reduce average skill attainment.*

Proof. Compare the value of $K_2(\bar{s}, s_M(\bar{s}))$ with $K_1(\bar{s})$, where $s_M(\bar{s})$ is the optimal level of the lower category, given the ideal $\bar{s}$ of the other category. (We conduct this analysis ignoring that $s_M(\bar{s})$ may be less than $I/t + m - \sigma/2$. The value of $s_M(\bar{s})$ puts a lower bound on what can be earned with two categories. For $s_M(\bar{s}) < I/t + m - \sigma/2$, the number of middle students and burnouts is the same as for $s_M = I/t + m - \sigma/2$, but the school could adjust up s_M to increase the skill attainment of the middle students.) We have

$$K_1(s_H^*) = s_H^* \left(\frac{1}{2} + \frac{m - s_H^*}{\sigma} + \frac{I}{t\sigma} \right) e(H)$$

$$K_2(\bar{s}, s_M(\bar{s})) = \bar{s} \left(\frac{1}{2} + \frac{m - \bar{s}}{\sigma} \right) e(H) + s_M(\bar{s}) \left(\frac{\bar{s} - s_M(\bar{s})}{\sigma} + \frac{I}{t\sigma} \right) e(M)$$

$$K_1(\bar{s}) = \bar{s} \left(\frac{1}{2} + \frac{m - \bar{s}}{\sigma} + \frac{I}{t\sigma} \right) e(H).$$

Recall that $s_M(s_H) = I/2t + s_H/2$. Using this to solve for $s_H(\bar{s})$, substituting and simplifying yields

$$K_2(\bar{s}, s_M'(\bar{s})) - \Pi_1(\bar{s}) = s_M(\bar{s}) \left(\frac{\bar{s}}{2\sigma} + \frac{I}{t\sigma} \right) e(M) - \frac{\bar{s}I}{t\sigma} e(H).$$

Substituting and simplifying further, this difference is positive when

$$\frac{2t\bar{s}I - t^2\bar{s}^2 + I^2}{4t\bar{s}I} > \frac{e(H)}{e(M)}.$$

Substituting for $\bar{s}$ we see that the left-hand side is always greater than one. Compare the numerator and denominator as follows:

$$2t\bar{s}I - t^2\bar{s}^2 + I^2 > 4t\bar{s}I,$$

which becomes, after substituting for $\bar{s}$ and simplifying,

$$\left[\frac{t}{2}\left(m + \frac{\sigma}{2}\right) - \frac{I}{2}\right]^2 > 0.$$

Note that the term inside the square brackets is always positive, since we have assumed that $I/t < (m + (\sigma/2))$. This inequality is always satisfied, and the left-hand side of our main inequality is always greater than one. Since the left-hand side of our inequality above is always greater than one, there is an $e(M)$ sufficiently large (i.e., close to $e(H)$) such that this inequality is satisfied, and it is better to have two categories than one. We can also see that the left-hand side of our main inequality is increasing in σ. $\qquad\qquad\qquad\qquad\square$

8.5 School policy to decrease the salience of social difference

In this section we consider school policy to create a school community and decrease the importance of initial social differences among students. In the earlier analysis, the school chooses its ideals taking as given the student population and the salience of social difference, t. But many school reform programs explicitly try to reduce salience of social difference. Schools strive to create a community, different from the social world outside the school. We see this strategy clearly in the Central Park East Elementary and Secondary Schools. In the account of the founder-director, Deborah Meier (1995), we see that from the very beginning school administrators set out to create a new type of school, with a strong sense of community and difference with the outside world. In her words: "[W]e committed ourselves openly and loudly to being different" (p. 30). We interpret the choice to create a school community as a choice about the allocation of resources within a school. Many school reform programs involve resources, such as teacher and staff time, training and special programs, devoted to this task. The model shows that when resources devoted to such a reform program will enhance educational attainment.

Suppose a school has resources $r = 1$ which it can divide into two uses. The first use, a proportion α, is teaching skills. The second use, the remainder $1 - \alpha$, is creating community within the school and reducing the social differences between the students and the school, t.[23] We assume skills increase directly in α: $k_i = \alpha s e_i$. On the other hand, social differences t also depends on α. We assume the parameter t depends on α as follows. First, $t(\alpha)$ is increasing in α. Then, we suppose the highest possible value of t is $\bar{t} > 0$, the lowest value is 0, and t decreases as more resources are devoted to changing it: we have $t(1) = \bar{t}$ and $t(\alpha) \to 0$ as $\alpha \to 0$, so $t' < 0$. Let t_0 be the initial value of t among the population served by a school.

The school's objective function (for $p = 0$) is now in the two-category and one-category case respectively:

$$K_2 = \alpha s_H \left(\frac{1}{2} + \frac{m - s_H}{\sigma} \right) e(H)$$

$$+ \alpha s_M \left(\frac{s_H - s_M}{\sigma} + \frac{I}{\sigma t(\alpha)} \right) e(M), \quad \text{2-category case}$$

$$K_1 = \alpha \cdot s \cdot e(S) \left(\frac{1}{2} - \frac{s - m - I/t(\alpha)}{\sigma} \right), \quad \text{1-category case.}$$

In the two-category case, the school chooses s_H, s_M, and α; in the one-category case it chooses s and α.

We conduct the following analysis supposing that t_0 is sufficiently high that it is initially optimal for the school to have two ideal categories.

The school's objective function is now

$$K_2 = \alpha \left[s_H \left(\frac{1}{2} + \frac{m - s_H}{\sigma} \right) e(H) + s_M \left(\frac{s_H - s_M}{\sigma} + \frac{I}{\sigma t(\alpha)} \right) e(M) \right]$$

for $s_H > s_M$

$$K_1 = \alpha \left[s_H \left(\frac{1}{2} + \frac{m - s_H}{\sigma} + \frac{I}{\sigma t(\alpha)} \right) e(H) \right] \quad \text{for } s_H \leq s_M$$

The school chooses s_H, s_M, and α. Let us consider this problem for K_2, where the school chooses two categories. Rewrite the objective function as follows:

$$K_2(\alpha) = \alpha f(\alpha),$$

where

$$f(\alpha) = s_H \left(\frac{1}{2} + \frac{m - s_H}{\sigma} \right) e(H) + s_M \left(\frac{s_H - s_M}{\sigma} + \frac{I}{\sigma t(\alpha)} \right) e(M).$$

We can solve for the optimum in two stages. We first solve for the optimal s_H and s_M as a function of α. We then solve for the optimal α.

Note that the optimal s_H and s_M could depend on α directly, and indirectly through $t(\alpha)$. Denote the optimal school positions as $s_H^*(t(\alpha), \alpha)$ and $s_M^*(t(\alpha), \alpha)$. To solve for these optimal positions, we differentiate the profit function with respect to s_H and s_M. Because skill attainment is proportional to α, we see that the $s_H^*(t(\alpha), \alpha)$ and $s_M^*(t(\alpha), \alpha)$ will depend on α only to the extent that α affects t. With some abuse of notation, we now write the optimal school types as $s_H^*(t(\alpha))$

and $s_M^*(t(\alpha))$, and we have:

$$s_H^*(t(\alpha)) = \left(m + \frac{\sigma}{2}\right)\left(\frac{2e(H)}{4e(H) - e(M)}\right) + \left(\frac{I}{t(\alpha)}\right)\left(\frac{e(M)}{4e(H) - e(M)}\right)$$

$$s_M^*(t(\alpha)) = \left(m + \frac{\sigma}{2}\right)\left(\frac{e(H)}{4e(H) - e(M)}\right) + \left(\frac{I}{t(\alpha)}\right)\left(\frac{2e(M)}{4e(H) - e(M)}\right).$$

We now have the following maximized value $f^*(\alpha)$:

$$f^*(\alpha) = s_H^*\left(\frac{1}{2} + \frac{m - s_H^*}{\sigma}\right)e(H) + s_M^*\left(\frac{s_H^* - s_M^*}{\sigma} + \frac{I}{\sigma t(\alpha)}\right)e(M),$$

and our objective function is $K_2(\alpha) = \alpha f^*(\alpha)$. By the Envelope Theorem, we have

$$\frac{dK_2(\alpha)}{d\alpha} = f^*(\alpha) + \alpha\frac{df^*(\alpha)}{d\alpha} = f^*(\alpha) + \alpha\frac{\partial f^*(\alpha)}{\partial\alpha}.$$

Hence, we have

$$\frac{dK_2(\alpha)}{d\alpha} = s_H^*\left(\frac{1}{2} + \frac{m - s_H^*}{\sigma}\right)e(H)$$

$$+ s_M^*\left(\frac{s_H^* - s_M^*}{\sigma} + \frac{I}{\sigma t(\alpha)}\right)e(M) - \alpha(t'(\alpha))s_M^*e(M)\frac{I}{\sigma t(\alpha)^2}.$$

The optimal level of α obtains where this first-order condition is equal to zero.

Here we see the costs and benefits of increasing spending α on reducing the salience of social differences t. The cost is a direct loss in skills – this is the first term. The benefit is an increase in the number of middle students, this is the second term. We always have an interior solution with appropriate conditions on $t'(\alpha)$. At $\alpha = 0$, the condition is always positive, hence we must have $\alpha > 0$. (If there is no spending on skills, no students obtain skills.) At $\alpha = 1$, the condition can be negative for $t'(\alpha)$ sufficiently large (recall that $t'(\alpha)$ is positive). In this case, it is optimal to spend some positive resources on changing this social parameter.

We record these insights in the following Proposition:

Proposition 7. *When t becomes sufficiently small, the school can maximize skills by promoting a single ideal category rather than two. Hence, the school can maximize average skill attainment by diverting resources from direct academic uses to reducing the social parameter t. The optimal α is less than 1 when there is a large decrease in t for a small expenditure on students' identity.*

Proof. The proof is contained in the above pages.   □

8.6   Conclusion

This chapter elaborates a new model of students and schools. The model departs from traditional economic analysis in two ways. First, the child is the decision maker and her motivation is primarily to fit in. Second, the school is a social institution that can promote particular ideals for its student population. The model integrates the standard sociological view of schooling into an economic model. The framework we suggest captures phenomena that could not be captured by standard economic modeling, such as how a school's curriculum might respond to a change in the demographics of the student population.

We see this outcome in the first of three possiblilities for school policy we examine in this chapter. We first consider a school that promotes a single social category and chooses an ideal to maximize students' average skill attainment. This model captures the situation of many public schools in the United States as new black and minority students entered their doors, beginning in the 1960s. The school faces a tradeoff. If it promotes an ideal that is closer to the ideal of the workplace, the school helps students acquire economically valuable skills. Students whose backgrounds differ from this ideal, however, will reject the school, adopt an alternative identity, and exert less effort in school. The optimal ideal balances this tradeoff. This simple model gives two important insigts on how schools might modify their policies and curriculum to better match student demographics. The more social differences matter to students' identities, the more the school must reduce its ideal to engage students in the school. Similarly, the greater the diversity of the student population, the more a school must reduce its ideal.

We consider a second scenario where a school promotes two social categories, providing students with more choice. As discussed earlier, this model captures educators' descriptions of a "Shopping Mall High School" in many contemporary US public school systems. Schools provide different alternatives to students, some emphasizing academic achievement, others not. Here the school faces two tradeoffs. First, raising the ideals directly increases skill attainment, but increases the number of students that reject the school. Second, there is competition between the two categories. Students can opt for the middle rather than the high category. These students will have lower levels of educational attainment. We show how a school chooses the ideals optimally to balance the education levels of the students at the top of the distribution with the education levels at the bottom of the distribution. When the student population is very diverse, the school finds it optimal to set high ideals that are close together. The students at the top of the distribution have higher educational outcomes, but the students at the bottom become burnouts. When diversity is low, on the other hand, the school finds it optimal to set a high and low ideal. There are no burnouts, but many students at the top of the distribution choose the middle category and have lower eduational attainment.

Finally, we consider a school that can invest to create a school community and reduce the importance of social differences to students' identities. This model captures the efforts of many school reform programs. There is a cost to diverting resources to this purpose; there can be a direct loss in students' skills. But the benefit is the increase in the number of students who identify with the school. When a school's student population is initially quite diverse, it can be optimal to spend resources to reduce the salience of social differences.

While we have focused in this chapter on the policies of a single school, the modeling could lend insight into the differences between public school and private schools. Educators describe public schools – in the wake of civil rights – as constrained in establishing strict ideals for students. Rather, they are shopping malls that provide students with choice. Private schooling can be seen as relaxing constraints on investments to establish identity.[24] Indeed private schools may have much more leeway, since parents agree upfront to abide by the school rules.[25] This ability to establish an ideal could be a benefit of private schooling. However, as we saw in the case of a single school, providing choice need not enhance skills. In a private market, many schools could emerge to serve different segments of a student population. Some parents and students would opt for schools with different ideals – just as students opt for the middle category inside a single school. Hence, when identity and students' social divisions are taken into account, private schools and school choice need not enhance overall academic achievement.

Acknowledgments

Rachel Kranton thanks The Pew Charitable Trusts for its financial support of this research, and the Research Program in Development Studies at Princeton University for its hospitality.

Notes

1 See, e.g., Christopher Jencks and Meredith Phillips' (1998) detailed work on the education and test score gap between black and white students.
2 This chapter draws on a wide literature outside economics by policy makers, educators, sociologists, anthropologists, and historians. Citations are distributed throughout the text. We believe the framework we present in this paper reflects a predominant framework in many fields, including schools of education. See, e.g., the Harvard University's Professor Sara Lawrence-Lightfoot's syllabus on the sociology of education: http://icommons.harvard.edu/~gse-a107/syllabus/Syllabus.html
3 See, e.g., Judith Harris (1998) who argues that a child's goal is success within his or her social world, and James Coleman's (1961) classic on adolescent social arrangements.
4 We develop this general model of utility and identity in Akerlof and Kranton (2000).
5 In a similar vein, Bowles *et al.* (2001) argue that much of the economic benefit of schooling results from "subjecting students to types of social interactions and systems of reward that replicate the social interactions and reward systems of the workplace, providing positive reinforcement for some behaviors and personalities and sanctions for others" (p. 1167).
6 See, e.g., John Ogbu's (1974, 1997) work on standard English in African American communities, Paul Willis' (1977) ethnography of working-class youth in Britain, and Douglas Foley's (1990) study of Mexican–American students in Texas.
7 See also Hampel (1986), Krug (1964, 1972), and Hollingshead (1949, 1975). Bloom (1987, p. 27) characterizes the social category of immigrant students as that of "traditional communities where myth and passion as well as severe discipline, authority,

and the extended family produced an instinctive unqualified, even fanatic patriotism," in contrast with the ideal of the schools: "the rational and industrious man, who was honest, respected the laws, and was dedicated to the family ...." For the purposes of this chapter it does not matter whether Bloom has given the correct interpretation of the contrasts; all that matters is that the protagonists believed in these differences.

8 See, e.g., Lisa Delpit's (1995) study which describes African American elementary school children in classrooms where teachers constantly correct their language, accents, and deportment. Foley (1990) describes Mexican–American high school students.

9 See, e.g., Grant (1988), and Powell *et al.* (1985).

10 Fliegel (1993) and Meier (1995) describe the CPESS program. Comer (1980, 1988) describes his New Haven program.

11 Following the human capital theories of Schultz (1960) and Becker (1964), a large body of empirical work in economics have examined the impact of resources on education outcomes. Prominent recent examples include David Card and Alan Krueger (1992a,b), Julian Betts (1995), Ronald Ferguson (1998), Eric Hanushek (1996), Caroline Hoxby (2000), and Krueger and Diane Whitmore (1999). These studies have variously viewed resources in terms of school expenditures, teacher – student ratios and teacher quality, and the returns to education in terms of earnings, as well as other intermediate measures such as enhanced test scores, continuation rates, and rates of college application. The sociological literature, in contrast, is remarkably silent on the return to resources devoted to education. The framework we develop suggests a synthesis of the sociological and economic viewpoints, providing insights into how resources can be effectively deployed.

12 The standard economic model of education and human capital originates with Theodore Schultz (1960) and Gary Becker (1964).

13 For review of social psychology and experiments see Margaret Wetherell (1996); for a basic social psychology text see Brown (1986).

14 Starting with Hollingshead (1949) and Coleman (1961), numerous scholars have spent extensive time in schools and demonstrate the importance of social divisions to student motivation. For more recent work see, e.g., Penelope Eckert (1989), Richard Everhart (1983), and Douglas Foley (1990).

15 We think of students' characteristics ϵ as correlated with a family's socioeconomic status, race, and ethnicity. We consider how these socially defined traits, rather than randomly distributed tastes as in a standard economic model, may affect effort in school.

16 Most ethnographies describe these interactions in fine detail. See the earlier citations. Foley (1990), e.g., tells how Mexican–American students felt like outsiders in the high school where most teachers and administration, not to mention football players and cheerleaders and students in the academic track, were "Anglo."

17 Again, see earlier citations for real or perceived conflict between academic and work skills and students' social backgrounds.

18 See Coleman (1961) and other ethnographies cited earlier. For example, in the high school described by Foley (1990, p. 101): "Most students came to school for extracurricular activities and the social scene." For all but a few "brains," academics was a sideshow.

19 This assumption, of course, reflects our own bias as economists. Many schools have other goals. Indeed it has been argued that "[E]very educational system ... wants to produce certain types of human beings" (Allan Bloom 1987, p. 26). Religious schools and military academies are obvious examples. However, public schools – following the directives of local school boards – reflect the character of their communities and their visions of what schools should accomplish.

20 This level of s is invariant to changes in σ and m when $m + \sigma/2$ is held constant. The optimal school after integration at Hamilton High would be the same as the optimal school before integration. However, if we included the many externalities of disruption, the school would lower s to account for the new students.

21 See Delpit (1995) for ideas on how to adjust the curriculum while minimizing the loss to students' skills. She suggests, e.g., that African–American students learn to speak standard English in drama class rather than in an English class. With this method, students are taught the skill without being told that their way of speaking is incorrect.

22 In the analysis we assume that all students located above s_H choose H. For $s_H = s_M$, we assume that students located strictly above $s_H = s_M$ choose H (and exert $e(H)$) and students located below $s_H = s_M$ that choose to identify with a school choose M and exert $e(M)$. This assumption prevents a discontinuity in the numbers of H and M students at $s_H = s_M$.

23 It is possible that resources devoted to reducing t are also directly complementary to skill acquisiton – as many would argue that CPESS' special curriculum enhances learning.

24 Chubb and Moe (1988, tables 4–8) find, e.g., in data from the Teachers and Administrators Survey supplement to High School and Beyond, that private school principals have less interference from school boards and other administrators over curriculum, instruction, and discipline. They face less constraints on school policy and procedures concerning personnel, and hiring and firing. They have more support from parents in setting their goals and set greater goal clarity for their schools.

25 Peshkin's (1986) account of a Christian school in Illinois provides an extreme example. Parents and children sign detailed contracts, where parents not only grant the school the right to enforce a firm Christian code of discipline, they promise to enforce the school's code at home.

References

Akerlof, George A. and Kranton, Rachel E. (2000) "Economics and Identity," *Quart. J. Econ.* 105 (August), 715–53.

—— (2002) "Identity and Schooling: Some Lessons for the Economics of Education," *J. Econ. Lit.* 40 (December), 1167–201.

Becker, Gary (1964) *Human Capital: A Theoretical and Empirical Analysis with Special Reference to Education.* New York: Columbia University Press.

Betts, Julian R. (1995) "Does School Quality Matter? Evidence from the National Longitudinal Survey of Youth," *Rev. of Econ. Statist.* 77 (May), 231–50.

Bloom, Allan (1987) *The Closing of the American Mind.* New York: Simon and Schuster.

Bowles, Samuel, Gintis, Herbert, and Osborne, Melissa (2001) "The Determinants of Earnings: A Behavioral Approach," *J. Econ. Lit.* 39 (December), 1137–76.

Brown, Roger (1986) *Social Psychology: The Second Edition.* New York: Free Press.

Card, David and Krueger, Alan B. (1992a) "Does School Quality Matter? Returns to Education and the Characteristics of Public Schools in the United States," *J. Polit. Econ.* 100 (February), 1–40.

—— (1992b) "School Quality and Black-White Relative Earnings: A Direct Assessment," *Quart. J. Econ.* 107 (February), 151–200.

Chubb, John E. and Moe, Terry (1988) "Politics, Markets, and the Organization of Schools," *Am. Polit. Sci. Rev.* 82, 1065–87.

Coleman, James S. (1961) *The Adolescent Society: The Social Life of the Teenager and Its Impact on Education.* New York: The Free Press.

Comer, James P. (1980) *School Power: Implications of an Intervention Project.* New York: The Free Press.

—— (1988) *Maggie's American Dream: The Life and Times of a Black Family.* New York: New American Library.

Delpit, Lisa (1995) *Other People's Children: Cultural Conflict in the Classroom*. New York: The New Press.

Eckert, Penelope (1989) *Jocks and Burnouts: Social Categories and Identity in the High School*. New York: Teachers College Press.

Evans, William N., Oates, Wallace E., and Schwab, Robert M. (1992) "Measuring Peer Group Effects: A Study of Teenage Behavior," *J. Polit. Econ.* 100 (October), 966–91.

Everhart, Richard (1983) *Reading, Writing, and Resistance: Adolescence and Labor in a Junior High School*. London: Routledge & Kegan Paul.

Ferguson, Ronald F. (1998) "Teachers' Expectations and the Black–White Test Score Gap," in *The Black–White Test Score Gap*, Christopher Jencks and Meredith Phillips (eds), Washington, DC: Brookings Institution Press, pp. 273–317.

Fliegel, Seymour (1993) *Miracle in East Harlem: The Fight for Choice in Public Education*. New York: Random House.

Foley, Douglas E. (1990) *Learning Capitalist Culture: Deep in the Heart of Texas*. Philadelphia, PA: University Pennsylvania Press.

Fordham, Signithia (1996) *Blacked Out: Dilemmas of Race, Identity and Success at Capital High*. Chicago, IL: University of Chicago Press.

Goldin, Claudia and Katz, Lawrence F. (1997) "Why the United States Led in Education: Lessons from Secondary School Expansion, 1910–1940," *NBER Working Paper 6144* (August).

Grant, Gerald (1988) *The World We Created at Hamilton High*. Cambridge, MA: Harvard University Press.

Hampel, Robert L. (1986) *The Last Little Citadel: American High Schools Since 1940*. Boston, MA: Houghton Mifflin.

Hanushek, Eric A. (1971) "Teacher Characteristics and Gains in Student Achievement," "Aggregation and Estimated Effects of School Resources," *Am. Econ. Rev. Papers Proceedings* 61 (May), 280–8.

—— (1986) "The Economics of Schooling: Production and Efficiency of Public Schools," *J. Econ. Lit.* 24: 3, 1141–77.

Harris, Judith R. (1998) *The Nurture Assumption: Why Children Turn Out the Way They Do*. New York: Simon and Schuster.

Hollingshead, August B. (1949) *Elmtown's Youth: The Impact of Social Class on Adolescents*. New York: John Wiley.

—— (1975) *Elmtown's Youth and Elmtown Revisited*. New York: John Wiley.

Hoxby, Caroline M. (2000) "The Effects of Class Size on Student Achievement: New Evidence from Population Variation," *Quart. J. Econ.* 115 (November), 1239–85.

Jencks, Christopher and Phillips, Meredith (1998) *The Black–White Test Score Gap*. Washington, DC: Brookings Institution Press.

Krueger, Alan B. and Whitmore, Diane M. (1999) "The Effect of Attending a Small Class in the Early Grades on College-Test Taking and Middle School Test Results: Evidence from Project STAR," mimeo., Industrial Relations Section, Princeton University.

Krug, Edward A. (1964) *The Shaping of the American High School: 1880–1920*. Madison, WI: University of Wisconsin Press.

—— (1972) *The Shaping of the American High School: 1920–1941*. Madison, WI: University of Wisconsin Press.

Meier, Deborah (1995) *The Power of Their Ideas*. Boston, MA: Beacon Press.

Ogbu, John U. (1974) *The Next Generation: An Ethnography of Education in an Urban Neighborhood*. New York: Academic Press.

—— (1997) "Beyond Language: Ebonics, Proper English and Identity in a Black American Speech Community," mimeo., University of California Berkeley, Dept. of Anthropology.

Peshkin, Allen (1986) *God's Choice: The Total World of a Fundamentalist Christian School.* Chicago, IL: University of Chicago Press.

Powell, Arthur G., Farrar, Eleanor, and Cohen, David K. (1985) *The Shopping Mall High School: Winners and Losers in the Educational Marketplace.* Boston, MA: Houghton Mifflin.

Schultz, Theodore W. (1960) "Capital Formation by Education," *J. Polit. Econ.* 68 (December), 571–83.

Sizer, Theodore R. (1984) *Horace's Compromise: What Works for the American High School.* Boston, MA: Houghton Mifflin.

Tajfel, Henri and Turner, John (1979) "An Integrative Theory of Intergroup Conflict," in *The Social Psychology of Intergroup Relations*, William G. Austin and Stephen Worchel (eds), Monterey, CA: Wadsworth, pp. 33–47.

Tyack, David (1974) *The One Best System.* Cambridge, MA: Harvard Universtiy Press.

Wetherell, Margaret (1996) "Group Conflict and the Social Psychology of Racism," in *Identities Groups and Social Issues*, Margaret Wetherell (ed.), Thousand Oaks, CA: Sage Publications, pp. 219–27.

Willis, Paul R. (1977) *Learning to Labour: How Working Class Kids Get Working Class Jobs.* Westmead, Farnborough, Hants., England: Saxon House.

9 Smallholder identities and social networks

The challenge of improving productivity and welfare

Christopher B. Barrett

9.1 Introduction

Poverty necessarily reflects relatively low productivity per capita. So perhaps the central challenge in the economics of development revolves around how to increase the productivity of the poor. Moreover, since most of the world's poor are engaged in agriculture, one might reasonably focus on understanding the economics of improving agricultural productivity. Slow and incomplete adoption of agricultural innovations has severely impeded productivity growth. A vast literature has therefore explored the factors that impede agricultural technology adoption in low-income agrarian nations, emphasizing in particular four general factors: (i) insufficient initial endowments of labor, land or finance necessary to make adoption attractive and/or feasible; (ii) natural resources management problems, especially those related to common property or open access resources; (iii) market failures that degrade the terms of trade faced by smallholders; and (iv) financial market failures that impede investment in improved production technologies or natural resource management practices characterized by significant sunk costs or higher production or price risk.[1]

Without detracting in any way from these appropriate foci, anyone familiar with rural areas of low-income agrarian nations is immediately struck by economists' general neglect of the social and psychological context in which smallholder make production decisions. It takes only a few hours' immersion in a village to become vividly aware that behavioral expectations, ritual embodied in ceremonies, tradition, and identity along dimensions of kinship, gender, ethnicity, religion, occupation, etc. play a central role in the myriad choices made by smallholders. Indeed, issues of identity and social relations seem to play a far more prominent role in low-income agrarian economies than they do in higher-income or more urban settings.[2] While much of the literature in anthropology, cultural geography, development sociology, and political science emphasizes the central role of identity and agents' social embeddedness in conditioning human agency, economists have been largely (and surprisingly) silent on these issues. This chapter proceeds from the premise that this silence may impede our capacity to understand and address the challenge of improving agricultural productivity, whether measured in terms of output per worker, yields per unit area cultivated or per head of livestock, or total factor productivity. Frictions related to identity and social networks may amplify the effects of the more conventional economic obstacles on which the technology adoption literature has tended to focus.

At a very coarse, unconditional level, casual observation suggests that productivity is lower and social embeddedness higher in low-income agrarian economies than elsewhere in the world, suggesting a negative association between technological change and social networks. However, such an observation verges on the heretical in contemporary development studies, conflicting sharply with a rapidly growing literature on social capital that posits a favorable, causal link from some indicator(s) of social cohesion and embeddedness – typically associational propensity – to economic performance, commonly measured in terms of expenditures or income, as in Narayan and Pritchett (1999). Knack and Keefer (1997), e.g., argue that social cohesion is more important for poorer economies because of imperfect contract enforcement capabilities via formal institutions of the state. Research that has focused more specifically on agricultural technology adoption has similarly emphasized the salutary effects of social relations, particularly in facilitating learning and borrowing from others (Foster and Rosenzweig 1995; Conley and Udry 2001, 2002; Bandiera and Rasul 2002; Isham 2002; Munshi 2003).

The preceding paragraph reveals the core puzzle that motivates this chapter: how do we reconcile the mass of recent evidence on the salutary effects of social capital at the individual level with the casual observation that social embeddedness appears negatively correlated with productivity and material measures of welfare at more aggregate scales of analysis? Put differently, can we formulate and empirically validate an analytical framework that not only explains individual productivity or technology adoption behavior as a function of the characteristics or behaviors of others, but that also explains the aggregate properties of social systems characterized by persistently low productivity?

This chapter proposes a general framework for beginning to address this puzzle. This framework, building on Akerlof and Kranton (2000), puts social and psychological phenomena on an equal footing with material considerations in trying to understand microeconomic behavior. In the second part of the chapter, we introduce a few empirical examples to illustrate the basic points. Ultimately, the objective of the chapter is to try to push for a more robust and useful understanding of why more productive technologies and natural resource management practices are often not adopted extensively or quickly in low-income agrarian societies where the benefits from adoption appear especially great and what, if anything, can and should be done to stimulate faster productivity growth in the socio-psychological context of such settings.

9.2 A general analytical framework

While economists have been increasingly taking socio-psychological phenomena into consideration in explaining behaviors observed in low-income agrarian societies, the dominant approach has tended toward treating these as having purely instrumental effects.[3] In the development economics literature, e.g., one learns that social networks have value because they provide access to information, credit, insurance or transfers that are imperfectly provided by markets and governments. They also reduce search and transactions costs and help with contract monitoring and enforcement in settings characterized by weak legal systems and high relative costs of market participation. These observations are all surely correct.

Yet, they are likely also to be incomplete. In particular, social networks also have intrinsic value because people care about their relationships and because those relationships help to define individuals' sense of self, the identity on which individual behavior is based. Furthermore, individuals' identity and their social networks may establish behavioral expectations – "norms" – that at least weakly constrain individual choice.[4] The concern motivating this chapter is that reducing the social dimensions of smallholder microeconomic behavior to their positive instrumental effects can lead to mistaken inferences about the role and value of social relations in productivity growth and thus to misguided prescriptions for development policy.

The general analytical approach introduced here aims to nest the various instrumental effects found in the extant economics literature into a more encompassing and realistic framework wherein individuals' self-image and social relations are endogenously affected by behavior. This builds on important recent contributions by Kevane (1997), Platteau (2000) and, especially, Akerlof and Kranton (2000), who each emphasize that individuals follow equilibrium strategies based on norms of prescribed or expected behaviors that are conditional on one's (potentially evolving) identity. This opens up possibilities of identity-based rents that accrue to members of particular groups, rents that can be maintained in equilibrium only through processes of social exclusion and hysteresis. This can result in self-reinforcing, separating equilibria that may keep some groups down while facilitating accumulation by others. It also opens up the possibility of rational substitution of social harmony for material gain associated with productivity growth when communities have difficulty coordinating behaviors so as to achieve a "big push" that carries everyone (or most everyone) along together.[5] Tying the results back to the core puzzle that motivates this chapter, in this framework, social capital may be positively correlated with economic outcomes in the small, within a community, yet also associated with a lower-level equilibrium in the large, at the level of regions or nations.

In this framework behavior has psycho-social foundations, rooted in one's identities. Individuals typically possess multiple, overlapping identities that jointly determine their self-image. A farmer may at once be male, belong to a particular ethnic group, live in a specific neighborhood, be a secondary school graduate, tall, honest, a good father, etc. Some identities are exogenous. Characteristics such as gender, birth cohort (i.e., age over time), birth family and its history, national origin, race, and other physical markings (e.g., deformities) shape one's sense of self and are inherited at birth and essentially immutable.[6] Other dimensions of identity are endogenous, effectively determined (with some lag) by the people with whom one associates and the behaviors in which one engages.

These are obviously interrelated, but, more importantly, they are repeatedly chosen.

Identities inherited at birth can have permanent consequences, whether positive (e.g., the son of the village chief, born into relative wealth and power) or negative (e.g., the crippled daughter of a lower caste, illiterate family). As in all systems with multiple equilibria, initial conditions matter. That is no less true with respect to identity and the social networks that flow from the exogenous components of individuals' identities.[7]

However, the endogenous component of identity is not only adaptable, it must be reproduced through social interactions and observable actions. Someone identified as a skilled farmer gradually loses that identity unless they continue to cultivate and produce (more often than not) above-average yields; someone's identity as so-and-so's friend gradually deteriorates unless they spend time with so-and-so, etc. People have to invest in the reproduction of those endogenous identities that bring them satisfaction. They likewise must invest in the transformation of those identities they dislike into some other form they prefer.

Collective, shared identities create groups and communities.[8] Indeed the etymology of the word "community" finds its origins in the Latin *communis*, meaning "shared by all or many." Within communities, affinities emerge that influence the sharing of resources (e.g., cash, food, labor), information (e.g., job leads, observations on third parties, tips on promising new technologies), and responsibilities. The community serves not only as a resource pool, but also as a mirror on oneself, confirming one's self-image, one's identity. Community relations are therefore not only *productive*, they are also *reproductive* in that they reinforce and thereby reproduce the collective identity that defines and sustains a community. Just as identity is multidimensional and multifunctional, so are the communities that are shaped by individuals' identities. People commonly belong at once to geographic, ethnic, religious, and other communities that intersect but do not duplicate each other.

Because communities serve as a mirror on oneself, an individual's actions impact not only their communities and their self-image, but also on those of others within their communities, generating effects such as pride or embarrassment. Individual decisions affect the collective identity, generating a type of pecuniary externality. As a result, communities commonly carry behavioral expectations of their members and enforce these through shared strategies, including sanctions on internal transgressors, discrimination against outsiders, and entry costs for new members.[9] Akerlof (1983), Coleman (1987), and Kevane (1997) identify these identity-based expectations and the associated constraints on behavior as social norms. Although collectively irrational, it may nonetheless be individually rational to adhere to such norms. As a consequence, there may exist multiple equilibria in which behavioral expectations become self-fulfilling, even for individuals adversely affected by the norms. Such patterns are often manifest in separating equilibria in which collective identity – race, gender, religion, caste – serves as a signal of expected behavior, even if the identity and the behavior are not intrinsically linked (Loury 2002; Hoff and Pandey 2003; Fang and Loury, Chapter 2, this volume).

Social networks are closely related to but distinct from communities. The key distinction between networks and communities is that while the latter are the natural byproduct of a shared identity, the former requires investment to establish and maintain relationships and, moreover, an individual's investment must be matched by her counterparts. Networks are thus the manifestation of a matching process in which people come together voluntarily, and at some gross cost to themselves, while communities are associations that exist irrespective of people's investments in links with others with similar identity. The two can obviously overlap to a large degree, not least of which because shared identities – i.e., common membership in a community – can reduce the search and transactions costs associated with matching with others. Networks likewise generate pecuniary externalities in the forms of club goods (e.g., for information that is nonrival but excludable) and demand-side network effects for many sorts of goods and services.[10]

9.2.1   A behavioral model

Consider the following dynamic optimization problem by a stylized small farmer, j. Individual j's well-being is a function in part of current expenditure, e_j, out of income earned through a chosen livelihood, savings and net borrowing, and transfers. Earned income results from her production technology, resource allocation and marketing choices, c_j. Net borrowing and transfers is a product of her identity and social network. Welfare also depends on others' choices, c_{-j}, that may either affect j's material consumption directly (i.e., pecuniary externalities) or influence the focal point against which she gauges the value of her own material consumption (i.e., positional externalities[11]). Well-being also depends on j's nonmaterial experiences, in particular, one's self-satisfaction, s_j, and social relations, r_j, over the period.

Farmer j possesses a stock of material (physical, natural, financial, and human) capital, represented by the composite asset A, expressed in the same units as expenditures. She also has a sense of self, an identity reflected in the vector I describing identification with a variety of characteristics such as gender, age, ethnicity, occupation, skills, and other attributes that define individual identity. Identity can be multidimensional and multiscalar; the elements of I are not, in general, mutually exclusive. The flow of self-satisfaction, s, one enjoys can be thought of almost as a dividend generated by one's self-image, I. Farmer j also possesses a stock of knowledge, K, about production technologies and marketing opportunities that affect her productivity, in part by affecting her propensity to adopt improved production or marketing methods. Finally, she is embedded in a set of social networks, N, represented by a vector describing links to others. This network also generates dividends in the form of desired social relations, r.

Using Bellman's method, we can collapse farmer j's dynamic optimization problem into just two periods: current (0) and all the future (1). Given a discount rate of δ, the farmer's problem can be represented as a value function, $V(\cdot)$, encompassing current period utility, $U(\cdot)$,[12] wherein she makes current period choices as follows:

$$\underset{c_{j0}, e_{j0}}{\text{Max}} \, V(A_{j0}, I_{j0}, K_{j0}, N_{j0}) \equiv U(e_{j0}, r_{j0}, s_{j0}) + \delta V(A_{j1}, I_{j1}, K_{j1}, N_{j1}).$$

$$(1)$$

This specification of the objective function incorporates several effects one finds in the literature, notably intrinsic valuation of identity or status and social relations and the possibility of interpersonal externalities due to altruism or positional externalities (Bernheim 1994; Frank 1995; Kevane 1997; Akerlof and Kranton 2000; Platteau 2000; Moser and Barrett 2003). Of particular importance to questions of technology adoption, mutual interdependence through pecuniary externalities can give rise to coordination problems and resulting multiple equilibria.

Individuals solve such dynamic choice problems subject to multiple constraints. First, as already indicated, the flows of social relations, r, and self-satisfaction, s, that j enjoys are a product of her *ex ante* stock of N and I, respectively, and the resource allocation choices she and others makes to exploit (or not exploit) those stocks:

$$s_{j0} = s(I_{j0}, c_{j0}, c_{-j0}),$$

$$(2)$$

$$r_{j0} = r(N_{j0}, c_{j0}, c_{-j0}).$$

$$(3)$$

Expenditures, e, are subject to the usual dynamic budget constraint. The generalized livelihood function, $\ell(c_{j0}, A_{j0}, K_{j0})$, yields physical output as a monotonically increasing function of each argument, where our interest focuses especially on j's choice of production technology.[13] Let c_{j0}^θ, an element of the broader c vector, represent an index of technology choices available that is, without loss of generality, ordered by technologies' total factor productivity, implying that productivity per unit land and labor is increasing in the technology index, or $\partial^2 L / \partial A \partial c^\theta > 0$. The standard findings of the technology adoption literature, that the probability and extent of adoption of improved technologies increase in farmers' *ex ante* asset holdings and knowledge, reflect the observation that $\partial c_{j0}^\theta {}^* / \partial A_{j0}, \partial c_{j0}^\theta {}^* / \partial K_{j0} > 0$, where $c_{j0}^\theta {}^*$ is farmer j's optimal technology choice.

Any expenditures in excess of current livelihood earnings and liquid assets, reflected in A_{j0}, must be financed through net borrowing or transfers, $B(I_{j0}, N_{j0})$. People receive loans, transfers, and insurance against adverse shocks that depend upon their identity and social networks, as the extant literature demonstrates (LaFerrara 2003; DeWeerdt 2004; Goldstein *et al.* 2004).

The net payoffs from assets or current livelihoods, $P(I_{j0}, N_{j0})$, generate monetary value that likewise depend upon j's identity and social networks. Women or members of certain ethnic or racial groups might receive lower wages than men from other groups for the same work. Those with a reputation for honesty or quality may receive premia for their products. People with good connections may get a discount on purchased inputs. Furthermore, payoffs depend on transactions, search and contract monitoring, and enforcement costs that are conditional on one's social network and identity (Fafchamps and Minten 2002). Because individuals differ in these dimensions, payoffs from otherwise identical decisions will vary in cross-section. Combining these different sources of disposable assets we get the following budget constraint for current expenditures:

$$e_{j0} \leq P(I_{j0}, N_{j0})[\ell(c_{j0}, A_{j0}, K_{j0}) + A_{j0}] + B(I_{j0}, N_{j0}) - F(c_{j0}). \quad (4)$$

where

$$F(c_{j0}) = \begin{cases} 0 & \text{for } L(I_{j0}) \leq c_{j0} \leq H(I_{j0}) \\ \Phi(c_{j0}, I_{j0}, N_{j0}) > 0 & \text{otherwise.} \end{cases} \quad (5)$$

The $F(c_{j0})$ term reflects fines or the monetary value of social sanctions imposed for choices, c_{j0}, perceived as transgressions of social norms. Those norms are reflected in identity-dependent higher and lower bounds on behavior, $H(I_{j0})$ and $L(I_{j0})$, respectively. Behavior within the bounds incurs no penalty. Out-of-bounds behavior, however, invites a fine or social sanction that is increasing in the offending choice's deviation beyond the expectational boundaries.[14] Sanctions from within one's own social network are increasing in network size. Punishment from outsiders is a function of one's identity; the same "deviant" actions may be punished differentially by outsiders who deem transgressions by some groups to be more threatening than the same transgression committed by another. This framework captures the fact that norms (and punishments for their violation) reflect the behavioral expectations associated with one's identity. For example, women may be expected to refrain from certain types of labor. Members of particular religious communities may be expected to avoid consumption of particular goods or services or not to work on particular days. Occupational identities likewise create behavioral expectations, as when self-identified organic farmers refrain from using chemical inputs.

Norms only weakly constrain behavior, however. They are not necessarily strictly binding constraints. One can typically violate the behavioral expectations associated with one's identity at a cost, perhaps in the form of social sanctions such as stigmatization, perhaps a physical penalty or a monetary fine.

Such penalties can be advantageous to a community in so far as they create a focal point to coordinate the selection of a relatively desirable equilibrium (Schelling 1960; Kandori *et al.* 1993). Consider, e.g., the penalties some hill communities impose on farmers – especially those near the top of slopes – who do not maintain terraces properly. Because terraces' effectiveness in soil and water conservation depends on the mosaic of structures along the whole toposequence, there are essentially two stable equilibria on a hillside: everyone terraces and enjoys superior productivity, or no one terraces. Penalties for those who fail to maintain their portion of the hillside can be understood as a means to focus all members of the community on the more desirable equilibrium. They are a coordination mechanism.

Of course, rule enforcement creates a second order free riding problem, in that everyone would rather that others enforce the rules than that they do it themselves, so long as their nonenforcement is not known to others. Hence, the place of public punishment. The social ritual of sanctions or fines ensures everyone knows not only who adheres to the rules, but also who enforces the rules. If adherence to and enforcement of rules helps define identity, the free riding problem gets resolved by making it in each person's interest to enforce rules.

In addition to the constraints on current expenditure, choice is made subject to an understanding of the laws of motion for the endogenous A, I, K, and N stocks. A central observation that undergirds this general framework is that the farmer's current choices affect the assets she carries into the next period, her sense of self, the accumulated knowledge on which she can draw, and the social networks of which she is a member. Put more succinctly, our choices have psychological and social consequences as well as informational or physical effects. Farmer j takes this into account, as discussion with virtually any small farmer in the tropics would confirm. The law of motion on A written here in quite general form, is quite standard:

$$A_{j1} = a(A_{j0}, e_{j0}, c_{j0}, c_{-j0}).$$ (6)

Asset stocks evolve in response to j's choices and those of others around her, with current expenditures having an especially prominent effect through both financial savings and consumption that doubles as an investment in productive assets, as is the case with food consumption that contributes to good health.

The more interesting dynamics for present purposes emerge from I, K, and N. One's future identity, I_{j1}, depends on not only one's self-image at the start of the current period, I_{j0}, but also on one's choices over the course of the period, others' choices and one's social relations, each of which could either reinforce or threaten one's sense of self. This implies

$$I_{j1} = i(I_{j0}, r_{j0}, c_{j0}, c_{-j0}).$$ (7)

If identity is mutable and well-being depends on one's sense of self, then this law of motion may limit farmers' willingness to choose new technologies that would conflict with one's self-image and social relations. Conversely, if others in one's social network are trying new production or marketing methods, one may be inclined to follow in the interests of social conformity.

The literature has increasingly admitted the importance of the endogeneity of social networks in villages. Let the law of motion for social networks take the form

$$N_{j1} = n(N_{j0}, I_{j1}, c_{j0}, c_{-j0}).$$ (8)

A significant empirical literature establishes that social networks form endogenously around collective identities associated with gender, church affiliation, ethnicity, kinship neighborhoods, etc. (Grimard 1997; Conley and Udry 2001; Bandiera and Rasul 2002; Hogset 2002; Murgai *et al.* 2002; De Weerdt 2004; Goldstein *et al.* 2004; Santos and Barrett 2005). So one should expect social networks to adapt in part to changes in individuals' identity, as when one changes churches, jobs or residences. Moreover, as was emphasized previously, the distinction between membership in different communities, which occurs cost-lessly as a by-product of the identities one shares with others, the size of one's social network depends on the resource allocation choices one makes and the corresponding choices others make, perhaps especially with regard to how peo-ple spend time. Those who allocate an increasing share of their labor to work on their own farm typically have to reduce the time they spend with others, implic-itly depreciating their social network capital in order to invest in greater on-farm physical output. If the value of maintaining network size is great, the opportunity cost of even uncompensated labor may be considerable and impede the adoption of labor-intensive technologies.

New technologies or management practices almost always require signifi-cant new learning in order to achieve maximal productivity. We capture this effect by endogenizing j's stock of productive knowledge about different liveli-hoods. K evolves in response to social relations that bring potentially informative interactions with others, one's own experiences and the activities of others:

$$K_{j1} = k(K_{j0}, I_{j0}, I_{-j0}, r_{j0}, c_{j0}, c_{-j0}) \tag{9}$$

with $k(\bullet)$ weakly increasing in K_{j0}, reflecting classic concave learning curve effects. Knowledge is produced in part through social interactions within a village as farmer j is exposed to experiments within her social network to the extent she relates with them (r_{j0}) and they innovate (c_{-j0}).[15] This formulation under-scores that social learning can have mixed consequences for an individual farmer's incentive to adopt more productive methods, as Foster and Rosenzweig (1995), and Bandiera and Rasul (2002) emphasize. People have better access to infor-mation about a new technology the more extensive their social interactions and the greater the similarity amongst them, *ceteris paribus* (Pomp and Burger 1995; Rogers 1995; Conley and Udry 2002; Romani 2002). But they also then have a greater incentive to delay their own costly experimentation with a new technology in order to free ride on others' experiments.

The quality of the communication, and thus of knowledge transmission, fur-ther depends on j's identity and the identities of the others in her social network because the nature of ties matters to the diffusion of knowledge.[16] Rogers (1995) emphasizes that more effective communication occurs when individuals are homophilous – possessing similar attributes – and that effective communication leads to greater homophily, in a reinforcing feedback loop. Homophily therefore accelerates the diffusion of innovations *within* a network.

Yet homophily may also limit initial innovation within networks because there are few openings through which new methods can enter the community. Consistent with Granovetter's (1973) notion of "the strength of weak ties," heterophilous interactions are essential to transmission of information regarding innovations *between* networks and to the organization of individuals into politically based movements to advance collective goals (Granovetter 1982). Yet a high degree of heterophily often implies less interpersonal trust, which may make interpersonal communications relatively inefficient and thus slow diffusion *within* a network.

This suggests a delicate balance in the nature of social networks and identity within villages. Innovation ought to occur more quickly and diffuse more broadly within relatively homophilous networks containing a few individuals whose multiple identities link them "weakly" to other networks, providing a bridge for information transmission between networks whose internal social structure – bonds or strong ties – then promotes rapid transmission. These bridges – labeled "opinion leaders" or "change agents" by Rogers (1995) – play a central role in diffusion by initiating change within their network(s). The early innovator benefits from reinforcement of his self-image as a leader, while members of his social network benefit from the information his experiments with the new technology generate. Early adoption and rapid diffusion are an equilibrium outcome in such networks. By contrast, a high degree of homophily in a system can inhibit information transmission between networks, generating something akin to autarky, manifest in separating equilibria, with some networks in a low-level equilibrium of low productivity. As Granovetter (1982, p. 106) puts it, "social systems lacking in weak ties will be fragmented and incoherent. New ideas will spread slowly, scientific endeavors will be handicapped, and subgroups that are separated by race, ethnicity, geography, or other characteristics will have difficulty reaching a *modus vivendi*."

The preceding system of equations (1)–(9) thus specifies a reasonably general dynamic behavioral model that nests within it all of the key instrumental effects attributable to individuals' social attributes and identifying characteristics that one can find in the literature on economic development. Such a general analytical framework is admittedly unwieldy for exploration of specific micro-level topics that require more structure and simplification to become empirically tractable. Nevertheless, this broader contextualization of the socially embedded choice problem faced by smallholder farmers in low-income agrarian settings, that takes seriously both the material constraints and incentives they face and the endogenous evolution and intrinsic valuation of self-image and social relations, enables some reconceptualization beyond the limits of much of the current literature. This is necessary if we are to begin to answer the core puzzle that motivates this chapter: how do we reconcile micro-level empirical evidence in support of the claim that social capital stimulates technology adoption and productivity with what seems a negative correlation between these outcomes and social embeddedness at the macro-level?

9.2.2 Some implications of the framework

The preceding behavioral model offers merely a reasonably precise structure for thinking through how individual identity and the social networks to which people belong influence individual behavior, especially with respect to choices to improve physical productivity. I leave detailed, formal exploration of the model for future work. Here, I merely want to highlight several intriguing and intuitive implications about the relationship between social embeddedness and smallholder agricultural productivity and welfare that merit brief comment.

(i) Productivity and expenditures are increasing in one's density of social networks and for those possessing particular identities (e.g., men, racial, or ethnic elites) that grant them preferential access to information, finance, or better net terms of trade. Differentiation of the system of equations (1)–(9) with respect to I_{j0} and N_{j0} yields these familiar hypotheses regarding the instrumental benefits of social networks and privileged identities. Productivity differences arise due to differences in net payoffs, $P(I_{j0}, N_{j0})$, and faster learning. Expenditure differences arise not solely due to productivity gaps, but also from improved access to informal finance in the form of loans, social insurance, and gifts. In low-income agrarian communities where formal financial systems routinely fail to provide the services needed by smallholders, this informal finance role of social networks and identity can generate significant benefits.

(ii) Social networks and identity nonetheless confer intrinsic benefits, not just the instrumental value manifest in increased productivity and expenditure. It is not only true that friends make gifts; it is equally true that gifts make friends, even family (e.g., through dowry payments). People routinely make tradeoffs between the two. For example, Osterloh (2002), studying microfinance institutions in rural Kenya, finds that local credit committees are commonly much more concerned about maintaining cohesion within the social network, and especially with not offending powerful members of the community, than with rejecting risky credit applications or enforcing loan repayment, as the theory of peer monitoring and group lending posits (Stiglitz 1990). People's desire for social acceptance and confirmation of their own self-worth affect behaviors. Behavioral change can create switching costs because of the endogeneity of social relations and identity. Many of the narratives assembled in the World Bank's recent *Voices of the Poor* project emphasize that material deprivation – poverty – may make affirmation of one's proper place in society, through costly religious rituals, gifts, entertainment, and others acts of hospitality, that much more important (Narayan and Petesch 2002).

(iii) Identity-dependent behavioral expectations constrain choice, especially where financial market failures constrain individuals' ability to absorb the short-term costs of both technology adoption and social sanctions. Farmer j's best response functions are thus necessarily based on her identity – how she and others see herself – and on others' subjective expectations on how those possessing her identity will act. Consider the following stylized example based on several real cases I have observed in different countries. An uneducated woman is expected to tend to her family's food crop. She is not expected to cultivate a high-value cash crop. Therefore, no one bothers to tell her about it or to help her learn how she might break into this promising new market. Knowing others' expectations, and not wanting to suffer the embarrassment of shocking or even offending people by asking about the crop or by struggling with it on her own, she rationally opts not to adopt the crop, even though there is no biophysical reason why she couldn't cultivate it and even though the returns to the crop are manifestly superior to the food crop she grows instead. Just as social networks can facilitate communication of valuable new information, so too can they facilitate the flow of erroneous or unnecessarily restrictive behavioral expectations that, when responded to rationally, effectuate precisely the anticipated outcome, even if they embody errors of judgment. Social networks can thus reinforce adverse equilibria associated with social control through identity, just as they can facilitate movement to superior equilibria.

This framework offers another lens through which to view the standard positive relationship between *ex ante* material wealth and one's propensity to adopt a new technology or product. As A_{j0} increases, j can better afford to incur the identity and social network costs associated with behavioral change, including necessary future investments in creating new social relationships and in reinforcing a new identity (e.g., as a French bean contract farmer for a European supermarket chain rather than as a maize producer like her neighbors). Those who start out poor may find it difficult to finance such change. As a consequence, the poor must often take their inherited identity as given and operate within that less remunerative and more restrictive nexus.

(iv) Movement to a higher productivity equilibrium then often depends on bold individual action or coordinated action among a critical mass of members within a community. People can and will break out of *ex ante* social norms when the associated sanction costs are low, their capacity to absorb those costs is high, or the attractiveness of breaking free of the behavioral bounds of their identity becomes too great to resist. If enough people violate behavioral norms, the shared identity shifts and social norms evolve endogenously.

This is a classic coordination problem. The key to coordination is communication, commonly through social processes such as public ritual (Chwe 2001). The value of public ritual comes not from unidirectional transmission of information, as we commonly think of information flow, but from the production of common knowledge, from letting all members know what the other members know, that they know that they know, and so on *ad infinitum*. If an individual's return to an action – weed or pest control, water management, terracing, starting up production of a high-value but perishable crop requiring coordinated, bulk evacuation, etc. – increases in the number of other people taking the same action, then multiple equilibria arise naturally. One equilibrium commonly involves no one adopting, because the action has negative payoff in isolation. Another involves coordinated adoption of the choice because the payoff to each individual participant is positive only so long as others do likewise.[17] Where networks based on "strong ties" are relatively weaker in accessing knowledge from outside the network, they function more effectively in generating common knowledge.[18] Common knowledge is essential to cooperative behavior to resolve collective action problems (Ostrom 1990; Baland and Platteau 1996; Chwe 2001; Bowles and Gintis 2002).

Yet one must guard against an overly romanticized view of social networks and common knowledge, since communities can equally prove exploitative or dysfunctional (Agrawal and Gibson 1999). The more bounded the network, meaning the greater the role of strong ties – also known "social closure" in the sociology literature – the greater the power conferred on individuals in position of internal authority. Such power can be exercised directly or indirectly through one's influence over third parties who independently interact with a partner (Basu 1986). The result may be unwanted regimes that persist because of interpersonal conjectures and an absence of outside contacts. Researchers and development practitioners have not yet developed any reliable rules of thumb for telling the difference *ex ante* between those communities whose social structures prove hospitable to promoting innovation and those that prove inimical.

In many low-income agrarian settings, public ritual is commonplace. Religious ceremonies, taboos, exacting social protocols, and the like have evolved over long periods of time as means to coordinate individual activity. The ritual life of villagers can create a strong focal point around established production practices, making it more difficult to coordinate mass movement to a different set of practices. Homophilous communities within which information flows relatively quickly and accurately can therefore be somewhat impervious to the introduction of new technologies if these are not individually rational in isolation from others' behaviors. This likely helps explain why it has been so difficult to promote many improved natural resources management practices – such as terracing, rotational grazing, biological control of pests, and weeds – that exhibit considerable pecuniary externalities without either (i) creating large group work parties that coordinate the work across many farms, (ii) securing the enthusiastic support of the community leadership, or (iii) relying on very large farms almost exclusively (Barrett *et al.* 2001).

(v) Strong social networks often contain within them the seed of egalitarian pressures that can impede investment by creating very high de facto marginal tax rates. Strong social networks depend on highly personalized relationships which naturally engender regular interpersonal comparisons to establish status. In such environments, relative positions commonly matter, perhaps as much as or more than absolute levels. Positional externalities permeate behavior within networks, but are commonly absent when comparing across networks. In the presence of positional externalities, socially inefficient equilibria can emerge as efforts to keep up with the neighbors induce mutually offsetting individual investment in the production of status, often through symbolic sacrifices in lieu of physically productive investments (Frank 1995; Platteau 2000). Positional externalities also naturally give rise to redistributive norms that "may be interpreted as a form of taxation designed to curb positional race for status, that is, as a device that compels them to take positional externalities into account in their choices" (Platteau 2000, p. 196).

Such social taxation creates an incentive to hold wealth in forms suboptimal for growth. Cash holdings tend to be most vulnerable to social claims, so members of egalitarian networks often consciously limit their liquidity as a means of defending themselves against claims from other members of the network (Platteau 2000). This can involve investment in relatively illiquid physical assets (e.g., land, livestock) or in extensive, costly ceremonial activities that seem excessive on their surface. The induced portfolio structure then exacerbates working capital constraints to production and investment, hurting productivity, and leaves few liquid assets with which to handle serious shocks.

In summary, when payoffs may depend on individual identity and social networks that also carry intrinsic value, there may be rents associated with membership in particular communities. These rents need not be equalized across communities because of nontrivial barriers to changing one's identity and leaving or joining new social networks. The social and psychological context of village life thus matters to the task of improving the material productivity of low-income rural communities. A serious challenge arises because the spontaneous introduction of new ideas, methods, practices, and technologies into a community depends on weak ties, as does individuals' freedom to seize new opportunities without either imposing welfare losses on others, due to positional externalities, or incurring prohibitive social taxation. Yet rapid and accurate transmission of such information within the community and resolution of coordination problems depends on strong ties. Maintenance of homophily can be valuable but can also come at a cost of parochialism because it implies barriers to trade – in ideas, finance, labor, and products – with other groups. Intuitively, there is some optimal balance of inclusion and exclusion, of weak and strong ties. From a practical standpoint, however, we currently know next to nothing about what the right balance is nor how to bring it about or maintain it once it is achieved.

The strong ties that typify many low-income agrarian communities can generate the puzzling pattern that motivates this chapter. Productivity and welfare can be increasing in the small, i.e., within a community, the larger an individual's social network density. Yet in the large, i.e., across communities and nations, homophilous communities with rich traditions of ritual that coordinate behaviors and impede communication with and trust of outsiders, productivity and welfare can be negatively correlated with social embeddedness. Since most econometric work (rightly) employs community-specific fixed effects to control for unobservable inter-community variation in prices, agroecological conditions, physical infrastructure and the like, these studies inherently estimate only the within-community effects of social networks, hence generating the customary, positive estimated effect of social networks on productivity or welfare measures. Yet, between-community variation – perhaps especially in preferences and expectations – may hold the key to understanding differences in performance more generally, as Henrich *et al.* (2001) suggest in studying variability in individuals' response to bargaining, dictator and ultimatum games played in 15 different communities in 12 different countries.

9.3 Some sample puzzles

The preceding approach is far too general to lend itself to specifying and estimating econometric models in an attempt to identify specific effects, especially given the considerable identification problems plaguing social interactions models (Manski 1993, 2000; Brock and Durlauf 2001). The framework is nonetheless useful as a guide for thinking through the prospective determinants of cross-sectional variation in agricultural productivity between households and villages and around the world and for informing more qualitative empirical research.[19]

In that spirit, I employ this framework to explore some particular puzzles I have encountered in rural Africa regarding adoption or nonadoption of improved technologies and natural resources management practices. The following examples help illustrate why people might freely choose not to engage in behaviors that could prove materially beneficial or to undertake others that cause manifest material loss, sacrificing predictable productivity gains due to the psycho-social context in which they find themselves. These are followed by examples of strategies I have observed that seem to facilitate the development of identity and social relations that help foster productivity gains.

9.3.1   Foregoing significant productivity gains

Smallholders' identities and the social networks in which they participate have an inherently complex relationship with the adoption of productivity-enhancing technologies or practices. The following two brief examples of large prospective gains foregone offer contrasting perspectives, the first illustrating how identity and social networks can impede adoption, the other how the absence of strong social ties can be a barrier to productivity improvements.

9.3.1.1   Conformity, tradition, and rice intensification in Madagascar

Madagascar is a rice economy, with more than half of all cultivated land planted in the grain and some of the world's highest rates of per capita rice consumption in spite of also being among the world's poorest countries. In spite of the Malagasy obsession with rice, yields are very low. As a consequence, the nation's rice farmers are in aggregate net buyers of rice (Barrett and Dorosh 1996). Quite a few different methods of rice intensification have been promoted in Madagascar over the past twenty or so years, but none has yet gained a sufficiently solid foothold to improve productivity appreciably. Over more than a decade of research in rural Madagascar, I have gradually come to the conclusion that Malagasy smallholder identities and social networks are one of several key factors that inhibit productivity gains.

Among rural Malagasy, the invisible is often more important than the tangible. They care not only about material satisfactions, but also about spiritual, social, and moral phenomena. And they willingly pay dearly for these. Although highland Malagasy farmers say they cannot afford inorganic fertilizers or improved seed, they routinely pay extraordinary sums to exhume and reshroud dead ancestors every 3–5 years – an elaborate ceremony known as *famadihana* – and to travel long distances and contribute significant sums for *famadihana* for even distant relatives' ancestors.

Further underscoring the social and spiritual importance of death rituals among the Malagasy, several ethnic groups have strong behavioral expectations that households will sacrifice cattle when a household member dies. But because rice productivity is strongly increasing in cattle ownership due to manuring and animal traction services that are imperfectly tradable, livestock sacrifice implies a long-term productivity decline for the household, thereby increasing the probability of subsequent undernutrition and illness leading to death, creating a vicious circle. Freudenberger (1999) describes the sorts of spirals into which families descend when infectious disease strikes a household, concluding that "[t]he practice of zebu sacrifice is a fairly certain guarantee that almost no families will be able to accumulate sufficient cattle to adequately fertilize their fields and almost all are condemned to a vicious circle of inexorable and (for some) deepening poverty" (p. 21). Perhaps most surprisingly, there is great resistance to change this behavioral expectation in spite of its obvious, and sometimes catastrophic, cost. The numbers of cattle sacrificed seems to have decreased very slowly over the years, as people have become poorer, gradually lowering the range of socially acceptable sacrificial behavior. But the strength of ethnic and spiritual identity has induced astonishingly high tolerance for productivity loss in the name of conformity with behavioral expectations.[20]

Malagasy rice cultivators have also resisted productivity improvements associated with Green Revolution technologies – improved seed and chemical fertilizer use – due to cultural practices that help reproduce collective identity.[21] The Malagasy practice elaborate systems of taboos (*fady*) regarding work rhythms, and these *fady* constrain adoption of improved rice technologies. For example, due to a precolonial history of extensive slavery on the island and a colonial history of forced labor by the French, manual labor for others is considered demeaning among some of Madagascar's ethnic groups, particularly the Sihanaka of the Lac Aloatra region, Madagascar's granary. Because its adverse effect on one's self-image and social standing made wage labor relatively unattractive, local labor supply was sparse and seasonal migrants from other ethnic groups – less averse to wage labor, more desperate, or both – began arriving in Aloatra. Landowners found cheap migrant workers to be very effective, gradually replacing reciprocal work groups with seasonal hired labor. But the commodification of labor dealt a blow to social interaction within the Sihanaka community, leading to the invocation of ancient taboos limiting the days one may work in rice fields and when outsiders may enter a village. Agricultural extension agents and researchers typically view such taboos as indicative of the backwardness of the Sihanaka because they impede adoption of improved production technologies that fundamentally change work rhythms, perhaps especially for women. But Jarosz (1994) makes a strong and logical case for the rationality of taboos as an instrument for enforcing the allocation of time to women's rainfed crops and, especially, to socialization. Taboos embody behavioral expectations and penalties for transgressions, as well as the intrinsic value of social relations, all of which serve to cement collective identity. As Jarosz (1994, p. 448) puts it, "[a]dherence to taboo days expresses what it means to be human: taking time to socialize at the market, to drink rum, to braid one another's hair, and to rest."[22]

Most recently, hopes for improvements in Malagasy rice productivity have hinged on adoption of the system of rice intensification (SRI), a suite of agronomic principles and practices requiring no purchased inputs (i.e., SRI uses standard seed and no chemicals). SRI was developed in Madagascar in the late 1980s by a French missionary priest and has been shown repeatedly to generate double (or more) the yields of traditional rice methods on farmers' fields.[23] Yet in spite of aggressive efforts to extend the technique around the island, adoption rates remain very low. While there are several economic explanations for this,[24] when I have posed this puzzle to Malagasy, even to scientists with western graduate training, by far the most common hypothesis I hear is that SRI's visibly different transplanting, weeding, and water management practices conflict with the "ways of the ancestors." Given the centrality of lineage to Malagasy self-image, tradition becomes important, reflecting one's ancestral identity, and may well impede sharp, rapid changes in cultivation practices, although I would expect these to evolve over time, much like practices of zebu sacrifice. Moreover, Moser and Barrett (2003) find economically and statistically significant social conformity effects once one controls for learning from one's neighbors and from extension agents. Malagasy smallholders appear to choose their cultivation practices in part to conform to local behavioral norms, even if it means sacrificing gains in expected rice output.

Because Malagasy patterns of material consumption and production indeed obey the basic laws of consumer and producer theory, respectively, it is tempting to rely exclusively on that framework, as I have in the past. Yet one cannot help but liken this to the problem of a fat lady in a corset;[25] the result may be sparse and elegant, but it is nonetheless so restrictive that it does violence to the underlying reality. So many different cases of persistently low rice productivity in Madagascar seem to have some partial explanation in the psycho-social context of village life in that wonderful island nation that it seems imperative to admit such phenomena into any credible economic model intended to inform agricultural productivity policy in the country.

9.3.1.2   *Striga control in Kenyan maize systems*

In contrast to the preceding case, let me now describe a case where the *absence* of strong social networks poses a serious barrier to improved agricultural productivity. Nutrient-depleted soils in sub-Saharan Africa are becoming infested with the parasitic weed *Striga hermonthica*. CIMMYT (2003), and Kim (1991) report estimated yield losses of 20–90% on fields blighted by *Striga*, generating cumulative productivity losses of more than US$1 billion annually from more than 100 million people in maize, millet, sorghum, and cowpea farming households across sub-Saharan Africa. Prevention of *Striga* encroachment depends on maintaining high soil fertility and moisture, which is difficult in rainfed lands with infrequent rotation or fallowing. Once established, "witchweed," as it is understandably called in the western and central Kenyan farms where I have most frequently encountered it, has proved resistant to conventional methods of weed control via herbicides and hand or mechanical weeding, not least of which because a single *Striga* plant produces thousands of seeds that can remain dormant but viable in the soil for many years. *Striga* is difficult to eradicate because a single surviving plant can recolonize a large area in a single season. And with so many seeds, it spreads readily from farm to farm.

The most promising current method of eradication involves planting a non-host crop, such as the multi-purpose fodder legume *Aeschynomene histrix*, which provides soil nutrient replenishment services through atmospheric nitrogen fixation, as well as nutritious feed for grazing livestock. *A. histrix* is, however, completely resistant to *Striga* and thus functions effectively as a "trap crop," inducing suicidal germination by witchweed seeds that cannot parasite it and thus die (Tarawali *et al.* 2003), cleansing the soil of the weed in fields that are planted wholly in *A. histrix*[26] for a fallow period of one or two years. A rotation of the leguminous fodder over the whole farm can substantially and sustainably reduce *Striga* infestation, thereby generating significant yield gains. Yet I have only seen a few farms try this and only one community where it was widespread.

Striga control poses a classic coordination problem that is difficult to resolve in heterogeneous communities because of households' differential incentives to invest in weed eradication (Hogset 2003). The efforts of an individual small farmer working to block the entry of (or to eradicate) *Striga* on his fields are an increasing function of neighboring farmers' efforts at weed control, either through maintaining soil fertility and moisture prior to the entry of *Striga* or through rotational planting of *A. histrix* to induce suicidal germination by established witchweed. It has proved exceedingly difficult to organize communities to combat *Striga* in spite of the weed's considerable costs. This seems to be especially true in villages with large numbers of recent immigrants, inter-clan frictions and other social phenomena that dampen the strong ties necessary to resolve such coordination problems. The one village in which I heard of widespread, coordinated (and seemingly effective) efforts at *Striga* control is an ethnically homogeneous community where a charismatic local elder gathered all the adult men to talk about the problem and to make each of them commit publicly to working in teams to seed a trap crop on a portion of every farm. Absent establishment of coordinated traditions of soil fertility replenishment and crop rotation involving a trap crop, it may be difficult to achieve considerable maize yield gains from improved cultivars or market access.

9.3.2 *Strategies to facilitate gains*

The preceding two examples underscore the nonmonotonic relation between social embeddedness and low productivity: too little social cohesion can lead to coordination failures while too much can impede uptake of novel cultivation practices. The next two examples similarly illustrate strategies I have seen smallholders follow to improve productivity, the first relying on the escape from incumbent social entanglements, the second based on exploiting social networks and reshaping farmers' sense of self.

9.3.2.1 *Boarding schools for poor children*

Poor rural families commonly spend stunningly large shares of their disposable income to educate their children. As a father of five children educated in free public schools, I have always been struck by the effort and resources many poor farm families put into funding their children's attendance at distant boarding schools when much cheaper, local options are available.

Surely, school quality differences are a part of that story. But some utterly unsystematic, qualitative empirical evidence suggests to me that school quality differences do not wholly explain this pattern, indeed they might not even be the most important explanation. I came to this realization in a conversation a couple of years ago with a farmer in central Kenya who expressed surprise at my assumption that the boarding school his son was attending must be markedly better than the nearby government school. No, he explained, the local school was quite good. But if his son had stayed here, he would become acculturated in local ways. The father wanted to remove his son from the local social environment and to embed him in one characterized by greater ambition and higher expectations for performance. In effect, he wanted to shape his son's emerging identity so that he would think of himself as productive and ambitious, measure his self-worth by material performance, and establish a social network of others with similar self-images and motivations. The cost to the father of breaking from his social milieu himself was prohibitive, so he dismissed out of hand the possibility of moving or breaking ties with family and friends. But he wanted to mark his son with an identity other than that of his birth community and in order to do so, he had to invest a significant sum in sending him off to a good-but-not-great boarding school.[27]

9.3.2.2   Farmer field schools

The field of adult and extension education has gone through dramatic philosophical change over the past two decades, owing in large measure to the disappointing performance of old transfer-of-technology models of agricultural extension in the low-income world.[28] Currently, there exists great enthusiasm for the "farmer field school" (FFS) model, although it seems to have been subjected to limited careful performance evaluation to date.

The FFS method emphasizes shared experiential learning and experimentation intended to boost people's confidence and their ability to learn about their own system. FFS methods have been employed widely in promoting integrated pest management (IPM) and integrated soil fertility management (ISFM) practices in southeast Asia. My experience with them has mainly come in east and southern Africa.

From my casual observation, and according to FFS philosophy,[29] FFS do not aim to impart new technologies to farmers, so much as to change farmers' sense of self, in particular to stimulate their eagerness to experiment on their own farms and to build their confidence in their own capacity to learn and adapt methods suitable to their specific circumstances. This, of course, is not an easy transformation to ignite. Part of the secret of FFS' apparent success in some places likely lies in the creation of common knowledge about experimentation within the community.

By drawing farmers together on a weekly basis for mutual discussion and observation, the FFS not only enables them to acquire first-order knowledge about others' experiments, but, perhaps more fundamentally, it transfers second-order knowledge that many others also know this, and that they know that they all know this, thereby validating a new approach to agriculture through the social ritualization of experimentation. Based on my limited observation of FFS in action and discussions with a number of agricultural researchers and NGO field staff with greater operational familiarity with FFS, most of the farmer instructors in FFS do not teach very well. So it seems unlikely that neighbors learn much in the way of new methods from one another directly, at least not more effectively than from trained extensionists under old transfer-of-technology methods.

Yet the evidence keeps pouring in that FFS work, albeit not in all settings.[30] Yields often appear to increase in the neighborhood of 10–20% or so among participants, as compared to control groups, while expenditures on inputs such as chemical pesticides and fertilizers fall, generating net gains in excessive of gross output gains (Barzman and Desilles 2002; Jones 2002). Moreover, measured rates of diffusion beyond FFS participants have been extraordinarily high. Jones (2002), e.g., reports that for each FFS participant introduced to IPM methods, roughly 13 were estimated to take up the practice ultimately due to the launch of the FFS program. If FFS indeed prove effective, as they often seem to, I hypothesize that much of the efficacy can be attributed not to first-order learning about technologies from others, but rather from the production of second-order learning associated with common knowledge that facilitates collective identity transformation with the support of extant social networks. FFS seem to create an effective coordination mechanism.

These few, brief, informal examples illustrate how social embeddedness can indeed foster significant productivity and welfare improvements, as in the examples of coordinated action for *Striga* control and FFSs. But they also illustrate how social embeddedness can impede productivity gains, in the cases of rice intensification in Madagascar and the social impetus to send children away to boarding schools. Smallholder strategies appear heavily conditioned by the psycho-social context in which they make crucial production, marketing and investment decisions, with that context as often as not impeding productivity growth in spite of the common finding of the salutary effects of "social capital" in the empirical literature.

9.4   Conclusions

The general analytical framework developed in this chapter has two key features that depart from more standard specifications in economics. First, individuals intrinsically value not just material well-being, but also the friendships that result from their social networks and the self-image that comes from their identities. People therefore routinely invest in the reproduction or transformation of identity and social networks. Second, identities mark people, creating expectations for others and for themselves. As a result, they may be cautious about behaving "out of bounds," creating a behavioral status quo bias that can retard uncoordinated transformation of production processes.

In this framework, as in many other formulations in the current development economics literature on social capital, payoffs are conditional on identity and networks, creating local gains to greater social embeddedness. These gains arise due to the various immediate, instrumental roles identity and social networks play in the lives of rural villagers around the world: as sources of altruism, credit, insurance, information, contract monitoring and enforcement services, in reducing search and transactions costs, establishing social norms, proscribing and reinforcing gender roles, and ethnic or racial discrimination. The social capital literature has documented such phenomena well, albeit with perhaps excessive focus on these instrumental values of social relations.

9.4.1   Implications for research

What we understand less well are (i) the degree to which people value identities and social networks intrinsically – and thus the material opportunity costs they are willing to pay for psycho-social benefits, (ii) how important coordination failures, conformity effects or power relations are as impediments to technology adoption, (iii) the degree to which degree behavioral expectations constrain individual activity and investment choice, and (iv) the dynamic effects of current behaviors on endogenous social networks and individual identity and how different social coordination mechanisms mediate their evolution. The framework laid out here points to these as key topics for future exploration if we are to enrich our understanding of how psycho-social factors condition productivity growth and poverty reduction in low-income agrarian societies.

Two major problems face economists wishing to explore these issues: definition of appropriate reference groups and observational equivalence. Exceedingly few data sets provide information sufficient to identify individual respondents' social networks accurately.[31] As a consequence, analysts have to rely on village averages or other crude proxies, although geographic proximity is only one factor – and, it seems, a relatively weak one (Conley and Udry 2002; De Weerdt 2004; Santos and Barrett 2005) – in establishing the interconnections between agents. Errors in defining networks bias the parameter estimates of models that assume correctly specified networks.[32] Moreover, even if network definition is correct, it is terribly difficult to disentangle (i) correlated effects due to unobserved or omitted factors (e.g., the quality of a local extension officer), (ii) effects exogenous to the social network (e.g., all members of the network graduated from the same elite school with a strong biology program), and (iii) effects that are truly endogenous to the social network (e.g., coordination due to interdependence or social learning from one another), as Manski (1993, 2000) emphasizes.[33] In econometric work, we commonly employ models that assume away one or two of these effects, leading to overstatement of the importance of the remaining one(s). As a consequence, the literature likely overstates somewhat the magnitude of social insurance – which is essentially identical in data to altruism, identity-based transfers, and gifts for the purpose of generating social relations – and of learning from others, which is observationally equivalent to mimicry or conformity.[34] In sum, it is difficult to identify the pathways of social influence in standard econometric studies. This puts a premium on (i) improved data collection that pays explicit attention to network definition and controls for confounding factors, and (ii) qualitative data collection to shed light where survey data regrettably keep us in the dark.

9.4.2 Policy implications

The framework mapped out in this chapter implies a potential role for policy to facilitate productivity growth, particularly through efforts to help communities coordinate activities, such as through FFSs or concerted efforts for *Striga* control. The policy opportunities arise from two basic features of the model. First, multiple equilibria arise naturally in this setting as social frictions (especially when combined with liquidity constraints) and coordination failures lead naturally to low productivity equilibria. Small, short-lived interventions can have persistent effects by inducing endogenous shifts from low-level to higher-level productivity equilibria. Absent appropriate interventions, social differences can persist indefinitely (Akerlof and Kranton 2000; Loury 2002; Hoff and Pandey 2003). Second, the existence of pecuniary externalities in a system characterized by market failures leads to significant but remediable inefficiencies (Greenwald and Stiglitz 1986). When individual choices are framed by others' decisions, modest changes to private incentives that induce behavioral change by just a few people can have significant effects on community-level behavior. Finding the tipping points or thresholds at which such changes can be induced is a central task for applied researchers.

The possibilities arising from the existence of such tipping points may be achievable through standard economic instruments: subsidies, taxes and similar finitely-lived interventions that can make it worth people's while to deviate from traditional practices, initially, after which time inertia will prevent reversal after the intervention ends. Improving poor farmers' access to financial services may also enable them to overcome the short-term costs of social sanctions in order to undertake desirable investment in long-term productivity gains.

The prospect of thresholds due to identity and social networks also raises crucial questions about targeting. In particular, one may want to employ community-based or indicator targeting without worrying excessively about traditional income-based indicators of targeting efficacy. If it takes a village to change a farmer's cultivation and husbandry practices, then the efficacy of community-level or indicator targeting may be high even if there is high initial leakage of short-term program benefits to unintended beneficiaries. In order to change the behavioral expectations associated with a particular collective identity, one needs to find change agents or opinion leaders (Chwe 2001) and they typically will not be the poorest members of a community.

Although this framework highlights the potential of assistance to communities that are having difficulty resolving coordination problems to realize available productivity gains within extant social networks and identities, it also casts some doubt on donors' current enthusiasm for creating groups in the expectation that this will build valuable social capital. If social networks are the endogenous product of matching processes between people drawn together by their identities and self-interest, then it seems unlikely that group creation could create durable communities capable of transforming production patterns. This is a hypothesis desperately in need of rigorous testing. Using creative partnership designs to reinforce extant groups with demonstrable-but-unrealized capacity to facilitate intra-community or inter-community coordination would seem to offer a higher likelihood of success.

One core prediction of the above model is that productivity will increase as identities become based more on innovativeness and material performance or as preferences adapt to place more emphasis on physical satisfaction and less on nonmaterial sources of well-being. The pace and desirability of such cultural transformations are open to question. This framework's emphasis on the intrinsic value of things nonmaterial underlines the need for caution in holding out productivity growth or advances in material measures of welfare as the sole metric by which we gauge well-being. By a simple revealed preference argument, if people choose not to adopt a technology that is manifestly more productive than that they presently use, we ought to explore whether that is because adoption would conflict with their sense of self or would threaten others with whom they identify closely. If so, then the sacrifice of material improvement may be a small price to pay for the non-material gains associated with the maintenance or reproduction of an individual's identity and social networks.

In this chapter I have attempted to broaden somewhat economists' conceptualization of the challenge of stimulating agricultural productivity growth within low-income agrarian communities. The analytical framework informally sketched out and the few brief examples offered are meant to provoke further, less speculative theoretical and empirical research. They nonetheless offer a first, tentative attempt at reconciling the puzzling inconsistency between widespread empirical findings of the beneficial effects of measures of social embeddedness in micro-level data sets and the casual empirical observation that social embeddedness appears negatively correlated with productivity at macro-level. Analytical frameworks that cannot reconcile these facts should be treated with some suspicion.

Acknowledgments

Department of Applied Economics and Management, Cornell University, Ithaca, NY 14853-7801 USA (Email: cbb2@cornell.edu). I have benefited greatly from conversations with Larry Blume, Michael Carter, Andrew Foster, Mark Freudenberger, Heidi Hogset, Ravi Kanbur, Rachel Kranton, Peter Little, John McPeak, Chris Moser, Sharon Osterloh, Max Pfeffer, Paulo Santos, Bill Schulze, and Chris Udry, and from comments on an earlier draft from David Amudavi, Janet Hou, Andrew Mude, Paulo Santos, Jacqueline Vanderpuye-Orgle, and participants at the 2003 annual meetings of the American Agricultural Economics Association. This work was generously supported by The Pew Charitable Trusts and by the United States Agency for International Development (USAID) through grants No. LAG-A-00-96-90016-00 to the BASIS CRSP and HFM-A-00-01-00132-00 to the Strategies and Analyses for Growth and Access (SAGA) cooperative agreement from Africa Bureau. These views, and any errors therein, are purely my own.

Notes

1 See Feder *et al.* (1985) and Sunding and Zilberman (2001) for surveys of the relevant literature.
2 Farmers in OECD nations appear relatively more socially detached in their production and marketing decisions than do smallholders in the tropics. For example, where smallholders in the South typically depend to a large degree on kin and neighbors for information, credit, insurance, and reciprocal labor, Northern farmers more commonly get information from public sector extension specialists or buy it – explicitly or implicitly, bundled with inputs – from private suppliers, borrow from banks, insure themselves with financial services firms and the government, and hire workers on the open market. As a coarse generalization, it seems accurate to describe economic decisions as more socially detached in the advanced market economies than they are in the low-income tropics. I do not explore the reasons for this here, but just take it as a maintained hypothesis.
3 See Barrett (2003) for a fuller discussion.
4 In the model developed in the next section, norms appear as constraints on choice, albeit constraints that can be violated at some cost in utility terms. One could alternatively model preferences as influenced by social norms, as in the recent literatures on process-regarding preferences and fairness (Fehr and Fischbacher 2002; Falk *et al.* 2003; Platteau 2003).
5 This view of multiple equilibria traces roots its roots back at least to Rosenstein-Rodan (1943) and Myrdal (1957).
6 In high-income societies, people can, at great cost, change gender, remake themselves to appear considerably younger than they really are, correct deformities, etc. In the context of rural, low-income communities, these options rarely if ever exist, so inherited characteristics are effectively exogenous and permanent.
7 LaFerrara (2003) offers a nice demonstration of the role immutably given kinship ties play in determining access to and terms of credit in rural Ghana.
8 One could draw a finer definitional distinction, that communities are groups that share not just an identity but also resources of value, although we set this issue aside here since it is not especially germane to the present line of inquiry.
9 One can even think of social sanctions as a form of optimal tariff, although development of that theoretical metaphor is left for future work.
10 The classic examples of goods characterized by network effects are fax machines, the value of which depends fundamentally on how many other people one might communicate with via fax, and software programs where compatibility with the application(s) used by others in one's network affects the value of the software to a prospective purchaser. See Katz and Shapiro (1986, 1994) for an introduction to the fundamentals of network effects.
11 See Frank (1995) or Platteau (2000).
12 As modeled here, preferences do not change over time. If one were to choose the alternative modeling strategy of having identity affect preferences directly (see note 4), rather than indirectly through (not strictly binding) constraints on choice, then preferences would necessarily become endogenous, varying as one's identity evolves.

13 This can equally encompass marketing strategies because markets are analytically equivalent to technologies, wherein prices and transactions costs are the "production function" transforming that which one sells into things one buys. This can be seen readily through a bit more formal treatment. Describe a general production technology mapping inputs, X, into output, Y, as $Y = f(X)$. Now, let there be another technology mapping X into another output, $Z = g(X)$. A market provides a medium of converting Z into Y according to the relative prices, p^Z and p^Y, respectively, and transactions costs, T, such that $Y = (p^Z Z - T)/p^Y$. Of course, substitution implies $Y = (p^Z g(X) - T)/p^Y$ and $f(X) = (p^Z g(X) - T)/p^Y$ satisfies all the usual characteristics of a production function.

14 See Akerlof (1980) and Bernheim (1994) for alternative approaches to thinking about how groups penalize individuals who deviate from social norms.

15 Feder and O'Mara (1982) and Feder and Slade (1984) provide some early economic evidence on social learning's role in technology adoption. Rogers (1995) provides a brilliant summary of the literature from other social sciences on the diffusion of innovations, emphasizing especially the importance of social relationships, norms, and intra-community similarity, which Rogers terms "homophily," defined as (p. 286) "the degree to which a pair of individuals who communicate are similar. The similarity may be in certain attributes, such as beliefs, education, social status, and the like." The opposite is "heterophily," the degree to which two or more individuals who interact differ.

16 Romani (2002) offers a nice empirical demonstration of this point, showing how rural Ivorien farmers' ethnic identity conditions access to information not only from extension agents bringing in information from outside the community, but also from neighbors with a different ethnic identity.

17 The industrial organization literature on network externalities revolves around similar phenomena and the existence of multiple equilibria. See Economides (1996) for a good survey.

18 Chwe (2001, p. 65) offers this insightful contrast, "[T]he idea that weak links are always better for communication relies on the assumption that communication is about 'first order' knowledge only and not about knowledge of what others know. Weak links might be better for communicating widely, but strong links are better at forming common knowledge locally. When there is no issue of coordinated action and hence common knowledge, weak links are better . . . . For social coordination, however, strong links have an advantage."

19 It can also help guide data collection so as to provide appropriate controls and instruments in order that quantitative researchers might properly test for particular social or psychological effects using model specifications sufficiently general so as not to conflate related but distinct phenomena (e.g., mimickry or social conformity) with hypothesized phenomena (e.g., social learning).

20 Cattle sacrifice for funerals has similarly been linked to productivity declines and households' fall into poverty in western Kenya (Kristjanson *et al.* 2004; Mango *et al.* 2004).

21 This paragraph draws heavily on Jarosz (1994).

22 Taboos, perhaps especially the keeping of a large number of days of religious observance during which it is forbidden to work, can be found in many other places as well. Ethiopian religious holidays, to pick just one example, are a notoriously great drain on household labor endowments.

23 Econometric evidence indicates that shifting to SRI, holding all field and farmer conditions constant, yields, on average, an output increase of more than 84% (Barrett *et al.* 2004).

24 See Moser and Barrett (2003) and Barrett *et al.* (2004).

25 Image drawn from Monroe (1994).

26 Another non-host crop (e.g., soybean) can serve the same function.

27 The contemporary literature on schooling in the US underscores some of these same patterns. For one recent example in the popular press, see the *New York Times* op-ed piece by Herbert (2003). The concern is that in some social communities, often defined by racial collective identity, investing effort in acquiring a good education can cost a child his identity and induce social sanctions. In this view, kids slough off at school because they face an identity-conditioned behavioral expectation – by others and themselves – that performance will be low. Peer effects and the biases of outsiders both create expectations to which people respond in equilibrium (Loury 2002; Hoff and Pandey 2003).

28 In a similar spirit to what follows, Munshi (2003) uses data on adoption of high yielding rice and wheat varieties in India to argue that first-order social learning is weaker in heterogeneous populations, especially when the performance of the technology in question depends on adopters' unobservable individual characteristics.

29 See, e.g., FAO (2000), Barrett *et al.* (2001), Barzman and Desilles (2002), Jones (2002), or any number of issues of LEISA magazine.

30 See Rola *et al.* (2002) and Feder *et al.* (2004) for studies that use quantitative survey data to question the efficacy of FFSs in the Philippines and Indonesia, respectively.

31 The data from Ghana used by Conley and Udry (2001, 2002) and De Weerdt's (2004) from Tanzania are important exceptions.

32 For example, Santos (2003) uses Monte Carlo methods to demonstrate the considerable bias in established econometric tests for intra-village risk-sharing when insured contracts are actually agreed within social networks that are not equivalent to the (typically geographic) sampling cluster and are not wholly interconnected.

33 See also the excellent review paper by Brock and Durlauf (2001).

34 Moser and Barrett (2003) offer one highly structured approach to try to disentangle social learning from social conformity in panel data with at least three periods.

References

Agrawal, A. and C.C. Gibson (1999) "Enchantment and disenchantment: the role of community in natural resource conservation," *World Development*, 27: 629–49.

Akerlof, G. (1980) "A theory of social custom, of which unemployment may be one consequence," *Quarterly Journal of Economics*, 94: 749–75.

—— (1983) "Loyalty filters," *American Economic Review*, 73: 54–63.

Akerlof, G. and R. Kranton (2000) "Economics and identity," *Quarterly Journal of Economics*, 115: 715–53.

Baland, J.-M. and J.P. Platteau (1996) *Halting Degradation of Natural Resources: Is There a Role for Rural Communities?* Oxford: Clarendon Press.

Bandiera, O. and I. Rasul (2002) "Social networks and technology adoption in Northern Mozambique," Centre for Economic Policy Research Discussion Paper No. 3341.

Barrett, C.B. (2003) "On social networks and economic development," *Faith and Economics*, 41: 1–8.

Barrett, C.B. and P.A. Dorosh (1996) "Farmers' welfare and changing food prices: nonparametric evidence from rice in Madagascar," *American Journal of Agricultural Economics*, 78(3): 656–69.

Barrett, C.B., F. Place, and A.A. Aboud (eds) (2001) *Natural Resources Management in African Agriculture: Understanding and Improving Current Practices,* Wallingford, UK, CAB International.

Barrett, C.B., C.M. Moser, O.V. McHugh, and J. Barison (2004) "Better technology, better plots or better farmers? Identifying changes in productivity and risk among Malagasy rice farmers," *American Journal of Agricultural Economics*, 86(4): 869–88.

Barzman, M. and S. Desilles (2002) "Diversifying rice-based systems and empowering farmers in Bangladesh using the farmer field-school approach," in N. Uphoff (ed.), *Agroecological Innovations: Increasing Food Production with Participatory Development*, London: Earthscan.

Basu, K. (1986) "One kind of power," *Oxford Economic Papers*, 38: 259–82.

Bernheim, B.D. (1994) "A theory of conformity," *Journal of Political Economy*, 102: 841–77.

Bowles, S. and H. Gintis (2002) "The inheritance of inequality," *Journal of Economic Perspectives*, 16(3): 3–30.

Brock, W.A. and S.N. Durlauf (2001) "Interactions-based models," in J.J. Heckman and E. Leamer (eds), *Handbook of Econometrics, Volume 5*, Amsterdam: Elsevier.

Chwe, M.S.-Y. (2001) *Rational Ritual: Culture, Coordination, and Common Knowledge*, Princeton, NJ: Princeton University Press.

CIMMYT (2003) "STRIGA: search for a long-term solution," available at http://www.cimmyt.org/whatiscimmyt/recent_ar/D_Foster/striga.htm

Coleman, J. (1987) "Norms as social capital," in G. Radnitzky and P. Bernholz (eds), *Economic Imperialism: The Economic Approach Applied Outside The Field of Economics*, New York: Paragon House.

Conley, T.G. and C. Udry (2001) "Social learning through networks: the adoption of new agricultural technologies in Ghana," *American Journal of Agricultural Economics*, 83: 668–73.

—— (2002) "Learning about a new technology: pineapple in Ghana," Yale, CT: Yale University working paper.

De Weerdt, J. (2004) "Risk-sharing and endogenous network formation," in S. Dercon, (ed.), *Insurance Against Poverty*, Oxford: Oxford University Press.

Economides, N. (1996) "The economics of networks," *International Journal of Industrial Organization*, 14: 673–99.

Fafchamps, M. and B. Minten (2002) "Returns to social network capital among traders," *Oxford Economic Papers*, 54: 173–206.

Falk, A., E. Fehr, and U. Fischbacher (2003) "On the nature of fair behavior," *Economic Inquiry*, 41(1): 20–6.

Feder, G. and G.T. O'Mara (1982) "On information and innovation diffusion: a Bayesian approach," *American Journal of Agricultural Economics*, 64: 145–7.

Feder, G. and R. Slade (1984) "Acquisition of information and the adoption of new technology," *American Journal of Agricultural Economics*, 66: 312–20.

Feder, G., R. Just, and D. Zilberman (1985) "Adoption of agricultural innovations in developing countries: a survey," *Economic Development and Social Change*, 33(2): 255–98.

Feder, G., R. Murgai, and J.B. Quizon (2004) "Sending farmers back to school: the impact of farmer field schools in Indonesia," *Review of Agricultural Economics*, 26(1): 45–62.

Fehr, E. and U. Fischbacher (2002) "Why social preferences matter – the impact of non-selfish motives on competition, cooperation and incentives," *Economic Journal*, 112 (478): C1–C33.

Food and Agriculture Organization of the United Nations (2000) *Guidelines and Reference Material on Integrated Soil and Nutrient Management and Conservation for Farmer Field Schools*, Rome: FAO.

Foster, A. and M. Rosenzweig (1995) "Learning by doing and learning from others: human capital and technical change in agriculutre," *Journal of Political Economy*, 103: 1176–209.

Frank, R.H. (1995) *The Winner-Take-All Society*, New York: Free Press.

Freudenberger, K.S. (1999) "Livelihoods without livestock: a study of community and household resource management in the village of Andraladranovao, Madagascar," USAID Landscape Development Initiative project report.

Goldstein, M., A. De Janvry, and E. Sadoulet (2004) "Is a friend in need a friend indeed? Inclusion and exclusion in mutual insurance networks in Southern Ghana," in S. Dercon (ed.), *Insurance Against Poverty*, Oxford: Oxford University Press.

Granovetter, M. (1973) "The strength of weak ties," *American Journal of Sociology*, 78: 1360–80.

—— (1982) "The strength of weak ties: a network theory revisited," in P.V. Marsden and N. Lin (eds), *Social Structure and Network Analysis*, London: Sage Publications.

—— (1985) "Economic action and social structure: the problem of embeddedness," *American Journal of Sociology*, 91: 481–510.

Greenwald, B.C. and J.E. Stiglitz (1986) "Externalities in economies with imperfect information and incomplete markets," *Quarterly Journal of Economics*, 101(2): 229–64.

Grimard, F. (1997) "Household consumption smoothing through ethnic ties: evidence from Côte d'Ivoire," *Journal of Development Economics*, 53: 391–421.

Henrich, J., R. Boyd, S. Bowles, C. Camerer, E. Fehr, H. Gintis, and R. McElreath (2001) "In search of homo economicus: behavioral experiments in 15 small-scale societies," *American Economic Review*, 91: 73–8.

Herbert, B. (2003) "Breaking away," *New York Times*, 10 July, p. A23.

Hoff, K. and P. Pandey (2003) "Why are social inequalities so durable? An experimental test of the effects of Indian caste on performance," Washington, DC: World Bank working paper.

Hogset, H. (2002) "Social insurance and adoption of a lumpy new technology with delayed and uncertain benefits," presented at the Northeastern Universities Development Consortium annual meetings.

—— (2003) "Externalities, free riding, and difficulties of coalition formation," Ithaca, NY: Cornell University unpublished paper.

Isham, J. (2002) "The effect of social capital on fertiliser adoption: evidence from rural Tanzania," *Journal of African Economies*, 11: 39–60.

Jarosz, L.A. (1994) "Taboo and time-work experience in Madagascar," *Geographical Review*, 84: 439–50.

Jones, K.A. (2002) "Integrated pest and crop management in Sri Lanka," in N. Uphoff (ed.), *Agroecological Innovations: Increasing Food Production with Participatory Development*, London: Earthscan.

Kandori, M., G.J. Mailath, and R. Rob (1993) "Learning, mutation, and long run equilibria in games," *Econometrica*, 61: 29–56.

Katz, M.L. and C. Shapiro (1986) "Technology adoption in the presence of network externalities," *Journal of Political Economy*, 94: 822–41.

—— (1994) "Systems competition and network effects," *Journal of Economic Perspectives*, 8: 93–115.

Kevane, M. (1997) "Can there be an 'identity economics'? Review of the literature with reference to Sudan," Santa Clara University working paper.

Kim, S.I. (ed.) (1991) *Combating Striga in Africa*, Ibadan: International Institute of Tropical Agriculture.

Knack, S. and P. Keefer (1997) "Does social capital have an economic payoff?," *Quarterly Journal of Economics*, 112: 1251–332.

Kristjanson, P., A. Krishna, M. Radney, and W. Nindo (2004) "Pathways out of poverty in Western Kenya and the role of livestock," International Livestock Research Institute working paper.

La Ferrara, Eliana (2003) "Kin groups and reciprocity: a model of credit transactions in Ghana," *American Economic Review*, 93(5): 1730–51.

Loury, G.C. (2002) *The Anatomy of Racial Inequality*, Cambridge, MA: Harvard University Press.

Mango, N., J. Cheng'ole, G. Kariuki, and W. Ongadi (2004) "Social aspects of dynamic poverty traps: cases from Vihiga, Baringo and Marsabit districts, Kenya," USAID BASIS CRSP research report.

Manski, C.F. (1993) "Identification of endogenous social effects: the reflection problem," *Review of Economic Studies*, 60: 531–42.

—— (2000) "Economic analysis of social interactions," *Journal of Economic Perspectives*, 14: 115–36.

Monroe, K.R. (1994) "A fat lady in a corset: altruism and social theory," *American Journal of Political Science*, 38: 861–93.

Moser, C.M. and C.B. Barrett (2003) "The complex dynamics of smallholder technology adoption: the case of SRI in Madagascar," Cornell University working paper.

Munshi, K. (2003) "Social learning in a heterogeneous population: technology diffusion in the Indian Green Revolution," Brown University working paper.

Murgai, R., P. Winters, E. Sadoulet, and A. de Janvry (2002) "Localized and incomplete mutual insurance," *Journal of Development Economics*, 67(2): 245–74.

Myrdal, G. (1957) *Economic Theory and Underdeveloped Regions*, London: G. Duckworth & Co.

Narayan, D. and P. Petesch (eds) (2002) *Voices of the Poor: From Many Lands*, Washington, DC: World Bank.

Narayan, D. and L. Pritchett (1999) "Cents and sociability: household income and social capital in rural Tanzania," *Economic Development and Cultural Change*, 47: 873–97.

Osterloh, S. (2002) "Microfinance in adverse environments: the experience of KDA among the pastoralists of Northern Kenya," presentation to the annual meeting of the African Studies Association, Washington, DC.

Ostrom, E. (1990) *Governing the Commons: The Evolution of Institutions for Collective Action*, Cambridge: Cambridge University Press.

Platteau, J.-P. (2000) *Institutions, Social Norms, and Economic Development*, Amsterdam: Harwood Academic Publishers.

—— (2003) "Solidarity norms and institutions in village societies: static and dynamic considerations," University of Namur Centre de Recherche en Economie du Developpement Working paper no. 250.

Pomp, M. and K. Burger (1995) "Innovation and imitation: adoption of cocoa by Indonesian smallholders," *World Development*, 23: 423–31.

Rogers, E.M. (1995) *Diffusion of Innovations*, New York: Free Press.

Rola, A.C., S.B. Jamias, and J.B. Quizon (2002) "Do farmer field school graduates retain and share what they learn? An investigation in Iloilo, Philippines," *Journal of International Agricultural and Extension Education*, 9(1): 65–76.

Romani, M. (2002) "Love thy neighbor? Evidence from ethnic discrimination in information sharing within villages in Côte d'Ivoire," Oxford: University of Oxford working paper.

Rosenstein-Rodan, P. (1943) "Problems of industrialization of eastern and south-eastern Europe," *Economic Journal*, 53(2): 202–11.

Santos, P. (2003) "Testing for risk-pooling in the presence of localized insurance," mimeo., Ithaca, NY: Cornell University.

Santos, P. and C.B. Barrett (2005) "Interest and identity in network formation: who do smallholders seek out for information in rural Ghana?" Cornell University working paper.

Schelling, T. (1960) *The Strategy of Conflict*, Cambridge, MA: Harvard University Press.

Stiglitz, J.E. (1990) "Peer monitoring and credit markets," *World Bank Economic Review*, 4(3): 351–66.

Sunding, D. and D. Zilberman (2001) "The agricultural innovation process: research and technology adoption in a changing agricultural sector," in B. Gardner and G. Rausser (eds), *Handbook of Agricultural Economics, Volume 1A*, Amsterdam: Elsevier.

Tarawali, S.A., M. Peters, and R. Schultze-Kraft (2003) "Forage legumes for sustainable agriculture and livestock production in subhumid West Africa," International Livestock Research Institute working paper.

10 Social networks in Ghana

Christopher R. Udry and Timothy G. Conley

10.1 Introduction

The design of economic policy in Africa has been, and continues to be, hampered by dependence upon misleading units of analysis inherited from venerable models that were developed in a radically different social context. We think about "firms" that produce, interacting through markets with "households" that consume, and about small enterprises in which the roles of the "household" and the "firm" are merged. It is increasingly clear, however, that the very definition of the core units of the "household" and "firm" are problematic in many African contexts and that the facile use of these concepts can lead to misleading judgments about the process of economic development.

In Africa, the boundaries of "household," "firm," and "market" are mobile and permeable. Things resembling market transactions occur within households, and family-like interactions take place across households and firms. Rather than conceptualizing membership in a household or firm as a zero-one event, it is fruitful to think of individuals as participating in numerous social relationships of varying qualities and intensities with a variety of different people. Important insights about the structure of African economies and the design of appropriate economic policy are gained by the recognition that people are embedded within social networks.

Some of these implications are apparent in the eastern region of Ghana. The region is one of the key foci of Ghana's development strategy of expanding non-traditional exports. It is experiencing a transformation of its farming system from the production of local foodstuffs to intensive cultivation of pineapple for export as fresh fruit to Europe. The salient aspects of this transformation include learning about a set of new technologies, alterations in established patterns of land resource management, a dramatic shift to more capital-intensive production, and important new risks. On each of these dimensions, patterns of change have been fundamentally conditioned by the composition of social networks.

For example, in Conley and Udry (2001, 2003), we find that information about the proper use of the new technology passes informally between farmers. Farmers experiment with varying levels of input intensity (particularly fertilizer) and they discuss the results of their experiments with a restricted set of peers. Farmers learn from these discussions. Our data show, e.g., that a given farmer will begin to use more fertilizer after a neighbor with whom he is linked in an information network uses high amounts of fertilizer and achieves surprisingly high profits. As a consequence, people who are strongly connected with many other pineapple farmers (call them central) have learned the contours of this radically new technology more rapidly than others. We hypothesize that, in turn, other farmers value information connections with these central farmers because of the value of the knowledge that central farmers have obtained from others. The particular structure of the information network in these villages has had a dramatic effect on the diffusion of these new techniques.

Similarly, we find that access to land is secured by way of informal channels of political power. Plots in Ghana, as in much of Africa, are controlled by individuals, not households. Goldstein and Udry (2004) show that profits on women's farms are much lower than those of their husbands. In these villages, land fertility is maintained by periodic fallowing, and we show that the reason for the much lower profits on wives' plots is the fact that they are left fallow for shorter periods than are the plots of their husbands. This, in turn, is a consequence of the fact that the ties of mutual obligation and political influence that undergird land tenure security – and thus permit extended fallow periods for men – largely bypass their wives. In Southern Ghana, access to land is based on negotiation, status and, identity within a corporate group. Those with relatively weak ties to the group leadership are reluctant to fallow their land for fear of finding it reallocated to a rival when it is time to re-establish cultivation. Women are disproportionately likely to inhabit the margins of this political network and so fallow relatively little. What is particularly striking about our findings is the extent to which the "household" is inconsequential for cultivation decisions. The political influence of the husband seems to be entirely irrelevant for the security of tenure of the wife. It is in those households in which the husband holds a political office and the wife does not that the gap in fallowing (and thus fertility and profits) between the husband's plots and the wife's plots is largest.

Political influence and thus security of access to land flows through networks that cleave households. Similarly, husbands and wives tend to participate in separate insurance networks. Goldstein (2002) shows that risk-sharing between husbands and wives is highly imperfect. Women pool risk with other women in their villages more than with their husbands, and men share risk with male members of their extended families. Other financial flows show a similar pattern. Rates of return on capital invested in this export-led rural economy are astonishingly high (Goldstein and Udry 1999a). However, net financial inflows are small and largely follow well-established paths between individuals with deep social connections: sometimes between husband and wife, but more often between siblings, long-term friends, and members of the extended family. It is clear that credit constraints apply at the level of the individual, not at the level of the "household": there were numerous instances during our fieldwork in which a wife was unable to make potentially profitable investments (say, in pineapple cultivation or a non-farm enterprise) as the husband was expanding his on-going enterprise. Once again, it is the individual's position in the relevant social network that is the crucial determinant of access to a valued resource.

Our work thus far has made it clear that economic development in this region is being shaped by the networks of information, capital, and influence that permeate these communities. The first goal of this chapter is to describe the patterns of information, capital, labor, and land transaction connections that are apparent in these villages. We discuss the interconnections between the various economic networks: how closely related are the functionally different connections between individuals? We then relate these functional connections between individuals to more fundamental spatial, kinship, migration, gender, and religious relationships between people. Finally, we propose an equilibrium model of multi-dimensional network formation that can provide a foundation for further empirical research. Our hope is that this chapter can serve as a resource for future data collection on social networks guided by economic theory.

10.2   Data and setting

The research was conducted in four clusters of villages in the eastern region of Ghana. Commercial agriculture is no recent innovation in the study area. Historically, the farming systems of the study area have undergone a series of significant changes. In the nineteenth century, oil palm production sparked the first inflow of migration to the area. This district was at the heart of Ghana's cocoa revolution at the turn of the twentieth century (Hill 1963). In 1930, swollen shoot disease devastated cocoa production and farmers adopted a system based on intercropped cassava and maize. Most recently (since the early 1990s), farmers in the area have moved toward intensive pineapple production for export.

The Southern Ghanaian forest-savanna transition zone has seen a dramatic reduction in forest cover since the 1970s (as evidenced by aerial photography (Gyasi *et al.* 1994) and satellite imagery (Hawthorne and Abu-Juam 1995), important reductions in fallow lengths over the same period (Amanor 1994; Gyasi *et al.* 1994) and increased evidence of soil deterioration and infestation by pests, particularly the virulent weed known locally as akyeampong) (Amanor 1994; Gyasi *et al.* 1995). Land rights, however, have not been transformed into anything close to individualized freehold tenure. Berry (2001) notes that land in Southern Ghana "is subject to multiple, overlapping claims and on-going debate over these claims' legitimacy, and their implications for land use and the distribution of revenue" (2001, p. xxi). Goldstein and Udry (2004) provide evidence that fallowing decisions are strongly influenced by the cultivator's political position in the village and lineage.

Within each village cluster we selected 60 married couples (or triples – a bit more than five percent of husbands have multiple wives) for our sample. Each member of the pair or triple was interviewed 15 times during the course of the two years. Each interview was carried out in private, usually by an enumerator of the same gender.

The survey was centered around a core group of agricultural activity questionnaires (plot activities, harvests, sales, and credit) that were administered during each visit. In addition, about 35 other modules were administered on a rotating basis. We also administered (once per field) an in-depth plot rights and history questionnaire, and mapped each plot using a geographical information system. We supplemented this with data on soil fertility: the organic matter and pH of each plot was tested each year.

Much of the analysis of this chapter is based on the data we collected on the social and economic interactions of our sample members with other people, and in particular with other people in our sample. We recorded data on the contacts that each of our respondents had with other individuals (in the data archive, this is the "individual roster"). "Contacts" include learning interactions, credit and gift transactions, sales/purchases of farm inputs and outputs, and labor and land market interactions. In the second year of the survey, for each such transaction we asked the respondent to provide certain information about the other party to the transaction. Data was recorded on the relationship and frequency of contact between the respondent and the contact, the residence and occupation of the contact, and the identification number of the contact if he/she is in the sample. Every contact has a unique identification number so we can trace them throughout the different questionnaires.

These contacts are reasonably well-defined for credit, gift, purchase/sale, and land and labor transactions. However, the nature of learning interactions is more subtle and subjective. We asked a long series of questions about specific tasks, ideas, and decisions. For example, "Did anyone advise you which particular crops to plant on your farm?", or "From whom did you first learn about the idea of using fertilizer?" Our list of information links for any individual includes anyone named in response to these questions. In principle, all pairs of respondents who learned about farming from each other should be listed. In fact, it is impossible to record the names of all individuals with whom respondents discuss farming, so enumerators were instructed to request the names of individuals with whom more than casual conversations took place. Two important issues arise as a consequence. First, different respondents interpret "casual" differently, and second, important information might be transmitted during quite casual conversation.

Therefore, we also collected complementary data on information interactions from questions about randomly selected *pairs* of respondents. We collected two such datasets. One was focused particularly on learning about pineapple. The other was more general. Consider the latter. Each sample respondent was questioned about a random sample (without replacement) of seven other individuals in the same village, and with three other predetermined individuals who appear to be focal in the village. Links for each respondent are defined according to his responses to specific questions about the relationship with the selected persons. For example, "Have you ever gone to . . . for advice about your farm?" For each pair of individuals we also record information on the frequency of contact, the period over which they have interacted, and the information on familial relations. This type of data has proven particularly useful for understanding the process of social learning through network connections. It is less useful for understanding the overall shape of social networks in the villages because it provides no information on interactions between individuals outside the random sample of seven for each respondent. Therefore, for the remainder of the chapter we utilize data from the "individual rosters" of each of the respondents.

In addition to the data on social and economic interactions, we will make use of the data on each respondent's family background, wealth, and education. Finally, we rely on our data on the spatial relationships between the plots of our respondents derived from the village and the plot maps.

10.3   Networks of information, finance, land, and labor in Southern Ghana

The data on network links provides us with a random sample from which we can infer some characteristics of the social and economic networks in our research villages. The data are "egocentric" in the parlance of network theory: we know (in principle) about the links from our sample individuals to other people. If one of these links happens to be another individual in our sample then we know a great deal about both nodes of that link, and about further connections along the network. However, if the individual at the other end of the link is not a member of our sample, then our information is quite limited. In particular, we know nothing about further links along the network.

A simple consequence of our fixed sample size across villages is that the probability that both nodes of a given link are included in our sample is lower in a large village than in a small village. This fact does not hinder inference about the relative densities of networks across villages. Let L_v^t be the number of links of type t in village v. The density of the t network in v is defined as

$$\Delta_v^t = \frac{2L_v^t}{n_v(n_v - 1)}, \tag{1}$$

(Wasserman and Faust 1994). Clearly, Δ_v^t ranges from 0 to 1 (for a complete network in which each individual is connected to each other individual). Consider two villages v and u with $\Delta_v^t = \Delta_u^t$. However, the sizes of the villages could differ ($n_v \neq n_u$). Since the densities are equal,

$$L_v^t = \frac{n_v(n_v - 1)}{n_u(n_u - 1)} L_u^t. \tag{2}$$

A link is observed in our data if *both* the involved individuals are in our sample. Therefore, if S is the fixed sample size across villages, the probability of observing any given link in village v is $(S/n_v)^2$. The expected number of links observed in village v is

$$\left(\frac{S}{n_v}\right)^2 L_v^t = \left(\frac{S}{n_v}\right)^2 \frac{n_v(n_v - 1)}{n_u(n_u - 1)} L_u^t \approx \left(\frac{S}{n_u}\right)^2 L_u^t, \qquad (3)$$

(for large n_u, n_v), which is the expected number of links observed in village u.

Our sampling was based on villages, and hence captures link only if both individuals reside in the village. It is commonly assumed that the village is the natural domain for the analysis of social and economic networks in rural West Africa, but that need not be true in all places and for all types of social network. These villages, in particular, have long been tightly integrated into the regional, national, and global economy. An analysis of connections entirely within the village may be profoundly misleading if the most important interactions generally cross village boundaries.

The data permit us to identify the relative extent of interactions within and across village boundaries by network type. For most of the interactions we consider the majority of the activity occurs within the village. Most of the individuals named by our respondents as sources of information about farming reside within the village. Sixty-six percent of the recorded cases of learning activity occurred with other people in the village. This proportion varies across villages, from a low of 53% in the smallest village to between 70% and 80% in the remaining three villages.

Financial interactions are similarly concentrated within villages. Fifty-nine percent of credit transactions and gift exchanges occur within village boundaries; virtually all the rest with relatives and friends outside the village. Only 13 of 719 loans were taken from formal or semi-formal sources. Again, the proportion rises with village size, from 54% in the smallest village to 65% in the largest. Sixty-two percent of the individuals from whom our respondents obtained land reside within the same village. This proportion ranges from 47% in the smallest village to 74%.

Labor transactions appear to be even more concentrated within villages. Seventy-six percent of identified non-household labor used on sample plots comes from within the village. However, this is likely to be an overestimate of the degree of concentration, because 40% of non-family labor is identified in our data simply as anonymous "no relation." For these transactions, we do not record the residence of the laborers, so we do not know if they originate from the village. Informal discussions and observation during the field research make it apparent that a substantial proportion of this kind of labor is brought in as daily wage labor from nearby towns. Moreover, most within-village labor transactions occur when a household head or spouse hires dependents in other households. When this is the case, we do not have information on the household identifier of the hired worker, so the link can not be included in much of the analysis that follows.

In dramatic contrast, only 7.6% of sales of farm output occur between residents of the village. Virtually the whole output is sold directly in regional markets, to itinerant traders or, in the case of pineapple, to specialized commercial exporters.

The predominance of intravillage interactions for information transfer, financial flows, and land exchange makes salient the analysis of their village-level networks.

Table 10.1 Incidence of network connections

	1 Information links	2 Credit/gift links	3 Land links	4 Labor links	5 Village population
Overall by village	0.015	0.013	0.005	0.006	—
1	0.013	0.011	0.002	0.008	1250
2	0.016	0.015	0.004	0.001	2000
3	0.018	0.012	0.010	0.009	450
4	0.013	0.013	0.004	0.003	1000

Note
Fraction of pairs of respondents within villages with network connections.

We are less confident of the importance of the within-village labor network and place less emphasis on this network. Within-village sales of output/purchases of farm inputs are unimportant. Therefore, we do not examine further the shape or determinants of this network.

All of the networks that we consider are sparse in terms of direct connections. Less than 2% of pairs of respondents are connected by any sort of direct link (this corresponds to a network density of approximately 0.04). Table 10.1 presents summary statistics on the frequency of the different kinds of links by village. In each case, the denominator of the proportion is the number of pairs of individuals in our sample in each village and the numerator is the number of observed links of a given type between sample individuals. There are few strong differences across villages in the density of the individual functional networks. Village 2 has a noticeably sparse network of labor connections, while the network of land transactions in village 3 is particularly dense.

There is a strong spatial element to these networks, and it is useful to be able to visualize their shape in real space (Faust *et al.* 1999). Figures 10.1 through 10.4 plot the geographic location and the various network links between our sample individuals. The geographic location of each individual is defined by the average position of the plots (s)he cultivates and is indicated by a node of the graph. Links between sample individuals in the various networks are indicated by the edges of the graphs.

There are individuals in each village for each network who appear isolated in these graphs. That appearance is a misleading consequence of the strategy of constructing these graphs based on "ego-centric" data from a random sample of the population. In fact, for each of these functional networks there is virtually no one in any of these villages who has no interactions with anyone. Virtually everyone in our sample has learning contacts, exchanges credit and/or gifts, hires labor, and has obtained land from someone. If none of those other parties happens to be in our sample, the individual appears isolated in the graphs.

The graphs do point in certain interesting directions. First, there is a substantial, but by no means complete, overlap between the different networks in a given village. Individuals connected along one dimension appear more likely

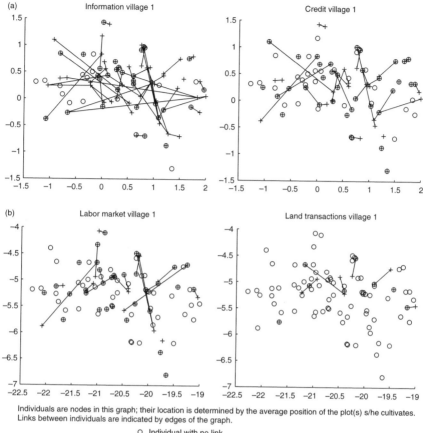

Individuals are nodes in this graph; their location is determined by the average position of the plot(s) s/he cultivates. Links between individuals are indicated by edges of the graph.

- O   Individual with no link
- +   Individual with at least one link in this network
- —   Network link

Figure 10.1 (a) Information and credit networks and (b) labor and land networks in village 1.

to be connected along the others. This impression is strongly supported by the statistical evidence that follows. Second, information networks appear to be more characterized than the other networks by the presence of focal individuals, who have multiple links in our sample. Third, it is apparent that connections are more likely between nearby farmers, but that links between more distant individuals are common, particularly for credit networks.

Links between individuals in the different functional networks are by no means independent. Tables 10.2 (A–F) shows that the presence of any kind of link between two individuals is much more likely conditional on the existence of any other kind of link. Credit and information links are the most closely associated: nearly half of the pairs connected by an information link are also connected by a flow of credit

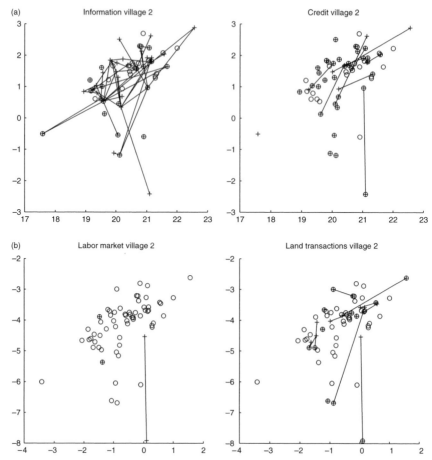

Individuals are nodes in this graph; their location is determined by the average position of the plot(s) s/he cultivates. Links between individuals are indicated by edges of the graph.

○ Individual with no link
+ Individual with at least one link in this network
— Network link

Figure 10.2 (a) Information and credit networks and (b) labor and land networks in village 2.

or gifts, compared to an unconditional probability of 1.25% for the existence of a credit link. The same general pattern, however, holds for all pairs of networks.

Careful analysis is required, therefore, to distinguish the consequences for behavior or outcomes of different kinds of connections between individuals. A finding, e.g., that adoption of a new technology is particularly likely for an individual who shares an information connection with someone who has recently had success with that technology might be attributed to social learning effects. However, because information links are correlated with financial links, this same

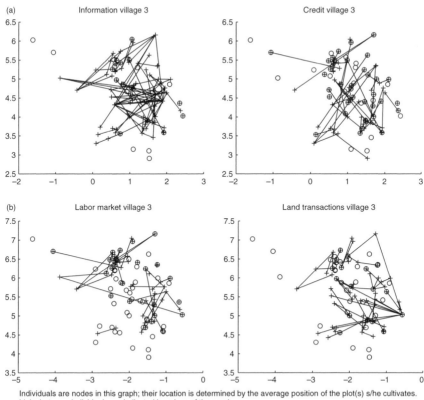

Figure 10.3 (a) Information and credit networks and (b) labor and land networks in village 3.

observation might arise if credit markets are imperfect and the success of the first farmer lowered the cost of capital to the second. Appropriate attention to the entire set of relevant networks may make it possible to distinguish between the different kinds of social interaction effects that influence behavior.

Alternatively, it might be appropriate to think of a single network of basic connections between individuals that can be mobilized for multiple purposes depending upon circumstances. Over some period, a connection might yield flows of finance; at others it might involve a land transaction. Recall how our data on links are constructed: the credit, land, and labor links are based on the existence of an exchange over the relevant period. Information links are defined somewhat differently because they look back at the whole history of learning interactions over a respondent's farming career. We believe that these are better-defined measures

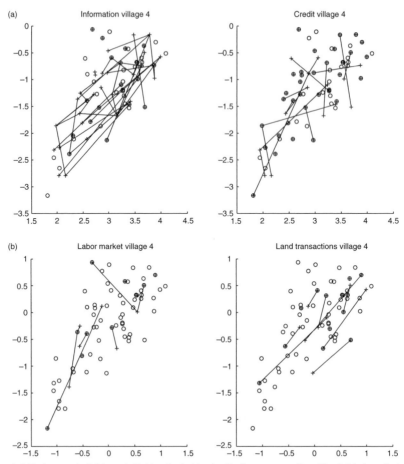

Individuals are nodes in this graph; their location is determined by the average position of the plot(s) s/he cultivates.
Links between individuals are indicated by edges of the graph.

○ Individual with no link
+ Individual with at least one link in this network
— Network link

Figure 10.4 (a) Information and credit networks and (b) labor and land networks in village 4.

than some loose notion of "who could you approach for credit," land or labor. However, it obviously has its costs because it provides no direct information about the potential (rather than realized) uses of a given tie between individuals.

Finally, close correlation between links of various types raises the possibility that the underlying determinants of network connections are similar for different types of links. If the different functional links really do have different purposes, this pattern tends to focus our attention on the costs of constructing and maintaining connections, which could well be similar for different types of links. We turn now,

Table 10.2 Incidence of network connections conditional on the existence of alternative links

(A)	Information link		Credit link	
			No	Yes
	No	n	47 860	274
		(Row pct)	99.43	0.57
	Yes	n	406	338
		(Row pct)	54.57	45.43
		Pearson $\chi^2(1) = 1.2e + 04$	Pr $= 0.000$	

(B)	Information link		Land link	
			No	Yes
	No	n	48 034	100
		(Row pct)	99.79	0.21
	Yes	n	602	142
		(Row pct)	80.91	19.09
		Pearson $\chi^2(1) = 5.3e + 03$	Pr $= 0.000$	

(C)	Information link		Labor link	
			No	Yes
	No	n	48 042	92
		(Row pct)	99.81	0.19
	Yes	n	556	188
		(Row pct)	74.73	25.27
		Pearson $\chi^2(1) = 8.1e + 03$	Pr $= 0.000$	

(D)	Credit link		Land link	
			No	Yes
	No	n	48 134	132
		(Row pct)	99.73	0.27
	Yes	n	502	110
		(Row pct)	82.03	17.97
		Pearson $\chi^2(1) = 3.8e + 03$ Pr $= 0.000$		

(E)	Credit link		Labor link	
			No	Yes
	No	n	48 176	90
		(Row pct)	99.81	0.19
	Yes	n	422	190
		(Row pct)	68.95	31.05
		Pearson $\chi^2(1) = 1.0e + 04$	Pr $= 0.000$	

(F)	Labor link		Land link	
			No	Yes
	No	n	48 444	154
		(Row pct)	99.68	0.32
	Yes	n	192	88
		(Row pct)	68.57	31.43
		Pearson $\chi^2(1) = 5.5e + 03$	Pr $= 0.000$	

Note
Fraction of pairs of respondents within villages with network connections.

therefore, to an examination of the correlations between current ties in the various networks and a set of arguably deeper social connections between farmers.

10.4   Predicting networks

Table 10.3 provides summary statistics about the social connections between (non-married) pairs of individuals in the villages. The sample is the set of all within-village pairs of sample individuals, except for pairs linked by marriage.[1] Approximately one-fifth of the pairs are members of the same religion. Again, one-fifth of the pairs are members of the same extended matrilineage (each village has two to three matrilineages that account for a collective 70–80% of the population, and five or six other, smaller matrilineages). For a further fifth of the sample pairings, at least one individual in the pair holds a traditional village or lineage office (e.g., is village elder). The two individuals have the same soil type (described as one of the three major groups of soil types) in one-third of the pairings. The average absolute value of the age difference between the paired individuals is a decade, while the average absolute non-land wealth difference is 750 000 cedis[2] (compared to average wealth of 670 000 cedis). The average distance between the plots of pairs of individuals is about $1\frac{1}{4}$ kilometers.

Logit estimates of the probabilities that a link exists in a pair are presented for each of the four networks (information, credit, land, and labor) in Table 10.4.[3] Let $\ell_{ij}^t = 1$ be an indicator variable that there is a link of type t between individual i and individual j. Let the notation $\Pr\{\ell_{ij}^t = 1\}$ refer to the probability that $\ell_{ij}^t = 1$ conditional on observable (to the econometrician) information. We estimate

$$\Pr\left\{\ell_{ij}^t = 1\right\} = \Lambda(X_{ij}\beta), \tag{4}$$

where Λ is the logistic Cumulative Distributive Function (CDF). Coefficients are presented as odds ratios (e^{β_k}), along with z-statistics for the test against the null hypothesis that the odds ratio is unity. The standard errors are heteroskedasticity consistent.

Table 10.3 Summary statistics of link characteristics

Variable	Mean	Std
At least one of pair holds office	0.22	0.41
Same religion	0.23	0.42
Same matrilineage	0.22	0.42
Same gender	0.52	0.50
Same soil type	0.32	0.47
Absolute value of age difference	10.61	11.61
Absolute value of wealth difference	0.75	1.29
Distance between plots (km)	1.27	0.78
Both members of 1st generation in village	0.05	0.21
Families trace origin to same region	0.55	0.50

Table 10.4 Predicting network links

	1 Information links		2 Credit/gift links		3 Land links		3B Land links		4 Labor links	
	Odds	z	Odds	z	Odds	z	Odds	z	Odds	z
At least one of the pair holds office	1.17	1.26	0.85	−0.78	1.46	1.92	2.30	4.09	2.17	2.62
Same religion	1.06	0.46	1.78	2.92	0.74	−1.19	0.74	−1.19	1.47	1.37
Same matrilineage	1.43	2.93	2.17	3.86	1.36	1.44	1.47	1.85	2.08	2.65
Same gender	7.29	11.57	3.95	5.75	2.54	4.42	3.41	5.56	3.89	4.41
Same soil type	3.09	8.44	1.36	1.55	5.40	6.75			3.39	3.70
Absolute value of age difference	1.00	−0.79	1.02	3.43	1.04	7.34	1.04	5.81	1.02	1.86
Absolute value of wealth difference	1.23	8.66	0.96	−0.62	1.29	5.22	1.29	6.05	1.08	1.25
Distance between plots (km)	0.56	−5.63	0.79	−1.68	0.30	−4.64	—	—	0.57	−1.90
Both members of 1st generation in village	0.37	−2.37	1.04	0.10	***	****	***	****	0.78	−0.33
Families trace origin to same region	1.09	0.65	2.20	3.22	1.26	1.01	1.31	1.21	1.26	0.75
Predicted probability of link										
Link = 1										
Mean	0.027		0.005		0.022		0.01		0.006	
Standard	0.026		0.003		0.033		0.005		0.006	
Link = 1 and less than 5 years										
Mean	0.014		0.005		0.004		0.003		0.002	
Standard	0.014		0.004		0.007		0.003		0.002	

Notes

Logit regressions – dependent variable = 1 if link exists.

Standard errors heteroskedasticity consistent, n = 40 960.

*** Both families migrants perfectly predict no land link.

The covariates and samples are identical across the different regressions, and the predicted probabilities of a link in the middle of the distribution of the covariates is very similar (always near 1–2%), so direct comparisons of the odds ratios are sensible.

In each case, gender is a crucial determinant of the likelihood of a link between individuals. It is very rare for non-married individuals of opposite genders to interact directly in any of these four dimensions. It is also the case that membership in the same matrilineage is strongly associated with the existence of any of these network links. This is particularly so in the case of credit links, and relatively less so in the case of information and land links. Given the informal enforcement mechanisms that can be brought to bear within the matrilineage, it is not surprising to find that credit and mutual gift exchanges are more common within lineages (Klingelhofer 1972). More surprising is the finding that among the four networks, land transactions are least positively affected by membership in the same lineage. Land rights in Southern Ghana are very strongly associated with the matrilineage (Goldstein and Udry 1999b; Berry 2001). It is possible that the relatively small increment to the likelihood of a land link associated with membership in the same matrilineage reflects the potential ambiguities of plot rights when land is transferred within the matrilineage. "The process of acquiring and defending rights in land is inherently a political process based on power relations among members of the social group" (Bassett and Crummey 1993, p. 20); the transaction may be less problematic when made on a more commercial basis across lineage boundaries.

The finding that membership in the same church is strongly associated with the presence of a credit link again may reflect the informal enforcement mechanisms that are available within religious groups. Religion is not strongly associated with the likelihood of any other type of network connection. Similarly, we find that credit links are much more likely when both the individuals share a family origin in the same region of Ghana. Region of origin can cross-cut matrilineages in these villages, so this may reflect the social enforcement mechanisms available to communities formed of migrants.

Farmers who share similar soil characteristics are much more likely to share an information link than others. This is naturally related to the potential gains from the information link, if optimal farming practices are variable across soil types in a non-systematic (or at least non-obvious) manner. We also find that land links are much more likely across farmers who share soil types; the simultaneity of this relationship makes even tentative interpretations problematic. In column 3B of Table 10.4 we remove this covariate and distance, which is subject to the same worry, and show that the remaining odds ratios are generally stable.

Differences in wealth are very strongly associated with the presence of information connections. Looking more closely at the individuals in the network maps of Figure 10.1, we find that several of the apparently nodal individuals are much wealthier than average, and they tend to be connected to individuals who are relatively less wealthy. There appears to be a surprising element of hierarchy in the information network. This is otherwise apparent only in the land network, where it is to be expected. Credit and gift exchange, on the other hand, appears to be more horizontally oriented. These exchanges do not often occur between rich and poor. The hypothesis that the provision of insurance is an important element of credit and gift exchange is consistent with this pattern.

Information and land links are much less likely between individuals who are members of the first generations of their families to reside in the village. For land links this effect is sufficiently strong that there are no instances of such links in our data.

All of these network interactions are more likely between farmers who are located near each other. One would expect the cost of social interactions to rise with distance, hence this is a pattern to be expected. In fact, it is this general pattern that underlies the decision by many researchers to use geographic location as a proxy for social connections. The relationship between proximity and the likelihood of a network linkage is sufficiently strong that location may indeed be a reasonable proxy for network membership for certain applications. However, it is clearly not an exact relationship, and the impact of distance on the likelihood of interaction varies in an interesting way across the networks. In particular, distance has a much less strong negative impact on the likelihood of a credit tie than on any of the other network connections. We have shown in the other work that there is a strong positive spatial correlation in agricultural shocks (Conley and Udry 2003; Goldstein and Udry 2004). This finding, therefore, points again to an important insurance motivation for the credit and gift exchanges.

Deeper social connections between individuals are strongly associated with the presence of connections in these four social networks. It is possible that information about these deeper relationships between people for predicting network connections is less useful for predicting relatively transitory connections. Unfortunately, our data is constructed in such a way that we can examine only one side of this question. We have no information regarding lapsed ties in these social networks. If two individuals once shared a connection and no longer do, this connection will not appear in our data. However, we do know for how long two individuals who do share a connection have interacted.[4] The last four rows of Table 10.4 show that the probability of correctly predicting a link to exist when the two individuals have known each other for less than five years is lower than when the two have been acquainted for longer period. This pattern is less evident for credit links, but is quite strong for each of the other types of connections. While the more fundamental social relations between people are important predictors of the likelihood of functional network connections, they are less useful in distinguishing more recent connections and will also be less useful to distinguish transitory links more generally.

10.4.1 Robustness

The simple logit estimates presented in Table 10.4 leave open the possibility that there are unobserved characteristics of individuals which influence the probability that they are linked with others. Put simply, it is plausible that certain individuals are more likely to build connections in a network than others. Consequently,

Table 10.5 Predicting network links, with 2-way fixed effects

	1 Information links		2 Credit/Gift links		3 Land links		3B Land links		4 Labor links	
	Odds	z	Odds	z	Odds	z	Odds	z	Odds	z
Same religion	1.38	2.09	2.78	3.67	1.33	0.84	1.22	0.69	2.78	2.59
Same matrilineage	2.10	4.65	1.55	1.34	0.26	−2.60	0.34	−2.31	2.97	2.46
Same gender	6.02	9.15	4.01	5.05	1.89	1.99	1.80	1.89	2.01	1.44
Same soiltype	2.14	3.23	2.23	1.76	11.69	3.33	—	—	0.29	−1.35
Absolute value of age difference	1.00	−0.19	1.00	−0.34	1.09	4.02	1.07	3.92	1.06	2.02
Absolute value of wealth difference	0.87	−1.90	0.93	−0.26	1.19	1.03	1.19	1.16	1.43	1.07
Distance between plots (km)	0.35	−9.25	0.55	−3.02	0.13	−8.34	—	—	0.31	−4.06
Both members of 1st generation in village	2.66	1.73	0.53	−1.12	***	***	***	***	1.75	0.28
Families trace origin to same region	1.98	3.22	1.38	0.63	2.49	1.51	1.09	0.18	9.73	2.82
Number of individuals dropped	247		338		335		335		358	
Number of observations dropped	24 696		33 711		33 463		33 463		35 786	

Notes

Logit regressions – dependent variable = 1 if link exists.

Standard errors heteroskedasticity consistent, $n = 40\,960$.

*** Both families migrants perfectly predict no land link.

we explore the possibility that the appropriate probability model takes the form

$$\Pr\left\{\ell_{ij}^t = 1\right\} = \Lambda(X_{ij}\beta + \lambda_i + \lambda_j),$$ (5)

where λ_i and λ_j are unobserved individual fixed effects. This model is obviously strongly related to the conditional logit model (Chamberlain 1980) but the standard conditioning approach is not available when there are two dimensions of fixed effects. Instead, we adopt a maximum likelihood (ML) approach to estimate β and λ_i. When there is a fixed number of observations per individual the conventional ML estimator of β is inconsistent. However, the median number of pairs including any individual in our data is 114, so we rely on the asymptotic consistency of the ML estimator. Estimates of equation (5) are presented in Table 10.5.

This estimation strategy implies that any individual who has no link of a particular type (i.e., any i such that $\ell_{ij}^t = 0 \; \forall j$) contributes no information to the estimate of $\hat{\beta}$. Such individuals and all of the pairs of which (s)he is a part are dropped from the estimation sample. The precise numbers are reported in Table 10.5. In addition, the variable "at least one of the pair holds office" is colinear with the individual effects and is dropped.

The remarkable feature of Table 10.5 is the overall similarity of the results to those reported in Table 10.4. The strong effect of gender is equally apparent in the table. Also, distance between plots is once again strongly negatively associated with the likelihood of a linkage in any of these dimensions. Once again, however, this effect is much less strong for credit links than for any of the other types of connections between individuals. As in Table 10.4, there is a very strong positive association between two individuals sharing the same soil type and the existence of an information link between them.

The strong positive relationship observed in Table 10.4 between the absolute value of the wealth difference between individuals and the likelihood that they share an information link is not replicated in Table 10.5. The result in Table 10.4 appears to reflect the fact that certain quite wealthy individuals are focal in the information network. Once this fixed effect is taken out, the wealth difference is negatively related to the likelihood of a linkage.

The very strong positive effect of membership in the same matrilineage for the likelihood of a credit link that we observed in Table 10.4 is not as apparent in Table 10.5. Instead, there is a much stronger effect of being a member of the same religion.

10.5 Modeling social networks

The long-term goal of this research program is an enriched understanding of individuals' behavior in the context of multiple and overlapping social networks and, in particular, to acknowledge the agency of the individuals embedded in social networks. The constituent links of the networks are chosen. They confer benefits, imply responsibility, and require effort to create and maintain. The choice to invest in social connections within and across conventional household boundaries is not so much a simple process of accumulation as of developing an appropriately complementary set of ties – "composition" is Belinga and Guyer's felicitous term (Guyer and Belinga 1995). While the shape of the networks moulds the pattern of economic development, economic change alters the value of particular network links and thus the shape of the networks themselves. Our goal is to understand this dynamic of network formation.

The reduced form analyses of the previous section provide clues as to the motivations that might be driving individuals' decisions as they compose a set of network connections. The results are consistent with the notion, e.g., that people are willing to pay a higher price for longer-distance credit connections than they are for information connections. However, in the absence of a model that incorporates both individuals' motivations for shaping the eventual structure of a particular social network and an appropriate equilibrium concept, these hints must remain just hints.

There is a large and useful literature that examines network efficiency, with the goal of characterizing the network configuration that maximizes a value function (Bolton and Dewatripont 1994; Hendricks *et al.* 1995; Economides 1996). This is appropriate for a planner (such as a telecommunications monopoly), but not for the decentralized process that governs the formation of social networks like those in the sample villages. Instead, we focus on the incentives of the individuals who build the links of the network (Coleman 1966; Granovetter 1973, 1992; Fafchamps 1999; Fafchamps and Minten 1999).

Consider for now just two networks: the network for information and that for credit/gift exchange. The links in these networks are bidirectional: if i and j converse about farming, then information flows in both directions. This is less obviously true of credit links, but to the extent that insurance motivations are central to these transactions, a bidirectional characterization is appropriate. Of course, this does not imply that the value of the link is identical to i and j. Bala and Goyal (2000) model the situation in which l_{ij}^t is costless to j, while in Jackson and Wolinsky (1996) both parties bear the cost and either can sever the link. It is not entirely clear what approximation is appropriate in these villages. In fact, costs are borne by both parties. But they are also asymmetric; the individual who approaches the other is likely to bear a larger proportion of the cost.

Let $N = \{1, 2, \ldots, n\}$ be the set of agents in the village. Agent i's strategy is a vector $\ell_i = \{\ell_{i,1}^I, \ell_{i,2}^I, \ldots, \ell_{i,n}^I, \ell_{i,1}^C, \ell_{i,2}^C, \ldots, \ell_{i,n}^C\}$, where $\ell_{i,j}^t = 1$ if i forms a type t link with j. Let the payoff to i for a direct connection of type t to j be V_{ij}^t. This represents the value to i of the information exchange or insurance contract between i and j.[5] V_{ij}^t varies across ij pairs.

The literature assumes exponential network decay (parameterized by δ), so that an indirect connection between i and j provides less value than a direct connection. The appropriate model for network decay would likely be very different depending upon the specific context and the type of network. Information, e.g., might be garbled when transferred between people, in which case exponential decay could be a natural assumption. The value of an indirect link in a financial network might be very different, however, depending upon the nature of the bilateral exchanges. At one extreme, there might be no decay so that everyone in a connected network shares complete insurance. One intermediate case would involve a limited commitment model, which might involve complete insurance for small shocks and incomplete insurance for larger shocks (Ligon 1998). It is clear that even if the decay in the value of indirect connections in a financial network can be approximated by an exponential process, δ would vary according to the type of network. We omit that notation for simplicity.

In a given network g, if the shortest path of type t between i and j is d, the value to i is $V_{ij}^t \delta^d$. The cost of forming links $\left(\ell_{ij}^I, \ell_{ij}^C\right)$ is $c_{ij}\left(\ell_{ij}^I, \ell_{ij}^C\right)$, where $0 < c_{ij}(0,1), c_{ij}(1,0) \le c_{ij}(1,1) < c_{ij}(0,1) + c_{ij}(1,0)$. The value of a network g in which $N(i; g)$ is the set of individuals with direct or indirect connections of any type to i in g is

$$\Pi_i(g) = \sum_{j \in N(i;g)} \left\{ V_{ij}^I \delta^{d(i,j;I,g)} + V_{ij}^C \delta^{d(i,j;C,g)} - c_{ij}\left(\ell_{ij}^I, \ell_{ij}^C\right) \right\}. \tag{6}$$

The obvious Nash equilibrium of this network formation game implies a series of inequality constraints that must hold. Let g_{-ijt} denote network g without a type t link between i and j, and g_{+ijt} denote the same network with the addition of this link. If $\ell_{ij}^t = 1$, then

$$\Pi_i(g) > \Pi_i(g_{-ijt}),$$
$$\Pi_j(g) > \Pi_j(g_{-ijt}),$$

while if $\ell_{ij}^t = 0$ then obviously enough

$$\Pi_i(g) < \Pi_i(g_{-ijt}),$$
$$\Pi_j(g) < \Pi_j(g_{-ijt}).$$

Heterogeneity in the characteristics of individuals (and their deeper social relationships to one another) can be introduced. Let $V_{ij}^t = V^t(x_i, x_j, \varepsilon_{ij})$ and $c_{ij} = c(\ell_{ij}^I, \ell_{ij}^C; z_i, z_j, \upsilon_{ij})$.

Bala and Goyal (2000) provide a characterization of the equilibria of a related model. The network in a village will be connected, and in the symmetric case ($V_{ij}^t = V^t$, and $c_{ij} = c(\ell_{ij}^I, \ell_{ij}^C)$) there are many Nash equilibria. This immediately raises very important questions about the feasibility of estimation (Jovanovic 1989). The problem is less severe in our application: since V and c vary across pairs of individuals in our model, the set of equilibria is made smaller. Nevertheless, it should not be expected that there would be a unique Nash equilibrium of this game, which complicates estimation of the parameters of V_{ij}^t and c_{ij} (Tamer 1999).

The most important intuition of this model for empirical work on network formation is that the expected benefit to i of a link with j depends upon i's opinion about the links that j has. Hence, i is more likely to pay the cost of linking to j if he thinks that j is linked to many people relevant to i. If j has characteristics (such as a common extended family or a common church) which make it likely that he will have links with individuals whose experience is valuable to i (e.g., with people who have plots similar to i for an information link), then i is more likely to pay for a link with j. The costs of a link between j and, say, k depend on the interaction between the aspects of their social backgrounds. Hence, i's prediction of the network resources available to j (and thus V_{ij}^{t}) need not be colinear with the costs of forming the link with j.

This model can in principle be estimated. However, the obstacles to be overcome are daunting. The amount of independent information available across individuals within a given network is limited because of the interdependence of each individual's actions. Data may be required on a large number of networks in order to distinguish the different equilibria that exist in the different villages (Conley and Topa 2003). The need for a broad cross-section of data is in tension with the simultaneous need for rather intensive collection of data from each individual, as described in the next section. We believe that the more promising direction is to study the dynamics of the networks directly, by observing changes in the composition of individuals' network ties. The problem then becomes one of understanding the *change* in ℓ_i conditional on the current existence of a particular equilibrium network g. It remains the case that plausible sources of exogenous variation in c_{ij} or V_{ij}^{t} are required in order to interpret any observed changes in the set of network links in the village. However, this appears to be the most promising strategy and it has important implications for the design of data collection.

10.6   Lessons for future research

We have argued that patterns of economic change in rural Africa are being shaped by the configurations of social networks in these communities. In turn, individuals' incentives to make and break network connections are influenced by economic transformation. The process through which individuals compose their various network connections, and the implications of these connections for economic and social activities are important frontiers for empirical research. The data generated by conventional surveys, however, are not well-suited for this task.

Equation (6) makes explicit the importance of a complete enumeration of any given social network within a community. It is not possible to calculate the value of the network – or of any of its constituent links – in its absence. Therefore, if an analysis of the dynamics of social networks is a goal of the research the basic strategy of ego-centric analysis based on a random sample is not appropriate. If the village is sufficiently closed to make it the relevant domain of the network, then a complete enumeration of the network connections will be required to make progress on understanding the determinants of network formation. This is a costly decision to make in planning data collection, because for most of the other purposes a complete enumeration would not be the optimal sampling strategy.

Data on the creation and dissolution of network connections are particularly useful to overcome some of the central technical challenges of analysing the determinants of the shape of social networks. Therefore, collection of panel data might be an appropriate strategy. Alternatively, it might be possible to collect retrospective data on the history of each individual's links to other individuals in the community.

The potential usefulness of retrospective data on network links is limited by the need for variation in the returns to or the costs of links between individuals that are driving the changes in the composition of people's networks. Data on network connections have to be integrated with more conventional socioeconomic data to begin to understand the implications of the network for behavior and outcomes, and thus to model the incentives individuals face for link formation and dissolution. It is not generally possible to collect retrospectively such data.

It is clear that functional network connections, like the information, credit, labor, and land interactions described in this chapter, are strongly influenced by background variables like geography and family history. In addition to these underlying social variables, any analysis of transitions requires data on exogenously changing factors that influence the costs or benefits of connections. For example, new market opportunities, new technologies, or changes in the returns to different kinds of assets could provide sources of variation to provide insight into the creation or collapse of network links.

A key advantage of the Ghana dataset discussed in this chapter is the relative precision with which it defines network connections. It is possible, e.g., to distinguish between social interactions that are focused on the exchange of farming information and those that are associated with credit or gift exchange. It is plausible that the incentives people face to develop and maintain these different types of connection are different, and in fact we have provided reduced form evidence that they are shaped by different underlying social connections between people. The weakness of data on realized interactions is that they do not necessarily reveal the potential utility of a given network link.

Acknowledgments

This research has been funded by The Pew Charitable Trusts through its project on Moral and Social Dimensions of Microeconomic Behavior in Poor Communities. The underlying field research received financial support from the NSF (grants SBR-9617694 and SES-9905720), International Food Policy Research Institute, Institute for the Study of World Politics, World Bank Research Committee, Fulbright Program, ESRC, and Social Science Research Council. We thank members of the Pew network for many helpful comments.

Notes

1 Married pairs are excluded from the analysis samples in Tables 10.4 and 10.5 as well.
2 The exchange rate during the survey period ranged from 1700 to 2300 cedis per US dollar.

3 See Anderson *et al.* (1999) for a discussion of logit models in network analysis.
4 The precise question is "How long have you known . . . ?" This is not necessarily the same as knowing the length of time the two individuals have shared this particular interaction.
5 Obviously, in general, V_{ij}^t depends upon the entire network configuration. In virtually any learning model, the value of an additional bit of information declines as the volume of information increases. The situation is even more complex with respect to credit, in which V_{ij}^C will depend upon the covariance of j's income with everyone else connected directly or indirectly with i. We assume that these effects are small so that we can approximate the value of the connection in this linear fashion.

References

Amanor, K.S. (1994) *The New Frontier: Farmers' Response to Land Degradation, A West African Study*. London: Zed Books.

Anderson, C., Wasserman, S., and Couch, B. (1999) "A p* primer: logit models for social networks." *Social Networks*. 21: 37–66.

Bala, V. and Goyal, S. (2000) "A non-cooperative theory of network formation." *Econometrica*. 68, 5 (September): 1181–229.

Bassett, T. and Crummey, D. (1993) *Land in African Agrarian Systems*. Madison, WI: University of Wisconsin Press.

Berry, S.S. (2001) *Chiefs Know their Boundaries: Essays on Property, Power and the Past in Asante, 1896–1996*. Portsmouth, NH: Heinemann.

Bolton, P. and Dewatripont, M. (1994) "The firm as a communication network." *Quarterly Journal of Economics*. 109, 8: 809–40.

Chamberlain, G. (1980) "An analysis of covariance with qualitative data." *Review of Economic Studies*. 47: 225–38.

Coleman, J. (1966) *Medical Innovation: A Diffusion Study*. New York: Bobbs-Merrill.

Conley, T. and Topa, G. (2003) "Estimating dynamic local interactions models." Manuscript. Chicago, IL: University of Chicago; New York, NY: New York University.

Conley, T. and Udry, C. (2001) "Social learning through networks: the adoption of new agricultural technologies in Ghana." *American Journal of Agricultural Economics*. 83, 3: 668–73.

—— (2003) "Learning about a new technology: pineapple in Ghana." Manuscript. Chicago, IL: University of Chicago; New Haven, CT: Yale University.

Economides, N. (1996) "The economics of networks." *International Journal of Industrial Organization*. 14, 6: 673–99.

Fafchamps, M. (1999) "Ethnicity and credit in African manufacturing." Manuscript. Oxford, UK: Oxford University.

Fafchamps, M. and Minten, B. (1999) "Relationships and traders in Madagascar." *Journal of Development Studies*. 35, 6: 1–35.

Faust, K., Entwisle, B., Rindfuss, R., Walsh, S., and Sawangdee, Y. (1999) "Spatial arrangement of social and economic networks in Nang Rong district, Thailand." *Social Networks*. 21, 2: 311–37.

Goldstein, M. (2002) "Chop time, no friends: intrahousehold and individual insurance mechanisms in Southern Ghana." Manuscript. London, UK: London School of Economics.

Goldstein, M. and Udry, C. (1999a) "Agricultural innovation and resource management in Ghana." Manuscript. London, UK: London School of Economics; New Haven, CT: Yale University.

—— (1999b) "Gender and land resource management in Southern Ghana." Manuscript. London, UK: London School of Economics; New Haven, CT: Yale University.

—— (2004) "Gender, power and agricultural investment in Ghana." Manuscript. London, UK: London School of Economics; New Haven, CT: Yale University.

Granovetter, M. (1973) "Strength of weak ties." *American Journal of Sociology*. 78, 6: 1360–80.

—— (1992) "Economic institutions as social constructions – a framework for analysis." *Acta Sociologica*. 35, 1: 3–11.

Guyer, J. and Belinga, S.L.E. (1995) "Wealth in people as wealth in knowledge: accumulation and composition in Equatorial Africa." *Journal of African History*. 36: 91–120.

Gyasi, E.A., Agyepong, G.T., Ardayfio-Schandorf, E., Enu-Kwesi, L., Nabila, J.S., and Owusu-Bennoah, E. (1994) "Environmental endangerment in the forest-savanna zone of Southern Ghana." Technical report. Tokyo, Japan: United Nations University.

—— (1995) "Environmental endangerment in the forest-savanna zone of Southern Ghana." Manuscript. Legon: University of Ghana.

Hawthorne, W.D. and Abu-Juam, M. (1995) *Forest Protection in Ghana With Particular Reference to Vegetation and Plant Species*. Cambridge, UK: IUCN/ODA/Forest Department Republic of Ghana.

Hendricks, K., Piccione, M., and Tan, G. (1995) "The economics of hubs: the monopoly case." *Review of Economic Studies*. 62, 1: 83–101.

Hill, P. (1963) *Migrant Cocoa Farmers of Southern Ghana*. Cambridge, UK: Cambridge University Press.

Jackson, M.O. and Wolinsky, A. (1996) "A strategic model of social and economic networks." *Journal of Economic Theory*. 71, 1: 44–74.

Jovanovic, B. (1989) "Observable implications of models with multiple equilibria." *Econometrica*. 57, 6: 1431–37.

Klingelhofer, A. (1972) "Agriculture." In D. Brokensha (ed.), *Akwapim Handbook*. Accra, Ghana: Ghana Publishing Corporation.

Ligon, E. (1998) "Risk sharing and information in village economics." *Review of Economic Studies*. 65, 4: 847–64.

Tamer, E. (1999) "Incomplete simultaneous discrete response model with multiple equilibria." *Review of Economic Studies*. 70, 1: 147–67.

Wasserman, S. and Faust, K. (1994) *Social Network Analysis: Methods and Applications*. Cambridge: Cambridge University Press.

11 Coping with disaster

Morals, markets, and mutual insurance – using economic experiments to study recovery from Hurricane Mitch

Michael R. Carter and Marco Castillo

11.1 Introduction

Hurricanes and other environmental shocks punctuate the lives of poor and vulnerable populations in many parts of the world. When Hurricane Mitch struck Honduras in 1998, poor rural households lost 30–40% of their crop income and measured poverty immediately increased 5.5 percentage points, rising from 69.2% of households to 74.6% (Morris *et al*. 2001). In addition to these immediate income effects, Mitch also destroyed productive assets, washing away land, livestock, and plantations, compromising future earnings and livelihoods for many house-holds. On average, these losses amounted to 15–20% of all assets held by lower wealth households according to Morris *et al*. (2001). While inflows of external aid to Honduras were substantial in the wake of Mitch, they amounted to less than 5% of the total losses suffered by households surveyed for this study, a finding confirmed by the Morris study. The long-term effects of disasters like Mitch on poverty depend very much then on households' ability to maintain and rebuild their depleted stocks of productive assets in the wake of the shock.

Unfortunately market mechanisms for protecting and rebuilding assets are often limited in poor rural communities like those of Honduras.[1] This chapter explores the efficacy of informal mechanisms of mutual aid and insurance in this con-text. A growing economic literature has explored informal insurance. Building on the pessimistic insights of Fafchamps (1992) and Coate and Ravallion (1993) about the viability of mutual insurance,[2] Ligon (1998), Ligon *et al*. (2002) and others have gone on to derive and test propositions about the limits to mutual insurance in the absence of moral norms that effectively compel the sharing and trustworthy behavior that would make mutual insurance commitments credible and effective. Empirical findings of incomplete insurance are interpreted to demon-strate the veracity of commitment constraints, private information, and, implicitly, the weakness of moral norms that might underwrite more ample mutual insurance.

This chapter's approach is somewhat different. Rather than assume that people operate in a moral vacuum and then evaluate observed mutual insurance against theoretical benchmarks, this chapter employs economic experiments to measure the degree to which altruism and trust shape people's economic behavior, and then explores the impact of such moral norms on the efficacy of mutual insurance. This approach complements Foster and Rosenzweig (2001) who show that mutual aid and insurance are more effective within than between families, a result they attribute to intra-family altruism. By directly measuring altruism and trust, this chapter is able to eschew universal assumptions of complete selfishness (or complete intra-family altruism) and is positioned to ask whether norms facilitate mutual insurance beyond the family. In addition, rather than exploring the impact of mutual insurance on coping with the immediate income impacts of shocks, this chapter explores its effect on the asset recovery that shapes long-term poverty and livelihood dynamics.

The chief findings of this chapter are threefold. First, there is notable variation in the degree of altruism and trust in the Honduran communities where the experimental work was carried out. Econometric estimates indicate the presence of endogenous social effects which serve to reinforce these distinctive, community-based normative environments. Second, post-disaster asset growth and recovery regressions (which account for the endogeneity of norms) indicate that higher levels of altruism promoted more rapid recovery from the shock of Hurricane Mitch. Indeed, the estimates indicate that absent these norms, recovery would be extremely modest. Third and finally, further exploration of the asset recovery relationship using quantile regressions reveals that mutual insurance mechanisms invigorated by norms work only for a small subset of the households. While demanding further analysis, this latter finding suggests that there may be a pattern of unequal access to socially mediated capital and insurance.

At the heart of the analysis lies a suite of experimental economic games designed to measure the strength of norms of altruism and trust. As explained in Section 11.3, these games were implemented in mid-2002 in a random sample of communities which were part of a panel living standards study which had last visited those communities in 2001. The 2001 living standards study – which took place 30 months after Mitch – collected detailed retrospective data on the effects of the hurricane, as well as on current household assets. It is the marriage of this real living standards data with the experimental results which makes possible the analysis of the impact of altruism and trust on asset recovery.

The remainder of this chapter is organized as follows. Section 11.2 lays out a framework for thinking about the economic anatomy of an environmental shock. After introducing the available living standards data, Section 11.2 then uses the framework to organize the Honduran data and articulates the basic hypotheses to be tested using an asset growth and recovery framework. Section 11.3 describes the experimental protocol and presents the basic experimental data. Section 11.4 puts forward a social interactions model of norms. An econometric strategy is then devised and implemented that permits the identification of endogenous social interactions that reinforce norms and also allows the unearthing of the pre-Mitch community norms that would have shaped subsequent recovery from the hurricane. Finally, Section 11.5 explores the impact of the norms on recovery from Mitch, while Section 11.6 concludes the chapter.

11.2   Economic anatomy of Hurricane Mitch

Figure 11.1 presents the stylized economic anatomy of an environmental shock from a household's perspective. The *x*-axis measures time and the *y*-axis measures asset stocks and income shocks. The time interval over which an environmental shock occurs could be very brief (as with a hurricane), or it could be an extended period (as in the case of a prolonged drought). Households can also be buffeted by a sequence of such events.

An environmental shock has two direct impacts. First, it may destroy assets (washing away land, killing livestock) by an amount Θ. In Figure 11.1, this first impact is shown by the sudden interruption of the household's asset trajectory as its assets decline from point A_0 to point A_1. The second direct impact is that it reduces disposable household income below its normal level (crops fail or households suddenly must devote income to medical expenses). This deviation from normal disposable income levels is shown in the figure by the negative shock ε. Different environmental events will be characterized by distinctive patterns of asset and disposable income shocks.

Once the shock is realized, the household enters the coping period. During the coping period the household must deal with the shock to its disposable income. One coping strategy is to reduce expenditures. Another is to redirect or increase work time (reduce leisure). The effectiveness of this strategy will depend on access to labor markets. Households with good financial market access can borrow against future earnings to smooth current consumption, or make claims on insurance policies. Informal finance and insurance arrangements (perhaps underwritten by norms of trust or altruism) can play the same role, as can receipt of disaster assistance.

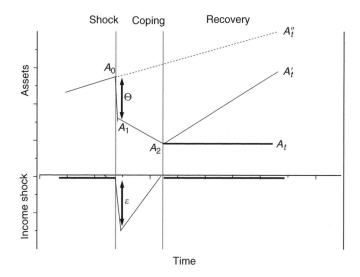

Figure 11.1 Coping and recovery from environmental shocks.

Finally, households can also cope by further drawing down on assets. This additional decline in household assets is shown in Figure 11.1 by the drop in assets from A_1 to A_2. Note that two factors will shape the severity of this secondary asset decline. The first is simply the household's ability to employ the alternative coping strategies listed earlier. The second is changes in the prices of assets relative to the price of food and other necessities. Unfavorable asset price swings (as would be expected to happen if all households in an area respond to a drought by selling cattle) will serve to further decapitalize households in the wake of a shock. Mutual insurance can, in principle, prevent households from further decapitalizing themselves in this immediate post-shock coping period.

The third and final stage is termed the recovery phase in Figure 11.1. The market and social mechanisms that broker access to employment and financial services will also shape the post-shock asset trajectory. A household with good access to capital (via social or market mechanisms) can borrow against future earnings to immediately rebuild asset stocks. A key question is whether or not the household is able to rebuild its asset base (shown in Figure 11.1 as the movement from A_2 to A'_t), or whether it gets trapped at a low asset level (shown by the A_2 to A_t trajectory). Note that point A''_t in Figure 11.1 indicates the asset level the household would have enjoyed had the environmental shock not occurred. Norms of altruism and trust that facilitate inter-temporal contracting could again be expected to bolster recovery.

11.2.1 Measuring the effects of Hurricane Mitch

In 2001, 850 producer households were surveyed in 5 departments in Honduras regarding the 2000 agricultural year. This sample can be broken into two distinct subsamples: panel and cross section. The panel households (500) originate from a study conducted in 1994 (Lopez and Valdes 2000) in which 450 farm households were interviewed to analyze the impacts of the initial land titling programs. The 2001 survey attempted to follow both these baseline households and the land they cultivated. Of the original baseline households, 362 were resurveyed. In addition, 138 "new" panel households were added. In 2000, these households were cultivating land that had been worked by the original panel households in 1994. The remaining 350 cross-sectional households were added in regions that were not covered in the 1994 study. The stratification process for this subsample was as follows. First, nine municipalities in three departments were non-randomly identified. Within each municipality, three towns (caserios) were randomly selected. A census of each town was conducted and used to classify households into five farm size categories. To ensure coverage across farm size, households were randomly drawn from each category.

In addition to standard income and asset data, the 2001 survey solicited detailed information on damages suffered during Hurricane Mitch, which hit Honduras in late October, 1998. Matching the concepts displayed in Figure 11.1, the data were aggregated into an asset shock measure (Θ, in the notation of Figure 11.1), and an income and expenditure shock (ε). Asset shocks include the value of land washed away, permanent crops (primarily coffee plantations) destroyed, as well the value of livestock and machinery that were killed or destroyed. Income and expenditure shocks include the imputed net value of crops that were washed away, costs of medical expenses, lost off-farm earnings and reductions in remittances. Assets were priced using median values by geographic locale, and all the values of asset and income shocks were inflated to the price level at the time of the 2001 survey. Using the data, it was possible to construct measures of the total value of productive assets immediately before Mitch (A_0) and again at the time of the survey, some 30 months after Mitch (A_t). Measures of intermediate asset reductions that may have taken place during the coping period are not available (i.e., we are unable to measure A_2).

Table 11.1 displays basic descriptive statistics on the Honduran household sample. The table distinguishes households based on whether they were located in low, medium, or high trust communities. The trust levels of communities was measured based on behavior by community residents in the Trust game.[3] Low trust communities are simply those in the lowest tercile of the trust distribution, with similar definitions used for medium and high trust communities. In low trust communities, the average participant in the Trust game entrusted 37% of his or her experimental budget endowment to an unknown trustee who was under no obligation to return any of it. The average budget share sent away in medium trust communities was 48%, while it was 62% in high trust communities. Low trust communities also exhibit lower levels of altruism – as evidenced by play in a Dictator game – than do medium and high trust communities.[4]

Table 11.1 Descriptive statistics on loss and recovery (median [mean] values)

	Community type		
	Low trust	Medium trust	High trust
Community characteristics (%)			
Households with losses	40	51	42
Altruism budget shares	28	42	53
Trust budget shares	37	48	62
Households with losses			
Productive assets lost (%)	7.6 [15.7]	7.7 [13.0]	7.5 [15.3]
Income loss ($US)*	84 [459]	0 [148]	139 [380]
External aid received ($US)*	0 [205]	0 [284]	0 [41]
Pre-Mitch assets ($US)*	13,315	14,523	10,124
Post-Mitch asset growth (%)	−6.0	−3.4	−0.6
Households without losses			
Income loss ($US)*	0 [55]	0 [196]	24 [149]
External aid received ($US)*	0 [87]	0 [83]	0 [196]
Pre-Mitch assets ($US)*	3061	1541	2736
Post-Mitch asset growth (%)	3.7	5.3	7.7
2001 Annual household income		794 [1776]	

Note
* Monetary values converted to 2001 US dollar using the market exchange rate.

For each of these community types, Table 11.1 displays basic information on loss and recovery from Hurricane Mitch. Data on households that suffered productive asset losses (which ranged from 46% to 59% of all households) are shown separately from data on households that did not suffer losses of productive assets. As the degree of loss is highly variable (and skewed), both median and mean values are shown for key indicators.

For those households suffering loss of productive assets, the median loss was about 7.5% of total household productive assets across all three types of communities. The mean percentage of assets lost was about twice as high, signaling that a number of households had substantially larger losses. As median household assets in the overall sample were about $12,000,[5] these figures indicate an absolute loss of around a $1000 for a typical household. To help place these figures in perspective, median (mean) household income in this sample was $794 ($1776) in 2001. Median income loss ranged from $0 to $139, while mean losses ranged from $148 to $380. Compared to these losses, external aid received was quite modest, averaging no more than $284 across the community types. In all cases, the median amount of aid received by households experiencing loss was zero.

Households that did not suffer productive asset losses still in many instances suffered income losses, as shown in the lower half of the Table 11.1.[6] Over the 30 months following Mitch, the stock of productive assets held by these households grew in total between 3.7% and 7.7% in real terms. These growth rates are roughly 10 percentage points higher than the −6.0% to −0.6% asset growth experienced by the households that had suffered losses. Put differently, as shown in Table 11.1, 30 months after Mitch, the median household that had suffered an asset loss had still not fully recovered to their pre-Mitch level. However, in high trust communities, the median household had almost recovered, as 2001 assets were less than 1% below pre-Mitch asset levels. The corresponding figures for medium and low trust communities were 3.4% and 6.0% below their pre-Mitch asset levels.

It is of course tempting to take these descriptive data as evidence that trust norms indeed facilitate coping with environmental shocks. Indeed, median asset growth for households that did not suffer losses is also strictly increasing in community trust. However, norms themselves are part of a broader social process. Among other things, the occurrence of a shock may itself enhance (or dampen) norms. In addition, norms may themselves be the product of a variety of contextual factors that may directly affect asset growth and recovery, including the economic health and history of a community. Devising a strategy to identify the portion of norms that is independent of these contextual factors is the topic of Section 11.3.

11.2.2 A model of asset growth

The following model of asset growth will be used to analyze the Honduran data:

$$A_{it} = A_{i0}e^{r(z_i,\Theta_i,\varepsilon_i,\beta_{g(i)})+v_i}, \tag{1}$$

where A_{it} is asset stock of household i at the end of the 30-month recovery period, A_{i0} is the pre-Mitch asset level, and the function $r(\bullet)$ is the 30-month rate of change (growth or contraction) of the asset stock expressed as a function of household characteristics (z_i), shocks received (Θ_i and ε_i), and the norms of altruism and trust of household i's community group, $\beta_{g(i)}$. The error term, v_i captures unobserved factors that also affect the rate of change of assets. Taking logs and rearranging terms yields:

$$\ln(A_{it}/A_{i0}) = r(z_i, \Theta_i, \varepsilon_i, \beta_{g(i)}) + v_i. \tag{2}$$

The key hypothesis to be investigated with equation (2) is whether a more favorable normative environment influences the growth rate of assets both directly and by dampening the impacts of shocks. However, in order to estimate this equation, two problems must be resolved. First, norms must be measured, and second, we must find a way to account for their endogeneity so that their impact on asset recovery and growth can be credibly inferred.

11.3   Experimental measurement of altruism and trust

This section reviews the experimental protocol devised to measure norms of altruism and trust in Honduran communities for which we have loss and recovery data from Hurricane Mitch. After presenting the experimental procedure and basic descriptive statistical results, the next section will consider how to model norms as a social and economic phenomena.

11.3.1   Experimental procedures

Experiments were based on modified versions of the Dictator game (Forsythe *et al.* 1994) and the Trust game (Berg *et al.* 1995). In the Dictator game, the proposer (or dictator) was endowed with an amount of cash that he had to decide to keep or share with an individual without an endowment. Each unit passed to the other was tripled before reaching the other person. In the Trust game, the proposer (the trustor) was also endowed with an amount of cash that he had to decide to keep or share with an individual without an endowment. The receiver of the tripled amount in the Trust game (the trustee) had the opportunity to send back none, part, or all the amount received. Because amounts sent by both dictators and trustor was tripled, the effective cost of giving money was the same in both games and equal to one-third.

Both Dictator and Trust games were played with complete anonymity. The games were also one-shot affairs, played with repetition and reputation. In their analysis of a similar experimental protocol in South Africa, Carter and Castillo (2003) argue that this game structure should permit the recovery of durable moral norms that characterize decisions that are not directly affected by considerations of punishment, reputation, or future strategic advantage. Moreover, because the games were played in long-standing communities (as opposed to the temporary and somewhat artificial social environment of a university campus), they should pick up characteristics of real social interactions in those communities.

These experiments were implemented in 31 separate Honduran communities. These communities were originally selected at random from a sample of communities studied in 1994 and 2001. One in seven of our experimental subjects were recruited from the respondents to these surveys, while the others were selected from other families in the same communities. Not more than one participant per household was allowed. All the participants were of 18 years of age or more and they were not told about experimental payments at the time of recruitment. The average age of participants was 41 years, with three out of five being male. Twenty five percent of the sample was at least 50 years of age and 25% was at most 31 years of age. Twenty five percent of participants had at most 5 years of education and 25% of them had at least 6 years of schooling. On average, there were 24 subjects per session. Two sessions were smaller (16 participants), and 3 sessions were larger (32 participants). All participants in each session belonged to the same community or neighborhood. On average, participants knew 88% of the people in the session by name. The average payment to a participant in the experiment was 90 Lempira (or around $5), which amounts to two days' wage in rural areas. Recruitment of participants was made with the help of local leaders, in particular, school principals, and, occasionally, the president of the local council (the *patronato*). These leaders were asked to recruit adults among families of different backgrounds.

Before the experiment, participants were given numbers at random. These numbers were used to divide people into groups and to assign experimental treatments at random. Subjects were divided across three rooms. In most cases, we had three school classrooms at our disposal, and only in two occasions did we need to accommodate people in different areas. Two rooms contained a quarter of the participants each and a third contained the remaining half of the participants. The third group was further divided into two.

The rooms containing a quarter of the participants each were labeled room *A* and room *B*. Room *C* contained the remaining 50% of subjects. In room *A*, people played the Dictator game first and the Trust game second. In room *B*, people played the Trust game first and the Dictator game second. The endowment for the Dictator game was 40 Lempiras ($2.50) and the endowment for the Trust game was 50 Lempiras ($3.10). Each Lempira sent to the other room was tripled in both games. In all rooms, instructions were read out loud, and then a series of questions were asked to make sure that the games were clear. In room *B*, participants were asked to make their decisions as dictators before the trustees' decisions were revealed. In this way, we prevented trustee actions from influencing choices by dictators. In rooms *A* and *B*, subjects were told that two different persons in room *C* were going to receive the first and second envelope sent by them. Moreover, it was made clear that a participant could be either a sender or a receiver, but not both. To make sure that different receivers did not receive envelopes from the same person, room *C* was divided in two sections. One section received the dictator's envelopes sent by room *A* and the trustor's envelopes sent by room *B*, and the other section received the dictator's envelopes sent by room *B* and the trustor's envelopes sent by room *A*. Sessions were run simultaneously. Finally, a post-experiment questionnaire was applied to collect background information on participants and their social organizations and networks.

11.3.2   *Experimental results*

Table 11.2 reports the summary statistics on the experiments. Participants sent around 40% of their endowment in the Dictator game, 50% in the Trust game, and returned around 40% as trustees. Note, of course, that the Nash equilibria for all these decisions – assuming purely selfish players – are zero budget shares. While obviously high compared to this selfish benchmark, these shares are also higher than those commonly found in experiments with college students (Forsythe *et al.* 1994; Eckel and Grossman 1996). The dictator share is especially remarkable given that amounts sent by dictators were tripled, meaning that dictators who sent 40% of their endowments allocated 54 Lempiras to their receiver and kept only 24 Lempiras for themselves. However, results from both games are consistent with previous results with non-college students (see Burks *et al.* 2005 for a survey). All decisions presented a high degree of variability. This variability is present at the community level also. The lowest average share passed in the Dictator game was 22% and the highest was 69%, and the lowest average share passed in the Trust game was 26% and the highest was 67%.

Decisions across games are correlated at the individual level as well as at the community level. For instance, the correlation between decisions made as dictator and as trustor equals 53%. Interestingly, this correlation is stronger in the Dictator–Trust sessions (63%) than in the Trust–Dictator sessions (44%). As found by Harbaugh *et al.* (2003), the order in which decisions are made seems to matter.

Table 11.2 Descriptive statistics for shares sent and returned

	Dictator	Trustor	Trustee
N	389	389	369
Mean (%)	42	49	42
SD (%)	29	29	30
Correlations at the individual level			
Dictator vs. trustor		0.53*	
Correlations at the community level			
Dictator vs. trustor		0.77*	
Dictator vs. trustee		0.37*	
Trustor vs. trustee		0.30	

Note
* Significant at 10% level.

The fact that decisions are correlated across games points to the potential ambiguities in the interpretation of the results of these games. While the Dictator game results stand as an easily defensible measure of an individual's willingness to unconditionally (or altruistically) share good fortune, Cox (2004), has suggested that any measure of trust elicited from games like ours must consider the fact that people are willing to reach very unequal distributions even without expecting any money in return (as in our dictator games). In their analysis of similar experiments in South Africa, Carter and Castillo (2003) argue that amounts sent by trustors and trustees in the Trust game will conflate the impact of altruism with pure norms of trust and/or reciprocity. While Carter and Castillo go some distance in showing how norms of trust and reciprocity can be recovered by combining play in both Dictator and Trust games, here we will content ourselves to note that the gross trust measure (defined as budget shares sent in the Trust game) is a noisy measure of the norm of interest.

In addition to correlation at the individual level, we also find significant correlations between decisions at the community level. Decisions as dictator and as trustor, and as dictator and trustee, are positively and significantly correlated at the community level. Dictator and trustee decisions were made independently and in separate rooms. Moreover, decisions by dictators and trustees are nonstrategic; they face no responders and they cannot affect the behavior of future game partners. Since we find that behavior at the community level is correlated even when no interactions are permitted, this shows that experimental data must be capturing factors other than a game equilibrium. While the analysis in the next section will more deeply probe the existence of distinctive community normative environments, this descriptive evidence is consistent with the notion of a common set of norms and expectations that shape economic behavior and relations between community members.

11.4 A social interactions model of altruism and trust

The economic experiments described in the prior section were designed to capture durable moral norms that shape and constrain real economic behavior. However, norms do not emerge from a vacuum, and are likely influenced by social and economic characteristics of both individuals and communities. Prior to estimating the impact of altruism and trust on economic recovery from Hurricane Mitch, we must first account for the endogeneity of norms and devise an estimation strategy that identifies the structural impact of norms shorn of simultaneity and other biases. The approach put forward in this section follows Manski (1993, 1996), Durlauf (2002), and Graham and Hahn (2003) and relies on a linear social interactions model of norms. In addition to laying the foundation for testing the impact of norms on economic recovery, our approach permits us to test the degree to which norms are self-reinforcing within communities. Evidence of such a reinforcement effect would indicate that communities constitute distinctive normative environments, such that it is meaningful to discuss more, vs. less, altruistic communities.

11.4.1   Modeling norms

Consider the following model of individual j's norm of altruism:[7]

$$\beta_j = [z_j b_1 + \theta_j b_2] + \bar{z}'_{g(j)} d + \bar{\beta}_{g(j)} c + u_j, \tag{3}$$

where β_j measures the individual's altruism, and the $g(j)$ subscript denotes the social reference group or community of individual j. Four types of factors are hypothesized to influence j's norms. First, the terms in the square brackets capture individual characteristics and experiences that shape j's altruism. We partition these factors into two components. The first component, denoted z_j, includes factors that affect j's altruism and also *directly* affect the altruism of other community members because they may influence the other's gains from being altruistic. An example of such a factor might be the extent of i's economic connectedness (e.g., ability to secure employment for others). Such connectedness may increase j's altruism as well as the incentives for others to be recognized as good, contributing altruistic community members. The second component in the square brackets, θ_j, captures private norm shocks that affect j's altruism, but do not directly affect the altruism of others. Symmetrically, private norm shocks experienced by other individuals do not directly influence the norms of j. Examples of θ_j include parental values and influences that shape j's morals, but do not directly affect others. The existence of such private norm shocks will be key to the econometric identification strategy developed here.

The second component in the model, $\bar{z}_{g(j)}$, measures average characteristics of the members of j's social group. Just as j's characteristics may shape incentives for others to act in a more or less altruistic fashion, so group characteristics may shape j's norms. In Manski's (1993) language, the parameter d measures contextual, or exogenous social effects.

The third component in equation (3) is the average level of altruism exhibited by members of j's community group, denoted $\bar{\beta}_{g(j)}$. A positive and significant influence of community norms on j's behavior ($c > 0$) would indicate that altruism is self-reinforcing within communities. A value of $c > 0$ implies that an individual matches or mimics the norms of other community members, controlling for individual and contextual factors. In Manski's language, a positive value of c signals the presence of endogenous social effects. The fourth and final component in equation (3) is u_j, which captures unobservable factors that affect j's altruism. While we scale u_j so that its unconditional expectation is zero, it may be correlated across individuals within the community.

The econometric difficulty confronting the analysis of norms can best be appreciated by considering the implications of equation (3) for the average or typical level of altruism in a community. Assuming that every community member's altruism is shaped by the analogue to equation (3), following Manski (1993) we can solve for the equilibrium expected community norm as:

$$\bar{\beta}_{g(j)} = \frac{b_1 + d}{1 - c} \bar{z}_{g(j)} + \frac{b_2}{1 - c} \bar{\varepsilon}_{g(j)} + \frac{\bar{u}_{g(j)}}{1 - c}. \tag{4}$$

As can be seen from equation (4), community norms of altruism will depend on both observed contextual factors, $\bar{z}_{g(j)}$, and any correlated unobservables measured by $\bar{u}_{g(j)}$.[8] To the extent that any of these contextual factors directly influence economic recovery after a shock, simple inclusion of the community level norm in the recovery regression equation (2) will conflate the influence of these factors with the influence of the norm itself. Clearly this is most problematic in the case of correlated unobservables.

In addition, equation (4) makes clear that simply including community altruism, $\bar{\beta}_{g(j)}$, as an explanatory variable in an ordinary least squares regression of the individual altruism, β_j, will not identify the endogenous social effects parameter, c. As can be seen from equation (4), even if $c = 0$, β_j will be correlated with $\bar{\beta}_{g(j)}$. Like the effort to identify the impact of norms on economic recovery, identification of endogenous social effects and the presence of community norm reinforcement requires an estimation strategy that accounts for the endogeneity of norms.

11.4.2 Econometric estimates of community norms and endogenous social interactions

In an effort to resolve these econometric problems, this section implements a two-stage approach, first estimating the determinants of community norms, and then using the instrumented value of community norms to estimate parameters in equations (2) and (3). As Durlauf (2002) has shown, identification of the impact of social variables like norms on economic outcomes requires instrumental variables that affect individual behavior, but are not themselves contextual variables. Private norm shocks – the θ_j in equation (3) – comprise one type of valid instruments for this purpose. Community social characteristics, which are unrelated to the current context which shape economic interactions, are another.

Table 11.3 shows the first stage community norm regressions. Identical specifications were used for both altruism and trust, with the community average amount sent in each game treated as the dependent variable. Parents' land wealth is included as a private norm shock variable on the grounds that parents' wealth and attitudes directly shape only the norms of their own children. Parent land wealth should also be uncorrelated with current economic outcomes. In addition to this private, norm-shaping variable, a number of community variables – also assumed to be unrelated to current economic outcomes – were included. The standard deviation of the parental wealth variable was included as a measure of the diversity of community backgrounds. In addition, 3 measures from the 2001 Honduran census (which took place a year before our experiments) were included: the average age of community members over 18 years of age; the proportion of men in the community; and, the average level of education. While the demographic characteristics of the people participating in our experiment are likely correlated with the current economic circumstances of the community, we expect that census data represent more permanent features of the community. Finally, we include the percentage of households that suffered housing losses from Mitch to see if such environmental shocks themselves directly influence the evolution of norms.

Table 11.3 First stage community norm regressions ($N = 30$)

	Altruism (Dictator budget share)	Trust (Trustor budget share)
Private norm shocks		
Parents' land wealth/10 (median)	0.08 (0.00)	0.3 (0.13)
Community characteristics		
SD of parental wealth/100	−0.04 (0.02)	−0.03 (0.04)
Average age (Census 2001)	−0.05 (0.00)	−0.02 (0.17)
Percentage of men (Census 2001)	−0.92 (0.14)	−1.63 (0.01)
Education level (Census 2001)	0.28 (0.00)	0.19 (0.02)
1 = urban, 0 = rural	−0.15 (0.02)	−0.13 (0.02)
Percentage of households with losses during Mitch	0.20 (0.07)	0.10 (0.28)
Constant	2.05 (0.00)	1.66 (0.00)
Adjusted R^2 (%)	55	43

Note
p-values in parentheses.

The estimation results in Table 11.3 are sensible. Parental wealth positively influences both altruism and trust, though only the former is statistically significant. Communities with older and more educated members tend to be more altruistic and trusting. Urban communities have a harder time building trust, perhaps due to the less personal nature of relationships. It is interesting to notice that behavior in the Dictator game seems to be more sensitive to factors affecting income. But trust and altruism are equally and negatively affected by the inequalities of community's member's backgrounds. The result on the proportion of males is more difficult to interpret. One possibility is that communities with a larger proportion of men experience more conflict. Another possibility is that communities with a larger proportion of men are communities with a larger portion of recent immigrants. Heterogeneity in the population would explain the lower levels of trust. Indeed, regression analysis of census data at the community level indicates that communities with larger proportions of men tend to be communities with larger proportions of non-locally born people. Finally, note that the proportion of households that suffered housing losses from Hurricane Mitch has a significant (at the 10% level) effect on altruism. While this shock is exogenous to the community, this impact of hurricane damage on norms threatens to create a (perhaps negative) spurious correlation between norms and economic recovery. This result suggests that it is important to try to unearth the norm levels that existed prior to Mitch. In the analysis of economic recovery in the next section, this Mitch loss variable will be eliminated from the set of instruments used to predict community norm levels for the recovery regression.

The first stage regressions reported in Table 11.3 could in principal be used to create instrumental variables estimates of community norms, the $\bar{\beta}_{g(j)}$, to estimate equation (3) and identify endogenous social effects. However, to further increase confidence in our identification strategy, we exploited the fact that our experimental design implemented simultaneous experimental sessions, yielding two measures of altruism and trust for each community. In order to avoid spurious correlation between individual and group behavior that may be induced by unobserved session-level experiment effects, the analysis of endogenous social interactions will use an instrumented measure of expected behavior based on the behavior in the alternate experimental session in the same community. This procedure eliminates any impact due to the existence of session-level correlated unobservables or endogenous social interactions at the experimental session level. Results of these regressions, which followed the same specification as shown in Table 11.3, are available from the authors.

To test for endogenous social effects, we then estimated equation (3), replacing the actual community norm with the instrumental variable estimate generated by this modified procedure. Table 11.4 presents the results from this second stage regression. Measures for community characteristics are the same as in the first stage regression in Table 11.3. We cannot include the individual norm shock measure

Table 11.4 Second stage estimate of social interactions

	Altruism	*Trust*
Endogenous social effect		
Instrumented community norm	0.36 (0.00)	0.38 (0.01)
Individual level variables		
Socioeconomic status		
Age	0.02 (0.16)	0.00 (0.37)
1 = man, 0 = woman	0.01 (0.77)	−0.03 (0.30)
Education level	0.02 (0.32)	0.01 (0.67)
Market dependency	−0.03 (0.12)	0.01 (0.77)
1 = evangelical, 0 = other	−0.03 (0.50)	0.02 (0.72)
Social capital		
Familiarity with participants	0.10 (0.20)	0.16 (0.03)
Trust in others	0.03 (0.15)	0.06 (0.00)
Community variables		
Age	−0.00 (0.43)	0.00 (0.67)
1 = man, 0 = woman	0.03 (0.24)	0.05 (0.07)
Education level	−0.00 (0.99)	0.00 (0.88)
Market dependency	0.01 (0.77)	−0.07 (0.02)
1 = evangelical, 0 = other	−0.14 (0.12)	0.01 (0.88)
Social capital		
Familiarity with participants	0.18 (0.26)	−0.03 (0.84)
Trust in others	0.05 (0.20)	0.03 (0.36)
Experimental Treatment		
1 = Dictator game first, 0 = otherwise	−0.02 (0.56)	−0.10 (0.02)
Constant	−0.09 (0.68)	0.03 (0.89)
Adjusted R^2 (%)	8	9

Note
p-values in parentheses.

as that variable was available only for experimental participants who were also included in the income and expenditure survey.

As seen in Table 11.4, in both Dictator and Trust games, the behavior of others is estimated to strongly and significantly affect individual behavior.[9] While this result signals the presence of strong endogenous social effects and community norm reinforcement, a caveat is in order. Insufficient control for unobservable factors at the community level could imply that our measures of community norms might be capturing community level characteristics not associated with norms *per se*. Despite this caveat, it is remarkable that the predicted behavior of people in different experimental sessions but in the same community might be at all related to individual behavior. This indicates that experiments do capture important information about communities, even if we cannot precisely pin down its origin. In any event, our identification strategy and choice of instruments reduces the effect of contemporaneous shocks on norms. The next section shows the impact of the strength of social norms on economic recovery.

11.5   The impact of trust on recovery

The direct, experimental measurement of the norms of altruism and trust, and the statistical confirmation that these measures capture systematic, self-reinforcing behavioral patterns within communities, permits us now to ask whether these norms bolster the effectiveness of informal financial mechanisms that provide insurance and capital. Table 11.5 displays regression results for equation (2), the rate of post-Mitch asset growth and recovery. The growth rate has been specified to be a function of the asset and income – expenditure shocks, where each of these has been normalized by the pre-Mitch level of assets. Shocks are measured as positive values (larger losses imply larger positive values). A negative coefficient on a shock variable would thus indicate that the household had been unable

Table 11.5 Second stage asset growth and recovery regressions

	OLS	Quantile regressions		
		25th	Median	75th
Shocks and aid				
Asset shock	−0.70 (0.04)	−1.57 (0.00)	−1.25 (0.00)	−0.91 (0.29)
Income shock	0.16 (0.01)	0.07 (0.30)	0.78 (0.10)	0.26 (0.42)
External aid	0.69 (0.00)	0.20 (0.56)	0.91 (0.00)	0.83 (0.03)
Trust*	1.23 (0.05)	0.08 (0.62)	0.15 (0.40)	0.80 (0.10)
Control variables		Included		
R^2 (%)	25	25	17	17
Observations		323		

Notes
* Instrumented and purged of the effects of Mitch.
p-values in parentheses.

to neutralize or fully recover from the shock. External aid, again normalized by the size of pre-Mitch value of assets, is also included in the regression. While much of the aid received was simply short-term consumption assistance, positive coefficients on aid would indicate that aid facilitated asset recovery (or perhaps prevented further asset alienation during the post-shock coping period).

Also included in the regressions is an instrumented community norm measure based on the analysis in the earlier section. Table 11.5 presents results only using the Trust game budget share measure of trust, instrumented with the pre-Mitch instrument set.[10] As discussed earlier, this measure is meant to capture the pre-Mitch level of community trust. This norm measure was entered directly into the regression as a factor that shifts the growth rate. In versions of the regression not reported here, the trust measure was also interacted with the asset shock variables to see if it effectively dampens the impact of the shocks on asset recovery. None of these collinear interaction terms proved to be statistically significant.

In addition, the regressions included household characteristics as control variables which might be expected to influence the post-Mitch asset growth rate. These variables included age and age-squared of the household head (to capture lifecycle patterns that might affect accumulation incentives), as well as the education and sex of the household head. Department level dummy variables were also included to control for basic market access and agro-ecological possibilities. Table 11.5 does not report the estimates of these control variables so as to eliminate clutter. Exclusion or modification of the control variable has little impact on the estimated coefficients for the variables of interest.

The second column in Table 11.5 presents the ordinary least squares (OLS) regression which explores the impact of trust on asset growth and recovery, controlling for the shock and aid variables. All the primary variables are statistically significant in this regression. The variables are scaled such that an increase in the assets lost by 10 percentage points decreases the 30 month, post-Mitch growth and recovery rate by 7.0 percentage points, indicating minimal recovery absent offsetting influences. By itself, this estimate signals the weakness of financial market-based responses to the shock.

Several factors, however, are estimated to be able to countermand the lingering impact of the shock. Higher levels of community trust significantly bolster the recovery rate, as every 10 percentage point increase in the budget share boosts the asset recovery rate by a hefty 1.2 percentage points. It is worth reiterating that this estimate comes from a norm measure that has been instrumented using parental characteristics and predetermined demographic features of communities. This estimated effect is striking evidence that when underwritten by pro-social norms, informal financial arrangements can play a large role in rebuilding stocks in the wake of a major environmental shock.

External aid flows also show a strong and positive effect on asset recovery. While total aid inflows were modest compared to asset losses (see Section 11.2), the estimated coefficient indicates that disaster assistance was very effective in protecting and rebuilding households' productive assets. This finding is especially striking given that much of the aid inflow was packaged as short-term consumption aid. Surprisingly, the OLS regression estimates that the income and expenditure shock positively affects asset recovery and growth. While these shocks have been normalized by pre-Mitch assets, it may well be that the largest shocks occurred when households were specialized in high-value plantation crops. Because these households might also enjoy the best access to formal capital markets, it may be that the positive coefficient on income shock is picking up the positive impact of access to capital on asset recovery and growth. Future work will explore this issue further.

While these results confirm the importance of local social norms in assisting growth and recovery, in prior work (Carter and Castillo 2003) we have argued that work on norms and social capital needs to pay more careful attention to the rules of inclusion and exclusion in social processes. To explore whether or not mutual insurance works better for some households than for others, we ran a suite of quantile regressions for the asset growth and recovery regression. The results, shown in Table 11.5 are striking. As expected, the constant term increases as we move up the regression quantile (coefficients not shown in the table). The coefficient on asset shocks is relatively stable across the regression quantiles.

In contrast, the coefficient on community trust is very unstable (and statistically different) across regression quantiles. As the quantile results demonstrate, the significance and magnitude of the coefficient on altruism is driven by the upper quantiles of the regression error distribution. In the regression for the 25th quantile, community trust has no impact of either economic or statistical significance. Even at the median regression, the altruism's effect is still small and insignificant at conventional levels. However, at the 75th quantile, altruism's effect has become large and significant at the 10% level. These quantile results imply that norms are working very well for households that do better than expected (in a regression sense). By contrast, the access to resources that can be brokered by trust and altruism within a community appears not to work at all for the subset that fares poorly.

There are at least two possible explanations for this result, one at the community level, and one at the individual household level. At the community level, it may be that norms only become effective once they pass a critical threshold level. In this case, it may be that it is only when altruism is high enough that households are able to sustain relationships of mutual insurance and capitalization. The alternative explanation at the household level is that the quantile results signal that unequal access to mutual insurance within communities is very much part of the story of disaster management and coping. While these quantile results are purely empiricist, future work will try to impose more structure on the problem in an effort to identify axes of inclusion and exclusion and/or threshold effects of altruism.

11.6   Conclusions

The damage wrought by Hurricane Mitch, which struck Honduras in late 1998, was substantial, with many households losing significant portions of their productive assets. Econometric analysis of norm measures, derived from a set of economic experiments, indicates that in communities with high levels of trust and altruism, recovery from asset loss was rapid and the longer term impacts of the Hurricane were significantly dampened. In contrast, in communities with low levels of trust, little recovery had taken place, and the effects of the Hurricane were still apparent in diminished levels of productive assets. These results flow from a regression strategy that attempts to account for the endogeneity of norms, and thus should not be the result of a spurious relationship between norms and economic possibilities. Moreover, analysis of norms through the lens of a social interactions model reveals the presence of endogenous social effects, meaning that community norm levels tend to be self-reinforcing.

Finally, while these results offer evidence that moral norms indeed enhance the effectiveness of mutual insurance, they do not resolve the question of whether all individuals enjoy similar access to mutual insurance, or if some individuals suffer a social exclusion that limits their ability to benefit from mutual insurance arrangements. To explore this question, the basic asset recovery model was reestimated using a quantile regression strategy. The quantile estimates signal substantial heterogeneity in the impact of trust on asset recovery, as they show that trust promotes recovery for only a subset of communities, or of individuals within communities. While further work is needed to tease apart this heterogeneous effect, the results presented here do indicate that mutual insurance underwritten by trust norms can function effectively for some households. However, social isolation, and ineffective risk coping, remain a reality for many households that continue to suffer diminished livelihood possibilities well after the experience of an environmental shock.

Acknowledgments

We thank The Pew Charitable Trusts and the BASIS Collaborative Research Support Program, The World Bank and the European Community for financial support. We also thank Ethan Ligon for helpful comments on an earlier draft.

Notes

1 Among the sample of 850 rural Honduran households which are studied here, only two reported receipt of insurance payments to offset Mitch-related damages (and the two cases were for medical costs covered by a health insurance plan). Buoyant capital markets could in principal substitute for these missing insurance markets. But in rural Honduras these markets are weak. Boucher *et al.* (2004) report that only 20% of the sampled Honduran households had accessed capital through formal market channels, while 40% of the sample indicated that there were rationed out of that market by non-price mechanisms.

2 The incentive problems of mutual insurance worsen when individuals can also self-insure by strategically building up private buffer assets as Ligon *et al.* (2000) and Carter and Zimmerman (1993) show with dynamic programming analyses.

3 As explained in more detail later, the trust game is comprised of two players, a trustor and a trustee. The trustor is given an amount of money which she may either keep or send to the trustee. Any money sent to the trustee is tripled. The trustee may keep all funds received from the trustor, but has the option of returning any or all of the funds

to the trustor. The notion of the game is that in communities with greater levels of trust, trustors will be more confident that funds will be returned to them and hence they will send larger budget shares to trustees.

4 The Dictator game is similar to the Trust game except that the person to whom funds are sent is unable to return any funds to the sender. Amounts sent in the Dictator game can thus be taken as an indicator of the degree of altruism within a community.

5 All amounts are expressed in 2001 US dollars, using the market exchange rate.

6 Some of these households also suffered loss of housing stock. These values have not been included in the measures of asset losses, as available data do not permit calculation of pre-Mitch housing values.

7 A symmetric discussion applies to trust norms as well.

8 Note that if the unobservables were uncorrelated across individuals, then $\bar{u}_{g(j)}$ would equal zero in expectation.

9 Using a panel data analogue method, Castillo and Carter (2004) show evidence consistent with the existence of endogenous social interactions at the session level in the experimental data used in this chapter. The existence of social interactions at the session level indicates the possible mechanism giving origin to norms. Unfortunately, this methodology cannot identify effects at the community level, which is the purpose of this section.

10 Given the strong correlation between trust and altruism in the experiments, repetition of the analysis with instrumented altruism yielded similar results, but with less statistical significance.

References

Berg, Joyce, Dickhaut, John, and McCabe, Kevin (1995) "Trust, Reciprocity, and Social History." *Games and Econ. Behavior* 10, 1 (July): 122–42.

Boucher, Stephen, Barham, Bradford, and Carter, Michael R. (2004) "The Impact of Market Friendly Reforms on Credit and Land Markets in Honduras and Nicaragua." Manuscript. Madison, WI: Univ. of Wisconsin, February.

Burks, Stephen, Carpenter, Jeffrey, and Verhoogen, Eric (2005) "Comparing Students to Workers: The Effect of Stakes, Social Framing and Demographics on Bargaining Outcomes." In J. Carpenter, G.W. Harrison, and J.A. List (eds), *Field Experiments in Economics*, Research in Experimental Economics, Vol. 10, Greenwich, CT: JAI Press.

Carter, Michael R. and Castillo, Marco (2003) "An Experimental Approach to Social Capital in South Africa." Ag. and Applied Economics Staff Paper 448 (revised): Univ. of Wisconsin, August.

Carter, Michael R., Castillo, Marco, and Zimmerman, Frederic (1993) "Mediating Risk through Markets, Rational Cooperation and Public Policy: Institutional Alternatives and the Trajectories of Agrarian Development in the West African Sahel." IRIS Working Paper: Univ. of Maryland, May.

Castillo, Marco and Carter, Michael R. (2004) "Identifying Social Effects in Economic Field Experiments." Manuscript. Madison, WI: Univ. of Wisconsin, May.

Coate, Stephen and Ravallion, Martin (1993) "Reciprocity without Commitment: Characterization and Performance of Informal Insurance Arrangements." *J. of Dev. Econ.* 40, 1 (February): 1–24.

Cox, James C. (2004) "How to Identify Trust and Reciprocity." *Games and Econ. Behavior* 46 (February): 260–81.

Durlauf, Steven (2002) "On the Empirics of Social Capital." *Econ. J.* 112, 4 (November): 459–79.

Eckel, Catherine and Grossman, Phillip (1996) "Altruism in Anonymous Dictator Games." *Games and Econ. Behavior* 16, 1 (October): 181–91.

Fafchamps, Marcel (1992) "Solidarity Networks in Preindustrial Societies: Rational Peasants with a Moral Economy." *Econ. Dev. and Cult. Change* 41, 1 (October): 147–74.

Forsythe, Robert, Horowitz, Joel, Savin, N.E., and Sefton, Martin (1994) "Fairness in Simple Bargaining Experiments." *Games and Econ. Behavior* 6, 3 (May): 347–69.

Foster, Andrew and Rosenzweig, Mark (2001) "Imperfect Commitment, Altruism and Family." *Rev. of Econ. and Statis.* 83, 3 (August): 389–407.

Graham, Brian and Hahn, Jinyong (2003) "Identification and Estimation of the Linear-in-Means Model of Social Interactions." Manuscript. Los Angeles, CA: UCLA.

Harbaugh, William, Krause, Kate, and Lidey, Steve (2003) "Children's Bargaining Behavior: Differences by Age, Gender, and Height." Manuscript. Eugene, OR: Univ. of Oregon.

Ligon, Ethan (1998) "Risk Sharing and Information in Village Economies." *Rev. of Econ. Stud.* 65, 4 (October): 847–64.

Ligon, Ethan, Thomas, Jonathan P., and Worrall, Tim (2000) "Mutual Insurance, Individual Savings, and Limited Commitment." *Rev. of Econ. Dyn.* 3, 2 (April): 216–46.

——(2002) "Informal Insurance Arrangements with Limited Commitment: Theory and Evidence from Village Economies." *Rev. of Econ. Stud.* 69, 1 (January): 209–44.

Lopez, Ramon and Valdes, Alberto (2000) "Fighting Rural Poverty in Latin Ameica: New Evidence of the Effects of Education, Demographics, and Access to Land." *Econ. Dev. and Cult. Change* 49, 1 (October): 197–211.

Manski, Charles (1993) "Identification of Endogenous Social Effects: The Reflection Problem." *Rev. of Econ. Stud.* 60, 3 (July): 531–42.

——(1996) "Identification of Anonymous Endogenous Interactions." Working Paper 96-04-019: Santa Fe Institute.

Morris, Saul, Neidecker-Gonzales, Oscar, Carletto, Calogero, Munguia, Marcial, Medina, Juan Manuel, and Wodon, Quentin (2001) "Hurricane Mitch and Livelihoods of the Rural Poor in Honduras." *World Dev.* 30, 1 (January): 49–60.

12 The role of ethnicity and networks in agricultural trade*

Evidence from Africa

Marcel Fafchamps

12.1 Introduction

It has long been observed that business has something to do with ethnicity. This is particularly true in Africa. In manufacturing, for instance, members of non-indigenous communities dominate business in specific countries in spite of the fact that they represent only tiny minorities in the population as a whole (e.g., Marris 1971; Himbara 1994; Fafchamps 2002a). Similar observations have been made by numerous authors regarding agricultural trade (e.g., Bauer 1954; Geertz 1963; Cohen 1969; Meillassoux 1971; Jones 1972; Amselle 1977; Geertz *et al.* 1979; Staatz 1979). In this respect, Africa is reminiscent of ancient trade practices in other parts of the world (e.g., Braudel 1986; North 1990; Greif 1993; Greif 1994). Similar comments have been made about gender and the conspicuous absence of women entrepreneurs in many parts of Africa (Spring and McDade 1998).

There are many possible explanations for this state of affairs. This chapter focuses on one – the functioning of markets – using original survey data on agricultural traders collected in Benin, Malawi, and Madagascar. African agricultural markets are such that few contracts between traders can credibly be enforced by courts. One reason is that most transactions are too small to justify court action. Another is that most traders are poor and have no fixed assets for creditors to employ the option of foreclosure. As a result, traders must trust each other to conduct business (Fafchamps 1996). For our purpose, trust can be defined as the belief that a commercial contract will not be breached in bad faith. Trust can originate in an interpersonal relationship, as when two people learn to trust each other through repeated interaction (Fafchamps 2004). Trust can also find its source in beliefs about differences between sexes, religions, or ethnic groups, as when people distrust others "not like themselves."

In this chapter we investigate the extent to which religion, ethnicity, and gender affects the functioning of markets through their effect on trust. We seek to assess the relative importance of the two possible origins of trust – or lack thereof: prejudice

* Originally published as: Fafchamps, Marcel (2003). "Ethnicity and Networks in African Trade." *Contributions to Economic Analysis and Policy*, 2(1), article 14. Reproduced with kind permission of Berkeley Electronic Press.

and statistical discrimination; and business networks. As in Fafchamps and Minten (2002), our concept of network is what the sociology literature calls subjective network, namely, the ties an individual has with others. An agent is defined as having a larger network if he or she has a larger number of ties with other agents. Network effects are identified using the number of ties reported by survey respondents, properly instrumented to account for possible endogeneity.

We also investigate the possible existence of location-invariant effects of religion, ethnicity or gender that make members of a particular faith, ethnic group or gender more or less trustworthy. The existence of such effects has been hypothesized in the literature under various guises. Max Weber explained, the economic success of the West as a result of Protestant ethics. In the old literature on East Asia, for instance, Shintoism and Confucianism were seen as value systems antagonistic to development. Greif (1994) argues that in medieval Europe, certain communities of traders developed a "culture" that was better able to foster trust. Other, less presentable ideas about the superiority of one group over others have yielded similar predictions about race and gender.

Such generalizations are suspect both on philosophical grounds and on the grounds that they are regularly disproved by counter-examples and subsequent historical events. One possible exception concerns gender. In nearly all human societies, parenting responsibilities fall primarily on the shoulders of women.[1] This is true in Africa also. In such a context, it is likely that men and women would differ systematically in the way in which they conduct business, particularly for women with children. We test for this possibility as well.

Results are mixed. In the case of domestic agricultural markets in the three countries studied, we find no strong evidence that either ethnicity or religion matter. Gender, however, has systematic effects that are constant across locations, irrespective of the gender make up of their trader community. The direct effects of ethnicity and religion generally disappear once we control for network effects. Ethnicity does not appear to have a significant effect on network formation. This suggests that whatever relationship is observed between success in trade and ethnicity is probably due to network effects, not to discrimination and prejudice in the conduct of everyday business.

The chapter is organized as follows. We begin by presenting the testing strategy in broad terms. A more detailed modeling exercise appears in Fafchamps (2002b, 2003). Next the data is, presented. In the first part of our empirical analysis, we focus on trust among traders. Trade credit is our yardstick for trust. We also examine whether traders share information about breach of contract by their respective clients. The first empirical section tests the significance of religion, ethnicity, and gender dummies. Having found no consistent relationship, except for gender, we switch to a location-specific definition of ethnic or religious dominance. We find no systematic effect of ethnicity on trust, but network contacts are significant in several regressions. The last part of our empirical analysis focuses on start-up conditions and accumulation of network and working capital over time. We test whether members of particular groups either are advantaged at start-up or grow faster and we find little or no effect of ethnicity.

12.2   Empirical testing strategy

We are interested in testing three alternative models of trade: a simple trust-based, relational contracting model; a statistical discrimination model; and a network model. These three models are derived in detail in Fafchamps (2003). We begin by noting that, by definition, in the simple trust-based model all traders have an equal chance of access to trade credit. Consequently, ethnicity or network links should not affect access to trade credit and firm growth. This is not the case in the other two models, which both predict that one group is more likely to have access to credit and to survive and grow. To test between the simple trust-based model and the other two, we therefore examine whether access to trade credit and business growth are correlated with group or network membership. If they are, this constitutes evidence against the simple model.

To test between the discrimination and network models, we note that there are important differences between them. In the statistical discrimination model, success in business and particularly access to trade credit are correlated with an observable characteristic such as ethnicity. In contrast, in the network model what matters is a trader's set of network contacts. It is possible, even likely, that the density of network contacts is correlated with ethnicity because it affects social links. But this need not be the case: networks that are not influenced by observable characteristics such as ethnicity can arise. We therefore begin by testing whether ethnicity is associated with trade credit and with firm entry and growth. If it matters, we cannot distinguish between the two models. But if ethnicity is not significant, this constitutes prima facie evidence against the discrimination model without necessarily rejecting the network model.[2]

The sign of the ethnicity effect also matters. Under fairly general conditions, an advantaged group eventually gets a large share of the trader population (Fafchamps 2003). Applied to individuals, this theoretical prediction implies that traders belonging to the ethnic group dominant in trade have better access to supplier credit and grow faster. In other words, supplier credit and firm growth should be higher for traders belonging to the ethnic group most represented among traders. This can easily be tested.

Supposing we find that ethnicity does not matter, we still need to distinguish between the simple trust-based model and a version of the network model in which network membership is not influenced by ethnicity. We do this in two steps. We first test whether individuals with better network have better access to credit. Because business networks are potentially endogenous to trade activity, we instrument the network variable. We also test another prediction of the network model, namely that better connected traders grow faster.

We complete the analysis with an investigation of start-up conditions. It is conceivable that ethnicity does not affect firm growth but influences the number of business acquaintances at start-up.[3] This is indeed what the network model predicts. Testing this prediction is undertaken at the end of the empirical section. Examining start-up conditions could also lead us to reject – or amend – all three models: if ethnicity affects start-up capital but not network links, this would suggest that our emphasis on transaction technology is misplaced and that all three models are wrong. A more promising line of enquiry then would be to investigate income and wealth differences across ethnic groups in activities other than trade – e.g., farming, civil service.

In our empirical implementation of the tests outlined above, we extend our analysis to include not only ethnicity, but also other external features most commonly associated with discrimination such as gender and religion. Everything we have said about ethnicity applies in a similar manner to religion. Gender is slightly different because male and female traders may also differ in motivation and entrepreneurial determination: men may enter trade as a career while many women may see agricultural trade as a temporary income-generating activity (Spring and McDade 1998). If this is the case, women traders may perform differently from men for reasons other than discrimination or networks. We also investigate this possibility when we examine the determinants of start-up capital and networks.

Having established our conceptual framework, we are now ready to turn to empirical analysis.

12.3   The data

Surveys of traders of domestic agricultural products were conducted in 1999/2000 in Benin (August–September 1999) and Malawi (August 1999–February 2000). A market-level survey was also conducted in order to obtain information on the marketing environment. The work was coordinated by the International Food Policy Research Institute (IFPRI), Oxford University and the World Bank. Data collection in the field was directed by the Laboratoire d'Analyse et de Recherche Economique et Sociale (LARES) in Benin, and by the Agricultural Policy Research Unit (APRU) in Malawi. A similar survey was conducted in Madagascar in the Fall of 2001. Survey work was undertaken in collaboration between Cornell University, Oxford University and the local Ministry of Scientific Research (FOFIFA). Funding for survey work was provided by The World Bank, USAID and the Pew project.

All three surveys focus on agricultural traders at both the wholesaler and retailer level.[4] Survey sites are market towns active in agricultural products. In Benin 24 markets were selected 30 in Madagascar and 40 in Malawi. Market selection is based on their trade importance and the availability of secondary price data. Due to the absence of reliable census information on the population of traders in both countries, a census of traders was conducted in each selected market.

In Benin, the survey team counted all traders present in the market on a given day. This count was supplemented by lists of traders obtained from the ONASA (Office National d'Appui à la Sécurité Alimentaire) and the regional bureaus of the Ministry of Commerce. These lists include larger traders who need not have a stall on the market itself. The two lists and the count were combined to construct a frame from which a sample was randomly drawn, resulting in a total sample of 663 agricultural traders.

In Malawi, a reconnaissance survey of traders was conducted in July–August 1999 to count and identify traders according to their status (independent, buying agent, or selling agent), their level (retail or wholesale) and the types of products they trade in. The information on the name, type, and location of traders from the reconnaissance survey were entered into a spreadsheet and the sample was drawn randomly from the census data using a computer algorithm. A total sample of 738 traders was interviewed in Malawi.

In Madagascar, three main agricultural regions were selected (Fianarantsoa, Majunga, and Antananarivo) and the sampling frame within these regions was set up as follows. Traders were surveyed in three different types of locations: big and small urban markets in the main town of every province (faritany) and district (fivondronana); urban areas outside urban markets; and rural markets at the level of the rural county (firaisana). Rural firaisanas were selected through stratified sampling based on agro-ecological characteristics so as to be representative of the various kinds of marketed products and marketing seasons. Traders operating in urban markets are mostly wholesalers, semi-wholesalers, and retailers. Urban traders located outside regular markets are bigger traders, processors (e.g., rice millers) and wholesalers. Traders operating on rural markets are mostly big and small assemblers and itinerant traders. A first trader survey was undertaken in 1997 in the same location. Only 30% of the surveyed 1997 traders were still operating in 2001. The 2001 sample is constructed so as to be representative of the trader population in 2001.

The questionnaire collects detailed information on the characteristics of the trader as well as on trade credit, contract enforcement and dispute settlement, information, and property rights enforcement. The characteristics of surveyed traders is summarized in Table 12.1. Traders are primarily middle-aged individuals with several years of experience in trade. Schooling is higher in Madagascar and lower in Benin where trade experience is higher. In contrast with the other two countries, a majority of Beninese agricultural traders belong to at least one trader organization. This results from a government effort to support trade by encouraging associations. Trade is a more common occupation in Benin, especially among women. This is reflected in the higher number of relatives in trade and the majority of mothers whose main occupation is trade. On average, surveyed traders have enjoyed a growth in their working capital and social networks since start-up.

In Table 12.2 we report the gender, ethnicity, and religion of surveyed traders. These characteristics are easily observable (e.g., name, attire) and are natural candidates for an investigation of discrimination. We see that agricultural trade is primarily a female occupation in Benin and Madagascar. For each sample, we distinguish among 6 major ethnic groups, plus a residual category. The determinants of ethnicity vary between the three countries. In Benin, language is the main criterion for deciding someone's ethnic group. In contrast, ethnicity in Madagascar is determined with reference to the region in which someone's ancestors are buried. There is considerable ethnic diversity in each sample. Of the three surveyed countries, Benin has the highest level of religious diversity, with Muslims and Christians on par and a large minority of respondents who describe themselves as

Table 12.1 Characteristics of surveyed traders

	Benin	Malawi	Madagascar
Personal characteristics			
Age	40.7	33.4	36.2
Number of languages spoken	2.7	2.1	1.3
Years of schooling	2.0	5.6	8.4
Years of experience in trade	20.9	9.3	6.0
Business characteristics			
Working capital (in US$)	1169	580	4479
Membership in trader organization (%)	62.4	3.1	10.5
Number of suppliers known	23.7	21.5	12.2
Number of clients known	28.4	25.5	13.6
Number of close relatives in trade	2.9	1.4	1.1
Start-up conditions			
Start-up working capital (in US$)	166	80	431
Number of suppliers known at start-up	8.8	3.6	4.3
Number of clients known at start-up	11.2	4.4	4.7
Family background			
Occupation of father			
Farmer (%)	72.2	64.8	76.3
Trader (%)	20.2	20.6	12.4
Wage worker (%)	7.6	14.6	11.3
Occupation of mother			
Farmer/housewife (%)	47.6	87.0	83.4
Trader (%)	51.9	11.0	14.4
Wage worker (%)	0.5	2.0	2.2
Father's years of experience in trade	4.0	6.1	2.8
Mother's years of experience in trade	20.8	5.0	3.1
Number of relatives	10.2	6.7	8.2

followers of traditional religions. In Malawi and Madagascar, the overwhelming majority of traders are Christian.

Each country sample covers between 20 and 25 districts, each with a slightly different gender, ethnic or religious make up. Discrimination and group membership are thus likely to operate differently in different districts. What matters is whether a trader is part of the "mainstream," i.e., is like the majority of traders in his or her immediate vicinity. To capture this idea, we construct a measure of membership in dominant local groups as follows. Within each district, we compute the proportion of each gender, ethnic, and religious group in the sample. We then construct a variable that takes the value one if a trader is of the same gender, ethnicity or religion as the majority of other traders in the district. Districts where no group has more than 50% of surveyed traders are regarded as having no majority group. Averages are displayed at the bottom of Table 12.2. We see, for instance, that in Benin some 44% of respondents are members of the locally dominant ethnic group albeit, in the sample as a whole, no group has more than 23%. The same is true for religion. This is because ethnicity and religion are geographically concentrated.

Table 12.2 Potential discrimination factors

	Benin (%)	Malawi (%)	Madagascar (%)
Gender			
Female	80.8	36.3	61.4
Ethnicity			
Ethnic group 1	18.9	23.9	45.5
Ethnic group 2	8.1	17.6	26.9
Ethnic group 3	22.5	4.7	4.7
Ethnic group 4	14.3	22.9	3.5
Ethnic group 5	3.5	4.9	8.6
Ethnic group 6	12.7	17.5	2.3
Other ethnic group	20.1	8.4	8.5
Religion			
Muslim	40.9	16.7	2.4
Christian	43.2	82.1	94.1
Other	15.9	1.2	3.5
Membership in locally dominant group			
Member of main gender group in district	78.0	69.9	63.8
Member of main ethnic group in district	43.6	43.1	54.7
Member of main religion in district	75.6	89.2	94.1

Table 12.3 Transaction technology

	Percentage of responses		
	Benin	Malawi	Madagascar
Whether credit is offered by suppliers			
Not offered	38.2	85.0	44.9
By some suppliers	56.8	15.0	43.6
By all suppliers	5.0	0.0	11.5
Whether respondent offers credit to clients			
Not offered	23.7	34.3	31.9
To some clients	73.9	64.3	67.5
To all clients	2.4	1.4	0.7
Information sharing with other suppliers			
Not shared	54.6	30.0	70.8
Some suppliers	37.3	70.0	27.0
All suppliers	8.1	0.0	2.1
Supplier credit (sample average)			
Percentage of purchases on credit	22.7	3.2	25.3
Percentage of sales on credit	23.3	10.9	15.6
Number of observations	662.0	738.0	885.0

Our main dependent variables are summarized in Table 12.3. Together they capture key dimensions of the transaction technology in each country. The first two variables are our measures of trust.[5] They are responses to questions "do any of your suppliers let you buy on credit?" and "do you let any of your clients buy on credit?" These questions basically measure whether credit is offered. This is credit of very short duration – in three quarters of the cases, the duration of the credit is seven days or less. We see that trade credit is much more likely to be offered in Benin and Madagascar than in Malawi. The next variable is a response to the question "if your client does not pay, will his or her other suppliers know it?" This is our index of information sharing. We see that in all three countries roughly two thirds of the respondents claim that some suppliers would get to know about non-payment, representing a moderate level of information sharing (e.g., Fafchamps and Minten 1999, 2001a). Our final two variables measure actual trade credit usage. We see that the average percentage of purchases and sales on credit is small, especially in Malawi.

12.4   Supplier credit and transaction technology

12.4.1   *Testing for ethnicity, gender, and religion*

Having familiarized ourselves with the conceptual framework and the data, we begin with the first part of our empirical strategy: we test whether gender, religion, and ethnicity affect the transaction technology. To this effect, we regress the five measures of transaction technology presented in Table 12.3 on gender, ethnicity, and religion. To avoid omitted variable bias – our variables of interest may be correlated with trader characteristics that affect transaction technology – we control for age and age squared, education, number of languages spoken, experience, and working capital.[6] We include district dummies as well to control for location-specific effects that are not due to gender, ethnicity or religion. This means that our regression coefficients are only identified by variation across traders within districts. Each regression is estimated for each of the three countries separately.

We are interested in whether the gender, ethnicity, and religion coefficients are significant. For each regression, we also conduct a joint significance test for ethnicity and religion dummies and we examine the signs of the coefficients. We expect women to be at an advantage in Benin and Madagascar since they represent the majority of traders, and both the discrimination and network models predict that the dominant group is also the most trusted. This follows from the fact that, in both models, traders in the good group become overrepresented over time. By the same reasoning, we expect minority ethnic and religious groups to receive and give less supplier credit.

An example of the kind of regression we estimate is given in Table 12.4 for supplier credit. The dependent variable is a categorical variable that measures whether credit is offered by all (highest category), some, or no supplier (lowest category). The estimator is ordered probit. Similar regressions were estimated for *all* variables appearing in Table 12.3. To save space, we only summarize them here.

We find that, once we control for personal characteristics and district dummies, gender is seldom significant. In the only regression in which gender is significant (percentage of purchases on credit in Benin), the coefficient is negative, contrary to expectations. Ethnicity seldom plays a significant role in trade credit. When

Table 12.4 Whether credit is offered by supplier (estimator is ordered probit)

	Unit	Benin		Malawi		Madagascar	
		Coef.	t-stat.	Coef.	t-stat.	Coef.	t-stat.
Possible discrimination factors							
Gender	female = 1	-0.227	-1.25	-0.238	-1.38	0.017	0.17
Ethnic group 2	yes = 1	-0.236	-0.64	0.376	0.96	0.420	1.51
Ethnic group 3	yes = 1	-0.344	-1.60	0.293	0.74	0.515	1.81
Ethnic group 4	yes = 1	-0.065	-0.20	0.037	0.07	0.221	0.66
Ethnic group 5	yes = 1	0.329	0.75	-0.022	-0.06	0.108	0.32
Ethnic group 6	yes = 1	-0.136	-0.45	-0.500	-1.09	0.253	0.51
Other ethnicity	yes = 1	-0.311	-1.17	-0.316	-0.67	0.686	**2.24**
Christian (Muslim is omitted category)	yes = 1	-0.106	-0.56	-0.710	**-2.71**	-0.895	**-3.00**
Other religion	yes = 1	-0.282	-1.25	—	—	-0.744	**-1.94**
Personal characteristics[a]							
Age of trader	log	0.003	0.09	-0.107	**-2.31**	0.096	**3.82**
Age of trader, squared	log * log	0.000	0.13	0.001	1.59	-0.001	**-3.88**
Number of languages spoken	log	0.245	**1.96**	0.120	0.66	-0.183	-1.18
Number of years of schooling	level	0.013	0.60	0.062	**2.39**	0.013	0.87
Years of experience	log + 1	0.209	**2.23**	0.441	**4.19**	0.175	**2.85**
Working capital (instrumented)	log	-0.359	**-3.81**	-0.299	**-3.12**	-0.115	**-2.74**
_cut1		-3.863		-3.314		2.150	
_cut2		-1.523		—		4.106	
Joint test of ethnicity variables							
Chi-square		5.42		9.71		8.54	
p-value		0.4908		0.1373		0.2014	
Joint test of religion variables							
Chi-square		1.69		**7.36**		**9.13**	
p-value		0.4305		0.0067		0.0104	
Number of observations		607		730		879	
Pseudo R^2		0.171		0.125		0.254	

Notes
a District dummies (20–25) included but not shown.
t-values that are significant at the 10% level appear in boldface.

it occasionally tests significant, individual coefficients do not have the expected sign (i.e., a small ethnic group is shown to have better access to credit). The only exception is information sharing, for which ethnicity is jointly significant in all three countries. In Benin, one ethnicity coefficient has the expected sign: the Nago, which represent close to one fourth of the Beninese sample, have a strong positive coefficient. But so do the Dendi, who are a small group. In the other countries, no clear pattern can be seen since none of the ethnicity coefficients are individually significant and many signs for minor groups are positive.

Religion is a different story. Muslim traders in Malawi and non-Christian traders in Madagascar more often report being offered credit by suppliers. Purchases on credit also represent a significantly larger share of total purchases. In contrast, non-Christian Beninese traders do not receive more credit but offer more credit to clients. While these results are not fully consistent (they apply to credit *from* suppliers in Malawi and Madagascar versus credit *to* clients in Benin; there is only a very small sample of non-Christians in Madagascar), they appear to suggest that Christian traders are less inclined towards trade credit and, by implication, less trusting and less trusted. These findings are consistent, for instance, with the work of Ensminger (1992) who reports that Islam penetrated cattle trade in Kenya because it fostered trust. Greif (1994) also emphasizes the role of religion in trade, but in his work on Genoese merchants, comes to a different conclusion regarding which religion is more emphatic to trade.

12.4.2   Testing for locally dominant groups

The lack of strong gender and ethnicity effects and the ambiguity of the reported religion effect may be due to an inappropriate aggregation scale. For dummies to be significant, a particular group – based on gender, ethnicity or religion – would have to be dominant over a very large geographical area. This need not be the case if the effect of networks and discrimination operate only at the local level. If this is true, what matters is not ethnicity per se, but whether a trader is a member of the locally dominant group.

To investigate this possibility, we construct an indicator variable that takes the value one if the respondent has the same ethnicity as at least half of the other traders in the district. In districts where no group dominates, the indicator variable is zero. With this definition, members of even a small ethnic group may have a local advantage. Similar indicator variables are constructed for gender and religion. Mean values of the variable were reported in Table 12.2.

We add these variables to our regressions. The results are mixed, and not shown here for lack of space. Whereas local group dummies are jointly significant in 5 out of 15 cases, they do not always have the expected sign. Whenever the local ethnicity dummy is significant, it has the wrong sign. The national ethnicity dummies themselves become largely non-significant. The local gender group variable is individually significant three times with the correct sign. But in Benin, when it is significant, gender itself has a negative coefficient. The local religion group dummy is individually significant four times, always with the expected (positive) sign. Its presence does not subtract from the significance of the religion dummies, with Muslims more likely to offer and be offered trade credit. Similar qualitative results obtain if we omit the national ethnicity dummies.

12.4.3   *Testing for network effects*

Albeit our results so far provide mild evidence that religion matters, they are in contradiction with the many sociological studies that insist on the importance of ethnicity in African trade (e.g., Cohen 1969; Meillassoux 1971; Amselle 1977). In an attempt to resolve this contradiction, we investigate the possible existence of network effects. Ethnicity may matter not because of general trust within ethnic communities and discrimination along ethnic lines, but because it is a determinant of membership in trade networks (Geertz *et al.* 1979).

To investigate network effects, we add four new variables to the regressions: the number of suppliers known, the number of clients known, the number of relatives in trade and membership in a trader association. The four variables are instrumented using start-up working capital, numbers of suppliers and clients known at start-up, the number of relatives and the average association membership in each district. Results are much more encouraging: network variables are jointly significant in 12 regressions out of 15, albeit in three cases with the wrong sign. Religion effects again remain unchanged.

The conclusion we draw from this exercise is that networks matter. To be offered and to offer trade credit, knowing people seems more important than being of the dominant ethnicity or gender. These results confirm earlier work on the effect of network membership on trader performance (e.g., Fafchamps and Minten 2001b, 2002). In turn, they raise the issue of how family background and ethnicity affect firm growth. We turn now to this issue.

12.5   Start-up and firm growth

Our analysis of the transaction technology is not fully conclusive: we find little evidence that ethnicity affects trust. Business networks, in contrast, appear to matter. To investigate this matter further, we turn to start-up conditions and firm growth. We first examine the determinants of business contacts at start-up. We then study the factors that affect the growth rate of an individual's business network over time. We also examine the role of working capital, in case ethnicity operates not through trade networks but through equity financing networks, i.e., parents and kin investing in the respondent's business.

12.5.1   *Start-up conditions*

Start-up networks are measured by the number of suppliers and clients known at start-up. We also investigate the determinants and role of start-up working capital as an alternative to our three models of business success based on trust. Means for all the variables were reported in Table 12.1. Regressors include gender, ethnicity, and religion dummies as before. We also include personal characteristics such as age at start-up (and age squared), number of languages spoken, and years of schooling. Family background variables, such as profession of the parents and experience in trade, are added to control for possible financial effects and prior exposure to trade.

We estimate the regressions without and with local group effects. Regressions without local group variables show no effect of ethnicity or religion, except an occasional significant coefficient, always with the wrong sign. Results with local group effects are reported in Tables 12.5–12.7. We see that ethnicity variables are never jointly significant, except in one case with the wrong sign: members of ethnic groups marginally represented in trade appear advantaged in start-up conditions, a result that contradicts the presence of ethnic favoritism. Religion is never significant. In contrast, gender is often significant and always negative: female traders start their business with less capital and fewer contacts. This is consistent with trade being a transient income generating activity for many African women, in which they enter and exit depending upon family circumstances (Spring and McDade 1998).

Being of the same ethnic group as half of the traders in the district has a negative effect on start-up contacts and capital in 6 out of 9 regressions – in one case, this effect is significant. Being of the same religion has a negative coefficient in 5 out of 9 regression and is never significant. In contrast, being of the same sex as most local traders has a significant positive effect on trade contacts in Benin. Combined with the fact that being a woman has a strong negative effect on start-up contacts, this suggests that Beninese male traders have more start-up contacts in districts where they represent the bulk of the traders.[7]

In contrast, family background is shown to have some effect on start-up conditions, especially trading experience. Better educated traders start with more working capital, possibly because they were able to save more money on earlier, better paid wage jobs. To summarize, we fail to find strong evidence that ethnicity affects start-up networks and capital.

12.5.2 Firm growth

Let us now turn to growth of networks and working capital after start-up. Both are important for firm performance (e.g., Fafchamps and Minten 2001b, 2002). If members of a particular gender, ethnic or religious group are advantaged in business, they should accumulate contacts and capital faster. Results are summarized in Tables 12.8–12.10 for known suppliers, known clients and working capital. As before, regressors include gender, ethnicity, and religion dummies together with district dummies. Personal characteristics include the age of trader at start-up (and age squared), number of languages, and years of schooling. Years of trading experience control for the time elapsed since start-up. Since both experience and the dependent variable are expressed in log, the (conditional) annual growth rate can be calculated as the coefficient of experience divided by years of experience.[8] Start-up conditions are included as well as the number of

Table 12.5 Number of suppliers known at start-up

	Unit	Benin		Malawi		Madagascar	
		Coef.	t-stat.	Coef.	t-stat.	Coef.	t-stat.
Possible discrimination factors							
Gender	female = 1	-1.643	**-3.80**	-0.166	-0.98	-0.112	-1.44
Ethnic group 2	yes = 1	0.085	0.21	-0.148	-0.45	0.644	**2.68**
Ethnic group 3	yes = 1	0.056	0.24	0.149	0.45	0.595	**2.47**
Ethnic group 4	yes = 1	0.472	1.23	-0.073	-0.22	0.599	**2.18**
Ethnic group 5	yes = 1	0.605	1.16	0.264	0.62	0.501	**1.71**
Ethnic group 6	yes = 1	0.484	1.31	-0.123	-0.34	0.933	**3.33**
Other ethnicity	yes = 1	-0.141	-0.44	0.310	1.06	0.375	1.52
Christian (Muslim is omitted category)	yes = 1	0.024	0.11	-0.067	-0.24	-0.141	-0.68
Other religion	yes = 1	-0.043	-0.16	—	—	-0.275	-1.06
Personal characteristics							
Age at start-up	level	-0.021	-0.74	-0.005	-0.21	0.010	0.80
Age at start-up, squared	level^2	0.000	0.59	0.000	0.10	-0.000	-0.90
Number of languages spoken	log	-0.203	-1.49	-0.160	-1.12	-0.299	**-2.93**
Number of years of schooling	level	0.008	0.38	0.035	**2.03**	-0.004	-0.41
Family background							
Father was a trader	yes = 1	0.251	1.21	-0.072	-0.47	0.110	0.67
Father was an employee	yes = 1	0.050	0.22	0.309	**2.12**	0.062	0.64
Mother was a trader	yes = 1	0.157	0.64	0.157	0.84	-0.339	**-2.07**
Mother was an employee	yes = 1	1.072	1.34	0.435	1.28	-0.095	-0.48
Father's years of experience as trader	log +1	0.029	0.42	0.090	**1.77**	0.015	0.25
Mother's years of experience as trader	log +1	0.034	0.50	0.025	0.48	0.163	**2.72**

Membership in local majority group[a]						
Member of main gender group in district	yes = 1	1.257	**2.69**	−0.120	−0.73	−0.102	−1.33
Member of main ethnic group in district	yes = 1	−0.142	−0.46	−0.050	−0.29	−0.001	−0.01
Member of main religion in district	yes = 1	−0.174	−0.97	−0.153	−0.65	—	—
Intercept		2.293	**3.35**	1.105	**1.80**	1.602	**1.78**
Selection-term		1.229	—	1.184	—	0.787	—
Number of observations censored at 0		156		237		96	
Number of uncensored observations		391		480		773	
Joint test of ethnicity variables							
F		0.97		1.01		**2.59**	
p-value		0.4443		0.4146		0.0171	
Joint test of religion variables							
F		0.04		0.06		0.58	
p-value		0.9568		0.8098		0.5584	
Joint test of membership in majority group variables							
F		**2.81**		0.40		0.88	
p-value		0.0389		0.7555		0.4148	
Number of observations		547		717		869	
Pseudo R^2		0.142		0.062		0.092	

Notes

a District dummies (20–25) included but not shown.

t-values that are significant at the 10% level appear in boldface.

Table 12.6 Number of clients known at start-up

	Unit	Benin		Malawi		Madagascar	
		Coef.	t-stat.	Coef.	t-stat.	Coef.	t-stat.
Possible discrimination factors							
Gender	female = 1	−1.007	**2.54**	−0.157	−1.19	−0.096	−1.29
Ethnic group 2	yes = 1	−0.058	−0.16	0.148	0.57	0.259	1.13
Ethnic group 3	yes = 1	−0.263	−1.21	0.220	0.84	0.262	1.14
Ethnic group 4	yes = 1	0.017	0.05	0.212	0.80	0.368	1.40
Ethnic group 5	yes = 1	0.133	0.26	0.230	0.68	0.282	1.01
Ethnic group 6	yes = 1	0.509	1.53	0.415	1.44	0.595	**2.22**
Other ethnicity	yes = 1	−0.026	−0.09	0.337	1.43	0.265	1.12
Christian (Muslim is omitted category)	yes = 1	−0.222	−1.13	0.101	0.47	0.004	0.02
Other religion	yes = 1	−0.006	−0.03	—	—	−0.106	−0.42
Personal characteristics							
Age at start-up	level	−0.009	−0.35	−0.010	−0.48	−0.003	−0.22
Age at start-up, squared	level^2	0.000	0.62	0.000	0.55	0.000	0.20
Number of languages spoken	log	0.072	0.58	−0.102	−0.90	−0.340	**−3.46**
Number of years of schooling	level	0.012	0.64	0.011	0.83	−0.002	−0.18
Family background							
Father was a trader	yes = 1	0.311	1.62	0.245	**2.00**	0.057	0.36
Father was an employee	yes = 1	0.170	0.83	0.385	**3.31**	0.167	**1.79**
Mother was a trader	yes = 1	0.291	1.27	−0.090	−0.61	−0.283	**−1.78**
Mother was an employee	yes = 1	0.819	1.10	−0.192	−0.70	−0.412	**−2.13**
Father's years of experience as trader	log +1	0.058	0.92	−0.028	−0.68	0.038	0.67
Mother's years of experience as trader	log +1	−0.031	−0.49	0.044	1.06	0.126	**2.18**

Membership in local majority group[a]						
Member of main gender group in district	yes = 1	0.807	**1.88**	−0.059	−0.46	−0.075	−1.01
Member of main ethnic group in district	yes = 1	0.253	0.90	0.125	0.89	−0.051	−0.47
Member of main religion in district	yes = 1	0.057	0.35	−0.118	−0.64	—	—
Intercept		1.370	**2.18**	1.227	**2.51**	1.874	**2.15**
Selection-term		1.140	—	0.975	—	0.761	—
Number of observations censored at 0		135	—	128	—	77	—
Number of uncensored observations		413	—	589	—	792	—
Joint test of ethnicity variables						
F		1.50	—	0.63	—	1.09	—
p-value		0.1772	—	0.7072	—	0.3660	—
Joint test of religion variables						
F		0.91	—	0.22	—	0.23	—
p-value		0.4050	—	0.6390	—	0.7962	—
Joint test of membership in majority group variables						
F		1.52	—	0.40	—	0.61	—
p-value		0.2076	—	0.7509	—	0.5448	—
Number of observations		548	—	717	—	869	—
Pseudo R^2		0.175	—	0.028	—	0.091	—

Notes
a District dummies (20–25) included but not shown.
t-values that are significant at the 10% level appear in boldface.

Table 12.7 Start-up working capital

	Unit	Benin		Malawi		Madagascar	
		Coef.	t-stat.	Coef.	t-stat.	Coef.	t-stat.
Possible discrimination factors							
Gender	female = 1	−0.001	0.00	−0.204	−1.17	−0.292	**−1.72**
Ethnic group 2	yes = 1	0.008	0.02	0.365	1.07	0.268	0.52
Ethnic group 3	yes = 1	0.353	1.44	0.270	0.78	0.306	0.59
Ethnic group 4	yes = 1	−0.146	−0.37	0.235	0.68	0.322	0.54
Ethnic group 5	yes = 1	1.119	**2.21**	−0.050	−0.11	1.033	1.63
Ethnic group 6	yes = 1	−0.268	−0.73	0.245	0.65	1.033	**1.70**
Other ethnicity	yes = 1	0.104	0.32	0.633	**2.05**	0.405	0.76
Christian (Muslim is omitted category)	yes = 1	0.253	1.17	0.154	0.53	−0.478	−1.06
Other religion	yes = 1	−0.099	−0.37	—	—	−0.248	−0.45
Personal characteristics							
Age at start-up	level	0.016	0.50	0.027	1.00	0.037	1.28
Age at start-up, squared	level²	0.000	0.08	0.000	0.11	−0.000	−0.86
Number of languages spoken	log	−0.043	−0.31	0.232	1.55	0.214	0.97
Number of years of schooling	level	0.081	**3.70**	0.075	**4.22**	0.088	**4.27**
Family background							
Father was a trader	yes = 1	0.111	0.50	−0.143	−0.88	−0.557	−1.56
Father was an employee	yes = 1	−0.094	−0.40	−0.027	−0.17	−0.220	−1.05
Mother was a trader	yes = 1	0.309	1.24	0.280	1.42	0.095	0.27
Mother was an employee	yes = 1	−0.387	−0.47	0.043	0.12	0.585	1.36
Father's years of experience as trader	log +1	−0.040	−0.54	0.114	**2.09**	0.081	0.62
Mother's years of experience as trader	log +1	−0.020	−0.29	−0.049	−0.89	0.263	**2.01**

Membership in local majority group[a]							
Member of main gender group in district	yes = 1	−0.671	−1.32	0.546	**3.22**	0.071	0.42
Member of main ethnic group in district	yes = 1	−0.114	−0.39	0.246	1.33	−0.688	**−2.82**
Member of main religion in district	yes = 1	−0.026	−0.14	−0.062	−0.25		
Intercept		3.938	**5.36**	0.133	0.21	0.462	0.23
Selection-term		1.309	—	1.310	—	1.723	—
Number of observations censored at 0		17	—	0	—	68	—
Number of uncensored observations		514	—	717	—	801	—
Joint test of ethnicity variables							
F		1.58	—	1.12	—	1.38	—
p-value		0.1496	—	0.3510	—	0.2211	—
Joint test of religion variables							
F		1.42	—	0.29	—	0.72	—
p-value		0.2429	—	0.5933	—	0.4859	—
Joint test of membership in majority group variables							
F		0.65	—	**3.98**	—	**4.09**	—
p-value		0.5829	—	0.0080	—	0.0171	—
Number of observations		531	—	717	—	869	—
Pseudo R^2		0.073	—	0.094	—	0.079	—

Notes

a District dummies (20–25) included but not shown.

t-values that are significant at the 10% level appear in boldface.

Table 12.8 Growth in the number of suppliers known

	Unit	Benin		Malawi		Madagascar	
		Coef.	t-stat.	Coef.	t-stat.	Coef.	t-stat.
Possible discrimination factors							
Gender	female = 1	0.347	1.26	−0.205	**−1.65**	−0.124	**−2.43**
Ethnic group 2	yes = 1	0.068	0.29	0.157	0.66	0.213	**1.76**
Ethnic group 3	yes = 1	0.151	1.08	0.180	0.74	0.314	**2.51**
Ethnic group 4	yes = 1	0.354	1.58	0.127	0.41	0.418	**2.92**
Ethnic group 5	yes = 1	0.162	0.61	−0.006	−0.03	0.093	0.63
Ethnic group 6	yes = 1	0.345	**1.68**	0.049	0.19	0.297	1.56
Other ethnicity	yes = 1	0.349	**2.07**	0.275	1.00	0.257	**1.93**
Christian (Muslim is omitted category)	yes = 1	0.339	**2.81**	−0.084	−0.41	—	—
Other religion	yes = 1	0.120	0.83	—	—	0.290	1.73
Personal characteristics							
Age at start-up	level	0.009	0.50	0.034	**1.73**	0.000	0.02
Age at start-up, squared	level²	−0.000	−0.63	−0.000	−1.49	0.000	0.31
Number of languages spoken	log	0.058	0.76	0.088	0.81	−0.131	**−1.99**
Number of years of schooling	level	0.016	1.27	0.008	0.59	0.008	1.23
Start-up conditions							
Years since start-up	log +1	0.081	1.37	0.173	**2.84**	0.196	**6.03**
Number of suppliers known at start-up	log +1	0.705	**18.19**	0.645	**13.04**	0.739	**22.11**
Number of buyers known at start-up	log +1	−0.073	**−1.89**	−0.184	**−3.58**	−0.029	−0.88
Number of relatives	log +1	0.136	1.64	−0.043	−0.45	−0.038	−0.84
Start-up working capital	log +1	−0.042	**−1.69**	−0.012	−0.42	0.007	0.66

Membership in local majority group[a]							
Member of main gender group in district	yes = 1	−0.558	**−1.91**	−0.015	−0.12	−0.024	−0.46
Member of main ethnic group in district	yes = 1	0.083	0.52	0.157	1.21	−0.002	−0.03
Member of main religion in district	yes = 1	−0.096	−0.96	−0.104	−0.60	0.047	0.35
Intercept		0.950	**1.94**	1.529	**2.72**	0.797	1.35
Selection-term		0.776	—	0.944	—	0.524	—
Number of censored observations at 0		59	—	32	—	34	—
Number of uncensored observations		552	—	698	—	848	—
Joint test of ethnicity variables							
F		0.81	—	0.55	—	**2.43**	—
p-value		0.5591	—	0.7664	—	0.0245	—
Joint test of religion variables							
F		4.37	—	0.17	—	**3.01**	—
p-value		0.0131	—	0.6812	—	0.0833	—
Joint test of membership in majority group variables							
F		1.59	—	0.52	—	0.11	—
p-value		0.1896	—	0.6669	—	0.9557	—
Number of observations		611	—	730	—	882	—
Pseudo R^2		0.323	—	0.109	—	0.411	—

Notes

a District dummies (20–25) included but not shown.

t-values that are significant at the 10% level appear in boldface.

Table 12.9 Growth in the number of clients known

	Unit	Benin		Malawi		Madagascar	
		Coef.	t-stat.	Coef.	t-stat.	Coef.	t-stat.
Possible discrimination factors							
Gender	female = 1	0.266	0.96	−0.147	−1.30	−0.116	**−2.37**
Ethnic group 2	yes = 1	0.044	0.19	−0.229	−1.05	0.241	**2.09**
Ethnic group 3	yes = 1	0.125	0.89	−0.278	−1.25	0.269	**2.26**
Ethnic group 4	yes = 1	0.174	0.78	−0.159	−0.56	0.381	**2.79**
Ethnic group 5	yes = 1	−0.077	−0.29	−0.173	−0.83	0.097	0.70
Ethnic group 6	yes = 1	0.084	0.41	−0.142	−0.58	0.328	**1.81**
Other ethnicity	yes = 1	−0.144	−0.85	0.083	0.33	0.263	**2.07**
Christian (Muslim is omitted category)	yes = 1	0.068	0.56	0.005	0.03	—	—
Other religion	yes = 1	−0.020	−0.14	—	—	0.311	**1.95**
Personal characteristics							
Age at start-up	level	−0.017	−0.91	0.029	1.64	−0.001	−0.10
Age at start-up, squared	level²	0.000	0.83	−0.000	−1.17	0.000	0.32
Number of languages spoken	log	0.094	1.23	0.167	**1.69**	−0.000	0.00
Number of years of schooling	level	−0.008	−0.68	−0.006	−0.52	−0.001	−0.25
Start-up conditions							
Years since start-up	log +1	0.064	1.08	0.164	**2.94**	0.182	**5.88**
Number of suppliers known at start-up	log +1	0.042	1.08	−0.036	−0.80	0.125	**3.92**
Number of buyers known at start-up	log +1	0.613	**15.86**	0.489	**10.38**	0.493	**15.49**
Number of relatives	log +1	0.263	**3.16**	0.104	1.19	−0.035	−0.81
Start-up working capital	log +1	−0.029	−1.16	−0.033	−1.32	−0.007	−0.66

Membership in local majority group[a]							
Member of main gender group in district	yes = 1	−0.431	−1.47	−0.089	−0.79	0.033	0.68
Member of main ethnic group in district	yes = 1	−0.060	−0.38	0.126	1.06	0.038	0.53
Member of main religion in district	yes = 1	−0.053	−0.53	−0.067	−0.42	0.071	0.56
Intercept		1.377	**2.81**	1.329	**2.58**	1.388	**2.45**
Selection-term		0.781	—	0.867	—	0.501	—
Number of censored observations at 0		47	—	8	—	24	—
Number of uncensored observations		564	—	722	—	858	—
Joint test of ethnicity variables							
F		0.65	—	0.80	—	**1.90**	—
p-value		0.6915		0.5665		0.0787	
Joint test of religion variables							
F		0.30	—	0.00	—	**3.81**	—
p-value		0.7396		0.9800		0.0513	
Joint test of membership in majority group variables							
F		0.87	—	0.61	—	0.36	—
p-value		0.4579		0.6073		0.7817	
Number of observations		611	—	730	—	882	—
Pseudo R^2		0.331	—	0.100	—	0.394	—

Notes
a District dummies (20–25) included but not shown.
t-values that are significant at the 10% level appear in boldface.

Table 12.10 Growth in working capital

	Unit	Benin		Malawi		Madagascar	
		Coef.	t-stat.	Coef.	t-stat.	Coef.	t-stat.
Possible discrimination factors							
Gender	female = 1	-0.333	-0.88	-0.807	**-6.09**	-0.405	**3.77**
Ethnic group 2	yes = 1	0.131	0.44	0.288	1.14	0.537	**2.04**
Ethnic group 3	yes = 1	-0.175	-0.98	0.279	1.08	0.632	**2.33**
Ethnic group 4	yes = 1	-0.079	-0.28	0.295	0.89	0.464	1.49
Ethnic group 5	yes = 1	-0.306	-0.87	0.409	**1.69**	0.553	**1.75**
Ethnic group 6	yes = 1	-0.104	-0.39	0.400	1.41	0.802	**1.97**
Other ethnicity	yes = 1	-0.234	-1.08	0.588	**2.01**	0.513	**1.79**
Christian (Muslim is omitted category)	yes = 1	0.122	0.80	0.020	0.09	-0.465	-1.57
Other religion	yes = 1	0.101	0.55	—	—	0.129	0.35
Personal characteristics							
Age at start-up	level	0.001	0.05	0.051	**2.45**	0.076	**4.07**
Age at start-up, squared	level²	0.000	0.41	-0.001	**-2.08**	-0.001	**-3.30**
Number of languages spoken	log	0.324	3.33	-0.066	-0.57	0.274	**1.95**
Number of years of schooling	level	0.046	2.93	0.077	**5.50**	0.023	1.76
Start-up conditions							
Years since start-up	log +1	0.733	**9.75**	0.434	**6.68**	0.497	**7.12**
Number of suppliers known at start-up	log +1	-0.005	-0.10	-0.026	-0.49	0.235	**3.31**
Number of buyers known at start-up	log +1	0.104	**2.13**	-0.070	-1.28	-0.072	-1.02
Number of relatives at start-up	log +1	0.223	**2.08**	0.213	**2.08**	-0.260	**-2.67**
Start-up working capital	log +1	0.371	**11.65**	0.441	**14.96**	0.501	**19.75**

		Model 1		Model 2		Model 3	
Membership in local majority group[a]							
Member of main gender group in district	yes = 1	−0.529	−1.33	−0.295	**−2.24**	−0.040	−0.38
Member of main ethnic group in district	yes = 1	0.175	0.87	−0.101	−0.72	−0.038	−0.25
Member of main religion in district	yes = 1	0.050	0.40	−0.106	−0.58	—	—
Intercept		7.714	**12.36**	4.492	**7.50**	0.221	0.18
Selection-term		0.981	—	1.010	—	1.089	—
Number of uncensored observations		592		730		828	
Joint test of ethnicity variables							
F		0.47		0.97		1.02	
p-value		0.8273		0.4458		0.4107	
Joint test of religion variables							
F		0.33		0.01		**4.17**	
p-value		0.7196		0.9249		0.0158	
Joint test of membership in majority group variables							
F		0.88		2.03		0.10	
p-value		0.4512		0.1085		0.9052	
Number of observations		592		730		828	
Pseudo R^2		0.218		0.222		0.254	

Notes

a District dummies (20–25) included but not shown.

t-values that are significant at the 10% level appear in boldface.

relatives. As before, local group effects are included to test for location specific favoritism.

Results show that the number of suppliers and clients known increases on average at 8–20% during the initial year, but rises more slowly in subsequent years. Working capital grows much faster, at 5% per year on average in Benin and Malawi, and 9% in Madagascar. Being a woman has a negative effect on the growth of working capital in all three countries; the effect is significant in two of them. The effect is also strongly negative and significant in Benin if either the district dummies or the local group dummies are omitted from the regression. Although we do not have information on why female traders accumulate capital more slowly, this finding is consistent with the often-made observation that African women use their personal income to pay for school fees and better child nutrition. Women also accumulate business contacts more slowly in Malawi and Madagascar, perhaps because their freedom to move from market to market is hindered by parenting responsibilities.

Ethnicity and religion dummies are occasionally significant, but usually with the wrong sign – ethnic groups that represent a smaller proportion of traders being shown to accumulate contacts and capital faster. The only exception is the Christian dummy in Benin, which is positive and significant for number of suppliers known. The same effect is not, however, observed for clients known, suggesting that the finding is not robust. Membership in locally dominant groups is never jointly significant. Individual dummies are occasionally significant, but always with the wrong (negative) sign.

There are some other results of interest. Education has a strong positive effect on the accumulation of working capital in all three countries, suggesting that better educated traders not only start with more capital but also accumulate faster. Traders who speak more languages tend to accumulate working capital faster in Benin and Madagascar.

12.6   Conclusions

In this chapter, we have examined the roles that gender, ethnicity, and religion play among agricultural traders. It is widely believed that these three factors play a paramount role in shaping African trade. African politicians and external observers commonly claim that trade is "in the hands" of a particular group and call for policy interventions to curb what they see as favoritism and discrimination.

We investigate these claims in detail using surveys conducted in three African countries (Benin in West Africa, Malawi in Southern Africa, and Madagascar in the Indian ocean). We begin with an examination of transactions practices, using the willingness to offer (very short-term) trade credit as a measure of trust. We also measure information sharing about breach of contract as the likelihood that other suppliers would learn about non-payment. The effects of ethnicity, gender, and religion are tested both at the national level and at the local level, that is, relative to other traders in the same district.

Contrary to expectations, we find no conclusive evidence that members of a particular sex or ethnic group are more easily trusted by suppliers or that they trust clients more easily. Non-Christians – particularly Muslims – appear to trust and be trusted more, but the effect is apparent only in the two countries where Christians are an overwhelming majority. In Benin, where Muslims represent 40% of the sample, no such effect is found. Perhaps it is being different from the rest (more devout?) that raises trust. This issue deserves more investigation.

We also investigate the effect of business networks, defined as the ties a trader has with other traders. Network effects are identified using the number of ties reported by survey respondents, properly instrumented to account for possible endogeneity. In contrast to gender and ethnicity, network effects are shown to have a strong and systematic effect on trust and information sharing – albeit occasionally with the wrong sign. These results are to be interpreted in the light of other work that has shown strong returns to network capital in African trade and business (e.g. Fafchamps and Minten 2001b, 2002; Barr 2003).

Finding network effects does not, however, fully eliminate the possibility of discrimination on the basis of ethnicity and the like. It is indeed conceivable that members of the dominant trading group start their business with better contacts and better access to equity finance. They may over time, also accumulate contacts and funds faster thanks to favoritism. To investigate this possibility, we examine whether ethnicity, gender, and religion affect start-up conditions and growth over time.

We find that women accumulate working capital much more slowly than men, but this appears to have little to do with their being marginalized: the effect is strong in two of the three countries, including in Madagascar where women represent 60% of surveyed traders. Women also start businesses with less capital. In contrast, better educated traders start with more capital and accumulate it faster. Ethnicity and religion appear to have little, if any, systematic effect on either start-up conditions or accumulation of network and working capital. Whenever a relationship is found, it is usually contrary to what would have occurred if belonging to the dominant trading group would lead to favoritism.

Taken together, these results suggest that ethnicity and religion only have limited effects on agricultural trade in the three countries studied. Whenever present, these effects tend to be country-specific so that it would be hazardous to extrapolate them to other countries. Gender matters more, but at least part of the gender effect reflect the different role women play in the household – particularly the tendency to initiate smaller, more transient businesses and to siphon funds off the business, possibly to finance investment in children.

The result presented here do not rule out the existence of strong ethnic, gender or religious bias in other African countries. But one should be cautious not to generalize these local situations to all of Africa. Our surveys suggest instead that, in the three countries studied, agricultural trade is open to all, irrespective of gender, ethnicity or religion. Networks matter, and better connected traders have larger and more prosperous businesses. But members of all groups start more or less from an equal footing to accumulate network and working capital. This ease of entry probably explains why scores of Africans, many of whom are women, flock into agricultural trade as an income-earning opportunity (Barrett 1997).

Acknowledgments

I thank The Pew Charitable Trusts for financial assistance with this research. Funding for data collection in Benin and Malawi was provided by the World Bank in collaboration with the International Food Policy Research Institute. Funding for data collection in Madagascar was provided by USAID and the Pew Foundation. I am particularly grateful to Chris Barrett and Gershon Feder for their assistance in funding the field work. Special thanks go to Bart Minten, Eleni Gabre-Madhin, Mylene Kherallah, Nick Minot, Soulé Bio Goura, and Richard Kachule for their help with data collection. I thank the participants for their excellent comments and suggestions to the Pew conference held in Rochester in May 2002.

Notes

1 Whether this is the result of women's choice or it is imposed upon them by society is irrelevant for our analysis.
2 One testable difference between the two models is that, in the case of statistical discrimination, members of the disadvantaged group also discriminate against members of their own group when deciding whether to grant trade credit. This is because members of their own group are more risky to screen. No such prediction arises from the network model: since members of the "out" group cannot afford to wait for a known agent to show up, they must screen everybody equally and thus do not discriminate against their own group. This prediction forms the basis of the econometric test performed by Fafchamps (2000) using data from African manufacturers.
3 The reader may have noted that, in our discussion of transition dynamics, ethnicity has a direct effect on survival in the discrimination model, but only works through profitability in the network model. It is therefore conceivable that the effect of network membership on firm growth is weak – and cannot be identified empirically.
4 Efforts to include agricultural inputs and cash crops into the survey were largely unsuccessful. In Benin, it became clear early on that fertilizer and seed trade are closely linked to the production of cotton. Cotton marketing is under the monopoly of a parastatal enterprise, the Societé Nationale de Promotion Agricole (SONAPRA). Input trading is done primarily through village cooperatives called Groupements Villageois (GV), rather than by individual traders. The GVs purchase inputs from 9 government-licensed fertilizer importers and distribute these inputs among their members. The marketing of cotton, the dominant export crop, goes entirely through SONAPRA.

   In the case of Malawi, the distribution of fertilizer and other agricultural inputs is dominated by few, very large firms, such as OPTICHEM and Norsk/Hydro. Inputs are distributed throughout the country by traders operating as selling agents for large corporations. A specific survey was organized for these selling agents, who do not conduct purchases, but who do sell independently. Results are not discussed here. A handful of independent tobacco traders are recorded in the Malawi survey.
5 Payment by check, another indicator of trust, represents only a minute proportion of all payments, thereby precluding any statistical analysis.
6 Because of possible endogeneity bias, working capital is instrumented using start-up working capital and the numbers of business contacts at start-up.

7 If local group effects are not included in the regression, the female dummy has the same sign and remains significant, but with a much smaller coefficient in absolute value.
8 A constant growth rate of the number of traders known was strongly rejected by the data: growth is faster initially.

References

Amselle, Jean-Loup (1977) *Les Négociants de la Savanne*. Paris: Editions Anthropos.
Barr, Abigail (2003) "Risk pooling, commitment, and information: an experimental test of two fundamental assumptions." CSAE WRS/2003–05, Oxford University, Oxford.
Barrett, Christopher B. (1977) "Food marketing liberalization and trader entry: evidence from Madagascar." *World Development*, 25(5): 763–77.
Bauer, P.T. (1954) *West African Trade: A Study of Competition, Oligopoly and Monopoly in a Changing Economy*. Cambridge: Cambridge University Press.
Braudel, Fernand (1986) *Civilization and Capitalism*. New York: Harper and Row.
Cohen, Abner (1969) *Custom and Politics in Urban Africa: A Study of Hausa Migrants in Yoruba Towns*. Berkeley, CA: University of California Press.
Ensminger, Jean (1992) *Making a Market: The Institutional Transformation of an African Society*. New York: Cambridge University Press.
Fafchamps, Marcel (1996) "The enforcement of commercial contracts in Ghana." *World Development*, 24(3): 427–48.
—— (2000) "Ethnicity and credit in African manufacturing." *Journal of Development Economics*, 61(1): 205–35.
—— (2002a) "The role of business networks in market development in Sub-Saharan Africa." In *Communities and Markets in Economic Development*, Masahiko Aoki and Yujiro Hayami (eds), Oxford: Oxford University Press.
—— (2002b) "Spontaneous market emergence." In *Topics in Theoretical Economics*, Vol. 2(1), Berkeley Electronic Press at www.bepress.com.
—— (2003) "Ethnicity and networks in African trade." In *Contributions to Economic Analysis and Policy*, Vol. 2(1), Berkeley Electronic Press at www.bepress.com, article 14.
—— (2004) *Market Institutions in Sub-Saharan Africa*, Cambridge, MA: MIT Press.
Fafchamps, Marcel and Minten, Bart. (1999) "Relationships and traders in Madagascar." *Journal of Development Studies*, 35(6): 1–35.
—— (2001a) "Property rights in a flea market economy." *Economic Development and Cultural Change*, 49(2): 229–68.
—— (2001b) "Social capital and agricultural trade." *American Journal of Agricultural Economics*, 83(3): 680–5.
—— (2002) "Returns to social network capital among traders." *Oxford Economic Papers*, 54: 173–206.
Geertz, Clifford (1963) *Peddlers and Princes: Social Change and Economic Modernization in Two Indonesian Towns*. Chicago, IL: University of Chicago Press.
Geertz, Clifford, Geertz, Hildred, and Rosen, Lawrence (1979) *Meaning and Order in Moroccan Society*. Cambridge: Cambridge University Press.
Greif, Avner (1993) "Contract enforceability and economic institutions in early trade: the Maghribi traders' coalition." *American Economic Review*, 83(3): 525–48.
—— (1994) "Cultural beliefs and the organization of society: a historical and theoretical reflection on collectivist and individualist societies." *Journal of Political Economy*, 102(5): 912–50.

Himbara, David (1994) "The failed Africanization of commerce and industry in Kenya." *World Development*, 22(3): 469–82.

Jones, William O. (1972) *Marketing Staple Food Crops in Tropical Africa*. Ithaca, NY: Cornell University Press.

Marris, Peter (1971) "African businessmen in a dual economy." *Journal of Industrial Economics*, 19: 231–45.

Meillassoux, Claude (1971) *The Development of Indigenous Trade and Markets in West Africa*. Oxford: Oxford University Press.

North, Douglas C. (1990) *Institutions, Institutional Change, and Economic Performance*. Cambridge: Cambridge University Press.

Spring, Anita and McDade, Barbara E. (1998) *African Entrepreneurship: Theory and Reality*. Gainesville, FL: University Press of Florida.

Staatz, John M. (1979) *The Economics of Cattle and Meat Marketing in the Ivory Coast*. Livestock Production and Marketing in the Entente States of West Africa, University of Michigan.

13 Altruism, household co-residence and women's health investment in rural Bangladesh

Andrew D. Foster

13.1 Introduction

In recent years there has been an increased analysis of the distribution of household resources, both within and across households, that are linked by family ties. This literature has addressed a variety of issues, such as the extent to which income shocks are redistributed across households, as might be expected in the presence of family-based altruism (Altonji *et al.* 1992, 1997), and whether the distribution of resources within households is importantly influenced by the bargaining position of individuals or groups within the household (McElroy 1990; Schultz 1990; Thomas 1990; Hayashi 1995). A common feature of this literature is that it has not generally accounted for the fact that co-residence by related sub-families is a choice that may both influence and be influenced by the resource allocation decisions. Of particular concern is the fact that the selection process associated with the decision to co-reside may bias statistical estimates, leading to inappropriate inference.

In this chapter, I posit a simple parametric model of family resource distribution and joint residence and use this model to examine the proposition that jointly resident family units care differently about the allocation of resources to each other than do otherwise equivalent family units living in separate households. In particular, I examine the extent to which differences in measures of parental human capital result in differences in the nutritional status of adult women in the household.

The focus on women's health is motivated by the longstanding concern about the vulnerability of women in rural Bangladesh given social constraints on activity and mobility, and the prominence of patrilocal residence (Cain 1985; Rahman *et al.* 1992). The latter feature is of particular interest because it implies that co-resident married women are, for the most part, biologically unrelated to other household members. Indeed, it has often been argued that daughters-in-law face particularly difficult circumstances when joining their husband's household if the husband remains co-resident with his parents or siblings. The relationship between a daughter-in-law and her husband's mother may also influence the degree of support provided to the latter, although this possibility has received considerably less attention in the literature. In any case, an analysis of the nutritional status of women and its relationship to living arrangements is likely to provide new insight into the position of women within the household, as well as to provide more general insights into behavioral differences between joint and non co-resident families.

Results indicate that unit-specific attributes have a limited influence on maternal outcomes net of household-specific effects in a joint household, while such effects are observed in recently divided households net of family-specific (across household) effects. While these results are consistent with the notion of greater altruism among co-resident units, it is also established that such a pattern might also arise from the selectivity associated with the household residence decision if the nutritional status of co-resident women from different family units are viewed as complementary. A simulation estimator that corrects for these selectivity effects is then developed. Identification comes from the characteristics of non-co-resident units in the case of the within household estimator and from the distribution of family unit characteristics within households for the across-household estimator. Application of this procedure indicates that the selection effect, while changing coefficient estimates substantially, is not entirely responsible for the observed differences between the within household and across household human capital investment equations. A second procedure is constructed that makes use of body size measures at two points in time separated by 16 years. The results conform closely to those obtained using the cross-sectional approach.

13.2   Theory

The theoretical model is designed to yield an analytical basis for the notion that selection associated with joint residence may importantly bias estimates of health investment equations, and to provide a foundation for the development of an econometric procedure that adjusts for potential selectivity. Necessary features of this model are that it should endogenize both the household residence decision and health investment in joint and non-joint household families, that it should produce relatively transparent predictions, and that it should account for the possibility that resources may be transferred across households as well as redistributed within households. The model is related in spirit to that developed in Foster and Rosenzweig (2002), extended to incorporate health as a household-specific public good and to allow for unobserved taste differentials across family units.

A central feature of the model relates to how decision making among distinct units and households is coordinated (i.e., who operates as the residual claimant, how reservation utilities are determined, and how any surplus is distributed). In particular, it is assumed that (1) the choice of the allocation of units to households, consumption, and human capital allocations for each unit, and a level of the public good for each household is efficient, and (2) the utility function exhibits transferable utility (see Bergstrom 1997). The first assumption seems a reasonable characterization of family behavior in that a group of related family units that live in close proximity to one another should have ample time to uncover and exploit existing opportunities to make one unit better off without decreasing the welfare of any other unit. The second assumption provides a substantial payoff in terms of analytical convenience but also imposes substantial structure on the model. The payoff is that given transferable utility, all distributional considerations both within and across households can be satisfied through the direct transfer of consumption, c_i, and thus distributional concerns do not affect the efficient choices of household residence patterns, human capital investment, or the level of the public good. The cost is that the implication that human capital investment is not affected by distributional concerns may not be, in fact, reasonable.

A general characterization of the model is as follows. Consider a family that consists of I distinct family units partitioned into K households. It is assumed that the head of each unit i has preferences defined over private-consumption c_i, the level of health in the units family h_i, the average health within the household, $\bar{h}_{k_i}$, where k_i denotes the household of unit i, and a household-specific public good, z_{k_i}:

$$u(c_i, h_i, \bar{h}_{k_i}, z_{k_i}; v_i), \tag{1}$$

where v_i is a unit-specific parameter reflecting intrinsic demand or taste for health for that unit.[1,2] Intra-family transfers across households are freely permitted so that the relevant budget constraint equates income and expenses at the level of the family:

$$\sum_{i=1}^{I} c_i + p_h h_i + \sum_{k=1}^{K} z_k = \sum_{i=1}^{I} y_i. \tag{2}$$

Under these assumptions the family's optimization problem involves the choice of the household allocations k_i, health investment h_i, and consumption levels c_i for each unit i, and of the level of public good z_k in each household k to maximize

$$W = \sum_{i=1}^{I} u(c_i, h_i, \bar{h}_{k_i}, z_{k_i}; v_i) \tag{3}$$

subject to equation (2). The health investment equation for family unit i that arises from this optimization problem then has as arguments total family income, prices, and the intrinsic demands of all units.

In order to use this model for econometric analysis, it is helpful at this point to impose functional forms. In particular, assume that the utility function is quadratic in its arguments with three exceptions. First, consistent with the assumption of transferable utility there are only linear terms in c. Because transferable utility would in general permit the marginal utility of consumption to be a function of public goods, one could in principle permit interactions with household-level health for the purpose of examining behavior in joint households. However, this would lead to violations of transferable utility when considering the behavior of families living in separate households, which would have different average levels of health. Second, assume that the intrinsic demand enters into the utility function in such a way that it appears as a linear term in the marginal utility of own-family health. This assumption makes the parameter readily interpretable as a measure of the taste for own health. Third, assume that utility is strongly separable in z. This requirement also imposes significant structure, but decreases the complexity of the problem yielding more transparent theory and simplified econometric analysis.[3] Given these assumptions the utility function is:

$$u(c, h, \bar{h}, z; v) = a_0 c + (a_1 + v)h + a_2 \bar{h} + a_3 z - \frac{1}{2} h^2$$
$$- \frac{a_5}{2} \bar{h}^2 - \frac{a_6}{2} z^2 + \frac{a_7 + a_5}{2} h\bar{h}, \tag{4}$$

where I have specified the parameters and incorporated an arbitrary normalization in such a way as to obtain relatively clean analytical expressions for the human capital investment in the following equations.

Given this functional form, it is relatively simple to show that the relative magnitude of the relationship between intrinsic demands and health investment that arises when differencing across or within households is critically related to the extent to which units care about the average health in their respective households. Consider first the case of a two-unit family. In this case health investment for unit i is, in the case of separate residence,

$$h_i = \frac{1}{1 - a_7}(a_1 + a_2 - a_0 p_h + v_i) \tag{5}$$

and, in the case of joint residence,

$$h_i = \frac{1}{1 - a_7}(a_1 + a_2 - a_0 p_h) + v_i + \frac{a_7}{1 - a_7}\bar{v}, \tag{6}$$

where $\bar{v}$ is the average intrinsic demand for the two families. Note that the average intrinsic demand only appears when units are jointly resident, reflecting the fact that one unit only cares about the health of the other when they co-reside.[4] Differencing these two equations across and within households, respectively, yields

$$h_2 - h_1 = \frac{v_2 - v_1}{1 - a_7}, \tag{7}$$

and

$$h_2 - h_1 = v_2 - v_1. \tag{8}$$

respectively. Because $a_7/4$ may be shown to be cross partial of the utility function with respect to h_1 and h_2, $a_7 > 0$ implies that own h and the h of the other unit are complementary (assuming $a_7 < 1$, which is required to ensure a local maximum). If this condition is met then a given within-family difference in intrinsic demand maps into a larger difference in health in the absence of co-residence than given co-residence. Conversely, $a_7 < 0$ implies that own and cross-partials of h are substitutes and thus differences in health are larger under joint residence.

The equation dictating whether joint or separate residence is preferred is also relatively straightforward and indicates that the effects of variation in intrinsic demand for health on joint residence depends again on whether own and cross-partials of health within the household are substitutable or complementary. Let $W(\mathbf{k})$ denote residence-pattern conditional total welfare (i.e., the maximum of equation (3) over resource allocations for given residence) where $\mathbf{k}$ is the vector of household indicators so that $\mathbf{k} = [1, 2]$ denotes separate residence and $\mathbf{k} = [1, 1]$ denotes co-residence. Then,

$$W([1,2]) - W([1,1]) = \frac{1}{4}\frac{a_7}{1-a_7}(v_1 - v_2)^2 - \frac{a_3 a_0 p_z}{a_6} + \frac{3}{4}\frac{a_0^2 p_h^2}{a_6}. \tag{9}$$

Note that if $a_7 > 0$ (complements) the first term is negative. Thus, if own and cross health are complementary then household division is more likely the higher the difference in intrinsic demands while the opposite result holds if they are substitutes.

Extending the model to three units is important because, as will be argued later, identification of the model cannot easily be achieved in two-unit households. Fortunately, although this somewhat complicates the analysis because of the increased number of potential residence patterns that must be considered, it does not alter fundamentally the nature of the problem. Indeed, although the level human capital equations become more complicated the predictions regarding within household differences (equation (7)) are identical and the equations regarding across-household differences (equation (8)) are identical if household averages are computed. For example, if units 1 and 2 are allocated to the same household and unit 3 is in a separate household then

$$h_2 - h_1 = v_2 - v_1, \tag{10}$$

and

$$h_3 - \frac{h_2 + h_1}{2} = \frac{1}{1-a_7}\left(v_3 - \frac{v_2 + v_1}{2}\right). \tag{11}$$

The welfare comparisons across residence patterns given a three-unit family are also readily interpretable. Consider first different ways of dividing up the three units into two households. Comparison of the case in which 1 lives with 3 with that in which 1 lives with 2 yields

$$W([1,2,1]) - W([1,1,2]) = \frac{1}{2}\frac{a_7}{1-a_7}(v_3 - v_2)\left(\frac{v_2 + v_3}{2} - v_1\right)$$

$$= \frac{1}{4}\frac{a_7}{1-a_7}\left[(v_1 - v_2)^2 - (v_1 - v_3)^2\right]. \tag{12}$$

The latter form of the expression, for $a_7 > 0$, implies that co-residence of 1 and 3 is preferred to co-residence of 1 and 2 if and only if the intrinsic demands of 1 and 3 are more similar than are the intrinsic demands of 1 and 2. Comparison of the case of separate residence of all three units with that in which 1 lives with 2 yields the RHS of equation (9):

$$W([1,2,3]) - W([1,1,2]) = \frac{1}{4}\frac{a_7}{1-a_7}(v_1 - v_2)^2 - \frac{a_3 a_0 p_z}{a_6} + \frac{3}{4}\frac{a_0^2 p_z^2}{a_6}. \tag{13}$$

Finally, comparison of the case of joint residence of the whole family and co-residence of 1 and 2 yields

$$W([1,1,1]) - W([1,1,2]) = -\frac{1}{6}\frac{a_7}{1-a_7}\left(v_3 - \frac{v_1 + v_2}{2}\right)^2$$

$$+ \frac{a_3 a_0 p_z}{a_6} - \frac{7}{12}\frac{a_0^2 p_z^2}{a_6}. \tag{14}$$

Thus joint residence is preferred to this particular two-household alternative for complementary health if the intrinsic demands in the third unit do not differ substantially from the average intrinsic demand in the first and second units.

In order to use this model to better understand the likely sorts of bias that arise when household residence is endogenous with respect to health outcomes it is necessary to posit a relationship between the v, which have heretofore been considered exogenous measures of intrinsic demand for health, and observable data. In particular, I assume that these intrinsic demands can be written as a linear function of a vector of observed characteristics, x_i, for each individual in the household, a fixed family-specific specific effect, η, that may be correlated with the x_i, and an orthogonal individual-level error term:

$$v_i = x_i \beta + \eta + \epsilon_i. \tag{15}$$

A key aspect of this model is that v_i cannot depend on household residence patterns or consequences of household residence patterns such as total household assets.[5] Note also that the effects of family-specific observables, as well as the family-specific unobservable η, cannot be identified from equations characterizing residence choice and differenced human capital investment given the assumptions of the model.

13.3   Empirical implementation

Substitution of equation (15) into the equations for differenced health investment and differences in residence-conditional family welfare provides an illustration of the bias introduced by the endogeneity of joint residence. In particular, equations (10) and (11) become

$$\Delta h_i = \Delta x_i \beta + \Delta \epsilon_i, \tag{16}$$

and

$$\Delta \bar{h}_k = \frac{1}{1 - a_7} (\Delta \bar{x}_k \beta + \Delta \bar{\epsilon}_k), \tag{17}$$

with Δ in equations (16) and (17) differencing within and across households in the same family, respectively. The bias arises from the fact that the conditional independence of ϵ given x in equation (15) is not retained when one examines data in which residence is chosen optimally. In particular, the implications of the model depend on the structure of preferences. Assume, for the moment that own, and cross-health are complementary. Then the model implies that units are most likely to co-reside when they have similar intrinsic demands for schooling. Thus, e.g., if two units have a large positive observable intrinsic demand difference, $\Delta x_i \beta$, and they nonetheless choose to co-reside, then one may infer that they have a compensating difference in the unobservable component of intrinsic demands, $\Delta \epsilon$, yielding $\sigma(\Delta x_i \beta, \Delta \epsilon_i) < 0$. Conversely, if two units have a large positive observable intrinsic demand difference, $\Delta x_i \beta$, and they live separately, then one may infer that they do not have a compensating difference in the unobservable component of intrinsic demand, $\Delta \epsilon$, yielding $\sigma(\Delta \bar{x}_i \beta, \Delta \bar{\epsilon}_i) > 0$. Thus, β estimates will tend to be biased toward zero for within household estimation and $\beta/(1 - a_7)$ estimates biased away from zero for across household estimation. Opposite effects will be observed if $a_7 < 0$: units with large differences in $\Delta x_i \beta$ who live separately will not have compensating differences in the unobserved component of intrinsic demand.

Given that the source of bias is joint residence and joint residence is determined, given the model, based on both the observable and unobservable components of v, instruments are unlikely to be available to construct a consistent instrument-variable estimator. Anything that is correlated with differences in the x variables will also tend to be correlated with the ϵ. A more promising approach is to treat this problem as one of selectivity bias, that is one in which the set of households that are in fact observed are a non-random sample of all potential households. Again, however, standard procedures do not easily apply because the nature of the relationship between unobservables determining the selection process and those determining the human capital process is not a simple linear one.

An alternative approach is the two-stage simulation approach of Foster (1997), which addresses selection bias arising from the process of matching in the marriage market. The procedure has two stages. During the first stage, a simulated method of moments procedure applied to individual-level longitudinal data on residence patterns is used to estimate the β and other parameters up to an arbitrary scalar.[6] In particular, let $I_j([1,2])$ denote the event that household j chooses separate residence. Then equation (9) implies that

$$E\left[I_j([1,2]) - \text{Prob}\left(\frac{a_7}{1+a_7}(\Delta x\beta + \Delta\epsilon)^2 + \tau_{12} > 0\right)\middle| x_2, x_1\right] = 0,$$
(18)

where τ_{12} is a household-size specific based on the second term in equation (9).[7] While in the case of family sizes of two this expression has a straightforward analytic solution for certain distributional assumptions such as the normal, the same cannot be said for larger families. I therefore adopt a simulation procedure in which the ϵ_i are drawn from a particular distribution (the standard normal) and then the value of the expression inside the Prob() function of equation (18) may be computed for given β and τ_{12}. Across many simulations this approach yields consistent estimates of the second term in equation (18). In practice, however, it has been established (Pakes and Pollard 1989) that consistency may be obtained for this type of problem with respect to the number of families, with the number of simulations per family held fixed. I therefore carry out the analysis with just two draws on the ϵ per family. I also adopt the standard procedure of using extreme value errors appropriately scaled to smooth the objective function to aid computation. Thus, the actual moment condition for a two-unit family is

$$E\left[I_j([1,2]) - \frac{1}{1 + \exp(-(a_7/(1+a_7)(\Delta x\beta + \Delta\epsilon)^2 + \tau_{12})/\delta)}\middle| x_2, x_1\right] = 0,$$
(19)

for small δ. For three-unit families there are five distinct household allocations, as noted, so four distinct moment conditions must be constructed.[8] For example, the moment condition for the probability that units 1 and 2 co-reside and 3 is in a separate household may be written using the expressions in equations (12)–(14) as

$$E(I_j([1,1,2]) - 1 \div [1 + \exp\{[W([1,1,1]) - W([1,1,2])]/\delta\}$$
$$+ \exp\{[W([1,2,3]) - W([1,1,2])]/\delta\} + \exp\{[W([1,2,1])$$
$$- W([1,1,2])]/\delta\} + \exp\{[W([1,2,2]) - W([1,1,2])]/\delta\} = 0.$$
(20)

The simulation of household residuals may also be used to construct consistent estimates of the human capital investment equations, given estimates of β obtained from the household residence equations. The approach rests on the recognition that equations (16) and (17) could be estimated consistently if the ϵ were actually observed. Let W denote a matrix consisting of the Δx_i and $\Delta \epsilon_i$, and let H denote the vector of Δh_i. Then consistent estimate of the column vector $B = [\beta 1]^T$, may be obtained using least squares

$$\hat{B} = W'W^{-1}W'h. \tag{21}$$

Alternatively, if there existed a vector Z of variables that predict $\Delta \epsilon_i$ given Δx_i a less efficient instrumental variables procedure may be used

$$\hat{B}^{IV} = (W'Z(Z'Z)^{-1}Z'W)^{-1}(W'Z(Z'Z)^{-1}Z'H). \tag{22}$$

Given the unobservability of the ϵ_i, $W'Z(Z'Z)^{-1}$ cannot of course be computed directly. A consistent estimate may be obtained, however, by computing this expression with a data set on household residence using the actual x_i but then simulating the ϵ_i, and then using the previous expressions inclusive of the estimates of the β and τ coefficients obtained from the first-stage of estimation.

Appropriate instruments for the within-household estimator are derived from the predicted values of $x_i \beta$ of the excluded unit or units. The intuition is straightforward. As noted, the model predicts that three-unit households will be sorted so that those with the most similar values of v_i will reside jointly. Suppose $x_1\beta > x_2\beta > x_3\beta$ and that units 1 and 2 co-reside. Then the closer $x_3\beta$ gets to $x_2\beta$, the more negative would have to be $\epsilon_1 - \epsilon_2$ in order for this choice to be optimal. Moreover, $x_3\beta$ is excluded from the differenced regression in equation (16). Thus levels of $x_3\beta$ and second and higher-order interactions of $x_3\beta$ with $x_1\beta$ and $x_2\beta$ can serve as instruments for the estimation of equation (16).[9] An analogous argument applies to the across estimator, equation (17), but in this case the appropriate instruments involve the variance of within-household observable indices. In particular, if $x_1\beta > x_2\beta > x_3\beta$, units 1 and 2 co-reside in household 1, and unit 3 is in household 2 then the smaller is $\bar{x}_1\beta - \bar{x}_2\beta$ the larger must be $\bar{\epsilon}_1 - \bar{\epsilon}_2$ in order that residence in two households is preferred to residence in one household.

13.4 Cross-sectional results

13.4.1 *Data*

The primary data for this analysis comes from the 1996 Matlab Health and Socioeconomic Survey (MHSS), which was designed by the author and three collaborators (Rahman *et al.* 1999). These data contain detailed information on household composition, assets and other household resources, and individual-level measures of adult and child human capital inclusive of schooling, body size, physical performance, and cognitive skills on 4539 households in the Matlab study area of the International Centre for Diarrhoeal Disease Research in Bangladesh

(ICDDRB). The data have been linked using individual registration numbers to the vital and census records for the Matlab study area, providing a longitudinal record on household formation and dissolution from the mid 1960s until the time of the MHSS. The data are well suited to the issues addressed in this chapter in that the longitudinal vital records permit tracking of family units over time, as required for the estimation of the household residence model, and the MHSS sample is designed to include non-co-resident family units, as required to consistently estimate the specified across- and within-household differenced health investment equations.

In order to ensure that any differences in the nutritional status of co-resident and non-co-resident individuals do not arise from differences in residence (and thus, e.g., differences in the prices faced), the analysis focuses on non-co-resident family units living in close proximity. Specifically, the data employed include information on multiple households within the same compound or "bari." This social unit, which is a prominent feature of life in that country, may be characterized as ". . . a cluster of households usually around a common yard accommodating households whose heads are related by blood or affinal connections" (Caldwell *et al.* 1982, p. 36). Most young men in rural areas that no longer co-reside with parents or siblings can be found in the same bari as these other members of their family (Foster 1993).

The bari in Bangladesh has been argued to play an important role as a source of support. Makhlisur Rahman (1986), e.g., notes that there is "a marked reluctance on the part of wealthy individuals . . . to permit (fellow) bari members to sink below a certain minimum level." It is not clear, however, how the extent of resource-sharing among households and, in particular, the relative well-being of married women in different households within the bari, compares with that that might be expected by co-resident family units. As might be anticipated if there are important differences in the degree of mutual support provided among those in the same bari and those in the same household, the process of household partition, in which two family units become separate households, is a prominent event in South Asia. As Caldwell *et al.* (1986, p. 218) reports, household partition is ". . . one of the central facts of social life, observed and discussed by all. There is little in the way of an intermediate or blurred situation: when partition occurs, division, somewhat ceremoniously and usually without rancour, is affected in eating arrangements, the family budget, land (if any), and residential arrangements." Indeed, the limits to within-bari support are also evident in Rahman's characterization of the bari as one in which a "minimum-level of support" is provided. The only empirical evidence on this question, of which I am aware, is that presented in Foster (1993), which reports evidence consistent with the notion that the bari provides less complete pooling of resources than does the household, but this evidence is subject to precisely the kind of selection bias discussed above.

Data preparation for this analysis involved two stages. The first stage was to select from the MHSS information on ever-married women, that is women who are currently married, divorced or widowed. The number and sex composition of co-resident children and the education and age of a husband, if present, were then linked to the women's records. The second stage was to determine the group of women that could reasonably be linked as family units that could have been co-resident. This grouping was done with close attention to the notion of the bari and the fact of patrilocal residence. In particular, all women living in a given bari in 1996 at the time of the MHSS who were ever married and co-resident with each other in 1982 were grouped together. In addition, women who had married since 1982 were grouped with other women from the same bari if their spouse was co-resident with other members of the group or their spouses in 1982. Groups with more than three women made up only 12% of all baris. These large groups were excluded for reasons of tractability and because typically only two households participated in the MHSS from any one bari. These procedures resulted in the selection of 1850 groups, 33% of which were one-unit families, 46% of which were two-unit families, and 21% of which were three-unit families. Among the three-unit families a majority co-resided in one household, but there was substantial representation of other configurations as well.

13.4.2   Results

The model described in the previous section is sufficiently general to capture two quite different sets of circumstances, based on the extent to which the health of members of other family units are viewed as substitutable or complementary to own health. In the case that health is substitutable, households tend to be formed of people who are different from each other in terms of their underlying intrinsic demand for health, while if health is complementary across family units then households tend to be formed of units with similar intrinsic demands for health. Because these indices are posited to be linear functions of observable attributes, one might expect to be able to distinguish these cases by examining within- and across-household variation in observables, recognizing that this is a somewhat imperfect test because of the presence of unobservable correlations among variables, and differences in the extent to which different variables affect intrinsic demands.

Measures of the standard deviations within and across households for the key variables of interest are presented in the first two columns of Table 13.1. For the most part these estimates suggest that the within variance is higher than the across variance. The largest difference is observed for women's education where the within-household standard deviation is 28% higher than the across standard deviation. There are three cases where the relative magnitudes are reversed: age, husband's education and the number of sons, although in no case is the across standard deviation more than 5% higher than the within.

The results from the structural household division estimation are presented in Table 13.2. Because of the inability to identify the magnitude of the parameter a_7 directly, it is helpful to assign a priori a sign for a_7, which captures the degree of complementarity or substitutability, before carrying out the estimation, thus yielding two sets of results. While the moment conditions are satisfied for both sets of criteria, the model with complementarity is a better fit to the data because it

Table 13.1 Standard deviations for actual and simulated data by assumed substitutability of own and co-resident's health

| | Actual residence | | Simulated residence | | | |
| | Within | Across | Substitutable | | Complementary | |
			Within	Across	Within	Across
Education	2.118	1.649	1.817	1.764	1.947	1.708
Age $(\times 10^{-2})$	0.064	0.070	0.085	0.080	0.092	0.082
Age^2 $(\times 10^{-4})$	0.079	0.066	0.088	0.078	0.090	0.083
Sons at home	0.715	0.740	0.770	0.691	0.737	0.731
Daughters at home	0.736	0.689	0.700	0.674	0.683	0.689
Husband's education	1.821	1.824	1.776	1.848	1.870	1.802
Husband was son in 1982	0.351	0.299	0.329	0.316	0.323	0.318
Currently married	0.349	0.266	0.327	0.298	0.325	0.308
Husband absent	0.338	0.291	0.334	0.316	0.344	0.314
Husband's age $(\times 10^{-2})$	0.092	0.072	0.079	0.076	0.080	0.076
Husband's age$^2 (\times 10^{-4})$	0.096	0.078	0.085	0.081	0.086	0.081
Index	—	—	0.296	0.247	0.270	0.277

yields a lower mean-squared error.[10] Moreover, by using the relevant coefficient estimates to simulate household division, it becomes clear that the use of the criteria of comparing standard deviations of individual attributes in Table 13.1 can be quite misleading. Columns 3–6 of Table 13.1, which present within and across standard deviations based on the simulated residence given the two sets of coefficient estimates in Table 13.2, show that both conditions generally yield higher within than across standard deviations for specific household attributes. While this may seem counterintuitive, it should be noted that both approaches attempt to fit the available data which exhibit this pattern, and that when the index $x_i \beta$ is computed based on the respective set of coefficients, the expected pattern is observed. The within standard deviation of this index is less than the across standard deviation given the complementary assumption, while the opposite result holds under the substitutability assumption. Given these results, subsequent discussion will focus on the complementarity results, unless otherwise stated.

The coefficient estimates of the household division model in Table 13.2, as noted, reflect the effects of the covariates on intrinsic demand for health investment, which in combination with the intrinsic demands of other family units determine household residence choices. Unfortunately, the direction of the effects cannot be inferred from these coefficients given the structure of the model. Instead, significant coefficients indicate, for the model with complementarity, that this variable is one for which variability predicts a lower likelihood of joint residence. Thus, e.g., the coefficient on husband's education indicates that households are unlikely to co-reside if household members have substantially different levels of schooling. Similarly, there is evidence that households with different numbers of sons and daughters do not tend to co-reside. Both the husband's age and wife's age exhibit

Table 13.2 Estimates of household division model by substitutability
of own and co-resident's health

	Substitutable	Complementary
Education	−0.083	−0.095
	(20.57)	(18.89)[a]
Age $(\times 10^{-2})$	0.661	−4.059
	(0.80)	(4.30)
Age^2 $(\times 10^{-4})$	−1.660	4.174
	(2.12)	(5.17)
Sons at home	−0.137	−0.120
	(9.87)	(6.32)
Daughters at home	−0.197	−0.186
	(14.12)	(7.95)
Husband's education	−0.121	0.041
	(17.34)	(4.81)
Husband was son in 1982	−0.165	−0.299
	(3.88)	(8.29)
Currently married	−0.181	−0.424
	(5.78)	(5.69)
Husband absent	−0.426	−0.092
	(7.77)	(1.28)
Husband's age $(\times 10^{-2})$	−0.995	−1.353
	(1.99)	(3.15)
Husband's age^2 $(\times 10^{-4})$	0.630	1.565
	(1.19)	(4.16)
κ_{111}	−1	−1
κ_{123}	−0.516	−1.530
	(16.85)	(39.18)
Criterion function[b]	0.182	0.148

Notes
a Absolute t-ratios based on heteroskedasticity-consistent standard errors in
  parentheses.
b MSE computed as the product of two errors from independent simulations.

strong quadratic effects, although over the relevant range the effects of husband's
and wife's age exhibit opposite signs.

The effects of the coefficients are moderate in size. Assume that there is a single
year of schooling differential between two ever married women in a given family.
Then a unit additional increase in schooling for the more schooled individual
decreases the probability of joint residence by 4.1 points. If one woman has one
more son than the other, then an additional son for the first woman results in a
4.7 point decrease in joint residence. One of the larger effects is associated with
whether a husband is present. If there is a one unit difference in the predicted index
for two women with the same marital status, then the change in whether a husband
is present (e.g., through the migration of a spouse) results in a 17 point decline in
the probability of joint residence.

Table 13.3 presents the estimates of the health investment equations. The
dependent variable is maternal body mass index (BMI), and the RHS variables

Table 13.3 Effects of family unit characteristics on maternal BMI equations by residence status with and without correction for the selectivity of the joint residence decision cross-sectional estimates

	Within households		Across households in same bari	
	Uncorrected	Corrected	Uncorrected	Corrected
Education	0.022	−0.216	0.075	0.026
	(0.41)[a]	(0.62)	(1.78)	(0.56)
Age ($\times 10^{-2}$)	3.61	3.915	0.021	5.573
	(0.71)	(0.77)	(0.00)	(0.88)
Age^2 ($\times 10^{-4}$)	−7.742	−10.986	−3.442	−7.056
	(1.58)	(1.61)	(0.56)	(1.12)
Sons at home	−0.053	−0.427	−0.063	0.13
	(0.42)	(0.76)	(0.77)	(1.16)
Daughters at home	−0.37	−0.858	0.012	0.218
	(2.69)	(1.19)	(0.14)	(1.83)
Husband's education	0.022	−0.296	0.023	0.195
	(0.48)	(0.64)	(0.69)	(2.55)
Husband was son in 1982	−0.033	−0.252	−0.456	−0.255
	(0.08)	(0.44)	(2.52)	(1.81)
Currently married	0.277	−0.365	0.899	2.066
	(0.45)	(0.33)	(1.81)	(3.03)
Husband absent	−0.464	−1.789	0.087	1.378
	(0.91)	(0.9)	(0.23)	(2.14)
Husband's age ($\times 10^{-2}$)	12.649	13.42	12.092	11.697
	(1.91)	(1.99)	(1.92)	(1.86)
Husband's age^2 ($\times 10^{-4}$)	−14.51	−15.637	−12.654	−14.733
	(2.32)	(2.41)	(2.2)	(2.54)
Selection term	—	2.968	—	2.421
		(0.69)		(2.49)

Note
a Absolute *t*-value in parentheses.

are the same attributes as used in the family residence decision. Note that although the model incorporates the assumption that these coefficients should be proportional to those obtained from the structural analysis, this restriction need not hold if BMI imperfectly measures health investment in the sense that the X variables influence BMI net of health investment as determined in the model. This might be the case, e.g., because BMI does not adjust for age although there may be important effects of aging on body size that are not themselves directly related to the provision of resources to the person in question. Under such circumstances, the coefficient on age in the health investment equation relative to that, say, for education, would be different than the same ratio taken from the residence-equation estimates.

The first and third columns contain estimates of the differenced health investment equations where differencing is carried out within and across households, respectively. While the precision of the estimates is not great, the overall impression that emerges is that the coefficients for the across estimator are somewhat larger and more likely to be significantly different from zero than are the within estimates. As noted, this might be evidence in favor of complementarity. It also could arise either because there are real differences in the effects of family-unit attributes on health within and across households, as posited by the model, or because of selectivity bias.

Selectivity correction for the within household estimator does not substantially change the results, a result that may in part be explained by the relative weakness of the excluded instruments in predicting the errors given family residence (p-value $= 0.31$). On the other hand, the selectivity corrected estimates for the across estimates, for which the excluded instruments in the first stage were significant at the 7% level, differ substantively from those obtained without this correction. In particular, the coefficients on key husband's attributes, including whether the woman is currently married, whether her husband is absent (likely reflecting earnings of a husband with employment in the city), and husband's schooling, increase significantly. The husband's schooling estimates, e.g., suggest that a 10% in husband's education at the mean level of 3 years results in a 0.3% increase in maternal body size given mean BMI of 18.8. Being currently married instead of being widowed or divorced results in an 11% increase in body size, a substantially larger figure than would have been obtained using the uncorrected estimates. Finally, daughters-in-law (i.e., those whose husband was a son of the head in 1982) appear to be disadvantaged in terms of intrinsic demand for health. The coefficient is negative for both the split and intact households once selection is accounted for, and it is significant for the split households. The sign of the bias is also as expected. The bias is away from zero for the split households and toward zero in the intact households.

13.5 Longitudinal data and results

An alternative approach to addressing the consequences of household division is to consider changes over time. By observing the same individual at multiple points in time, fixed attributes of the individual that are correlated with the possibility of joint residence are thus controlled and that the problem of endogenous household residence is thus substantially diminished. It is clear in the context of the earlier theoretical framework that this argument may fail for two reasons. The model clearly indicates that both individual outcomes and household residence depend not only on the characteristics of the individual but also in the distribution of characteristics in the family.

To address the possibility of change over time in intrinsic demand for household public goods one may add a time sub-script to the β in equation (15):

$$v_{it} = x_i \beta_t + \mu + \epsilon_{it}. \tag{23}$$

The change in health for the member of an intact two-unit family is thus,

$$\Delta_t h_{it} = -\frac{a_0}{1 - a_7} \Delta_t p_{ht} + \left(x_i + \frac{a_7}{1 - a_7} \bar{x} \right) \Delta_t \beta_t + \Delta \epsilon_{it} + \frac{a_7}{1 - a_7} \Delta_t \bar{\epsilon}_t, \tag{24}$$

while the change in health for the member of a two-unit family that divides is

$$
\Delta_t h_{it} = -\frac{a_0}{1-a_7}\Delta_t p_{ht} + \frac{a_7}{1-a_7}\beta_t x_i + \frac{a_7}{1-a_7}(x_i - \bar{x})\Delta\beta_t
$$

$$
+ \frac{a_7}{1-a_7}(\epsilon_{it} - \bar{\epsilon}_t) + \frac{1}{1-a_7}\Delta_t\epsilon_{it}. \tag{25}
$$

Notice that in the absence of changes in the ϵ_{it} over time there is no bias from estimating equation (24) using least squares. Moreover, even with such change it is not a priori clear what the sign of the bias will be given these changes. If intrinsic demands for unit i increase, then this may increase or decrease probabilities of joint residence depending on i's initial intrinsic demand relative to that of the other members of the household.

In contrast, for split households, bias arises even in the absence of changes in the shock. The reason is that household composition changes over time and thus the unobservables at two points in time enter in a different way as a result of the fact that the allocation across family units will be different under co-residence. In this case, if both the difference in the x_i between i and the household average and the corresponding difference in the ϵ_i are both positive for positive β, then a household split is likely and there is thus a positive correlation induced between the observable and unobservable components of the difference between own and average effects in equation (25). To address this problem one may again make use of simulated errors – intuitively, if there is a great deal of variation in the unobservables across family units at time t, and the household nonetheless stays together, then it is likely that the residual differences compensate for the differences in the observables.

To implement the analysis I use the Determinants of Natural Fertility Survey (DNFS) sub-sample of the MHSS. The DNFS was a survey of 2441 women aged 11–50 in January 1975 from 14 of the Matlab Study villages. These women were included in the MHSS framework and thus permit the analysis of body size change over a period of 21 years, a sufficiently lengthy period for a substantial degree of household division to have taken place. Of the original 2441 women, there are 1213 who lived in multiple-unit households in 1975 and were reinterviewed as part of the MHSS in 1996.

For the purpose of this analysis, household family units were constructed based on the DNFS. Then women from the co-resident family units were followed through 1990 using the MHSS records where possible and the Matlab Demographic and Surveillance System records otherwise. Body size data at two points in time were only available for primary respondents in the DNFS who were also interviewed in the MHSS. For other women co-resident with these respondents in 1975 one could construct measures of demographic chracteristics but not outcomes. Thus, one can estimate the impact of household co-residence by differencing either across time or across individuals at a point in time as above, but not both.

Results appear in Table 13.4, in which a pared down specification is used. Other variables presented in Table 13.3 were not significant and thus are excluded so that

Table 13.4 Effects of family unit characteristics on maternal BMI by residence status
with and without correction for the selectivity of the joint residence decision
longitudinal estimates

	Intact households		Split households	
	Uncorrected	*Corrected*	*Uncorrected*	*Corrected*
Individual x				
Husband was son in 1982	0.134	0.065	−0.028	−0.062
	(1.79)[a]	(0.69)	(1.54)	(2.56)
Education	0.005	0.004	0.007	0.0071
	(2.22)	(1.84)	(2.91)	(2.82)
Individual minus household average				
Husband was son in 1982	0.011	0.056	−0.0003	0.022
	(0.36)	(1.13)	(0.01)	(0.76)
Education	0.0005	0.001	−0.0002	−0.000
		(0.86)	(0.34)	(0.33)
Selection term		0.323		−0.215
		(1.13)		(2.15)

Note
a Absolute *t*-value in parentheses.

the principle results might be highlighted. This is not surprising given that one is
differencing over time for the same individual. Particularly in the case of an intact
household, it is only possible to identify changes in coefficients over time.

Of particular interest are the coefficients in the fourth column, which correspond
to split households. Comparison to equation (25) indicates that the coefficients on
the individual variables in this specification indicate changes in the effects of the
coefficients over time. Thus the coefficient on whether one's spouse was the son
of the head in 1982 is negative and significant, indicating that intrinsic demand for
health of daughters-in-law in the family (whether co-resident or not) declined over
this period. Given that the coefficient on the difference in this variable between the
individual and family average is not different from zero, this result suggests that in
fact daughters-in-law are allocated fewer resources than other women. This indeed
seems consistent with the results from Table 13.3, in which the corresponding
cross-sectional coefficient is negative. This result corresponding with the finding
that body size is complementary within households suggests that the process of
household division lowers body size for these women relative to others, particularly
the spouse and mother of the original head. By contrast, educated women tend to
have higher intrinsic demands for health, with this difference rising over time.
Thus, given redistributive effects of joint residence, educated women are better
off when separately resident as one might expect.

Interestingly the magnitude of the coefficient on daughters-in-law (the individual coefficient for women whose husband was the son of the head in 1982) becomes
more negative once household division selection is controlled for. Evidently,
daughters-in-law who split off from the original households are less disadvantaged

than those in the intact households so the daughter-in-law effect is biased toward zero. This direction of the effect is as expected if bias from the levels of the residuals dominates that from the change over time. To understand this note that it was argued above that $x_i - \bar{x}$ is positively correlated with $\epsilon_{it} - \bar{\epsilon}_t$ in this sample. Thus the coefficient on the former is biased downward, which is what is observed. But one would anticipate that x_i is positively correlated with $x_i - \bar{x}$ so this induces a positive bias on the x_i term. Bias from the level differences is not present for the intact households so it is not inconsistent to see that the selection term is marginally significant and the bias operates in the opposite way in that case. For these households bias can only arise due to change in the ϵ.

13.6   Conclusions

In this chapter, I have examined the determinants of the nutritional status of ever married women in rural Bangladesh, giving particular attention to potential selectivity bias arising from the fact that joint residence is potentially endogenous with respect to health investment. In addition to examining the extent to which a woman's health is sensitive to the characteristics of a woman's spouse as well as the number and composition of her children, the results generally support the notion that individuals care differentially about the welfare of co-resident and non-co-resident family members. Specifically, it appears that the health status of co-resident family units are viewed as complementary to the health of one's own family. The results also suggest that intrinsic demand for health is lower for daughters-in-law than other female members of the household. Evidently joint residence is protective for these women given the complementarity of health allocations in the joint household.

Acknowledgment

This research supported in part by NIH Grant HD10379 and by The Pew Charitable Trusts.

Notes

1 Arguably one might also want to include, in addition to household-specific average schooling, the family-specific average health. Inclusion of this argument has a small effect on the interpretation of parameter estimates but does not alter the econometric approach. Thus, for notational simplicity this possibility has been ignored.
2 I use the term intrinsic demand to reflect the idea that this parameter is an indicator of the demand for health in the family unit if it were autarchic and thus could, in principle, be derived from an underlying model of health demand under autarchy. In this chapter, however, I will treat this component of health demand as a reduced form so that I can focus on the implications for health of combining family units.
3 Given this restriction and the previous one, it is shown here that only the difference in the v across and within households affects the returns to joint residence. Without this restriction the levels of v would also affect these returns because they would then influence the demand for z. The primary econometric implication of relaxing this restriction

would be that one could not permit, without further assumptions, family heterogeneity in intrinsic demands that is correlated with unit-specific observables. If these effects were assumed to be absent then it would be straightforward to test the implied exclusion restriction.

4 If average family health were also an argument of the utility function then the average family intrinsic demand would also appear in the former equation.

5 I do not at this point need to take a position on whether the β may be interpreted structurally. If there is unobserved heterogeneity that influences intrinsic demands for human capital and is correlated with the "x"s then the "β"s may be thought of as a result of projecting these demands on the set of observed variables.

6 As is typically the case for limited-dependent variable models the variance of ϵ cannot be separately estimated from the regressor coefficients.

7 Note that the term $a_7/(4(1 - a_7))$ has been absorbed into τ_{12} as it cannot be separately identified using only residence data.

8 The fifth moment condition is implied by the other four.

9 Note that the assumption of an ordering is not innocuous. Without such an assumption and if the ordering of units within the family were random, $x_3\beta$ would not be correlated with $x_2\beta - x_1\beta$. But of course as the $x_i\beta$ are observable, units may be ordered in any desirable way. Or, interactions between the differenced $x_i\beta$ and $x_3\beta$ may be incorporated into the instrument set.

10 Because a small number of simulations per family are drawn, the mean-squared error is estimated using the product of the prediction error of two independent simulations for each family. It may be shown that this yields an expression with the same probability limit as would be obtained with a large number of simulations per family.

References

Altonji, Joseph G., Hayashi, Fumio, and Kotlikoff, Laurence (1992) "Is the extended family altrusitically linked? Direct evidence using micro data," *American Economic Review*, 82: 1177–98.

—— (1997) "Parental altruism and inter vivos transfers: theory and evidence," *Journal of Political Economy*, 105: 1121–66.

Bergstrom, Theodore (1997) "A survey of theories of the family," in Mark Rosenzweig and Oded Stark (eds), *Handbook of Population and Family Economics*, New York: Elsevier.

Cain, Mead (1985) "The fate of the elderly in South Asia: implications for fertility," IUSSP International Population Conference, Florence, 4: 279–91.

Caldwell, J.C., Immerwahr, G.L., and Ruzicka, L.T. (1982) "Illustrative analysis: family structure and fertility," *WFS Scientific Reports* No. 39, Voorburg: International Statistical Institute.

Caldwell, J.C., Reddy, P.H., and Caldwell, P. (1986) "The determinants of family structure in rural South India," *Journal of Marriage and the Family*, 46(1): 215–29.

Foster, Andrew D. (1993) "Household partition in rural Bangladesh," *Population Studies*, 47(March): 97–114.

—— (1997) "Marriage-market selection in rural Bangladesh," Manuscript, Providence, RI: Brown University.

Foster, Andrew D. and Rosenzweig, Mark R. (2002) "Household division, inequality and rural economic growth," *Review of Economic Studies*, 69: 839–69.

Hayashi, Fumio (1995) "Is the Japanese extended family altruistically linked? A test based on Engel curves," *Journal of Political Economy*, 103: 661–74.

McElroy, Marjorie (1990) "The empirical content of Nash-bargained household behavior," *Journal of Human Resources*, 25: 559–83.

Pakes, Ariel and Pollard, David (1989) "Simulation and the asymptotics of optimization estimators," *Econometrica*, 57: 1027–57.

Rahman, Makhlisur (1986) "Tradition, development and the individual: a study of conflicts and supports to family planning in rural Bangladesh," in Penny Kane and Lado Ruzicka (eds), *Asian Population Changer Series No. 1*, Canberra, Australia: Australian National University.

Rahman, M. Omar, Foster, Andrew D. and Menken, J. (1992) "Older widow mortality in rural Bangladesh," *Social Science and Medicine*, 34: 89–96.

Rahman, M. Omar, Foster, Andrew D., Gertler, Paul and Menken, Jane (1999) *Matlab Health and Socioeconomic Survey*, Los Angeles: RAND.

Schultz, T.Paul (1990) "Testing the neoclassical model of family labor supply and fertility," *Journal of Human Resources*, 25: 599–634.

Thomas, Duncan (1990) "Intra-household resource allocation: an inferential approach," *Journal of Human Resources*, 25: 635–64.

14 Self-help groups and income generation in the informal settlements of Nairobi*

Eliana La Ferrara

14.1 Introduction

Recent years have seen a growing interest on behalf of economists and other social scientists in the role played by *groups* in the process of economic development. Drawing upon the conceptual framework of Putnam (1993), some studies have looked at civic engagement in a variety of associations, including recreational and socio-political ones, to argue that the mere participation in such groups can have an economic impact by providing opportunities for members to share information, enforce informal transactions, and coordinate on cooperative outcomes.[1] Other studies have focused on the role of groups in the informal credit market and have analyzed their incentive schemes and economic performance.[2] For some of the poorest individuals in developing countries, however, groups are more than socio-political associations or saving devices: they are "employers." People who do not have access to the formal labor market and whose options in the informal market are relatively unattractive can often benefit from pooling resources and working in groups. To what extent can informal groups constitute a reliable source of income for the poor? What factors affect group performance, and in particular, how does the "social" composition of the group affect the organization of production and the allocation of resources to members?

This chapter attempts to address the above questions by employing a unique dataset on "self-help" groups with income-generating activities collected by the author in the informal settlements of Nairobi in 1999. Information has been collected on *each and every member* of the surveyed groups, which allows us to construct exact measures of the composition of the group in terms of income, education, age, and ethnicity. This is particularly important when investigating the impact of heterogeneity on group performance. The advantage of this methodology compared to the studies that infer within-group heterogeneity from the heterogeneity of the population at large is that it accounts for the possibility that people sort into groups that are more or less heterogeneous than

* Originally published as: La Ferrara, Eliana (2002) "Self-help Groups and Income Generation in the Informal Settlements of Nairobi." *Journal of African Economies*, 11(1): 61–89. Reproduced with kind permission of Oxford University Press.

the whole population. By having a "census" of the entire group, the matching between group composition and individual outcomes can thus be estimated more precisely.

The main findings of the empirical analysis can be summarized as follows. First, within each group, individual earnings increase with age and decrease with the number of years the individual has been living in the current place. The time spent in the group, as a proxy for experience, has a positive but insignificant impact on earnings, suggesting that the notion of "seniority" rewarded by these groups is strictly related to age. Second, women and young people are relatively more dependent on group activities for their living, while adult males often have an alternative source of income. "Dependency" is also negatively correlated to the income that the individual was earning before joining the group, suggesting that group production serves a particularly crucial function for members with low "outside options." Third, giving access to loans to otherwise credit constrained individuals is among the most valuable functions of these groups. About 64% of the respondents say that in case of need they borrow from the group as a whole or from individual members. The most important factor to gain access to such loans seems to be speaking the same language of the chairperson: *ceteris paribus*, members of the same ethnic group as the chairperson are 20–25 percentage points more likely to borrow from the group or from other members. Fourth, while ethnic fragmentation and wealth inequality do not affect the likelihood of borrowing, inequality in group earnings has a negative and significant effect. The effect is particularly strong in groups that experienced financial losses, suggesting that when the available capital to lend is particularly scarce and members are not remunerated "uniformly" it may be difficult to reach a consensus on who should get a loan. This hypothesis is corroborated by the fact that when loans from the group as a whole are distinguished from loans from individual members, earnings inequality negatively affects the former but not the latter. Finally, apart from affecting the allocation of loans, heterogeneity seems to influence the organization of production. In more ethnically heterogeneous groups it is less common for members to specialize in different tasks and more likely that everyone does the same job. Also, ethnic fragmentation seems to be associated with remuneration schemes in which every worker gets the same fixed amount, rather than being paid on the basis of the number of hours worked or the number of items produced. Again, this may be due to the relative difficulty of reaching a consensus in heterogenous groups. The ability to sanction free-riding behavior on contributions to the group is also negatively related to ethnic fragmentation, while that of sanctioning absenteeism and other irregular behavior is not. Finally, no pattern emerges between group composition and the criteria for recruiting new members.

The remainder of the chapter is organized as follows. Section 14.2 briefly reviews the related literature. Section 14.3 describes the setting, starting with a description of the informal sector and of self-help groups in Kenya and then moving to the specific data used in this chapter. Section 14.4 contains econometric results on income generation, access to credit, and the organization of production. Section 14.5 concludes.

14.2 Background literature

The issue of heterogeneity and group participation has received increasing attention in recent years. Alesina and La Ferrara (2000) analyze the impact of racial, ethnic, and income heterogeneity on individual propensity to join socio-political associations in the US and find that it has a negative effect. La Ferrara (2002) models the role of wealth inequality in villages where people have the choice of joining groups that provide different net benefits to the rich and the poor, and shows that when access is unrestricted, higher village inequality translates into lower participation because the relatively rich opt out of the groups. Both chapters differ from the present work in two respects. First of all, they address the question of how groups form (what determines the likelihood that an individual will join), and not how they function. Second, they relate group formation to "society wide" heterogeneity as opposed to within-group heterogeneity. In fact, the link tested by those papers is from inequality (or racial fragmentation) in the "pool" from which members are drawn, to individual choices regarding group participation. While this chapter employs exact indexes of within-group heterogeneity, it has the limitation of taking membership as exogenous, without accounting for the motivations that may induce people to join homogeneous vs. heterogeneous groups. Developing a comprehensive framework (and suitable data) to account for both group formation and internal group composition and functioning seems an important task for future work.

A strand of the literature which is closer to the current chapter is the one on heterogeneity and group performance. This has been explored in the context of project maintenance by Khwaja (2000), who uses project level data on 132 community-maintained infrastructure projects in the Himalayas. The author finds that, *ceteris paribus*, socially heterogeneous communities have poorly maintained projects, and that the relationship between maintenance and inequality in projects returns is U-shaped. Miguel (2000) and Gugerty and Miguel (forthcoming) analyze the effect of ethnic diversity on school funding and school organization in Kenyan villages. Both the studies find that ethnic fragmentation is associated with worse outcomes, and suggest mechanisms though which this effect may be generated. In particular, Gugerty and Miguel find that the more racially heterogeneous the pupils' population, the lower are parental participation in school activities, school committee attendance, and teacher attendance and motivation. The authors suggest that these results may be due to the fact that social sanctions apply within ethnic groups, hence fragmented communities have lower scope for sanctioning non-cooperative behavior. In a recent study, Karlan (2001) examines the impact of members' composition on savings and repayment performance in group lending programs offered by a Peruvian organization. The author focuses on geographic and "cultural" dispersion (Western vs. indigenous) and finds that both types of heterogeneity increase the probability of defaulting on group loans. As for savings, which can be viewed as a form of "collective" good to the extent that capital is lent back to the members, geographic distance among the members significantly reduces saving rates, while cultural dissimilarity has a negligible effect.

Finally, Wydick (1999) estimates the determinants of repayment performance and of intra-group insurance in a sample of 137 borrowing groups from Guatemala, and finds that "social ties" (as measured by the number of years that the members have known each other and by the degree of friendship and social interaction before and after joining the group) have a negligible impact on group performance. What seems to matter most is the availability of sanctioning mechanisms and the possibility of monitoring (as proxied by geographical distance and knowledge of each other's business).

The present study builds upon this literature with a few significant modifications. First, it considers groups that provide the main source of income for most of the members. In other words, individuals' stake in these groups is particularly high in this case as compared to project maintenance groups or school committees, and possibly even to borrowing groups, in that members mostly depend on production activities organized within these groups for their daily living. As such, it is important to investigate what determines individual earnings and the "dependency rate" on group income, as well as group performance. And even when the attention is on the latter, we may expect the effects of characteristics such as heterogeneity to be amplified – and possibly different – in this context. Second, as will be described in the next section, the setting in which these groups operate is as precarious and socially disrupted as one may conceive, due to the virtual absence of property rights in the squatter communities and to the high degree of in- and out-migration. This can also be expected to have an impact on group functioning. Finally, compared to some of the studies described earlier in which the degree of heterogeneity and other group characteristics were estimated based on the leaders' evaluation, a key ingredient of the survey methodology in this study was to interview *all* members of each group and to compare their "subjective" assessments with "objective" measures of group composition. This reveals some interesting differences, e.g., in the case of wealth and income inequality.

Before turning to the description of the setting in which the data was collected, it is useful to compare this study to the earlier work by Abraham *et al.* (1998). The authors surveyed 510 households from one of the most populated informal settlements of Nairobi, Kibera, collecting data on participation in different types of groups and on the socio-economic background of the respondents. The groups were then divided into several categories, such as rotating savings and credit associations, burial societies, health groups, etc. and their main characteristics in terms of organizational structure, contributions, and composition were examined. While similar for the context, the present chapter differs from the work of Abraham *et al.* in three respects. First, their approach was purely descriptive, while this chapter employs multivariate analysis. Second, among their respondents some were members of a group and some were not, so they could estimate participation rates but not know who else was in the same group of a respondent. In this chapter no participation regression can be run, because every respondent is by definition member of some group, but the identity and characteristics of all other group members are known. Finally, the data of Abraham *et al.* had a broader coverage, including groups with and without investment or production activities, while in this chapter the focus is on groups with income-generating activities.

14.3 The setting

14.3.1 *Informal settlements and self-help groups in Nairobi*

It is estimated that in 1993 more than 55% of the population of Nairobi lived in "informal settlements," i.e., squatter communities where inhabitants have no legal right or at most a quasi-legal right, in the form of temporary occupation right from the Local Authority or a letter from the Chief.[3] These informal settlements in turn cover less than 6% of Nairobi's residential area, which leads to an average density of 250 dwellings and 750 persons per hectare as compared to about 10–30 dwellings and 50–180 persons per hectare in upper- and middle-income areas (Alder *et al.* 1993). Until the late 1970s the government policy was to demolish informal settlements throughout the country, while since the early 1980s they gradually became tacitly accepted, with occasional episodes of demolition and resettlement of the population to other areas (e.g., in Nairobi Muoroto and Kibagare in 1990, Mitumba in 1993). Uncertainty over basic property rights adds to that over land tenure to generate a pattern of extreme insecurity where almost no investment is made in infrastructure and local public goods. Dwellings are entirely made of temporary materials such as mud, wattle, and timber offcut, and waste disposal is done on the street and in the rivers. Most sites have virtually no sewerage systems and hygienic conditions are extremely poor.

The inhabitants of squatter communities usually work in the informal sector. Most of them are involved in hawking, are occasionally employed for the day, or operate small businesses without licenses. A non-negligible fraction is also involved in illegal activities. Particularly relevant are small businesses known as "*jua kali*," which encompass manufacturing activities, repair, and services, and employ a large number of mechanics, carpenters, and construction workers that serve other areas of Nairobi as well.[4] The attitude of the City Council has historically been that of discouraging this type of employment, but in recent years the official stand on this issue has shifted, possibly in recognition that the lack of employment opportunities in the formal sector for many slum dwellers called for alternative forms of employment. Public opinion and policy makers have thus started to view the *jua kali* sector as a valuable opportunity for unemployed youth to enter the (informal) labor market and contribute to domestic product generation (Otieno Okumu 1999).

Jua kali workers may have formal education, but they often receive informal training on the job, for which they may have to pay their employer (Ng'ethe and Ndua 1985). In addition to training costs, people who want to start their own business need start-up capital which, though limited compared to licensed businesses, may be far beyond the possibilities of a typical slum dweller. For this reason it is becoming increasingly common among the urban poor to join resources and form the so called "self-help" groups, which operate in the informal sector with income-generating activities similar to those of individual *jua kali* workers, but are organized approximately as a production cooperative. The degree of formalization of these groups, as well as their stability and the scope of their activities, vary a lot. It seems therefore valuable to undertake a first step toward a quantitative assessment of the economic potential of these groups and of the determinants of their economic performance.

14.3.2   The data

The data used in the empirical analysis was collected by the author in the months of July and August 1999 in five of the most populated informal settlements of Nairobi: Dandora, Gikomba, Kayole, Korogocho, and Mathare Valley. In consultation with local community workers, a list of the self-help groups active in these areas was prepared and 20 groups were selected to be interviewed, based on their location, type of activity, size, age, and sex of the members.[5] A key requirement was that the group had some type of income-generating activity (though not necessarily the *only* activity of the group). Income-generating activities in the sample span as different fields as crafts-making (wood carving, basket weaving, etc.), tailoring, garbage recycling, education and health services, informal lending, etc. Preliminary meetings were set-up with the chairperson and secretary of each group, and a list of all active members was obtained. Based on this list, individual interviews were scheduled with each member for the survey modules on demographics, income, and personal assessment of group functioning. An additional module was administered separately to the chairperson, the treasurer, and the secretary of each group to gather information on the history, organizational structure, and costs and revenues of the group. Given that the methodology of this study required a complete survey of *all* participants in the group, only groups for which at least 90% of the members were successfully interviewed were retained in the sample. This leaves us with 18 groups for a total of 303 individual members. While the sample is certainly not representative of all groups in the informal settlements of Nairobi, it can provide a reasonable representation of small and medium-sized groups with a focus on income generation and a low degree of formalization.

As can be seen from Table 14.1, the groups in the sample differ substantially in terms of size and of the number of years they have been in place. The smallest group has 6 members and the largest has 30, with an average of 14 members per group. The average group has been in place for almost 5 years, with a minimum of 9 months and a maximum of 16 years. Groups are mostly mixed in terms of gender, with 33% of them being all-women and 11% being all men. These figures are not surprising, given the prominent role of women groups in the informal sector of most developing countries. The average group member is 31 years old, but this figure hides substantial differences in the sample: the "youngest" group has a mean age of its members equal to 19, and the "oldest" group of 60. Approximately 10% of the respondents has no formal schooling, 48.4% has Class 1–8, and the rest

Table 14.1 Basic group characteristics

	Fraction (%)	*Mean*	*Min.*	*Max.*
Size (regular members)	—	14.22	6	30
Duration (yrs)	—	4.92	0.8	16
% Female members	—	50	0	100
Only men	11.1	—	—	—
Only women	33.3	—	—	—
Mixed, mostly men	33.3	—	—	—
Mixed, mostly women	22.2	—	—	—
Members' age	—	31.09	15	73
Group avg. median	—	28.68	—	—
Group avg. min.	—	19.53	—	—
Group avg. max.	—	60.22	—	—
Members' education	—	—	—	—
Class 1–4	7.3	—	—	—
Class 5–8	41.1	—	—	—
Form I–II	12.9	—	—	—
Form III–IV	25.8	—	—	—
Form V–VI	0.0	—	—	—
Educational college	2.0	—	—	—
Technical institute	0.7	—	—	—
Basic adult education	2.3	—	—	—
No schooling	7.9	—	—	—
Members' wealth (Ksh)	—	7379.1	350	197 300
Group avg. median (Ksh)	—	5134.4	—	—
Group avg. min. (Ksh)	—	2450.0	—	—
Group avg. max. (Ksh)	—	24 192.3	—	—

has higher education. This is an important piece of evidence because it shows that in the reality of urban informal settlements with strong barriers to entry in the formal labor market, self-help groups cater not only to unskilled workers. Finally, members' wealth was assessed on the basis of ownership of a basket of durable consumption goods such as radio, TV, camera, bike, car, stove, electric or gas cooker, clock, sofa, bed, and mattress, weighted by an estimate of their prices in the informal market.[6] Based on this index, the average respondent owned durables for 7379 Kenyan Shillings (Ksh), which amounted to US$99.60 in August 1999 prices. Groups differed substantially in wealth, though, with the average member of the "poorest" group having 2450 Ksh, and that of the richest having 10 times as much.

In what follows we turn to multivariate analysis to investigate how individual and aggregate characteristics affect the economic performance of these groups.

14.4   Empirical results

14.4.1   Income generation

The first aspect to be considered is the potential for income generation provided by these groups. One can estimate the following earnings function:

$$y_{ij} = X_{ij}\beta + D_j\gamma + \varepsilon_{ij} \tag{1}$$

where y_{ij} is the log of hourly earnings of individual i in group j, X_{ij} is a vector of individual characteristics, D_j if a set of group dummies, and ε_{ij} is an error term. Individual characteristics, which should capture labor productivity, include sex, marital status, age, education, and experience (proxied by the number of years the respondent has been in the group), as well as language dummies. A nonlinear specification is chosen for age, education, and experience, to allow for nonlinearities in the returns to human capital. Group fixed effects are introduced to control for differences in remuneration schemes across activities.

Table 14.2 reports coefficient estimates for (1), with White-robust standard errors in parenthesis. Group dummies are omitted from the table, but a standard F test in all cases rejects the null that their coefficients are jointly equal to zero. When a small set of demographic controls is included (column 1), the only significant determinant of hourly earnings is age: within each group there are positive but decreasing returns to age. Surprisingly education is not significant (the omitted category is people with no formal education), nor are sex and marital status. Column 2 introduces two more regressors: the number of years the respondent has been working in the group (and its square), and the number of years he or she has been living in the current place of residence. The coefficients on the former variable are positive but not statistically significant: in these groups there seem to be returns to "seniority" in the sense of age, but not in the sense of experience. As for the latter variable, residential stability has a negative and significant effect on individual earnings. This is not surprising if we consider that the areas of study are probably the poorest and the most degraded of urban Nairobi, so having resided somewhere else probably means higher "unobserved ability." This interpretation may also help explain why the experience variable is not significant. On the one hand, spending more years in the group increases job-specific skills; on the other hand, to the extent that high ability workers may be the first ones to quit for formal jobs, length of work within the group may end up capturing low ability. In an attempt to control for this, column 3 introduces among the regressors individual earnings before joining the group (in log). The previous results remain virtually unchanged and past earnings are insignificant, indicating that this variable is a poor proxy for unobserved ability.[7]

In column 4 a set of language dummies is introduced to control for whether the respondent is Kikuyu, Luo, or Kamba (the omitted category is Luhya and other ethnicities). Furthermore, the dummy "Dominant language" takes value 1 if the

Table 14.2 Earnings functions

Dependent variable	Hourly earnings from group (ln)				
	[1]	[2]	[3]	[4]	[5]
Female	−0.134	−0.130	−0.123	−0.136	−0.135
	(0.116)	(0.119)	(0.121)	(0.119)	(0.119)
Married	−0.094	−0.087	−0.085	−0.092	−0.086
	(0.070)	(0.069)	(0.070)	(0.073)	(0.073)
Age	0.056**	0.059**	0.054**	0.059**	0.060**
	(0.019)	(0.019)	(0.023)	(0.019)	(0.019)
$(Age^2)^a$	−0.065**	−0.069**	−0.063**	−0.069**	−0.070**
	(0.023)	(0.022)	(0.026)	(0.023)	(0.023)
Education 1–8	0.001	−0.001	0.018	0.014	0.021
	(0.173)	(0.169)	(0.184)	(0.180)	(0.179)
Education Form 1–4	−0.223	−0.228	−0.204	−0.221	−0.204
	(0.179)	(0.175)	(0.196)	(0.183)	(0.183)
Education advanced	−0.097	−0.093	−0.063	−0.091	−0.071
	(0.195)	(0.192)	(0.203)	(0.198)	(0.199)
# years in group	—	0.018	0.004	0.012	0.022
		(0.052)	(0.053)	(0.053)	(0.054)
$(\text{\# years in group}^2)^a$	—	−0.008	0.064	0.024	−0.034
		(0.318)	(0.321)	(0.322)	(0.327)
# years resident	—	−0.009**	−0.008**	−0.009**	−0.008*
		(0.004)	(0.004)	(0.004)	(0.004)
ln income before group	—	—	0.011	—	—
			(0.012)		
Kikuyu	—	—	—	0.081	−0.066
				(0.135)	(0.141)
Luo	—	—	—	−0.054	−0.115
				(0.146)	(0.170)
Kamba	—	—	—	−0.113	−0.089
				(0.160)	(0.157)
Dominant language	—	—	—	−0.158	—
				(0.130)	
Chair's language	—	—	—	—	0.128
					(0.125)
Constant	1.665**	1.652**	1.691**	1.795**	1.686**
	(0.407)	(0.440)	(0.454)	(0.419)	(0.428)
Number of observations	301.0	301.0	298.0	301.0	301.0
Adjusted R^2	0.72	0.72	0.73	0.72	0.72

Notes
Table reports estimated OLS coefficients. Robust standard errors in parenthesis.
All regressions include group fixed effects.
a Coefficients and standard errors multiplied by 100.
∗ Significance at the 10% level; ∗∗ Significance at the 5% level.

individual speaks the same language as the majority of other group members, and 0 otherwise. This is aimed at capturing possible ethnic favoritism, as discussed, e.g., by Collier and Garg (1999) and by Barr and Oduro (2002) for the Ghanaian labor market. As can be seen from the table, the coefficient on this variable is not statistically different from zero. A possible explanation is that when the decision process is not democratic, what counts is not belonging to the majority, but being the same ethnicity as the leaders. The last column introduces a dummy for whether the respondent speaks the same language as the chairperson of the group when decisions are reported to be made by leaders as opposed to democratically, but the conclusion remains the same. The coefficient on this variable is positive but not statistically significant.[8]

A second aspect to consider in order to assess the role of these groups for income generation is to what extent they offer better earning opportunities compared to individual jobs in the informal sector. When asked what was the most important reason for joining the group, 39% of the respondents said that they did not have another job, 25% said that they had a job but the job in the group was better, 19% indicated the access to side benefits such as health or training opportunities, and the rest gave other reasons. At first sight, then, the answer to this question is not obvious. A possible way to rephrase the question is to ask to what extent people are dependent on these groups as their main source of income, and estimate the determinants of this "dependency ratio" through multivariate analysis.

The dependent variable in Table 14.3 is the ratio of individual income earned in the group over total individual income, expressed in percentage. The sample average for this variable is 75%, indicating a fairly high dependence on group earnings. The controls in columns 1–3 are the same as those introduced in Table 14.2. The single most important correlate of group dependency is gender: other things equal, the share of women's income coming from the group is about 11 percentage points higher than that of men. Though not statistically significant at conventional levels, the coefficients on the age variables show that group dependency declines as members become older, suggesting that these groups may serve a particularly valuable function for young people who do not have access to alternative jobs. Column 4 attempts to control for alternative employment opportunities by introducing among the regressors the income that the individual was earning *before* joining the group. Interestingly, this variable is negative and highly significant: people who were earning more in the past are less dependent on the group to earn a living. Notice also that from column 4 dependency decreases with education up to Form 4 level, as one should expect.[9]

14.4.2   *Access to credit*

Aside from the cash flow provided by the group in the form of earnings, responses to the survey suggest that many members value the possibility of resorting to the group for help in case of need. This section will examine to what extent this occurs with respect to credit, i.e., what factors affect members' access to group loans.

Table 14.4 estimates the probability of borrowing from the group or from individual members in case of need as a function of the respondents' characteristics plus group fixed effects. The dependent variable takes value 1 if, when asked "If you need a loan, who do you borrow from?" the respondent answers "Group as a whole" or "Individual group member." It takes value 0 if the answer is "Bank,"

Table 14.3 Dependence on group for income

Dependent variable	% of total income coming from group			
	[1]	*[2]*	*[3]*	*[4]*
Female	11.44**	11.06**	12.35**	11.14**
	(4.84)	(4.84)	(5.05)	(5.06)
Married	−1.58	−1.39	−1.39	−0.80
	(2.97)	(2.92)	(3.00)	(3.08)
Age	−1.05	−1.05	−0.94	−0.34
	(0.73)	(0.73)	(0.54)	(0.74)
Age^2	0.011	0.012	0.011	0.005
	(0.008)	(0.008)	(0.008)	(0.009)
Education 1–8	−3.88	−4.05	−5.21	−6.84
	(4.52)	(4.54)	(4.81)	(4.94)
Education Form 1–4	−4.72	−5.14	−6.70	−9.45*
	(5.11)	(5.19)	(5.39)	(5.50)
Education Advanced	−7.84	−8.02	−9.51	−12.34
	(10.55)	(10.37)	(10.50)	(9.71)
# years in group	—	−0.53	−0.48	−0.60
		(2.14)	(2.17)	(2.17)
# years in group^2	—	−0.07	−0.07	−0.06
		(0.16)	(0.16)	(0.16)
# years resident	—	0.266	0.24	0.19
		(0.191)	(0.20)	(0.21)
Kikuyu	—	—	2.70	1.68
			(7.62)	(7.47)
Luo	—	—	8.09	7.43
			(6.05)	(6.02)
Kamba	—	—	5.62	5.86
			(6.35)	(6.35)
Dominant language	—	—	−3.06	−1.75
			(6.87)	(6.81)
In income before group	—	—	—	−1.26**
				(0.46)
Constant	96.06**	94.90**	91.29**	87.69**
	(14.77)	(15.05)	(15.39)	(15.44)
Number of observations	299.0	299.0	299.0	296.0
Adjusted R^2	0.60	0.60	0.60	0.61

Notes
Table reports estimated OLS coefficients. Robust standard errors in parenthesis.
All regressions include group fixed effects.
∗ Significance at the 10% level; ∗∗ Significance at the 5% level.

"Relative," "Friends *not* in the group," or "Nobody." The regressors are meant to control both for demand and for supply factors, as will be clear from the discussion. Column 1 reports marginal probit coefficients on demographic variables only. It is surprising that only the language dummies are statistically significant. An interesting regressor is the dummy identifying respondents that speak the same language as the chairperson when leaders make decisions. *Ceteris paribus*, speaking the

Table 14.4 Ability to borrow, individual determinants

	Probit		OLS	2SLS[c]
	[1]	[2]	[3]	[4]
Female	−0.097	−0.097	−0.063	−0.043
	(0.105)	(0.105)	(0.085)	(0.087)
Married	0.002	−0.003	0.004	−0.027
	(0.069)	(0.069)	(0.068)	(0.069)
Age	−0.021	−0.021	−0.015	−0.024
	(0.018)	(0.018)	(0.016)	(0.017)
$(Age^2)^a$	0.016	0.016	0.010	0.018
	(0.020)	(0.020)	(0.020)	(0.021)
Education 1–8	−0.007	−0.013	−0.016	−0.035
	(0.124)	(0.124)	(0.128)	(0.137)
Education Form 1–4	−0.135	−0.142	−0.114	−0.025
	(0.141)	(0.141)	(0.140)	(0.155)
Education Advanced	−0.151	−0.171	−0.138	−0.045
	(0.253)	(0.249)	(0.197)	(0.211)
# years in group	−0.003	−0.008	0.001	−0.019
	(0.045)	(0.045)	(0.037)	(0.045)
(# years in group^2)^a	0.003	0.033	−0.014	−0.001
	(0.265)	(0.272)	(0.246)	(0.003)
# years resident	−0.003	−0.002	−0.002	−0.001
	(0.005)	(0.004)	(0.004)	(0.004)
Kikuyu	−0.206	−0.197	−0.142	−0.240*
	(0.135)	(0.138)	(0.100)	(0.132)
Luo	−0.346**	−0.342**	−0.227*	−0.329**
	(0.165)	(0.167)	(0.124)	(0.158)
Kamba	−0.241	−0.230	−0.170	−0.293*
	(0.161)	(0.162)	(0.130)	(0.168)
Chair's language	0.201*	0.196*	0.215*	0.251**
	(0.085)	(0.086)	(0.126)	(0.133)
Own house	—	−0.061	−0.049	0.152
	—	(0.102)	(0.084)	(0.180)
Wealth^b	—	0.253	0.059	−1.81
	—	(0.424)	(0.073)	(1.59)
Constant	—	—	1.251**	1.457**
	—	—	(0.312)	(0.356)
Number of observations	278.0	278.0	278.0	275.0
Adjusted R^2	0.21	0.21	0.14	0.14
Predicted p	0.69	0.69	0.64	0.64
Observed p	0.64	0.64	0.64	0.64

Notes

Dependent variable = 1 if borrow from whole group or group member.

All regressions include group fixed effects.

Columns 1–2 report marginal probit coefficients calculated at the means; column 3 reports OLS coefficients; and column 4 reports two stage least squares.

Robust standard errors in parenthesis.

a Coefficients and standard errors multiplied by 100.

b Coefficients and standard errors multiplied by 10 000.

c Instruments for wealth are: income earned before joining the group (in logs), number of other groups to which respondent belongs, dummy = 1 if group is main source of income.

* Significance at the 10% level.

** Significance at the 5% level.

language of the chairperson increases the probability of borrowing from the group or from members by 20 percentage points, which is a very sizeable effect. Column 2 adds two measures of individual wealth, to control for the need to borrow. The first is a dummy equal to 1 if the respondent or a relative owns a house, which for the reasons explained in Section 14.3.1 is rather uncommon in the informal settlements under investigation. The second is the index of durable goods described in Section 14.3.2. Neither index turns out to be significant in column 2. While home ownership can be considered exogenous given the small size of group loans, one could argue that ownership of durable assets is an endogenous variable or that it is measured with error. Column 4 of Table 14.4 reports two stage least squares estimates of a linear probability model when wealth is instrumented with three variables: income before joining the group (in logarithm), the number of groups to which the respondent belongs (excluding the current group), and a dummy equal to 1 if group work is the main source of income for the individual. Column 3 reports the uninstrumented linear probability model for comparison. When wealth is instrumented, its coefficient becomes negative but is still insignificant. The Hausman test fails to reject the joint null of weak exogeneity and no measurement error in wealth (p-value is 0.24), and according to the Sargan overidentification test our instruments are valid (p-value of 0.36). This seems to suggest that the concerns about reverse causation and measurement error are not warranted empirically. Notice that the "Chair's language" variable remains significant in all cases and its coefficient is even bigger in the 2SLS regression.

Apart from including group fixed effects, the analysis so far has not attempted to relate ability to borrow to any specific group characteristic. Table 14.5 addresses this point by adding to the individual controls listed in column 2 of Table 14.4 (not displayed) a number of group level controls. The first two are measures of resources available in the group: group profits per capita (which may serve as capital to advance loans) and average wealth of group members (in case members draw upon their own personal capital to lend to others). Neither variable has a significant impact on access to credit. The remaining variables are indexes of heterogeneity within the group.

Fragmentation indexes measure the likelihood that two randomly drawn members belong to different "categories" and are computed as follows:

$$\text{Fragment}_j = 1 - \sum_k s_{kj}^2 \qquad (2)$$

where j represents a group, k a category, and each term s_{kj} is the share of category k in the total membership of group j. For ethnic fragmentation, e.g., the categories are Kikuyu, Luhya, Luo, Kalenjin, Kamba, Kisii, Meru, Mijikenda, Masai, Somali, Nubian, and other. In this case, s_{kj} is the fraction of group members speaking each of the above languages. The other fragmentation indexes are computed in a way analogous to equation (2) but instead of using ethnicity we use the fraction of individuals in a group with the same education level (no formal education, Class 1–8, Form 1–4, technical or college) and residential location.[10]

Table 14.5 Ability to borrow, group determinants

	[1]	[2]
Group profits per capita[a]	−0.769	−0.853
	(1.30)	(1.27)
Avg wealth of group members[a]	2.41	3.09
	(2.72)	(2.99)
Ethnic fragmentation	−0.172	0.019
	(0.336)	(0.321)
Education fragmentation	0.654*	0.792**
	(0.382)	(0.357)
Residence fragmentation	−0.102	−0.087
	(0.236)	(0.228)
Gini wealth	0.497	−0.103
	(1.02)	(1.20)
Gini income from group	−0.735**	—
	(0.375)	—
Gini income from grp$\vert$grp profits>0	—	−0.266
	—	(0.423)
Gini income from grp$\vert$grp profits≤0	—	−1.04**
	—	(0.453)
Number of observations	278.0	278.0
R^2	0.20	0.21
Predicted p	0.67	0.67
Observed p	0.62	0.62

Notes
Dependent variable = 1 if borrow from whole group or group member.
Marginal probit coefficients calculated at the means. Standard error in parenthesis are corrected for heteroskedasticity and clustering of the residuals at the group level.
Controls include all those listed in column 2 of Table 14.4.
a Coefficients and standard errors multiplied by 10 000.
* Significance at the 10% level
** Significance at the 5% level.

All indexes are constructed in a way that increasing values correspond to more heterogeneity.

From the studies reviewed in Section 14.2, both ethnic and geographic fragmentation can be expected to play a significant role to the extent that they capture possibilities for information flows, monitoring and enforcement. Education fragmentation instead is usually not employed in the literature, but becomes relevant in the present study because different education levels may represent complementary production skills. As can be seen from the table, of the fragmentation indexes, only that related to education is significant: members of groups in which widespread education levels are represented are more likely to borrow, possibly because of complementarities among members themselves.

The last two regressors in column 1 are Gini coefficients of inequality either in wealth (durable assets ownership) or in earnings from the group. It is noticeable that the latter has a negative and highly significant coefficient, indicating that when members earn very different amounts from group activities it is less likely that loans are advanced either by the group as a whole or by individual members. Column 2 expands on this result by allowing the coefficient on group income inequality to differ depending on whether the group has positive or negative profits. Interestingly, the negative effect of inequality on credit is found in groups that have financial difficulties but not in those that make positive profits. In other words, having members who earn very different amounts does not harm their ability to borrow if the pie is large enough for a number of them, while it does undermine lending by the group or among individuals when members have to struggle over resources.

Borrowing from the group as a whole or borrowing from individual members could make a difference, especially in the light of these results. Table 14.6 reports the estimated coefficients from two multinomial logit regressions in which the explanatory variables are the same as in Table 14.5, but the dependent variable is a categorical variable taking value 1 if in case of need the individual borrows from the group as an "institution," 2 if he or she borrows from a single member, and 0 if the lender is outside the group. The latter is the omitted category in the table. Inequality in group earnings decreases the likelihood of both types of loans, but is statistically significant only for "group" loans. This suggests that allowing for differences in remuneration of the members does not significantly undermine their willingness and ability to lend to each other, but it does undermine the ability to use the group as a source of credit, especially when the group runs in financial difficulties (see column 2). This may be due to the difficulty of agreeing on how to allocate the common funds when these are very limited. The next section will look more closely at the various forms of heterogeneity among group members and at the relationship between heterogeneity and group organization.

14.4.3 Heterogeneity and group organization

One of the clear patterns that emerged from the previous analysis was that certain types of heterogeneity had a stronger impact than others. In particular, inequality in individual earnings from the group significantly reduced the ability to borrow from the group as a whole, while inequality in "wealth," as measured by the index of durable goods, did not. It is useful to investigate why this is the case.

In addition to asking about "objective" wealth, the questionnaire asked each respondent the following question: "Leaving aside the income from this group, do the members have the same wealth?" and prompted the following responses: "Mostly the same," "Some differences," "Very different." Figure 14.1 relates this "subjective" notion of inequality to the objective ones used in the regressions.

The vertical axis in each panel measures the fraction of members of each group saying that members' wealth is "very different." The horizontal axis reports for each group the Gini coefficient for individual wealth (top panel), the Gini for earnings from the group (middle panel), and the ethnic fragmentation index (bottom panel). For example, a point such as (0.23, 0.54) in the top panel represents a group in which the Gini coefficient for wealth is 0.23 yet 54% of the members

Table 14.6 Borrowing from group vs. members

	[1]	[2]
Source = whole group		
Group profits per capita[a]	−0.160**	−0.168**
	(0.076)	(0.068)
Avg wealth of group members[a]	0.079	0.136
	(0.142)	(0.180)
Ethnic fragmentation	0.108	1.35
	(1.79)	(1.75)
Education fragmentation	2.78	2.74
	(3.00)	(2.94)
Residence fragmentation	−1.24	−1.21
	(1.22)	(1.15)
Gini wealth	3.45	−1.56
	(6.04)	(8.89)
Gini income from group	−4.01**	—
	(1.92)	—
Gini income from grp| grp profits > 0	—	−0.811
	—	(2.30)
Gini income from grp| grp profits ⩽ 0	—	−5.94**
	—	(2.61)
Source = individual group member		
Group profits per capita[a]	0.219**	0.154
	(0.091)	(0.095)
Avg wealth of group members[a]	0.108	0.207
	(0.151)	(0.176)
Ethnic fragmentation	−4.09	−2.74
	(3.80)	(3.70)
Education fragmentation	−4.07	−2.59
	(5.46)	(5.18)
Residence fragmentation	−1.87	−0.390
	(1.95)	(2.02)
Gini wealth	−3.56	−10.30
	(6.28)	(8.27)
Gini income from group	−3.14	—
	(2.93)	—
Gini income from grp| grp profits > 0	—	1.42
	—	(3.97)
Gini income from grp| grp profits ⩽ 0	—	−11.01
	—	(7.01)
Number of observations	247.0	247.0
Pseudo R^2	0.36	0.37

Notes

Table reports estimated multinomial logit coefficients. Omitted category is "Source = other." Standard error in parenthesis are corrected for clustering of the residuals at the group level.

a Coefficients and standard errors multiplied by 1000.

* Significance at the 10% level.

** Significance at the 5% level.

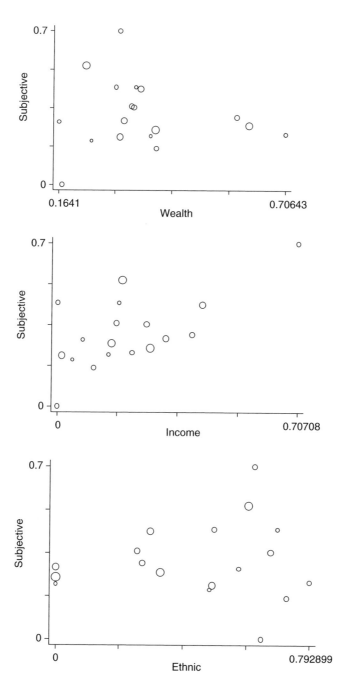

Figure 14.1 Subjective and objective heterogeneity.

think that differences in wealth among them are substantial. The size of the circles in the figure is proportional to group membership: points identified by larger circles correspond to larger groups.

It is quite striking how in the top panel no relationship at all emerges between the actual level of wealth inequality and that *perceived* by the members. On the contrary, the middle panel shows that subjective inequality is positively correlated with the extent of inequality in income received by different members from the group (the correlation between the two is 0.64). This result can be rationalized by presuming that people have limited information about each other's personal belongings, but that they have fairly accurate information about how much each member is paid, which matches the environmental conditions of the informal settlements and the groups surveyed pretty closely. If subjective beliefs are formed this way, then, it is not surprising that inequality in earnings affects group functioning more than wealth inequality: members' ability to agree on collective outcomes may depend more on their beliefs than on their objective conditions.

The bottom panel in Figure 14.1 plots the fraction of people who think that members differ a lot in wealth against the likelihood that two randomly drawn members of the group belong to different ethnicities. The link between ethnicity and wealth is not obvious in this context, but it may be that simply by considering a member as an "outsider" leads an individual to label him or her as very different in terms of wealth. The figure suggests a weak positive association between the two dimensions (the correlation coefficient is 0.10). Finally, in no case the heterogeneity indexes considered vary systematically with size, which means that higher heterogeneity does not simply capture a larger group of participants (which may be considered a source of collective action problems).

In the light of these discussions it is useful to examine the impact of various dimensions of heterogeneity on the organization of production within the group. The first column of Table 14.7 reports summary statistics on the percentage of groups that fall into different forms of organization: this provides a broad idea of the way these groups function. The same statistics are then computed splitting the groups into "High" and "Low" heterogeneity depending on whether their degree of heterogeneity is above the median or not (where the median is the index of heterogeneity of the median group). The dimensions of heterogeneity considered are ethnic, in wealth, and in education. Inequality in earnings from the group is omitted because it is endogenous to the organization of production chosen. Comparing the incidence of the various organizational forms in high and low heterogeneity groups can be a first step toward understanding how heterogeneity affects group functioning, though such interpretations will have to be taken with caution, given the small number of observations on which Table 14.7 is based (there are only 18 different groups in the sample).

Starting from the division of labor, on average 33% of the groups assign the same task to everybody, 45% allow for specialization, and 22% have different tasks in which the members alternate, so that no one is systematically assigned to

Table 14.7 Organization of production and heterogeneity

	% of groups with						
	Full sample	Ethnic heterogeneity		Wealth heterogeneity		Education heterogeneity	
		High	Low	High	Low	High	Low
	[1]	[2]	[3]	[4]	[5]	[6]	[7]
Division of jobs							
Everyone same	33.3	45.4	14.3	22.2	44.5	22.2	44.5
Specialization	44.5	36.4	57.1	44.5	44.4	66.7	22.2
Alternate	22.2	18.2	28.6	33.3	11.1	11.1	33.3
How members paid							
# items produced	33.2	22.2	33.3	22.2	33.3	22.2	11.1
# hours worked	5.6	11.1	11.1	0	11.1	11.1	11.1
Fixed amount, same for all	55.6	66.7	44.5	66.7	44.5	44.4	66.7
Their contributions	5.6	0	11.1	11.1	11.1	0	11.1
Penalty for missed contributions	0.38	0.14	0.67	0.20	0.50	0.60	0.25
# times applied	3.7	9.0	0.6	8.3	1.0	1.2	6.2
Penalty for irregular behavior	0.47	0.55	0.37	0.37	0.55	0.44	0.50
# times applied	3.2	2.9	3.5	2.6	3.7	3.3	3.1
How members recruited							
Ability	22.2	22.2	22.2	22.2	22.2	22.2	22.2
Need	22.2	22.2	22.2	11.1	33.3	22.2	22.2
Commitment	50.0	55.6	44.5	55.6	44.5	55.6	44.5
Friendship	5.6	0	11.1	11.1	0	0	11.1

a given task. When we split the sample according to their ethnic fragmentation (columns 2 and 3) the pattern is different. Highly fragmented groups tend to be ones in which everyone does the same job, while in relatively homogeneous groups it is more common to observe specialization in tasks. A possible explanation, which will be further advanced later, is that when members are heterogeneous it is more difficult to reach consensus on something that would generate disparities in economic treatment or in responsibilities, hence a "flat" rule becomes more attractive. Notice that this does not hold for heterogeneity in wealth, which, as argued, is likely not to be common knowledge among the members. As for education levels (columns 6 and 7), more heterogeneous groups display more specialization, while in homogeneous ones everyone tends to do the same thing. This seems reasonable, given that people with different education are "naturally" suited to different tasks.

Turning to remuneration schemes, groups tend to fall into two broad categories: those that pay a fixed amount equal for everyone (55.6%) and those that pay in proportion to the number of items produced (33.2%). Occasionally, they pay according to the number of hours worked (5.6%) or to the contributions made by the members when the group started (5.6%). When the sample is split according to ethnic fragmentation, more heterogeneous groups tend to pay a "flat rate," while more homogeneous ones pay in proportion to output. As discussed earlier, this can be interpreted as resulting from problems in reaching agreements that involve differential treatment of heterogeneous members. Results for wealth inequality go along the same lines, while those for education heterogeneity again follow the expected allocation of "competence."

Previous studies (e.g., Gugerty and Miguel (in press)) indicate the sanctioning technology as the key mechanisms through which ethnic fragmentation affects group functioning. The third panel of Table 14.7 reports data on the fraction of groups that employ a penalty (monetary fine or suspension) in case of missed contributions and in the case of absenteeism and other irregular behavior. The average number of times in which the given punishment was applied in the past year is also reported. In the full sample, the percentage of groups imposing a penalty for missed contributions is 38%, and that for irregular behavior is 47%. When these statistics are computed separately for "high" and "low" heterogeneity groups, we find that only 14% of the ethnically heterogeneous groups penalize missed contributions, while 67% of the homogeneous ones do. Wealth inequality works in the same direction, though the discrepancy is somewhat smaller. As for education heterogeneity, the pattern is reversed but we have already seen that this index seems to capture skill complementarities more than "conflict." From the number of times in which the penalty is applied, it seems that when ethnically fragmented groups do envisage a penalty, they apply it more often than others (though this may be due to a higher *need* for punishment due to increased tension, as opposed to greater effectiveness).[11] Sanctions for absenteeism and irregular behavior seem more or less equally likely and uniformly applied between high and low heterogeneity groups, suggesting that the effect of fragmentation may be closely related to control over economic resources.

Finally, the last panel of Table 14.7 explores whether there is a relationship between the criteria for recruitment and the composition of the group. For example, if new members are chosen on the basis of their ability we may expect groups to be more heterogenous than if they are chosen because they are "friends" of other members. In the aggregate, group leaders say that the single most important criterion to select new members is "commitment" (50% of the groups), indicating the degree of uncertainty faced in their everyday work. The remaining criteria are ability (22%), need of the member (22%), and only in rare cases friendship (5.6%). Interestingly, no clear relationship emerges between the recruitment criterion and the heterogeneity of the group, which may be due to the limited importance of the "friendship" factor in determining who joins. When individual members were interviewed about the main reason for joining the group, only 6% said that they had friends in the group. All this is comforting because it is consistent with the interpretation that the causal link goes from heterogeneity to decision making and group performance, and not the opposite. In fact, if group composition were the result of a "biased" decision-making processes, we should expect the method of recruitment to be correlated with the degree of heterogeneity, which from Table 14.7 is not.

14.5   Conclusions

Overall, the empirical evidence in this chapter suggests that self-help groups are an important source of income for certain categories of people, e.g., women. Individual earnings within the group seem to increase with age more than with job experience (as proxied by the number of years spent in the group), and are negatively correlated with the time spent in the current place of residence. This probably reflects the precarious living conditions of the slums, which induce most skilled people to leave if they have the opportunity to do so. Production groups also serve an insurance function by giving access to informal credit: 64% of the respondents borrow from the group or from individual members in case of need. An important channel to gain access to such loans seems to be the ability to speak the same language as the chairperson, leading to a probability increase of 20–25 percentage points at the mean. Group composition affects both the extent to which borrowing can be carried out within the group, and the organization of production in terms of division of labor, compensation schemes, and sanctioning technology. The data at hand do not allow to estimate these effects precisely, nor do they give insights into how groups get to be more or less heterogeneous. However, they seem to suggest that fragmented groups may be limited in their choices by the need to curb the higher potential for conflict within the group. To the extent that the resulting choices (lower access to group loans, simpler production and compensation schemes, lower ability to sanction) are suboptimal from an efficiency point of view, the case for understanding the roots of social cohesion and "social capital" within these groups is strengthened.

Appendix

Table 14A.1 Summary statistics

Variable	Number of observations	Mean	SD
Age	303	31.09	11.66
Age^2	303	1101.98	939.98
Avg wealth of group members (Ksh)	303	7367.46	5675.09
Borrow	302	0.64	0.48
Chair's language	302	0.06	0.22
Dominant language	302	0.74	0.44
Education 1–8	302	0.48	0.50
Education Form 1–4	302	0.39	0.49
Education Advanced	302	0.03	0.16
Education fragmentation	303	0.63	0.11
Ethnic fragmentation	303	0.35	0.27
Female	303	0.50	0.50
Gini income from group	303	0.22	0.15
Gini wealth	303	0.38	0.13
Group profits per capita (Ksh)	280	3271.96	7367.66
Hourly earnings from group (Ksh), ln	302	2.50	1.06
Income before group (Ksh), ln	300	4.32	3.86
Kamba	302	0.36	0.48
Kikuyu	302	0.38	0.48
Luo	302	0.14	0.35
Married	303	0.43	0.50
Own house	303	0.26	0.44
Wealth (Ksh)	302	7379.14	19221.42
# years in group	303	3.14	3.37
# years in group^2	303	21.19	45.65
# years resident	303	11.64	7.69
% of total income coming from group	300	76.43	37.55

Acknowledgments

I wish to thank an anonymous referee, Jean-Marie Baland, Abigail Barr, and participants at the 2000 Conference on "The role of micro-institutions in economic development" in Milan and at the 2002 CSAE Conference in Oxford for useful comments and suggestions. I also thank Paolo Ghia, Ignatius Mayero, Peter Warui, Fabrizio Floris, and the staff of WAC-Dandora and of ICS Africa for invaluable help during the fieldwork. Luca Opromolla provided excellent research assistance. Financial support from Centro Studi "Luca d'Agliano" and from The Pew Charitable Trusts is gratefully acknowledged. The usual disclaimer applies.

Notes

1 In the context of developing countries, see e.g., the work of Narayan and Pritchett (1999), Grootaert (1999), and Isham (2002).

2 See the surveys by Besley (1995) on ROSCAs and other nonmarket institutions, and by Ghatak and Guinnane (1999) on group lending.
3 Technically, when some form of legal rights exists these may not be viewed as "squatter communities," but in this chapter that term will be used interchangeably with "informal settlements" and "slum."
4 The term "*jua kali*" was originally created to indicate people who work "under the sun" with no permanent structure, but has extended to represent the whole informal small business sector.
5 The criterion was to have some degree of diversification among the groups in terms of size, productive activities, and location, as well as age and gender of their members.
6 The average prices for these items on the second hand market at the time of the interview were as follows (in Ksh). Byke: 4000, car: 180 000, electric cooker: 4800, gas cooker: 4500, stove: 400, charcoal burner: 200, sofa: 4500, bed: 2000, mattress: 1100, mat: 350, radio: 700, TV: 4000, camera: 2000, wall clock: 900.
7 This is not too surprising, given the heterogeneity of the sample in terms of age: for young respondents low pre-group earnings may simply reflect an out-of-the-labor-force status during school years, while for older ones the same is not true.
8 The variable "Chair's language" is an interaction between a dummy equal to 1 if the language of the respondent is the same as that of the chariperson, and a dummy equal to 1 if the respondent declares that "leaders decide" in the group. Using only the former dummy also yielded an insignificant result.
9 The cofficient on Advanced education cannot be estimated precisely due to the small incidence in the sample (only 2.6%) of respondents with a technical or college degree.
10 The different "categories" in the residential fragmentation index were the sub-areas where members resided within each slum. For example, Korogocho was divided into Grogon, Gitadhuru, Highridge, Nyayo, Kisumu Ndogo, Ngomougo, and so on for the other settlements.
11 The apparent inconsistency between the presence of a penalty for missed contributions and the number of times in which it is applied may be due to measurement error, but it may also indicate that, even when in place, sanctions in heterogeneous groups do not deter deviations, while in homogenous ones they serve a pre-emptive role.

References

Abraham, A., Baland, J.-M., and Platteau, J.-P. (1998). "Groupes Informels de Solidarité dans un Bidonville du Tiers-Monde: Le Cas de Kibera, Nairobi (Kenya)." *Non-Marchand* 2: 29–52.

Alder, G. *et al.* (1993). *Nairobi's Informal Settlements: An Inventory*. Nairobi: Matrix Development Consultants.

Alesina, A. and La Ferrara, E. (2000). "Participation in Heterogeneous Communities." *Quarterly Journal of Economics* 115: 847–904.

Barr, A. and Oduro, A. (2002). "Ethnic Fractionalization in an African Labour Market." *Journal of Development Economics* 68: 355–79.

Besley, T. (1995). "Nonmarket Institutions for Credit and Risk Sharing in Low-Income Countries." *Journal of Economic Perspectives* 9: 115–27.

Collier, P. and Garg, A. (1999). "On Kin Groups and Wages in the Ghanaian Labour Market." *Oxford Bulletin of Economics and Statistics* 61: 133–51.

Ghatak, M. and Guinnane, T. (1999). "The Economics of Lending with Joint Liability: Theory and Practice." *Journal of Development Economics* 60: 195–228.

Grootaert, C. (1999). "Social Capital, Household Welfare, and Poverty in Indonesia." Local Level Institutions, Working Paper No. 6, Washington, DC: The World Bank.

Gugerty, M.K. and Miguel, E. (2000). "Community Participation and Social Sanctions in Kenyan Schools," mimeo. University of California at Berkeley, CA.

——(in press). "Ethnic Diversity, Social Sanctions, and Public Goods in Kenya," *Journal of Public Economics*. Available online 6 November 2004 by Edward Miguel and Mary Kay Gugerty.

Isham, J. (2002). "The Effect of Social Capital on Fertilizer Adoption: Evidence from Rural Tanzania." *Journal of African Economies* 11: 39–60.

Karlan, D.S. (2001). "Social Capital and Group Banking," mimeo. Massachuessett Institute of Technology at Cambridge, MA.

Khwaja, A. (2000). "Can Good Projects Succeed in Bad Communities? Collective Action in the Himalayas," mimeo. Harvard University at Cambridge, MA.

La Ferrara, E. (2002). "Inequality and Group Participation: Theory and Evidence from Rural Tanzania." *Journal of Public Economics* 85: 235–73.

Miguel, E. (2000). "Ethnic Diversity and School Funding in Kenya," mimeo. University of California at Berkeley, CA.

Narayan, D. and Pritchett, L. (1999). "Cents and Sociability: Household Income and Social Capital in Rural Tanzania." *Economic Development and Cultural Change* 47: 871–97.

Ng'ethe, N. and Ndua, G. (1985). "*Jua Kali*." Research Report No. 55, Undugu Society of Kenya.

Otieno Okumu, C. (1999). "Promotion of Micro Enterprise Activities among the Youth as a Practical Alternative to Formal Employment: Focusing on Youths in Korogocho Slums, Nairobi," mimeo. Catholic University of Eastern Africa.

Putnam, R. (1993). *Making Democracy Work: Civic Traditions in Modern Italy*. Princeton, NJ: Princeton University Press.

Wydick, B. (1999). "Can Social Cohesion Be Harnessed to Repair Market Failures? Evidence from Group Lending in Guatemala." *The Economic Journal* 109: 463–75.

15 Community ties and land inheritance in the context of rising outside opportunities

Evidence from the Peruvian Highlands

Tatiana Goetghebuer and
Jean-Philippe Platteau

15.1 Introduction

In lineage-based societies, a social norm commands that every household, by virtue of being a member of the community, be granted access to the amount of productive resources, land in particular, that it requires to meet basic needs (see, e.g., Cohen 1980, p. 353). Here is a "general right" that is "an inseparable element of the status as member of the tribe," and can only be lost through formal expulsion from the group (Boserup 1965, p. 79). The relationship between such right of access and social identity is actually reciprocal. On the one hand, group membership and identity are the basis upon which land entitlements are defined and, on the other hand, access to a share of the corporate assets of the group or community serves to validate or confirm membership in the group (Berry 1984, p. 91). Paraphrasing Karl Marx, Shlomo Avineri writes that tribal property "appears as a relationship signifying social identification" (Avineri 1968, p. 112). The fact of the matter is that rights and obligations associated with land form "a guarantee of relational existence" in the sense that land is "the basis of social networks that enable people to access a whole series of material and nonmaterial resources" (Ng'weno 2001, p. 118).

The land system in tribal communities is characterized by multiple tenure, meaning the coexistence of different tenure rights corresponding to various modes of exploiting the land. In particular, individualized use rights may exist side by side with common property resources, and the extent of individualization of private tenure rights also may vary between different portions of the village resource base. The mix of land rights depends on the balance of benefits and costs of land tenure individualization. More precisely, we expect a common property regime to prevail when or where partition of the village natural resources would involve large transaction costs (because these resources are highly spread out, and/or of a low quality or value), or large opportunity costs in terms of lost scale economies and/or foregone insurance benefits. Insurance benefits arise whenever the returns to a common property resource (CPR) are highly variable across time and space. In such circumstances, a common property system offering access to a large area within which rights-holding users (think of herders or fishermen) can freely move appears as a desirable arrangement from a risk-reducing perspective (Dasgupta 1993, pp. 288–9; Baland and Platteau 1998; Platteau 2000, chap. 3; Breusers 2001).

At the other extreme, fertile or well located lands, such as the intensively cultivated garden lands situated near rural dwellings, tend to be subject to a comparatively high degree of tenure individualization. This implies that rights over these parcels tend to be granted more or less permanently to individual member households, and these rights can be bequeathed to children. The more the balance of land allocation shifts in favor of these privately held portions, mainly as a result of growing population pressure and the resulting intensification of agricultural activities, the more the villagers come to depend on the family rather than the community for securing their access to land. This is part of the process of land tenure individualization that is under way in many rural economies subject to the forces of population growth and market integration (e.g., Bruce and Migot-Adholla 1994; Platteau 2000, chap. 4). However, the role of the community does not vanish altogether, if only because participation in communal activities may remain a prerequisite for enjoying access to collectively provided services that are critical for agriculture.

A question that naturally springs to mind is how lands placed under the responsibility of family heads are being allocated among members and, more particularly, how they are divided among children upon or before the parents' death. This question has two components. First, are daughters entitled to inherit their parents' land in the same way as sons are and, second, are the sons (or the daughters) entitled to inherit an equal share of the land earmarked for them? Daughters' rights actually vary from one region to another: thus, while daughters have no right to inherit the father's land in all the patrilineal systems of Sub-Saharan Africa (even in societies influenced by Islam, the right of a daughter to inherit one-half the share of a brother, as it is prescribed in the Koran, is rarely applied in practice), their rights are usually identical to those of their brothers in Andean societies. As for the second aspect, the division that prevails in many lineage-based, patrilineal societies is based on the principle of equal sharing among all the sons subject to the following proviso: if a son takes special care of his parents in their old age – often, but not always, the eldest or the youngest son – he is entitled to a larger share than his brothers (Platteau and Baland 2001).

An interesting issue is whether the above principles are resistant to deep changes in the social and economic environment, such as the emergence of new outside employment opportunities involving the permanent migration of some family members. What economic theory predicts here is not clear. For one thing, if migrants have benefited from more schooling and education, and/or if their migration experience has been successful, one could expect parents to lower or cancel their share in the family land to the benefit of members who have stayed on this land. But, for another thing, migrants can render useful services to their relatives remaining in the native village (whether through remittances or through in-kind services provided in the resident city), or they (or their children) may be confronted with the risk of losing their urban employment. These two considerations could actually justify that migrants continue to be put on an equal footing with their brothers in matters of land inheritance, which implies that they maintain ties with the native community. Which of these two sets of factors predominates is an empirical question that cannot be sorted out without recourse to detailed micro-evidence from the field.

In this chapter, we examine inheritance patterns in Andean communities of the Peruvian Highlands, to see how they evolve under new circumstances shaped by the expansion of education possibilities and the opening of new employment opportunities outside the agricultural sector. Our sample consists of three Indian communities belonging to the district of Sicuani, a city located in Cusco department in the southern part of the Peru.

The outline of the chapter is as follows. Section 15.2 gives general information about the three sample communities, the sample respondents, and the structure of the data collected. Section 15.3 is devoted to reviewing the most salient literature on the subject of choice of bequest rules and highlighting the theoretical underpinnings from which a number of testable hypotheses can be derived. In Section 15.4, key descriptive statistics are then presented about land inheritance sharing practices and various possible determining factors. Moreover, the respondents' perceptions regarding these determining factors are examined. In Section 15.5, econometric evidence is reported with a view to assessing the separate impact of various factors, including education and migration, on the mode (egalitarian or discriminatory) of bequeathing land. Section 15.6 concludes.

15.2 Sample, data, and methodology

15.2.1 The sampled communities

Our inquiry has taken place in three communities belonging to the region of Cusco, and located at various ecological levels and at varying distances from Sicuani, a small town of about 28 000 inhabitants situated on the railway line between the cities of Cusco and Puno. These two factors are strongly correlated. Within each of the three ecological levels or measures of distance from the nearest urban agglomeration, our choice of sampled communities was not random. As a matter of fact, they were selected because a local non-governmental Organization (Intermediate Technology Development Group – ITDG) had carried out projects of irrigation development in them, thereby providing us with a convenient way to enter into contact with the local population and to establish the necessary degree of trust. We are, of course, aware that such a non-random (stratified) sampling procedure is liable to cause selection biases. Nonetheless, since Indian communities, especially the more distant ones, are very hard to penetrate for outside researchers, we could not think of an alternative to using ITDG's entry points in pre-determined locations. Even then, getting acquainted with the people enough to extract reliable information from them proved to be a slow and exacting experience, particularly in the most distant community.[1]

The first community, called Sunchochumo (henceforth labeled Suncho), comprises around 70 families and is situated at an altitude (between 3530 and 3700 meters) corresponding to the first ecological level ("Piso de valle," at the bottom of the valley). It is rather close to Sicuani since it takes only 20 minutes by bus and between 10 and 30 minutes' walk to connect the two places. Note that the exact connecting time depends on the location of the houses, which are highly scattered.

The second community, named Pumaorcco (henceforth labeled Puma), comprises about 120 families and is situated at an intermediate altitude of between 3820 and 4350 meters (in the so-called "Piso de ladera"). It is located further away from Sicuani since it takes 45 minutes by bus (but the bus service is rather irregular) or about 2 hours by foot to shuttle between Puma and Sicuani. The third community, named Pataccalasaya (henceforth labeled Pata), has about 130 families and is situated on the third ecological level ("Piso de Puna") at an altitude of 4000–4780 meters. To reach Sicuani, an inhabitant of Pata has to walk between 1 hour and 4 hours and 30 minutes till Puma, and thereafter take the bus (45 minutes) to Sicuani.

As expected, the average land area available per family (whether cultivable or not) increases while going from the lowest to the highest ecological level: 2.70 hectares in Suncho, 8.50 hectares in Puma, and 27.31 hectares in Pata. This perceptible increase in average land area mirrors the fall in average land quality, and therefore productivity, when moving from lower to higher altitudes. However, that land is highly sloped in the intermediate community of Puma whereas fields are relatively flat in the comparatively low-lying and high-lying communities of Suncho and Pata. In Pata, moreover, the raising of alpaca on vast natural pastures allows inhabitants to make up for the disadvantage of their low fertility lands.

The sampled communities, moreover, differ in terms of educational achievements and incidence of (permanent) migration: average education levels and rates of permanent migration, two correlated phenomena, are the highest in Suncho and the lowest in Pata (see infra Table 15.1), thus determining a monotonic inverse relationship between these two variables and remoteness of location. The foregoing picture confirms the view that disadvantages tend to be compounded in remote locations: education and migration levels are low and, in so far as group effects exist, these have negative spillover effects on all member households (remote communities tend to have a more traditional outlook and to be more resistant to change); costs of communication are high and all sorts of transaction costs that narrowly depend on them impede trade expansion and market integration. Since there are significant inter-family variations in inheritance practices, it will be interesting to see whether we observe different patterns of land inheritance in Suncho (or Puma) compared to Pata (or Puma), after duly controlling for relevant household characteristics.

The important role of the community is also reflected at the political level. As is typical in many Andean communities, assuming administrative and political responsibilities (in the so-called "junta directiva") is considered a duty that each member with the appropriate age and status must carry out at least once in his life. A refusal to take up one's turn in the periodic rotation of administrative-political functions is thus deemed equivalent to reneging on one's obligations as a community member.

We need to say a few words about the land tenure regime in the three sampled communities. The first thing to note here is that only two of the three communities still possess communal lands in the form of permanent collective pastures: Suncho, which has a compact land area earmarked for collective grazing, and Pata, which has vast areas of non-cultivable land owing to excessive elevation as well as substantial portions of fallow land. Some parts of the latter community's local territory (known as "tierras de secano," or drylands) are still subject to periodic rotations according to a pattern resembling the open-field system. Lands are individually cultivated during a few years, following which they become fallow and are transformed into collective pastures. These communal pastures are subject to strict rules of access and use, such as the number of animals allowed in per family, the times of the year during which grazing is allowed, etc. All members must abide by these rules lest they should expose themselves to sanctions from their community.

Since theft of animals by outsiders during the night is a high risk, guards are posted near the pastures. While in Suncho these guards rotate every night and all families are expected to take their turn in the sequence, in Pata guards are appointed for longer periods by the community leaders and they are usually chosen among the poorest or most land-hungry families.

In Peru, village communities are treated as such by the state. Collective, rather than individual titles to land are established by the national land registrar (the "registro publico") when Indian-inhabited areas are concerned. Each community is requested by the state to write down its bylaws where the main internal rules governing relations between members and the land (the members' rights and obligations in land matters), as well as relations amongst members themselves, are reported in a clear manner. When land was abundant, the rules crafted by the community comprised provisions regarding periodic redistribution of communal lands among members families (according to needs) so as to make them available for individual cultivation after the fallow period was over. Nowadays, land has become scarce due to population pressure and, as a result, families tend to enjoy permanent rights, at least over the most valuable lands (the irrigated lands, known as the "tierras de riego").

As far as the less valuable drylands are concerned, once the fallow period is over, families are allowed to return to the same parcels as those cultivated before the "opening of the fields" to communal grazing uses. This illustrates the sort of institutional evolutionary trajectory sketched by Ester Boserup (1965). In Suncho and Puma, the process of individualization of land tenure is even more advanced. Most of the land parcels are under the continuous control of the same family even during the fallow period. Such a clear move towards individualization has been propelled by coordination failures that caused animals belonging to one family to encroach upon the land of a neighbor whose harvest was not yet completed. Parallel to this institutional evolution, animals have increasingly been put on a stake. In permanent collective pastures, on the other hand, animals freely graze under the supervision of shepherds during the daytime while, during the night, they are concentrated in more compact flocks to make their guarding easier.

Peasants are officially entitled (but not compelled) to write down a document in which they bequeath parcels over which they hold permanent rights. Such a document must then be inscribed on the community's "book of deeds" ("libro de actas") to have full validity. On the other hand, the national law provides that lands belonging to peasant communities may not be disposed of through sale or mortgaging. Only usufruct rights may be transmitted or acquired. In practice, however, sale and other transactions do occur, and peasants often go to a notary in town to have them sanctioned by an appropriate contract (or testament). Although such deeds have no legal validity, peasants believe that they give them adequate guarantee in case their rights are being disputed by others. Their belief is strongly sustained by the fact that communal authorities tend to attach a high value to documents certified by notaries. It is therefore evident that communities increasingly tend to accept sale transactions, but only to the extent that they take place among community members. In other words, sales of land to outsiders are not considered legitimate and, as a consequence, they may be actively opposed even when they are supported by a sale deed signed before a notary.[2] This confirms the view that formalized rules and procedures work only to the extent that they crystallize existing informal rules and practices (North 1990).

Finally, even though rights over irrigated lands are strongly individualized, peasants remain dependent upon the community for the irrigation of these valuable parcels. Indeed, as is typical in mountainous areas (Hayami and Kikuchi 1981), irrigation is collectively provided through a communal infrastructure that needs to be continuously maintained, and water is to be shared in an orderly and equitable manner. Rules are therefore laid down that (i) prescribe participation of all irrigators (in proportion to their irrigated land area) in collective maintenance works organized under the traditional form of local "faenas," and (ii) specify a sequence of turns to regulate the irrigators' access to the available water. When these rules are violated, punishment is meted out to the breakers in a gradual fashion. After repeated lapses, an irrigator is deprived of access to the water system.

15.2.2   *The sampled households and data structure*

Since we are interested in inheritance practices, our data gathering strategy consisted of collecting family stories (FS) by interviewing couples with children. Husband and wife respondents were queried about the inheritance patterns followed by their own respective parents, as well as the patterns they have adopted or intend to adopt *vis-à-vis* their own children. Such a strategy can therefore be expected to produce information about a maximum of three FS per parental couple interviewed, or 1.5 FS per person interviewed. These ratios are maximum values because parents may be too young to have carefully thought over how to share the land amongst their children (they may not even know how many children they will eventually have) and they might still enlarge their landholding by purchasing or inheriting additional parcels. Also note that because spouses belonging to different age categories were interviewed, our information spans more than two generations. Our FS actually concern as many as four successive generations.

The collection of objective information about the exact way family land has been divided among the children, as well as about the timing of land bequests, is obviously a time-consuming process. In order to restrict the time of interview to manageable limits, we decided to require such data regarding only the children of the sample parental couple (or the sample single parent). In other words, the complete details about the total amount of land in the hands of the parents before division takes place, and the manner in which it has been, or is planned to be, divided among the children (including the timing of land transfers), have been obtained only for the sample couples considered as parents. As far as the ascendants are concerned, we limited our query to the following: (i) the exact amount of land received by a sample spouse from his or her parents; and (ii) essentially qualitative information about the land portions inherited by his or her siblings, so we know whether a particular child has been positively or negatively discriminated, or whether all children have been treated equally.[3]

Overall, 80 households were visited, implying that 80 three-part question-naires were administered. This coverage corresponds to 78 men and 80 women (158 individuals), as 2 households were female-headed. Information could thereby be gathered on a total of 230 FS: 78 stories about the husbands' parental family, 80 stories about the wives' parental family, and 72 stories about the children of the spouses. The number of FS per respondent thus turns out to be remarkably close to 1.5. Since 12 FS are actually redundant (in 12 instances, the same FS was told by 2 different persons, a father and a son, or 2 siblings), the real sample size is 218 FS.

Moreover, removing the FS in which a unique child is involved (some siblings may have died before being married, or before having given birth to children) so that the issue of equal or unequal inheritance does not arise, we are left with a reduced sample of 208 units.

On the other hand, there are two different kinds of stories in our sample: those for which the inheritance process has been completed, typically because the parents are dead, and those for which it is still ongoing or has not started yet. The latter possibility is especially likely to occur with respect to the children of the sample respondents, but it also happens that the respondents' parents have not completely distributed their land to their children, usually because they are alive and retain some land for themselves. Out of 218 FS, 84 (38.5%) stories report completed inheritance processes (either the 2 parents are dead, or at least one of them is still alive but they have already bequeathed all their land property), while 134 stories (61.5%) report partially completed inheritance processes or bequest plans.

Decomposition of the full sample (except for the redundant cases) by community is shown in Table 15.1.

The figures displayed in rows (2) and (3) are not strictly comparable since they do not measure the same thing. Bearing in mind that each living couple goes through three different FS, we obtain the maximum number of FS for a given community (see row (4)). These figures, however, grossly exaggerate the set of FS available because the existence of consanguineous ties between many resident families actually makes many FS redundant. We tried hard to avoid visiting related

Table 15.1 Sample sizes of family stories (FS) decomposed by community

Name of the community		Suncho	Puma	Pata	Total
# of visited households	(1)	26	30	24	80
# of sample FS[a]	(2)	67	83	68	218
		(65)	(80)	(63)	(208)
Population of households	(3)	70	120	130	320
Maximum # of FS	$(4) = (3) \times 3$	210	360	390	960
Relative sample size	$(5) = (2)/(4)$	31.9%	23.1%	17.4%	22.7%
# of sample FS referring to the community	(6)	53	74	63	190
# of sample FS referring to a different community	(7)	14	9	5	28
# of sample FS per household in the community	$(8) = (6)/(3)$	75.7%	61.7%	48.5%	59.4%

Note

a Between brackets are indicated the corresponding figures once FS with a unique child have been removed.

families, especially in Suncho where we are confident of having reached almost all existing FS. The percentages shown in row (5) of Table 15.1 are therefore clear underestimates of the extent of our coverage of each community. Yet, on the assumption that the incidence of family ties between households does not significantly differ across the three communities (so that the extent of underestimation can be thought to be roughly similar from community to community), the ordinal ranking emerging from row (5) is meaningful and the coverage of FS appears to be better in Suncho than in Puma and, a fortiori, Pata. This is confirmed by row (8), which shows the ratio of the number of sample FS referring to a community to the total number of households residing in that community.

The monotonic relationship between the degree of remoteness of a community and the incidence of coverage is not coincidental. The two more distant communities have comparatively scattered populations, as a result of which respondents were more difficult to reach, a difficulty compounded by bad weather conditions in Pata. Moreover, distance has a psychological dimension as well, and this dimension is reflected in the fact that people are less easy to approach in more remote communities (particularly Pata), which are also less educated (see earlier). Consequently, the more remote the community the longer the time spent per interview.

Measuring the extent of our coverage is further complicated by the fact that not all FS recorded in a given community actually refer to family events that have occurred there. Indeed, when reported by a spouse originating from another community who tells the story of his or her parental family, events concern a different community from the one where information has been collected. From row (6) in Table 15.1, it is apparent that we have available 53 FS referring to events that happened in Suncho, whereas the corresponding numbers for Puma and Pata are 74 and 63, respectively. The FS referring to another community will

Table 15.2 Sample size of individuals concerned by the FS collected, as per community

Name of the community	Suncho	Puma	Pata	Total
# of individuals concerned by sample FS	326	383	302	1011

Table 15.3 The age structure of sample respondents

Age category of respondents	Percentages
≥70 years old	8.16
≥50 and <70	26.53
≥35 and <50	35.37
<35	29.94
Total	100.00

nevertheless be retained in our sample for all relevant analyses because they do not turn out to influence the results.

Inquiring about a particular FS implied that we collected information regarding all the children involved in the bequest. Depending upon the generation considered, the beneficiaries of land bequests are either siblings or children of the sample respondents. The total number of individuals thus concerned by the FS collected works out to 1011 (after removing redundant cases). Their breakup by community is shown in Table 15.2.

That the collected FS span a long time period stretching over (at least) four successive generations is evident from the breakup of the sample respondents by age category as presented in Table 15.3. What emerges from these figures is that the sample respondents are divided more or less equally between three categories: older than 50 years, between 35 and 50 years, and below 35 years. Moreover, the presence of respondents older than 70 years guarantees that inheritance rules dating back to almost a century have been reported in our sample data.

From our database, we have constructed two separate files, one which treats the individual as the unit of analysis, and the other which treats the family (concerned by a FS) as the unit of analysis. In the latter case, we have used individual data to construct indicators pertaining to the family, e.g., the average number of years of schooling, the proportion of migrants, whether land has been divided equally among all children or not, etc.

15.3   Theoretical underpinnings and hypotheses

There is not much economic literature dealing with the problem of choice of inheritance rules. Yet the available contributions give an adequate idea of the sort of factors that economists think influence such a choice. Two main questions arise in this context. First, there is the question as to whether a fixed inheritance rule is preferable to discretion. Second, in the event that the former solution is deemed preferable, should one favor equal sharing or some form of asymmetrical division of the parents' assets, which includes the possibility of exclusive or impartible inheritance such as primogeniture or ultimogeniture?

To the former question, Baker and Miceli (2002) answer in terms of the following tradeoff between rules and discretion. On the one hand, a fixed inheritance rule prevents wasteful competition (or rent-seeking) among the potential heirs but, on the other hand, potential gains are surrendered if talents in using the land are not equally distributed between children and information about those talents takes time to be revealed to the testator. The prediction is that discretion leading to the granting of land to the best-qualified child will be observed when rent-seeking is not expected to be severe and ability is an important factor for efficient land use. This assumes that inheritance shares are chosen to maximize the productive potential of the family (which, in turn, implies that each family freely decides which practice to follow, as no social norm prevails), and that no effective land market exists to allow reallocation of the family land as a function of the children's relative skills. The existence of a perfect land market obviously renders the inheritance rule irrelevant.

The latter question assumes that a fixed inheritance rule prevails. What are then the factors underlying the choice between preferential and equal shares? The standard explanation for exclusive inheritance, dating back to Adam Smith, is the presence of scale economies and any belief that land property is indivisible in some physical or symbolic sense (Gagan 1976; Alston and Schapiro 1984; Platteau and Baland 2001; Baker and Miceli 2002). The latter includes, on the one hand, considerations of farm size viability in the context of acute land scarcity and, on the other hand, the indivisibility of authority and the desire to perpetuate the family name, or the power and prestige associated with compact landed property. This sort of considerations can thus account for the historical dominance of primogeniture among European aristocracies and in the large plantations of the southern United States. Notice that, in the presence of scale economies, rich families are more likely to adopt unigeniture than poorer families because the excluded children are better able to find alternative employment and income opportunities (Bergstrom 1994), or because the children who are deprived of land can be more easily compensated through other forms of transfers made by the parents or by the privileged child (Platteau and Baland 2001, pp. 46–8).

In the same line, Chu (1991) argues, with special reference to China and Japan, that parents may choose to concentrate their bequest on one son so as to maximize his chances of becoming rich and reaching a great position from which he will then be able to help the rest of the family. The prediction here is that primogeniture or, at least, an unequal division of bequests, is more likely to be observed if capital markets are imperfect and income mobility is rigid.

Another line of thinking is developed by Bernheim *et al.* (1985) who view bequests as "a medium of exchange" (p. 1057), or as a means of payment used by parents for services rendered by children: "parents reward more attentive children with family heirlooms," as they are willing to forego other forms of consumption or, alternatively, to hold their wealth in bequeathable rather than annuitized forms (pp. 1046–7). A central assumption underlying their analysis is that testators, although altruistic, use bequests to influence the behavior of potential beneficiaries so that they adopt appropriate actions (attention levels). The influence is strategic: in the words of the authors, "the testator *intentionally* manipulates the behavior of his beneficiaries through his choice of a rule for dividing his estate" (p. 1048), and it is when he can successfully threaten to disinherit a potential beneficiary that he extracts the full surplus generated through interaction with him (p. 1057). Of course, in order that the prospect of inheritance can induce children to take better care of their parents, there must be more than one potential beneficiary to whom the testator can credibly plan to leave the bulk of his estate (he cannot, e.g., credibly threaten universal disinheritance).

The above model makes no prediction that bequests should be equal across children, except if beneficiaries are identical (p. 1071). As a matter of fact, the optimal division of the parental land property should vary with the characteristics of the children as well as with the attitudes and preferences of the parents. In this respect, the "strategic exchange" model differs from the Becker-type altruistic model in which perfectly altruistic parents maximize a utility function in which the utility of their children also enters, but they engage in no strategic behavior (Becker 1974, 1981). The implication of the latter type of model is, indeed, that "bequests should be used to equate as closely as possible the utilities of various offspring" (Bernheim *et al.* 1985, pp. 1071–2).

Some recent works have allowed for the possibility of inter vivos transfers to children in addition to bequests (McGarry 1999; Bernheim and Severinov 2003). Treating the two sorts of transfers as part of the same decision-making process, they yield different predictions about the expected patterns of giving. While inter vivos transfers are made in response to liquidity constraints and therefore depend on current income, bequests are based on permanent incomes of the children. Such models aim at explaining the empirical finding (based on US data) that bequests (including the division of estates) tend to be divided equally among children, in contrast to inter vivos transfers which are typically unequal and tend to go disproportionately to less well-off children.

Close in spirit to the paper by Bernheim *et al.* (1985), but allowing for inter vivos transfers in addition to bequests, and centering explicitly on the issue of land division, is the recent work of Platteau *et al.* (2004). In their model, choice of the rule to divide land arises in an environment where outside economic opportunities are available which drive young members of rural households to opt for permanent migration. The authors assume an (imperfectly) altruistic parent who cares directly about attention supplied by children. The parent has two sons, one who has chosen to stay in his native village and the other who has migrated (these decisions are exogenous). The employment and income prospects of the migrant child are uncertain, and he is therefore potentially interested in maintaining contact with the parent (and the native community) so that his right of access to the family land is not forfeited. Maintaining contact is achieved by sending remittances or providing services to the parent.

The parent decides how to allocate the land between the two sons, both *pre mortem* and *post mortem*. The staying son receives *pre mortem* a certain share of the family land while the parent keeps the rest for his own use. Out of this land kept by the parent, a portion can be transferred *pre mortem* to the migrant child, but only if the latter loses his outside employment and returns to the native village after having maintained the necessary contact with the parent. Benefiting from the *post mortem* share of the parent's land is also conditioned on the persistence of this contact. The *pre mortem* and *post mortem* shares accruing to both sons are endogenously determined in this two-agent model where the parent and the migrant child interact strategically. (This is in contrast to the model of Bernheim *et al.* where inter vivos gifts are ruled out.) Note that, by fixing the *pre mortem* share to which the migrant son is entitled in the event of employment loss, the parent sets the value of the fall-back option available to this son.

An important implication of the way the problem of choice of the bequest rule has been modeled by Platteau *et al.* is that the decision to opt for unequal sharing of family land property is ultimately made by the migrant son and not by the parent. Because the migrant thinks it is not worthwhile to keep a fall-back option in his native community, he deliberately chooses to sever his links with it and thereby lose his land bequest. Exclusive inheritance thus appears as the outcome of self-renunciation by the potential beneficiary rather than of discriminatory behavior on the part of the parent.

This said, the model also explains why unequal land bequests come into being even though the migrant son chooses to maintain contact with the parent and the community. The parent chooses the share accruing to the migrant son with a view to inducing him to render valuable services. If circumstances are such that this son is eager to maintain contact with the parent, the incentive share to be offered to him will be lower. For instance, a higher probability of losing the outside employment will lead the parent to lower the share of the migrant son relative to that of the staying son. The same effect is predicted if the migrant son attaches a higher value to his *post mortem* share of inheritance. On the other hand, greater benefits accruing to the parent (and the other son) from the presence in town of a migrant son have the opposite effect. Furthermore, and this is perhaps the most valuable insight provided by the model, increased land scarcity also requires the parent to supply a larger share of the land bequest to the migrant son compared to that given to the other son, thereby leading to more equal land bequests (assuming that the share of the staying son may not fall below that of a migrant son). Indeed, as the land base is smaller, the migrant son needs to receive a larger share of it in order to be induced to render services to his parents.

In the light of the earlier survey of the most salient literature on the subject, the following hypotheses can be put forward for testing in the subsequent sections:

Hypothesis 1   based on the theory proposed by Platteau *et al.* (2004), unequal land bequests are more likely to be observed when a child has migrated.

Hypothesis 2   based on the model by Bernheim *et al.* (1985), unequal land bequests are also more likely to prevail when some children are devoting more attention and taking better care of their parents.

Hypothesis 3   based on Platteau *et al.* again, a smaller amount of bequeathable land should result in more equal land bequests, at least if there are migrants among the children. Yet, if the family land holding is so low that a migrant child may not be interested in keeping access to it (however high the share earmarked for him/her) one would expect the opposite result, namely that inheritance is more unequal within poor families with migrants. A non linear effect in the above model is thus responsible for the reversal of the perdicted outcome.

Hypothesis 4   in the presence of indivisibilities, family size should have the effect of increasing inequality of land bequests because parents are willing to avoid excessive fragmentation of their family property, and/or because some children lose interest in their right of inheritance when their share becomes too small.

Note that, inasmuch as daughters often leave their native village to join their husband upon marriage, they are treated as migrants within the analytical framework proposed by Platteau *et al.* The risk which they are incurring and against which they may wish to insure is not the loss of an employment but a failure in their marriage. The implication is, therefore:

Hypothesis 5   once migration is properly controlled, daughters should not appear to be treated differently from their brothers in matters of land inheritance.

The independent effect of wealth, i.e., the effect of wealth regardless of whether there are migrants or not in the family, is difficult to predict because there are potentially several forces pushing into opposite directions. It is thus possible that considerations of farm size viability play a more important role among poor households which have little land available, than among richer households which can better afford to grant equal shares of family land to all their children. Yet, on the other hand, land bequests are expected to be more unequal among richer households which possess several types of assets to be bequeathed to their children or whose children can more easily find alternative employment opportunities outside agriculture. Some children may thus receive their bequests under the form of land while others are compensated by receiving other types of assets, such as animals. In addition, more educated children may receive less land or no land because their parents have financed their education expenditures.

Finally, we are interested in knowing whether community-specific cultural factors, such as social norms, have an independent influence on inheritance patterns. In keeping with the above framework of an economic approach to inheritance practices, we want to test the following hypothesis:

Hypothesis 6   once the possible influence of various elements of the economic environment facing families is controlled, there is no remaining impact associated with communities which are differently located and not exposed in the same manner to urban influence.

15.4   Descriptive statistics and key definitions

To present descriptive statistics summarizing key evidence for the testing of the above hypotheses, we will proceed in four steps. In the first one, evidence about the incidence of various types of migration will be examined. In the second step, we will use detailed figures to form an idea about education levels prevailing in the surveyed areas. These levels will be differentiated according to the migration characteristics of the individuals. Attention will then be turned to various measures of wealth or wealth rankings among the sample households in each community. The relationship between such measures and the migration and education variables will be investigated. Finally, patterns of inheritance will be the focus of the last and most crucial fourth step where different characteristics of inheritance practices will be highlighted and related to migration, education, and wealth variables. The ground will then be laid for a more rigorous econometric treatment of our data in Section 15.5.

15.4.1   Migration

Migration can be either temporary, when a villager works outside the native community for a limited period of time, or more permanent, when the villager has established himself or herself durably in another location. We will consider only the latter type of migration since the former characterizes a great majority of rural households and cannot be presumed to influence inheritance patterns in any significant manner. More permanent migrations can be either to another rural area, or to a town or city, either close or distant. A nearby place is defined as a place which is within walking distance of the native community. Notice that a woman who marries a man of another community and goes to live with him in his own native village is counted as a permanent migrant, typically, to another rural location. Hence the importance of distinguishing migration patterns on the basis of gender.

Given this last clarification, it is not surprising that the proportion of (permanent) migrants among women (45%) is larger than that among men (almost 40%). According to ancient custom a woman is required to live in her husband's community, yet changing circumstances have altered that custom. A couple tends increasingly to settle down in the community where land availability and living conditions are more favorable, which is not necessarily the community of the husband. Bear in mind that, in computing these averages (see Table 15.4), we have removed all the children below the age of 15 on the ground that they have not yet made their choice about migrating or not.

Table 15.5 further shows that, as expected, men and women differ essentially in two respects: women tend to migrate more to nearby rural communities (usually on the occasion of their marriage), and less to distant towns or cities. The other major observation is that as many as three-quarters of the migrants have moved to towns or cities while almost 62% have opted for living and working in rather remote locations.

Table 15.4 Permanent migrants as a proportion of the total sample population, as per community

	Men	Women	Total
Total number of (permanent) migrants	170 (39.5%)	192 (45.1%)	362 (42.3%)
Total number of non migrants (or temporary migrants)	260 (60.5%)	234 (54.9%)	494 (57.7%)
Total number of sample individuals	430 (100.0%)	426 (100.0%)	856 (100.0%)

Table 15.5 Proportions of sample individuals above 15 years who are involved in various types of migrations

Type of migration	Men	Women	Total
To a nearby rural community	15 (8.8%)	43 (22.4%)	58 (16.0%)
To a distant rural community	15 (8.8%)	17 (8.8%)	32 (8.8%)
To a nearby urban location	38 (22.4%)	43 (22.4%)	81 (22.4%)
To a distant urban location	83 (48.8%)	72 (37.5%)	155 (42.8%)
To plantation (distant tropical) areas	19 (11.2%)	17 (8.8%)	36 (10.0%)
Subtotal: rural migration	30 (17.7%)	60 (31.3%)	90 (24.9%)
Subtotal: urban migration	140 (82.3%)	132 (68.7%)	272 (75.1%)
Subtotal: nearby migration	53 (31.2%)	86 (44.8%)	139 (38.4%)
Subtotal: distant migration	117 (68.8%)	106 (55.2%)	223 (61.6%)
Total number of (permanent) migrants	170 (100.0%)	192 (100.0%)	362 (100.0%)

The villagers' propensity to migrate is not uniform across the sample communities. While the proportion of migrants exceeds 54% in Suncho (152 out of 281 individuals), it works out to 41% in Puma (135/328), and only 30% in the more remote area of Pata (75/247). In the latter area, almost 40% of the migratory moves are toward other rural areas, compared with only 15.5% in Puma and 26% in Suncho. Relatedly, as expected, the proportion of wives originating from the same community or from a nearby rural location is highest in Pata (86.5%) and lowest in Suncho (68.2%) with Puma standing in between (79.8%). Another finding evident in Table 15.6 is the incidence of (permanent) migration that has markedly increased over time, yet seems to have stabilized in recent years. Note, however, that the figure shown in the last column is likely to be an underestimate because people barely older than 15 years may not yet have made their decision about whether to migrate or not.

15.4.2   Education

Table 15.7 below gives a decomposition per education level of the sample population of individuals distinguished on the basis of gender. We have removed all

Table 15.6 Proportions of (permanent) migrants according to the present age of the individuals

	≥70 years	70 ≥ 50 years	50 ≥ 35 years	35 ≥ 15 years
Proportion of migrants belonging to that age cohort (%)	10.6	33.5	48.5	45.7

Table 15.7 Decomposition of sample population according to education level and gender

Education level	Men	Women	Total
No education	45 (11.5%)	129 (32.9%)	174 (22.3%)
Primary school started but not completed	73 (18.8%)	71 (18.1%)	144 (18.4%)
Primary school just completed (6 years)	115 (29.6%)	95 (24.2%)	210 (26.9%)
Secondary school started but not completed	58 (14.9%)	42 (10.7%)	100 (12.8%)
Secondary school just completed (5 years)	73 (18.8%)	41 (10.5%)	114 (14.6%)
High school started but not completed	10 (2.5%)	1 (0.3%)	11 (1.4%)
High school completed	15 (3.9%)	13 (3.3%)	28 (3.6%)
Total	389 (100.0%)	392 (100.0%)	781 (100.0%)
Average number of years of study per individual	6.5	4.6	5.6

individuals who are still at school or have not yet reached the age of starting school.

The average level of education is low since four-fifths of all individuals have not reached the end of their secondary school curriculum. But average figures conceal large difference between genders. In particular, almost one-third of the sample women have never gone to school while this holds true of barely more than one-tenth of the sample men. Significant differences also separate the three communities (see Table 15.8). The picture here is quite consistent. In all respects, Suncho comes out as the most educated community whereas Pata, the remotest area, is the least educated one, and Puma occupies an intermediate position. The inter-community differences in the average number of years of study per individual are statistically significant.

Not surprisingly, there exists a clear time pattern in education: in particular, the proportion of people who never went to school falls markedly, and the average level of education (as measured by the average number of years of study per individual) rises regularly as we move from older to younger generations (see Table 15.9). These trends are observable in each of the three sample communities, but educational progress is actually more rapid in the intermediate community of Puma

Table 15.8 Incidence of formal education as per community

	Suncho	Puma	Pata	Total
Proportion of individuals with no education at all (%)	14.9	24.1	28.2	22.3
Proportion of individuals who have not completed secondary schooling (%)	68.6	81.6	92.1	80.4
Average number of years of study per individual	7.2	5.5	4.0	5.6

Table 15.9 Time trends in formal education

	≥ 70 years	$70 \geq 50$ years	$50 \geq 35$ years	$35 \geq 15$ years	Total
Proportion of individuals with no education at all (%)	78.7	44.5	14.2	8.0	22.3
Proportion of individuals who have not completed secondary schooling (%)	98.0	95.1	79.6	69.8	80.4
Average # of years of study per individual (all communities)	0.8	2.8	6.1	7.4	5.6
Average # of years of study per individual (Suncho)	1.7	4.4	7.9	8.8	6.9
Average # of years of study per individual (Puma)	0.3	2.5	6.0	7.5	5.3
Average # of years of study per individual (Pata)	—[a]	1.4	3.0	6.4	4.3

Note
a There is no individual in this category.

which has been able to catch up with the most advanced one of Suncho in recent years.

To what extent is the cost of schooling (beyond primary school, which is essentially free) borne by the parents or by the pupil concerned. In other words, are there transfers from parents to children on the occasion of the latter's studies? To answer that question, we have computed the equivalent number of study years financed by the parents, counting as one full year a year of study entirely financed by the parents, and as half a year a year of study partly financed by them. We wish to compare this figure with the actual number of study years, and to construct an index measuring the relative difference between the two figures.

For a given individual, we thus have $I_j = (a_j - f_j)/a_j$, where a_j stands for the actual number of study years which individual j has gone through, and f_j for the equivalent number of years financed by the parents. This index therefore indicates the measure of self-financing of study costs by the individual concerned. It equals zero when parents have entirely borne the cost of the studies, and to one when they have not intervened at all. An average value of the index can then be computed on the basis of family, gender, or community. Tables 15.10 and 15.11 report average values computed on the basis of the last two criteria.

From Table 15.10, two interesting findings emerge. First, the aggregate value of the self-financing index is rather low since it hardly exceeds 20%. But, second, this average conceals a wide gender difference: the rate of self-financing for girls is indeed twice as large as for boys. Clearly, parents offer significantly less financial support for post-primary schooling when their child is a girl than when the child is a boy. This marked discrimination of daughters in matters of education is confirmed by the additional observation that the proportion of girls who had to bear at least part of the cost of their post-primary schooling is much larger than the corresponding proportion for boys (see the last row of the Table 15.10). Evidence of such financial discrimination is to be combined with the previous observation that school enrollment is much smaller for girls than for boys. The two phenomena may in fact be related in so far as lack of financial support from the parents may discourage girls from undertaking post-primary studies.

Table 15.10 Index values measuring the degree of self-financing of post-primary school studies, and percentages of pupils who bore at least part of the resulting cost, as per gender

	Gender		All individuals
	Men	Women	
Index measuring the degree of self-financing of post-primary school studies (%)	14.8	29.6	20.6
Proportion of pupils who had to bear at least part of the cost of their post-primary schooling (among those who went beyond primary school) (%)	22.4	30.9	25.7

Table 15.11 Index values measuring the degree of self-financing of post-primary school studies, and percentages of pupils who bore at least part of the resulting cost, as per community

	Community		
	Suncho	Puma	Pata
Index measuring the degree of self-financing of post-primary school studies (%)	28.7	12.5	15.9
Proportion of pupils who had to bear at least part of the cost of their post-primary schooling (among those who went beyond primary school) (%)	40.5	12.7	17.5

Table 15.12 Evolution over time of the index measuring the degree of self-financing of post-primary school studies, and of the percentage of pupils who bore at least part of the resulting cost

	Age cohort of the individuals concerned (years)			
	$\geq 70^a$	$70 \geq 50$	$50 \geq 35$	$35 \geq 15$
Index measuring the degree of self-financing of post-primary school studies (%)	—	12.8	33.7	23.5
Proportion of pupils who had to bear at least part of the cost of their post-primary schooling (among those who went beyond primary school) (%)	—	33.3	39.1	16.1

Note

a Note that only one year of post-primary schooling has been performed by a person belonging to the oldest age category, and that the individual concerned had to partly bear himself the cost of that year of study. To compute percentage figures on that basis is, of course, meaningless.

Table 15.11 shows that the rate of self-financing of post-primary schooling is the highest in the most educated community (Suncho), while the difference between the other two communities is not statistically significant. This means that it is a current practice for children who want to pursue their study curriculum through the secondary school cycle (which is especially true in Suncho) to contribute to the financial cost involved. (Bear in mind that only in Suncho is the average number of years of study exceeding the duration of primary schooling.)

The evolution over time of the values of the self-financing index *I* is described in Table 15.12 from which no clear pattern emerges.

Finally, Table 15.13 is designed to explore whether there exists a relationship between educational achievement and migration decision. It compares the average number of years of formal schooling for the migrants with that of the villagers who have stayed on in their native community. Note that the sample size is more restricted than the one used in the earlier computations because, in addition to removing individuals who are still at school or are too young to go to school, we had to keep out (i) those who are not old enough to make a migration decision (i.e., those below 15 years), and (ii) those who live in one of the three sample communities yet have been born in another community (since they have gone through a migration experience).

The results are striking. As expected, migrants are far more educated than non-migrants, and the difference between the two figures is highly significant statistically. At the same time, it is revealing that the level of schooling does not differ significantly between inhabitants residing in Suncho, Puma, or Pata, and

Table 15.13 Differences between educational levels of migrants and non-migrants, as well as between educational levels of various types of migrants (in years)

Non-migrants	4.2
Migrants	7.4
Total	5.5
Migrants to a close community	4.6
Migrants to a distant community	5.4
Migrants to a close urban location	8.5
Migrants to a distant urban location	8.0
Migrants to plantation areas	7.0

Table 15.14 Coefficients of correlation between within-family average educational levels and proportions of migrants

Correlation coefficients between	*Within-family average educational level*
Proportion of migrant children in the family	0.45
Proportion of children emigrated to distant locations	0.33
Proportion of children emigrated to urban locations	0.54

those who have migrated to a nearby community.[4] This finding is again in accordance with intuition. It is actually between non-migrants and migrants to distant places or, even more so, between non-migrants and urban migrants that significant educational differences are found. Confirmation is readily obtained when we correlate the average level of formal education per individual in a family, on the one hand, with the proportion of migrants in the same family, on the other hand (see Table 15.14). All three correlation coefficients displayed in Table 15.14 are statistically significant at the 1% confidence level, yet the correlation is particularly large when education is related to the proportion of urban migrants.

15.4.3 Wealth

Let us now look at our wealth indicators. The subjective indicator consists of a ranked assessment made by the president of the community concerned in the presence of the enumerator, an educated person drawn from the same community, and one of the authors. The president was asked to sort all the sample households into one of the three following categories: relatively rich, intermediate, and relatively poor. It was carefully explained to him that his rating had to take into account all the dimensions of wealth (land, cattle, quality of housing, consumption levels, etc.). The president was willing or able to appraise the relative wealth of most, but

Table 15.15 Comparing subjective wealth rankings and irrigated land owned (measured in square meters), as per community[a]

	Suncho	*Puma*	*Pata*
Relatively rich households	9226	—	12 410
	(4)		(4)
Intermediate households	3704	1591	6563
	(11)	(17)	(9)
Relatively poor households	2051	478	3102
	(9)	(5)	(11)
All households	4005	1338	5951
	(24/26)	(22/30)	(24/24)
F-statistics	0.0013	0.1370	0.0050
Prob > *F*			

Note
a Figures between brackets indicate the number of households for which subjective wealth rankings are available. In the row reporting information for all households, the figures between brackets indicate the number of households for which such rankings are available compared to total sample sizes.

not all, of our sample households. Interestingly, the average number of children does not differ significantly between the three categories.

On the other hand, we have recorded the amounts of irrigated land owned by each sample household (essentially, the amounts inherited and the amounts purchased). In Table 15.15, we compare the two earlier indicators by computing the average amount of land owned for each category of subjectively assessed household wealth (see column (1)). This is done for each community separately: indeed, since both land quality and subjective appraisals of wealth ranking are community-specific, it is not meaningful to compute aggregate averages over the whole sample.

It is evident from Table 15.15 that the expected relationship exists between the subjective categorization of a household by the community president, on the one hand, and the amount of irrigated land owned by that household, on the other. The relationship is somewhat weaker (it is not statistically significant at the 10% confidence level, yet not far from being so) in the intermediate community of Puma where no household is considered to be rich by the local president. There, indeed, the variance of land wealth within the intermediate category is quite large. Yet, households in this category still own more than three times as much irrigated land as those considered poor in the subjective assessment exercise.

The same monotonic relationship emerges if, instead of the amount of land owned, we consider the amount of land purchased (see Table 15.16). (Note that land purchased makes a significant part of the total land owned, yet this part is much smaller than the part inherited from parents.) However, in this case, statistical significance is obtained only for the community of Suncho.

The convergence between the subjective measure of wealth and the amount of irrigated land owned is good news. While we have information about subjective rankings for all our sample FS, our quantitative information about owned land is

Table 15.16 Comparing subjective wealth rankings and land purchased (measured in square meters), as per community[a]

	Suncho	Puma	Pata
Relatively rich households	2860	—	4012
	(4)		(4)
Intermediate households	716	547	2749
	(11)	(17)	(9)
Relatively poor households	535	18	1203
	(9)	(5)	(11)
All households	1006	427	2251
	(24/26)	(22/30)	24/24
Land purchased as a % of land owned	23.19	27.32	34.48
F-statistics Prob > *F*	0.0000	0.3079	0.2710

Note

a Figures between brackets indicate the number of households for which subjective wealth rankings are available. In the row reporting information for all households, the figures between brackets indicate the number of households for which such rankings are available compared to total sample sizes.

Table 15.17 Relationship between subjectively assessed wealth migration and education

Wealth subjective category	Proportion of urban migrants (%)	Average number of years of study per individual
Rich	42.3	7.6
Intermediate	32.2	6.0
Poor	22.8	4.2
F-statistics Prob > *F*	0.0031	0.0001

limited to the households which we have personally interviewed. This is due to the aforementioned fact that the complete details about the total amount of land in the hands of the parents before division takes place, and the manner in which it has been divided among the children, have been required and obtained only for the sample spouses considered as parents (see Section 15.2). The availability of a subjective measure of wealth therefore allows us to overcome this data constraint and to use our full FS sample when we will attempt to assess econometrically the impact of household wealth on inheritance patterns.

By relating our subjective wealth indicator with migration and education variables, we can check whether the usual relationships are obtained, thereby providing an additional test of its reliability. In this respect, too, we have good news to tell: as a matter of fact, Table 15.17 confirms that, as expected, there appears to be a positive monotonic relationship between our subjective measure of wealth and the level of education measured by the average number of years of study per individual.

Another interesting observation is that the proportion of (permanent) migrants is higher among the rich households than among the middle-ranked ones, and there are relatively more migrants in the latter category than among the poor.

15.4.4 *Inheritance*

In the following discussion, two objectives are pursued. First, we want to get a clear idea of the incidence of unequal inheritance sharing across the three communities, and of its evolution over time. Second, we aim at gaining preliminary insights into possible factors influencing the adoption of equal or unequal sharing practices, particularly migration and education. Bear in mind, moreover, that our data comprise information not only about the way the family land has been actually divided among children or is planned to be divided (henceforth called actual division of land), but also about whether parents perceive the inheritance to have been equal or unequal (henceforth called perceived division). The two indicators do not necessarily coincide as parents may consider an equal division process while, in the light of the objective information at hand, we have decided to consider it unequal. A typical instance of such divergence arises when a son has permanently migrated and stopped maintaining ties with his family in the native community: in these circumstances, he has forsaken his right to a share of the family land, yet the parents consider that division has been equal precisely because of the existence of this right.

To begin with, let us look at the actual incidence of unequal land division across the three communities. Land division or inheritance is defined as equal when the individual shares of the family land inherited by all the children are strictly similar. Otherwise, it is defined as unequal. The number of sample cases where inheritance has been unequal represents as much as 72% of the total number of recorded cases (208 FS), which is significantly larger than the parents' perceived incidence of 58%. If we remove the irrelevant cases of FS in which children haven't started or finished school yet and/or in which all the children are less than 15 years old – in such instances, indeed, no division of the family land has occurred and the possible plans of the parents may well be disproved when the children will have completed their education and decided whether they stay in the community or migrate, the proportion does not vary much. In addition, the incidence of unequal sharing does not significantly differ between the three communities. For the complete sample of FS, this incidence works out to 73% in Suncho, 75% in Puma, and 68% in Pata. This is a somewhat surprising finding in so far as we know that education levels and migration rates, two important possible causes of discrimination, are higher in Suncho than in Puma and, a fortiori, in Pata.

On the other hand, it is evident that the incidence of unequal inheritance has increased over time. The proportion of cases of unequal inheritance in the total corresponding to a given age category (as measured by the mean age of the family's children) has thus risen from 67.4% for the oldest generation (more than or equal to 50 years), to 79.0% for the intermediate generation (between 35 and 50 years), and 83.3% for the younger generation (between 15 and 35 years).

Table 15.18 Reasons adduced by parents to justify unequal division of family land, as per community and per decreasing order of importance in the whole sample

Reported reasons for unequal division of family land	Relative frequencies according to community (%)			
	Suncho	Puma	Pata	Total
Preference for non-migrant children	41.7	52.0	52.5	49.2
Migrants are not entitled to receive any land	19.4	32.0	42.5	31.7
Migrants are entitled to a smaller share	22.3	20.0	10.0	17.5
Preference for caring children	44.4	34.0	22.5	33.3
Preference for less educated children	16.6	28.0	25.0	23.8
Preference for sons over daughters	5.5	16.0	35.0	19.8
Preference for eldest or youngest child	30.5	16.0	10.0	18.2
Personal preferences	13.9	8.0	12.5	11.1
Other reasons	5.5	4.0	5.0	5.5
Cumulating preference for caring children with preference for eldest or youngest child[a]	63.9	46.0	30.0	46.0

Note

a Relative number of cases where one of these motives, or both, have been mentioned.

We have information on the justifications given by spouses for unequal inheritance practices whenever they actually occurred. In particular, we can see whether some factors other than migration or education play a role and, if yes, whether they have a varying impact between communities. The list of the reasons adduced, as well as their relative frequencies presented for the whole sample and for each community separately (by decreasing order of importance in the whole sample), are displayed in Table 15.18. The relative frequency for a given reason is defined as the proportion of cases of unequal inheritance for which this reason has been mentioned, alone or jointly with some other reason(s). Since respondents have sometimes mentioned more than one motive, the percentages do not add up to 100%.

Migration and education are among the three most important reasons mentioned by the sample spouses to justify discrimination in dividing family land. In particular, discrimination against migrant children is mentioned in almost half of the instances of unequal inheritance (see Hypothesis 1). Discrimination in favor of children who support their parents is the second most important justification overall, being mentioned in one-third of the cases (see Hypothesis 2). Once we decompose the answers according to the community of the respondents, some significant variations are observed. First, if migration is an equally important source of discrimination in all three communities, a noticeable difference is the following. Migrants are more likely to be deprived of any inheritance share in the family land in Pata than in the other two communities where the prospect of receiving a smaller share than the other members of the family is another possible outcome of the inheritance process. A plausible explanation for this observation is that it is more difficult or costly for migrants to maintain ties with the native community when the latter is remote than when it is within relatively easy reach.

Second, preference for caring children turns out to be the most important justification for unequal sharing in Suncho (mentioned in 44% of the cases), coming even before migration. And, in the same locale, preference for the eldest or youngest child is the third most important reason mentioned (in 30% of the cases). By contrast, preference for sons over daughters appears as the second most important justification in Pata (mentioned in 35% of the cases).

If preferences for sons over daughters, or for the eldest or the youngest child, are considered as the hallmark of a traditional society, our findings are only partly surprising. While preference for the eldest or youngest son seems to prevail in the most opened and the most educated community, preference for sons mainly characterizes the remotest community.[5]

The prevalence of preference for the eldest or the youngest child in Suncho needs not be as anachronistic as it may appear at first sight, however. This is because it is in fact not independent of the preference for caring children. In many village communities, the custom usually demands that the eldest or the youngest child take special care of the parents in old age. A larger share in land inheritance is then a compensation that a child receives for making a special contribution toward ensuring the well-being of his or her old parents. To the extent that the two answers are thus interdependent (in one case, the support given by a child is mandatory, and in the other case it is the outcome of a free decision), it is interesting to calculate a cumulative frequency indicating the number of times where at least one of these preferences has been stated by the household. For that purpose, we add up the two separate frequencies as they appear in Table 15.18, and then subtract the cases where they have been cited together. We then obtain the figures displayed in the last row.

The outcome of this exercise is striking: at least one of the two earlier preferences has been cited in 46% of the answers, which makes this combined motive to come very close to migration as a justification for unequal land inheritance (see Hypothesis 1 and 2). By an ample margin, it even appears as the most important rationale in Suncho, which is the community where migration is the most widespread. Upon reflection, this is an intuitively understandable result. In families where many children have settled down outside the community, parents are expected to be eager to identify a child who is ready to assume responsibility for taking care of them in old age. The view of bequests as being "exchange-motivated" appears to be well validated by such results which are usefully added to the kind of evidence adduced in the aforementioned paper of Bernheim *et al.* (especially, pp. 1072–3).

On the basis of our data, it is possible to see whether the motives discussed earlier for unequal sharing have changed over time. The way to do this is to compute the relative frequency of a particular motive for several age categories representing successive generations of villagers. To determine the "generation" of a household, we compute the arithmetic mean of the ages of all the children involved in a FS. An expected but clear result is the following: the relative frequency of education as an acknowledged source of discrimination in land inheritance rises neatly over successive generations, passing from 0% for the people falling in the oldest category to 72% for those belonging to the youngest one (see Table 15.19).

Table 15.19 Evolution over time of the relative frequencies of education and migration as sources of discrimination in land inheritance

Reported reasons for unequal division of family land	Relative frequencies according to mean age of children (%)			
	≥50 years	50 ≥ 30 years	30 ≥ 15 years	<15 years
Relative frequency of education	0	9.1	26.6	72.0
Relative frequency of migration	55.6	56.8	40.0	40.0
Preference for caring children	29.6	38.6	30.0	32.0
Preference for sons over daughters	18.5	25.0	26.7	4.0
Preference for eldest or youngest child	22.2	18.2	20.0	12.0
Personal preference	7.4	20.4	6.7	4.0

The evolution has been especially rapid during the last decades owing to rapid increase in school enrollment. Note that we have adjusted our age categories to take account of the answers given by relatively young parents (whose children have a mean age smaller than 15 years). In their case, obviously, the inheritance process has not been completed, let alone started, and their answers therefore refer to intentions rather than actual practice. The lesson emerging from Table 15.19 is thus that a large proportion of those parents intend to give lower shares of the family land to their more educated children.

Regarding preference for sons, for the eldest or youngest child, and personal preference, no clear trend emerges, there is a broadly downward trend for migration. This may seem surprising in the light of accelerating rates of migration, yet it should not be so. It must, indeed, be borne in mind that what we consider here are justifications mentioned by the parents, which do not necessarily coincide with objective facts of discrimination. The most obvious reason for divergence lies in the fact that children themselves may be responsible for the unequal character of land division, such as when a migrant child decides not to maintain ties with the native community and thereby forsake his or her share in the family land. This is actually confirmed by the evidence brought in Table 15.20, where we directly compare perceptions by the parents with our own assessments based on data reporting actual facts. The information displayed is in the form of a discrepancy index intended to measure the relative number of diverging cases, and calculated as follows:

$$d^i = (\text{Per}^{eq,i} - \text{Actual}^{eq,i})/(\text{Per}^{un,i} + \text{Per}^{eq,i})$$

$$= (\text{Per}^{eq,i} - \text{Actual}^{eq,i})/(\text{Actual}^{un,i} + \text{Actual}^{eq,i}),$$

with $i = m, nm$, and where $\text{Per}^{eq,i}$ is the number of FS with either no migrant ($i = nm$) or at least one migrant ($i = m$) for which inheritance has been perceived

Table 15.20 Rates of discrepancy between perceptions by parents and data-based assessments about the equal/unequal character of land inheritance

Types of families	Families without any migrant	Families with at least one migrant	Families without any urban migrant	Families with at least one urban migrant
Rates of discrepancy (%)	+3.8	+20.0	+5.2	+21.3

as equal by the parents concerned; $Per^{un,i}$ stands for the number of FS with either no migrant ($i = nm$) or at least one migrant ($i = m$) for which inheritance has been perceived as unequal by the parents concerned; $Actual^{eq,i}$ is the number of FS with either no migrant ($i = nm$) or at least one migrant ($i = m$), for which inheritance has been considered equal on the basis of fact-reporting data; and $Actual^{un,i}$ is the number of FS with either no migrant ($i = nm$) or at least one migrant ($i = m$), for which inheritance has been considered unequal on the basis of fact-reporting data.

Clearly, when the sign is positive, the value of the discrepancy index indicates the extent to which parents have overestimated the equal nature of the land inheritance process.

From Table 15.20, it is evident that, when there is no migrant in the family, the parents' perception hardly differs from the facts (it does in less than 4% of the FS concerned). By contrast, when there is at least one migrant in the family, parents have perceived land division as equal while facts indicate the opposite in as many as 20% of the relevant FS. Such a contrast also obtains if, instead of considering all the migrants, we limit our attention to urban migrants. As hinted earlier, this finding suggests that, when migrant children do not inherit a portion of the family land or inherit a smaller share than their siblings who remained in the native community, their discrimination does not necessarily result from a denial of their inheritance right by the parents, but may be the outcome of their own decision to forsake their right. In 25 out of 28 cases of diverging assessments of the inheritance process, migrant children have received no land at all, while in the remaining 3 cases they have obtained a smaller share than their siblings.

An important task remains to be completed before embarking upon the econometric analysis, namely to examine whether our key variables, migration, education, and wealth, have an impact on actual land inheritance practices. Table 15.21 sets out to assess the impact of migration, which is done in two different ways, continuous and discontinuous. For the first measure, we compute the proportion of migrant children in the family while, for the second measure, we make a comparison between families with no migrant child and families with at least one.

When assessed continuously, the impact of migration on land inheritance patterns is statistically significant, especially so if all migrants are taken into consideration. Moreover, there exists a highly significant difference between families which have no migrant child and those which have at least one, whether we take all migrants into account or only those who have migrated to urban locales. This

Table 15.21 Assessing the impact of migration on land inheritance patterns

Land division	Proportion of migrants in the family	Proportion of urban migrants in the family	No child has migrated in the family[a]	At least one child has migrated in the family[a]	No child has migrated to an urban location[a]	At least one child has migrated to an urban location[a]
Equal	33.7%	25.6%	19 (52.8)	23 (16.9)	21 (38.9)	21 (17.8)
Unequal	45.2%	34.0%	17 (47.2)	113 (83.1)	33 (61.1)	97 (82.2)
Total	42.4%	32.0%	36 (100.0)	136 (100.0)	54 (100.0)	118 (100.0)
Statistics						
Prob > F	0.0267	0.0918				
Chi-square				0.000		0.003

Note

a Figures between brackets are percentages.

Table 15.22 Assessing the impact of children's education on land inheritance patterns

Land division	Minmax difference in education levels in years	Minmax difference in years financed by parents[a]	Variance of education levels in years	Variance of years financed by parents[a]	Average no. of years of education	Average no. of years of education financed by parents[a]
	(1)	(2)	(3)	(4)	(5)	(6)
Equal	2.3	2.2	3.7	3.5	4.3	4.2
Unequal	4.1	3.4	6.5	5.1	6.0	5.6
Total	3.7	3.1	5.9	4.7	5.6	5.2
Statistics						
Prob > F	0.003	0.0277	0.1094	0.3251	0.0121	0.0337

Note

a A year financed partly by parents and partly by the child himself or herself is counted as half a year.

latter result is certainly expected: indeed, if migration is a source of discrimination, the presence of only one migrant among the children should be sufficient to cause land inheritance to be unequal. The fact that it is essentially driven by urban migrants is also according to expectation: rural migrant children who live rather close to the native community are more likely to maintain narrow ties with the parents and, therefore, they tend to benefit from the same share of the family land as their siblings who remained in that community.

Let us now turn to the influence of education by looking at Table 15.22.

The most important finding is that land inheritance tends to be more unequal when the difference between the education levels of the different children is larger. This is especially evident when we measure education differentials by computing minmax differences between the most and the least educated child of each sample family (see column (1)). When we instead use the variance of education years, the same relationship obtains, yet it is now hardly significant statistically (see column (3)). If we consider the number of years of education financed by the parents (based on the aforementioned convention of counting as 1/2 year any year which has been partly financed by the parents and partly by the child himself or herself), we have the results displayed in columns (2) and (4). It is striking that the expected positive relationship between dispersion of financed education and the probability of an unequal division of family land obtains only with the minmax indicator of dispersion. Equally worth noting is the fact that the degree of statistical significance decreases when years financed, rather than total years of education, are considered (compare columns (1) and (2), and columns (3) and (4)), while we assumed the opposite to be true.

We have seen earlier (see Table 15.14), that a high correlation exists between average family-level education and the proportion of migrant children. At this stage, it bears emphasis that the correlation between within-family dispersion of education levels and the proportion of migrant children is much smaller: thus, the correlation coefficient has a statistically significant value of 17% when dispersion is measured by the minmax and a non-significant value of 9% when it is measured by the variance (regardless of financing considerations). Therefore, we have some ground to believe that educational differentials have an independent effect on the inheritance pattern. This will be tested rigorously in the next section with the help of the econometric approach.

Another result emerging from Table 15.22 is that the average education level of children appears to exert an influence on the manner in which family land is apportioned between them (see columns (5) and (6)). Since the correlation between average education levels and their dispersion, albeit significant, is not quite large (26.6% when dispersion is measured by the maxmin criterion, and 17.2% when it is measured by the variance, financing considerations left aside), the tendency for inheritance to be more unequal when children are more educated on an average is unlikely to be spurious.[6] A plausible explanation is that, when children are more educated, they are more able and willing to accept differences in inheritance shares aimed at correcting unequal endowments (non-observable for us) among them.

The effect of wealth is investigated in Table 15.23, from which no neat relationship can be discerned. On average, however, poor households (as assessed by the community president) divide the family land more equally than the other categories of households, and the difference is statistically significant ($\chi^2 = 0.038$). The fact that wealth is strongly associated with education and migration (see earlier),

Table 15.23 Assessing the impact of subjectively assessed wealth on the inheritance pattern (in %)

Inheritance pattern	Rich	Intermediate	Poor
Equal	22.2	16.2	32.2
Unequal	77.8	83.8	67.8
Total	100.0	100.0	100.0

however, precludes us from inferring any relationship at this stage. Econometrics will help clarify the matter.

A few other observations deserve to be made. First, families with a comparatively large number of children tend to practice unequal inheritance more often. While the mean number of children is 5.4 for unequal inheritance events, it is only 4.1 for equal ones (Prob $> F = 0.0003$). Second, does the presence of girls in a family tends to increase the parents' proclivity to divide their land unequally? To highlight this issue, we differentiate between mixed FS in which sons coexist with daughters, on the one hand, and FS in which only sons or only daughters (unisex FS) are found, on the other hand. When this is done, no significant variation is observed in the inheritance patterns. More precisely, 78% of FS of the former type are characterized by unequal sharing, compared to 68% for the FS of the latter type, yet the value of χ^2 is a disappointing 0.30. Hence discrimination against girls in land inheritance does not seem important when assessed over the three communities.

Our next and last two points are methodological. Each respondent is simultaneously involved in two FS, one as a parent and the other as a child. This approach could create a bias in the answers in so far as a respondent may be influenced by his or her position in the family when reporting facts about it. To test for the presence of such a bias, we have compared FS reported by a child with those reported by a parent.[7] We find that the incidence of unequal inheritance practices does not significantly vary between the two categories. In conclusion, the generational position of our informant does not influence the way in which the inheritance pattern has been reported.

On the other hand, there is a possibility that the reported pattern of land division varies according to whether the inheritance process has been completed or not. One can imagine that parents who have not completed the division of the family land tend to answer our questions in a biased manner. Comparing the answers about the (a)symmetric nature of land inheritance reveals, however, that the proportion of equal inheritance in FS where inheritance has been completed (25.4%) is not significantly different from the proportion observed in FS where it is incomplete (32.1%).

15.5 Econometric results

We know that some of the potential determinants of land inheritance practices are correlated, making it necessary to go beyond simple descriptive statistics and testing in order to disentangle the separate effects of the dependent variables of interest. The dependent variable is a dummy which differentiates between FS in which land division has been strictly equal (the dummy is then equal to zero), and those in which some asymmetry has been observed in the sharing (the value of the dummy is one). We estimate a logit model in which we assume the existence of an underlying latent variable for which we observe a dichotomous realization.

A potential problem with our estimation procedure is the existence of an endogeneity bias resulting from simultaneous decisions regarding migration, education, and the inheritance rule. Thus, a plausible scenario is one in which parents, acting as heads of the household, would jointly determine whether and which children will migrate, whether and which children will be educated, and what rule to follow for the division of the family land. For instance, they would choose to encourage the education and migration of some gifted child or children, and agree on an unequal division of the land as a form of compensation for the other children. If this were true, the coefficients of the explanatory variables in a simple one-stage logit regression would obviously be biased. Nonetheless, we have solid reasons to believe that the earlier scenario does not fit our facts. Thus, fragmentary evidence shows that children who migrated often made their decision individually. Furthermore, the sense of disarray expressed by many parents faced with the departure of some of their children and the resulting anxiety for their future subsistence (both physical and psychological) confirm that, as a rule, migration decisions are not collectively planned within the family.

In order to make the econometric analysis relevant, the sample has been restricted. We have excluded all the FS in which there is a unique child, those in which all children are less than 15 years old (and, therefore, not yet in a position to decide whether to migrate), those in which some children haven't completed their studies yet, and, finally, those for which no rating of the wealth situation is available.

We are interested in examining whether several effects highlighted in the Section 15.4 are confirmed by the econometric analysis. In particular, we want to answer the following central questions: (i) do migration and education have a separate impact on the inheritance division pattern; (ii) does the wealth of a household influence the way it divides the land among children; (iii) is the effect of wealth possibly conditional on the presence of migrant children in the family; (iv) does the presence of girls change the sharing rule chosen by the parents; (v) does the number of children influence such a rule?

Let us now establish the list of our independent variables. To assess the role of migration, we wish to compare FS in which there is no migrant with FS in which there is at least one migrant: for this purpose, we use a dummy denoted by *migrant*, which is equal to one when there is at least one migrant child in the family, and to zero otherwise. Moreover, because we hypothesize that the effect of the migration variable is susceptible to variation according to whether the household is rich or poor, we refine this distinction by constructing three categories: families, poor or rich, where there is no migrant (the reference category); poor families with at least one migrant (denoted by the dummy *migrant poor*); and rich families with at least one migrant (identified by the dummy *migrant rich*). Note that the *poor* category is composed of all the households considered poor according to the subjective assessment measure, whereas the *rich* category includes all those considered rich or intermediate according to the same measure. The lack of observations in the "rich" category (remember that there was not even a single household considered rich in one of the communities) compelled us to make such a regrouping for the purpose of econometric analysis.

To measure the impact of education, we use variables reflecting intra-family education differentials, namely the minmax difference (*education differential minmax*) and the variance of education levels (*omitted results*), two variables which are measured in years and are therefore continuous. Alternatively, we measure the impact of education differentials by taking into account the contribution of the parents toward financing the (post-primary) studies. Again, we wish to check whether the influence of education on the inheritance sharing rule is conditioned by the level of wealth of the household. In this case, we use any of the four above-mentioned variables and multiply it by a *wealth* dummy that is equal to one when the household is intermediate or rich, and to zero when it is poor. The independent effect of wealth is tested by including in the regression the *wealth* dummy that we have just defined.

Next, in order to determine whether daughters are discriminated against in the land inheritance process, we define a new dummy, called *gender bias*, which takes on value one when all children in the family belong to the same sex (they are all boys or all girls), and value zero when both sexes are represented (boys coexist with girls). If discrimination prevails against daughters, the coefficient of that variable should be negative, meaning that land inheritance tends to be more equal when children are all of the same sex, or, conversely, that inheritance tends to be more unequal when the division is to be made between sons and daughters.

We also have a continuous variable measuring the number of children (*number of children*) to examine the influence of family size on the sharing rule. Two binary variables, the dummies *Puma* and *Pata*, stand for the sample communities, assuming that Suncho, the location closest to a city, is the reference category. In addition to the impact of location, we are interested in knowing if inheritance rules have changed over time for reasons that have nothing to do with the growing incidence of migration and education. To test for this possibility, we identify the generation to which the family concerned belongs. This is done by computing the mean age of a family's children and classifying it into one of the three following categories: more than 49 years (≥ 50), which is chosen as our reference category; between 30 and 49 years ($30 \leq \ < 50$); and less than 30 years (< 30). The latter two categories are denoted by *intermediate generation* and *younger generation*, respectively.

Finally, we test for the aforementioned possibility that inheritance rules, as reported in our study, differ according to whether the respondent occupies the position of a parent or a child in the FS concerned, or according to whether the division process has been completed or not. To address the first issue, we add a dummy called *position of respondent*, with unit value when the respondent is a parent, and with zero value when he or she is a child of the family inquired about. And to address the second one, we include a dummy labeled *division process*, with unit value when the inheritance process is complete and zero value when it is not.

In the first column of Table 15.24, we present the estimates of our basic logit model. Note that the coefficients have been transformed (through the Dprobit stata procedure) so that we can directly assess the effects of changes in any of the explanatory variables on the probabilities of any observation belonging to the

Table 15.24 Estimations of logit models to identify the determinants of unequal land inheritance*

Explanatory variables	Basic model (1)	Variant 1 of basic model (2)	Variant 2 of basic model (3)	Variant 3 of basic model (4)	Alternative model (5)
Number of observations	155	155	155	155	155
Migrant poor	0.282***	—	—	—	0.360***
	(0.079)				(0.091)
Migrant rich	0.116	—	—	—	0.235*
	(0.115)				(0.131)
Wealth	0.269**	—	—	—	0.265**
	(0.132)				(0.138)
Poor family and no migrant	—	Reference variable	−0.337** (0.182)	−0.437*** (0.146)	—
Rich family and no migrant	—	0.174** (0.054)	Reference variable	−0.078 (0.139)	—
Poor family and $1 \leq$ migrant	—	0.282*** (0.079)	0.069 (0.108)	Reference variable	—
Rich family and $1 \leq$ migrant	—	0.351*** (0.096)	0.116 (0.115)	0.048 (0.083)	—
Education differential minmax	0.007 (0.116)	0.007 (0.012)	0.007 (0.012)	0.007 (0.012)	0.053 (0.033)
Migrant and education differential	—	—	—	—	−0.054 (0.035)
Number of children	0.051** (0.024)	0.051** (0.024)	0.051** (0.024)	0.051** (0.024)	0.052** (0.024)
Intermediate generation	−0.006 (0.103)	−0.006 (0.103)	−0.006 (0.103)	−0.006 (0.103)	−0.043 (0.109)
Younger generation	0.064 (0.131)	0.064 (0.131)	0.064 (0.131)	0.064 (0.131)	0.024 (0.145)
Puma	−0.025 (0.086)	−0.025 (0.086)	−0.025 (0.086)	−0.025 (0.086)	−0.017 (0.086)
Pata	−0.001 (0.089)	−0.001 (0.089)	−0.001 (0.089)	−0.001 (0.089)	−0.011 (0.091)
Gender bias	−0.041 (0.102)	−0.041 (0.102)	−0.041 (0.102)	−0.041 (0.102)	−0.028 (0.101)
Division process	0.043 (0.103)	0.043 (0.103)	0.043 (0.103)	0.043 (0.103)	0.008 (0.106)
Position of respondent	−0.158 (0.116)	−0.158 (0.116)	−0.158 (0.116)	−0.158 (0.116)	−0.186 (0.122)
LR chi^2 (12)	35.29	35.29	35.29	35.29	37.96
Prob > chi^2	0.0004	0.0005	0.0005	0.0005	0.0003
Pseudo R^2	0.2100	0.2100	0.2100	0.2100	0.2259

Notes
Standard errors are shown between brackets.
* 10% level of confidence.
** 5% level of confidence.
*** 1% level of confidence.

category of unequal inheritance. The coefficients displayed are not odd-ratios but can be interpreted as standard regression coefficients.

The central result is that there is a strongly significant impact of migration on the inheritance division rule, and that this impact is conditioned by the wealth position of the household.[8] The direction of these effects is that predicted by the theory discussed in Section 15.3 (see Hypothesis 1). More precisely, the sharing of family land tends to be more unequal when there is at least one migrant among the children, but this effect is apparently observed only when the household is poor (the coefficient of *migrant poor*, which is positive, is significant at the 1% confidence level). When the household is relatively rich, the presence of migrants (at least one) among the children does not seem to affect the inheritance rule (the coefficient of *migrant rich* is not significant).[9] In terms of our theory, the interpretation is as follows: when land is scarce, migrants from poor families tend to forsake their inheritance rights owing to the paucity of the available land base (see Hypothesis 3). Moreover, there is a wealth effect irrespective of the migration phenomenon (the coefficient of *wealth*, which is positive, is significant at the 5% confidence level): the probability of unequal inheritance is higher among richer than among poorer families, probably because the former are better able to compensate non-beneficiaries through other forms of capital, or because non-beneficiaries have better alternative income opportunities when they belong to well-to-do families.

Bear in mind that the reference category used in this first model is composed of families with no migrant, whether rich or poor. In order to refine our understanding of the various effects at work, it is useful to specify other econometric models in which all possible interactions between the migration and wealth variables are explicitly tested, so that the *wealth* variable becomes redundant. Three alternative models can thus be specified depending on the way we define the reference category: (i) poor families with no migrant; (ii) rich families with no migrant; and (iii) poor families with at least one migrant. In each attempt, three additional categories need to be defined, each corresponding to a dummy variable in the regression. For example, in the first exercise, these categories are the following: rich families with no migrant; poor families with at least one migrant; and rich families with at least one migrant. The results obtained from these new specifications (see columns (2), (3), and (4) of Table 15.24) can be summarized as follows:

- poor families with at least one migrant child tend, other things being equal, to practice unequal inheritance sharing more often than poor families with no migrant among the children (a migration effect);
- poor families with no migrant child tend to follow rules of equal division more often than rich families with no migrant child (a wealth effect);
- a rich family with at least one migrant child does not behave differently from a rich family with no migrant child in matters of land division;
- a rich family with at least one migrant child does not behave differently from a poor family with at least one migrant child.

In other words, there is a migration effect, but only among poor families, and there is a wealth effect, but only among families with no migrant child. Note, however, that an important qualification concerning the former effect will be made later.

Turning to the role of education, we find from Table 15.24 that the inheritance sharing rule is unaffected by education differentials among children, once the influence of other factors with which education is associated (migration and wealth, in particular) has been duly controlled for. This result continues to hold when we measure education differentials by the variance rather than the minmax criterion, and when we base the computation of the two statistics on the years of studies financed by the parents rather than on the years performed regardless of the financing source (results not displayed here). In conclusion, parents do not try to correct inequalities in education among children by adjusting the shares of family land bequeathed to them.

We have also tested for the possible presence of interaction effects between education differentials and wealth position, hypothesizing that correcting for unequal endowments in human capital could depend on the wealth level of the household. This attempt has proven unsuccessful, however: the estimated coefficients of the interaction terms are never statistically significant in the new regressions and, furthermore, the size as well as the significance level of all other variables present in the regression are unaffected.

On the other hand, when we test for the existence of an interaction effect between education differentials (measured by *education differential minmax*) and migration (measured by *migrant*), a variable denoted by *migrant and education differential*, the above-reported results are slightly modified and the significance of the entire regression improves somewhat (see the last rows of Table 15.24). More precisely, as is evident from column (5) of Table 15.24, the coefficient of *migrant rich*, which is positive, becomes statistically significant, suggesting that the effect of migration on the inheritance pattern is characteristic of all households, and not only of the poorer ones. Yet, the impact of migration appears to be larger for the poor than for the rich households.

Also, the coefficient of *education differential minmax* is getting very close to significance (it is significant at the 11% confidence level), and the same holds true of the interaction effect itself (significant at 12% confidence level). Since the value of the coefficient of the interaction effect (−0.054) is almost exactly the opposite of that of the coefficient of education differentials (+0.053), these results taken together imply that education differentials influence the inheritance pattern only when there is no permanent migrant among the children. In other words, parents would not tend to correct unequal endowments in human capital when at least one child has gone to live outside the community. The influence of education is thus independent of the phenomenon of migration.

Two important points must however be made to qualify these new results. First, the significance level of the coefficient of *migrant rich* is just 10%. Second, it reaches that level only in the specification reported in column (5), where we use the minmax criterion to measure the education differences, and these differences are measured in terms of years of studies rather than years financed by the parents.

When other measures are used, the result is no more significant. This said, since our sample size is small for reasons that are beyond our control, we should not perhaps require too high levels of statistical significance in order to decide whether an effect exists.

The number of children has a significant influence on the inheritance rule, and the sign of the coefficient is positive, as expected (see Hypothesis 4): bigger families tend to practice unequal land inheritance more often than smaller ones. Like that of migration, the effect of family size is extremely robust to any conceivable alternative specification of the econometric model. In interpreting this result, caution is needed since we actually control for wealth in the regression. The implication is that larger families, whether they belong to the category of relatively poor or relatively rich families, have a tendency to practice asymmetrical sharing when dividing land assets among the children. In other words, parents seem eager to avoid excessive fragmentation of the family land irrespective of the size of landholding (remind that land owned is correlated with our wealth subjective indicator), or the children themselves are more willing to give up their inheritance share when it is a smaller part of the whole.[10]

The coefficients of all the other variables present in the regression turn out to be non-significant, usually by a wide margin, and their non-significance resists all kinds of changes in the specification of the econometric model. Some of these non-significant effects are quite interesting and deserve to be emphasized. First, there is no evidence that inequality in the division of family land can be explained by discrimination against daughters: the coefficient of *gender bias* is not significantly different from zero (see Hypothesis 5). This result confirms the observation by Malengreau (1999, pp. 128–9) that, in the Andean communities of Peru, parents divide their bequests equally among their sons and daughters. In addition, testing for interaction between migration and the gender composition of children reveals that the effect of migration on the inheritance pattern is not to be ascribed to discrimination against daughters who leave the native locale upon marriage in order to join their husband's community.[11] Preferential treatment of non-migrants in the division of family land is also observed in families where there are only boys and, in those where boys and girls are present, boys tend to obtain differential shares depending on whether they are migrants or not. To sum up, the observed impact of migration on inheritance is not driven only, or even mainly, by considerations of marriage and the associated mobility of daughters. In this regard, it is worth bearing in mind that the custom of uxorilocal marriages is increasingly abandoned in favor of more flexible practices: spouses, indeed, tend to settle down in the locale, whether the community of the man, the woman, or another locale, where economic opportunities are best.

Second, once we control for the fact that migration and education expand over time, we find no remaining effect attributable to some sort of generational effect. In other words, the growing incidence of unequal inheritance that is observed in the three sample communities does not seem to have anything to do with cultural or social changes unrelated to migration and education. Note that this result continues to hold if we measure the mean age of the children continuously rather than categorically. Third, there is no community-specific effect even though the sample communities are located at varying distances from an urban center. This means that only variations of observed characteristics reflected in the regression (especially, migration and education) account for inter-community differences in inheritance practices. In conformity with Hypothesis 6, despite differences in location and in the degree of exposition to urban influences, there are no variations in inheritance practices that can be ascribed to location-specific cultural or social norms. The absence of cultural effects or community-specific norms is perhaps not surprising given the fact that the sample communities belong to an area within which communications (through the markets and schools in Sicuani) and exchanges (including marriages) are frequent. When we remove respondents (both men and women) who have been born in a different community, all our results stand unaltered and, in particular, no community-specific effect emerges.

Finally, one may note that there is no apparent bias in reporting sharing patterns due to the status, child or parent, of the respondent. Moreover, there is no perceptible difference in land inheritance depending on whether the process has been completed or not.

15.6   Conclusion

According to the statements made by the respondents, (permanent) migration of some children is the main rationale for departing from equal land inheritance. This is confirmed by the econometric analysis. Because migration has noticeably increased over the last decades, it is not surprising that the practice of unequal land inheritance has also been on the rise. Furthermore, the influence of migration has been found to be conditional on the household's level of wealth: the division of family land tends to be more unequal when there is at least one migrant among the children, but this effect apparently obtains mainly when the household is relatively poor.

To the extent that migration is responsible for the unequal sharing of family land and that rates of discrepancy between justifications adduced by parents and hard facts are higher when there is at least one migrant child in the family, we may draw the implication that the initiative for departing from the equal inheritance pattern lies with children rather than with parents. Indeed, migrant children, especially when they belong to poor families, tend to voluntarily forsake their inheritance rights owing to the paucity of the available land base. Adoption of such a behavior results from the realization that it is not worth maintaining ties with the family and the native community and incurring the costs involved (e.g., sending regular remittances to parents and relatives, returning more or less regularly to the native locale to participate in collective activities such as maintenance of the irrigation system, and to manifest one's interest in community affairs, or, at least, doing so in a vicarious manner) when the subjective probability of losing one's employment in the city is not high and the expected income of the fall-back option in the countryside is comparatively low. To sum up, in the presence of migration, the practice of unequal land inheritance is not imposed by parents on the children. Instead, it is the latter who appear to induce the deviation from the egalitarian norm by voluntarily foregoing their due share of the parental land.

This interpretation, suggested by qualitative interviews with local people as well as by the finding that migrants are more likely to be deprived of any inheritance share in the most remote community,[12] does not imply that parents always refrain from deliberately choosing to favor some children while dividing the family land. Behind migration, the second most important justification invoked to explain unequal inheritance is the fact that children who take special care of their parents in old age receive a special reward under the form of larger portions of the family land. This is especially true in the community that is closest to an urban center and where the incidence of migration is the highest.

Now, taking care of old parents is either mandatory or left to the free decision of the children themselves. The first possibility occurs when attending to old parents is a task devolved upon children occupying pre-determined positions in the family (usually, the eldest or the youngest child), a practice prescribed by the custom in many communities. As for the second possibility in which any child can assume special responsibility for old parents, it seems to be a more recent phenomenon, which can be explained by the fact that migration has the effect of disturbing customary prescriptions (if the eldest or the youngest child migrates).

While parents decide to favor some children in the former instance, it is the actions of children strategically interacting with parents which determine the rule of bequest in the latter. The analogy between this latter case and that of migrants choosing to cut off their ties with the family is evident. Unfortunately, our data do not allow us to objectively measure the influence of caring on inheritance using the econometric approach. True, we have evidence that granting preferential land shares to more caring children does happen in some of our sample FS, yet we do not have a systematic recording of the occurrence or nonoccurrence of that practice.

Notice carefully that in the earlier two instances unequal land inheritance cannot be considered an unfair practice. Under the first sort of circumstances (migration), inequality is willingly accepted by the children who receive smaller or zero landholdings, whereas in the second sort of circumstances (differential contribution of children to the welfare of old parents) parents adjust the inheritance sharing rule so that more caring children get a return for their kindness.

Whether parents adjust the sharing rule to allow for unequal endowments of their children in terms of human capital is less clear. Once we control for migration, a phenomenon with which education differences are tightly associated (migrant children are comparatively more educated than those who stay behind), education does not exert an independent influence on inheritance in the basic econometric model that we use. Yet, when we change the specification of the regression by introducing an interaction term between education differentials and migration, the coefficient of the variable measuring education differentials gets rather close to statistical significance. Since our sample size is small, we should perhaps not require too high levels of significance in order to decide that an effect exists.

Systematic discrimination against daughters in the matter of land inheritance is absent in our sample areas. Unlike what is observed in other (patrilineal) lineage-based societies, such as those of sub-Saharan Africa, daughters are considered to enjoy the same rights to family land as their brothers. (By contrast, girls are neatly discriminated in their access to education.)

A wealth effect clearly exists that operates independently of migration: the probability of unequal inheritance is higher among richer than among poorer families. The most plausible explanation for this effect is that richer households are better able to compensate children deprived of land through other forms of capital. For example, they may give more land to children who make their living from agriculture and more financial capital to those who start a business in town.

The inheritance pattern is influenced by the size of the family, and this effect holds true when we control for the wealth level of the household. In other words, larger families, whether they belong to the category of relatively poor or relatively rich families, have a tendency to practice asymmetrical sharing when dividing land assets among the children. Parents thus seem eager to avoid excessive fragmentation of the family land, however large or small is their land endowment, or the children themselves are readier to give up their inheritance share when it is a smaller part of the whole.

Finally, there is no community effect that persists in the presence of the measured influences of education and migration, in particular. In other words, there is no evidence of the operation of cultural factors.

Notes

1 For readers interested in knowing more about the methods followed to win the confidence of the people, see Goetghebuer (2002).
2 A commonly used tactic of opposition consists for community authorities and members to physically prevent stranger-owners from taking hold of their newly acquired land and putting it into cultivation.
3 Of course, when children have been treated equally, since we know the amount of land inherited by one of them (the sample sibling), it is straightforward to infer the total amount of family land owned by the parents. When such is not the case, however, derivation of the parents' land endowment may prove much more hazardous. This is especially true when the shares inherited vary between almost all children.
4 This result is confirmed by the following complementary finding: the average level of schooling among residents of the sample areas who have migrated from another community in the past works out to 4.65 years, which is remarkably similar to the figure obtained for the subjects who have left the native community for another, rather close, community (4.6 years).
5 Note that the rather widespread prevalence of preferences for sons in Pata is a plausible explanation for the aforementioned fact that the incidence of unequal sharing practices is not lower in Pata than in Suncho and Puma despite the relatively low levels of education and rates of migration in the former community.
6 As we know, education levels are higher in some communities than in others, and what seems to be an education effect could therefore be a community effect. Yet, as we know also, communities do not differ in terms of the incidence of unequal inheritance

practices. Here is another reason why the relationship between average education levels and the inheritance pattern is unlikely to be spurious.

7 It cannot be objected that we actually test for a generational effect rather than for the mentioned bias. Indeed, there is considerable overlap between the age categories of the two types of respondents: an informant answering as a parent might thus be younger than another informant answering as a child.

8 When migration is measured continuously by the proportion of migrants among all the children, the results continue to hold but are less significant than when we use the more meaningful dummy variable.

9 When we use the dummy *migrant*, instead of *migrant poor* and *migrant rich*, the coefficient comes out as significant at the 1% level of confidence.

10 Note that, when no wealth variable is present in the estimated equation, whether in interaction terms or as a separate variable, the coefficient of *number of children* remains remarkably stable and the level of statistical significance is unaffected.

11 More precisely, we have introduced the interaction term *migrant and gender bias* in the regression (after removing *migrant poor* and *migrant rich* to avoid too much collinearity). What we find is that families with at least one migrant child, whether they are unisex (families where there are only boys or only girls) or mixed (with both sons and daughters), tend to practice unequal land inheritance more often than unisex families with no migrant children (the reference category). Both effects are statistically significant, and the effect is even stronger for unisex families. As for mixed families with no migrant children, they do not behave differently from those in the reference category (the coefficient associated with the corresponding dummy is not significant). We can therefore conclude that the effect of migration on inheritance operates independently of the gender composition of the children in the family.

12 A plausible explanation for this observation is, indeed, that it is more difficult or costly for migrants to maintain ties with the native community when the latter is remote than when it is within relatively easy reach.

References

Alston, Lee J. and Schapiro, Morton Owen. (1984) "Inheritance Laws Across Colonies: Causes and Consequences," *JEH* XLIV (June): 277–87.

Avineri, Shlomo. (1968) *The Social and Political Thought of Karl Marx*, Cambridge: Cambridge University Press.

Baker, Matthew and Miceli, Thomas J. (2002) "Land Inheritance Rules: Theory and Cross-Cultural Analysis," Working Paper 43, Department of Economics, University of Connecticut.

Baland, Jean-Marie and Platteau, Jean-Philippe. (1998) "Dividing the Commons – A Partial Assessment of the New Institutional Economics of Property Rights," *AJAE* 80 (August): 644–50.

Becker, Gary S. (1974) "A Theory of Social Interactions," *JPE* 82 (November/December): 1063–93.

——(1981) *A Treatise on the Family*, Cambridge, MA: Harvard University Press.

Bergstrom, Theodore C. (1994) "Primogeniture, Monogamy and Reproductive Success in a Stratified Society," Technical Report, Department of Economics, University of Michigan, Ann Arbor, MI.

Bernheim, B. Douglas and Severinov, Sergei. (2003) "Bequests as Signals: An Explanation for the Equal Division Puzzle," *JPE* 111: 733–64.

Bernheim, B. Douglas, Shleifer, Andrei, and Summers, Lawrence H. (1985) "The Strategic Bequest Motive," *JPE* 93 (December): 1045–76.

Berry, Sara. "The Food Crisis and Agrarian Change in Africa: A Review Essay," *Afr. Stud. Rev.* 27: 59–112.

Boserup, Esther. (1965) *The Conditions of Agricultural Growth: The Economics of Agrarian Change under Population Pressure*, London: Allen and Unwin.

Breusers, Mark. (2001) "Searching for Livelihood Security: Land and Mobility in Burkina Faso," *JDS* 37: 49–80.

Bruce, John W. and Migot-Adholla, Shem E. (eds) (1994) *Searching for Land Tenure Security in Africa*, Dubuque, IA: Kendall/Hunt Publishing Company.

Chu, C.Y. Cyrus. (1991) "Primogeniture," *JPE* 99 (February): 78–99.

Cohen, John M. (1980) "Land Tenure and Rural Development in Africa," in R.H. Bates and M.F. Lofchie (eds) *Agricultural Development in Africa – Issues of Public Policy*, New York: Praeger, pp. 349–400.

Dasgupta, Partha. (1993) *An Inquiry into Well-Being and Destitution*, Oxford: Clarendon Press.

Gagan, David P. (1976) "The Indivisibility of Land: A Microeconomic Analysis of the System of Inheritance in 19th Century Ontario," *JEH* 36 (March): 126–46.

Goetghebuer, Tatiana. (2002) *Règles d'héritage de la terre dans les communautés andines (Pérou)*, Master Thesis, Department of Economics, University of Namur, Belgium (mimeo).

Hayami, Yujiro and Kikuchi, Masahiko. (1981) *Asian Village Economy at the Crossroads*, Tokyo: University of Tokyo Press, and Baltimore, MD: Johns Hopkins University Press.

McGarry, Kathleen. (1999) "Inter Vivos Transfers and Intended Bequests," *JPE* 73: 321–51.

Malengreau, Jacques. (1999) *Structures identitaires et pratiques solidaires au Pérou – Gens du sang, gens de la terre et gens de bien*, Paris : L'Harmattan.

Ng'weno, B. (2001) "Reidentifying Ground Rules – Community Inheritance Disputes among the Digo of Kenya," in A. Agrawal and C.C. Gibson (eds) *Communities and the Environment*, New Brunswick, NJ and London: Rutgers University Press, pp. 111–37.

North, Douglass C. (1990) *Institutions, Institutional Change and Economic Performance*, Cambridge: Cambridge University Press.

Platteau, Jean-Philippe. (2000) *Institutions, Social Norms, and Economic Development*, London: Harwood Academic Publishers.

Platteau, Jean-Philippe and Baland, Jean-Marie. (2001) "Impartible Inheritance Versus Equal Division: A Comparative Perspective Centered on Europe and Sub-Saharan Africa," in de Janvry, Alain, Gordillo, Gustavo, Platteau, Jean-Philippe, and Sadoulet, Elizabeth (eds) *Access to Land, Rural Poverty, and Public Action*, Oxford: Oxford University Press, pp. 27–67.

Platteau, Jean-Philippe, Gaspart, Frédéric, and Lemay, Philippe. (2004) "A Theory of Unequal Land Bequest in Opening Societies," Working Paper, Centre for Research on the Economics of Development (CRED), Department of Economics, University of Namur, Belgium.

Index

Note: Page numbers in italics refer to figures and tables.